W9-ANH-851

First published in Germany in 1985, *Geschichte der deutschen Literaturkritik* was quickly recognized as the most original and comprehensive study to date of a proud critical tradition including such giants as Lessing, Goethe, and Heine. Now translated into English, it will serve as a model for a new approach to literary history in America and elsewhere, one emphasizing the connections of criticism with other public discourse.

In *A History of German Literary Criticism, 1730–1980* five scholars concentrate not merely on aesthetics and intellectual history, as previous writers have done, but on the development of literary theory and criticism in its social context. They seek to connect the evolution of critical discourse with larger developments occurring at the same time in the economic and political sectors of society, developments that in turn have a profound effect upon mass communications. Hence, this history takes into account the wide range of variables that influence literary production, consumption, interpretation, preservation, and taste.

The editor, Peter Uwe Hohendahl, is a professor of German and Comparative Literature at Cornell University and is the author of *The Institution of Criticism* (1982) and other works.

Modern German Culture and Literature

General Editor
Peter Hohendahl, Cornell University

Editorial Board
Russell Berman, Stanford University
Jane Caplan, Bryn Mawr
Sander Gilman, Cornell University
Martin Jay, University of California, Berkeley
Sara Lennox, University of Massachusetts, Amherst
Klaus R. Scherpe, Freie Universität, Berlin

A History of German Literary Criticism, 1730–1980

. . . .

Edited by Peter Uwe Hohendahl with contributions
by Klaus L. Berghahn, Russell A. Berman,
Peter Uwe Hohendahl, Jochen Schulte-Sasse,
and Bernhard Zimmermann
Translated by Franz Blaha, John R. Blazek,
Jeffrey S. Librett, and Simon Srebrny

. . . .

University of Nebraska Press   *Lincoln and London*

Copyright © 1988 by the University of Nebraska Press
All rights reserved
Manufactured in the United States of America
Originally published as *Geschichte der deutschen Literaturkritik (1730–1980)*, © J. B.
Metzlersche Verlagsbuchhandlung und Carl Ernst Poeschel Verlag GmbH in Stuttgart
1985
The paper in this book meets the minimum requirements of American National
Standard for Information Sciences—Permanence of Paper for Printed Library
Materials, ANSI Z39.48–1984.
Library of Congress Cataloging in Publication Data
Geschichte der deutschen Literaturkritik (1730–1980). English.
A History of German literary criticism / edited by Peter Uwe
Hohendahl; with contributions by Klaus L. Berghahn . . . [et al.];
translated by Franz Blaha . . . [et al.].
p. cm.
Translation of: Geschichte der deutschen Literaturkritik
(1730–1980)
Bibliography: p.
Includes index.
Contents: From classicist to classical literary criticism.
1730–1906 / by Klaus L. Berghahn — The concept of literary
criticism in German Romanticism, 1795–1810 / by Jochen Schulte-Sasse
— Literary criticism in the epoch of liberalism, 1820–70 / by Peter
Uwe Hohendahl — Literary criticism from empire to dictatorship,
1870–1933 / by Russell A. Berman — Literary criticism from 1933 to
the present / by Bernhard Zimmermann.
ISBN 0-8032-2340-4 (alk. paper). ISBN 0-8032-7232-4 (pbk.: alk.
paper)
1. German literature—History and criticism. 2. Criticism—
Germany—History. I. Berghahn, Klaus L. II. Hohendahl, Peter
Uwe. III. Title.
PT47.G4713 1988
801′.95′0943—dc19   87-30178

BURGESS
PT
47
.G4713
1988

Contents

. . . .

Preface

. . . .

THIS study was originally written for a German-speaking audience—taking into account and critically responding to the specific viewpoints and interests of German students of literature. While the history of criticism has conventionally been considered an integral part of literary history in the United States, this has not been the case in Germany; there, a rather narrow concept of literary criticism has discouraged scholars from devoting much energy to the history of criticism. Since in Germany "literary criticism" (*Literaturkritik*) has *grosso modo*, at least since the late nineteenth century, been understood as a specific form of journalism, thus excluding rather than including literary theory and academic criticism, a comprehensive treatment of the history of German literary criticism in the broader Anglo-American sense of the term was not available before the original publication of this study in 1985.

The American edition means to make this work available to English-speaking students of literature outside the narrow circle of experts of German literature. Hence, numerous smaller changes had to be made in order to adapt the presentation of the material to an audience less familiar with the facts of German literary and social history. Among other things, the translation of the German terminology—especially that of the eighteenth and nineteenth centuries—proved to be a difficult task. Therefore, in some instances the original German term is given in parentheses to indicate that the English word can only approximate the meaning of the German term.

With respect to its content, the American edition is unabridged and follows the original German text rather closely. Its purpose is twofold: first, to provide the English-speaking reader with a comprehensive overview of German criticism; second, to introduce a distinct approach to the more general problem of conceptualizing literary evolution. While traditional histories of literary criticism either focused on the development of literary theory and aesthetics or emphasized the achievements of individual critics, our study underscores the institutional grounding of criticism: that is, its embeddedness in the literary public sphere. This approach, we believe, has certain advantages. It has enabled us to go beyond a purely descriptive presentation of facts, concepts, and ideas; in particular, it has allowed us to explore the social and political dimensions of criticism without forcing them into a rigid base/superstructure model. Our viewpoint encourages a more serious and more concise analysis of the structure of literary communication in the public sphere.

We want to thank Franz Blaha, John R. Blazek, Jeffrey S. Librett, and Simon Srebrny for their considerable labor as translators, which required not only excellent linguistic skills but also a great deal of familiarity with the subject at hand. Also, without the generous support of Katharina Gerstenberger, the project assistant at Cornell University, it would have been far more difficult to complete the manuscript.

PETER UWE HOHENDAHL

. . . .

Introduction

I N Germany today it is still not obvious why or how one would write a history of literary criticism. To be sure, German historians of literary criticism no longer need to justify themselves explicitly, but they cannot assume—as can those working in the Anglo-American or French traditions, for example—that their readers will immediately acknowledge and comprehend the importance of their project.[1] If the history of literature has itself become a problematic genre, hardly noticed beyond the academic public sphere, the history of literary criticism is that much more problematic. Not even professional critics seem to be interested in it more than occasionally. This is intimately tied up, of course, with the present status of literary criticism. As long as texts that refer to other literary texts are regarded as "secondary," one cannot expect that their representation in literary history will be granted more than a modest corner.[2] The situation is aggravated by the split—customary since the nineteenth century—between literary criticism (*Literaturkritik*) and literary scholarship (*Literaturwissenschaft*), between feuilleton (newspapers and magazines) and university.[3] Literary scholarship has, of course, pursued its own history in the attempt to shed light on contemporary methodological discussions, even if a considerable number of lacunae remain.[4] But journalistic criticism is not, apparently, worthy of becoming the object of scholarly historiography. The feuilleton, written for the moment, seems too fleeting and weightless to merit remembrance. The limitation of the German term "literary criticism" (*Literaturkritik*) to the evaluation of current literature in the mass media (newspapers, magazines, radio) by no means corresponds to the entire spectrum of what it claims to name. The history of literary criticism is not identical with the history of the feuilleton or even of the reviewer's trade. But this insight is not yet a sufficient answer to the question, how do we define "literary criticism"? What are the objects to which our investigation refers?

Historians of literary criticism are faced with a double difficulty: first, they cannot unthinkingly adopt *today's* linguistic usage for the definition of the field of their investigation; second, the history of literary criticism cannot be modeled on the history of genres. These two problems are of course intertwined. For example, it would be possible to treat the history of criticism—as one treats the history of comedy or of the short story—as the history of a particular genre. This approach has its own seductiveness, for it would allow us to integrate criticism into literature as a whole, of which criticism would constitute one component genre. The historical analysis of criticism would then become an intraliterary task, dealing with the considerable but also reassuringly familiar difficulties of the history of genres. A closer look, however, reveals that this approach underestimates the heterogeneity of its materials. The forms in which literary criticism has historically appeared—review, commentary, polemic, essay, dialogue, reportage, and finally also literary history—hardly permit its conceptualization as a single genre. Perhaps the history of the review could be written as the history of a particular genre—but not the history of criticism. The category "criticism" is not even a generic term for a range of subgenres but rather—to introduce a preliminary definition—*public communication on literature* comprising both description and evaluation. And it is not necessarily a disadvantage that this definition includes literary history.

So abstract a definition remains unsatisfactory, however, because it doesn't say anything about the medium and function of communication. We all think we know what literary criticism is, because we are familiar with its contemporary forms and problems, but can we universalize this "knowledge"? Does it correspond to criticism in the seventeenth and eighteenth centuries, for example? These questions allude to the historicity of the concept. As soon as we admit that the category of literary criticism is not transhistorical and immutable, we can no longer describe the history of criticism as the unfolding of an

Idea that merely expresses its essence in various forms. We can neither arbitrarily project the contemporary concept of literary criticism back into the past nor erect the texts of a particular past epoch—for example, the epoch of Romanticism—as the origin and standard of all criticism. In our time, such constructions would face considerable difficulties of self-legitimation.

As long as the institution of literary criticism possessed unquestioned legitimacy, teleological conceptions of its history seemed appropriate. Historians either declared the present to be the culmination of all prior developments or chose a particular historical epoch other than their own as the center with respect to which all prior history became ascent and all posterior history became decline. The crisis of literary criticism between 1967 and 1976, which shook the foundations of the institution, meant the end of these teleological conceptions.[5] The criticism of criticism desolated and thus laid bare the institutional foundations that everyone had blindly considered self-evident. If "bourgeois criticism" was abruptly declared dead, this did not mean—as the New Left had prophesied—the end of German literary criticism but was rather an incentive to interrogate the institution critically.[6] The interrogation concentrated on the relationship between the function of criticism and the social structure of the Federal Republic of Germany. Our project presupposes and in part arises out of this crisis of literary criticism and the lively debate that at once manifested and aggravated it. The object of our study is accordingly *the genesis and transformation of a literary institution.* The new perspective required by our object induces us to push traditional questions of the history of ideas into the background in order to foreground questions that were not traditionally posed: What is the status of literary criticism within the literary system in general? What specific tasks are assigned to it? Which media are considered appropriate to these tasks? What procedures does criticism develop for the analysis and evaluation of literature? Who takes part in this communication? Which particular social groups or classes dominate the discussion in a given place and time, and which others are excluded? These are some of the questions a history of literary criticism must confront today.[7]

If we approach the material with these questions in mind, the field of investigation widens considerably. The history of the institution of criticism can by no means be described on the basis of literary documents alone. Rather—and this is one of its most difficult problems—it must coordinate literary, social, and political data. Both traditional literary history and reception aesthetics have been aware of this problem, but they have not been able to arrive at any satisfactory solutions, because they have treated extraliterary data as mere "background" material. The treatment of context as "background" certainly enables one to write a social history of the critic or his public. It also sanctions specific investigations of the influences of the book market on the goals and strategies of criticism or of the connection between political ideology and the evaluation of artworks. However, although dissection of the problem into partial problems makes these isolated problems easier to solve, it does not necessarily lead to a satisfactory history of criticism. For such a history cannot content itself with establishing a *monocausal* relation between extraliterary data and literary-critical texts; rather, it must demonstrate literary-critical communication *itself* to be a social phenomenon.

The project of demonstrating the specific communicative sociality of literary criticism requires first of all the investigation of the literary-critical discourse: that is, the argumentative and rhetorical strategies by means of which critics attempt persuasively to evaluate and organize literary works and authors. The analysis of discourse allows us to witness the interpenetration of linguistic communication and social function. But it allows us to witness this interpenetration only if it explains in terms of sociohistorical, communicative function why a certain period privileges certain forms of criticism (for example, the authorial portrait or the polemic) and why at a given place and time particular argumentative structures predominate (for example, the associative procedure of the feuilleton of the late nineteenth century). Historical transformations frequently become visible at this level which remain invisible at the level of general aesthetics or literary theory. (On the other hand, historical transformations in the theory of art and literature do not necessarily express themselves at the level of the literary-critical discourse.) In other words, by means of the analysis of literary-critical procedures, the difference between literary theory and literary criticism becomes more strikingly apparent than by means of traditional analyses. We take our distance from a model in which critical practice is nothing but the application of theoretical insights, in which the history of literary criticism recounts nothing but such insights and their applications. The relation between theory and criticism proves, in fact, to be decisively more complex. Although theory and criticism seldom fail to interact in some manner or other, theory by no means predominates over criticism in all literary-historical periods. Whereas classical periods prefer to submit literary-critical practice to aesthetic laws, this is not the case at all for other historical phases.

Once we analytically separate literary theory from criticism, we may be tempted to write the history of criticism as the *history of taste*. The literary taste of the recipients, as represented by the critic, would then take the place of aesthetic theory. But this approach to the history of criticism, invoking as it does eighteenth-century notions of criticism, is as reductive as a model that operates in terms of the history of theory. Such an approach reductively and anachronistically restricts the notion of critical discourse to the mere reflection of the opinions and feelings that predominate among the public. The problem is the same whether one takes these opinions and feelings to be irreducibly and opaquely given data or reduces them further to group mentalities. In both cases one must fail to conceptualize the specific communicative function of criticism.

A similar reduction results when one equates the social history of criticism with the sociology of the critic. We do have to take the social position of a critic into account if we want to understand the function of a literary-critical text. But it is not sufficient to classify the critic socially—for example, as the member of a particular social group. Such crude classifications can at best contribute to the preliminary delineation of a communicative sphere's borders. One cannot arrive in this manner at concrete functional analyses.

Functional analyses do, of course, require the formal description of composition, rhetoric, and argumentation in literary-critical texts. But this procedure can arrive at sociohistorical insights only when it is combined with considerations of the contexts of such texts. For example, both the Enlightenment and realism preferred to argue from literary norms and then measure the literary work against these norms; however, we cannot infer that this preference functioned the same way in both contexts. As soon as we take into account the specific historical situation, we can easily show that the functional status of the deductive procedure differed considerably in the two cases. But how can we determine further the connection between text and context without having recourse to the vague notion of "background"?

At present, various models are available whose mutual compatibility is certainly not beyond question: systems theory (Niklas Luhmann), ideology critique (Louis Althusser), and critical communications theory (Jürgen Habermas, Karl Otto Apel). Whereas systems theory conceives literary criticism as a subsystem within the cultural system, ideology critique conceives literary criticism as an apparatus of determinable social function within the system of ideological state apparatuses.[8] Finally, for communications theory, literary criticism is one of the institutions that helps constitute and articulate the public sphere (die Öffentlichkeit). We assume ideology critique and communications theory to be potentially compatible.

The following study is essentially determined by the sociohistorically based model of the public sphere. We hardly need to emphasize that this model is indebted to Jürgen Habermas's pathbreaking investigation, Strukturwandel der Öffentlichkeit (Structural change of the public sphere; 1962). The fruitfulness of the category of the public sphere for the analysis of the history of literary criticism was already recognized in the early 1970s. And Peter Gebhardt has recently reemphasized the central significance of this category for the historical interpretation of literary criticism. Of course, one must take into account that Habermas's model, which developed further the earlier work of Reinhart Kosellek, has been criticized and modified by later research.[9] Habermas's critics have attacked above all his notion of the genesis of the bourgeois public sphere but also his theory of structural "deterioration." Not without reason, Strukturwandel der Öffentlichkeit has been accused of failing to distinguish adequately between the theory of the public sphere and its historical reality.[10]

For example, Jochen Schulte-Sasse has recently pointed out that the literary public sphere did not simply, as Habermas argues, prepare the political public sphere by promoting public communication. Schulte-Sasse shows that this literary public sphere simultaneously represents a "publicly organized and accepted experience of subjectivity which not only renounces its supplementation by critical-rational discourse but directs itself precisely against this discourse as against the alienated will-to-domination characteristic of instrumental rationality."[11] This objection points out a problematic element of Habermas's early theory.

Habermas assumed that the genesis of the bourgeois public sphere was closely involved with the genesis of capitalism. From this assumption comes his strong emphasis on rationality as the critical instrument that dissolves traditional society. The purpose of public discourse is for Habermas the rational communication between mature (*mündigen*) private individuals (in a modern society). Habermas thus fails to consider—in contrast to Max Horkheimer and Theodor Adorno in the *Dialektik der Aufklärung* (Dialectic of enlightenment)—that this rationality had already become the object of criticism in the medium of literature during the Age of Enlightenment. This difficulty would dissolve if we assumed that it was precapitalist conditions that brought forth the classical model of the bourgeois public sphere. Thus Annette Leppert-Fögen, building on Hans Medick's interpretation of Adam Smith, has taken the position that the classical model of the public sphere is based predominantly on the life of the petty bourgeoisie and craftsmen under precapitalist conditions.[12] If we accept this argument, we can understand the critique of capitalist instrumental reason—which was already formulated by the second generation of the Enlightenment—as a defensive strategy against the incursion of the rational capitalist calculus. The classical public sphere is not merely, as Habermas assumed, concerned with overcoming feudal life practices but is equally directed against capitalist purposive rationality, which is interested not in maturity (*Mündigkeit*) and humanity but in social effectiveness.

The history of literary criticism must take these objections seriously. It will have to distinguish between the model of the public sphere and the structure of the public space in which literary-critical communication actually happens. Above all, it has become clear that the abstract conception of the bourgeois public sphere offers a frame that is much too crude for the description of finer historical nuances. The significant alterations of the literary-critical discourse between 1830 and 1840, for example, cannot be explained merely by reference to the model of the bourgeois public sphere.

The theory of the public sphere can be used, then, only in modified form. Its enduring value lies in its capacity to explicate the context of the literary-critical discourse without reducing this context to an aggregate of sociological data. If we understand literary criticism since the Enlightenment as an institution within the public sphere, we can decode its forms and contents. At the same time, we continue to face the problem of its contemporary crisis, which became visible in 1967 and which is not suspended or overcome merely by virtue of the fact that the literary trade continues to operate. Norbert Mecklenburg has rightly warned against turning the history of literary criticism into a neutral description of the past, against viewing history as a purely objective semiotic realm: "As a supertheory named semiotics of literature, it describes—more or less in terms of the theory of games— literary communication, and therefore also literary criticism and the genesis, expansion, and alteration of notions of literary value. But in this way it falls prey to the illusion of being able to remove itself from its object, instead of reflecting on its role as one of the players in the game."[13] There are two reasons why such a semiotics is inadequate to its object. First, it overlooks the fact that literary scholarship (academic criticism) is itself part of the institution of literature—specifically, a subinstitution which in the early nineteenth century was largely identical with literary criticism and which remained in later periods in a close, if also tense, relation with literary criticism. Second, the historian who writes about the literary criticism of the past is always also an actor in the contemporary configuration, and it is this configuration that determines his interest in the past. Mecklenburg is therefore right to underscore the necessity of a reflective procedure (which of course must not be confused with a mere dialogue with the great critics of the past).

The extensive discussion about the contemporary fate and the future of criticism in the 1960s and 1970s both addressed the failings of the contemporary institution and presented proposals for the correction of these failings. These proposals included the reintroduction of theory and aesthetics (Heinrich Vormweg), the intensification of the dialogue with the reader (Peter Glotz),[14] and the pursuit of rhetorical forms (Norbert Mecklenburg). The connection of these themes with the history of literary criticism was, however, only seldom mentioned. As a result, the reform of literary criticism remained strangely ahistorical—as if contemporary problems had fallen from the heavens— whereas any serious consideration of the history of the institution makes clear that we are faced with accumulated questions that cannot be solved merely by manifestos nor even merely by intensive reflection. On the other hand, some contemporary critics have called for a renaissance of certain high points of past criticism, such as the work of Friedrich Schlegel, Ludwig Börne, or Theodor Fontane, as if one could overcome the contemporary malaise by repeating the work of these men. But such appeals are based on problematic inferences, for these critics wrote in and for a form of literary public sphere that no longer exists. A literary-critical practice that does not reflect on this will not be able to grasp its own situation in a late-capitalist (if not postindustrial) public sphere and will thus either make unrealizable demands or overlook new tasks that did not present themselves to the criticism of the nineteenth century. If anything is to be learned from the history of the institution of literary criticism, it is the experience of the *difference*, the discontinuity between the material and ideal conditions of the present and those of earlier phases. The insight into this difference should make us skeptical about the attempt to posit our own standpoint dogmatically as the center of history, as is still implicitly done in René Wellek's comprehensive history of literary criticism (the standpoint there being that of the New Criticism). Such constructions, in which the past becomes the precursor of the present, tend to shove aside whatever does not fit into the desired frame. In contrast, the reflection on historical difference holds open both the present and the past.

If in the 1960s the aesthetics of modernity (such as the aesthetic theory of Theodor W. Adorno) could still be seen as the telos of the history of criticism, the constellation had changed by the 1970s so utterly that this aesthetics no longer seemed self-evident. The extensive debate over postmodernity[15] has shown that the presuppositions of avant-garde aesthetics, which have so strongly influenced most of the advanced literary criticism of the present, have become problematic. These reservations concern above all the assumption—propagated by the neo-avant-garde and also partly by experimental literature—that aesthetic innovation and political change go hand in hand. The dissolution of this assumption inaugurates the postmodern configuration. With the arrival of this configuration, the function of literary criticism is altered in a manner that has as yet hardly been explored. If we assume with Karl Heinz Bohrer[16] that postmodernity consists among other things in the growing proximity of avant-garde and popular culture (distinguished from traditional culture), then not only do new tasks emerge for literary criticism but also a new standpoint for the treatment of its history. Evidently, texts and documents of popular culture cannot be judged on the basis of the aesthetics of autonomy—which is the reason they could be described only negatively by Adorno. The same is true for the literature of the Baroque and Enlightenment periods. In other words, the institution of literary criticism can no longer dogmatically depend on the aesthetics of autonomy that has been dominant since the late eighteenth century; it has good cause to interrogate its own historicity more thoroughly than heretofore.

Precisely this is the reason the hermeneutic procedure no longer suffices for the conceptual analysis and presentation of the history of literary criticism. It is doubtless correct, as Mecklenburg and Gebhardt have pointed out, that the interest in this history is determined by the present and hence that little is to be gained by the ostensibly neutral descriptive presentation of an only seemingly uninvolved historian. Moreover, hermeneutics—as a dialogue between subject and text—is not in a position to disclose the institutional presuppositions that determine this process. This is true also of the critical variant of hermeneutics that Adorno proposed, which essentially limits itself to modernity (1750–1930) and tends to reject or ignore older (Baroque, for example) forms of artistic production. Evaluation, intimately bound up with understanding, can be legitimated neither by recourse to the immediate insightfulness of feelings of value nor by reflection upon material adequacy (*materiale Sachgemässheit*) as Adorno still hoped. It is, in fact, based on and situated within socio-cultural systems of norms determined by interests, which are in turn grounded in concrete historical social formations. The entry into these systems of norms lies on a level other than that of the hermeneutic dialogue between reader and text, or between aesthetic reflection and artwork. To this degree, the history of literary criticism moves on two levels. Where it establishes the relation between present and past, it operates within the frame of hermeneutics (and stands thus in the context of contemporary systems of norms); where it refers to institutionalization, it operates with materialist and communications-theory procedures.[17] The metahermeneutic discussion of institutionalization does not of course relieve literary scholarship of the need to incorporate the results of historical reconstruction into the practice of literary-critical writing and evaluation. The insight into the history of the institution—that is, into the historical difference between present and past institutionalization—ensures that past literary-critical texts do not become a dogmatic burden.[18]

TRANSLATED BY JEFFREY S. LIBRETT

KLAUS L. BERGHAHN

· · · · · · · ·

From Classicist to Classical Literary Criticism, 1730–1806

We are in agreement that criticism per se is a science which deserves
every effort at cultivation.
—GOTTHOLD LESSING

MODERN literary criticism began during the Enlightenment, and the institution of bourgeois criticism still reflects
the aspirations and contradictions of its period of origin.
Beginning its history with the Enlightenment accords with the views
of most scholars. As early as 1915, Albert Dresdner noted with amaze-
ment: "It is remarkable that after thousands of years during which the
world had gotten along very well without it, art criticism suddenly
made its appearance in the middle of the eighteenth century."[1] In the
foreword to his monumental work on European literary criticism,
René Wellek writes: "The middle of the 18th century is a meaningful
point to start, as then the neoclassical system of doctrines, established
since the Renaissance, began to disintegrate." Farther along, he adds:
"In the later 18th century there emerge, and struggle with one another, doctrines and points of view which are relevant even today."[2]
Historical (if not radical) change and contemporary interests ground
his periodization and determine the manner of his presentation as
intellectual history. Hans Mayer too begins his four-volume anthology,
Deutsche Literaturkritik, with the year 1730; and Peter Uwe Hohendahl
has recently affirmed: "The history of literary criticism is briefer than
generally assumed. As an institution, it developed firm contours only
during the Age of Enlightenment."[3]

Demonstrating such unanimity is one thing; finding any deeper agreement is something else altogether. A closer look at these various presentations makes it apparent that even issues so basic as the definition of literary criticism remain clouded. The *Reallexikon der deutschen Literaturgeschichte* contains the following definition (or attempt at one): "Literary criticism originates in a direct reaction to literary stimuli." Today, criticism principally means "contemporary reviews of new literary publications, and theater criticism."[4] Hans Mayer interprets the concept much more broadly; his documentary volumes contain first reviews as well as treatises on poetics, and scathing parodies side by side with literary theories. On this point Mayer finds himself in agreement with Wellek's Anglo-Saxon understanding of "literary criticism," as presented in his foreword: "The term criticism I shall interpret broadly to mean not only judgments of individual books and authors, 'judicial' criticism, practical criticism, evidences of literary taste, but mainly what has been thought about the principles and theory of literature, its nature, its creation, its function, its effects, its relations to the other activities of man, its kinds, devices, and techniques, its origins and history."[5] Since at times Wellek also wishes to embrace aesthetic theory, his concept of literary criticism de facto encompasses everything belonging to the theory of literature.[6]

It is quite unreasonable to be forced to choose between the extremes of ephemeral journalistic criticism on the one hand and a comprehensive theory of literature on the other. And the *Reallexikon* offers little help when it distinguishes between "criticism (in the newer, narrower sense) and literary studies (as in the old, comprehensive meaning of literary criticism)." There appears to be no satisfactory mediation between universal literary theory and a level of journalistic response which, according to the *Reallexikon,* scarcely deserves notice as a form of serious study. Instead of settling for either of the two definitions, it seems wise first to explore the concept's history, to determine whether the dichotomy between scholarly and journalistic literary criticism can genuinely be sustained. For it might well prove in both cases that methodological blinders have restricted historical understanding. In the definition of the *Reallexikon* one hears the apparent arrogance of a literary scholarship that has abandoned literary criticism to the despised journalists, whereas Wellek equates the concept with his Anglo-Saxon understanding of "literary criticism," thus lending it historical legitimacy.

That, at any rate, is suggested by his article "The Term and Concept of Literary Criticism." In that essay Wellek briefly explores the Greco-Latin etymology of the word, but what actually interests him is simply the question, how and why has the term "criticism" (*critica, la critique*) expanded to embrace all study of literature and thus replaced "poetics" or "rhetoric"? This development began in the Renaissance with the rediscovery of Aristotle's *Poetics*. Yet initially, it was not the countless commentators on the *Poetics* who were named "critics" but rather the grammarians who developed the philological methods used to test the genuineness of classical works. Then, during the era of Humanism, philological textual criticism (*ars critica*) became an important tool of biblical exegesis. J. C. Scaliger's *Poetics* (1561) had already contained an entire book bearing the title "Criticus," a critical comparison between the Greek and Latin literatures. But it was Nicholas Boileau, in his *L'art poetique* (1687), who first "used the term as a matter of course" by detaching it from textual criticism and applying it purely to a work's literary aspects. Of course, Wellek is fully aware of the degree to which Boileau was still obligated to the old rules of rhetoric and poetics. It was the debate concerning taste at the start of the eighteenth century that first truly liberated literary criticism from the tutelage of ancient authorities and conceded the public the right to a say in the matter. The development was similar in England, from philological through biblical to literary criticism. In his *Advancement of Learning* (1605), Francis Bacon had already drawn a distinction between pedantic textual criticism and criticism in the sense of interpretation, comparison, and judgment of literature. According to Wellek, John Dryden was the first author to use the neologism "criticism" in the sense of general theory—"By criticism, as it was first instituted by Aristotle, was meant a standard of judging well"[7]—and since Alexander Pope's *Essay on Criticism* (1711), the usage has remained so constant "that it is superfluous to follow it any further."[8]

Wellek fails to pursue the German development of the concept in comparable detail. He limits himself to the observation that the concept was imported from France and showed up in 1730 in Johann Christoph Gottsched's *Versuch einer kritischen Dichtkunst*. He cites neither the dictionaries of the eighteenth century (Zedler, Sulzer, Adelung) nor the programs of the numerous "critical" journals. Instead, he is interested only in the question of why the concept narrowed during the course of the nineteenth and twentieth centuries: "In Germany something happened to dislodge the term and concept and to narrow it more and more till it came to mean only day-by-day reviewing, arbitrary literary opinion."[9]

This conclusion needs to be more carefully examined, since it is not at all certain that German literary criticism in the eighteenth century had the comprehensive significance that Wellek speaks of, only to become restricted in the nineteenth century to journalistic book criticism. There is much to suggest that the designation *Kriticus und Kunstrichter* (critic and art judge), which entered the language in the eighteenth century, referred specifically to book criticism—which was by no means "arbitrary literary opinion" but instead had an important function in the opinion formation process within a literary public sphere. Since Wellek limits his conceptual history semantically and rests content, having established the earliest appearance of the word "criticism" (simultaneously giving the New Criticism an air of tradition), his investigations remain historically abstract. For the same reason, his intellectual-historical presentation of European criticism remains peculiarly restricted to exclusively literary matters. This does not mean, however, that he is altogether oblivious to larger historical connections. On the contrary, his introduction explicitly states that criticism should be part of general cultural history: "[Criticism] is thus set in a historical and social context." Yet because he concentrates on describing the development of European literary theory since 1750, he neglects to portray the historico-social processes that function as a substrate for and exert influence upon literary criticism. Wellek says expressly: "The specific influence of social and general historical causes on criticism is much harder to grasp and describe."[10] In however sketchy a fashion, that is precisely what this essay in historiography attempts to do.

The Age of Criticism and the Emergence of a Literary Public

"Ours is the true age of criticism, an activity to which all else must be subordinated," wrote Immanuel Kant triumphantly in the preface to the First Critique of 1781.[11] He therewith gave expression to one of the most important tendencies of the Enlightenment, in a concept which took aim at "illusory knowledge" (*Scheinwissen*) and simultaneously grounded the universal claim of Reason. For only that which had proved itself before Reason, through "free and public examination," could earn our respect. Three years later, during the famous discussion in the *Berlinische Monatsschrift* concerning J. F. Zöllner's question, "What is Enlightenment?" Kant demanded that every mature adult take cognizance of the "most harmless" of all freedoms and "make open use of his Reason in all his affairs." What Kant discussed only theoretically (and rendered even more innocuous by the characterization "harmless") is nothing less than the claim to authority of public criticism, which would ultimately raise the political issues of freedom of speech and opinion formation in late eighteenth-century Prussia. Of course, in the same breath Kant recalled the judgment of Frederick II, a man who knew something about power politics: "You may indeed reason as much as you wish, and on any subject. But never forget to obey."[12]

While the political praxis of Reason was thus rigorously restrained, both Kant and the French Encyclopedists took the opportunity to test enlightened absolutism's thresholds of tolerance in such areas as philosophy, morality, and art, which did not stand directly under state control. Under conditions that were anything but liberal, Kant made the wise tactical distinction between the public use of Reason, which "must be free at all times," and the "private use," which is limited. Thus, in order to discuss the possibility of public criticism at all, he found himself compelled to develop a theory of the "double life": in their social roles as citizens, the officers, clergymen, and civil servants must obey; but as human beings who conceived of themselves as "citizens of a cosmopolitan society," they "may of course use their Reason." As a citizen of the state, the individual must subordinate himself; as a citizen of the world, he assumes the standpoint of freedom and behaves like a scholar offering his thoughts for public discussion. Through this peculiar dualism, typical of Absolutism, Kant secured intellectual freedom for critical Reason, making of it a public authority which by its very nature would extend its claim to authority to areas such as religion and the state. For critical Reason did not merely test the conditions of possibility for knowing, acting, and feeling but also triggered processes of consciousness that would ultimately rock social and political institutions and throw the Absolutist state into crisis.

Reinhart Koselleck has interpreted this connection between Enlightenment critique and the crisis of the polity of estates as a subterranean dialectical process of morality and politics. In particular, the *république des lettres* accelerated the process, to which the polity of estates ultimately fell victim. This republic, the homeland of philosophical and literary criticism, differentiated itself vis-à-vis the political sphere of the state, establishing itself as a purely moral authority, "in order then (precisely on the *basis* of this detachment) to expand with apparent neutrality and subject the political sphere to its judgment." To demonstrate this process of the increasing politicization of criticism, Koselleck too turns to the history of concepts—though with a perspective different from Wellek's. Both agree that before Humanism, "criticism" had developed as a philological method for objectively evaluating ancient texts; then the two thinkers part ways. Whereas Wellek is principally interested in the term's history, as well as the process whereby criticism separated itself from the tradition of ancient rhetoric and poetics and by the eighteenth century became a theory of the understanding and judgment of literature, Koselleck concentrates on the universalization (and the accompanying politicization) of the concept of criticism, a process particularly well illustrated by literary criticism. He follows *le règne de la critique* paradigmatically by focusing on four developmental steps of French criticism. In Richard Simon's *Histoire critique du Vieux Testament* (1678), textual criticism was applied to the Bible, a practice that would lead to the separation of reason and revelation. True, Simon still used reason to defend the church's teaching of salvation, but over the next century the difference between revelation and critical thought ripened into open contradiction, ultimately placing the authority of the church in question. This was already intimated in Pierre Bayle's *Dictionnaire historique et critique* (1695). For Bayle, too, criticism—narrowly construed—still meant textual criticism, but in its more comprehensive significance of critical method; he extended it to all areas of knowledge. Critique becomes the true activity of reason, and in the "continuous performance of criticism" it becomes the true motor of historical progress. In Bayle's writings, the separation of religion and reason was already complete, although the state was still expressly excluded from criticism: "Reason, inwardly critical, remains outwardly loyal to the state." In the republic of scholars, evidently, one strove exclusively for the truth—that is, the criticism of philosophical error, not (yet) of government iniquities. This state of affairs first changes with Voltaire, who pretends to be criticizing art only in a completely apolitical way. Yet under the cover of aesthetic, literary, and historical studies "he indirectly criticizes both the Church and the state." Political criticism comes out of the closet altogether with Denis Diderot and the Encyclopedists, becoming the voice of public opinion. While they still recognize the divisions (constitutive for Absolutism) between human being and political subject, morality and politics, their acceptance of this dualism is only tactical—a means of giving stronger expression to their moral criticism and defying the king's claims of sovereignty until, during the Revolution, they would try him as a mere human being.[13]

In Germany, the political situation did not come to such a head, and criticism was consequently not influential enough to establish itself as a political public sphere. Yet even here criticism was by no means subaltern. Toward the end of the century it even raised claims to authority, as Kant's example illustrates. Just how political criticism can articulate itself in the innocent medium of literary theory is illustrated by Friedrich Schiller's essay on the theater, "Die Schaubühne als eine moralische Anstalt betrachtet" (1784), which climaxes with the famous sentence: "The jurisdiction of the stage begins where the realm of secular law comes to its end."[14] In his lecture Schiller radicalized the thesis (formulated earlier in France by Diderot and Louis Sébastien Mercier) that the theater as an institution propagated bourgeois virtues and, as political morality, also criticized the dominant social relations. The theater as cultural institution, according to Kosellek, became the "antipode of existing authority."[15] As a "supplement to the law" (Lessing), the theater already possessed a critical potential that could be further actualized and amplified through literary criticism. Even in Germany, moral criticism could be articulated (as a substitute for political action) in the free space of the literary public sphere.

Here it is appropriate to mention Jürgen Habermas's study *Strukturwandel der Öffentlichkeit*, which offers a historico-philosophical reinterpretation of Kosellek's conservative criticism of the Enlightenment.[16] While Kosellek leaves no doubt about his rejection of the Enlightenment critique, since it leads to the crisis of the well-ordered polity of estates,[17] Habermas (out of concern for contemporary society) emphatically defends the political category of the "bourgeois public sphere" as it has developed since the eighteenth century. It developed gradually out of the decay of the representative public sphere, which polarized into a public and a private sphere. The representative public sphere of government power, as it appeared to the people during the Middle Ages in the self-presentation of the ruler (enthronement, insignia, rites of authority), in the regional exercise of authority (Palatinates), and in court celebrations transformed itself over the course of several centuries into the modern administrative state. Although the basis of Absolutism continued to be feudalism (with the monarch atop the social hierarchy), an apparatus established itself between ruler and ruled, one that administered the state and appeared before the people as public power. As Lessing once put it, the state became "a far too abstract concept for our emotions."[18] It became alien to its citizens, confronting them with demands through taxation and administrative decrees and thus rendering them subjects. Excluded from the arcane politics of governmental power, citizens formed a contrasting category—the private sphere of civil society, which organized itself into the nuclear family and the private economy. Between this private sphere of bourgeois intimacy and activity and the political sphere of the state, a literary public formed, composed of "private individuals who coalesce into a public." Initially, the public reasoning of its intellectual spokesmen circled around philosophical, moral, and literary themes considered politically neutral, because private individuals were expressly forbidden to discuss or criticize the government or its decrees publicly. The censorship authorities were there to ensure that the intellectuals obeyed this rule. Yet the latter were not intimidated and gradually began testing the limits of the literary public sphere in order to exert an influence on Absolutism, which in Germany considered itself rather enlightened. The public use of reason served the "jointly promoted process of Enlightenment," and the outcome of this process was the bourgeois public, before which governmental power had to legitimate itself. The literary public that emerged in the eighteenth century needed only a slight readjustment in order to be transformed into a sphere of political public opinion. "Even before the 'public' quality of public power is disputed (and ultimately renounced) by the political reasoning of private individuals, a public sphere is covertly developed, in an apolitical form—the literary, preliminary form of a politically functioning public sphere."[19]

Even though this development—as is well known—was conducted with much more conscious intent and can be more clearly demonstrated in England and France than in Germany, Habermas points out one central sociopolitical aspect of literary life that is crucial to understanding literary criticism in the eighteenth century. The rising bourgeois society used art and criticism not just to reassure itself of its own values and projections of life; indirectly, the self-reflection of art in criticism also aided in the formation of political opinion. Thus the journals for the maturing bourgeoisie had an important function: they became the true instruments of criticism and of a literary, critical public. "Ultimately, the critical journals themselves were to bring to an end that which the works had been criticizing."[20]

Literary criticism in the eighteenth century, then, is *not* merely an intraliterary phenomenon of comprehensive theory and taste formation; rather, it contributes to the very constitution of a bourgeois public. As valuable as Wellek's history of European literary criticism is for presenting (in enormous comparative detail) the processes by which modern criticism detached itself from the strictures of Classicist poetics and by which literary theory emerged, his concept of literary criticism must be narrowed on the one hand, and brought into a larger sociopolitical framework on the other. For in the eighteenth century (truly the Age of the Journal), literary criticism was above all *book* criticism, criticism that renders judgment.[21] One need only recall that one of the Enlightenment's most important cultural-pedagogical intentions was to review *all* new publications in order to steer critically the development of literature as well as to form the public's taste. The institution of criticism, as developed during the Enlightenment, mediated between the work and the public in such a way that the critic was speaking on behalf of individuals who, through constant discussion, formed a *literary* public, with the intention of better understanding both themselves and the constitution of a rational life. This literary reasoning, as Koselleck and Habermas have shown, is always covertly political and aims at the production of a bourgeois public sphere. Ignoring the reciprocal relationship between criticism and the public prevents adequate understanding of either the political function of criticism or its social relevance for the process of Enlightenment.

The emergence of modern literary criticism was very closely connected with a comprehensive structural transformation of literary life, one inseparable from the sociohistorical changes that occurred during the eighteenth century. Without going into these complex connections in detail,[22] and also without reducing criticism to a mere reflection of these changes, one must nevertheless pay attention to the ways in which literary production, distribution, and reception are interconnected. For without considering the material preconditions of literary life, one can scarcely hope to understand the emergence of modern literary criticism, an event that presupposes the development of literacy among broad layers of the population, the commercialization of the book market, and an altered role for the writer. The publisher replaced the wealthy patron in providing assignments for freelance writers, who after 1770 had to orient themselves increasingly to the reading needs of the public and to the laws of the market. Information about literary production was afforded by the literary journals that emerged around this time: it was within these very journals that criticism was in the process of constituting itself.

There were concrete reasons why the spread of the Enlightenment throughout Germany was very slow and why the process displayed considerable regional difference. One of these was the backward state of general schooling. The populace was for the most part still illiterate, and a wide public able to enlighten itself through reading had yet to be formed. Even the use of the term "public" is quite problematic, since the concept was unknown until the middle of the century. As late as the 1760s, Gottsched found it odd that theatergoers in Berlin were "now called the *Publikum.*"[23] It is thus worthwhile to examine more closely the development of the reading world into a public, and, in doing so, to distinguish further between the real and the ideal public.

"Empirical reconstruction of the 18th century readership is as good as impossible": thus Helmuth Kiesel's lapidary conclusion.[24] And indeed, controversy reigns concerning the documentary value of the small amount of data we possess. Most of this information derives from contemporary writers and publishers, and much of it is contradictory. Yet slowly, over the course of the eighteenth century, efforts by Enlightenment writers to educate the people produced results. The introduction of obligatory schooling[25] and catechism instruction in the church contributed to the reduction of illiteracy. The reading ability of the public grew to such a degree that by the end of the century there were even complaints about the "reading mania" that had seized the lower classes. Research estimates regarding the extent of this "reading revolution" (Rolf Engelsing) vary considerably. While Rudolf Schenda assumes that by 1770, around 15 percent of the population (from an estimated 25 million) could be considered potential readers,[26] Kiesel is significantly more cautious: "However much it grew during the 18th century, the reading public remained disappearingly small."[27] He assumes that not more than 1 percent could actually read, probably only the educated elite who took an interest in contemporary literature. His supposition receives support from Friedrich Nicolai, who in 1773 noted sarcastically: "This minuscule scholarly world comprises not more than 20,000 teachers and students: they so heartily despise their 20 million German-speaking fellows, that they don't even bother writing for them."[28] Such an observation on literary life, stemming from a publisher and leading Enlightenment figure, is of interest in two respects. Evidently, around 1770 the republic of scholars still remained largely off by itself, reading and writing almost exclusively for one another. The rest of the population, inasmuch as it found the leisure to read at all, sought entertainment and instruction elsewhere, and what these classes read was surely not what the leaders of the Enlightenment had hoped for. What was here already discernible would become still clearer as the century neared its end: the polarization of the literary public sphere into an educated elite and a broader "popular" readership.

In opposition to this, the leaders of the Enlightenment held firm to the notion of a homogeneous public that could be shaped by criticism and expand without limit. Although their ideal never coincided with social reality, and the project of criticism ultimately shipwrecked on this very contradiction, it nevertheless possessed the power of a regulative idea and continued to have an impact on the literary life of the Enlightenment. The optimism concerning progress (shared by those who wanted to enlighten the people and who were pushing for popular literacy) corresponded with the postulate of criticism, that public literacy would be advanced through the holding of public discussions.

Habermas describes the institutional framework, within which "the private individuals who have joined to form a public" find themselves as a society, in the following terms: at least theoretically, "the measure of equality" rules.[29] Class, office, and privileges were stripped of their power; the only thing that counted was an argument's power to convince. Everything having to do with the common good was held worthy of discussion. Debate was not limited to the products of culture but also covered economic, legal, and theoretical problems. Even though membership in most of these circles was quite exclusive, each one nevertheless spoke on behalf of a greater public, presupposing the existence of a general interest. Clubs, coffeehouses, reading societies: all these were sites for discussing matters that concerned everyone. This sense of mutuality would become particularly clear when a society inaugurated a journal in order to bring its internal discussions to the attention of the public. The moral weekly *Der Patriot* (1724–26) emerged in this way from the "Society of Patriots" in Hamburg, a group of councilmen, businessmen, scholars, and writers who had met weekly since 1723. Their journal was addressed to their "fellow citizens in and around Hamburg."[30]

Of course, this idea of a "general public" and its "principally unbounded nature" (Habermas) must be qualified in one crucial respect: de facto, the concept encompassed only the small number of scholars, art lovers, and educated individuals—a social composition restricted to the bourgeois middle class and the lesser nobility. To take part in literary life, one had to be educated enough to understand the cultural products one read or saw and to follow the cultural discussion; and one had to be wealthy enough to be able to afford books and theater tickets. Yet by far the greatest part of the urban and rural population lacked both education *and* property, and it is this broad class which, toward the end of the century, formed a second, more diffuse public. Its members took a greater interest in entertainment and distractions than in discussions about literature, and publishers who understood the market soon began to respond to their taste.

The growing need for reading matter had an impact on the book market, which after 1764 experienced an incredible upswing in northern Germany, thanks to rapid commercialization. The trade-fair city of Leipzig became the center of the book trade. Business converted from an exchange to a cash basis, and the tasks of publishing and selling—earlier often done by the same outfit—became separate specialties.[31] Improvements in paper production and printing processes led to the "factorylike" production of books—to an "industry," as Kant soberly observed: "Book production is hardly an insignificant commercial branch in a community which (with respect to culture) is already far advanced, one in which reading has become an almost indispensable and universal need."[32] The figures alone tell the story: book production between 1763 and 1805 expanded at ten times the rate of the period between 1721 and 1763.[33] For the years 1780 to 1782, 1,582 works of the "fine arts and sciences" were registered: 648 poetry collections, 352 plays, 266 novels, 230 theoretical writings, and 86 "miscellaneous."[34] The enormous jump in novel production during the second half of the century makes it quite clear that the new entertainment literature was finding its consumers.[35]

The capitalization of the book market caused the Enlightenment to fall into contradiction with itself. On the one hand the rise in book production corresponded perfectly to the wishes of Enlightenment theoreticians: to educate the people through books and reading in order to combat superstition and prejudice. As a commodity, the book became generally accessible, losing its earlier aura of precious object: that anyone could buy and read it could only help to spread the Enlightenment—or so it was thought. On the other hand Enlightenment figures were forced to "look on in horror, as the dynamic of the autonomous market increasingly withdrew itself from their idealistic control."[36] The business of Enlightenment was turning into a business *with* the Enlightenment. Leaders initially responded to this challenge from the emerging entertainment literature with an intensification of criticism, later only with polemics.[37]

The development of a journal culture paralleled the differentiation and expansion of the book market. Indeed, it was only in the eighteenth century that literary journalism (and with it, criticism) emerged. The literary journals became the most important "medium of the Enlightenment":[38] in them, Enlightenment ideas were popularized and publicly discussed. As Robert Prutz noted early on, in their variety and liveliness they constituted the "monologue that the age held concerning itself."[39] The journals were often the only way to survive for freelance writers who had struggled to break free of dependency upon a patron or single employer. More than 3,000 periodicals were begun between 1730 and 1790; if, following Jürgen Wilke, we select from these the most important literary and critical journals relevant to our interests, we still find 323, of which 224 began appearing between the years 1766 and 1790 alone.[40] As early as 1768 Just Riedel, in his "Letters concerning the Public," praised the accomplishments of the literary journals: they provided a reading guide for the public, led it to the more demanding literature, and shaped its taste.[41] Moreover, they offered the bourgeois public a forum in which to gain clarity about itself and about the irrationality of the dominant relations in society. In Germany, of course, despite the political journals, the public sphere remained primarily literary-critical; as late as 1790 Georg Forster complained that there existed "no German public opinion" and that indeed this term was itself "so new, so strange . . . that everyone demands explanations and definitions."[42]

The scholarly journals, many of which had been founded during the seventeenth century, consisted primarily of monologues addressed to the republic of scholars. Patterned after Denis de Sallo's *Journal Scavans* (1665), the *Acta Eruditorum* (1682–1782) was published in Leipzig; it both reported on all areas of knowledge and reviewed new publications. As usual in the universities and among scholars, the Latin language was used. The first German language literary journal in Germany was the *Monatsgespräche* (1688–89), edited by Christian Thomasius.[43] Utilizing the conceit of a "conversation among good friends," it wittily and entertainingly instructed the reader about the latest from the world of the learned. As an educated man of the world after the French style, Thomasius also took an interest in belles lettres and reviewed eighteen literary works, an activity that the scholarly world at that time considered "unserious." His standards of literary criticism were still derived from Baroque poetics, yet as an *homme de bon gout* he no longer allowed himself to be restricted by pedantic rules.

The moral weeklies (following the English pattern) that soon began to emerge in Germany played a special role in the literary life of the early Enlightenment.[44] As in England, these developed out of bourgeois conversational circles, which turned outward to seek a wider, like-minded public. The themes dealt with in the essays were intended to stimulate discussion, which was continued in letters from readers: "In these journals, the public encountered itself as a theme of discussion."[45] In the case of Germany, it would seem premature to speak at this point of a "self-representation" of the bourgeoisie. Yet the research of Wolfgang Martens has convincingly shown that the editors, public, and themes of the moral weeklies all point unambiguously to the sphere of the bourgeoisie, not just in their criticism of the life ideal of courtly gallantry but also in the presentation of bourgeois life values as a universal ideal.[46] These values include industry, thrift, and prosperity; social virtues (such as concern for others), honesty, and a sense of duty; and education. As one example among many, Martens quotes from the fictive life history of the merchant Pasitiles: "Everything about his external appearance was decent, proper, and in good taste, but it was also totally bourgeois. He understood, and placed great emphasis upon, the distinction between bourgeois prosperity and a noble or courtly way of life."[47] The degree to which such practical guides to life (which often went on for many pages) corresponded to the bourgeois self-understanding can be estimated by the success of the *Patriot*, which at times attained the unheard-of circulation of 6,000 copies.

To the degree that one can speak of it at all, the literary criticism of the German moral weeklies was comparatively backward. It was still necessary to defend the usefulness of literature (and of reading) against those who despised such practices on religious grounds. While Joseph Addison, in *his* publications, had already relativized the judgments of the art experts and was defending the taste of the public, in the German weeklies one finds, at best, recommendations for reading or "beginning instruction in poetics" (Martens). Germany still awaited the formation of something that already existed in England— a literary public sphere. It was this contradiction (as we shall see) that triggered the opposition of Gottsched, who in his journals and in *Critische Dichtkunst* (1730) defended Classicist-rule poetics against those championing public taste.

In Germany, literary journalism and criticism began with Johann Christoph Gottsched. He was active in journalism for more than thirty-five years, founded five journals, and was a key figure in the establishment of several others. The very titles of many eighteenth-century journals signalize their concern to serve in the formation of taste or literary criticism. Besides the literary-critical journals (which supplied information, theorized, and debated about literature), others—emerging in tandem with the expansion of the book market—exclusively reviewed books.[48] By means of these critical journals "even the broader public found a way to enlighten itself through the critical appropriation of philosophy, literature, and art; indeed, they allowed the public to conceive of itself as the living process of Enlightenment itself."[49]

From Rhetorical to Rationalistic Criticism

Of course, judgments had been made about literature long before the eighteenth century. Poets, patrons, and scholars had held precise notions about what they expected from literature, and they inquired whether it was socially, ethically, and poetically appropriate to their respective situations. Their judgments were based on the rules of ancient rhetoric and poetics, and they took as models the works of ancient authors. Up to the start of the eighteenth century, literary taste appealed to this system of norms and its models: to justify a judgment, one drew upon authorities such as Aristotle, Cicero, and Horace, whose works were the subject of countless commentaries after the Renaissance. Poetry was considered a form of eloquence and therefore subject to the rules of the *ars bene dicendi,* even though (because of its ingenious mode of production and its fictionality) it was granted greater freedoms (*licentia*).[50]

Without exploring in greater detail the possibilities of rule violations (*vitia*), which could disturb the enjoyment and effect of literature, one can nevertheless class them under the central category of "appropriateness" (*aptum*). This category is concerned with both internal harmony of the verbal expression and external agreement with the given social situation. The older, rhetorical criticism (as we may label it in contradistinction to the modern form) had based itself on the capacity to judge the verbal-formal as well as the political-social appropriateness of literature (*judicium*). The *aptum* was "the true regulative category in the rhetorical system, and the basis of all valuations, mistakes, and licenses, of every rhetorical activity in theory and practice."[51] Hence, it was expected from oration and poetry that they would appropriately reflect their objects and also, in doing so, respect the social and political circumstances. Stylistic failures were believed to have an effect on the public, just as a misestimation of the public, the place, or the time could destroy the effect of even the finest speech. Thus, language and public, style and society, art and life were connected: they reciprocally conditioned each other. This is made even clearer in the theory of style (*genera dicendi*), which from the time of the Renaissance had set style and social class in relation. The Breslau "Primer" could still say in 1725: "Accordingly, a shepherd must not speak in too elevated and splendid a fashion, nor a hero too timidly or vulgarly; a melancholic must not speak too affectedly, nor a lover too sharply and sensually."[52] Verbal expression must correspond to social position and the situation: a shepherd should not use a sublime style, nor a hero a vulgar one. Thus the *genera dicendi* prescribed what was stylistically appropriate, and these style ideals corresponded to the social divisions of higher and lower. Naturally, this also held for literary genres such as pastoral poetry and tragedy. The estate structure of society demanded that tragedies involve only royalty and utilize the sublime style, which corresponded to the public significance of the action, whereas comedy was located among the commoners, in the private realm. Style, genre, and class were to be in harmony, and criticism kept watch to see that formal and social expectations did not fall into conflict. The rigid rule criticism of Classicism, which faithfully observed these precepts, corresponds to the representative public sphere, which presented itself equally in art and etiquette.

Goethe, who no longer felt himself bound by the domination of the "appropriate," once characterized it this way: "The various categories of literature are treated as though they were different societies, each having a specific, 'appropriate' procedure."[53] For him, the distinctions among genres were located within poetry itself, and only the artist could genuinely intuit them. What Goethe articulated as the demand for autonomy and an individualistic attitude in art marked a functional transformation of literature in the eighteenth century, which for the moment can be described this way: poetry had freed itself from the rules of ancient rhetoric and poetics; the requirements of the three-style theory and of representative *decorum* no longer corresponded to a society in the process of differentiation, one whose tastes were changing; the Beautiful was no longer what corresponded to the rules and was suitable at court but what was universally pleasing and stood up to public criticism. The embourgeoisement of literary criticism had begun.

At the intersection between old and new criticism stands Gottsched, who hoped to realize his bourgeois-pedagogical intentions by means of French Classicism. Gottsched's cultural-historical achievement on behalf of the Enlightenment is no longer disputed, and the polemical devaluation of his work from the perspective of Lessing and Goethe has yielded to a more objective assessment.[54] The only remaining point of dispute is Gottsched's historical position in the development of poetics and criticism. Some see him in the tradition of rhetoric and Baroque poetics;[55] others already interpret him as a bourgeois representative of a literary-critical public.[56] Researchers have not yet sufficiently attended to Gottsched's literary journalism (which comprises an imposing thirty-four volumes of his complete works); hence, he is scarcely known as a critic of literature.[57]

Advocates of the continuity thesis can cite a few things in their favor, especially when they evaluate Gottsched from the standpoint of Classical aesthetics or see his *Critische Dichtkunst* as still in the tradition of Baroque poetics. From this vantage, one can indeed find connections with the still-powerful rhetorical tradition, which is perhaps not so astounding for a thirty-year-old professor of "worldly wisdom and rhetoric." His views on the poet (*ingenium* theory), his concept of imitation (*inventio*), and his theory of style (*elocutio*) were still unquestionably obliged to rhetoric and Humanist poetics.[58] Yet one should do more than merely recognize the older elements; one must also see the new approach, which absorbs the old and thus allows for the *possibility* of something new. The very structure of the *Critische Dichtkunst* shows a clear division between rhetoric and poetics: the "first, general part" is still divided according to rhetorical categories; the second part contains a theory of genres that can no longer be so unambiguously aligned with the ancient tradition. Further, the book lacks the theory of verse that was obligatory in all Baroque poetics; Gottsched explicitly refused to equate the essence of poetry with the theory of rhyme and verse, as though "poetry were nothing more than a constrained eloquence." This move was aimed equally at the late Baroque methodical poetics and the predominance of rhetoric within poetics. Also, it would be pointless to seek in the old poetics a separate chapter on "taste"—which does appear in Gottsched's book. In this, as in the comments on the "judges of art," new tendencies were becoming discernible which are of particular interest to us.[59]

Gottsched understood his *Versuch einer Critischen Dichtkunst* to be both the foundation of a "fruitful, essential concept of poetry" and a guide for the critic. "Over the last several years, the practice of criticism has become more common in Germany than it had been hitherto," notes the preface to the second edition (1737), and "thus the true concept of criticism has become more familiar. Today even young people know that a critic or judge of art deals not just with words but also with ideas; not just with syllables and letters but also with the rules underpinning entire arts and artworks. It has already become clear that such a critic must be a philosopher and must understand something more than the mere philologists, who only collect variant texts, or (more plainly expressed) assemble vast lists of penmanship and printing errors."[60] This passage shows that the concept of criticism had by this time taken hold in Germany also and signified a quite specific judgment of literature, written by professional critics for an interested public. The respect accorded the learned critic was no longer inferior to that granted the philosopher, a fact that attests to criticism's claim of universality. The practice of criticism was no longer limited to philological textual criticism, which Gottsched deprecatingly referred to as "the judgment of splinters." Likewise, verse theory's fetishistic counting of words and syllables now fell beneath the critic's dignity. As Gottsched defined him in the preface to the first edition, "a critic is . . . a scholar who has acquired philosophical insight into the rules of the free arts and thus is in a position to rationally examine and correctly judge the beauties and flaws of any masterpiece or artwork he should encounter."[61] Clearly, Gottsched's intention was to provide a philosophical grounding for criticism.

The standards of the new criticism are set down in the *Critische Dichtkunst*. This work is not (as is still frequently alleged) merely a formalistic rule poetics; rather, it is a scientifically grounded theory of poetry and, as such, a basis for literary production and criticism. Substantively, it may display similarities to rhetorically based Renaissance poetics and at times even to poetry instruction manuals of the "poetry funnel" (*Poetische Trichter*) type. But the traditional rules receive a new foundation: they are subject to critical examination and must justify themselves before the court of reason. Appeals to the authority of Aristotle or the ideal character of ancient authors no longer suffice to ground a literary judgment. Rather, each work must correspond to rational rules that possess general validity. "For only to the extent that the rules of the ancients are in agreement with Reason can they claim unchanging validity. The authority of age alone cannot protect them from critical doubt."[62] This loss of authority, which began in France with the "Querelle des Anciens et des Modernes," is well illustrated by Gottsched's Homer criticism. The occasion is the famous description of Achilles' shield, a passage that Gottsched criticizes because Homer "did not pay the proper respect to probability." He criticizes the presentation of gods and heroes on the same basis, although with different conclusions, already familiar from the *querelle* discussion: while the presentation of humanlike gods is excused by the moral customs of the Greeks, the affects of the heroes violate human nature, "which has at all times been the same."[63] The rationalistic argument that all human beings are anthropologically equal, and the concept of naturalness grounded on this principle, become standards of criticism.

The rationalistic critique appeals to a rule system in conformity with reason, one claiming universal normative validity: "These laws, discovered and confirmed only after long searching and contemplation, now stand solid and undiminished." Gottsched's critical poetics gives the critic general criteria with which he can determine in the manner of a cognitive judgment what is beautiful. The beauty of an artwork rests on its perfect organization, which can be analyzed and objectively defined. "The exact relation, the order and symmetry of all the parts of which a thing is composed, is the source of all beauty."[64] Thus, the pleasure caused in the observer by a work of art is rooted in the work's purposiveness, which can be demonstrated by means of poetic laws. "After all, the rules are merely a healthy Reason's expression of what is proper, what is fitting (or not) in a work of art."[65] This still distantly recalls the rhetorical *aptum*, which oriented itself on what was socially proper, yet Gottsched places his emphasis on the regularity and completeness of the artwork. Judgments about art are no longer guided by the precept of *decorum* (which demanded conformity with the expectations of a courtly taste) but rather by a system of norms that are universally binding. Hans Mayer has compared this universal claim of the laws of poetics to the division of powers in Montesquieu's theory: "The artist belongs to the executive, the critic is the judge. But both are subordinate to the laws of the beautiful, a legislature whose laws claim eternal validity." It is the function of the critic to judge the concrete work of art according to the norms and rules of the genre, yet he himself has "no legislative power whatsoever."[66] Naturally, a criticism that appeals to unchanging laws and renders normative judgments always runs the danger of degenerating into dogmatism and formalism. Gottsched, like many who followed him, did not always successfully escape this danger, and with respect to several of his judgments (or misjudgments) of contemporary literature (such as his views on Friedrich Gottlieb Klopstock's *Messias*), the development of poetry went its own way without taking further notice of him.

Gottsched liberated literary criticism from its restriction to philological textual criticism and from tutelage to ancient authority. He thus turned it into a matter of relevance to *everyone* interested in literature, not merely to scholars. "True criticism," he said, was not "some sort of scholastic spelling bee, no ill-digested book reading," of relevance only to the scholarly world; rather, it was a meaningful occupation of interest to men of the world possessing taste. Therefore, criticism did not belong in the *Acta Eruditorum*, with its long-winded summarizing reviews, but in literary journals designed for educated laymen. Gottsched's literary journals served this goal. With them, he strove to advance "the acceptance of German literature and the purification of the taste of his fellow countrymen."[67] The learned critic speaks for the taste of the public, without allowing himself to be guided by it. He turns to the educated bourgeoisie and (as a judge of art, an expert, and a guardian) raises it to the level of literary maturity. A contradiction begins to be felt between judges of art and laymen, between rule criticism and judgments of taste. The competent critic, who bases his judgments on reasonable norms, will concede that laymen knowledgeable about art *could* render intuitive judgments of taste that would be in fundamental agreement with critical judgment, but the critic would *not* take his direction from the tastes of the existing public. The manner in which Gottsched resolved this tension (of which he was fully aware) within the framework of his theory deserves to be more fully discussed.

Even as it was first being articulated in Germany, the apparently impregnable position of rationalistic literary criticism was shaken by the initiation of the taste debate. Gottsched, who was an attentive observer of trends in foreign literary theory, could not evade this discussion and the degree to which it contradicted his system. Therefore he dedicated one chapter of his *Critische Dichtkunst* to the problem.

At its start he writes: "Recently much has been said and written about good taste. Certain poets have been said to possess it; some others apparently do not; and from all this the rule has been derived that a poet simply must have good taste. To explain this rule (after my own fashion), and to prove it, is the object of the present chapter." Very much after his own fashion, then, Gottsched proceeds to integrate taste into his own system—by neutralizing the concept altogether. Characteristically, he sets up the problem in a manner that suits his own purposes: he proceeds not from the good taste of the reader but from the "good taste of the poet" in order to commit him to the objective rules. The poet may "never take his direction from the taste of the world: that is, from the great mass or the uncomprehending mob. This many-headed idol often judges things in a most perverse manner. The poet must instead try to purify the taste of his fatherland, of his court, of his city."[68] Certainly, these sentences also express his nationalistic, pedagogical concerns, but when it comes to judging literature, Gottsched vehemently refuses to make concessions to the taste of the readers. The taste of the "narrow-minded people" would open the floodgates to subjective, arbitrary opinion, thereby endangering his concept of criticism. Therefore, he turns decisively against the sensualist aesthetic of effects, which had been gaining influence after importation from France and England. Indeed, the whole chapter seems to be Gottsched's answer to Jean Baptiste Dubos's position, since it is precisely the emotional response of the public that Dubos elevates to become *the* standard of criticism: "But whether a work is stirring and makes the right impression on us is something our own emotional responses can tell us better than all the treatises of the judges of art."[69] Against this "inner feeling" (which Dubos also calls a "sixth sense"), Gottsched argues from the standpoint of judgmental reason: "That taste is good which conforms to the rules which have been established by Reason."[70] That is Gottsched's antithesis to the sensualistic theory of taste.

He repeated his argument several years later in a critique of Addison, who in issue 592 of the *Spectator* makes fun of "rigid critics" who only form judgments according to rules, ignoring the approval of "the town": "Whatever dramatic performance has a long run, must of necessity be good for nothing; as though the first precept in poetry were, not to please."[71] Gottsched answers that for the true critic, the fact that a theater piece pleases its audience *cannot* be determinative: "He only examines whether a play is correct according to all the rules; having done so, it is a matter of indifference to him whether the play has been performed a hundred times or only once. . . . The true critic will always condemn a play that fails to observe the rules."[72] What is pleasing must prove itself before "judgmental reason" and be in agreement with the rules. Good taste is the prerogative of the poet, who structures his play in a fashion so faithful to the rules of the genre that it both produces the intended moral effect on the public and develops the public's good taste.

It would scarcely be original to heap scorn once again on Gottsched's objectivistic solution to the problem of taste. Moreover, it would be historically unjust. His theory is nothing less than one of the first attempts in Germany to overcome the antinomy between subjective pleasure and objective validity in judgments of taste. He believed that he had solved the problem in explaining that the pleasure given by the beautiful was derived from the completeness or perfection of the artwork. Good taste, he asserted, distinguishes itself in that it can recognize the beauty of a work of art "according to the pure perception of correctly judging Reason." The "touchstone" of the correctly perceived judgment lies "in the rules of completeness."[73] Taste judgments of educated laymen are thus taken quite seriously, even though (as intuitive, "merely" emotional responses) they are granted only a prescientific character. By means of the rules, good taste can be justified post facto and transformed into a cognitive judgment. The learned critic assumes this mediating function by demonstrating the beauty of particular works of art.

There are understandable reasons why Gottsched made concessions to the cultivated taste which he refused to make to the diffuse taste of the general public. Not only did the judgment of taste endanger the claims of rationalistic rule criticism, which (as opposed to the case in France or England) had just established itself in Germany. Germany also lacked the broad educated class that could have produced a consensus in public discussion of taste questions. The literary life still needed considerable development before this could happen, and a literary public had yet to emerge. By tying good taste to the rules of art, Gottsched made the law of taste generally binding. He thereby withdrew judgments of taste equally from the still diffuse public *and* from the claims of the aristocracy, which prided itself on having the final word in such matters. Both theoretically and sociologically, he assumed an intermediate position between the court-influenced ideal of taste and the aesthetic concept of taste, which (in terms of art theory) was to generalize the old concept and thereby socially neutralize it.

Between Leipzig and Zurich there were no fundamental differences of opinion regarding the conception of taste and the task of literary criticism. For all the divergences in the theory of imagery, in the estimation of the miraculous, or the power of the imagination (differences that had only grown sharper in the literary debates following 1740), it is impossible to overlook the points in common in the respective theories of literary criticism. Although Johann Jakob Bodmer and Johann Jakob Breitinger polemicized (in a journal they founded especially for the purpose) against Gottsched's rule dogmatism and his "monopoly on poesy and eloquence,"[74] both camps combatted the influence of Dubos's sensualistic aesthetic. Despite their other controversies, in this they were fully united.

Bodmer's standpoint within the taste debate is most clearly expressed in his correspondence with the Italian Count Conti. Three aspects in particular, because of their fundamental significance and their agreement with Gottsched's conception, should be stressed. Bodmer adopted the then usual distinction between sensual and "figural" taste. Their *tertium comparationis* was the fact that both could distinguish and compare; their *differentia specifica*—and he stressed this—was that sensual taste was passive (the "tools" of sense perception only "mechanically" perceived an impression), while the "metaphoric" taste was an active capacity of the soul. The latter distinguished "qualities of speech" and judged them "according to certain fundamental rules." The two types of taste were also distinguished by their differing objects: "The one is physical and materialistic, the other spiritual and active." The former acts upon the senses, the latter "through the understanding." While this discussion already silently introduces the opponent Dubos, the line of demarcation becomes even clearer when Bodmer characterizes taste as "a so-called sixth sense" and proceeds to criticize this conception. This sense, he points out, could be deceived, or it could be ambiguous. Experience alone speaks against its infallibility, for the very same work can be judged differently at different times. Yet a sensation so contradictory that it is praised at one time and damned at another can hardly serve as the foundation of taste. And it is of little help to appeal to the "unanimous agreement of the greater part," for the majority can be wrong and a minority right. Here, too, public approval is rejected as any sort of standard. It is less astonishing to see the Swiss reject it than Gottsched, for in Zurich there was still no public theater, and even wandering groups of players were denied permission to perform. The absurdities of the sensualistic judgment of taste could be effaced for Bodmer only by putting "reason and investigation" in its place. The deceptive senses must answer "before the judicial bench of Reason."[75] Thus, the sensualistic judgment of taste is rejected, and with it the judgment of the "majority." Only the educated specialist can judge the true value of an artwork, since only he is familiar with the "fundamentals of science." The scholar is the true judge of art.

Five years later, in his preface to Bodmer's treatise *Über die poetischen Gemälde der Dichter* (1741), Breitinger defined the "office of a proper critic" along these very lines. Although it initially appears as if the reader (and thereby the layman's judgment) is given a say, this "majority of voices" is more and more suppressed, until ultimately only the scholar is suited for "the office of judging and meting out punishment." He is the only one who can judge impartially and with an expert's knowledge, according to the "rules of art" and the "nature of the beautiful." More rigorously than other Enlightenment writers, Breitinger emphasizes the "punitive function of the critic" and binds judgments of taste to the laws of art. The critic should, "just like the police," improve through punishment and deter by setting examples. Here, criticism indeed becomes a "scourge for poetic sinners."[76]

The Taste Debate of the Eighteenth Century and Its Consequences

Gottsched's discussion of the taste problem makes sufficiently clear how greatly the taste debate complicated the situation of a still-fledgling literary criticism. Not only did the concept of taste place the rule-interpreting authority of the critics in question, thus rendering them uncertain (since judgments were always easier to make with the help of a canon of rules than on the basis of taste), but there was still no satisfactory explanation of how individual judgments of taste could be generally binding. Gottsched resolved this problem only provisionally and with difficulty, by subordinating mere emotional response to the correctly judging understanding; for him, good taste and agreement with the rules of art were identical. But this transformation of taste judgments into cognitive judgments soon proved problematic, as did the assumption of universally valid poetic laws. Above all, under the influence of the sensualistic aesthetics of effect, the public's right to have a say in the matter could no longer be dismissed. "Where taste is elevated to become the standard of aesthetic judgment, reception and consequently the role of the public become integral components of the theoretical debate."[77] Since 1750, two tendencies had been operating against the rationalistic rule poetics and its form of criticism, and favoring taste as a new basis of criticism: the rise of a new taste-bearing social group, and the emergence of modern aesthetics.

Even today, taste has the double meaning of enjoyment and judgment, whether of food or art. In spite of Kant, who distinguished culinary enjoyment (as the pleasurable) from the enjoyment of art (as the beautiful), this Janus-faced character of taste has persisted. Additionally, if one takes note of certain common figures of speech (for example, when we say that someone has taste or "that certain something"), one sees that the concept of taste extends over the whole of the culture that it represents and judges. Even for Immanuel Kant, before he made judgments of taste the basis of aesthetics, taste was a phenomenon of the "good society," a matter of how its members ate, dressed, and appointed themselves: "Taste is the capacity to choose with general validity."[78] Taste belongs to mankind's forms of social intercourse, and since its first formulation by Balthasar Gracian it has been a form of wise life practice. From the start it has been a "social phenomenon of prime importance."[79]

Now, one could once again raise the objection that the concept of taste is not really so modern, that it can be found in ancient rhetoric as innate *judicium* (Cicero) or *gustus* (Quintilian).[80] Cicero writes that the orator, both in his speeches and in his life, must respect that which is fitting and proper.[81] *Decorum* guarantees, as we have seen, a symmetry between the formal and social appropriateness of art. In representative art, artistic appearance must correspond to social existence. Thus, the *decorum* concept displays certain similarities to the concept of taste; in any event, the former anticipates the latter. Yet all the emphasis on continuity should not mask the fundamental discontinuity, for between *decorum* and taste runs the fault line separating the representative and the bourgeois conceptions of art: taste "connects and divides courtly and bourgeois culture."[82] If one wished to clarify the distinction typologically, one would want to compare the educational ideal of Baldassare Castiglione's *cortegiano* with that of Balthasar Gracian's *discreto*, whereby precisely the taste of the educated man of the world would be an important distinguishing characteristic. As long as one followed the ancient authorities and knew exactly what was beautiful and proper, one didn't actually need taste. Only as doubts began to arise concerning the ideal character of the ancients and as the once-compulsory classical rules were called into question could taste (as the emotion-directed judgment of art) make its appearance and become the basis of aesthetics and criticism. The taste of the bourgeois public no longer corresponded to the decorum of the courtly society, nor did it coincide with the prescribed theory of style. Gadamer sees the distinguishing characteristic of the modern judgment of taste precisely in the fact that it has liberated itself from class-based expectations and raised a claim to universal validity: "The history of the concept of taste follows the history of Absolutism from Spain to France and England, and coincides with the prehistory of the Third Estate. Taste is not just the ideal that a new society establishes. Rather, for the first time, matters are reversed: what was thereafter called the 'good society' forms itself under the sign of this ideal of 'good taste.' Members of the 'good society' no longer recognize one another and legitimate themselves by birth and rank. Fundamentally, this is now achieved by nothing other than their shared judgments or, better, by the fact that they alone knew how to elevate themselves above the narrow-mindedness of interests and the privateness of preferences and lay claim to true judgment."[83]

At the beginning of this development, which is still inseparable from courtly society, stands Gracian's *El Discreto* (1646), a treatise on the complete man of the world. To his art of worldly wisdom and life practices in the court environment belongs taste (*gusto*), the skill of making the right choice in all areas and situations of life. Thus Gracian's taste is not originally an aesthetic category but rather belongs to the realm of social and political life, where the individual must constantly prove himself. For this he needs mental acuity and keen judgment, qualities that cannot be based on the understanding or on learning. Therefore, neither are there behavioral norms or rules that make the correct choice easier. Everything depends on the intuitive ability of the actor. For Gracian, taste is a subjective capacity to judge, to choose in a generally valid manner, without orienting oneself by rules or concepts.

Between this social significance of the taste concept and its later aesthetic formulation lie numerous intermediate steps (in France, England, and Italy), none of which need detailed recounting here.[84] Yet structural similarities can be established between Gracian's taste and the aesthetic judgment, similarities that may explain the transposition of the taste concept into aesthetic theory.[85] The analogy between the two taste categories can be defined as follows: As subjective capacities to judge, both are free from any sort of oversight by social conventions or preestablished rules. The category of *decorum*, as the intersection of social and aesthetic expectations, is rendered powerless. Whoever acts or judges with taste does so intuitively, with a natural certainty that can be grounded only post facto, if at all. The correct choice is based on "instinct" or feelings, and yet the taste judgment claims to be a cognitive judgment. This tension between subjective feeling and objective claim becomes a central problem in the aesthetic discussion of the eighteenth century. Finally, aesthetic taste also resembles Gracian's in that an assured tradition with its rules no longer suffices to ground it.

In the seventeenth century, taste in Gracian's sense was still an expression of the aristocratic life style, and to the extent that it was applied to artworks, it was the prerogative of court culture, which articulated itself in the patron's judgment.[86] The court's claim to cultural leadership was first shaken when bourgeois critics were able to appeal to the taste of the public. This took place in England, where Addison supported himself on the taste of the "town," and in France, where Dubos made the applause of the *parterre* into the standard of criticism. In these countries, the bourgeoisie's demand for equality proclaimed itself, mediated by the judgment of taste. The "Beautiful" was no longer that which corresponded to the expectations of representative art but what (after public discussion) was found to be generally pleasing. Consequently, in grounding this judgment, one no longer made use of the classical rules but instead appealed to the feeling that the artwork triggered in the viewer.

In Addison's *Spectator* essays, the bourgeoisie appears for the first time as the key taste-bearing social group. As already mentioned, he concedes more authority to the approval of the public than to the rigid critics, who only judge according to rules. What they lack is taste, which Addison defines as a "Faculty of the Soul, which discerns the Beauties of an Author with Pleasure, and the Imperfections with Dislike." Only those with taste can perceive the Beautiful with pleasure. According to Addison, beauty can no longer be objectively defined except as a reflex of the perceiving subject. The viewer reacts to the Beautiful with surprise and concern: "We are struck, *we know not how*, with the Symetry [*sic*] of anything we see, and *immediately* assent to the Beauty of an Object, without enquiring into the particular Causes and Occasions of it."[87] Here we encounter that ominous *je ne sais quoi* typical of the judgment of taste: one feels something without being able to give it a name. The pleasurable sensations experienced in the presence of the Beautiful can no longer be reduced to "mechanical rules," which inevitably break down when confronted with the works of a genius; the prime example Addison adduces is Shakespeare. Addison's contribution to the taste debate is important in three respects: (1) he defines taste as subjective pleasure, thus making it an aesthetic problem; (2) since he puts into question the authority of rules in the act of creation and in the judgment of art, the genius problem becomes acute; and (3) taste for Addison no longer being the prerogative of an aristocratic or educated elite (of "fine gentlemen"), he pays far more attention to the taste of the public (the "town"), which no critic can any longer afford to ignore.

In France just a few years later, Jean Baptiste Dubos comes to wholly similar results. In his *Réflexions critiques sur la poésie et sur la peinture* (1719) he defines the purpose of art as emotionally moving the reader/spectator. Subjective response (sentiment) becomes the standard of the artistic judgment, for whether we are moved by a work of art is a matter of feeling, not understanding. The latter might post facto provide grounds for the pleasurable response, but the taste judgment is and remains a capacity of the feelings, which is why Dubos calls it the "sixth sense." Therefore, the judges of art (with all their rules) can no longer decide by themselves what is beautiful and pleasing: "The decision does not belong before the court of reason. Instead, reason must subordinate itself to the claims of feeling, as the more fitting judge in such disputes." If the taste judgment is to avoid falling victim to arbitrary subjectivity, its universal validity can be mediated only via the anthropological equality of human beings. This is exactly the approach taken by Dubos, however simple and vague it may seem: "Every individual can render judgments concerning verse and painting, because verse and painting are intended to affect the emotions, and these are common to all men." On the basis of a uniform human nature all men are deemed principally capable of rendering judgments of taste; however, Dubos does anticipate real differences in their *actual* taste judgments. Family background, milieu, education, and nationality influence taste, and even Dubos carefully differentiates himself from the "common mob."[88] In a similar connection, Peter Hohendahl has also established that for David Hume, "already at this early point, the contradiction of the bourgeois public sphere is indicated: it does not fulfill its own concept. The capacity to render a suitable judgment of taste (which in principle had been conceded to all human beings), is covertly restricted to the educated class."[89]

Dubos's aesthetics of effect has been described as a "revolt of healthy common sense" against classicist metaphysics and logic.[90] It is still more important to see in it evidence for the maturation of the bourgeoisie, which was no longer willing to accept outside supervision in matters of art. Dubos writes programmatically: "Our century is far too civilized to believe that it needs judges of art to tell it what to think of a given work which is intended to stir the emotions. One can read the work for oneself, just as thousands of others have done." The *parterre*, as Dubos labels the educated public, becomes the new taste-bearing social group in France, and its judgment attains a dignity that can no longer be ignored.[91] Moreover, one should not lightly underestimate the taste of the new public, nourished for over half a century on the works of French classicism. Even if Dubos ultimately cannot philosophically ground the general validity of the taste judgment and also must sociologically limit the circle of those who can enjoy art, he nevertheless demands a decisive right of participation for the educated public. For the critic this means that he now truly mediates between the work and the audience, reasoning openly before the public.

Until the middle of the eighteenth century, Germany lacked virtually all the preconditions necessary for taking over this advanced concept of taste from abroad: there was no Classical literature on which a national taste could have developed; Classicist literary criticism, against which the *new* concept of taste had arisen in opposition, was itself just in the process of emerging; and finally, the condition of society was still so desolate that until the middle of the century the concept of a public didn't even exist. One would look fruitlessly in Germany for an educated public like the one that interested itself in literature in England, or for a bourgeois *parterre* like the one that existed in France. Therefore, the taste discussion itself assumed completely different contours. The missing social backing was compensated for by pedagogical and theoretical efforts, so that out of the taste discussion there developed an independent "Science of the Beautiful" (*Baumgarten*), which philosophically grounded the judgment of taste.

Gracian's ideal of a man of the world as one possessing wide life experience and wisdom became known in Germany through Christian Thomasius. In his Leipzig lecture on the question "To what extent should we imitate the French in everyday life?" (1687), he is concerned not with the aping of French manners but with certain pleasing forms of living that have proved their worth in all life situations. For him, taste is that "certain something" which distinguishes the man of the world and is grounded in the sureness of his feeling. Thus, for Thomasius, it is a category of aesthetic life practice, one revealed in clothing, behavior, and particularly in conversation. This gallant educational ideal is recommended to the bourgeoisie as worthy of imitation.

The literary-theoretical discussion opens in 1727 with the "Examination of Good Taste," from the court poet of Saxony, Johann Ulrich König. König solves the problem that endangers the foundations of his poetics in a typically rationalistic manner, by demanding a "taste of the understanding." He specifically distinguishes between taste and judgment. Taste is the immediate emotional reaction to "sensual works," while judgment is an activity of the understanding that proceeds in a strictly logical fashion and leads to the truth: "People possessing more healthy understanding than they do learning judge by their feelings, and those who unite learning with a healthy reason judge on the basis of logical chains of reasoning. Thus, if this spontaneous emotional response, or taste, wishes to be considered good, the judgment must hold up to both logical examination and comparison to the rules of art."[92] Taste (and, consequently, the layman's judgment) is taken seriously, but it is only a lower form of knowledge, characterized by spontaneity and pleasure, that still needs to be converted to the clarity of a cognitive judgment. A precondition for having the sense of taste is, basically, that one already be in possession of good taste: that one be well-read, cultivated, and witty, so that one's provisional judgment need only be brought into alignment with the rules of the particular art. That is the German answer to the challenge of the sensualist aesthetic, which had protested against rules criticism precisely in the name of subjectivity and the public. Taste is once again tied down to rules and turned over to the judge of art.[93]

König and Gottsched after him did make some concessions to a feeling for art, but for them, ultimately, judgments concerning the Beautiful were rendered by the examining understanding. Taste is understood as a metaphorical variant of sensual taste, a concept which, thanks to its indeterminacy, no one knew quite what to do with. Therefore, taste was treated as a prescientific judgment that still needed to pass the test of a cognitive judgment. This treatment expressed both the uncertainty caused by the new category of taste and the struggle to fit subjective responses (which no one could deny) into the system of art. Such a solution soon proved to be no more than temporary. What was needed was a new theory of sensual knowledge, which would also philosophically ground the enjoyment of art. That is the moment that gave birth to modern aesthetics.

Its founder is generally held to be Alexander Gottlieb Baumgarten, whose *Aesthetica* appeared in 1750. But given the background of the taste debate, it is surely clear that many attempts were already being made in this direction. Were we to present the philosophical and historical context in more detail, it would also become clear how deeply Baumgarten himself was still indebted to rationalistic philosophy, which he enriched by adding the new discipline of aesthetics. To exaggerate somewhat, one could say that his object was to *complete* the rationalistic system by going on to investigate the lower cognitive faculties (such as feelings, imagination, taste) and integrating them into the system.

This systematization and "logicization of the taste problem"[94] is already expressed by the fact that he understands aesthetics as the analogue of logic. Even for Baumgarten, the higher cognitive powers are still more important and determinative, but sense knowledge takes its place next to the rational; it is granted a relative autonomy. The task of aesthetics is to recognize (by means of the senses) beauty as perfection. Beauty is thereby still bound to the work of art, but the aesthetic impression no longer needs to be converted into a cognitive judgment. Aesthetic experience possesses its own laws, which are similar to those of reason. "The aesthetic object unites individuality with uniformity [Gesetzlichkeit]. That is what is meant by the formula: Beauty is the perfection of sensual cognition."[95]

For our interests, the philosophical grounding of the new discipline is less important than the question of the *function* of taste. Taste belongs among the lower cognitive faculties, although this was evidently not enough to give it major significance for Baumgarten. Taste is the capacity to judge the perfection or imperfection of beautiful objects. In the sense of the rhetorical *judicium* it is the *presupposition* of criticism, but it is not constitutive for the foundation of aesthetics. Only later, in the thought of Baumgarten's student G. F. Meyer, did taste (as the "art of judging") receive practical aesthetic importance, because it distinguished between the beautiful and the ugly. For this, the power of judgment no longer needed to be subsumed under the understanding; it was established as an autonomous faculty. Yet it was still an open question how aesthetic criticism could raise a claim to universal validity. How could an individual judgment of taste be generalized? Kant was the first to give a satisfying answer to this question.

For the precritical Kant, taste is still what it was for Gracian and Thomasius, primarily a question of sociability and society: "Taste is sociable" and "the judgment of taste is a social judgment."[96] Kant, who personally laid great emphasis on clothing, deportment, and conversation, esteemed the life style of the man of the world, the man who knew how to behave in every sort of society and always maintained "good form." Even in the *Kritik der Urteilskraft*, one catches echoes of this in such passages as the following: "Empirically, the Beautiful is interesting only in society."[97] In a narrower sense, taste also means for Kant the sensual enjoyment afforded by eating and the capacity to compare and select foods: the good host is distinguished by knowing how to select with general validity. It is this sensual pleasure which, as the "merely" pleasurable, is excluded from the aesthetic realm in *Kritik der Urteilskraft*, since Kant's transcendental inquiry is specifically set up to disregard heteronomous influences on the taste judgment.

Kant's *Kritik der Urteilskraft* (1790; until 1787 it bore the working title "Critique of Taste") also asks, from a transcendental perspective, about the conditions of human knowledge, specifically about the binding nature of aesthetic judgments. He demonstrates that even emotional judgments regarding the Beautiful can be traced back to an a priori principle, and this allows him to resolve the contradiction between the subjectivity of taste judgments and their claim to objectivity. For our purposes, the deduction of the pure aesthetic judgment is of less interest than those aspects of the taste judgment that legitimate criticism and an aesthetic, critical public sphere.

Given his transcendental method, Kant took the subjectivity of taste more seriously than did many of his aestheticizing contemporaries, and he reacted testily to their rationalistic, psychological, or empirical pseudosolutions. From the very start, Kant emphasizes that the aesthetic composition of an object is "purely subjective"; even if one speaks of an object's beauty as though it were a quality of the object itself, nevertheless, "strictly speaking, beauty without relation to the feelings of a subject is nonexistent." With this, Kant turns against the rationalistic theory of taste, which post facto converted spontaneous taste judgments into cognitive judgments by binding the Beautiful to rules and demonstrating them on a beautiful object. For Kant, no objective principle of taste exists. For the same reasons, he rejects English empiricism, which explained taste judgments anthropologically, from the equality of human nature (David Hume), or investigated their psychological presuppositions (Edmund Burke). While with this mode of analysis one could indeed *begin* to understand "how judgments are formed,"[98] the method was inadequate for resolving deeper concerns: for example, why aesthetic judgments should be considered "unconditional." Thus Kant defends the subjectivity of aesthetic judgments, yet he is far from surrendering them to the merely subjective and pluralistic. Instead, he makes considerable effort to ground the universal validity of aesthetic judgments. How can the binding nature of aesthetic judgments be proved, and what consequences for literary criticism can be derived from the analysis of the taste judgment?

Taste is the "capacity to judge the Beautiful." Kant sees its distinguishing quality in the fact that judgments regarding the Beautiful are rendered "disinterestedly."[99] This "disinterested pleasure" of the taste judgment initially serves to distinguish the Beautiful from both the pleasurable and the good: both of the latter are bound to an interest, inasmuch as they desire to appropriate (or realize) that which they find pleasurable, whereas aesthetic pleasure is "purely contemplative." In the aesthetic state the viewer feels himself liberated from physical constraint and moral demands; the experience of the Beautiful yields a special feeling of pleasure, one that does not press for satisfaction. For this reason, all metaphysically or socially defined purposes are banished as heteronomous from the experience of art. The consequence of this declaration of art's autonomy is that taste is no longer the prerogative of noble patrons or an educated elite. What is beautiful is no longer what is suitable for the court or what corresponds to the rules, but what pleases universally and without interest.

From this derives the claim of the taste judgment to "subjective general validity." Since the taste judgment should not be dependent on the subjective inclinations or interests or other heteronomous grounds of determination, its validity for everyone can be presumed. Here, too, the distinction from the "merely pleasurable" quality of sensual taste is illuminating: in the judgment of foods, we all have our own tastes; when we judge the Beautiful, however, we do so not as private persons but rather as though all human beings should agree in our judgment. We impute the same pleasure to all. In this connection of subjective experience and generally valid assertion lies the true problem of the aesthetic judgment, for only when I communicate my subjective pleasure do I raise the claim that *everyone* would experience a similar feeling in the face of the Beautiful. When we judge, we speak "as though beauty were a quality of the object, and our judgment were purely logical,"[100] although it cannot be reduced to concepts or proved by rules. The person rendering a taste judgment transcends his private subjectivity: he communicates with others and thereby adopts a standpoint from which he speaks for all. That would be the social aspect of the taste judgment, which exists alongside its aprioristic grounding and which leads us back to art criticism.

The general communicability of the aesthetic mental state and the regulative idea of a shared aesthetic sense form the bases of practical art criticism. What else is criticism but a judgment of the Beautiful from a universal perspective? When rendering a taste judgment, the critic does not speak of his private feelings but rather proceeds on the assumption that the Beautiful affects everyone similarly. Since the taste judgment cannot be proved in the manner of a cognitive judgment, its validity can only "be labeled exemplary, i.e., a necessity of the agreement of all to a judgment that is seen as exemplifying a general rule which one cannot adduce." The critic can communicate his feelings generally only as though he were speaking for all, so that a consensus appears possible. His judgment demands that everyone assent to it and that there exist a shared aesthetic sense (*sensus communis aestheticus*).[101] For Kant, this shared sense is only a regulative idea, which derives from the taste judgment's claim to necessity and universal validity. Since no objective principle of taste can be adduced, according to which what is beautiful might be defined once and for all, Kant presents mankind with the task of *realizing* the shared aesthetic sense as a cultural ideal.

Three things are demanded of the critic, who always proceeds inductively: "(1) He must think for himself; (2) he must think on behalf of everyone else; (3) he must at all times think in a manner that is self-consistent." The first maxim is one that is constitutive for the Enlightenment and demands unprejudiced thinking. It is aimed at that sort of passive thinking which accepts being watched over by church and state. According to Kant, the only remedy against such a comfortable way of thinking (which even in matters of taste subordinates itself to fashion or foreign models) comprises thinking for oneself, criticism, and the public use of reason. The second maxim is aimed at narrow-minded thinking, "incapable of going beyond the private, subjective conditions of judgment."[102] This way of thinking judges in a dilettantish manner, as though the Beautiful were merely pleasurable, enticing, or useful; it never elevates itself to the "universal standpoint" that is necessary for the judgment of the Beautiful. The "consistent manner of thinking," finally, which Kant assumes is the most difficult requirement to satisfy, presumes that the other two have already been reached. It is this level that makes possible the communication of one's aesthetic responses.

Thus, Kant's theory of taste again confirms the intentions of the Age of Criticism, inasmuch as he liberates taste from oversight by court, church, or state and makes it a matter of concern for everyone. The concept of taste is thereby socially neutralized and aesthetically universalized. "While it is true that the individual taste judgment of the critic is subjective, it nevertheless legitimates itself before the forum of readers, who have joined to form a public sphere."[103] The critic reasons openly before the public and on its behalf, and he stimulates public discussion, the goal of which is to arrive at an aesthetic consensus.

Lessing as Critic and Polemicist

Attentive contemporaries recognized that Gotthold Ephraim Lessing's literary arrival marked the start of a new epoch of literary criticism. "A new critic has appeared on the scene," reported Johann Georg Sulzer in 1751 to Zurich, "but he still seems a bit too young."[104] Johann Gottfried Herder wrote of Lessing in his 1781 obituary essay: "I believe that no recent writer has had more impact in Germany concerning matters of taste and the finer basic judgment of literature than Lessing."[105] And in 1804 Friedrich Schlegel wrote: "Everything that Lessing did, attempted, or desired can be most accurately embraced by the concept of criticism."[106] In the Age of Criticism, his significance for practical literary criticism was equivalent to Kant's significance for theory.[107] Between the compulsive systematization of rules and dogmatic Aristotelianism on the one hand and a scientific aesthetics on the other, Lessing developed a new literary criticism, one that did equal justice to both the principles of art *and* the emotional responses of those who enjoyed it. The sort of transformation that was wrought in the literary-theoretical discussion after 1750 and the consequences it had for literary criticism can best be recognized in hindsight. In 1766 Lessing introduced his *Laokoon* with the following words:

The first to compare painting and poetry was a man of fine sensibility, who noted that both arts had a similar effect on him. Both, he found, present to us absent things as though they were present, and appearance as though it were reality; both deceive, and both deceptions are pleasant.

A second sought to penetrate to the interior of this enjoyment, and he discovered that in both cases it flowed from the same source. Beauty, whose concept we first derive from physical objects, has general rules that can be applied to various things; to actions and ideas, as well as to forms.

A third, who pondered the value and the distribution of these rules, noted that some tended to be more dominant in painting, others more in poetry; and that therefore with the latter rules, poetry could assist painting with explanations and examples, and for the former rules painting could help poetry.

The first man was a connoisseur in the true sense; the second, a philosopher; and the third was a judge of art.[108]

This passage shows clearly how far the judgment of art had removed itself from Gottsched's standards of criticism. The arts were now to be judged according to their effects on the emotions of the art lover, and no longer by objectivistic rules. Thus, the sensualistic aesthetics of effects had triumphed over Classicist rule poetics in Germany, too. But unlike the situation in France and England, where taste could already appeal to a bourgeois public, in Germany the layman's judgment received a *philosophical* justification. The philosophers from Baumgarten to Kant grounded the "inwardness of enjoyment," asked after the conditions of possibility of sense knowledge, and established "general rules" for the Beautiful. It was the critic who mediated between the emotional responses of educated layman and aesthetic principles; it was the critic who "applied himself to the individual case" and universalized the subjective feeling in order to produce a consensus.[109] In all this, the critic was both an advocate and an educator of the public.

Lessing was less a theoretician of the "beautiful sciences" than he was their attentive critic. He was more interested in the practical question of the possible *effects* the arts could have than in their systematic theoretical grounding. He followed the taste debate without taking part in it, just as he presupposed the results of aesthetics without studying the subject in detail. The various aesthetic theories—up to and including Kant's—were too little occupied with the general theory of art; they scarcely concerned themselves with artistic practice and most definitely not with problems of genre. But it was precisely these things that interested Lessing as a critic, one who inquired into the artistic possibilities of the different genres, their means and effects. *Despite* his theoretical treatises on literature and art, Lessing never desired to be a systematician of aesthetics and poetry. Thus, having just concluded a genuinely lasting contribution to the theory of the bourgeois drama, he reminds the reader of the *Hamburgische Dramaturgie* "that these pages contain nothing in the way of a system of drama." Lessing is a critic, even in (and precisely in) the *Hamburgische Dramaturgie,* a point that is generally overlooked. As such, he wishes neither to prescribe for the dramatists how they should write their plays nor to force his own taste on the public. Rather, he conceives of his theater criticism as *fermenta cognitionis,* the yeast of knowledge, meant to stimulate independent thinking.[110]

As a judge of art, Lessing is neither a legislator nor a disciplinarian for the poets. He examines only the individual work, to see whether it has achieved the effects belonging specifically to its genre. As his "Literary Letter" 105 states: "It is the duty of the critic, whenever he undertakes to judge a work, to concentrate on that particular work alone . . . and to simply tell us candidly what sort of concept one can justifiably derive from this present work alone."[111] Without wishing to conclusively identify Lessing's literary criticism with the inductive method, we can at any rate provisionally distinguish it from the deductively operating rationalistic rule criticism.[112] The distinction between inductive and deductive methods doesn't say very much by itself, of course, especially not when they are stylized into a pair of ahistorical, opposing forms of thought. But in connection with the taste problem, inasmuch as it was important for criticism in the eighteenth century, the distinction has a historical and heuristic function: precisely in the case of the taste judgment, the issue is how the feeling of art in the face of the beautiful object can be generalized. For the critic who speaks on behalf of the public, this is the true problem, since with his judgment he raises the claim to articulate and ground the emotional responses of the layman and to produce a general consensus.

That Lessing was aware of this problem is illustrated by the beginning of a fragmentary reflection from the year 1767, headed "The reviewer need not be better able to do that which he criticizes":

> To criticize means to let one's displeasure be known.
> Given this displeasure, either one can appeal to pure emotional response, or one can support this response with reasons.
> The man of taste does the former; the judge of art does the latter. Which of them must understand how to make that which he criticizes better?
> One is not master of his feelings! but one *is* master over what he finds to say. When a man of taste is displeased by something in a poem or painting, need he first go out and become himself a poet or painter before he may say: that displeases me? I find my soup too salty: have I no right to call it too salty unless I am able to cook? What are the reasons of the judge of art? Conclusions that he has drawn from his own feelings, compared among themselves and with the feelings of others, and led back to the fundamental concepts of the Perfect and the Beautiful. I can't see why a man should be more reticent about his conclusions than he is about his feelings. The judge of art not only senses that something displeases him; he also adds his own *because*. And this *because* should oblige him to be able to do better? This very *because* ought rather to *exempt* him from having to do better.[113]

The distinction between the "man of taste," who appeals "to pure emotional response," and the "judge of art," who "supports his feelings with reasons," is already familiar. Therefore what is of interest here is to observe how Lessing proceeds in grounding the response of the judge of art and then universalizing it. That Lessing relieves the critic of the know-it-all task of performing as the artist's conscience is clear from the title and content of this brief fragment. It simultaneously rejects the deductive method of normative criticism, if for no other reason than that Lessing proceeds (after the manner of the aesthetics of effect) from the emotional responses. The critic goes beyond the intuitive responses of the layman's judgment by grounding his feelings and communicating them generally: he is the master with the right to say what he feels. He imputes his judgment to the general public, on whose behalf he speaks, and thereby stimulates public discussion. In brief, as a critic he assumes the standpoint of the shared aesthetic sense that needs to be made a reality.

This still does not answer the question of *how* the critic gets from the emotional response to the judgment, which of course cannot be a judgment of the understanding. Lessing wishes to draw conclusions from his own feelings, which he has "compared among themselves and with the feelings of others," and then lead these conclusions back to the "fundamental concepts of the Perfect and the Beautiful." That is less discursive than Kant's formulation and stands even closer to Baumgarten than to Kant, yet it corresponds to the inductive method and agrees with Lessing's actual practice. The comparison and differentiation of emotional responses is the presupposition of every judgment of taste. With the inductive method, which must proceed empirically, the general conclusions are first arrived at from the comparisons. Similarities and distinctions can be determined in a comparativist manner, which allow orders and genres to be recognized and lead to an exemplary universal validity.

Finally, Lessing also considers the judgment of others: that is, he refers to the ideal totality of the literary public sphere. One can usefully speak with Keller of a "triple division" as the fundamental structure of Lessing's criticism: "His criticism aims at the most concise example, which is then made the basis of the critical comparison and judgment."[114] This procedure not infrequently leads to prolix digressions, such as those in the *Hamburgische Dramaturgie*, in which, for example, he compares Voltaire's *Merope* with Maffei's original and finally discusses the ideal form of Euripides.[115] Using an inductive, comparativist approach, Lessing ultimately arrives at a judgment that formulates his ideal; this contains the concept of a genre, which he passes on to his contemporaries as a model worthy of discussion.

The "fundamental concepts of the Perfect and the Beautiful"—particularly with respect to literary genres—were of course already given through tradition and contemporary discussion. It is true that Lessing the critic orients himself toward the individual case, but that by no means excludes the possibility that prototypes, conceptual ideals, and generic expectations prejudice his criticism. Yet unlike Gottsched, with his objectivistic rules system, Lessing had no fixed system of norms by which he measured every work of art. He preferred to make concessions to the genius rather than force him onto the Procrustean bed of rules poetics. "In textbooks the genres are separated from one another as exactly as possible," Lessing once wrote, "but when a genius, with higher intentions, lets several of them flow together into a single work, one should forget the textbook and just look to see whether these higher intentions have actually been realized." Dogmatism and hair-splitting are alien to Lessing. Yet at the end of the *Hamburgische Dramaturgie* he distances himself from the genius mania of critics who want to place themselves above *all* rules.[116]

What precisely was Lessing the critic's stance vis-à-vis rules of art? He criticized them to the degree that they rested solely on the authority of tradition and convention, and he utilized them to the degree that they were in accord with nature and reason. "It is true that I wished quickly to have done with Aristotle's authority," he wrote in his discussion of catharsis, continuing in the true rationalistic manner, "if I had to give up on his principles." In the same sense he polemicized against the "tyrannical rules" that the French followed only outwardly, without fulfilling their spirit.[117] Above all, he sharply criticized those rules that transposed the conventions of the court and traditional class society onto poetry. Thus he attacked the class limitations on tragedy and the courtly tone of conversation in drama; both offended against naturalness and were therefore unsuited for moving the emotions of an audience: "I have long been of the opinion that the court is precisely the *wrong* place for a poet to study nature. When pomp and etiquette have made human beings into machines, it is the job of the poet to turn these machines back into humans." When even kings appeared on the stage as mere human beings, acting privately instead of in their official capacity in order to move the public, then it became quite clear that the standard of "naturalness" is of bourgeois origin. Lessing relied on rules only after first critically testing them to see whether they corresponded to his notion of a bourgeois literature. Yet the normative aspects of Enlightenment poetics interested him far less than those having to do with the aesthetics of effect, to which the formal means are logically subordinate. Thus he was not so much concerned with the formal regularity of the tragedy as with its purpose: "The dramatic form is the only one in which pity and fear can be aroused." When Gottsched reduced the objective of the drama to the presentation of a moral thesis, Lessing countered by pointing out that this would hardly be worth all the expense of creating and operating a theater; an Aesopian fable would suffice. It was not enough for a work to have noble intentions; it must also produce those responses "appropriate to it, by virtue of its genre." The following passage indicates how important he found economy of form and the proportionality of means to ends: "Why all the thankless work of the dramatic form? Why build a theater, stitch together costumes for men and women, torture their memories, invite the whole city to descend on a single place? Why all this effort, if all I want to achieve with a work and its performance is to bring forth a few of the emotions which anyone could have more or less experienced reading a good short story at home?"[118] Obviously, Lessing believed that it *was* worth the effort, and that no literary institution had a more important public function than the theater. He therefore strove through his criticism to help the theater onto its feet and to win over a still largely indifferent public.

Of course, this describes Lessing's critical method only in its most general form; the description would fit many Enlightenment critics in the period following 1750. The quality that made him unique remains to be specified. Lessing's criticism was characterized by Friedrich Schlegel as "a crushing eloquence" and by Walter Jens as "rhetorical didacticism"; both saw him as a speaker who "constantly formulates for the public,"[119] who wanted to convince, who sought someone whom it was *worthwhile* to dispute. A feel for the public (Schlegel also called it "popularity") and polemic are the essential characteristics of Lessing's criticism, qualities that make it as lively as it is combative.

Anyone who relies on the sensualist aesthetic, who as a critic speaks on behalf of the general feeling and hopes to educate his public, must write rhetorically and in a generally understandable style. Here Lessing was a master from the moment he made a name for himself as a young man in the reviewer's trade.[120] It is precisely in his critiques that the dialogical moment in Lessing's thought and writing emerges most clearly. He argues with the reader, formulates objections for him, or interrupts himself in the middle of imposing on the reader a long-winded digression; he is always aware that he is speaking before a public. When in 1759 he edited (together with Moses Mendelssohn and Friedrich Nicolai) the *Briefe, die neueste Literatur betreffend*, his introduction styled the review as a collection of letters to a "meritorious officer" who had been wounded in the Seven Year's War. Their putative intent was to "fill in the gaps which the war has left in the officer's knowledge of the latest literature," and to distract him from his boredom and disgust over political events with a more pleasant diversion.[121] The form of the reviews corresponds to this fictive situation: utilizing the fabricated addressee, the critics speak to the reader as a friend, in a familiar, conversational tone.

The "prospectus" to the *Hamburgische Dramaturgie* indicates how important Lessing found the public's right to a say in these matters and how strongly he battled to create a general level of taste. He expected that the public would not merely passively enjoy the theater but would also contribute to its improvement: "The public's voice should never go unheard; its judgment should never be listened to without submission." Though Lessing was ultimately to complain that the public had contributed nothing to the creation of a national theater, this expressed the bitterness of a disappointed critic who had hoped for a bourgeois theater and an ideal public.[122] The real public behaved differently than he had expected. Even in Hamburg the public interested in literature scarcely extended beyond the narrow class of the educated.

Wit and polemical rigor made Lessing's criticism famous and notorious in equal measure. Friedrich Schlegel, who appreciated such qualities, pointed out early that "Lessing's temperament was thoroughly polemical, that his entire career as a writer, from the first essay to the last incomplete fragment, whatever the subject or outward form, had a wholly polemical tone and direction, and the low esteem in which he held those for whom the polemic was neither an art nor a science: all this is so obvious in everything we have from him that it would be superfluous to spend another word on the subject."[123] For Schlegel, Lessing the critic and polemicist was clearly more important than Lessing the poet. Even if one cannot follow him in this judgment, what he wrote on Lessing's polemical style still provides one of the best characterizations of its subject, without thereby having said everything about him.

For Lessing, criticism was a sort of "mental gymnastics" (Mendelssohn), and the polemic was its ideal form. "We seem to forget," he once wrote, "that the Enlightenment owes not a few important points to pure contradiction, and that human beings still wouldn't agree about *anything* if they hadn't even gotten to the point of *arguing* about *something.*"[124] Enlightenment as contradiction, and polemic as method: this is perhaps the most precise characterization of Lessing's criticism. Even so, the polemical tone disturbed more tender minds, who feared that such criticism would destroy the enjoyment of art and harm the genius. Thus the first reviewer of the *Hamburgische Dramaturgie* offered the reproach that "our theater is at still too tender an age to bear the monarchical scepter of Lessing's brand of criticism."[125] "But that's altogether wrong!" Lessing would reply, for it was the intent of his criticism to *promote* the still-young German literature. Following his "scale for the judge of art," he dealt gently with young talents, encouraged writers of middling talent, and was implacable only against famous poets or those held to be such. Lessing viewed his criticism—and that includes his polemic—as indisputably productive. In a discussion of method he cited a "little saying" from Lactantius: "Primus sapientiae gradus est, falsa intellegere; secundus, vera cognoscere": essentially, to recognize and refute what is false for the sake of truth. Thus he recommended to the writer that he "first seek out someone with whom he can argue: by this means he will gradually get into the subject matter, and the rest will take care of itself." That sounds arrogant, but it was not offered lightly; in fact, it perfectly captures Lessing's approach, which is inductive and dialogic. He needed a sparring partner with whom he could trade a few punches in order to help him get into the material. Those whom he chose as conversational partners or opponents offered a starting point: for him, polemic was just a means to reveal the heart of the matter in dispute and to advance toward new insights. As he remarked in his theory of fables: "I would have learned little from the great judges of art, if I had found them all to have been perfectly correct."[126] The authorities were in any case to be examined critically, and the maturity of the Enlightenment writer also received confirmation, if necessary, in the polemical, independent thought that had left the classroom. The rigor and radicality of Lessing's argumentation was an act of enlightenment and of public reasoning.

Lessing's polemical tone is therefore *not* just a stylistic feature that can be formally analyzed. It is rather to be explained (as Koselleck and Habermas have demonstrated) by the political and social situation of the German Enlightenment. The separation (compelled under Absolutism) between the state-political sphere and the private-moral sphere necessitated criticism's restriction to the apparently apolitical realms of philosophy, art, and literature. Yet the criticism of the politically powerless intelligentsia always displayed a tendency to transgress these narrow boundaries, even offering moral-political criticism under the cover of literary criticism. Lessing's criticism can be taken as representative of this compensatory form of thought. When at the end of the *Hamburgische Dramaturgie* he complained of the absence of a national consciousness among the Germans, who couldn't even manage to create a national theater, he continued in the style of that moral criticism: "I am not speaking of the political constitution but purely of their moral character," which (he then sarcastically concludes) "apparently consists of their not wishing to have one."[127] He forgoes political criticism (which in any event would never have gotten past the censor) and limits himself to literary-moral criticism, which nevertheless is intended politically. Since the relations of social domination cannot be criticized, much less effectively changed, it is necessary to settle for alternative actions of the mind—which, of course, also helps account for the polemical sharpness of his criticism.

Conservative opponents of the Enlightenment understood this perfectly well, and they called out early for preventive measures from the censor. The reaction of Hamburg's Chief Pastor Johann Melchior Goeze, in his capacity as the authorized defender of Christian truth, is sufficiently well known; less so is the attempt of Johann G. H. von Justi to thwart publication of the *Literaturbriefe*. In a "most subservient advertisement" in 1761 he brought it to the attention of the king of Prussia that "the authors of the Letters Concerning the Latest Literature, in disregard of the censorship laws, have (in the most irresponsible and discourteous way) mistreated the most famous learned writers in every land." Under the "pretext of criticism," the letters "publicly" attack writers like Voltaire, Rousseau, Gottsched, von Moser, Cramer, and the king himself, as if there were "no censor" in Prussia. Nor was religion spared from their "tasteless mockery," a state of affairs for which probably a "certain Jew named Moses" was said to be responsible.[128] In March 1762, Nicolai did in fact receive a ban on publication bearing the royal seal: the *Literaturbriefe* had been found to be "a book against religion and the state." When he complained to Attorney General Uhde (since he indeed *had* presented the "Letters" to the censor for approval), he received the answer that it was known what "unforgivable and highly punishable things were contained therein." The items referred to were probably Lessing's critique of the *Nordischer Aufseher*, a moral weekly edited by Danish Court Chaplain Johann Andreas Cramer, and Mendelssohn's critique of Friedrich II's poetry.[129] Both reviews were attributed to Moses Mendelssohn, who a short time later also had to justify himself before Uhde—which, in his situation as a protected Jew (*Schutzjude*) in Berlin, was incomparably more dangerous. Yet the threats remained a gesture, and the ban was lifted five days later. This episode may suffice to indicate how dangerous the Berlin Enlightenment writers were considered to be and how opponents like Justi and Uhde saw fit to deal with them. In retrospect, Nicolai saw it as necessary that the Enlightenment writers undergo these tribulations in order to "advance and defend freedom of thought, through which better opinions could be introduced."[130] If this connection between criticism and the public sphere is ignored, the function of literary polemic and its political content is also misunderstood.

Literary criticism not only reviewed the latest literature; it also examined the value of tradition and engaged the influences of neighboring cultures in order to determine their function for contemporary literature. In the moment of criticism, the demands of the present became so important in the judgment of works of the past that new literary positions and a new canon resulted from the engagement. The critic thereby became a critical historian who scrutinized authorities from the past and the exemplary status of foreign models. In this trait, too, Lessing typifies the Enlightenment. Even when relying on tradition (for example, Aristotelian poetics), he utilized it for something new: namely, for a "bourgeois, humanitarian theory of drama that owed much to 18th-century ideas."[131] Lessing's critique of French Classicism must also be understood in this way. It was precisely with the "French scribblers," particularly Voltaire and Pierre Corneille, that he fought pitilessly, challenging the notion that their dramas should have exemplary status for German literature. His polemic was aimed at fundamental matters, even if the prestige of some of the persons he trained his sights on occasionally sustained damage. He wished to prove that a century of admiration for Corneille had "probably been without foundation." Presenting the Germans with the socially obsolete relic of a foreign court theater culture, as Gottsched had done, meant imitating the culture of another nation and society instead of creating an independent, contemporary theater. Lessing's criticism is therefore to be understood as historical and functional throughout but by no means "chauvinistic"; he explicitly emphasizes in section 81 of the *Hamburgische Dramaturgie*: "Now, do I mean by this that no Frenchman is capable of writing a truly moving tragic work? . . . I would be ashamed of myself if such a thought had so much as crossed my mind. . . . For I am quite convinced that no single people has received any spiritual gift to a higher degree than the other peoples on Earth."[132] His critique of Voltaire was aimed at the epigonal dramatist, not the historian and leader of the Enlightenment. He praised the "clear and pure Diderot," whose plays he translated in 1760, and ranked him as a modern theoretician on a par with Aristotle. Significantly, he did *not* criticize the *comédie larmoyante*, out of which developed the bourgeois tragedy. Only Corneille, with his "Discours" of 1660, gave him a sufficient occasion for polemical refutation and the development of his own conception of a bourgeois drama.

Lessing dealt similarly with Gottsched, whose struggle on behalf of a "German stage" he supported (and later carried on himself) but whose rule dogmatism he criticized—not for the first time—in the notorious seventeenth "Letter on Literature" (1759). In 1751, as the young editor of the *Berliner Privilegierte Staats-und Gelehrten Zeitung* (later the *Vossische Zeitung*), Lessing was publishing a monthly supplement of "The Latest from the Realm of Wit," containing contributions and reviews written almost entirely by himself.[133] Along with reviews of Rousseau, Charles Batteux, Diderot, and Klopstock, one also finds there a scathing critique of the second edition of Gottsched's "Poems," which already displays the previously unheard-of tone of Lessing's criticism: "The first part is old: indeed, only the order is new, which would do honor to the most severe court etiquette." Gottsched's numerous dedicatory poems are termed *Jubeloden* (exultation odes), and the evaluation of the "poetical spirit of the Herr Professor" closes on the same jeering note. The poems cost 2 thaler and 4 groschen: "The 2 thaler pay for the laughable parts; the 4 groschen just about cover what's worthwhile in the volume."[134]

However, his early turn against Gottsched by no means leads Lessing into the camp of the Zurich opponents. On the contrary, as early as 1749 he had also taken aim at that school in the didactic poem "An den Herrn Marpurg." This poem, "concerning the rules of science, particularly poetry and music," is a major attack on the dictates of rule poetics, which strangle the "spirit and fire" of poetry. It reads like a settling of accounts with Gottsched's still-dominant conception of poetry, against which enthusiasm and feeling are set in opposition. Yet surprisingly, it is not Gottsched's name that is mentioned, but Bodmer's: "O, poor poetry! Instead of enthusiasm and a sense of Gods housed in one's breast, rules are now held to be enough. Just one more Bodmer, and a lot of pretty nonsense shall fill the minds of the young poets, instead of spirit and fire." This only confirms what we asserted earlier about the literary criticism of the Swiss: it is no less rationalistic than that of Gottsched. As further proof one could draw on Bodmer's preface to Breitinger's *Critische Dichtkunst* (1740) to show that their theory of poetry and criticism "despite some appearance to the contrary, is not sensualist but intellectualistic."[135]

At the start of the 1750s, this "double front" (Karl Guthke) procured independence and authority for the young critic Lessing, so that by 1754 he was considered a "famous writer" whose critical judgments Leipzig and Zurich grudgingly had to take into account. Christoph Karl Reichel, a student of Gottsched, was of the opinion that contempt would be "the best punishment for a young upstart like Lessing."[136] But such tactics were already inadequate as a means for getting at him; he and his Berlin "sect," as Bodmer was forced to realize, had already firmly gotten the upper hand. By the middle of the 1750s Lessing, Mendelssohn, and Nicolai had long since assumed the heritage of Leipzig and Zurich. With their new review journals they dominated criticism and were shaping the general taste.[137] "The authors of the Letters on Literature caused Gottsched to be forgotten along with Bodmer"; as Justus Riedel put it in his letters "Über das Publikum," "they alone hold the scepter, and the other judges of art are either laughed at, or they devoutly repeat the opinions dictated by their masters."[138]

As Riedel wrote these sentences in 1768, that epoch of literary criticism was already coming to an end; at least, a "fermentation of taste"—as Lessing called it—was endangering the achievements of Enlightenment criticism, which was now distrusted in the name of genius. Lessing (in his turn) took grudging account of this new criticism and polemicized against it at the end of the *Hamburgische Dramaturgie:* "Now, thank heavens, we have a generation of critics whose best criticism consists of—having made all criticism suspect. 'Genius! Genius!' they cry. The genius transcends all the rules! What the genius does *is* the rule!" Even worse, these critics consider *themselves* geniuses, or at least the equals of geniuses. Lessing himself had made use of the "genius" (and that exemplary figure, Shakespeare) against French Classicism and Gottsched, in order to protect art from dogmatic and social rigidification: "The genius laughs at all the lines so exactingly drawn by critics," he wrote at the start of the *Hamburgische Dramaturgie,* in order to add later, as the reason, "because he carries the test of all rules within himself." Now the concept of the genius was being turned against Lessing's *own* criticism: reasoning was easier than inventing for oneself; rigorous criticism harmed the genius; and the German theater could be more swiftly improved through encouragement or example than through overly demanding criticism. Such were the arguments of the countercritique, with which one stood protectively before the genius to defend his irregularities. But for Lessing, this appeared to be merely a position complementary to Gottsched's, "the edge of another abyss"; he rejected it vehemently, for it entailed nothing less than "arrogantly forfeiting all the experience of the past, and demanding of the poets that each one reinvent the whole art by himself."[139] For Lessing, "genius" is not synonymous with an absence of rules or with the new beginning of a cultural revolution; rather, the genius guarantees art's continued development at the highest level of his age. Thus Lessing was skeptical of the beginning genius movement, and even more so with respect to critics who evidently sought to abolish criticism. This crisis, which would call into question the Enlightenment's concept of criticism, cannot be explained only in terms of intraliterary causes; it is also a symptom of the first crisis in the *institution* of literary criticism.

The Late Enlightenment in Berlin and the Contradictions of the Literary Public Sphere

Paradigmatically reducing the literary criticism of the High Enlightenment to Lessing's individual achievement could probably be justified as a heuristic device, yet it would be a historical injustice to the many critics who with their treatises, reviews, and journals first helped establish a literary public sphere. Focusing exclusively on Lessing casts a shadow on many equally engaged Enlightenment partisans who, long after Lessing's death, continued to defend the achievements of the Age of Criticism, among them Christlob Mylius, Johann Georg Sulzer, Karl Wilhelm Ramler (*Critische Nachrichten aus dem Reich der Gelehrsamkeit*, 1750–51); Friedrich Nicolai, Moses Mendelssohn, Christian Felix Weisse (*Bibliothek der schönen Wissenschaften und der freyen Künste*, 1757–65; *Neue Bibliothek*, 1766–1805); Johann Benjamin Michaelis, Georg Christian Lichtenberg (*Göttinger Anzeigen von gelehrten Sachen*, from 1739); Christian Adolf Klotz (*Bibliothek der schönen Wissenschaften*, 1767–71); Christoph Martin Wieland (*Der Teutsche Merkur*, 1773–89; *Neue Merkur*, 1790–1810); Heinrich Christian Boie, Wilhelm von Dohm (*Deutsches Museum*, 1776–88); Johannes E. Biester, Friedrich Gedike (*Berlinische Monatsschrift*, 1783–1811).[140]

The name of Friedrich Nicolai (1733–1811) stands out among this group of important Enlightenment figures. His career as a writer and critic exemplifies the aspirations of Enlightenment literary criticism and its dilemma at the end of the century. He was undoubtedly one of the "most important representatives of the Enlightenment," one whose achievement and influence Goethe and Schiller disparaged in the *Xenienkrieg* (the Xenia war; 1797) and who was so ridiculed by the Jena Romantics that he was thereafter forgotten—unjustly, for as a publisher and book dealer, as a writer and critic, he was the leading organizer and promoter of the Enlightenment in Prussia. It is scarcely an overestimation to place him next to Lessing in significance. What the latter achieved for the development of literary criticism, the former did for the literary life. As the editor of three literary journals he exercised great influence on the literary public until 1805. Even if he was not Lessing's equal as a critic, he nevertheless enjoyed great respect as a writer, and he never shied from controversy with famous contemporaries.

Nicolai started making a name for himself as a literary critic in 1755, when he debuted with the *Briefe über den itzigen Zustand der schönen Wissenschaften in Deutschland*. In the seventeenth letter he explained his concept of criticism: he saw it as a means toward the betterment of taste. Although the taste discussion had long been underway and Baumgarten's *Aesthetica* had meanwhile appeared, Nicolai didn't want to turn over the judgment of art exclusively to taste, since the obstinacy of some individuals would prevent them from ever reaching a thorough and harmonious judgment. It is true, he said, that emotional responses are considered in rendering a judgment of art, but they must first be critically examined and rationally grounded. Thus, the critic grants validity to spontaneous emotional reactions, but he purifies them by bringing taste into agreement with the rules of the various arts. With this, Nicolai finds himself halfway between the taste concept of the early Enlightenment (König) and the aesthetic of effects. He never ultimately gets beyond this standpoint, which wavers between normative and aesthetic criticism.[141]

Yet he is far from having made himself a "critical messenger-boy from Leipzig or Zurich." Even if his concept of criticism is not very distant from either school, that debate belongs to an earlier era, which was transcended by scientific aesthetics. Therefore, he criticizes both camps because they moralize too much and fail to take aesthetic criteria sufficiently into account. "It requires no elaborate proof to realize that a mediocre moralist and a great poet are two different things," he notes, and adds derisively that they wrote poetry "with the sleepiness of a judge of art." He in no way disputes how important their theoretical works have been in giving the Germans "proper concepts of the truly beautiful in poetry,"[142] but now the "sharpest criticism" is needed to promote the improvement of taste.

He himself practiced such criticism together with Lessing and Mendelssohn in the *Literaturbriefe* (1759–65). Yet after the founding of the *Allgemeine Deutsche Bibliothek* (1765) he found less and less time for literary criticism. When he later focused satirically or polemically on contemporary literature and philosophy, the accent of his judgment had shifted from aesthetic to moralistic criticism. He engaged in famous critical skirmishes with Herder, Goethe, Schiller, Kant, and Fichte, obviously formidable opponents, against whom he defended his Enlightenment concept of the general intelligibility and social usefulness of literature and philosophy—very much to his own detriment, for he increasingly gained the reputation of being an out-of-date Enlightenment advocate and a moralizing pedant. Two controversies, of interest from both literary and social-historical perspectives, should at least be briefly sketched here.

Nicolai's well-known Werther parody, *Freuden des jungen Werthers*

(1775), is generally treated as a curiosity piece in the reception history of Goethe's work. Its moralizing social criticism of Werther-mania goes unremarked. Contrary to his own concept of criticism as formulated twenty years earlier, Nicolai neither attended to the poetic form of Goethe's epistolary novel nor offered an aesthetic critique. Instead, he used the introductory dialogue between "a boy and a man" to focus attention on the moral and social dangers of the work. This introductory dispute makes it clear that he also saw the Werther controversy as a generational problem. It is well known that (besides Nicolai) Christian Garve, Christoph Martin Wieland, and Lessing also feared that "such a heated project could be more disastrous than beneficial," and Lessing recommended a "brief, cool closing speech" as a warning.[143] In *disputatio* and parody, Nicolai criticized Goethe's work only with respect to its content, which makes quite clear how strongly Werther's subjectivism, his rejection of society, and above all his suicide called into question the bourgeois ideology on behalf of which Nicolai became an apologist.[144] Yet the success and impact of the original work allowed the critic to be forgotten, especially as the subsequent history of the bourgeoisie proved Goethe's critique to be correct.

Fundamental problems of the literary public lie at the root of Nicolai's controversy with Friedrich Schiller, for the respective representatives of Enlightenment and Classicism proposed different solutions, each having consequences for the function of literary criticism. Nicolai published a critique of the *Horen* in 1796, admonishing the journal for the incomprehensibility and esoteric nature of its contributions. In his book-length *Anhang zu Schillers Musen-Almanach für das Jahr 1797*, he summarized his critique of the previous year:

> The journal *Die Horen* has been praised with an unseemly amount of self-satisfaction. Herr Schiller's prospectus indicated that the journal was intended for the public mind (or more plainly, for the healthy common sense) and for the fine public. I would have thought that essays full of scholastic sophistry, presented in an impenetrable style, were ill suited for such a purpose. . . . I spoke on that occasion of the many philosophical blockheads who are ruining German literature with a multitude of supposedly "deeply meaningful" writings, full of transcendental fantasies. I talked generally about the misuse of Critical Philosophy . . . and di-

rected attention to the many embarrassments which have resulted since Herr Schiller began using the driest terminology of
Kantian philosophy even in his poetry.[145]

The philosophical poems of the "Kantian poet" Schiller particularly
aroused Nicolai's ire, since he found them unpoetic and esoteric.
Moreover, he polemicized against the *Briefe über die ästhetische Erziehung des Menschen*, which in its abstractness and obscurity he felt must
remain incomprehensible to a wider public. The fault lay—this was
Nicolai's leitmotif—in the "misuse of Critical Philosophy," which had
degenerated to a mere fad and was doing more harm than good,
thanks to the elitist arrogance of the "Kantians."

After Schiller's rude *Xenien*, directed against him, it would be easy to
dismiss the elderly Nicolai's critique as a case of wounded vanity or to
minimize it as the resentment of a philosophical autodidact toward the
pretentions of Critical Philosophy. But that would be dealing unfairly
with the argumentative significance of his criticism. Furthermore,
many of Schiller's contemporaries had offered similar judgments of
the *Ästhetische Briefe*, if not all with the same concern for educational
politics. Nicolai was pointing to the danger of an intellectualization of
literature that no longer took into account the general public's powers
of comprehension. He called into question the use value of the *Horen*
and the utility of Schiller's treatise because he thought them too self-
satisfied to concern themselves with advancing the public mind and
too elitist to stimulate a reasoned *public* discussion of literature.

On the contrary (one might object along with Schiller), it had been
precisely Schiller's hope that the *Horen* would bring together a "literary
association" of the nation's best writers in order to unify "a public
which until then had been widely dispersed." Through this "society,"
the "things that had pleased the best could make their way into the
hands of everyone." Their taste would become a model for the "entire
world of readers."[146] By means of an aesthetic education guided from
above, art would be used to cultivate the public *to* art. Schiller was
eager to see "whether the public has its way with us, or we with the
public."[147]

We know how this test of strength came out: after less than two
years the *Horen* had to cease publication. Contrary to its "prospectus,"
the journal offered little entertainment or instruction for average

readers, who were forced to seek their rest and relaxation elsewhere. Nicolai and Schiller's publisher, Johann Friedrich Cotta, realized how "inappropriate" the journal was and became advocates of the public, which Schiller now despised and abandoned: "Evidently there are readers who prefer the watery soup of other journals to the heartier fare offered up by the *Horen:* now that is a most unfortunate situation, but I have not the slightest idea what to do about it."[148]

The dominant question in Nicolai's literary life was how a truly *popular* Enlightenment could be brought about. As a publisher and critic, he championed the popularization of the sciences and stressed the intelligibility and utility of literature. But even his efforts ultimately foundered on the Enlightenment's insurmountable contradiction between an intellectually advanced elite and the backwardness of the general public. This contradiction did not escape Nicolai—it had occupied him since the beginning of the 1770s. One need only recall the bitter criticism aimed at writers and scholars in his *Sebaldus Nothanker:* "The class of writers in Germany deals only with itself. . . . A scholar writes only for his immediate audience. . . . The twenty million uneducated accordingly repay the contempt of the learned with indifference, scarcely aware that the scholars exist."[149] These "uneducated," therefore, sought their entertainment and instruction in the moral weeklies, devotional books, almanacs, and trivial novels. Even Nicolai was incapable of bridging this gap. Indeed, it grew wider after 1770; the rapid capitalization of the book market led to a permanent schism within the public, which disintegrated into an educated elite (with its art literature) and a mass public (with its trivial literature).

Nicolai's answer to this phenomenon of literary life—so typical of the modern age—was the organization of a comprehensive review. The *Bibliothek der schönen Wissenschaften und freyen Künste* (1757–65) had already devoted great attention to literary criticism; the *Briefe, die neueste Literatur betreffend* (1759–65) was the first reviewing journal intended to offer—however incompletely—a critical overview of contemporary literature. But the *Allgemeine Deutsche Bibliothek* (*ADB,* 1765–92; *NADB,* 1793–1806) was actually the first journal to set itself the ambitious task of giving "a general report of the whole year's literature."[150] As editor and publisher between 1765 and 1805, Nicolai became the true promoter of the Enlightenment. This monumental undertaking (264 volumes), which in its aspirations and comprehensiveness deserves comparison with the French *Encyclopédie*, still testifies to the Enlightenment idea of the perfectibility of human society. Nicolai hoped that public criticism could rectify the failings of the book market, raise the intellectual level of literature, and create a homogeneous public. Literature must here be understood in the broadest sense, for Nicolai wanted to review the *whole* of German book production, comprehending all areas of knowledge and including translations. Given their proportional share of the market,[151] the "beautiful sciences" could claim at most a quarter of the total volume. In fact, the *ADB*, during the forty-odd years of its existence, reviewed some 80,000 books. If one considers that during this period 433 scholars and writers worked for the journal, one can describe Nicolai's "reviewing institution" (Horst Möller) as the most important integrating factor of the Late Enlightenment. "Only now could Germany discover what was going on literarily within its borders; it finally got to know itself."[152] Even if on average no more than 2,000 copies of the *ADB* were sold per year, it still created a transregional critical forum. For Nicolai, it was even a "profitable undertaking" (Günther Ost), so that his publishing and critical achievement can be most succinctly characterized with these words: He lived for the Enlightenment, and from it.[153]

The gradual disintegration of the literary public sphere can be traced through the history of the *ADB*. This inexorable process of decay can hardly be blamed on the institution of criticism: the *ADB* itself is an imposing monument to its achievement. The reasons must instead be sought in the rapid expansion of the book market in the last third of the eighteenth century. As early as 1769 the journal was scarcely able to keep pace with a production rate of 1,300 new books a year, and the contradiction between the ideal and the reality of the *ADB* grew more striking over time, until Nicolai finally had to content himself with reviewing only half the new publications. By 1768 he had already rejected Herder's proposal to tone up the *ADB* by a tighter selection. Nicolai wanted above all to offer sharp critiques of the "mediocre trash which many people still think has merit."[154] But by 1770, criticism was already limping hopelessly behind a market oriented toward rapid turnover; the Enlightenment idea of a homogeneous literary public that could be guided by criticism proved a fiction: "The model of the bourgeois public sphere was an ideal to which social reality never corresponded."[155]

Intimations of this problem were already in the air during the late Enlightenment, and attentive observers of literary life criticized the symptoms even then, though without being able to identify the underlying causes. Like Nicolai, a schoolmaster named Laukhard held writers primarily responsible for the fact that the greater part of the population was still not enlightened. He mockingly commented about Weimar, which "adorned itself with the most dazzling minds of Germany," that "here one sees quite plainly that even the best writers have no effect on the lower classes, even those in their immediate vicinity."[156] They remain off by themselves, write in a manner not generally comprehensible, and take little heed of people's own desires in the matter of their education. By contrast, Nicolai attempted, through the popular and popularizing literary criticism of his journals, to reach a broader readership and have a socially beneficial effect, so that as many as possible could take part in the process of Enlightenment. As literature was converted into a commodity, however, this desire to enlighten was quickly rendered questionable. Literature was no longer aimed at an ideal and still knowable readership, with which one could communicate via the subscription lists, but rather at an anonymous, consuming readership whose needs could be stimulated and satisfied by canny publishers. The emerging mass entertainment literature could still be criticized, as Nicolai attempted to do in *ADB*, but it could no longer be effectively controlled.

The disintegration of the literary public sphere, which in reality had never been more than a postulate, expresses one moment in the dialectic of Enlightenment. "The Enlightenment's literary efforts at educating the people supplied a vital precondition for the subsequent rapid capitalization of the book market. Thus the movement ultimately brought on its own ruin."[157] The Janus-faced character of the book as spirit and commodity was openly welcomed by Enlightenment leaders as long as the book market could be steered by criticism. Only when the spirits they had conjured up could no longer be controlled and their belief in the education of a homogeneous, mature public had been shaken did they react with moralizing criticism. They cursed the profit-hungry publishers and book dealers, the "writing factories," and the "reading addiction" of the public.[158] Yet such helpless criticism cast attention only on symptoms without being able to combat the causes effectively. In light of this schism of the public, institutionalized criticism also had to reorient itself: should it take the taste of the broader public into account, or defend works of higher literature *against* exactly this taste?

The Storm and Stress Period

One easy way to deal with the literary criticism of the "Storm and Stress" (*Sturm und Drang*) period would be to accept Lessing's opinion that this generation had rendered criticism suspect—indeed, that it wished to abolish criticism altogether in the name of genius.[159] Its hostility to criticism, based on an emphatic genius cult, turned the poet into a highhanded legislator of art while reducing the critic to the role of congenial interpreter of the works. Lessing resisted such a move because it threatened to invalidate the control function of criticism. Yet if the opposition between the Enlightenment and the beginning genius movement is overdramatized, one is left with that familiar schematism that plays the irrational off against the rational—something that by no means corresponds to the historical process. Much of what sounded so hostile to criticism was still aimed at French Classicism or dogmatic Aristotelianism. Moreover, Lessing's fears were *not* confirmed: there was no abolition of criticism; at most, one can speak of a paradigm shift. In some respects the genius movement continued and even sharpened certain Enlightenment tendencies.

The literary criticism of the Storm and Stress period can no longer be presented from a unitary perspective: it is too multivoiced and too self-contradictory. If one considers the period only from the point of view of the genius movement, it is too easy to overlook its plebeian-populist and political tendencies. And an understanding of this epoch that orients itself too one-sidedly on this generation's own self-understanding and its poetic manifestos will underestimate the continuity with the Enlightenment and the overall complexity of the era.

The continuity and the paradigm shift in literary criticism can be most clearly observed in the case of Johann Gottfried Herder, more precisely in his collection of fragments, *Über die neuere Deutsche Literatur* (1767), which he characterizes in the subtitle as a "supplement" to the *Briefe, die neueste Literatur betreffend*. The book provides important passages excerpted from the "Letters," with commentary and criticism from Herder. It is a continuation of the literary conversation, now completed by Herder in his own way. These fragments touch on all the themes that became important in the Storm and Stress period and that shaped literary criticism for the next two decades. Three aspects should be highlighted here: Herder's understanding of criticism, his concept of taste, and the new category of popularity (*Volkstümlichkeit*).

"The first judge of art was nothing more than a reader of sensitivity and taste." For Herder, too, the basis of criticism is the sensualistic aesthetic of effects. Even if he distances himself from this naive state of criticism by shifting it to a "golden age," he nevertheless speaks from the perspective of the Enlightenment, when "instead of learning what others thought, human beings arrogated the right to think for themselves."[160] At the next stage of development the philosophers explain the impression that the Beautiful makes upon us: "And thus the man of feeling becomes a philosopher."[161] The modern critic may have lost his original naiveté and is also no longer creative himself, but as one who knows and observes literature he can examine, teach, and improve. The "true judge of art" serves the reader, the writer, and literature: "For the reader, first as a servant, then confidant, then doctor. For the writer, first as a servant, then friend, then judge. And for the whole of literature, either as smelter, or handyman, or as the masterbuilder himself."[162] This passage and Herder's further commentary illustrate both the continuity and the expansion of Enlightenment criticism. As in the Enlightenment, the critic writes for the reader, whom he hopes to guide toward proper reading and whose taste he wishes to shape. Obviously, in Herder's time, too, the public is still immature, either not knowing how to read or having a corrupted taste. The critic functions as the delegated representative of an immature public, still incapable of articulating its wishes. Criticism first produces the publicity that forms a necessary presupposition for an improvement of cultural and political life.

More striking and central is the interest Herder devotes to the critic in his relationship with the writer, if only because he obviously encounters writers more as a servant and friend then as a critic. This stands in open contradiction to the early Enlightenment, for unlike Gottsched, Herder wants to be neither a teacher nor a taskmaster for the poet; he does not want to "think against, but always *with* and *for* his author." Such a notion would scarcely have occurred to Lessing; he wanted to criticize and convincingly ground his judgment but not—like Herder—"put himself in the mind of his author and read from his very spirit." Lessing criticized from the standpoint of the reader and a critically examined genre poetics; Herder's "true judge of art" is supposed to empathically receive the impress of the artwork and fathom its spirit. The critic becomes an understanding interpreter of the artwork and an advocate of the artist. That is a significant shift of accentuation within the aesthetics of effect. The critic is no longer primarily speaking for the public, whose feelings he makes generally communicable; instead, he immerses himself empathically in the work and attempts to understand the genius and his ideal intentions: "The best way to judge an author is by means of his own plan: this should be examined, improved, and brought to completion." Empathic knowledge of the artwork and its originating conditions (a knowledge possibly indicating a genius equal to the author's) is more important for Herder than any amount of judicious criticism. Despite his respect for Lessing and the *Literaturbriefe*, that sort of criticism seems to him too carping, polemical, dissecting. "Unfortunately, this sort of dissection contributes nothing to the awakening of genius."[163] Herder's positive and creative criticism wants to bring a work's originality closer to a like-minded reader. He is the interpreter and prophet of the genius, whose creations draw his poetical praise.

William Shakespeare is the ideal paradigm for this sort of enthusiastic criticism. Herder becomes his "interpreter and rhapsodist" and accordingly mixes intuitive insights with rapturous apotheosis: "When I read him, it is as though theater, actors, and stage have vanished! Only individual pages blown about by the storm of time, pages torn from the book of events, of providence, of the world!—individual impresses of peoples, classes, souls! all the most various and separate machines, all—what we are in the hand of God—unknowing, blind tools in the creation of a theatrical image, of a great event, which only the poet sees whole."[164] This is no longer criticism but revelation. Herder duplicates the work of art by interpretively poeticizing it and interpreting it like an oracle. Goethe becomes even more hymnlike in his speech "Zum Schäkespeares Tag" (1771). Here, one genius is ignited by another; Goethe's appropriation is the self-discovery of another genius. But this is no longer criticism, either; rather, it is a secularized veneration of saints.

Herder's Shakespeare essay is interesting from yet another point of view. It by no means limits itself exclusively to dealing with the great Englishman but is in fact primarily a comparative study of "Greek and Nordic Drama." True, Herder feels himself closer to Shakespeare than to the Greeks, but he is also interested in the historical question of the genesis and transformation of the dramatic genre. (The fact that in discussing these issues Herder expends a lot of energy criticizing Classicism, especially French drama—"puppet, imitation, ape"—ought merely be noted in passing.) His comparison again proves the value of the historico-genetic method, which uses the specific originating conditions to explain the variety of forms, without deriving generic poetic norms that would be binding for the critic. This approach also has consequences for the taste problem, which Herder can conceive of only as a historical problem. Obviously, from what has been said thus far, the rationalistic taste of the understanding, with its rule dogmatism, is necessarily alien to him. Attempts at theoretical explanation that ground taste anthropologically or aprioristically are too abstract for his liking. Instead of explaining taste as a general principle, he considers it a historical phenomenon whose "materials and purposes are different in every period." The flowering or decay of taste depends on how freely a genius can unfold within his nation's culture. The classical Greek and Roman cultures offer proof that political freedom and the flowering of taste go hand in hand. The sunken taste of the present day indicates a lack of free productivity. Whoever hopes to better contemporary taste "must get at the causes"; that is, political freedom and a sense of nationhood must first be created. That is why good taste in Germany, according to Herder, has "always remained on the surface of the nation" and could never achieve full flowering.[165] In the taste debate of the eighteenth century these are new and uncommon thoughts that transcend purely aesthetic arguments. Herder is no longer asking about the ideal taste, or about the conditions of possibility of taste, but rather about its political and historical presuppositions in each respective epoch. This sort of questioning opens new perspectives which point beyond Kant's solution of the taste problem.

Herder's contemplations on art, as one could label his style of criticism to distinguish it from that of the Enlightenment, had a galvanizing effect on that circle of like-minded thinkers who found themselves in Strasbourg in 1770–71. The "flying pages" of *Von deutscher Art und*

Kunst (1773) are generally considered to set forth their artistic program, but equally significant is their critical journal, the *Frankfurter Gelehrten Anzeigen* (*FGA*), particularly the famous volume of issues from 1772, containing no fewer than 400 reviews.[166] They can be taken as representative of the criticism of this bourgeois avant-garde. That, at least, is how Goethe saw it, who looking back wrote in the *Annalen* (1815): "The reviews in the *Frankfurter Gelehrten Anzeigen* of 1772 transmit a perfect notion of the state of our society and personality as it was at that time. One notes an unconditional striving to break through any and all barriers."[167] That is certainly true not for all the reviews (which, in the characteristic *Gelehrten Anzeigen* manner, were also scholarly, thorough, and objective) but for many of the reviews devoted to new art-theoretical or belletristic publications. In them one notes a new tone, antispeculative and antiacademic, and therefore correspondingly temperamental and lacking in respect. Thus, Goethe's review of Johann Georg Sulzer's *Allgemeine Theorie der schönen Künste* (1771) begins with an anti-Classicist jab: "The book is very easy to translate into French; for that matter, it may well have been translated *out* of French." Sulzer's principles of the fine arts are useless for anyone "except the student seeking a basic primer, and the quite superficial fashionable dilettante." Goethe is also disturbed by the fact that Sulzer, "in traditional fashion, draws conclusions from nature about art"; even more disturbing is the way Sulzer trivializes the "indefinite principle: imitation of nature" into a "prettification of things." Against such an idyllization, Goethe opposes the great, monstrous, and violent aspects of nature—its "power," the "counterpart" of which is art. He wishes neither to follow Sulzer into the "empyrean of transcendental virtue-beauty" nor to hear any talk of a "theory of sensuality." The only things that interest him are the "true influence of art on the heart and mind" and what the genius is capable of. Given such new standards, it is not surprising that even Salomon Gessner's *Idyllen* (1772) is no longer satisfactory. In his first published pieces of literary criticism, Goethe appears self-confident and sometimes even pitilessly polemical, as in his critique of Friedrich Heinrich Jacobi, annihilating in its brevity: "Herr Jacobi and his goodly heart; the goodly heart and Herr Jacobi: a large part of the public shares our feeling of being heartily sick of both."[168]

Herder, who many assumed was the head of the whole *FGA* undertaking and the author of the sharpest critiques, actually contributed only reviews of new works from the fledgling science of history, in which he polemically represented his organic conception of history against those of the academic guild. He avoided theological disputes. Yet it was precisely in this area that the *FGA* caused its greatest uproar, provoking the wrath of the orthodox clergy with its critique of religious fanaticism and intolerance. Once again, the controversy centered on Chief Pastor Goeze of Hamburg, whose *Erbauliche Betrachtungen über das Leben Jesu auf Erden* (1772)—which, on top of everything else, was dedicated to the Magistrate of Frankfurt—had been received in the *FGA* with scornful derision.[169] Whereupon the Frankfurt Senate stepped in, threatened to take the journal to court, and finally extracted an agreement that the *FGA* would no longer review theological works. "Our spectacle with the clerics grows larger all the time," Goethe reported to Albert Kestner. "They prostitute themselves a little more each day, and we are constantly getting the better of them."[170] This episode again illustrates (as would Lessing's quarrel with Goeze a little later) the restrictions on public discussion. In Germany, Enlightenment as the production of a critical-rational public sphere was feasible at best only in the philosophical and literary sector; as soon as religious dogma or orthodoxy came under fire, the state would intervene, sensing that its governmental authority was also being indirectly attacked. In the eighteenth century no writer could transgress the limits on the political public sphere with impunity.

Yet the "Frankfurters" took every opportunity, even after the ban, to criticize religion and the state indirectly, as is illustrated by a review of an anonymously published satire, *An meine Landesleute* (1772). In the book a king makes himself a speaker on behalf of enlightened Absolutism, pointing out to his co-regents that (as the review puts it) "an educated people would be more obedient than an ignorant one, for they would better understand their relationship with the state." The clergy is reproached for "happily leaving the people in a state of ignorance and stupidity" and "blocking all the outlets for healthy common sense." The despot is criticized for failing to realize that "religion, politics, and legislation must be much simpler, and must have far different purposes, than they currently are (and have) in our land, if it is hoped to make the people wise."[171] Here, by actualizing the satire in a review, criticism succeeds in making it even sharper.

What one catches in many reviews from the *FGA* is the interest these writers had for the people, whether for their poetry or for their justified demands for education. Hans Mayer sees in this the true tendency of literary criticism during the period: "In a certain sense one could say that, during the German Storm and Stress, the bourgeois liberation movement widened out into a general plebeian emancipation, with the concept of the 'people' more and more taking the place of the concept 'bourgeois.'"[172] The populist-plebeian direction of Storm and Stress (represented by Herder, Gottfried August Bürger, Jakob Michael Reinhold Lenz, and Christian Friedrich Schubart) sought, in association with Rousseau, its standards of criticism in the people. *Volkstümlichkeit* (popularity) now became a category of literary criticism in two senses: "Whatever makes up the unique essence of the people, that is, its national character. Harmony with the essence, the conception, the feelings of the uncultivated, naive people, its lower strata."[173] Standards for poetry and criticism should no longer be exclusively based on the taste of a small educated elite; rather, they should also take their direction from the feelings and intellectual capacities of the simple people in order thus to create a homogeneous, national culture, one that is rooted in the past and that can develop a literary public mind in the present. When the critic conceives of his task as expressing the literary feelings and needs of the people, and relies on popular poetry and *Volkstümlichkeit*, one can say farewell to the judge of art who spoke on behalf of a literary elite.

This emphatic concept of *Volkstümlichkeit* is inseparable from Herder's thoughts on popular poetry, as set down in his essay "Briefwechsel über Ossian und die Lieder alter Völker" (1773). Even though Herder reaches far back into history for the legitimation of popular poetry, his understanding of *Volkstümlichkeit* must not be confused with that odious concept of *Volkstum* that has been utilized by all proponents of the *Volk* since Ludwig (*Turnvater*) Jahn. For Herder, the higher valuation of popular poetry and *Volkstümlichkeit* has social and aesthetic reasons that are connected with his understanding of his own age. Like Rousseau, he finds contemporary social relations contrary to nature, repressive and "artificial." "Polished" society, with all its conventions, strangles what is natural and distinctive in a people. In popular poetry he still finds that evidence of naive and unspoiled feeling, which he has fruitlessly sought in his own day. The folksong, which Herder conceptualizes in very broad terms, preserves the natural originality that he believes absent from conventional book poetry. With this essay, Herder not only contributed to the rediscovery of an almost forgotten tradition; his enthusiasm also awakened the creative powers of the younger generation. Concerning Herder's influence during the Strasbourg period, Goethe recalled: "Folk poetry . . . the oldest documents of poetry, offered eloquent testimony to the fact that poetry was a gift of the whole world and of every people, not just the private inheritance of a few fine and cultivated men."[174]

For Gottfried August Bürger, who had read Herder's Ossian essay with enthusiasm, *Volkstümlichkeit* became "the axis around which my entire poetics turned." All his theoretical and artistic works are determined by the poetic "confession of faith" with which the essay "Von der Popularität der Poesie" (1784) breaks off: "All poetry should be in harmony with the *Volk* [*volksmässig*], for that is the seal of its perfection." He *wants* to write for all classes and to be read in both cottage and palace, but his tendency toward *Volkstümlichkeit* keeps breaking through, a tendency actually oriented toward the petty bourgeoisie, the artisans, and the farmers: "And poetry shouldn't be for the people, but only for a few pepper merchants? Ha! As if not all human beings were—human beings." Like Herder, Bürger seeks a model for his poetic practice in folk poetry, polemicizing against learned poetry with all its formal conventions: "Come down from the peaks of your cloudy learning, and don't demand that we, the many who live on the earth's surface, should ascend to regions only you few find a fit habitation."[175] He wants to base his work on the taste and intellectual capacities of the simple people, for whom he writes as a "folk poet." This plebeian-populist tendency bursts out of the framework of the purely literary, since it validates the demands of the people against political and cultural repression from above. Even if the postulate of equality finds only theoretical formulation in Bürger's work, his protest against all educational and cultural privilege is clearly perceptible. Here, something that will soon appear on the political agenda is being demanded for poetry.

In France, what had begun with the weapons of criticism was carried to its end by the Revolution; in politically splintered Germany, where counterrevolutionary preventive measures sharpened the censorship, republican-minded forces couldn't even carry the day in the

literary public sphere. Under the pressure of dominant social relations, the function of criticism also changed after 1789: it lost its bour-
geois-enlightening impetus, shook itself free of all practical ties to life,
and became aesthetically immanent. Thus began the "art period,"
whose criticism established new standards that were to become controlling for bourgeois criticism.

Weimar Classicism: Autonomous Criticism and the "Fine Public"

When Friedrich Schiller in 1791 reviewed the second and expanded
edition of Bürger's poems,[176] the élan of Storm and Stress had evapo-
rated, and Schiller himself had long since distanced himself from the
movement. His political and philosophical standpoint had changed to
such a degree that he confronted Bürger's antitheoretical and plebeian
position with skepticism, if not outright rejection. His merciless review is still often apologetically interpreted as Schiller's "radical renunciation of his own youthful beginnings."[177] Such renunciation
may well have played a role, even if this psychological explanation can
base itself only on a single sentence in the review.[178] Yet that marginal
perspective does not do justice to the paradigmatic significance of the
text, which has been described as a "turningpoint in the conception of
literature and its function."[179] What separates Schiller from Bürger is
less personal resentment than the objective tendencies of the age that
Bürger evidently either could not or would not see. The oppositions
that seem to assume personal form in this controversy have their basis
in that change in the historical tides symbolized by the French Revolution. In his review, which *in nuce* already contains his whole program
of aesthetic education, Schiller clearly alludes to the tendencies that
define his age and find expression in the literary theory and criticism
of the Classical period.[180]

Schiller's culture-critical analysis of his own epoch and of the literary
market is, despite its fragmentary nature, immeasurably more philosophical and skeptical than Bürger's naive conception of *Volkstümlichkeit*. At the outset he points to the dangers of "our philosophizing
age," which seems to make poetry almost superfluous, and to the
consequences of "the progress of scientific culture," which threatens

the totality of the human being. If one also takes note of the "cultural differential" that now exists "between the *elect* of a nation and its *mass*,"[181] one begins to realize that the bad times are not limited *just* to lyric poetry. Yet Schiller's cultural criticism doesn't slip into cultural pessimism; instead, he derives from negativity the impetus for his aesthetic demands. Thus, the Kant-influenced philosophical interpretation of the world is not merely a challenge for poetry; Schiller also owes to it the foundations of his aesthetic theory, which first opened to him the possibility of responding to the cultural crisis with his aesthetic-utopian project.[182] In light of the self-alienation of human beings, due to the one-sided development of reason at the expense of nature, "poetry alone is able to reunify the divided powers of the soul . . . to reproduce the *whole human being* within us." Yet these two important tendencies of the age are only touched on here; Schiller devotes more detailed analysis to the structural transformation of the market and its consequences for both art and criticism.

Schiller, who as a freelance writer was more than familiar with the laws of the literary marketplace, judges the disintegration of the public more realistically than does Bürger. He rejects the emphatic ideal of *Volkstümlichkeit* (with which Bürger hoped to overcome the literary schism from below, as it were) as inadequate to the times: "Ours is no longer the Homeric world, in which every member of society had attained approximately the same level of feeling and belief." For Schiller, the conjuration of *Volkstümlichkeit* is incapable of recreating the lost cultural unity. If a poet is nevertheless unwilling to abandon the concept, he has a choice "only between the *easiest* and *most difficult* of its forms; either to accommodate himself exclusively to the intellectual capacities of the great mass, and renounce the approval of the educated class—or to transcend the huge gap that exists between these two classes by the very greatness of his art." Bürger wants the former; Schiller demands the latter. He would like to satisfy the "delicate taste of the connoisseur, without thereby being unenjoyable for the great mass." This passage alone is enough to make clear the standpoint from which (and the social group for which) Schiller is writing. The critic no longer speaks on behalf of a general public, and certainly not for the "people," but for a literary elite. However, this group is *not* to shut itself off in an elitist fashion; rather, as "spokesmen for the people's feelings," its members should lower themselves to the people's level in order to "laughingly and playfully draw it up to their level," so that ultimately the divided public will again be unified. Schiller interprets *Volkstümlichkeit* accordingly: unlike Bürger, he sees in it not the "seal of perfection" but, instead, a happy *addition* to poetry. For Schiller, the "perfection of a poem is the first, indispensable condition," possessing an absolute, inner value completely independent of the various intellectual capacities of its readers.[183] This appears to be only a minor correction of Bürger, setting the demands of art higher than that of *Volkstümlichkeit*. Yet wide-ranging consequences for literary criticism result from the shift of emphasis: criticism is uncoupled from reception; the artwork possesses an absolute value, one existing independent of the readers' ability to comprehend it intellectually. The critic examines only whether a work corresponds to "the highest demands of art," not whether it is generally pleasing. Art becomes autonomous, and the critic defends it against the leveling taste of the public.

Beyond this, the review contains a catalogue of criteria that have inarguable consequences for the history of criticism. Bürger's lyrical poetry inevitably fails against these new standards of Classical aesthetics. This part of the critique begins with a sentence that is as famous as it is misunderstood: "The only thing the poet is capable of giving us is his *individuality*." What at first reading appears nothing more than a tired truism proves to be a great deal more. However cryptically, the sentence already contains the Classical ideal of individuality and culture. After Schiller it is no longer enough for a poet simply to exhibit his unpolished genius and subjective experiences; he must "refine and purify them to the purest, most magnificent humanity" before he can hope to interest others (that is, the educated) in his poetry. "To refine" means for Schiller first of all striving for moral and spiritual perfection; the old-European cultural-educational ideal of the *vir bonus*, later of the complete courtier and man of the world who is particularly suited for the role of orator/poet,[184] is also implicated in the term. Finally, "to refine" can also mean "to elevate the local and the individual to the level of the universal." Here the ethical quality is transformed into an aesthetic one, for the aesthetic synonym for refinement is idealization. The artist refines the real into beauty: "Idealization is one of the first requirements of the poet."[185]

Today, "idealization" has a bad connotation, in both its general and its aesthetic sense. Distorted by the history of bourgeois society, it is understood as a flight from reality, as prettification or concealment; in short, it is distrusted as ideology. For Schiller, by contrast, idealization was (next to the aesthetic appearance) constitutive for his conception of art. It is true that in the review of Bürger this key concept of Classical mimetic theory is discussed only by way of suggestion, but two aspects of the theory can already be clearly made out. It is demanded of the poet that he idealize reality, so that everything individual, private, and local is eradicated, in order to bring the universal into appearance. It is only through this "operation of the idealizing artist," as Schiller calls it in his "Defense of the Reviewer," that the individual is elevated "to the universal character of humanity." The ideals represented in this manner spring from the "soul of the poet," who must have purified himself up to this level of idealized humanity. Refined individuality and idealization are complementary concepts. How is it possible to represent ideas and to move the reader by means of ideas? This central problem of the sentimental poet is first solved by Schiller in a later famous essay, but even at this point it is clear to him that only "idealized emotions" belong in the realm of poetry.

It is precisely in the presentation of emotions that such an "art of idealization" requires *more* than mere directness or enthusiasm. Schiller writes: "The poet must beware not to sing of pain, while still in its midst"—both a warning and a criticism. What is here demanded for the first time is familiar to us from modern poetics as artistic distancing.[186] Schiller is by no means against feelings in lyric poetry, or against enthusiasm, which played an important role in eighteenth-century theory. But he *does* oppose the direct expression of feelings; he *is* against a lyric of experience that (over)flows from a plenitude of the heart. Here, too, one finds a departure from the "Storm and Stress" conception of poetry. This bad immediacy, which still stands "under the current domination of the affects," harms the quality of lyric poetry. Precisely with poems that are meant to express love and sorrow, joy and pain, the poet must "grow distant from himself," so that the feelings presented achieve a universal validity. The poet should write about feelings and passions from a temporal distance, "out of his gentler and distancing memory," so that the objectified enthusiasm is taken up and sublimated in the poem.[187]

Measured against such idealistic standards, neither Bürger's concept of *Volkstümlichkeit* nor his lyrics of personal experience could be found satisfactory. It is arguable whether Schiller's withering critique was justified, or whether he wanted to force his idealistic concept of poetry onto the epoch; but it is undisputed that both his concept of aesthetic distance and his conception of *Volkstümlichkeit* were generally accepted and entered the arsenal of criticism, where they have remained in use to the present day.

Goethe reportedly said of Schiller's anonymously published review that "he wished he had been the author of the piece."[188] Even though Goethe, who had just returned from Rome, was still maintaining his distance from Schiller, there is no reason not to take this compliment seriously; Goethe himself had just published a short essay that served to underscore the change marked out by Schiller. In the February 1789 issue of Wieland's *Teutscher Merkur,* Goethe's essay "Einfache Nachahmung der Natur, Manier, Stil" offered a new perspective on the problem of mimesis.

The first two concepts in Goethe's typology can be briefly summarized, since they treat the older mimetic theories in a simplifying manner, while the truly new element is to be found in his understanding of style. The simple imitation of nature can call upon a long tradition that reaches from the ancient world to Goethe's own age: from the painted cherries of Zeuxis, which deceived the sparrows, to Lessing's *Laokoon,* in which the limits of pictorial art and the distinctions between it and poetry are unambiguously defined. Yet in spite of Lessing, Goethe does not problematize this tradition; instead, he lets it stand as one possible, if also naive, method of art. The artist as artisan keeps to certain "limited objects," such as flowers, fruits, and still lifes, which he copies with meticulous precision.[189]

With respect to mannerism, things are a bit more complex, since Goethe neglects to clarify the concept historically. Although "mannerism" had been negatively valued since Classicism, Goethe uses the word "in an elevated and respectable sense." For him, to imitate in a manneristic way means to produce a fanciful invention, "without having Nature herself before you." The artist creates his own language "in order to express in his own way that which has moved his soul." Of course, the characteristic expression must subordinate itself to the "great whole" of the artwork, a requirement that already points to Goethe's morphological conception of art. If this category is transposed onto Schiller's review, one may conclude that Bürger's poems are quite mannered, since they are the characteristic expression of a subjective emotional experience; but for Schiller, it is precisely as such that they lack style. For him, as can be seen in his short treatise "Das Schöne der Kunst," style is a "total elevation above the accidental to the universal and necessary."[190] With respect to substantive matters, Schiller and Goethe are already in accord, although Goethe is the less rigorous critic.

By style, Goethe means the "highest degree that art has ever attained and ever can attain." However aphoristically, this is the first sign of Goethe's new understanding of art. Its foundations are Goethe's natural scientific observations and his study of ancient art. In Rome he experienced the classical perfection and ideality of ancient art. With Johann Joachim Winckelmann's writings as a guide, he learned the laws of beauty through direct exposure to Greek sculpture: simplicity and stillness, the harmony of the parts that make up a living whole, the sensual appearance of the idea. That undoubtedly was the intuitional basis of Goethe's style concept, while his empirical researches into nature form the epistemological foundation: "Through a deep and exacting study of the objects themselves," art finally arrives at "an exact and ever finer knowledge of the qualities of things and the manner of their existence. Art is then able to survey the series of forms and is able to set the various characteristic forms next to one another and imitate them." This already anticipates Goethe's theory of the Urphenomena and their metamorphoses, particularly when he concludes: "Style rests on the deepest foundations of knowledge, on the essence of things, inasmuch as we are allowed to know it in visible and tangible forms." Art rests on a deep knowledge of nature, which is the analogue of art. It is produced by the artist "in accordance with true and natural laws," as he had already written in 1787 during his second Roman visit. In great art, everything arbitrary, accidental, and individual must be expunged, to the benefit of the regular and universal, so that beneath the surface "the essence of things" appears. Several years later, clearly under the influence of Schiller, Goethe also describes style as "idealizing" representation: "The objects presented in this way appear merely to stand for themselves, and yet they are at the same time deeply significant, and they are so because of the ideal, which always carries a universal with it."[191] From style, as the "genuine method" of great art, is born the Classical symbolic form.

Yet even at the time of Weimar Classicism, symbol theory was by no means monolithic. While Goethe's understanding of the symbol rests on an object-related knowledge of essences, which "sees the universal in the particular,"[192] Schiller (following Kant's theory of subjectivity) asks how emotions and ideas can be represented.[193] Both agree that spiritual and intellectual matters attain expression in symbolic representation, without being reducible to a theory or a concept. But whether this lawfulness of art is grounded in the nature of things or in subjective reflection is an issue concerning which "fine differences" existed between them, a situation that produced some fruitful misunderstandings—not just between the two friends but also within the field of criticism itself. From this time on the symbol concept was to become a central category of bourgeois literary criticism, which generally lent it an aura of atemporal validity and classical normativity, as if it had arisen neither historically nor philosophically from a concretely comprehensible situation of consciousness.

That the symbol concept of Weimar Classicism, when detached from its historical originating conditions, can also be distorted and misused (as an "ontological contemplation of essence") is something that cannot be fully explained just by looking at the history of bourgeois criticism. It also has to do with the ambivalence at the heart of the Classical symbol concept itself. Goethe's symbols are undoubtedly more concrete and objective than Schiller's, although this by no means makes their significance easier to grasp, for as far as their intellectual content is concerned, they are ambiguous and mysterious, "living, momentary revelations of the ineffable."[194] Schiller's theory of symbols, by contrast, is philosophically more ambitious, which makes its poetic realization more difficult, for the "symbolizing power of the imagination" must in reality seek material that corresponds to its ideas and appears analogous to it. Both see a "language for humanity" in the new symbol form, a language that allows them to elevate themselves above the "mean, narrow reality" (Schiller) in order to represent the "purely human," beyond the sphere of contemporary political events and social contradictions. The real conditions of life are thereby poeticized and their contradictions reconciled.

The foregoing criteria of literary theory, which were to become decisive for criticism, express a new relation to reality and to the public. Even more than this, they mark a functional transformation of

art, from a bourgeois-enlightened to an autonomous concept of literature.[195] It had been self-evident during the Enlightenment that literature had a moral-social and critical-emancipative function, one that
could permanently influence the life practices of the readers or audience. During Weimar Classicism a momentous change occurred: art
separated itself from life, aesthetics detached itself from ethics, and an
elite distanced itself from the real public. As one might suspect, this
had rather serious consequences for literary criticism. To borrow again
Mayer's analogy with Montesquieu's division-of-powers model,[196] literary criticism became "legislative": that is, Goethe's and Schiller's
literary-theoretical maxims became normative exemplars. A provisional and aphoristic enumeration of the leading reasons (there were
undoubtedly many others) for this functional transformation of art
and criticism would surely emphasize the French Revolution, Kant's
aesthetics, and the structural transformation of the literary market as
dominant tendencies of the age.

Of course, this transformation occurred neither quickly nor smooth-
ly; in fact, quite the opposite was the case. Goethe and Schiller had to
defend their new understanding of art against bitter criticism from the
"republic of scholars," and they literally had to force it on the public.
One should take care not to imagine Weimar Classicism as a harmonic,
restful epoch triumphantly closing a period that had seen the blossoming of German literature. It would be wiser to represent German
literature in that period as being in a state of development and still
controversial. This is also true of the literary criticism of Weimar Classicism, the standards of which attained dominance only slowly and
against considerable resistance.

Just how controversial the Weimar literature program still was
around 1795, especially as it was presented in the "prospectus" of the
Horen, can be well illustrated by an episode that provoked Goethe to
write the essay "Literarischer Sansculottismus," which (characteristically) appeared in the *Horen*. In the March 1795 issue of the *Berlinisches
Archiv der Zeit und ihres Geschmacks* appeared an essay by Daniel
Jenisch, dealing with the theme "Prose and Eloquence of the German
People." The essay demanded a "classical" prose for Germany, one
that would orient itself toward ancient, republican rhetoric and modern French journalism. What he missed in German prose was any
practical and political intent of having an impact on life and society,

something that *could* be found in France. If read as a program for a political journalism, the essay can also be understood as an answer to the consciously apolitical and aestheticizing *Horen*.[197] With this criticism from the republican camp, Jenisch struck a raw nerve, as the sharpness of Goethe's reply indicates. We owe to it Goethe's definition of a classical national author and lively depiction of the still miserable state of literary life in Germany.

"When and where does a national author arise?" The answer to Goethe's question casts light on the self-understanding of Weimar Classicism. As the historical preconditions for a Classical national literature, Goethe names a great national past, national unity, and a high level of culture; further, a national spirit, a mature public, and a supply of exemplary works; and finally, a "center point for the formation of social life." Measured against such conditions, which in France and England had led to great national literatures, "no German author can consider himself to be classic." To give his thesis even more weight, he compares the ideal with reality, and his portrait of literary life in Germany and the misery of its writers is truly appalling. But since critical negation isn't Goethe's style (even when he is annoyed), he leaves the reader with a healthy dose of hope: in the last half-century "a sort of invisible school has developed," and the "critical journals and newspapers" have also done their part in raising the general taste. "It's break of day," he writes optimistically, "and we shall not close the blinds again."[198]

Goethe's essay is interesting in yet another respect. It shows his unconcealed abhorrence of revolutionary overthrow, an attitude expressed by the very title of the piece. He turned strongly against the "ignorant arrogance" with which certain elements of society repressed their betters in order to take over their positions, just as the sansculottes had done in Paris. This carrying-over of the abusive political term into the realm of taste not only shows where Goethe stands with respect to the French Revolution; it also shows how he, like Schiller in his review of Bürger, opposes the plebeian tendencies in literature. Goethe and Schiller presented their idealistic art program in opposition to the "literary sansculottes." Goethe's political confession of faith went one step further: if political unity and a national culture could only be had at the price of a revolution, then he would rather forgo a national literature: "We would not wish for the upheavals which in

Germany could pave the way for classical works." When he wrote
that, the danger of the revolutionary wars for Weimar had been eliminated by the Peace Treaty of Basel (April 5, 1795). This may suffice as a
brief (but for our purposes sufficient) characterization of Goethe's relationship to the French Revolution and to the "revolutionary mob."[199]

Even if Schiller in 1795 would largely have agreed with Goethe's
political philosophy, his relationship to the French Revolution is nevertheless more complex and his proposed aesthetic solution for the
cultural crisis more interesting. The dramatist was viewed as a revolutionary, and on August 26, 1792, he was made an honorary French
citizen along with eighteen other foreign personalities.[200] The conditions that had led to the Revolution were familiar to him from his
youth in Württemberg; he shared its hopes and ideals but shrank from
the harshness of revolutionary methods and was horrified by the rigor
of their bloody logic. When he learned of the execution of Louis XVI
(January 23, 1793), in whose defense he had intended to write a
memoir, he turned away in disgust: "These miserable slaughterhouse
boys sicken me."[201] His altered and newly thought-out attitude toward revolution was formulated for the first time in a famous letter of
July 13, 1793, to the Prince of Augustenburg. There he again summarized his political hopes that in France "political legislation will be
given over to reason, human beings will be respected and treated as
ends in themselves, law will be elevated to the throne, and true
freedom will be made the foundation for the edifice of the state." Yet
Schiller's dream of a truly enlightened "monarchy of Reason" in which
the happiness of the citizens could be reconciled with Absolutism,
were not to see fulfillment: "It is exactly this fact which I dare to
doubt."[202] Out of this disappointment, which converts into general
cultural criticism, he proceeds to develop his aesthetic theory, in
order—through utopian thought—to give to contemporary events a
perspective that would make a revolution in Germany superfluous.

The aestheticization of the political with historico-philosophical intent now replaces political reasoning and leads to a conscious turning-
away from political reality. Schiller's close association with Goethe
after 1794 only serves to strengthen this tendency, so that one can
speak of a revocation of the pragmatic Enlightenment concept of literature. This is further confirmed by a letter to Herder in which Schiller
takes issue with his Enlightenment axiom "that poetry should derive

from life, from the age, from reality, in order that it can flow back into these." Schiller disputes this connection of art and society, for it is exactly the "predominance of the prosaic" in bourgeois, political, religious, and scientific life that is damaging—indeed fatal—to poetry. "Therefore, I know no other means of salvation for the poetic genius than to withdraw from the real world . . . since reality would only soil him."[203] The "most stringent separation" from contemporary reality corresponds in two ways to the Classical principle of distancing: it is demanded of the artist that he objectivize and idealize both his subjective experiences and contemporary events, in order thus to create works of timeless universal validity.

The aesthetic legitimation for such a depoliticization of art and for its turning away from reality is delivered by Kant's concept of autonomy, which now gathers effect: what is beautiful is that which pleases generally, in a disinterested manner. Or, in Schiller's words: "Art is absolved from everything that is positive or that has been introduced by human convention." This declaration of art's autonomy is Schiller's answer to the historical crisis following the French Revolution. He distances himself from both the "barbaric constitution of the State," which allows for no cultural renewal, and from the dominant culture, which is characterized by division of labor, specialization, and alienation—all of which threaten the totality of the human being. Finally, this declaration of autonomy is directed against any state or religious control over art. "Poetry never carries out a specific task for human beings," reads another programmatic passage. "Its sphere of effect is the totality of human nature."[204] That Goethe shared this conception is suggested by passages underlined in his copy of Kant's *Kritik der Urteilskraft*[205] and by a letter to Karl Friedrich Zelter, in which he praised Kant for the "immeasurable merit" of having declared art to be autonomous.[206]

Art as the "pure product of isolation" (Schiller) is opposed in the broadest sense to the dominant social relations, whereby it contrafactually keeps alive the hope for a more human world. Of course, it also belongs to the dialectic of the autonomy concept not only that it affords resistance against the reality principle, but also that this resistance becomes abstract, through the renunciation of the social practice. The beautiful illusion compensates for the bad reality. The result can be an affirmative culture that internalizes the sufferings of human beings and accepts the existing order.[207] The same ambivalence is shown in literary life. Undoubtedly, the Classical authors use the autonomy postulate to defend the highest level of art against the market-dominating entertainment literature and the crudity of the public taste. But they thereby alienate themselves more and more from the real public. Indeed, over time they exclude the real public from the enjoyment of art. It is their answer to the fragmentation of the bourgeoisie after the French Revolution and to the crisis of the literary public sphere.

Schiller offered various explanations for this, sometimes irritably polemical but at other times coolly theoretical. When Fichte during a controversy in 1795 taunted him by noting that the public understood his writings better and therefore he had a greater impact, Schiller responded that he had a "hearty disgust for the German public" and had never taken his lead from it; that his writings had been engendered in direct opposition to the spirit of the age.[208] The corresponding theory can be found in "Über naive und sentimentalische Dichtung," in which Schiller (among other things) reflects on the value of literature. From poetry, he says, one expects pleasure, relaxation, and refinement, expectations which "by themselves are fully correct but which often receive a completely false interpretation," for everything depends on how one defines relaxation. According to Schiller, there are two kinds of relaxation: one derives from the "needs of the *sensual nature*," while the other restores the "autonomy of the *human nature*." After "exhausting work," the former seeks mere relaxation and "can only restore itself in emptiness"; the latter seeks the ideal of restorative relaxation, "the reproduction of our natural wholeness after one-sided tensions." Here Schiller obviously means nothing less than the aesthetic condition. The necessary precondition for genuine relaxation through art would be the bringing to it of "an open mind, an expansive heart, a fresh, unweakened spirit"—indeed, of having one's "entire nature in a state of unity." Only a few persons are in this fortunate state and thus capable of true enjoyment of art—certainly not the "working class," which Schiller must write off as "victims of their jobs." He is therefore forced to look around for "a class of human beings who, without working, are nevertheless active. . . . Only such a class can preserve the beautiful wholeness of human nature, which every labor temporarily disturbs, and which a laboring *life* permanently destroys."[209] This is the "circle of the select few," as it is called in the "Aesthetic Letters," who represent the ideal of the harmonious human being and among whom he found his ideal public.

Obviously, Schiller had abandoned as a hopeless illusion the Enlightenment ideal of a homogeneous public. As in his review of Bürger, he here presumed the disintegration of the bourgeois public. In light of the capitalization of the literary market, he detached himself from the real public and turned toward an ideal public that had scarcely been formed. Since he was no longer guided by the taste of the market, and since the ideal public was a privileged minority, Schiller had manuevered himself into such an extremely marginal position that he had to champion his ideal of art *against* the literary public. With Goethe, he proceeded to position himself "against the spirit of the age": that is, they became Classical, and those wishing to understand them and to ascend to their level of cultivation had to make an effort.

This attitude toward literary life had serious consequences for literary criticism. To the degree that the "art judges of handiwork" were not simply laughed at (because they could formulate only "technical but not *aesthetic* judgments"), they were freed from their Enlightenment task: namely, to speak for the public and to act as mediators between public and work. Since the autonomous artwork is completely independent of public taste and contemporary interests, aesthetic criticism limits itself to offering understanding interpretations. As a "genetic method" (Schiller), criticism supplements theory by theoretically justifying and completing the work. The detailed correspondence between Goethe and Schiller concerning *Wilhelm Meisters Lehrjahre* can serve as a paradigm of such criticism; it was supplemented by further letters and interpretations from others in their circle.[210] This confirmed Schiller's maxim that only a few "possess correct judgment in aesthetic matters" and that therefore, "in order to have their works interpreted," they ought to expose them only to the critique of such connoisseurs. Criticism thus became a conversation about art, conducted within a literary elite, a "literary association" that defined the taste ideals of the epoch in contrast to the needs of the public. Here the criticism of Weimar Classicism agreed with the reflexive criticism of Romanticism, the foundation of which was the autonomy of art and which stood "with its back to the public."

The journalistic organ of his "literary association" became Schiller's

Horen, whose programmatic "prospectus" can be regarded as the manifesto of Classicism. Here the Weimar circle organized itself (albeit loosely) as the journal's editors,[211] and its ideas received an institutional framework. The founding conception is interesting in its own right. In an "invitation to participate" written by Schiller (with the assistance of Fichte and Wilhelm von Humboldt), artists, writers, and scientists are called upon to form a "society" to stimulate the interest of the educated public. If each writer would bring his readers to the journal, Schiller speculated, the *Horen* would have "the entire reading world as its public."[212] In fact, the list of co-editors that appeared with the "prospectus" of the *Horen* in the *Allgemeine Literatur-Zeitung* (*ALZ*) in December 1794 would have done honor to any academy. Yet unlike the scholarly and literary societies of the Enlightenment, whose journals published internal discussions in order to advance criticism and general reasoning, Schiller was primarily interested in an effective attention-getting device to arouse the interest of the "widest possible circle of readers and buyers." As an adept publisher who knew the laws of the market only too well from personal experience, Schiller didn't shy from unusual measures in order to secure the highest possible market share for his literary journal. It has been correctly observed that he "used a publicist's methods to advance positions that were against the expectations of the public."[213] He was without scruple about utilizing criticism for the purpose of advertising: a deal was made with the *ALZ* editor (who by fortunate coincidence happened also to be a member of the "society") to review each issue of the *Horen* immediately after its appearance. As if this weren't enough, the review was also to be written by a "member of our society" in order that it be properly "enthusiastic."[214] Schiller wrote to Cotta that this "preferment," which had never before been enjoyed by any journal, made "any further advertisement in the other learned newspapers" unnecessary.[215] Literary criticism as literary advertisement illustrates once again how important it was to Schiller to win at least the educated public for the new Weimar art program, if not to "compel" their allegiance.

The first issue of the *Horen* appeared in January 1795, still during the period of the revolutionary wars. In the middle of such martial tumult, the journal was intended to form an enclave that defended the "ideals of a refined humanity" against an "impure spirit of partisanship."

According to the prospectus, the journal intended to remain apolitical and far from contemporary events, but "the more the limited interest of the present tenses, narrows, and subjugates our minds, the more pressing becomes our need both to return our minds to freedom and to reunite the politically divided world under the flag of truth and beauty through a universal and higher interest in what is *purely human* and sublimely above all temporal influences."[216] The aestheticization of political reality, which from this point on would be Schiller's "confession of political belief," is already clear: "Through beauty toward freedom," as he wrote at the end of the second letter on "Aesthetic Education." Significantly, the *Horen* begins with this major theoretical work of Schiller's. An education toward art, attained by means of art, is introduced through reflection on art and with exemplary works of the highest artistry.

In the same way, "the previously dispersed public" should be reunited in a manner typical of Schiller's view: "that which had pleased the best" should make its way "into everyone's hands." As in the review of Bürger, it is that "classical popularity" (as Thomas Mann once called it) which through education from above combats the "frivolous taste" in order to make the taste of the literary elite a model for the entire "reading world." True, contributions to the journal were intended to be entertaining and "comprehensible to the public mind," but this meant "an entertainment of a completely different kind," one that corresponded to Schiller's aesthetically demanding "relaxation." Despite his national-pedagogical intentions, the gap between elite and educated public could not be bridged, even by publicistic manipulations. The "classical" journal remained an organ for the internal discussion of the "society" and ignored the entertainment needs of the broader readership. This fact was clear even to observant contemporaries who still oriented themselves toward the Enlightenment's concept of literature and who sharply criticized the esotericism and distance from life of the *Horen:* "In fact one can see clearly here what relations our writers entertain with the public. Precisely in this journal, which should quite properly be dedicated to the German people, one finds a coterie of idiosyncratic writers, running around in a tight circle, one to which the 'uninitiated' have no means of access. . . . Unfortunately, the journal perfectly substantiates the old saw that our public and our writers are essentially disparate, making up two separate classes that will always *remain* alien to one another, since they have fundamentally divergent interests."[217] Schiller nevertheless stuck to his ambitious program—and lost the general public.

Goethe's art journal *Propyläen* (1798–1800) forms a sort of pendant to Schiller's *Horen*—less in its themes, which mostly concentrate on the pictorial arts, than in its tendency: "In these times of general dissolution," Goethe seeks to preserve the lawfulness of human nature and of the development of humanity in the "sanctuary of art." As the programmatic title of the journal at once signalizes, the ancient world is the vanishing point that should afford a perspective to the present: "Which modern nation does not owe its artistic formation to the Greeks? And in certain areas, which more so than the German?"[218] Although Goethe by no means understood his Classicism normatively, the writings in the *Propyläen* (particularly the prize assignments for pictorial artists) were so interpreted by his contemporaries.

Yet for our purposes, the obvious Classicism, which literally tried to *wrest* acceptance as an aesthetic model, is less significant than Goethe's grounding of the autonomy of art, which he clarified by using the distinction between art and nature. The "Introduction to the Propylaeum" states flatly: "The prime demand made of an artist is always that he should stick to nature, study it, and imitate it." Yet in the same connection Goethe also emphasizes that "nature is separated from art by an enormous gap." How can this contradiction be resolved? Obviously, Goethe is no longer content with the naive axiom of the "simple imitation of nature," which as recently as 1789 he had considered the bottommost level of art. Or, more exactly, a naive and uneducated lover of art may enjoy "a work of art as though it were a work of nature"—he does not allow himself to be deceived like the "real sparrows who flew toward the painted cherries"—yet the genuine connoisseur knows that "what is true in art and what is naturally true are two completely different things." Although the artist remains bound to nature and reality, the artwork is a "product of the human spirit": it "goes beyond nature," becoming "second nature." The simple imitation of nature yields at best a superficial description of appearances, while true art transcends nature, lending it depth and significance. These reflections are of great importance for the art theory of the mature Goethe.

The struggle against the "eternal lie of the connection between nature and art"[219] also had a more immediate literary-sociological cause. It was aimed against "naturalism," with its "demands of reality and usefulness." The simplified mimetic principle had long since been pressed into service to legitimate trivial literature, with its naturalness, sentimentality, and quotidian banality. Goethe saw in market-dominated entertainment literature a danger for art and for the intellectual culture of the nation. Without penetrating the economic causes, he criticized writers who "slide along on the broad surface of dilettantism and bungling, between art and nature," and the public which, "for its money and applause, demands works that please it."[220] Of course, Goethe's essays in *Propyläen* placed such high demands on the public that it was neither able nor willing to follow him.

Like Schiller's *Horen*, Goethe's *Propyläen* also quickly ceased publication, because Cotta couldn't sell more than 450 copies. Schiller, who after his disappointment with the *Horen* no longer took much stock in the German public, took this as evidence of its "unparalleled wretchedness." Now it came to a radical drawing of fronts against the public: a state of war was the only relation that would not be regretted later.[221] Accounts had been settled with the "land of the philistines" two years earlier in those poisonous gifts known as the *Xenien*, by means of which Schiller and Goethe polemicized in the *Musenalmanach für das Jahr 1797* against all those who did not share their new conception of art. The *Xenien* could be understood as an epigrammatic critique of literary relations in Germany, even as a substitute for literary criticism, a critique that polemically personalized whatever opposed them ideologically or literarily in this matter. They were directed against the enthusiasts of revolution (most of whom in the meantime had either died off or been effectively isolated); against the late Enlightenment and its journals, which insisted on the intelligibility and social utility of literature; against the reading mob and the public taste, which was too philistine to understand them; in short, against everyone who couldn't understand them or who had criticized them—and this also included, besides the broader public, many writers and scholars who weren't inclined to subject themselves to Weimarian dictates about art.

Such "true poetic devilry" (Schiller), which allowed instruction to follow upon satire and ridicule, called forth a storm of indignation, one that gives an idea of how isolated the Classical writers were in their own epoch. Moreover, the "Xenia War" signaled a crisis in the literary public, whose contradictions were becoming visible. The contemporary reaction to the provocation from Weimar cannot be played down as simply the protest of a few envious writers left behind by the course of progress. The debate involved considerably more: namely, "the struggle among various institutionalizations of literature,"[222] a struggle that in 1797 was still not decided. The sharp criticism that the *Xenien* received from many quarters again accentuates how strongly the Enlightenment-bourgeois conception of literature was, and how greatly it corresponded to the expectations of the public interested in literature. In light of the massive opposition, even Goethe and Schiller came to doubt whether their autonomous concept of art could gain general recognition. They drew from this the consequence that it was necessary to realize their ideals of art against the older expectations. "After the mad and daring deed of the Xenien," wrote Goethe to Schiller, "we now have to set to work producing greater and more dignified artworks, and transform our protean natures, to the shame of our opponents, into the form of the noble and the good."[223] Schiller brought his phase of theoretical creativity to a close and turned back to dramatic poetry; both withdrew from ongoing literary discussions and devoted criticism only to each other's works in progress.

This privatization of criticism into workshop conversations corresponds exactly to the functional transformation of literature. The literature of the Enlightenment supplied the bourgeoisie with meaningful entertainment and moral orientation in the world, and it was this bourgeoisie that made up the public; literary criticism (the forum of which was the literary journals) mediated between works and the public on whose behalf it spoke; in its permanent discussions and debates it constituted a literary-bourgeois public sphere. In Weimar, this Enlightenment-bourgeois public was transformed through the declaration of art's autonomy and the aestheticization of life into a "fine public," which at points reassumed a courtly-representative form.[224] To sum up, the criticism of Weimar Classicism rested on new aesthetic norms largely detached from social practice; it defended the level of the highest art against entertainment literature and the public taste; it gathered support from a like-minded literary elite. In consequence, "the binding quality and universal validity can no longer be legitimated by the literary public sphere."[225] Autonomous literary criticism operated from a position of marginality and aimed for an aesthetic consensus, which could then serve as the basis of a new political public sphere.

The functional transformation of literature can be more clearly traced in the institution of the theater. The bourgeois drama of the Enlightenment understood itself as a "supplement to the laws" (Lessing) or even as a tribunal that functioned as a "podium of the bourgeois public" (Habermas). This public function of the stage, to which Schiller remained faithful until *Don Carlos,* proved illusory in light of the social and literary relations in Germany after 1789. In Weimar Classicism the theater developed into a site of worship (*Kultstätte*) for the "fine public" and an institute of aesthetic education. The theoretical manifesto of this shift is Schiller's preface to the *Braut von Messina* (1803), "On the Use of the Chorus in Tragedy." This essay once again summarizes the main points of Classical aesthetics and can be considered an "organon" of Classical criticism.

Its basis is the principle of autonomy: art should "totally shut itself off from the real world" in order to preserve its "poetic freedom." Only in this way can it succeed in opposing to the "oppressive constriction" of reality a "possible" world that in the mode of potentiality criticizes the real existing world and demands a better one. Like Goethe, therefore, Schiller "openly and honestly declares a war upon naturalism in art." The "lowly concept of the natural" is damaging to art because it adheres to the surface of appearances, and the "loyal painters of the real" never grasp the "spirit of nature" that lies beneath the "cover of appearances." Moreover, these writers ruin the taste of the public, which becomes accustomed to what is inferior and does not demand that which is superior. True art distances itself from the reality it idealizes and poeticizes, so that ultimately "everything is only a symbol of the real." Yet art wishes to achieve more than mere temporary deception through illusion; in the appearance of art the truth is taken up and preserved, since in it the idea comes to appearance. This synopsis of aesthetics is the foundation for Schiller's new functional determination of the theater.[226]

Even in this, some Enlightenment substance shimmers through, as when he writes that the viewer hopes to find "on the stage the moral government of the world which he misses in real life." But with the introduction of the chorus in modern drama, Schiller discovers an "organ of art" that transforms the "common constricting reality" into a poetical reality, thus guaranteeing the separation of art from the prose of life. It is a fact that contemporary reality does not appear directly in any of Schiller's Classical dramas: everything political or bearing contemporary relevance is eradicated in favor of an "ahistorical Classicism" (Peter Szondi), as in the *Braut von Messina*. Yet not completely—for Schiller hopes with this chorus drama to achieve no less than the aesthetic "reproduction" of "everything immediate" in public life, as it had been known to the ancient Greeks. Schiller sees the distinction between the ancient and the modern conditions of life in the fact that in the old tragedy "the actions and fates of the heroes and kings were already in and of themselves public," and the accompanying chorus represented the public; the political public of the present has become abstract "through the artificial arrangements of real life": "The palaces of the kings are now closed, the courts have withdrawn from the gates of the cities to the interiors of the houses, writing has repressed the living word, and the people itself, the sensual living mass, where it doesn't act as naked force, has been transformed into the state: that is, into an abstract concept." The unnatural state of modern life is demonstrated by the polarization of society into a public-political sphere, in which the citizen has no influence, and a private sphere, in which morality and humanity are preserved. The individual and the people have become alienated from the state, or, as he put it elsewhere: "The state remains perpetually alien to its citizens, since feelings cannot reach it."[227] Through the introduction of the chorus, Schiller wants at least to hint poetically at what modern life is missing in the way of public representation: "The poet must rebuild the palaces; he must lead the courts back out into the open air." He wants to compensate for the lack of a public life with the appearance of a *possible* public sphere. "The world of the stage thereby becomes a contrasting image to the present condition of the world, a *terra utopica*."[228]

Yet one must not overlook the exaggeration contained in this idealistic experimentation with form. Schiller's aesthetic public sphere is, *qua* "aesthetic state," an artistic and pedagogical maxim which, although it possesses the appearance of an ideal that is close to life, in fact has hardly anything further in common with the literary-critical public sphere of the Enlightenment. Because Schiller, unlike the Greeks, cannot derive the chorus from real life and its public forms, this also fails to become "a concrete representation of the public."[229] The choir, as an "organ of art," can at best "extend itself to the human in general in order to draw the great conclusions of life and to express the teachings of wisdom." Certainly, this expresses the aspirations to humanity of Weimar Classicism, aspirations which—faced with a deforming society and its politics—keep alive the Utopia of the "whole human being" and a harmonious society. Yet the art figure of the chorus brings no direct bourgeois, critical reasoning into the drama; it has neither public relevance nor resonance, at any rate not in the Enlightenment sense.[230] If, despite the renunciation of the real public, one wishes to speak of a public in Weimar Classicism, it can only be characterized as a counterpublic. The criticism of the epoch reflects these tendencies: it becomes autonomous and serves a "fine public."

TRANSLATED BY JOHN R. BLAZEK

JOCHEN SCHULTE-SASSE

. . . .

The Concept of Literary Criticism in
German Romanticism, 1795–1810

Art and Criticism in Romanticism: A Retreat into the
Esoteric World of an Aestheticist Praxis?

T H E disintegration in the last quarter of the eighteenth century
of the Enlightenment project to establish a bourgeois public
sphere—a process described in the previous chapter—reached
its apex in Romanticism, where the notion of a bourgeois public
sphere completely relinquished its regulatory power over the practice
of politics and literature.[1] Disturbed and sensitized by the experience
of a mass literary market and repelled by the development of a new
bourgeois ethos grounded in economics, the Romantics retreated
more and more into an aesthetic praxis, which still claimed to be
socially critical but held that a meaningful social critique could be
made only from the unalienated position of what proved to be an
increasingly esoteric aestheticism. A plethora of novels thematizing
the artist's alienation from society's superficial business orientation
(*Künstlerromane*) exemplified this literary stance. In order to illustrate
the obvious parallels between literary production, critical practices,
and theoretical reflections, and to make my introductory characterization somewhat less theoretical, I will first deal briefly with two such
novels.

The hero of Ludwig Tieck's *Franz Sternbalds Wanderungen*, published
in 1798, is a painter whose repeated confrontations with a society
ruled by bourgeois economics impress upon the reader the themat-

ically dominant antagonism between the artist and the bourgeoisie. For example, while traveling through the Netherlands, Franz is supposed to deliver a letter from Albrecht Dürer, whom he reveres, to a Flemish businessman. At a dinner hosted by the businessman, Franz encounters the city's bourgeois society, which is interested only in economic questions: "Only a few people noticed him, and those who started conversations accidentally broke them off once they learned he was a painter." His host, in whom he had hoped to find a like-minded partner, "rambled on about how he had gradually improved his factory and made it more profitable. What particularly troubled Franz was that all the rich people present were spoken of with the greatest respect; he felt that money was the only thing anyone paid attention to and valued." To heighten the antagonism between art and society at the level of narration, Tieck allows the single-mindedly success-oriented host, who is convinced he has Franz's best interests at heart, to attempt to dissuade him from his plan to devote his life to art: "You're young, so let me give you some advice. When I was young I occupied myself from time to time sketching, but as I got older I realized that it wouldn't get me anywhere. I therefore shifted my attention to serious pursuits and devoted all my time to them; and look, they made me what I am now. I control a large factory and a large number of workers, and I always need loyal people to supervise them and to keep track of my accounts. If you want, you could start with me at a very good salary, because my chief supervisor just died."[2]

It hardly need be mentioned that the artist Franz distances himself from such profane, blasphemous opinions. For him such experiences are merely occasions to reflect upon the unartistic, egoistic business orientation of this world, which forces the individual into an isolated, agonistic existence: "There is something sad about the fact that the whole of human life . . . is driven by the shabbiest of mechanisms; pitiful worries about tomorrow set everyone in motion . . . they are all martyred, plagued by drudgery, envy, selfishness, plans, and worry, so that they lack the heart to see art and literature [*Poesie*], the heavens and nature as something divine."[3]

Here art is no longer determined by any practical connections with everyday concerns, as was the case during the Enlightenment; it is no longer supposed to shape bourgeois society by portraying its norms and values, thereby providing a medium in which those who experience art in their role as members of society have an opportunity to view and perceive the most important and the most desirable social norms aesthetically and, on the basis of their perception, to reflect on them critically. Art has ceased to be an agent of the public interest; on the contrary, it has segregated itself from society, which it views as thoroughly unartistic. Nothing illustrates this more clearly than the effect of one of Europe's largest commercial cities on Franz:

> All the commercial activity in Antwerp was a completely new show to Franz. It seemed to him miraculous how these people moved about among themselves like a restless sea, and every one of them with only his own advantage in mind. Not a single artistic thought occurred to him here; in fact, when he saw the multitude of large ships, the bustle directed at making money, everyone's attention to business, the meetings at the exchange, it seemed to him impossible that anyone from this confused mass could dedicate himself to tranquil art. . . . He did not fail to notice that the businessmen continued their commercial conversations and speculations even when they took a walk, and he was too depressed by this new view of life to be able to ignore it.[4]

It is certainly not accidental that Tieck chose Antwerp as the paradigm of an alienated industrial society. In the early fifteenth century, when the novel takes place, Antwerp under Charles V was the wealthiest trading city in the world and had already developed distinct capitalistic features. In addition, many eighteenth-century writers considered the Netherlands rather than England to be the prototypical embodiment of bourgeois economic ideas. As the most powerful city of the Spanish Netherlands, Antwerp therefore bore a considerable semiotic value for Tieck. As a capitalist city of the late Middle Ages, it signaled the disintegration of an era highly valued by the Romantics and could thus signify their anticapitalistic sentiments.

The "Romantic anti-capitalism" (Georg Lukács) that Tieck's novel embodies was characteristic of the generation born around 1770. Novalis portrayed the similar experiences of an artist amid a society of merchants in his *Heinrich von Ofterdingen*, in which the merchants with whom the protagonist travels use art only to compensate for their everyday activities. As Friedrich Schlegel wrote in one of his *Athenäum* fragments, summarizing the sentiment of his generation: "Triviality—

economy—is the necessary supplement of all people who aren't absolutely universal [that is, who only foster their selfish interests]. Often talent and education are lost entirely in the process."[5] And in his *Ideen* he said: "Wherever there are politics or economics no morality exists" (*FS*, 250).

The Romantics' anticapitalism and their opposition to the bourgeoisie were driven to new heights by the disappointment they experienced at the hands of the literary market in their attempt to influence society. The Romantics contrasted the bourgeoisie's ties to "particular" interests, such as greed, with an artistic ethos supposedly free from all such interests; while the bourgeois seems narrow-minded, agonistic, provincial, and egotistical, the artist appears to be an exceptional, morally superior outsider who can claim special rights. As a result of this newly won moral self-confidence the Romantics felt compelled to polemicize against every literary movement (like the Enlightenment) that, in spite of its contemporaries' narrow horizons and limited comprehension, still clung at all costs to a project in which the medium "literature" was given the political or philosophical task of educating its public, even when this meant that writers had to curtail their artistic ambitions in order to be understood. In the Romantic view, those contemporaries who were still partisans of the Enlightenment preferred to close their eyes to the increasingly visible contradictions within bourgeois society; they still maintained the fiction of a uniform bourgeois public sphere that merely needed to be educated, even after the representatives of both Classicism and Romanticism had recognized this fiction to be fiction.

It is immediately apparent that the Romantics' view of social reality would have to have a direct effect on the concepts underlying Romantic literary criticism and praxis. The Romantics had no intention of founding periodicals aimed at mass circulation and critiquing all new publications for a broad readership, as did Friedrich Nicolai's *Allgemeine Deutsche Bibliothek*, a characteristic embodiment of the Enlightenment project. Consequently, the traditional genre of the book review, aimed at mediating standards to a general public, had to disintegrate. Nevertheless, in the history of literary criticism, Romanticism is rightly seen as a period of culmination. To understand the nature of its mode of criticism, one must ask whether Romantic criticism aimed at an esoteric exchange of ideas among like-minded individuals voluntarily residing in their respective ivory towers, or whether the Romantic project itself was the product of a social analysis that did not remain external to its concept of criticism and its critical (and literary) praxis, thus presupposing the possibility of affecting society through, and *only* through, a seemingly aestheticist criticism.

In order to answer these two questions one must decide how to judge the Romantic tendency of aestheticist retreat from society. From the perspective of the Enlightenment (or from a contemporary perspective that has been shaped by the tradition of Enlightenment thought, such as the liberal-leftist literary criticism of more "progressive" Germanists), this tendency is *in and of itself* negative. Yet there can be no doubt about its existence. One of the first and most important Romantic literary documents, Wilhelm Heinrich Wackenroder's *Herzensergiessungen eines kunstliebenden Klosterbruders*, written in 1796, glorifies the artist's aestheticist retirement from the world in vibrant colors: "The essence of works of art is as unsuited to the common flow of life as thoughts about God." Here, art seems to provide an opportunity to distance oneself from life, an ascent to pleasures that are distant from society and hostile to it. Wackenroder writes of the artist-hero Berglinger: "Heaven had created him in such a way that he was always striving toward something higher; he was not satisfied with the mere health of his soul, that it conducted its business on earth, working and performing good deeds, in an orderly fashion—he wanted it to dance in luxurious wantonness, rejoicing to heaven, its place of origin." Wackenroder's description of Berglinger's reaction to the regular musical performances in a church functions like the iconography of an otherworldly, as yet unconstituted religion of art. At the same time, this passage is one of the first examples of the motif of aestheticist *élévation*, which was so characteristic of nineteenth- and early twentieth-century symbolism and aestheticism—an elevation that liberated the artist from the dross of reality:

> Before the music started, while standing in the midst of a softly murmuring crowd, he felt as if he could hear the confused, discordant buzz of the ordinary and base life of people at a fair all around him; his head was dazed by the empty, earthly trivialities. He waited expectantly for the first tone from the instruments— and by appearing, extended and powerful, from the dull silence it

broke over him with the force of a wind from heaven, carrying the collected force of the music over his head—then it seemed as if large wings had been affixed to his soul, as if he were being lifted from a dry heath; the sad curtain of clouds before his mortal eyes disappeared, and he wafted toward the bright heavens. He used his body to keep himself quiet and immobile, and he fixed his gaze unwaveringly at the floor. The present moment sank before him; his core was cleansed of all the earthly trifles that are the dust on the soul's shining surface.[6]

That Wackenroder is not unique in his esoteric conception of artistic production and reception is shown by a brief reference to Friedrich Schlegel, who was the most important theoretician of early Romantic criticism: "What am I proud of, and what can I be proud of as an artist? Of the decision that separated and isolated me forever from everything ordinary . . . of the awareness that I can stimulate my fellows to do their best, and that everything they create is my gain" (*FS*, 254). Artists as a group are closely linked here to an elitist circle of art recipients, for the ascent to the lofty heights of art on the part of its creators corresponds to the ability and readiness of a closed group of insiders to recognize the essence of art. Reacting to the bifurcation of the public by the marketplace,[7] Friedrich Schlegel talks of readers who "are always complaining that German authors write for such a small circle, and even sometimes just for themselves. That's how it should be. This is how German literature will gain more and more spirit and character" (*FS*, 201).

The direct, experiential connection between art and social reality is in far greater jeopardy here than in Goethe and Schiller. To be sure, as Schiller grew increasingly pessimistic about the present and the possibility of influencing it through art, he pushed the social goals to be achieved by art more decidedly into the distant future, but the tension in his thinking between the present and the future, between reality and the ideal, remained essentially historical; his art was intended to work concretely toward overcoming the difference. Criticism was therefore, at least in Schiller's own understanding of it, embedded in a praxis based on the notion that the artistic portrayal of a historically and philosophically grounded ideal society can provide a preview of a better world, one that can be realized gradually. Because Schiller's displacement of the social goals of art into the too distant future limited the number of concrete references to social experiences he could make in his work, his late conception of aesthetics implicitly runs the risk of allowing art to degenerate into an emotional refuge detached from reality—that is, into a merely compensatory medium—despite his declared intentions. Nevertheless, Schiller's declared purpose was still direct influence. By way of contrast, the Romantic theory of art consciously altered the (historical) character of the tension between the real and the ideal. Schiller himself presented the clearest expression of this difference in a letter to Goethe, dated September 14, 1797: "Out of desperation that he cannot reduce the empirical nature that surrounds him to an aesthetic one, the newer artist [i.e., the Romantic] with a lively phantasy and spirit prefers to abandon it completely and looks to the imagination for help against things empirical, against reality. He implants a poetic content in his work, which would otherwise be empty and inadequate, because he lacks the content that has to be drawn from the depths of an object."

The fact that both the production and the reception of art became esoteric in Romanticism led to a radical restructuring of the concept of criticism predominant in the eighteenth century. As we have seen, Enlightenment criticism owed its institutionalization to a practical interest in constituting and shaping a public sphere. The Romantic concept of criticism lacked not only the link with a concrete, contemporary public sphere but also every inclination to engage in detailed negation: that is, to condemn a literary work on the basis of a reasoned argument. For the Enlightenment concept of criticism, oriented as it was toward a progressional form of argument, the element of evaluative, analytic differentiation of the positive from the negative was so constitutive that it governed critical praxis even in its details. Merely pointing out the negative was not sufficient; its existence had to be proved and analyzed in order to achieve criticism's purpose: namely, to have a permanent influence on the analytical quality of public argumentation. This was already true of Pierre Bayle, the first important theoretician whose theory of criticism was rooted in a teleological philosophy of history, in a concept of progress. For Bayle, Enlightenment criticism "did not bring forth the truth directly; instead, it began the destruction of appearances."[8] In the eyes of the Romantics, as we will see later, it was just this moment of methodologically controlled analysis and negation that caused Enlightenment literary criticism to be caught affirmatively in the snares of social modernity.

In Romantic criticism, by contrast, "the negative is completely atrophied" (Walter Benjamin). As Friedrich Schlegel wrote in 1804 in *Lessings Gedanken und Meinungen*, it wants to be a "literary organon, that is, a form of criticism that would not just enlighten and preserve but would itself be productive, at least indirectly through guidance, direction, inspiration."[9] It consciously intends to be positive and constructive in its attitude toward the individual work in order to assist in the development of the spirit that exists in every work but also transcends its boundaries, so that the work of art is brought to full fruition in the critic's reflections. The critic thus is actively involved in the process through which not only the individual work but art in general is completed. For a particular work of art, every reading can be only an approximate realization of the infinite reflexive continuum contained in it. In delving into this continuum, the critic completes the work of art as a work. Critical reading, seen as an act of genius, reaches its historical high point here, with the consequence that everyday criticism—critiquing new books in short reviews—loses its importance. The preferred form of Romantic criticism is the long philosophical essay. In addition, the critique of recently published books is perceived as being of less importance than the critique of established works of world literature, even though they may be thousands of years old. In contrast to Nicolai, whose *Allgemeine Deutsche Bibliothek* appeared in 268 volumes without interruption between 1765 and 1806 and attempted to review every new book that appeared on the market, the Romantics increasingly turned their attention to the great literature of the past. A. W. Schlegel is a typical example of the development of this sort of reviewing practice; his *Jenaische Allgemeine Literaturzeitung* published nearly 300 reviews between 1796 and 1799, but after about 1801 it ceased reviewing contemporary works entirely.

The artist's and the literate cognoscenti's self-imposed aestheticist isolation from society is reflected in this development, as well as in the philosophical anchoring of the Romantic concept of criticism. "Criticism" acquires a new meaning in the Romantic period. Where the Romantic "concept of criticism remains historical" (*KA*, 3:81)—that is, where criticism still refers to the practice of reviewing carried on in the Enlightenment, and where the "total reversal" or conceptual reorientation envisioned by the Romantics has not yet occurred—the paradoxical result is a situation in which the best critics use their reviews to polemicize against *Kritik* and the practice of reviewing books. Clemens Brentano, for example, whom Wilhelm Grimm ironically but quite justifiably labeled "one of the best critics" of the era,[10] wrote in 1815: "Furthermore, wanting to use public, sensible criticism to improve theaters and actors would be an extremely incomprehensible project. . . . Since the Hamburger Pastor Goeze's condemnation of the theater (an opinion we almost completely subscribe to), since Lessing's vital dramaturgy . . . not a single theater critic . . . has produced even the slightest change in European theater, any more than the voices of publicly political writers will ever be able to exert an active, effective influence on the course of history."[11] Here the rejection of the traditional Enlightenment institution of literary criticism is very clearly linked to the rejection of a public function for art in general.

Friedrich Schlegel's revaluation of criticism, which originated in the "theoretical conviction that all criticism should be extremely positive,"[12] corresponded to the logic of this development. However, when he asserted that "true criticism need take no notice whatsoever of works that do not contribute to the development of art and science" (*KA*, 2:411) and in this connection maintained that bad art was not amenable to criticism, he did not mean that the critic should refrain completely from dealing critically with literature written for the masses in order to concentrate on the unfolding of the beautiful and providing support for it. The negative moment in literary judgments is constitutive of another form of literary praxis—namely, the "polemic," whose difference from criticism reflects the dichotomy between art and society: "In order to create a space for the seeds of something better, all sorts of mistakes and figments of the imagination have to be cleared away. One can agree with Lessing in calling this a polemic" (*KA*, 3:58). Polemics directed against "non-art" (*Unpoesie*)—that is, widely distributed popular literature—which were part of the Enlightenment as well as the contemporary concept and practice of criticism, can also be found in Romantic criticism, although the Romantics would have denied that name to such a critical activity. In their polemics against the mass market and popular literature, the Romantics used the same biting tone that had become common after the bifurcation and commercialization of the book market.[13]

Whenever the realms of art and social reality confront one another as antagonistically as they do in Romanticism, the confrontation results in two differing critical practices for which different names have to be found; the qualitative split among works of literature depends on whether the literature in question is able to rise above the particular interests governing social reality or is immersed in them. For Schlegel, art and "non-art" (popular literature) form the basis for two opposing spheres of value among books, which scarcely impinge on each other: "Two completely different types of literature exist right now alongside one another . . . each has its own public, and each proceeds without worrying about the other. They take no notice whatsoever of each other, except when they meet by chance, to express mutual contempt and derision—often not without a secret envy of the one's popularity or the other's respectability."[14] In summary, *criticism* is the technical term for dealing with the esoteric sphere, while the criticism that deals with popular literature is called *polemic*. A few lines after remarking that one should take no notice of works whose "nonexistence" and "nullity" contribute nothing to the development of art, Schlegel continues in the same vein:

It can be the case that one should not avoid the proof of this nonexistence and nullity, and this allows us to deduce the necessity for polemic in a manner that is bound to garner relatively general agreement, because all the individual examples and their urgency make it extremely evident. It seems to me, however, that the polemic is much more than that, much more than a necessary evil; when it is what it is supposed to be, then it is the crown on the most vital effect of the divine in mankind, the touchstone of a mature mind. Should it not be the beginning of all comprehension to be able to separate the good from the bad? At least that is my belief; and when I see that a man is content to be easily and superficially tolerant in his own particular sphere, that he lacks the heart to unconditionally reject something that has been honored [by popular approval] and to posit [such approval] as an evil principle, then I can only maintain, on the basis of my way of thinking, that it is simply not clear to him, even when outward appearances would indicate that things are perfectly clear to him. (KA, 2:411)

By pointing out the insurmountable antagonism between art and social reality, the polemic becomes social criticism, because it condemns
the literature produced in accordance with the fashionable dictates of
the marketplace. Such literature responds to readers' emotional needs
and, as a result, corresponds to the economic spirit of the time (which
was beginning to realize that these needs could be profitable). Polemic
practiced as a form of Romantic annihilation is an act of aesthetic
liberation for artists, who are not as interested in rising above reality as
in freeing themselves from it. As a matter of principle therefore,
polemic is just as important as criticism: "Every honest man, every real
cynic starts with an absolute polemic. I started in the same way—
decisively opposed to my situation and to all of modernity" (*KA*,
18:80).

Three Interpretations of the Romantic Critique of Civilization

My introductory section was intended to provide a general characterization, to be elaborated and clarified below, of the Romantic critique
of society and its effect on the theory and praxis of literary criticism.
The use of notions like "making artistic production and reception
esoteric" and "aestheticist retreat" from social reality (that is, as the
Enlightenment had perceived that reality) was meant to present a set
of facts, not to evaluate them. Actually, the circumstances in question
can be evaluated from three radically different perspectives. If I judge
correctly, these three viewpoints, in various mixtures and colorations,
have determined recent research into Romanticism.

To begin, there is the leftist-rationalist method of dealing with Romanticism, which is still firmly attached to Enlightenment traditions
and regards the aestheticist reorientation described above as a kind of
political original sin. According to this position, even current literature
would do well to provide a medium in which members of a society
could perceive and reflect upon various constellations of norms and
values. This position intellectualizes literature's emotional component
(its ability to foster sensate, intuitive cognition) by coupling literature
to a public process of opinion formation (preferably in the form of
literary studies in high schools and universities, in cultural publica-

tions, and in the arts sections of newspapers) and by making the medium "literature" part of a rational political project whose goal is the systematic realization of a humane society. Such a project, including the function it ascribes to literature, is premised, first, on an extremely optimistic, basically unmaterialistic belief in the ability of people to plan and, second, on confidence in the cleansing potential of an enlightened public discourse, through which people could rid themselves rationally of all the undesirable inscriptions on their psyches or bodies, without leaving any traces. As we shall see, it is just this optimism that the Romantics were no longer able to share. Thus the Romantic change in the concept of criticism was the result of an analysis of society that has to be explained much more thoroughly than was done above.

Works of literary historiography that share the premises and political interests of this first perspective often rely on the historical and theoretical results of Jürgen Habermas's *Strukturwandel der Öffentlichkeit* (Structural change in the public sphere). Ironically, however, most of Habermas's major work can be assigned to a different tradition. He increasingly takes the category of rationalization, with which Max Weber attempted to describe the essence of modernity, as his starting point. But if Weber judges modernity—that is, the results of the process of rationalization—ambivalently (he is very much aware of the loss of freedom that came with social rationalization and of the emotional loss connected with cultural rationalization), Habermas seems increasingly ready to regard the functional dissociation of ideological, economic, and emotional reproduction within autonomous institutions as an indispensable accomplishment of modernity, in spite of its negative side effects. According to Habermas:

> From the perspective of the individual, the absolute and the objective spirits appear to have taken on a structure through which the subjective spirit can emancipate itself from the organic form [*Naturwüchsigkeit*] of traditional life. In the process the spheres in which the individual lived as *bourgeois, citoyen,* and *homme* [roles that correspond to the economic, ideological, and emotional realms of reproduction] increasingly diverge from one another and become independent. The separation and the independence, when viewed in historical and philosophical context, open the

way for an emancipation from ancient forms of dependence, but at the same time they are experienced as abstraction, as alienation from the totality of a traditional way of life.[15]

Habermas seems to conclude that the negative side effects of rationalization mentioned toward the end of the passage can be mitigated or sublated by the resultant order itself. His optimism is apparent, first, because he ascribes functions within modernity to one of the three spheres (material or technological, political or moral, aesthetic or emotional reproduction of society), which this sphere alone can undertake—namely, the aesthetic; second, because the fulfillment of these functions identifies the aesthetic sphere as a constitutive and functionally autonomous subsystem within a rational order: "Only bourgeois art, which has become autonomous in the face of demands for employment extrinsic to art, has taken up positions on behalf of the victims of bourgeois rationalization."[16] The dissociated realm of art makes it possible for individuals to experience the integration they long for into a community of sympathetic human beings—an integration that, although it takes place in the medium of fiction, is nevertheless actual (imaginary experiences produced by aesthetic identification are actual, too). Aesthetic pleasure is in this case a forgetting of the self in the process of an aesthetic reprieve from social constraints to behave like a selfsame identity; it is thereby a sublation of alienation in a happy, even if imaginary, human community. The Enlightenment project of coupling art and life through the graphic presentation of contextually (also politically and economically) important constellations of norms and values totally neglects or contradicts the dissociation of different, independent spheres within society and the accompanying institutionalization of art as a compensatory medium.

Habermas sees the greatest threat to the project of an apparently rational differentiation of society in the complete purging of practical experience from the aesthetic realm while *at the same time* the aesthetic principle is being extended to other spheres. When the critique of bourgeois society immanent in the aesthetic realm (immanent in regard both to the content of individual works and to the medium as such, although the content-oriented critique of society in an individual work is always already defused by the functionally differentiated institutionalization of art) attempts to transgress the boundaries of its own sphere, it necessarily has to confront the status of theoretical and practical reason in modernity. According to Habermas, such a dangerous project marks the "entry into postmodernity," the attempt to overcome the rational organization of society in modernity that began in Romanticism and attained its first programmatically consistent formulation in Nietzsche: "Nietzsche continues the Romantic purging of the theoretical and moral dimension from aesthetic phenomena. In aesthetic experience Dionysian reality is sealed off from the world of theoretical comprehension and moral activity, from everyday life, by a gulf of forgetting. Art allows entry into the Dionysian world only at the price of ecstasy—at the price of a painful undifferentiation or dissolution [*Entgrenzung*] of the individual, his or her melting internally and externally into amorphous nature." By giving up its complementary functional role as a "pendant [*Gegeninstanz*] to reason" aesthetic experience—according to the postmodern project as Habermas sees it—is supposed to assist in the practical and effective "self-unveiling of a decentered form of subjectivity freed from all the limits of cognition and purpose, from all the imperatives of usefulness and morality."[17]

Among other reasons, these ideas are important for an assessment of Romanticism because they allow critics to interpret the process discussed above, in which art became esoteric, as a necessary yet positive result of the process of rationalization described by Weber. According to this view, the consignment of art to an aestheticist, esoteric realm was part of the project of modernity as long as art was restricted to that institutionally separate realm. If it could be shown that Romanticism contained elements that linked it to the postmodern project of undoing the differentiation of social organizations—that is, if the Romantic project saw the extension of aesthetic principles into reality as its goal—then the assessment of Romanticism would have to become negative, but from this perspective the Romantics could no longer be blamed for abandoning the Enlightenment project of mediating socially important norms through art.

Habermas himself now seems to have been influenced by literary scholarship that places Romanticism closer to the Enlightenment, at least ideologically (although not in regard to the autonomous institutionalization of art in modernity, which gains a new quality with Romantic art), which has recently led him to try to link Romanticism more closely to the project of modernity. (He quotes Manfred Frank; one could add Klaus Peter, among others.)

Interestingly enough, no matter what Habermas is now up to, the third position is attempting to uncover the anarchic, postmodern strands of early Romanticism. In this connection Gisela Dischner speaks of the "polit-aesthetic aspect" of early Romantic theories of art, which is expressed in the project of a "synthesis of art and life."[18] In fact, when Friedrich Schlegel talks about the "unification of poetry and life" in his lectures *Geschichte der europäischen Literatur* (The history of European literature), which he delivered in Paris in 1803, he defines Romantic art as a kind of poetry "that tries to unite itself with life, where life is completely poetic and poetry completely alive" (*KA,* 11:156; see also 11:181). His definition seems to contain the very elements that Habermas finds characteristic of postmodernity: namely, an undoing of the differentiation of social organization in modernity, and the claim that aesthetic principles ought to apply to other, functionally autonomous spheres of life. According to this third line of reasoning, the polit-aesthetic program of early Romanticism, which was an attack on the Enlightenment project of modernity, was the critical epistemological precipitate of social and historical developments in the course of which individuals came to see society as an increasingly impenetrable set of relationships. On the basis of their critical assessment of society the Romantics are supposed to have concluded that only a strategy of anarchic dismantling—that is, deconstructive disengagement—had any chance of success. In this sense the French historian Henri Brunschwig characterized Romantic politics as the politics of miracles, because the belief in the possibility of gradual change through reform had been lost: "The new mentality generates political methods into which the Romantics plunge haphazardly in every country—the revolutionary rising to bring a new order suddenly into being."[19] The same mentality is reflected in the early Romantics' reaction to the French Revolution; without exception they praised it, and their support generally continued long after the Jacobin terror had reversed public opinion in Germany. Since the events in Paris are usually interpreted historically as an attempt to realize Enlightenment ideas on the part of the bourgeoisie, the question arises how Romantic enthusiasm for the revolution could coincide with the deliberately antibourgeois, esoteric position of art in Romanticism discussed above. The answer may lie in the individualist, activist character of that enthusiasm, which was inspired by actions that transcended the individual, thus freeing him from the dross of an unsatisfactory reality and at the same time dismantling it.

Apparently all three critical positions (I have omitted a fourth, conservative one) vary considerably in their assessment of the Romantic concept of criticism. The *"enlightened" leftist-rationalist* perspective finds there an aestheticist escapism that undermines the political potential of literature; the *leftist-liberal, system-theoretical* standpoint accepts what it sees as a critical praxis involved with humane self-realization, a praxis that complements the realm of the state (politics) and that of bourgeois society (economics) as long as it recognizes the differentiation and restricts itself to an institutionally autonomous aesthetic realm; the *deconstructive-anarchic* position sees in Romantic criticism the formulation of a program that allows the members of society to free themselves at least momentarily from the repressive, alienating intellectual pressures of modernity, thereby creating a critical potential that is a prerequisite for every intervention in social reality. We can decide which of these assessments comes closest to Romantic intentions only after we have mapped out the constitutive features of the Romantic critique of society and observed their influence on the Romantic theory of art in general. As Karl Solger once wrote in a review, "If I am supposed to express my provisional opinion of the *Wahlverwandtschaften*, I have to act like a critic, which is not really my preferred way of doing things, and start with some general theoretical considerations."[20] The same is true here.

The Romantic Critique of Civilization and the Functional Autonomy of Art

In the introduction to his *Vorlesung über schöne Literatur und Kunst* (Lectures on fine literature and art), which Hans Mayer rightly calls one of the masterworks of German literary criticism, A. W. Schlegel quotes the following assertion by the English philosopher Henry Home: "Since the beautiful is often useful, our preference for the beautiful gives us an additional incitement to plant our fields and improve our manufactures." The statement is from the same Lord

Home whose considerable influence on Schiller, particularly in Schiller's differentiation of grace (*Anmut*) and dignity (*Würde*), was still positive. Schlegel, in contrast, viewed him with nothing but scorn: "The beautiful should also perform economic services, and God is already supposed to have worried about the blossoming of English manufacturing at the time of the creation."[21] Nothing about the social usefulness of the beautiful proclaimed in the Enlightenment had repelled the Romantics as much as the economic aspect of what Joseph von Eichendorff had ridiculed as the "doctrine that usefulness alone was the key to happiness."[22] According to the Romantics, thinking in economic categories in modernity had exerted such a profound influence on the overall human ability to think that thinking itself had degenerated to mere instrumentality; in other words, reason was used only as a technical means of solving problems that were, in the end, economic.

In a review of Johann Gottlieb Fichte from the year 1808, Friedrich Schlegel accuses contemporary philosophy of having accommodated itself to "that vulgar mathematical-dialectical scientism" that is one of the "fundamental mistakes of the age" and whose influence "surfeits and oppresses . . . the speculative spirit more than it enriches it." Opposed to this, he demands a "higher form of knowledge" that would abandon the "vulgar objectivity of knowing" and not just "prefabricate the history of the self-annihilation of reflection out of the principle of splitting and separating."[23] Schlegel contrasts the merely analytical with the reflexive-practical use of reason and blames the atrophy of the latter on the instrumentalization of thought in the course of economic development. In a letter to Friedrich Schlegel, Novalis calls this atrophied reason "petrifying and petrified reason."[24] And in the introduction mentioned above, A. W. Schlegel contrasts the useful with the beautiful in such a way that it becomes clear what the Romantics feared most about a functional appropriation of the beautiful: namely, the subjugation of the beautiful to the principles of "petrifying reason," or instrumental rationality.

According to Romantic opinion, the critical potential of the aesthetic realm, which the Romantics viewed as being able to "negate" the social reality of modernity, was lost completely in the functional appropriation of the beautiful. A. W. Schlegel, for example, wrote that "many have had good intentions with regard to art, but they misunderstood it when they attempted to recommend art on the basis of its usefulness. This is to demean art totally and stand the thing on its head. It is the essence of the fine arts not to want to be useful. In a certain sense the beautiful is the opposite of the useful; it is that for which usefulness has been waived."[25] Schlegel continues his polemic with a classification of the useful, which apparently presupposes a critical understanding of the tendency in the economic realm to subjugate everything to its standards and reduce it to a measurable quantity. This polemical classification is fundamentally determined by a search for a locale that is removed from the quantifying conditions and relationships of modernity: "Something must exist that is itself an ultimate or inherent purpose; otherwise we would constantly employ usefulness to refer to something else in an endless chain of references, and the concept of usefulness would finally have no reality whatsoever." Interestingly, the status of "reality" is here attributed only to that which can maintain and assert its own identity rather than having that identity undermined and finally disposed of in an endless succession of exchanges and instrumental calculations.

One can surely characterize the Romantics' search for a locale that is removed from the quantifying conditions and relationships of modernity, and can thus help humans to secure a selfsame identity in the face of the dissipating forces of modernity, as a search—however secularized—for a metaphysical guarantor, a transcendental anchor in a world of fluctuation, and criticize it as such. As a matter of fact, recent attempts to move the philosophical project of early Romanticism closer to the critical project of Theodor W. Adorno and to current poststructuralist philosophies[26] overlook the Romantics' place in the history of secularization, which is a history of constant displacements of the transcendental anchor from God to the absolute ruler, the state, the world as substance, nature, the generic definition of reason, art, the genius, text/meaning, and so on. What all these displacements have in common is that they leave a major premise of occidental metaphysics untouched: namely, that there must be a steady locale transcending the world of change, from which firm meanings and stable norms and values can be derived.

From this perspective, the Romantics' struggle against instrumental reason is not per se "progressive," for the Romantics' intent in establishing the superiority of reflexive reason and their belief in the generic nature of reason must surely be interpreted, at least in part, as a traditional search for a new transcendental anchor. The Romantics pursue a philosophical project that still tries to argue for the normative *and* ontological importance of the spirit in fundamentally the same way as the scholastics, who viewed God as the *summum bonum et verum* (the highest good and truth). Reflexive reason is a secularized, world-immanent locale in whose philosophical characterization ontological and moral ideas are just as indistinguishably merged as in the characterization of God as *summum bonum et verum*. No matter how immanent reflexive reason was meant to be, its function as transcendental anchor breaks up its immanence and establishes a transcendence within immanence. Like the Enlightenment and German idealistic philosophy, the Romantics do not conceive of reason as the empirical reason of specific human beings; they always perceive it as a transpersonal, normative agency that transcends all empirical forms of reason. Reflexive reason is the transcendental focal point for all instrumental—that is, merely empirical—forms of reason; it is the "ontological source of an ethical imperative."[27] Its location is a fictive metasubject.

Romantic thinking cannot simply be reduced to the traditional metaphysical drives implicit in it, however. It can be characterized more precisely by the tension between the traditional, metaphysical roots of some of its figures of thought and its attempts to use these figures to comprehend the nature of emerging modernity. If we emphasize the cognitive motives organizing Romantic thinking, then the opposition to those endless chains of exchanges and calculations that are regulated and governed by atrophied instrumental reason, and dominate modern society, is a stronger motif in Romantic thinking than the desire to reestablish a transcendental realm that can serve as an anchor in questions of legitimacy.

To return to A. W. Schlegel's analysis of the endless chain of meaningless references that would result from exchanges not anchored in something transcendental—the regulatory principles of those exchanges threaten to dissipate and particularize human nature and human modes of experience according to special interests and will, once they have achieved full command over society, eliminate the possibility of ever establishing an epistemological vantage point outside their jurisdiction. The early Romantics always held—no matter how much they revolutionized the notions of subjectivity and of language[28]—that the possibility of critique presupposes the existence of a platform from which that critique can be launched, even if that platform is nothing more than the realm of a nonalienated imagination.

The impact of the Romantics' analysis of social modernity on their overall philosophy is also visible in their attitude toward rationality. To be sure, they still acknowledged that logical argumentation can help free people from those instances of control sanctified only by tradition; the Enlightenment's use of logic in its successful critique of feudal absolutism was something the early Romantics still valued. However, since the rationality of logical argumentation merely dissects problems, it cannot prevent an individual from falling into the snares of instrumental reason and quantifying exchange and becoming lost there, once capitalism and instrumental reason have established themselves in society and made logical argumentation the only valid form of thought. This inability to resist a prevalent feature of modernity—not an unqualified inclination toward the irrational on the part of the Romantics—is the aspect of "enlightened" rationality that undermines its status in Romantic thinking. As Karl Solger wrote in his review of Goethe's *Wahlverwandschaften*, "Whoever understands his own individuality falsely . . . and follows cunning rationality [*dem klügelnden Verstande*] is lost."[29]

Once technical rationality has been legitimated as a form of argumentation, there is no longer any space within the "endless chain" of logical steps where the discussion of all a society's norms and values can be legitimated. Instrumental reason can locate such a discussion of norms and values only in the irrational "no-place" of selfish needs, without ever being able to uncover the motivational power of those needs in a critique of society—which is one reason why the category of self-interest as a negative and critical category became so important in Romanticism. Self-interest is the necessary result of the atrophy of practical reason—which reflected on social norms—in the course of modernity. As Fichte wrote in 1806, in his *Grundzüge des gegenwärtigen Zeitalters* (The characteristics of the present age), where he clings emphatically to the historical and philosophical importance of reflective reason, "Once [reflective] reason has been suspended and eradicated, nothing remains but merely individual, personal life. Consequently, in the third epoch brought about by reason," which Fichte on the basis of his philosophical reconstruction of history regarded as his own age, "nothing but this latter form of life is left. Wherever it has achieved dominance and attained consistency and clarity, there is nothing besides sheer, pure, and naked egoism. The completely natural result is that the form of reason created and existing in this third epoch can be no other than, and contain nothing else but, cleverness, which always attempts to promote its own advantage." This cleverness is determined "by the drive for self-preservation and well-being." Fichte was already able to see clearly what Max Horkheimer and Adorno later worked out in their *Dialectic of Enlightenment*, that humanity's attempt to control nature, which is manifested in technological exploitation, also affects human nature by reshaping it in a repressive fashion: "In its attempt at influencing nature by using its forces and products, such an epoch [for Fichte, the present] sees only what is immediately and materially useful for shelter, food, and clothing. . . . It [this alienated epoch] does not recognize any higher form of dominion over nature through which the majestic feature of humanity as a species, I mean that of ideas, is imposed upon a resistant nature. In such dominion lies the true essence of the fine arts."[30] In a society that allows the motivation behind actions to be determined by instrumental reason and individual self-interest, interaction with nature that is independent, free, and mimetic—that is, in which representations of nature continue to be related to reflections upon norms and values constitutive of social interaction—is no longer possible. In this sense Friedrich Schlegel's critical moral statements are also motivated by considerations of artistic theory, as when he asks, for example, in a review of Georg Forster's writings, "Can't one even hope for the ultimate overthrow of the universally dominant egoism?"[31]

In Romantic thought the morally critical category of self-interest corresponds to the socially critical idea of money. The principle of usefulness that is constitutive of the social system of modernity leads to a complete quantification of qualities; that is, human cognition under the spell of usefulness needs to transform everything into units that will allow the comparison of otherwise incomparable qualities. In the economic realm the unit is money. Only with the guaranteed comparability of qualities that money makes possible can exchange function. In a philosophical fragment from the year 1799, Friedrich Schlegel compares two possible opposing principles of centrality (constitutive principles for the whole of society): "The prin[ciple] of this [positive] centrality is enthusiasm—energy—universality. Where it is money, lust and so on = − [minus] univ[ersality]" (*KA*, 18:307). Since universality here does not refer to a process of universalization in the sense of leveling or quantifying qualities (which results from money's power to abstract) but rather to humankind's generic and therefore universal ability to employ practical reason in freely reflecting upon the rules governing our existence (through which people can liberate themselves from their particular interests and make themselves "universal"), the equation "money = − (i.e., lack of) universality" implies the same critical assessment of modernity as Fichte's critique of the times. In the eyes of the Romantics, money's power to abstract leads on the one hand to a dequalification of human life (for example, preventing love from being a socially constitutive principle) and on the other hand to self-alienation, a loss of individuality in the exchange process. To repeat one of Schlegel's central ideas: "Wherever there are politics or economics no morality exists" (*FS*, 250). In Novalis's *Heinrich von Ofterdingen* the same kind of statement is made in a more positive fashion because it is from the perspective of businessmen and their interests: "Money, activity, and commodities produce each other mutually and promote each other's circulation, and the countryside and cities prosper" (*N*, 1:206).

The Romantics' conviction that this circulation led to a dissipation of selfsame identities directly affected their attitudes toward newly published books and toward the era's reviewing practices. One could even claim with some justice that the Romantic-idealist critique of society was not applied analogously—after the fact, so to speak—to the literary market, to reviewing, and to reading habits but rather that it *resulted from* observations of structural changes in the book market. In the eighteenth century the marketplace for books was one of the most important sectors of the economy. Authors who saw to what extent the principles of profit maximization had taken hold in the publishing and sale of books—mainly in the development of a separate market for popular literature and the corresponding realization that "high" literature was not profitable enough—had to rethink their own social role. Such introspection, and the socially critical categories that grew out of it, had profound ramifications both for artistic theory and for the new concept of criticism.[32]

The extent to which the mass market for books and the business of reviewing such books was viewed as an aspect of the circulation of commodities can be seen clearly in Fichte's *Grundzüge des gegenwärtigen Zeitalters*.[33] Fichte insisted that the transformation of the book into a commodity had to suffocate every literary quality because such qualities were long-lasting, while the marketplace needed a "stream" of fashionable, novel, surpassable products. "This stream of literature is always renewing itself and bursting forward so that every new wave will push aside the one that preceded it; hence the reason why things were printed in the first place is thwarted, and the immortalization that the press represented is suspended. It is of no help to have held an opinion openly in print if one does not have the ability to continue having opinions unceasingly, because everything that is past will be forgotten." Fichte sees the "advantage in erecting the apparatus of criticism" sarcastically in criticism's relation to the world of commodities; namely, "that the person who has no particular desire [to read], or doesn't have a great deal of extra time, no longer needs to read any books whatsoever . . . in this system books are printed only so that they can be reviewed, and there would be no need for books if there could be reviews without them." The readers who are sucked into this circulation of novelties can find no place "in their restless flight to stop to consider by themselves [!] what they are really reading." According to Fichte, this self-alienation in the act of reading, which is forced upon readers by the market and its principles of profit maximization, produces "a specific mood unlike any other emotional state, one that is extremely pleasurable and that can become an indispensable need. Just like other narcotic substances it transports one into the comfortable semi-state between sleep and being awake and lulls one into a sweet oblivion without any necessity of doing anything at all." The category of alienation (*Entäusserung*)—which I am using throughout not in the sense of the idealist philosophy of identity but in its Marxist sense—corresponds at the psychological level to that of (regressive, reminiscent of pre-oedipally experienced) oblivion. Fichte already saw that the institutionalization of this form of oblivious reading, a process fostered by the development of the marketplace, compensated for the efforts demanded by the instrumentalization of reason and by the consequences of the division of labor—in short, for what was demanded of members of society by its rationalization in the course of modernity. That the *book* as a medium would have to undergo a fundamental change in its character and that the public institution of literary criticism had therefore become pointless was seen quite clearly by Fichte and the Romantics: "There is no more educating the aforementioned pure reader through reading, or relating any clear ideas to him, because everything printed quickly lulls him into a quiet tranquillity and sweet oblivion. In the process he is also cut off from every other means of instruction."

Anxiety at the power of commodity circulation to disperse individual identities moved the Romantics again and again to reflect, anthropologically and from the perspective of semiotics, on the possibility of an unconstrained, unalienated form of identity within modernity. In their assessment of what art and being an artist should mean in an age of commodity exchange, they were led to a valorization of the individual characteristics (*das Charakteristische*) of artists and artworks: the characteristic is that which remains identical with itself. In the realm of the sign the result was a valorization of pictorial or metaphorical expressions that were not easily integrated into logical semantic fields. I will return to both of these problems.

So far my interpretation of the Romantic critique of society might allow one to conclude that this critique was directed only at the developing bourgeois, capitalist society and as such represented a "flight from bourgeois routine into the realm of art."[34] Or, as Marx wrote, it expressed only "the hysterical irritation which a sensitive soul who has been snubbed feels" in its use of "great illusions" to combat "petty trade."[35] However, the precision in the categories with which early Romantics carried out their criticism of contemporary society should make one doubt that that criticism can be reduced to the expression of "hysterical irritation" felt by a "sensitive soul." The references to specific German conditions call its supposedly antibourgeois, anticapitalist character even more into question. For what has been diagnosed as the "double affront against the old feudal order and the new bourgeois society"[36] is not contradictorily "doubled" but rather directed quite precisely and consistently at the historical coalition of interests represented by the ruling aristocracy and the capitalistic bourgeoisie in enlightened absolutism. In the early eighteenth century the aristocratic rulers of numerous German kingdoms and dukedoms, particularly of Prussia and Saxony, recognized the economic superiority of the bourgeois capitalist system found in England and the Netherlands, and they wondered how the same conditions could be brought about in Germany through centralized planning. As a result, what Henri Brunschwig maintained for Prussia was really true of all the absolutistically ruled principalities in Germany: "Nowhere else, indeed, is the economic system so closely welded to the political system; the two systems have grown up together like the branches of a single tree. The same officials administer both of them: graduates of the national universities."[37] *One* result of the Enlightenment project of centralization was the establishment of two new university disciplines: cameralism (that is, economics) and police science (which then meant administrative theory). Centralized, scientific planning was supposed to produce the greatest happiness for the greatest number of people in any given society. Cameralist writings define "happiness," a concept that was frequently ridiculed by the Romantics, as that social state brought about by the provision of internal and external security politically, by an increase in the population (read "laborers"), by the creation of additional sources of income in agriculture and industry (the income accrues directly to ordinary citizens and indirectly through taxation to the nobility), by the promotion of exports and the restriction of imports, and so on.[38]

Just how important the shift away from the position of centralism was, even superficially, for Romantic literary criticism can be seen in the following section of Friedrich Schlegel's review of Georg Forster: "To be sure he could be viewed in some of his earlier writings . . . as appearing to maintain that procuring general happiness was the purpose of the state. But if one looks at his ideas, as is necessary with him, in general, it is clear that nothing was further from his heart and mind than the doctrine that the judicious ruler could force his subjects to be happy according to the dictates of his whim."[39] The precondition for rescuing Forster's literary value in a work of criticism is being able to distance him from Enlightenment centralism.

The ideologues of enlightened centralism transferred the machine metaphor, which had often been used in the discourses of natural philosophy since the early seventeenth century, to the political realm. Johann Heinrich von Justi, for example, one of enlightened centralism's leading theoreticians, believed that a well-led and well-organized state would work like a machine in which all the cogs and drive shafts had been precisely coordinated with one another and that the absolute ruler set the whole machine in motion like a mainspring.[40] However, all of this was possible only on the basis of a well-conceived plan.

The early Romantics were certainly not the first to turn against Enlightenment centralism in politics and philosophy. One can already find the basic elements of their critique in Christian Fürchtegott Gellert and Gotthold Ephraim Lessing.[41] Under the influence of Rousseau, in whose critique of civilization the machine metaphor signaled only the negative aspects of modernity, "Storm and Stress" writers expanded on this line of criticism. But only with the early Romantics, who found features of modernity in the Enlightenment that could *not* be sublated by a bourgeois revolution, did the critique of the Enlightenment's philosophical and political centralism become constitutive. In their eyes the centrally administered enlightened state proved an obstacle to the use of reflective, practical reason, because the state was interested only in fostering a mode of reason that could function instrumentally in planning. For the early Romantics the enlightened state was therefore the most effective adversary of freedom. Freedom was inconceivable to them without a value-creating use of reason closely linked with critical reflection and questioning of the means and ends implicit in prevailing norms and values. Reflective reason does not just work intrinsically with a given set of norms and values, as instrumental reason does, but *produces* ideas. As a result a philosophically important anonymous fragment known as the "oldest system proposal of German idealism" can claim "that no *idea* of the state exists, because the state is something mechanical, just as there can be no idea of a machine. Only objects of freedom can be called ideas. We therefore have to go beyond the state! For every state has to treat free human beings as mechanical cogs; a[nd] it should not do so; therefore it has to come to an end."[42] Naturally, the state referred to here is the absolutist state, the first modern state with a developed and consolidated administrative apparatus.

A passage from Novalis's *Glauben und Liebe* makes it clear to what extent the socially critical categories discussed above (self-interest, money, instrumental reason, quantification, self-alienation, machine, state) are connected with Romantic thought and are intended to provide a consistent analysis of the German form of modern society: "No state has been administered more like a factory than Prussia since the death of Frederick William I. However necessary such a regime might be for the physical health, strength, and efficiency of the state, when handled solely in this manner, the state will essentially perish. The principle behind the famous old system is to bind everyone to the state through self-interest" (N, 2:494).

Mention of the mechanistic administration of the state, along with distaste for every form of centralization and planning, already hints at another motif in Romantic thought that unfolded in its social criticism as well as in its theories of signs, philosophy of art, and literary criticism—namely, its critique of processes of abstraction. The Romantics clearly understood abstraction (or generalization) not simply as a mental operation but rather also (and most importantly) as a sociohistorical process in which the increasing historical prominence of generalized principles of behavior had the effect of homogenizing human thoughts, feelings, deeds, and appearances. In Romantic terminology, those contemporaries whose thought and actions reflected the constitutive principles of modernity (self-interest, instrumental reason, and so on) were labeled "philistines." In 1811 Clemens Brentano published a satire on the circumstances of the time, *Der Philister vor, in und nach der Geschichte* (The philistine before, in, and after history), in which the philistines' leveling drive—which corresponds to modernity's quantification of the world—is characterized as follows: "Their ultimate plan to bring happiness to a country is to turn it completely into a squared-off checkerboard, which makes it easier to reduce everything to smaller units. They would like all the houses to be painted white and periodically relettered and renumbered, just as they want to make progress, or not fall behind their neighbors even in literature. All the tollgates and tollbooths are striped but the other public buildings of the state are checkered so that everyone knows where he can get help."[43] Generalizing or homogenizing existing modes of behavior is historically not just the rather accidental result of an economic process in which the functional prominence of exchange value, its power to abstract, leads to an absence of specific qualities but also the conscious goal of new policies like the codification of laws. There were functional reasons why the development of the market-place enforced equality before the law for as many people as possible; it was only when social and economic interaction within society could occur on the basis of legal principles applicable to all that the calculations of economically oriented citizens, whose decisions formed the basis of capitalist exchanges, became reliable.

For Reinhart Koselleck this indicates that the attempts at codifying Prussian law, which continued throughout the eighteenth century, were part of a process (although as a result of numerous compromises, a somewhat watered-down one) of "abstracting" the legal system to the extent that individual statutes would apply to *all* citizens. The actual laws of the early eighteenth century when those attempts began were not, by and large, universally valid; rather, they were an accumulation of individual legal precedents in the form of privileges. Special laws that frequently applied only to individual estates (*Stände*) were the rule, and legal traditions that were centuries old made it difficult to introduce a uniform legal system. The struggle over a uniform code of laws continued even after the Prussian General Code (*Allgemeines Landrecht*) was promulgated in 1794.

According to Koselleck, the internal history of Prussia in the era of Romanticism was "the history of the enforcement of this code as opposed to ancient estate, local, and regional laws and legal customs and, at the same time, the history of successive changes in the code brought about by general laws that increasingly applied to the entire state." The authors of the code were interested in "first, binding the monarch to a system of reasonable goals . . . and otherwise in transforming the estates' independence into state service, so that every subject entered into a direct relationship with the state." Both the citizens' direct subordination to the state (compare the legal term *Staatsunmittelbarkeit*), which eliminated the estates' traditional rights to control their own affairs, and the existence of a universally applicable code of law were prerequisites for a society based on commodity production. Koselleck points out that the expression "manufacturer" (*Fabrikant*), which, along with "factory," played such a significant role in Romantic social *and* literary criticism, originally designated not the bourgeois owner of a factory but this newly determined status of direct legal subordination to the state—a status that applied only to that select group of citizens who worked in the "capitalist" segment of the economy. Other citizens—members of traditional corporations, guilds, and trades, or inhabitants of certain provinces—were still subject to various regional laws that existed alongside the *Allgemeine Landrecht*. "Manufacturer," in other words, was the name for those citizens to whom the statutes of the new codified law were applicable. Since factory workers had the same legal status as the factory's owner, the word could designate both worker and owner. The word signaled that Prussia, as well as other German principalities, was in the midst of a transition from a form of society organized according to crafts and estates, each with its own particular legal privileges, to a society of "free" citizens engaged in capitalist production and defined by a new, direct relationship with the state—a relationship that the Romantics interpreted as "abstract." In the eyes of contemporaries the new legal status of direct subordination to the laws of the centralized state was more important than membership in a particular class. "Manufacturers" were citizens of the centralized state, which meant that their citizenship was direct and not dependent on their being integrated into one of the regional estate systems. As citizens, they viewed themselves "not as political members of the state but rather as participants in the free market—in modern society. "Citizen" essentially meant *homo oeconomicus;* a person was a citizen of the state only to the extent that it was economically liberal."[44]

For those engaged in production and distribution, being subject directly to the state—which necessarily undermined the old estate society, with its regional laws that often applied only to particular groups—had become essential, because the commodity exchange characteristic of bourgeois society could prosper only with markets that ignored regional boundaries, and because this new form of interaction required legal codes and moral ideologies that could regulate the exchange of commodities, people, and information in ways that were calculable and binding on everyone involved. One high judicial authority by the name of Wentzel saw the connection early in the nineteenth century: "One of the differences between the old and the new age that is seldom seen is that in the former people existed without much communication, without much mobility within narrow geographic boundaries, and were therefore satisfied with their local laws, whereas now there is so much communication and such a high level of mobility" that "local laws" would be obstacles to progress.[45] Without an awareness of these connections it is impossible to understand the Romantics' high regard for a society based on estates; it was a critical gesture determined more by its absent adversary than by its affirmative content.

Although individual accents changed radically between early and late Romanticism, contempt for the sociohistorical process of abstraction is common to all Romantics. Fichte had laid the groundwork for them; in his *Grundzüge*, for example, he wrote: "The intention behind constitutions for states and legal governments for nations in such an age [Fichte is again referring to his own time] . . . is fueled by hatred for the old, by plans to construct constitutions from airy and empty abstractions, and by reverberating phrases, without having the resolute and pitiless outward power necessary to undertake the government of degenerate tribes."[46] This already makes it clear why forms that were traditional and seemed to have developed organically could have been valorized at the expense of the all-encompassing, leveling power of abstraction characteristic of capitalist society; they represented what this society had destroyed and what was opposed to it. In late Romanticism this aspect was even more heavily accented. Eichendorff's *Der Adel und die Revolution* (The nobility and the revolution) reflects the tendency: "From all possible and impossible virtues a fabulous citizen's crown had been fashioned for the whole of humanity; it was supposed to fit on every head, as if mankind were a mere abstraction. . . . The nobility, however, was thoroughly historical. . . . This barbaric leveling, this pruning of the fresh tree of life according to some imagined (unitary) norm was the purest slavery; for what could freedom be if not the spiritual development of individual peculiarities with as few hindrances as possible." In a society grounded in capitalist economics, in which "base materialism" (= greed) wages war with "incorporeal abstractions," individuality—so goes Romantic reasoning—is always suppressed.[47]

To oppose this sociohistorical process of abstraction—in which the tendency was to base all thought and every activity on the rules of logical and economic calculations and circulations, thereby standardizing them—the Romantics attempted to define a space that was u-topian: that is, a no-place in relation to social reality, a place outside this vicious circle. There, the particular could maintain itself and, in its unyielding otherness, provide the force necessary to shatter the socially conditioned, transsubjective logic of society. They believed they had found this space in art. In his early *Gespräch über die Poesie* (Conversation on poesy; 1800) Friedrich Schlegel had accorded art a redeeming power in the face of "deadly generalizing. . . . For all poetry begins by suspending the process and the laws of logically thinking reason and by transporting us again to the beautiful confusion of fancy, to the original chaos of human nature" (*KA*, 2:319).

The Functional Dissociation of the Aesthetic Realm and Its Effect on the Concept of Criticism

The Romantic concept of art criticism was determined socially and historically, as discussed above, by the process of differentiation during which the aesthetic realm became functionally independent or dissociated, a process whose pace was particularly forced in the second half of the eighteenth century until it reached a temporary conclusion. This process was caused by the increasing acceptance of social norms, which had been around since the late Middle Ages, involving the disciplining of desires and the rational planning of existence; these in turn entailed constraints on behavior and thought—social constraints that grew in the course of modernization and gave rise to the need for a separate, functionally autonomous realm in which such one-sided pressures could be suspended in a compensatory manner, all of which was immanent in the system as it developed. The connection between modernization and the dissociation of the functionally autonomous realm called "art" first became absolutely clear with the publication of Kant's *Critique of Judgment* in 1790: "Beautiful art must be free art in a double sense. It is not a work like a mercenary employment [*Lohngeschäft*], the greatness of which can be judged according to a definite standard, which can be attained or paid for; and again, though the mind is here occupied, it feels itself thus contented and aroused without looking to any other purpose (independently of reward [*"Lohn"* which more often means "wage," an important connotation at this point])."[48] Work, which can be quantified "according to a definite standard"—one that is at the same time cognitive (technical reason "judges"), based on the principles of the division of labor (this division, along with rationalization, can be used to "attain [*erzwingen*]" production), and economic ("paid for": money is the universal, itself insubstantial sign of equivalence)—is being transformed by the principles of economic circulation; this new form of wage labor alienates individuals and tends to enslave them. The dissociated realm of art, in which art is no longer technically useful, is radically opposed to quantifiable "mercenary employment," because art's functional autonomy is the sole guarantee of the compensatory "satisfaction" it provides. Kant's formula concerning "the disinterested pleasure in the beautiful" reflects precisely the dissociation of the aesthetic realm (in the eighteenth century the term "interest" referred primarily to the economic realm, something often overlooked in interpretations of Kant's aesthetics, since the German term *Interesse* has lost its economic or financial connotation in the meantime).[49]

The process in which art became functionally autonomous was, to use Niklas Luhmann's terminology, part of a larger historical transition from stratified to functionally differentiated societies.[50] This transition had a number of consequences for literary criticism. In a stratified society where the social status of the individual was determined by his or her birth and where cultural representations had to "reproduce" traditional hierarchies rather than general ideologies, art was integrated into the whole of social praxis. The social integration of art was thus not just functional, as it is in modern societies where art's primary role is to provide compensatory experiences; rather, it penetrated both the form and the content of individual works of art. In other words, art played a much more concrete and direct role in the reproduction of such societies than is the case today (a conclusion that holds true even in comparison with today's popular literature). One aspect of this development merits particular attention: since traditional societies were characterized by a rigid system of social hierarchies, their ideological reproduction cannot be reduced to the transmission of ideologemes, which are defined only by their specific content. It must also include the purely formal components of society, such as those modes of social interaction that distinguish members of different levels of the social hierarchy from each other and from all kinds of other traditions, because this kind of social control was legitimated not by public argumentation within certain standards of rationality but by the general acceptance of the sheer weight of accumulated convention. Criticism in such stratified societies therefore centered on poetic rules that upheld social customs and represented the legitimizing power of tradition. The defeat of normative poetics or *Regelpoetiken* in the eighteenth century was not the achievement of individual geniuses, as some critics still maintain, but a historical event related to changes in the overall organization and reproduction of society. Hans Mayer pointed this out in the introduction to his *Meisterwerke deutscher Literaturkritik:* "It was not just the case that since Storm and Stress the poetic 'genius' wanted to create his own rules rather than to accept those that were already there. There was always a particular set of general social norms behind the 'rules' that were rejected. . . . A poet who submitted to a given set of rules accepted at the same time the socially determined task of incorporating the rules of the society in which he lived into his work and of reflecting those rules as consistently as possible by observing and fulfilling their demands in questions of form and social convention."[51] The relation between aesthetic and social rules in stratified societies explains, among other things, the importance of the discipline of rhetoric for literature and literary criticism in traditional societies.

The functional dissociation of art, which made normative poetics obsolete, at the same time necessitated a standardization and restriction of the concept of art in the eighteenth century. There never had been a concept of art in today's sense; different arts existed, but because they included mechanical arts and crafts, it was difficult to unite them under the single heading of "art." To be more precise, the need for such unification and universalization of the concept of art was not felt before the eighteenth century. Consequently, one spoke of "the arts," not of "art." As long as the aesthetic realm had not been functionally dissociated, the various arts could be related to different realms of praxis, which reinforced their conceptual independence.

The functional separation of the aesthetic realm produced not only a unified concept of art but also a theory of aesthetics, which henceforth replaced rules as the basis of criticism. As a result, critical practice became more abstract and more philosophical, as well as more subjective. Whereas aesthetic philosophy reflects on the *status* of the particular and of the individual within modernity in general terms, criticism reflects on the particular as it is portrayed in individual works. Criticism's treatment of the particular, though, always remains related to the reflection carried on in aesthetic theory, without being able to use aesthetic theory's conclusions to systematize its critical praxis. As an individual representation of the particular, art is not amenable to systematic forms of criticism. As Friedrich Schlegel wrote: "The critical method is really no method at all, or, to put it differently, criticism needs no method; the business of criticism can be carried out according to every method; it depends only on the genius of a penetrating mind . . . on qualities that do not lie in laws and methods but in the individual" (*KA* 12:313). Schlegel's conclusion is also directed against deducing judgments logically from rules based on common sense. The transition from art's concrete reference to reality to the abstract functionalism of art in modernity, which is the historical prerequisite for Schlegel's statement, is also reflected in the following polemic against the term "rules": "Critics are always talking about *rules*, but where are the rules that are really poetic rather than just gr[ammatical], metr[ical], log[ical], or that would apply to every work of art?—The only pragmatic art lesson for the artist is the lesson of Classicism and of Romanticism."[52]

From the perspective of Romanticism, the Enlightenment's attempt to institutionalize art as a mediator of socially important norms and values—thus rejecting the traditional idea of a representative function for art (that is, the representation of *forms* of social interaction through art) but nevertheless expanding art's role for the ideological reproduction of society—appears to have been a transitory phenomenon. Art as a mediator of "morally superior" norms and values proved powerless when confronted with the process of modernization, which soon imposed its own norms on narratives still organized around traditional normative configurations. The individual interpellated (to use Louis Althusser's term) by the dissociated realm of modernist aesthetics, a realm defined in opposition to social modernity, ceases to be a member of society during his or her solitary encounter with art. In moments of aesthetic pleasure we momentarily affirm a form of individuality that longs to be emancipated from the constraints of society, a pleasure allowed us as compensation for suspending that longing at other times.

Autonomous, functionally differentiated art can, however, take on two radically different tasks within modernity. On the one hand, artists can interpret the freedom accorded art as a critical potential vis-à-vis negative reality (but, in spite of criticism at the level of *content*, functionally dissociated art cannot rid itself of the affirmative elements implicit in its *institutional* relationship to society, for the manner in which art is institutionalized defuses any criticism of contemporary issues that it might contain); on the other hand, artists can accept totally the functional appropriation of art for its compensatory potential (which is the rule for popular literature produced according to the dictates of the marketplace). The Romantics, however, believed that they could escape this functional appropriation of art by living *completely* for art rather than just integrating it into everyday life as a compensatory force. The latter is what philistines do. As Novalis wrote in *Blüthenstaub* (Pollen): "Philistines only lead an everyday life. The most important means [= earthly existence] seem to be their only purpose. They do everything for this earthly life. . . . They mix in some poetry only when the need becomes urgent [*zur Notdurft*],[53] because they are used to certain interruptions in their daily routine. Normally, the interruption occurs every seven days, and could be called a poetic sept-fever. . . . The philistine achieves the highest level of his poetic existence on a trip, at a marriage or baptism, or in church. . . . Their so-called religion works like an opiate: stimulating, anesthetizing, soothing wounds caused by weakness." Art here provides the compensatory satisfaction of desires because "a mind [*Verstand*] that is trained per force by external circumstances" is "the clever slave" that "broods and worries" about the philistine's "lusts" (*N*, 2:447ff.).

For Brentano, the prototypical form of dissociated art is the theater: "I believe that the philistinism of modern times scarcely appears more openly than at the theater; where else would it ever be possible for an ordinary person to be as enraptured by costumes and paintings, as separated from everyday life by lighting and music, as the enthusiast who can isolate himself in the theater's charmed circle." The theater contains "everything loathsome and all the diseases, scandals, and poverty in history in itself and appears to the better class of spectator as nothing but the clearest sign of the general condition of the world."[54]

The Concept of Criticism in the Context of Romantic Theories of Art

If we want to assess the Romantic concept of criticism in terms of social history, we first have to explain its relationship to the Romantic philosophy of history, for at least the *early* Romantic concept of criticism is anchored in a philosophy of history. In 1798 Friedrich Schlegel noted:

"Classical and progressive are historical ideas and critical opinions—There c[riticism] and h[istory] are joined."[55] Just as the opposition of classical (= antique) and progressive (= modern, Romantic, mannered, and so on) has to be understood from the point of view not only of the history of art but of history in general, so too is its critical content not only artistic but also socio-analytical. An explanation of these ideas is all the more important because Schiller developed a critique of society that was similar in many respects without, however, giving up the hope embodied in the Enlightenment's philosophy of history and its linear model of progress. In spite of all the ambivalence previously discussed, the cultural and political status of art in Schiller's theory was defined by its social function; art was to alter not only individuals but also the whole of society—concretely and within the chronological dimension. Numerous statements proposing similar projects can be found in early Romanticism. One of Friedrich Schlegel's *Athenäum Fragments* provides a good example: "The revolutionary desire to realize the kingdom of God on earth is the elastic point of progressive [i.e., Romantic] civilization [*Bildung*] and the beginning of modern history" (*FS*, 192). In the previous fragment he had assigned criticism rather than art the major burden in the poiesis of this golden future: "Christianity seems to me to be a fact. But only a fact in its beginning stages, one, that is, that can't be represented historically in a system, but can only be characterized by means of divinatory criticism" (*FS*, 192). The characterization of criticism as divinatory (able to foresee or foretell future events, thus accelerating their arrival) recurs frequently. Criticism alone can locate the contemporary and timely as well as the historico-philosophical content of Romantic art, whose "primal strength in predestining and apprehending the future is so essential" (*KA*, 18:311); by unfolding the content of art in a reflexive and divinatory fashion, criticism alone can raise art's historico-philosophical potential to the level of consciousness: "Without criticism, indeed without divination, no progression" (*KA*, 18:14).

Thoughts like these seem to lessen the distance between early Romantic views of history on the one hand and the views of the Enlightenment and German Classicism on the other. However, on closer examination, one sees that in the historico-philosophical formulations themselves the concrete historical tension between the present and the future has already been transformed into an ahistorical opposition (even if that opposition is motivated by a critique of social conditions) between social reality and art, criticism, and philosophy. As Novalis wrote in 1798–99 in his *Allgemeiner Brouillon* (General scratch pad): "Philosophy is basically antihistorical. It advances from the future and from necessity to the real—it is the s[cience] of the universal sense of divination. It explains the past from the perspective of the future, which is the opposite of what history does. (It views everything in isolation, in the state of nature—unconnected)" (*N*, 3:464f.). What is decisive is Novalis's characterization of the future as *philosophically* necessary (which robs the category of its historical content) and the isolation and separation of the object to be observed and judged from history, a method he addresses directly in his parenthetical remark. Unlike Friedrich Hölderlin, whose Hyperion finds only "an infinite emptiness" in ideas devoid of history and who burdens his protagonist with the task of "discovering new meaning *within* limits . . . i.e., within history,"[56] the Romantics insist that the gulf between philosophically deduced ideal and social, historical reality cannot be overcome simply through cultural policies.

That the Romantic critical impulse is constantly in danger of being transformed into culturally pessimistic esotericism is shown by Friedrich Schlegel's critique of Fichte's *Die Grundzüge des gegenwärtigen Zeitalters* (1808): "To see the reference contained in Fichte's characterization of the epoch one need only recall the basic division between the great majority of those unable to see beyond ordinary enlightenment and the small minority of those who aspire to traverse those boundaries somehow in order to reach a higher or highest pretersensuality [*Übersinnliches*], or who think they already possess it; since their spirit is the remnant of a past age, the forerunner of a future one, or since it has risen above time, it no longer belongs exclusively to their era."[57] First of all, a philosophical, historical, and temporal tension is transformed here into a pessimistic (and static) cultural opposition between the masses who have fallen victim to the instrumental reason associated with the baser form of enlightenment and an intellectual aristocracy that wants to elevate itself to pretersensuality, the opposite of social-sensual reality. The shift appears quite openly in Schlegel's concluding phrase that is superficially reminiscent of "enlightened" historico-philosophical discourses: "or since it has risen above time, it no longer belongs exclusively to their era." The early Romantic philosophy of history aims, as Gisela Dischner aptly puts it, at "transcendence or surpassing instead of progress or advancement."[58]

The extent to which this shift in accent had already led the Romantics to favor a cyclical model of history over the linear one characteristic of Enlightenment philosophy is shown clearly by A. W. Schlegel's *Vorlesungen über schöne Literatur und Kunst* from 1801–2; these lectures have to be seen as a programmatic attempt to explain early Romantic theories of art in a relatively "popular" and accessible form. For Schlegel, it remained "problematical whether in the longest span of time in the most extensive history . . . one could identify more progress or retrogression. . . . [François] Hemsterhuis describes the waxing and waning of culture quite ingeniously as an elliptical motion, in which humanity finds itself near the sun in one age and far from it in another." Of interest here is Schlegel's discovery of the principle that turns every essentially linear model of history into a chimera; it is human individuality, which he does not regard as historically determined: "No matter how early [history] begins to deal with the individuals who intervene in events in order to show . . . that their characters were determined in this way or that, and thus to regard them again as effects, it necessarily leaves some original kernel in them inexplicable. For the creation of individuals is the secret that nature has reserved for itself, and here is the basis for the wonderful magic of history, in which otherwise no unexpected roles could appear."[59] Consequently, what can be analyzed and planned—that is, the feasible in history—is invaded by something synthetic and organic that undermines this feasibility. For the Romantics, though, that which can only be negative in the eyes of Enlightenment thinkers turns into a positive critical tool. The critical force of organic, genial individuality is based on the fact that it does not allow itself to be subjugated by the spirit of analytic, instrumental reason controlling modernity.

Art represents the synthetic-organic and the individual par excellence. In terms of production aesthetics, art is the expression of the artist's individuality. From the point of view of reception aesthetics, art provides individuals with the opportunity to perceive and contemplate the sociocritical principle of individuality in concrete form and to strengthen that principle in themselves. However, such a conception leaves the Romantics with a dilemma: how can one justify the practice of criticism and the concept of artistic completion through criticism when art is conceived of as the expression of individuality? Organic individuals cannot be analyzed, nor is a comparative criticism of individuals legitimate, because any critical analysis would destroy their organic nature. Furthermore, any concept of complete and perfect individuality is itself contradictory if completion refers to a (general) ideal of perfection as it does here, for perfection cannot unfold itself thousands of times into (particular) individuals if these individuals are supposed to be "individual" at all.

The Romantics attempted to eliminate this dilemma by introducing the notion of an art history, which would, on the one hand, sublate the contradiction between the particular and the general in the ideal of art and, on the other, form the basis for a higher form of history in which history and individuality would be reconciled. In his 1801–2 lectures, A. W. Schlegel outlines the dilemma as follows: "The object of history" in a general and specific sense "can only be that in which infinite progress takes place," but if one transfers this concept to the history of art, then in art history every "individual manifestation of art . . . has to be shown to be an indeterminate distance from absolute perfection, and yet we only call something a real work of art when it is in itself complete." For Schlegel, the solution to this apparent contradiction lies in considering "a given work of art from its own perspective . . . it need not achieve an absolute height, it is complete when it is the best of its kind, in its sphere or its world. And this explains why it can, at the same time, be one link in an infinite chain of progressions and nevertheless satisfactory and independent in itself." This kind of progress could, however, be labeled more precisely as the mere cumulative succession of historical events. Accepting such a progressive concept of art history, one not centered on notions of qualitative developments, allows the Romantics to treat the history of both art and criticism (which for A. W. Schlegel "is not only the indispensable organ of theory and art history but also the link between the two") as the potentiation of art: "Perfect, apprehensible art history would, although in prosaic form, raise poesy to the second power"; in other words, the discourse of art history can "square" the mere existence of individual works. All the individual works taken together constitute *art* (in the singular), which is the highest form of human expression. But art needs the discourse of art history for its artistry to become visible. For A. W. Schlegel the "whole species" of humanity is not an abstraction; it is rather nothing less than "the immortal individual" himself.[60]

And for Friedrich Schlegel, in his Forster review, this humanity "extends beyond the genius." The practice of criticism is concerned with this broader tribunal, "the immortal individual," whereas for the genius and his products the following is true: "No literary artist can be so worthy of imitation that he will not someday have to be considered obsolete and surpassed. The pure value of the individual continues forever, but particularity, even of the greatest [genius], is lost in the universal stream."[61] Only art history, with "criticism" as its organ, is able to cross the stream of history to the unity of the whole. Criticism here is the constitutive instrument for a form of art, not yet realized, that is no longer viewed in terms of works but rather as aesthetic reflection through the medium of individual works. That such a conception of art can (but need not) undermine a critical attitude toward individual works of art, as well as toward criticism and art history, is shown by a remark A. W. Schlegel made in this connection: "However much we are repelled by the barbarism and non-art [Unpoesie] produced in many epochs, perhaps including our own, who can know if the genius [God] will not take all these thousandfold deviant forms and figures of humanity and shape them into a great work of art."[62] This would mean that all historical events, whatever they are, are justifiable.

In comparison with the Enlightenment, the accent here is on aesthetic contemplation rather than on the critical representation of a different, better world. The latter is nevertheless a dominant aspect of early Romanticism. Novalis, for example, stressed the power of graphic, perceptually present symbols as "the means of education for a distant goal" (N, 2:489): "All of representation is based on making things present—the not yet present and so on—(the miraculous power of fiction). My Glauben und Liebe is based on representative faith [i.e., faith that leads to the representation of the not yet present; Novalis is fully aware of the paradox that he wants to re-present something that never has been present]. So, too, the assumption— perpetual peace is already achieved—God is with us—here is America or nowhere—the golden age is here—we are magicians—we are moral and so on" (N, 3:421).

Novalis knew that unless a poetic work expresses an ideal in its representations—an ideal defined by its opposition to the really existing conditions of social life—it unfortunately loses any historico-philosophical importance and cultural-political relevance. The artistic representation of that ideal, however, can never represent anything real; it is, in other words, necessarily speculative because it cannot be deduced from any total conception of history. In 1800 the Enlightenment philosophy of history was still so effective and so much in control of public discourse that Novalis apparently believed he could make his own project comprehensible only with conscious, reformulated references to the discourse of an "enlightened" philosophy of history: "Nothing is more poetic than remembrance and conjecture, or a mental image of the future. The lowly present links the two [past and future] through limitation—Contiguity arises through ossification—crystallization. There is, however, a spiritual present—that identifies both by dissolving them—and this mixture is the poet's element, his atmosphere" (N, 2:468). The lowly present is what really exists, where instrumentalization has ossified or crystallized reason and where a critical discourse, including its "enlightened" references to history or to the future, can only be narrow and accidental. In opposition, Novalis posits a spiritual present brought about by the use of reflexive reason; in this present the past and future have dissolved into one another and are identical. That means, however, that the spiritual present, since all time is sublated there, is no longer present in a historical sense; it has become a historically transcendent ideal world. For this reason Hans-Joachim Mähl correctly speaks of the "transcendent reality [Überwirklichkeit] of the future" in Novalis.[63] The historico-philosophical tension between a negative present and a better future that intrinsically structured the literature of the Enlightenment shifts in Romanticism into a tension between poetry and reality. The Romantics avoided articulating this tension in poetic language in order to permit literature to retreat totally into the ideal world and thus to remain untainted by the ossification of all thought pervading everyday life. The symbolic presence of the ideal world in poesy should be a thorn in the side of the present: "Ideal language belongs to the realization of the ideal world" (N, 2:561).

Both the retreat of the better world into an "infinite, fairytale distance" (Mähl) and the representation of this world in Romantic art (in such characters as the poet, woman, lovers, or the child and in the ideal situation of Romantic communication) doubtlessly contributed to the process of institutional dissociation of art, described above, and therefore to making the function of the entire medium a compensatory one. However, one should not overlook the fact that at least the early Romantics intended (and in so doing they could be regarded as the first avant-garde movement in art)[64] to reconnect art with life: that is, to return art to the realm of experience. The beautiful appearance of art was not just supposed to remind people of a better world; the re-presented modes of communication were supposed to be present, to be acted out, in Romantic groups. The formation of such groups was an essential part of the Romantic aesthetic program, not a mere side effect, and this was another reason that criticism and not the individual work of art became the most important activity in the realm of art. For in the eyes of the Romantics, communication through art was the only form of praxis able to free itself from the reified relationships of society. The Romantic project "was therefore not limited to the 'reconciliation of truth with reality' (Hegel) only in the realm of ideas; rather it aimed at changing people's lives, but without giving up its speculative character in favor of day-to-day political pragmatism."[65] The ultimate failure of this project was connected with the Romantics' insufficient insight into the functional dissociation of various subsystems within modernity; a real understanding of the institutional character of art was not yet historically possible. Only such insight would have allowed them to see the dialectic inherent in the process: namely, that the institutional organization of modernity changed the function of art in such a way that even the most radical criticism contained in individual works was defused by the medium in which it was expressed.

The Romantics thought of their analysis of social totality not in terms of institutions and system theory but in categories that were essentially epistemological or concerned with a critique of the nature of knowledge. In their analysis of the increasingly universal dominance of the principle of exchange value in modern societies, they recognized that the constitution of subjectivity would have to become a problem in modernity. For if this principle actually had a universalizing effect, it could no longer simply be supposed epistemologically that individuals are able to act vis-à-vis social totality in the way that idealist theories of knowledge conceived of cognizing subjects: that is, as free centers of knowledge (centered in themselves) confronted by objects that they can take cognizance of without being influenced by them. Hence, the Romantics were interested in the conditions necessary for the possibility of an independent constitution of subjectivity in the face of social totality (which tended to incorporate and generalize everything): that is, the conditions for the possibility of a form of individuality that, in the confrontation with social totality, would prove itself to be free. Totality viewed as the "slowly disintegrating and destructive force of conditions"[66] is "absolutely incomprehensible" (N, 2:152) to the individual, because adequate understanding, in according cognitive power over its content to a knowing subject, would call the totalizing effects of social structures themselves into question and suspend the effect these structures have on individuals. However, if this effect exists, as the Romantics claimed, the basic problem is as follows: how can subjectivity constitute itself free from the domination of society if the structures of this society are already inscribed on the individual through socialization, and if subjectivity can never experience itself as originally free? The question is also broached in terms of a philosophy of language; in their eyes a society's language is not an independent, immutable, readily available tool but is structured and determined by the communicative interaction that takes place in a given society. Language, existing only in a historically concrete form, muddles human thought. The question then becomes, how is it possible for us to free ourselves from the social and ideological contamination of language?

In answering this question the Romantics started from the problematic posed in Fichte's *Wissenschaftslehre*, even though they corrected and varied his results. Fichte had assumed that the fundamental act of positing an other (*Nicht-Ich*)—that is, the positing of intentional objects or mental images (*Vorstellungen*) in our minds—is an absolutely necessary precondition for human thinking, an act that happens unconsciously or preconsciously and that forms the basis or starting point for our intellectual identity. This means that the concrete, always already existing difference between a thinking ego and its intentional objects can be neither eliminated nor sublated and that the ego exists only when it is already filled with mental images. The chain of intentional objects that make up human thinking cannot be traced back to its origin and thereby overcome, because, according to Fichte, an ego empty of intentional objects is inconceivable. All we can do is remain within such chains of intentional objects, merely comparing different intentional objects and deciding for one group of them as opposed to another according to rules prescribed by an accepted formal and ideologically bound logic.[67] Fichte's philosophy therefore stays within the realm of a (logocentric) mode of thinking that reflects upon and works with "identities." For a theory of literary criticism this approach means that we can criticize, favor, or reject the norms and values represented in literature in an open discussion; that these norms and values are identifiable; and that our conclusions, based on a critical comparison of these "identities," are justified by the persuasive force contained in our arguments. This philosophy does not concede the possibility that we can transcend the process of argumentation in an epistemologically meaningful fashion, thus freeing ourselves radically from the logical constraints of always already existing mental identities; nor would it *grant us permission* to transcend the realm of rational argumentation, even if that were possible in a meaningful sense. This epistemological model also underlies Kant's conception of criticism, as well as his notion of the public sphere and of progress: "The critique . . . arriving at all its decisions in the light of fundamental principles of its own institution, the authority of which no one can question, secures to us the peace of a state governed by rules, a state, in which our disputes have to be conducted solely by the recognised methods of *lawful action*." A necessary precondition for such action, according to Kant, is the freedom "to submit openly for discussion the thoughts and doubts with which we find ourselves unable to deal, and to do so without being decried as troublesome and dangerous citizens. This is one of the original rights of human reason, which recognizes no other judge than that universal human reason in which everyone has his say."[68]

Can the very process of forming an opinion be guided by a form of reason that is not dependent on a gesture of force and is not always already entangled in the interests of a society based on exchange value? The early Romantics answered this question in the negative. They realized—and here they attacked the epistemological presuppositions of both Kant and Fichte (which, by the way, are the same presuppositions implicit in most ideology-critical interpretations of literature published in the 1970s)—that they were incapable of providing and justifying a praxis of writing and reading with whose help individuals could remove the inscription of social totality from their minds and bodies. The Romantics saw that such an approach raises logocentric thought to the only form of thinking, whereas it was the specific goal of the Romantic project to destroy the universal power of "petrifying and petrified reason" (Novalis), so that freely reflecting subjects could constitute themselves in spite of social totality. As Novalis wrote in 1795–96 in his *Fichte-Studien*, which can be read as an assault on Fichte's epistemological presuppositions: "I do not exist to the extent that I posit myself but to the extent that I sublate (suspend) myself—I do not exist to the extent that I am in myself and apply myself to me [i.e., stay within the limits of my already established identity]" (*N*, 2:196). Sublation (suspension) refers to an emancipation from those preordained (ideo)logical deductions that were inscribed on our consciousness during the process of socialization.[69]

The Romantics believed that they could reach this goal with the help of a program emphasizing critical readings of art in which the individual work would become the starting point for infinite reflection; they spoke of art as the occasion, incitement, vehicle, beginning, or pivotal point in this process. The way they put the question epistemologically forced them to develop a new reception aesthetics (*Wirkungsästhetik*) in which art would not achieve its effect automatically and almost necessarily—as was the premise of the aesthetics of Sentimentality and the Enlightenment—but rather attain its effect through self-activating individuals who, in the medium of art, free themselves from all petrifying and petrified inscriptions in their minds. Unlike the reception aesthetics of Sentimentality and Enlightenment, which held that a work of art was the sole source of positive aesthetic effects (the reader needed only to react passively if the work was of high quality), even unlike German Classicism's dialectical notion of an appropriate understanding's dependence on the quality of both the individual work and the individual reader, Romanticism completely shifted the accent to the critical recipient: "Nothing is to be done with the object; it is a *medium*, nothing more" (*N*, 2:142). Art mediates free subjectivity. The ego that is able to use art in this sense, becomes him- or herself a work of art: "The ego is not a natural product—not nature—not a historical being—but an artistic one—an *art*—a work of art" (*N*, 2:253).

This is why, for Romantic art criticism, the work itself and the notion of value immanent in works and existing independent of their reception are no longer constitutive. What is decisive is that particular characteristic of art that the Romantics attempt to describe in such terms as infinite, inexhaustible, and the like—a characteristic that refers to the reader's state of mind rather than to an objective feature of the work. An individual work can nevertheless be centered in itself and formally closed, so long as it does not present the reader with an ossifying interpretation of the world and prevent him from thinking further, beyond the formal and ideological limits of the work. For Friedrich Schlegel in one of the *Athenäum Fragments*, "A work is cultivated [*gebildet*, which also means well-formed] when it is everywhere sharply delimited but within these limits is still limitless and inexhaustible" (*FS*, 204). For Tieck, every "genuine work of art" makes "an infinite description possible."[70] A work need not, however, be well-formed or cultivated, "sharply delimited," to be aesthetically valuable; the infinity contained even in a sharply delimited individual work must be activated by the critic. Since for early Romanticism the essence of art lies precisely in the *act* of infinite reflection, there is no difference in the value of a closed narrative work, a fragment, or a group of more or less independent works that merge in the act of aesthetic reception; they can all become the "incitement" of or occasion for infinite reflection. As Friedrich Schlegel wrote in his *Philosophische Fragmente*, "Fr[agmentary] forms are perhaps the most correct for everything ct. [central]"; and "Fr[agments] [are] t[he] spirit and t[he] form of universality" (*KA*, 18:359f.).

The notion that continuums of aesthetic reflection are inexhaustibly interpretable can be traced to Kant's concept of the aesthetical idea. In his *Critique of Judgment* Kant wrote: "By an aesthetical idea I understand that representation of the imagination which occasions much thought, without however any definite thought, i.e. any *concept*, being capable of being adequate to it; it consequently cannot be completely compassed and made intelligible by language."[71] One can describe the history of mentalities from the sixteenth to the eighteenth century as the gradual disciplining and instrumentalization of human thought ("instrumentalization" meaning the reduction of reason to an instrument for the exploitation of nature). If human thought in the sixteenth century still tended, as Michel Foucault argued in *The Order of Things*, toward erratic, "illogical" associative thinking based on vague similarities, during the seventeenth and eighteenth centuries such thought was gradually replaced by a form of thinking that proceeded step by step according to rules. However, the logification of thought in the course of the modernization of Western society also produced a variety of problems. What sort of theoretical and institutional basis is there for innovative thinking when the ideal is step-by-step, rule-governed thought whose absolute dominance would, however, lead to a short-circuiting or sterilizing of thinking in general? Attempts to differentiate between the positive and negative sides of imagination led to the conceptual bifurcation embodied in the negative term *fancy* (*Phantasie* as well as *Phantasterei*) and the positive term *imagination* (*Einbildungskraft*), in which the imagination was further defused by limiting all its positive activities to the functionally dissociated aesthetic realm.[72]

This limitation did not mean, however, that the healthy effects of its use should be confined within the boundaries of the aesthetic realm. To the contrary, the productivity that reflexive reason is allowed to develop there supposedly helps it maintain its productive ability for those instances outside the aesthetic realm when instrumental reason is insufficient. Kant therefore called the imagination "a productive faculty of cognition," in whose use "we feel our freedom from the law of association (which attaches to the empirical employment of imagination)." This means that such freedom has to be guaranteed freedom from logic. A chain of aesthetical ideas that "takes the place of logical presentation" in aesthetic cognition not only transforms an idea into another mode of representation—namely, into a sensate or graphic one, as the thinkers of Enlightenment asserted; they promoted the sensate (*anschauliche*) mode of representation as an adequate means of educating the masses—but also "enlivens the mind by opening to it the prospect into an illimitable field of kindred representations."[73] In other words, the chosen mode of representation does not remain external to its content; transforming ideas from one mode of representation to another and leaving them otherwise unchanged is impossible. In contrast to their function during the Enlightenment, each mode now fulfills a completely different function within the discursive organization of society.

The prospect Kant speaks of becomes visible only to the extent that the individual is successful in freeing himself from the strangulating corset of instrumental reason. For Kant, such acts of emancipation were only sporadically necessary, so that the individual could, when the need arose, momentarily overcome instrumental reason. In other words, he derived its necessity in functional terms. For the early Romantics, on the other hand, such acts of emancipation were the basic condition necessary for the *possibility* of subjectivity; they were supposed to lead to a permanent and fundamental emancipation from instrumentality.

This is another reason why Romantic art criticism had to oppose all codifications and uses of rules. As I pointed out above, the validity of rules is always an indication of the degree to which art has been integrated into social communication. In addition, the application of a fixed canon of rules in criticism fosters the instrumentalization of the critical process, which makes it unsuitable for sublating the technical reification of thought. All criticism that is bound by rules has to pay close attention to the details of aesthetic structures, which are commonly ideological configurations as well; in psychohistorical and psychological terms such criticism and its correspondent literature tend to be an integral part of a society emphasizing the value of strong superegos, whose intellectual identities closely reflect norms and values characteristic of that society. Criticism emancipated from the rules of poetics can associate freely. A. W. Schlegel therefore wrote:

> Of course, there were many who claimed to be critics and who wrote exhaustive evaluations of art, although they were not capable of doing so. That is particularly true of those who preferred to judge, or who judged exclusively, on the basis of so-called correctness. . . . [With this term] they referred . . . to perfection of individual elements of a work of art, including the smallest details, which supposedly could be achieved without reference to the work as a whole. One could label this form of criticism atomistic . . . in that it views a work of art as a mosaic, a laborious assemblage of minute, dead particles, even though everything that earns the name [of art] has an organic nature, in which individual elements exist only through the mediation of the whole.[74]

The reflective continuum of art that sublates logical, instrumental thought has an organic nature. Such a conceptual framework, filled as it is with metaphor, originates logically in the binary opposition of the two semantic fields that structure Romantic thought. Since everything mechanical or machinelike is relegated to the negative field (discussed above), the infinite reflective continuum intended in (to use Schlegel's term) "progressive universal poesy" is interpreted to be organic.

That the Romantic concept of art as an infinite reflective continuum was not the result of an escapist attitude—that is, of an aestheticistically motivated fear of taking sides in the struggle for cultural or ideological hegemony (as one could still read until recently)—is repeatedly made clear by the structure of the arguments used in Romantic discourse: the opponent against whom the argument is directed, who therefore structures the Romantics' own discourse *ex negativo*, is the instrumentalization of culture. As A. W. Schlegel put it: "The products of mechanical art are dead and limited; the products of the higher, spiritual arts are alive, internally mobile, and infinite. The former serve some external purpose, whose achievement they do not transcend, and the reasoning that proposed them can understand them at every level."[75] It becomes obvious here that notions of infinity and inexhaustibility were conceived of together with the concept of the living or the organic; the aspects of art covered by these concepts, which are activated in the act of criticism—that is, brought to life from a state of mere potentiality—are supposed to protect art (in its double sense of artistic objectifications and the critical, subjective act) from reification.

Of course, conceiving of art's radically critical nature in such terms threatens it with *semantic* atrophy—semantic in the sense of identifiable, even if unstable, units of meaning. When Friedrich Schlegel refers to Romantic poetry in the famous 116th *Athenäum Fragment*, where he calls it "progressive, universal poetry," he says that it must be "free of all real and ideal self-interest, on the wings of poetic reflection, and can raise that reflection again and again to a higher power, can multiply it in an endless chain of mirrors" (*FS*, 175). This comes close to propagating a mode of aesthetic writing that is empty of content. As Heinz-Dieter Weber put it, Schlegel formalizes "the text into a substratum of the occasion for reflection," because a text is valuable not when it can be read for various semantic effects but only "when, in the interest of openness and of establishing a [reflexive] progression that is impossible to halt, it devotes itself to 'promoting self-reflection' . . . so that, in the final analysis, every text that permits this is equally

valuable. As a result the demand for an apparently progressive reflective continuum can be met in such a way that the impulse behind new
productive creations no longer exists."[76]

The question is whether any mode of reading of works of art, which
will always remain self-contained (semantically delimited in one sense
or another), can ever transcend the individual work's ideological structure: that is, whether the semantic structure of any work of art can ever
be so "infinite" and "inexhaustible" that all its ideological delineations
are necessarily sublated by the aesthetic mode of presentation claimed
for "universal poetry." The Romantics themselves noticed that the idea
of reflexive infinity does not necessarily contradict the idea of self-
containment. Novalis, for example, envisioned the possibility that
closure and infinity exist concurrently in art: "Something is absolutely
at rest when the external world regards it as absolutely immobile.
However much it may alter itself internally, in the view of the external
world it remains at rest. This sentence refers to all self-modification.
The beautiful therefore appears to be so immobile. Everything beautiful is a self-illuminated, completed individual" (*N*, 2:461). The question arises whether, in spite of its internal, conceptual "inexhaustibility" (see *N*, 3:664), the border that separates it from the external world
does not force a definite ideological dimension onto the text—whether
the fluctuation involved in aesthetic reflection, which sublates conceptual certainty, does not always take place *within* a definite and defin-
able ideological framework, which would mean that although the
reflective flux Friedrich Schlegel speaks of cannot be halted, it is nevertheless ideologically specific.

Again, the early Romantics apparently saw this themselves. At
least, such an insight would provide an explanation for why on the
one hand they retreated from the concept of the closed work of art and
favored as poetic genres the open novel and the fragment, and why on
the other hand they tended to free the critic's aesthetic reflections from
the limits placed on them by the internal structure of a work. The
category of wholeness already makes this clear, because in Romantic
thought wholeness is never a merely objective characteristic; it never
refers to an evaluative quality emanating from the act of artistic production that is present for all times. In Romantic thinking, aesthetic
wholeness tends to be something that the recipient produces for himself, independently. As Friedrich Wilhelm Schelling wrote in his *Philo-*

sophie der Kunst: "For someone who, when confronted with art, does not succeed in contemplating it freely, that is, contemplating it at the same time passionately and actively, enthusiastically and deliberately, all the effects of art are merely natural effects [which is how the era of Sentimentality viewed aesthetic effects]; he behaves like a being in nature, and he has never really experienced or recognized art. What moves him are, perhaps, individual beauties, but in a true work of art there is no individual beauty; only the whole is beautiful. Therefore, whoever does not bring himself to comprehend the idea of the whole is completely incapable of judging a work."[77] During the High Enlightenment, Moses Mendelssohn and Lessing still held that even if the work as a whole did not possess any aesthetic qualities, the "individual beauties" contained in a work of art possessed a completely positive validity.[78] In the meantime the book market had developed into an important industry; as such, it was subject to the principle of profit maximization, which led to an ever-increasing rationalization of the writing process—including the establishment of so-called writing factories in which writers specialized in different modes of writing, to the exploitation of various literary effects used to influence the public, and to the harmonization of the literature written for the marketplace with the normative demands imposed upon social life by the process of modernization.[79] In this emerging context the new emphasis on wholeness as a central criterion in art criticism was intended to be socially critical. Concentrating on the whole aesthetic structure—a critical adjustment demanded for an adequate reading—was supposed to give the reader the strength to free himself from the emotive mechanisms of the culture industry. Schelling wrote in just this sense when attacking the culture industry's writing strategies: "Serious, theoretical instruction in art is all the more necessary in this age of the literary Peasant War being waged against everything elevated, great, theoretical, yes, even against beauty itself in poetry and art; where what is frivolous, emotional, or, in a base sense, aristocratic is idolized and accorded the greatest honor."[80]

The Romantic aesthetic of effect (*Wirkungsästhetik*) therefore aimed at an intellectualization of aesthetic reception without ever allowing that reception to arrest its motion within a conceptual framework. According to Romantic terminology, this intellectualized reading of art remained "organic," "free-floating," and "infinite" because it never fell prey to "petrifying reason." The project claimed for itself that it wanted to deconstruct not only the reification of thought but also the rigidity of *emotional* reactions (and thereby the social inscriptions on the body, the psyche, and the intellect) brought on by the culture industry. The failure of this project as a result of its idealistic presuppositions is discussed below. Still, it is doubtlessly true that the Romantics were conscious of the social dimensions of their project. As Schelling concluded from his own deliberations: "Part of general social education (*allgemein gesellschaftlichen Bildung*) should be . . . to have formed in oneself the ability to grasp the idea of the whole, as well as the reciprocal relationship of the parts to the whole and, in addition, that of the whole to the parts." In an almost Adornean argument Schelling then proceeds to deduce the necessity of a synthesis of philosophy, artistic production, and criticism: "But this is possible only through science and especially through philosophy. The more exactly the idea of art and the work of art is constructed, the more it becomes possible to influence not only laxness in critical judgments but also frivolous attempts in producing art or poetry, which are generally made without any idea of what art is. . . . Only philosophy can reopen those ancient productive wellsprings of art, now generally sealed shut, for reflection."[81]

How the critic is to be freed from a one-sided dependence on the inner structure of the work of art becomes clearer after an examination of the way Friedrich Schlegel linked the following two ideas in his *Charakteristik des "Wilhelm Meister"*: in artistic reception it is necessary (and here he begins by repeating a Romantic idea that I documented above with A. W. Schlegel and Schelling) "to be able to abstract from individual features in order to comprehend the totality while hovering above those [individual features], to be able to survey a mass and retain the whole while listening for its most hidden elements and connecting those most disparate. We have to raise ourselves above our own loves and become capable of annulling in our thoughts those things we cherish; otherwise, no matter what other abilities we have, we will be without any feeling for the universal."[82] The intellectual annihilation of what we cherish—that is, of the beautiful—is necessary because liberation from society's "text" cannot take place within the semantic and ideological borders of an individual work; it can occur only while contemplating "infinity" or "the universe" in a way that encompasses all possible points of view. When Walter Benjamin says that "the moment of self-annihilation, the potential negation through reflection, cannot outweigh the thoroughly positive aspect of raising the level of consciousness in the person engaged in reflection,"[83] he fails to realize that the negation advocated by Schlegel is the *precondition* for the critic's elevation in the act of reflection. The intellectual annihilation of the beautiful has nothing to do with the critical negation of a failed work, and it is completely consistent with the fundamentally affirmative nature of Romantic criticism. Intellectual annihilation means a mode of thinking that sublates what it negates; that subsumes and includes specific, concrete ideas—that is, potentially all possible semantic "identities"—while at the same time floating between these "identities," never arresting their meaning; that keeps those ideas in a constant state of flux, thus creating a semantic zero point at which our attention is not focused upon individual, identifiable ideas. Such a state of reflection is both complex and protected from naive, positional thinking; it is intended to permit thinking that is not constrained by always already existent social inscriptions.

This concept is radically different from Fichte's early position. Fichte assumed that thinking was possible only as a process of proceeding from one mental content to another. For him, the "infinity of reflection" could exist only as endless human argumentation, as a set of logical steps from content to content. However, for the early Romantics, as Walter Benjamin has shown, what is important is "not the infinity of process but the infinity of correlation. . . . Fichtean reflection means reflection within the absolute Thesis [i.e., within the positing of the other, which for the individual has always already taken place]; it is reflection that is supposed to remain within the Thesis, and is not intended to have any meaning outside it, because there it would lead nowhere."[84] The early Romantics wanted to rescue the ego's capacity for *self*-limitation, its capacity to transgress the realm of the always already posited; for Fichte, these limitations predate the ego. As a result, Romantic literary criticism scarcely concerns itself with plot structure and character constellations. Criticism of character always has to discuss the figures as ideological paradigms, while criticism of plot has to view the shift from narrative configuration to narrative configuration as a temporal and figurative unfolding of semantic strategies. That kind of critical practice would be possible only on the basis of Fichte's epistemological presuppositions, which in this regard are closer to the late Enlightenment than to Romanticism. By way of contrast, Romantic literary criticism, because of its sociocritical and epistemological presuppositions, by and large has to abstract from the specific sets of semantic oppositions immanent in a work of art, for "criticism is far more than the merely aesthetic form of explicating art" to which it is so frequently "denigrated" (*KA*, 2:14). The mode of argumentation in Romantic reviews reflects this idea with formulations such as Friedrich Schlegel's observation about Georg Forster: "However, it is not just this or that view but rather the dominant tone of *all* his works that is really moral." On the one hand, Schlegel disassociates himself from the concept of morality based on positional thinking in terms of opinions, in which one opinion *in contrast to another* is moral: Forster is moral on the basis of his unique personal stance, not because of his specific convictions. On the other hand, Schlegel also distances himself from the practice of reviewing that concentrates on individual works: "It is just as absurd to attempt to get to the bottom of a particular work without already knowing [all the other works of] an author; only by repeatedly studying all the works that were produced by and in one mind can one find the real [individual] point of view, which is what matters in the end."[85]

Since Romantic criticism is not interested in evaluating individual works, it remains "without an answer to the question of art's meaning."[86] For poetry as "the high art of constructing transcendental health" (*N*, 2:535) is initially supposed to provide only the preconditions for arriving at meanings that are not merely restatements of those established in a reified and alienated public discourse. Poetry is supposed to rejuvenate that discourse. As a result, Novalis can write: "Poetry is the basis of society, just as virtue is the basis of the state" (*N*, 2:534). For Friedrich Schlegel, the functional effect achieved by poetry as a medium is actually its most important task; its success guarantees that humanity will empower itself: "Education's most important task is to empower one's transcendental [i.e., reflecting] self, to be the ego of one's ego."[87] Criticism makes it possible to achieve this state.

We constantly have to remind ourselves that Romantic criticism was not interested in judging or ordering objective values. In fact, the concept of (objective) value did not interest the Romantics in the least. Friedrich Schlegel's early and isolated formulation, that the critical genius's only task "is to determine the value or lack of value of poetic works of art" (*KA*, 2:14)—which is often quoted out of context and is thus easily misunderstood—does not alter this view. The Romantics were equally uninterested in the concept of judgment, which is so constitutive for the current notion of critique. In their eyes an act of judgment that attempts to establish the value of a literary work is a reification of the critical process, the ossification of activity. "At the stage of mere judgment the individual feels himself to be *passive*," wrote Novalis in 1797 (*N*, 2:363). Friedrich Schlegel's *Gespräch über die Poesie*, for example, makes it clear that the early Romantics regarded this form of reification as part of the quantifying process they associated with acts of exchange. Antonio, one of the characters in Schlegel's work, attacks his friends by claiming that, "the principles underlying their criticism . . . were to be found in [Adam] Smith's writings about the wealth of nations. They were happy only when they could put another classical writer into the public treasury. . . . For the same reason, and in the same manner, they were just as proud of the fabrication of the best pairs of scissors as they were of the best poetry" (*KA*, 2:289). The Romantic concept of literary criticism implies a process taking place within the subject and acting upon him: "Being critical means elevating thought so far above all constraints that a magical insight into the falsity of these constraints will result in the concurrent comprehension of the truth."[88] In Romanticism, as Walter Benjamin has already emphasized, critical and reflective attitudes toward art are fundamentally the same.

In an early essay, *Über das Studium der griechischen Poesie* (1795), Friedrich Schlegel used the ancient-versus-modern opposition to argue that in contrast to its modern counterpart, ancient art was "beautiful," which for him meant "disinterested" (*interesselos*). He reproached modern art for having a one-sided interest in cognition; as "interested" art it preferred the typical and the general. The early Schlegel, for whom the term "modern" had not yet become the positive, historico-philosophical concept it was in his later writings, was apparently thinking of the semiotic, ideological function of art in the Enlightenment and its integration into the public discussion of norms and values. He accused modern art of "aesthetic heterogeneity" and compared it unfavorably to the autonomy of ancient art. The semiotic and ideological utilization of the institution of art in the eighteenth century

(a form of utilization that has since been continued in popular literature) was what made it possible for Schlegel to view ancient art as the
ideal reflection of a better society. His assessment expressed the socially critical desire for a world freed from particular interests, a world
not ruled by the abstract principles of exchange. In the *Lyceum Fragments* Schlegel criticized his earlier study by speaking of its "revolutionary rage for objectivity" (*FS*, 150); the phrase refers to the intellectual gesture with which the early Schlegel projected everything
positive into the distant past, without conceiving of a strategy for
overcoming the social negativity of the present. Once this "rage for
objectivity" is overcome, his strategy changes, but his goals remain the
same. At this point he starts to believe that a redefined form of modern
poetry—namely, ironic poetry—could shoulder the burdens he had
previously placed on (what was interpreted as objective) beauty in
premodern poetry. Carl Schmitt's criticism of Romanticism, that it had
attempted to "use the past as a negation of the present,"[89] is basically
true only for the short initial phase of early Romanticism and for late
Romanticism, not for the most productive and most important period
between approximately 1798 and 1806. Following this initial phase,
the early Romantics postulated a concept of "universal poetry" that
was generally *not* interested in using the past as a mirror in which their
contemporaries could discern the negative aspects of the present. On
the contrary, with their concept of universal modern poetry they intended to intervene actively in social reality to "make poetry lively and
sociable, and life and society poetical" (*FS*, 175). Irony in art and in
criticism was an important means to that end.

The concept of Romantic irony converges with the concept of criticism, just as it does with the concept of reflection. All three aim at
overcoming the classical aesthetic of representation with an aesthetic
of production, in which what is to be produced is not so much a work
as an ability or an attitude that can induce a more humane praxis. In
Lyceum Fragments 42, Schlegel defines irony "internally," that is, as a
subjective potential rather than the objectified irony contained in a
work (which is not as important to him): it is "the mood that surveys
everything and rises infinitely above all limitations, even above its
own art, virtue, or genius" (*FS*, 148). Irony involves a free-floating
condition, which is not positive per se (that would lead to a new form

of ossification in aesthetic indeterminacy) but rather implies a momentary liberation from "dependency": that is, from the system of social acts of (communicative or material) exchange. While floating free of the dictates of reality, the ironic critic can supposedly make decisions that are not predetermined by the relations of dependency inherent in society. The reference to reality always has to be preserved; otherwise, the dialectical tension between ironic reflection and social reality would be lost. If it is lost, there are only two possible modes of existence left: the existence of the philistine, who is completely under the sway of reality; and the existence of the aestheticistically isolated artist. Consequently, Schlegel says that irony "contains and arouses a feeling of indissoluble antagonism between the absolute [*Unbedingte*] and the relative [*Bedingte*]" (*FS*, 156). This indissoluble antagonism and irony's anarchic, deconstructive relationship to that pole of this opposition where everything is "determined" by the intricate web of social totality are the result of the Romantic analysis of society.

The Romantic discourse was structured by three questions to which the Romantic concepts of criticism, irony, and reflection were supposed to provide answers: (1) How is it possible for subjectivity to be constituted freely? (2) How can the relations of dependency in society be breached? (3) How can free subjects interact with one another humanely in modern society? This fact is inadequately dealt with whenever (as has repeatedly been the case since Rudolf Haym's influential monograph *Die romantische Schule*, 1870, and Carl Schmitt's studies) Romanticism is accused of subjectivism or egocentricity with a resultant loss of objectivity. Carl Schmitt was certainly correct in writing: "Irony and intrigue are not ideas around which society can crystallize, nor can a universal social order be structured around the need not to be alone, but rather to be a free-floating participant in an energizing discussion."[90] However, Schmitt's conclusions presuppose an analysis of society and an epistemology that the Romantics no longer accepted: namely, mental activity as the crystallizing point for political activity, and subjects as powerful centers of cognition and action—which in turn implies the possibility of constructing society on the basis of rational judgments. The degree to which the failure to reconsider such presuppositions can hinder an understanding of both the Romantic project as a whole and individual concepts becomes clear when Lothar Pikulik, for example, in his study of "Romanticism as an experience of normality's insufficiency," writes in affirmative reference to Schmitt that for "the Romantics reality was only an occasion for the development of the subjective play of fantasy."[91] Aside from the fact that the statement inadvertently allows Schmitt's pre-Fascist notion of political order to show through, the intended direction of the effects exercised by irony and fantasy are reversed: Schmitt's formulation, "the Romantic keeps avoiding reality, but ironically," eliminates the strategic, deconstructive dimension in the relationship of irony and fantasy to what exists.

It is certainly true that one can find statements—taken out of context—that make the Romantic project look like a flight from reality. To add a further example to the ones presented at the beginning of this essay, in A. W. Schlegel's *Vorlesungen über schöne Literatur und Kunst* one can read: "The fantasy removes this disturbing medium [reality] and submerges us in the universal; it creates and activates within us a magic kingdom of constant change in which nothing exists in isolation, rather where, through a miraculous creation, everything becomes part of everything else."[92] However, interpreting such statements as obvious calls for a flight from reality is false. The disturbing medium of reality is, in fact, the purely quantitative utilitarianism that has been drilled into us; it has to be deconstructed before "active reason" can become "productive imagination" (N, 3:460) and initiate discussions of norms and values that are freed from the ostensible constraints of reality. Fantasy is revealed to be nothing other than productive imagination operating in the face of ossified reality. Fantasy, reflection, and irony are the constitutive components of the critical discourse on art, whose primary function is to allow the critic to enter into a productive relationship with reality, one that is freed from instrumentally crippled reason. It is interesting to note how Novalis introduces the category of productive reason in his *Allgemeiner Brouillon:* "What if *understanding* [*Verstand*] were not a sense of qualities but only of quantities—and *active memory* in contrast only a sense of qualities." He begins the fragment with this question, before explaining his use of the term "memory" shortly thereafter: "*Categories of memory—categories of reason—active* reason is *productive imagination*" (N, 3:460). The Romantics radicalized Kant's distinction between Ver-

stand (understanding) and *Vernunft* (reason) by turning the terms into sociocritical categories fundamentally opposed to each other and by aestheticizing the concept of reason. Fantasy liberates reason from thinking only in quantities.

With such ideas, the early Romantics come astonishingly close to anticipating similar ideas in Horkheimer and Adorno's *Dialectic of Enlightenment*. This is also true of their reflections on language. For just as the subject, through his or her socialization, is always already integrated into the conditioned relationships of modernity, so too has the language available to writers always already accommodated itself to the structure of modernity. Whereas Horkheimer and, even more, Adorno therefore concluded that the import of any statement, especially in philosophy, has to be surrendered to an unconventional, obtuse style, which is intended not only to impede easy reading but also to generate new meaning, the Romantics viewed their own ironic, fanciful playing with language as a means of breaking out of a language deformed by instrumental reason: "A *pure* thought—a *pure* image—a *pure* sensation are all thoughts, images, and sensations—that were not *awakened* by a corresponding object [such as a sign] but rather *emerged* outside so-called mechanical *laws*—outside of the mechanistic sphere. Fantasy is one such extra-mechanical force" (*N*, 3:430). Art that is saturated with this force, as Schelling wrote in his *Philosophie der Kunst* (a book that was very influential in early Romanticism), "impresses [*einbilden*] the infinite on the finite, the ideal on the real."[93]

In his 1808 review of Fichte, Friedrich Schlegel dealt with that author's attacks on the concept of fantasy and on the "fanciful" playfulness of modern writing; Schlegel argued against Fichte's avowed intention of "rooting out fantasy from the human mind, because it can degenerate into raving fanaticism." In spite of all of Fichte's insightful criticism of the contemporary situation, Schlegel accuses him of ultimately viewing social reality affirmatively. In an ironic reference to Fichte, Schlegel contends "that many otherwise extremely intelligent men were absolutely unable to transcend their own age; no matter how much effort they expend to rise above it, no matter how decisive the rigor they turn against it, they nevertheless fall back under its sway, because they lack . . . an anchor outside their own era." The result of this affirmative attitude is that "the vast majority in any age, the legitimate elite of its sensible and well-educated members, . . . just like Herr Fichte, [regard] art as nothing more than the portrayal of reasonable and moral life. For them nature is dead material, the means and a tool for the realization of goals prescribed by reason; that state is best developed [*ausgebildet*] where the state has inculcated all its citizens to the greatest degree [with the desire to unite] their customs and efforts in its one purpose."[94]

In the eyes of the Romantics, uniting society into one interdependent network—which would suffocate every "qualitative" difference while pressing art into its customary service of reproducing that society ideologically—robs art of its sociocritical potential, which can be guaranteed only through its use of deconstructive, anarchic fantasy and irony. It is interesting that Schlegel's argument connects the institutionalization of art that took place in the Enlightenment with the exploitation and subjugation of (external and internal) nature in the economy and with the organization of the modern state for the purpose of gradually improving economic (re)production. It is also interesting that he does not see any difference between so-called high literature, in those instances when its role within the institution of art was limited to portraying moral life, and popular literature. Both of them (and this view is historically accurate; ever since Romanticism, popular literature has continued the institutional tradition begun with the Enlightenment's functionalization of art as a mediator of life-practical norms and values, although it is increasingly in the service of the easily assailable interests of the culture industry) fall victim to the dialectic of Enlightenment. As a result of their voluntary integration into the process of social communication, both "high" and "low" literatures reproduce established modes of speaking and thinking; even the critique of contemporary conditions, if it accepts the rules of public discussion, remains locked within the system of binary oppositions inherent in the system. In the "age of books" (*KA*, 2:332) it is generally true that "paper cement . . . glues people together" (*N*, 2:488). Reading popular novels, as Antonio puts it in Schlegel's *Gespräch über die Poesie*, "really serves no purpose other than killing time and destroying the imagination" (*KA*, 2:330). Reading that has become a "necessity" (*KA*, 2:330)—that is, an addiction—produces a uniform set of human reactions; the "paper cement" unites people by leveling their differences for the purpose of more easily achieving the aims of the modern state.

The project behind Romantic art and art criticism is an attempt to break out of this set of relationships. The "original chaos of human nature," which fantasy is supposed to recreate (*KA*, 2:319), refers to a free-floating condition directed against a one-sided systematic order and against hierarchical thinking. The "infinity" that art is supposed to represent symbolically, while criticism activates it, thus actualizing its functional goal, refers to that which is not ossified in (semantic, ideological, linguistic, psychological, and so on) identities. If fantasy and irony can introduce "infinity" into reality, the ossifications of social reality will dissolve. It is precisely this thrust behind the Romantic project that is overlooked when Romanticism is decried for its egocentricity and its loss of objectivity.

What is decisive in the Romantics' conception of their own project, however, is not the destructive but the productive moment in this free-floating state.[95] To be sure, Friedrich Schlegel, who wrote in his *Transzendentalphilosophie* in 1801 that absolute freedom for the fantasy was "the ultimate goal of everything" and "the most valuable possession," also asserted in the same context that "a society organized in accordance with this concept of freedom would be anarchy—one could call it *the kingdom of God* or the golden age. Essentially it would be complete anarchy" (*KA*, 12:84). Yet at the same time he wrote: "The essence of humanity consists of *understanding* [*Verstand*, i.e., reason as an instrumental tool in the material reproduction of society] and *fantasy*." In the same context he had defined understanding (*Verstand*) as "the highest power of consciousness [as long as the latter is merely] concerned with the notion of lawfulness in the relationship of the whole to individual elements": that is, as the indispensable form of thought that operates with well-defined identities, while fantasy is that which "propels the finite into the infinite, where lawfulness ceases." The early Romantics' idealistic anthropology allowed them to imagine both the liberation of humanity from the inscriptions of social totality and the construction of new, socially untainted identities as a process originating in the free-floating state of liberated consciousness created by irony and fancy. They viewed imagination as a human capacity untouched by and independent of the social process. They assumed "that lawfulness [i.e., the production of new modes of lawful thinking in this condition] would [then] be determined by freedom, which would result in a relative freedom; whoever promulgates the laws himself is relatively free" (KA, 12:85).

For the Romantics the reconstruction of "transcendental health" is impossible as long as individuals remain agonistically isolated. In isolation the individual cannot think difference; he or she can only think in traditional terms, can only proceed along the chain of preexistent identities. In other words, in order to communicate meaning successfully in the usual sense, the individual has to disregard the Other, suppress difference, and attempt to fit him- or herself into an already functioning, preexistent semantic structure. In playing with the components of the German for "to ponder" (nachdenken: nach = after, and denken = think), Schlegel says that what we call thinking "is really more thinking 'after' [i.e., a thinking that is dependent on the thinking that preceded it] than [self-active] innovation [Dichten]" and therefore "a particularly wrong-headed form of individuality" (KA, 19:95). The result is that the individual who sticks to the ideal of linguistic transparency, and therefore tends to suppress difference, ossifies in his "delimited individuality" (KA, 19:95); or he constantly and inadvertently falls back into a state of ossification if he is always unable to "transcend his own identity anew, in order to search out and find a supplement to his own most personal essence in the depths of an other," thus sublating his subject-centered thinking in a "play of [real] communication and approximation," which leaves difference intact and which, for Schlegel, is "the business [i.e., purpose] and the force of life" (KA, 2:286). Novalis expresses the same idea in Fichtean terminology, while correcting Fichte: "Instead of a non-ego—thou" (N, 2:430). But if the "thou" remains a mental image for the ego—a non-ego in the Fichtean sense—the individual who does not accept the otherness of the other as challenge to his own identity reifies that other by relegating it to the realm of already established mental images.[96]

In the eyes of the Romantics the encounter between "I" and "thou," which changes the identity of both for the better, is possible in only one medium, the medium of poetic language. Novalis, for example, developed a theory of the interchangeability of the center (I, or the ego) and the periphery (thou), which was oriented toward a theory of mediation that leaves difference intact. Poetry as mediator of otherness offers the individual an opportunity for reflection that is not delimited by the boundaries of his or her own identity. Whereas Fichte held that cognitive freedom can be found only in the form of a subject-centered reflection, in which the individual turns the attention of his reflexive reason to his own identity, thus questioning it, the Romantics were convinced that such self-reflection on the transcendental rules under which we act was not enough to guarantee that the ego would accept an other in its otherness. According to Novalis, the latter becomes possible only in an "appropriate state of dialogue" (N, 2:649), in which we recognize the reflecting other as a reflecting self—that is, as a (different) free center; this supposedly is the state that poetry engenders in humans. Poetry thus becomes a precondition for the possibility of a dialectical—nonsolipsistic—self-constitution of subjectivity. In his Fichte studies, Novalis characterizes the dialectical nature of this "appropriate state of dialogue" as follows: "The first designator interacts with the second. The former is guided by the signs of the latter, while the latter is guided by the signs of the former—a quasi-free contract." As soon as the first designator, the creative artist or the critical writer, "thinks in terms of signs and signifieds, he anticipates in his imagination the other's will. . . . The other's will has to occur concurrently with the action that takes place within the former" (N, 2:110f.).

Art results from and initiates mimetic assimilations of otherness. This concept of approximating the other's will in mimesis also has hermeneutic consequences for criticism. From the perspective of the Romantics, any attempt to come up with a "correct" interpretation of what an individual work of art "means," an ideal that still underlies most academic interpretations, implies an agonistic stance that corresponds to the social principles of a society based on competition. As in the agonia of antiquity, interpretations compete hermeneutically by claiming victory—that is, truth. However, as Novalis says, poetry should initiate "the most intense sympathy and interaction [Coactivität]" (N, 2:533). Its criticism, exhausting itself hermeneutically by constantly trying to comprehend the otherness of the other, should develop interpretative categories that are not always already determined by the agonistic praxis of society. The act of interpreting texts therefore converges with criticism in a dialogical ideal the Romantics called symphilosophein, which is the act of philosophizing together, an ideal that shrinks at the thought of formulating any final doctrine. "The only complaint I have regarding the attempt to interpret Goethe," says Antonio toward the end of the first version of the *Gespräch über die Poesie*, "is that the judgments it contains are often expressed too peremptorily [*imperatorisch*]. It may very well be that there are people living in the boondocks who hold completely different views on one thing or another" (*KA*, 2:349).

For the Romantics, the relativity of artistic judgments has nothing to do with an epistemological skepticism. "The aforementioned subjectivity in even the most thorough judgments in no way justifies," according to A. W. Schlegel, "a general skepticism regarding art. Various people could, in fact, have the same center in front of them, but because each of them is standing at a different point along the circumference, they would describe differing radii leading to it."[97] The philosophical perspectivism that Schlegel advocates here, which was at the root of the early Romantic concept of the characteristic—that is, that which is distinguished by an unmistakably individual perspective on things—and of criticism as a genre characterizing the characteristic, is derived from Leibniz.

This historical reference to Gottfried Wilhelm Leibniz is interesting because it helps to explain the relationship among the concepts "organic," "individuality," and "characteristic" and their common connection to the Romantic critique of civilization. In his *Monadology* Leibniz had written: "And as the same city looked at from different sides appears entirely different, and is as if multiplied *perspectively;* so also it happens that, as a result of the infinite multitude of simple substances, there are as it were so many different universes, which are nevertheless only the perspectives of a single one, according to the different *points of view* of each monad."[98] Interpreting individuality as an indivisible substance was a reaction to the process of modernization. In the seventeenth century this process was most visible in the development of scientific and analytic thought, which attempted to explain everything according to the model of mechanics; the machine was a common metaphor in all kinds of discourses. Claims for the universal validity of this mode of explanation threatened the qualitative unity of subjectivity. Leibniz therefore tried to prevent the dissociation of subjectivity as a unity of cognition and consciousness by proclaiming the ego to be an indivisible substance. In his view, these substances or monads were centers of meaning and analysis, and they could in turn comprehend and explain totality from the point of view of their own (particular) perspective and maintain their individuality within this perspective. Interpreting individuality as a substance implicitly contains a critique of the penetration of calculation into the sphere of experience. Organic individuality was conceived of as a fortress that would be able to withstand the negative side effects of modernization.

It was precisely this aspect of Leibniz that was taken up by the Romantics. They hoped that what was individual and characteristic in art and art criticism would be able to resist both the sociohistorical and the intellectual process of abstraction. In his review of Goethe's novel *Elective Affinities*, Karl Solger wrote: "Here [in the modern world] the first-born is the individual, who carries the image of God within himself. And to be sure, he does not carry an image of a universal or an absolute God, but rather one that endows this particular element of finite appearance (which we now call the individual) with his very own essence, belonging only to him. Today, therefore, everyone can find his own God only within himself, and also his philosophy and his art, or whatever he would like to call it."[99] Solger says respectfully that even when Goethe reflects on particular things, he remains "characteristic": that is, individual in his perspective.

Early Romanticism's valorization of what is characteristic of an individual testifies to the strategic, anarchic-deconstructive character of its project. Although German Classicism, which was far more concerned with using beauty to present an ideal image to the present, classified the characteristic above simple imitation (see, for example, Goethe in *Der Sammler und die Seinigen* from 1799), it relegated the characteristic to a position far below beauty as a representation of the ideal. Friedrich Schlegel's early essay *Über das Studium der griechischen Poesie* contained the same negative judgment of the characteristic; for the reasons outlined above he complained of "the absolute profusion of the characteristic, the individual, and the interesting in the whole mass of modern poetry."[100]

With the Romantics' transition from an aesthetic of representation to one of the production of subjectivity, this judgment changes quite decisively. From this point on the early Romantics turn against the ideal of an objectively beautiful object implicit in representational aesthetics, because objective beauty can also suppress the individuality threatened by modernity. Now that the "mode of representation" is considered to be an ideal through which "even the most limited object" can gain "a totally unique and independent essence," and through which "yet another aspect, a new variation of universal and, in spite of all the changes, authentic human nature, a small part of the infinite world" can be portrayed, Friedrich Schlegel would like "to see the doubtful and ominous attribute of immortality completely eliminated from our concept of what is classical."[101]

The notion of the characteristic introduces an (apparent) paradox into the Romantic project of art criticism. Within the history of art criticism in general, the central concepts of Romantic art criticism, which structure Romantic theory as well as individual reviews and interpretations of works of art, are, of course, thoroughly specific and historically unique instances (that is, characteristic) of the group known as the Romantics. At the same time, however, the Romantics claim that their insights into art and their own "characteristic" products in art criticism possess a universal validity, which—strictly speaking—recognizes only their own criticism as real criticism. But this obviously contradicts their concept of criticism as the poetry of poetry and their concept of criticism as characterization, because both these concepts presuppose the existence of histories in which otherness cannot be sublated: a history of criticism that consists of "characteristic" (that is, incompatible) critiques, and a history of art that also consists of "characteristic" (that is, historically specific) works of art. In other words, the historicity of their own categories would make logically impossible a history of criticism (which A. W. Schlegel described as a collection of the "most impudent, witty, direct expressions of the mind") based on these categories. Either the evaluation of historical instances of art and art criticism would occur according to the "characteristic" perspective of the Romantics, thus destroying the otherness of other "characteristic" perspectives, or it would end in an absolutely tolerant relativism, which would be too shallow to comprehend otherness. This apparent paradox becomes visible, for example, in Schlegel's critique of Forster when he denies that Forster has "any real feeling for the artistic representation of the beautiful" but nevertheless highly praises his judgment in artistic matters: "Even the most perfect representation could not reconcile him to a content that injured his sensitivity, offended his morality, or failed to satisfy his intellect. . . . Forster's unique theory of art is interesting as a specific opinion if for no other reason than that it is so completely his own and so much the product of his emotions, but above all because it regards its object from the indispensable point of view of cultured society, which will never achieve such a degree of connoisseurship that artistic merit will allow it to forget justice and the demands of morality and reason."[102]

How is it possible to resolve the paradox between the respect for the artistically positive "uniqueness" of Forster's critical judgment and the accusation that he is missing a feeling for art, especially if both art and judgments about it *should* be characteristic? And what of the "demands of morality and reason" on art, which the Romantics generally regarded as a sign of the reviewer's rationalistic limitations and his relapsing into the strictures of instrumental reason, as well as an indication that art was mistakenly made to serve some social function?

The resolution of this apparent paradox, in the Romantic mind, is that the concept of the characteristic is used at two different levels: first and foremost with reference to individual works and individual judgments, but also with reference to the "universal-poetic" characterization of something "characteristic," a characterization to the second power, which transcends specific instances of art and art criticism by relating them to the infinite continuum of history. In other words, "characterization" as a critical genre exists at both levels of reflection. According to Friedrich Schlegel in his *Charakteristik des "Wilhelm Meister,"* any characterization, at whatever level, "is not supposed to function like a mere epigraph reporting what a thing really is, where it is located in the world, and where it is supposed to be; that would simply require a complete, undivided human being who would make the work the center of his activity as long as was necessary." A real characterization "crosses the borders of the visible work with conjectures and assumptions" and "supplements, rejuvenates, and reshapes the work" from its own peculiar perspective.[103] At any rate, a higher mode of characterization will add to critical reflection "by relating it to the universe" and establishing a connection between the individual work and its history, including the history of its reception, as a higher continuum of aesthetic reflection. "On the other hand, our own efforts are directed," as A. W. Schlegel wrote: "at forcing artistic criticism to adopt a historical point of view, i.e. at regarding every work of art, no matter how closed upon itself that work might be, as belonging to a chain determined by the conditions of its production and existence, and at comprehending it on the basis of what existed before, what followed it, and what is still to come." Shortly thereafter he also called the historical point of view the "disinterested viewpoint [*Indifferenz-punkt*],"[104] in which identifications with specific moral positions are sublated by focusing on the complexity of history. History here is apparently being aestheticized—without necessarily being depoliti-cized at the same time. Reflecting on the characteristic within the endless continuum of history is the highest form of aesthetic reflec-tion; it is criticism as the poetry of poetry, in which the first level of poetry can be a characteristic work or an artistic judgment.

What is interesting about the dialectical relationship of the two levels of reflection is that literature promoting "justice and the de-mands of morality and reason" can be an extremely valuable instance of art on the first level. The early Romantics have no complaints about socially engaged literature if it is permeated by the consciousness of its own historicity and contextuality. To be sure, such literature is not an expression of the highest form of consciousness (which is reserved for Romantic universal poetry, poetry written from the second level of reflection), but it is still necessary in particular eras—presupposing, of course, that it does not completely exclude the higher form of con-sciousness. Forster, according to Friedrich Schlegel, "respected . . . the value of universal receptivity,"[105] which means he remained open to other positions. For the Romantics, the necessity of such openness did not follow from an "enlightened" model of open, public discussion but rather from the traps of modernity in which everything is con-trolled by "the purposes of the state" and the hegemony of instrumen-tal reason.

The ideal of openness inherent in the Romantic project is not con-nected with a linear concept of historical progress as was the case in the Enlightenment; it is epistemological in nature and contains a latent readiness to engage in "infinite" aesthetic reflection outside of the traditional boundaries of the aesthetic. The Romantics held that such openness does not necessarily exclude a latent disposition to make morally unequivocal, "finite" judgments—that is, to engage in politi-cal issues and choose sides; they were convinced that the latent dis-position to reflect prevents engaged judgment in specific cases from ossifying into merely positional thinking. The Romantics were arguing against the agonistic identification of and with one's own position, which usually leads to a systematic fortification of that position and remains unproductively intolerant of any contradiction. As Friedrich Schlegel wrote in his Forster review: "In a system of doctrines complete freedom even from the smallest contradiction might be an important virtue. For an individual, whole person taking an active part in society, however, such uniformity and rigidity are generally the result of blind one-sidedness and obstinacy, or even of the complete lack of unfettered personal opinions and perceptions."[106] The latter, however, are aesthetic qualities that predispose one to the aesthetic use of critical reflection. That the deconstruction of agonistically ossified identities (the term "identities" always refers here to the dialectic between "semantic" identities in language and personal identities) was viewed as an *aesthetic* process was related to the fact that the eighteenth century interpreted the mimetic concern for the particular and the individual—that is, a collection of "vivid impressions through observing an object"[107] that did not precipitously subsume the individual in some general category—as an aesthetic stance. The deconstruction of "generalized" identities was viewed as a recovery of the particular, which by definition is an aesthetic procedure. To be sure, the Romantics removed the cognitive moment, affirmatively connected with an overall concept of cognitive progress that had previously been considered constitutive of the aesthetic perception of objects, and replaced it with a strategic aspect: the deconstructive, rescuing force of aesthetic reflection. Since in their view this reflection is an absolutely necessary precondition for a life that is neither reified nor alienated, the epistemological equality attributed to sensory-aesthetic and conceptual perception in the Enlightenment was dropped in favor of the valorization of art. However, one has to be constantly reminded that in this instance "art" does not refer to works but to their perfection in criticism, viewed as the poetry of poetry; in the shadow of this critical reflection the logical operation of instrumental reason loses its petrifying character and can be sublated, or overcome, without being eliminated.

Before examining the increasing deterioration of the critical potential of the Romantic concept of criticism after 1808 (in the final section of this chapter) and also before turning to late Romanticism, I would like to attempt a historically critical assessment of the early Romantic concept of criticism, dealing more thoroughly with several negative aspects of that concept. My own presuppositions, which I can naturally only hint at, obviously influence the way I view these problems. The enriched "point of neutrality" (*Indifferenzpunkt*) or free-floating state, to which the Romantic subject is transported through criticism, is supposed to be a state in which the individual, on the strength of what he or she has achieved through reflection, has freed him- or herself from the inscriptions of social totality. But the Romantics never discussed the possibility of *material* inscriptions on the minds and bodies of individuals by social praxis—inscriptions that are not completely amenable to cognitive analysis.

In the first instance, their failure is connected with the fact that the Romantics perceived social totality too statically—that they did not see it as a social process whose interactions also both follow and produce a "text," which is inscribed on individuals. Liberation from this text would have to occur through means other than a form of reflection that is exclusively and inherently linked to reflection on language, if one were actually to achieve the free-floating state the Romantics strove for (which would also have to allow for the construction of social praxis on new lines). Their idealistic presuppositions become visible precisely where the Romantics seem to argue materialistically: "All states are based on *money*; but money originated accidentally; it could just as easily disappear again, which would deprive states of their foundation. All present states would collapse" (*KA*, 12:47).

In addition, their difficulty is related to their conception of human consciousness as a homogeneous, undifferentiated, and noncompartmentalized entity, evenly filled with mental images and their linguistic representations. Yet consciousness is apparently intertwined with social praxis in such a way that only clearly delimited segments of the whole are engaged in specific realms of praxis, without our ever suffering too severely from this fragmentation. This segmentation of human consciousness reflects the institutionalized segmentation of various realms of social praxis, which is the result of the differentiation of society into social subsystems in the course of modernization. We fail to recognize the contradictions inscribed in our behavior and in our consciousness precisely because they correspond to the "rational" organization of society and are therefore defused and made to appear normal.

The conception of a homogeneous, undifferentiated consciousness is also a precondition for the anarchic-deconstructive features of the Romantic project, with its production-oriented aesthetic, in the sense that it assumes that the effects of aesthetic reflection on consciousness would be the same for all consciousness. The segmentation of consciousness that corresponds to the institutional differentiation of society can, however, hinder the transference of the effects of aesthetic reflection to nonaesthetic areas of consciousness. In other words, the institutional autonomization of the aesthetic realm in modernity aids in the compensatory functionalization of art, which in turn defuses the potential impact of art's critique of society by aestheticizing it.

For the Romantic concept of criticism the result is the collapse of the constitutive dichotomies of criticism and polemics, good and bad, art and the culture industry. For if one cannot escape the inscriptions of social praxis with a language-based strategy of deconstructing instrumental reason, then reflection on such inscriptions, especially on the products of the culture industry, is inherently necessary for cultural criticism to raise society's "writing" to the level of awareness. Of course, this kind of critical praxis could be institutionalized only as a collective, social praxis, not as the esoteric practice of a literary group. Annihilating the "bad" in order to devote oneself to infinite reflection on the "good" essentially means that the opportunity for a liberation from material inscriptions is lost. As a result of their idealistic presuppositions the Romantics basically return to Fichte's position and share his contempt for the masses. Contrasting the masses' addiction to prevailing ideas with the independence gained by the elite in a free-floating state of critical intelligence, Fichte held that "Just as Penelope's suitors, already caught up in the destruction planned for them, caroused in darkened houses and laughed with alien cheeks [i.e., they belong to the world spirit; see below], so too do they [the masses addicted to the times] laugh with alien cheeks; for in their laughter the eternal wit of the world spirit is laughing at them. In general, we are happy to allow them their pleasures, and we are careful not to remove their blindfolds."[108] In the early Romantic project one can nevertheless detect attempts at institutionalizing the criticism and evaluation of art as social processes that would have been in a position to dislodge the inscription of social totality on subjects. In this sense the Romantics were the idealistic forerunners of the materialist critical praxis later formulated by authors such as Bakhtin, Benjamin, Brecht, and Negt/ Kluge.

The Deterioration of Romantic Criticism's Critical Potential

After 1807–8 the critical potential of Romantic criticism was increasingly repressed, but this development was already implicit in the ambivalence contained within the early Romantic concept of criticism. I have already pointed out that in Germany the eighteenth century was a period marked by an increasing social disciplining of the populace in general. (In other countries, most notably Spain, the process had begun much earlier.)[109] Under the pedagogic influence of various social institutions, including the state, the whole of a person's life was regarded as a period of productive labor. The rationalistic demands of modernization were making the rhythms of everyday life more mechanical. Regarding leisure time as the necessary, regenerative side of the labor process was part of the new relationship to time; historically speaking, the emerging necessity of maintaining a productive balance between work and leisure was a precondition for the functional differentiation of the aesthetic realm. According to Achim von Arnim in his essay *Von Volksliedern,* the estate made up of industrial manufacturers "wanted active hands, wanted factories, wanted people to wear their products. For them festivities were exclamation points and dashes [within everyday life] that were far too long; a comma, they said, would certainly be enough. Furthermore, his [the manufacturer's] needs should become a law enforced on every estate (everyone should be medicated into society)": that is, welded into a social body of citizens who are subject only to the authority of a unified state (see above). The way the statement continues shows why the literary motif of the good-for-nothing was so beloved in late Romanticism: "Since the producing estate [*Nährstand*] needs a firm and solid house, everyone who wandered about without any particular business in mind was banished as a good-for-nothing, completely disregarding the fact that the state and the world need these wandering troopers and lost knights the most . . . to carry out their best, and most difficult undertakings."[110] At the end of the quotation, however, one aspect of late Romanticism, which would be even more obvious following a detailed analysis of the whole essay, becomes apparent: the socially critical discourse of early Romantic poetry loses its strategic and concrete reference to the present in late Romanticism; the better times this literature often portrays are now identified with a concrete, historical time: namely, the late Middle Ages.

The Romantics' reaction to the increasing social disciplining of society's subjects (as Arnim said, "In the city physical training is giving way to repressive mental exertions, so that children can be forced into men's jobs")[111] was to a large degree exactly that: a re-action, not intellectual comprehension. This was already particularly true of those aspects of early Romanticism that can only be explained psycho-historically or psychoanalytically. Manfred Frank has recently demonstrated in detail the Romantics' astonishing valorization of Dionysus, the god of intoxication, ecstasy, and fertility.[112] The same valorization can be observed with other motifs that call up an image of a free-floating state or of dissolution (*Entgrenzung*): the Venus motif, the Orpheus motif, woman as a symbol of non-male (that is, non-agonistic, non-rational) principles, erotic ecstasy, the desire to experience time as "timeless," traces of the mother-child symbiosis in the memories of adult heroes, and so on. Many of the human desires portrayed in Romantic narratives can only be explained psychoanalytically as desires for experiences similar to our experience with reality in the phase of primary, pre-oedipal narcissism: that is, in the state of a mother and child's libidinal unity. In psycho*historical* terms the increasing disciplining of the population in the course of modernization led to a reinforcement of the patriarchal reality principle. The Romantics' socially critical intentions were at the base of their opposition to this principle, but the nature of their deconstructive strategies led all too easily to the valorization of opposing experiences and antitheses. What was missing was the realization that the poetic representation of such oppositional experiences not only did not hinder the functional differentiation of the aesthetic realm into a compensatory institution; it actually hastened the process.

Limited as I am to the context of Romantic criticism, I cannot examine these poetic motifs in greater detail. The psychohistorical aspects of the Romantic project are of concern to us here only to the degree that they permeated the theoretical and critical discourse of the Romantics. In this sense the "golden age" as a code word for the melancholy memory of lost harmony is not just a historico-philosophical category; its meaning also has an ontogenetic and individual-psychological dimension. Even the image of a conceptually diffuse, free-floating state achieved in the infinite reflective continuum of art (criticism) is undeniably associated with the psychic desire for dissolution. In fact, most of the metaphors contained in Romantic discourse are extremely revealing in psychoanalytic terms. Friedrich Schlegel's *Gespräch über die Poesie*, for example, begins as follows: "Poetry reconciles all the souls who love it and binds them together with unbreakable cords. Even though they strive for the most disparate goals in their own lives, absolutely despise what others hold to be the holiest, misunderstand and fail to inquire about each other, and thus remain eternally alien, in this one particular sphere a powerful, magical force nevertheless unites them and keeps them at peace. Every muse seeks and finds another, and all the streams of poetry flow together into the great universal ocean" (*KA*, 2:284). This paragraph strikes a careful balance between words that vary the motif of strife and alienation and those that formulate a desire for dissolution in the medium of poetry ("streams . . . flow"). The metaphor of the ocean, which in Symbolism and Aestheticism became a common cipher for the desire for dissolution in people tired of civilization, already pointed in the same direction in Romanticism.

The early Romantics' desire for harmony, which was initially an aspect of an anarchic, deconstructive, culture-revolutionary strategy directed against the present, hardened noticeably in late Romanticism into a restorative utopia. In a certain sense the late Romantics were trapped by the image of a better past, which arrested their critique of the present—although that image still was supposed to function as a critical mirror for the present. But when that past became too concrete and historical, it lost both its active, strategic connection to the present and its historico-philosophical reference to the future.

The concept of the folk (*Volk*) and of folk poetry (*Volksdichtung*) played an important role in this development. The concept of the folk expressed a political, antimodernist desire for national harmony, because the idea was intended to overcome "the boundaries of class with the help of a utopian preview of an intact community [*Gemeinschaft*] composed of a synthetic union of citizens, who would *communicate* with one another and *understand* each other, not just superficially through the medium of the state but in an unmediated fashion through the system of common language [*Umgangsprache*]."[113] What is remarkable is that as soon as the desire for harmony lost its psychic and political ambivalence (one could also say as soon as Romanticism lost the narcissistic individualism condemned by Carl Schmitt), it turned into a regressive utopia. In the discourse of Romanticism "the people" or "folk" is primarily a historical category; the concept refers to a time that predated the "fragmentation" brought on by modernization: "In an era when there was one universal set of beliefs, one national character, and one specific goal," as Wilhelm Grimm wrote in a review of Arnim's *Armut, Reichtum, Schuld and Busse der Gräfin Delores*, "every extraordinary force had an opportunity to express itself. . . . But in these times of infinite division an extraordinary force can hardly express itself otherwise than in eccentricity."[114] Left to its own devices, and threatened by modernization, the modern "folk" suffers from "poetic exhaustion and disharmony."[115] In this context collecting folksongs (*Volkslieder*) was a cultural-political act of conservation: "Virtually forgotten among the people, we stumble painfully to find their roots. Once a lofty mountain peak is completely deforested, rain washes the soil away; no trees grow again. Our goal is that Germany's resources will not be squandered in this way in the course of economic development [*Verwirtschaftet*]."[116]

Since real popular poetry (*Volksdichtung*) is an expression of a people's spiritual unity, it could thrive only in premodern times. As Joseph Görres wrote in his *Einleitung zu den Volksbüchern* (Introduction to people's literature): "If we look for the universal character that all these writings have in common, we have to convince ourselves that these creations are rooted in the masses and find their own, independent existence there, and that an internal sympathy must exist between them and the nation itself. There has to be a moment of elective affinity within them, and the same moment has to exist within the people. In a process of give and take everything is then united in love and is harmonized in a general spirit of joy and intimacy."[117] Behind the publication of folksongs and folk literature in the age of modernity was the hope of re-creating the collective harmony they expressed; Achim von Arnim put it as follows: "If the German peoples were linked by one common spirit, they would not need this collection; oral transmission would make it superfluous." Collections like the famous *Des Knaben Wunderhorn* were therefore intended not to provide scholarly documentation of a tradition but rather to create this "common spirit." The point becomes particularly clear in the debate about whether the poems were genuine, which was unleashed by J. H. Voss with his attacks in the newspaper *Morgenblatt für gebildete Stände*. Voss claimed that the editors of *Des Knaben Wunderhorn* "were guilty of fraud, forgery, smuggling, and malicious fakery." In the course of the dispute, which lasted for more than a year, Jakob Grimm wrote to Brentano in 1809 that he should not "publish an index of what was true and false [i.e., authentic and inauthentic] in Wunderhorn as a part of a history of popular poetry," because calling attention to what was not authentic would detract from the collection's main purpose: namely, "making all the poems universally valid"[118] for the purpose of recreating a "common spirit."

Folk poetry that was thought to express "the ancient, pure feeling for life"[119] was scarcely open to criticism. Since it was an organic product of the people, and positive in and of itself, it could not be improved upon. Görres therefore separated a more valuable, natural poetry from less valuable art: "We believe quite frankly in the existence of a real natural poetry, which comes to those who practice it like a dream, which is neither learned nor earned, nor acquired in a school, but which is like a first love, which even the most ignorant person comprehends completely in an instant; whoever practices it effortlessly does best when he studies it the least, and does ever worse to the degree that he attempts to understand it. We have a high regard for art, which it deserves, but there is more demand for nature. And that is only right, because, although we are surrounded by art, nature has made itself rare." Görres continues in a manner that illustrates the typically binary structure of the Romantic arguments critical of civilization. Modern art, he says, which is based on the quantifying exploitation of effects, is no longer able to resist its own times: "These mint supervisors have assayed and standardized the whole language, determined the value and validity of every word, and tested every combination. . . . How many gears are necessary for a machine, how many teeth each gear has, how many axles are in the gearbox, how the casings in which the axles go are built, and where the openings are supposed to be. All this has been calculated exactly, and talented workers only assemble works according to rules that divide heartbeats into thirds."[120]

Görres's critique of modern literature is reminiscent of eighteenth-century criticism of popular literature; both evaluate art against the background of a fundamental dichotomy. But for Görres, the dichotomy is no longer one within the present, no longer a synchronic dichotomy between "high" and "low" art, but a historical, antimodern dichotomy between the good art of the past and modern art. This allows him simultaneously to historicize and to biologize the notion of the good—that is, natural—poetry for the purpose of a critique of civilization. However, what is biologically good loses every active, critical meaning for cultural politics; it either exists or doesn't exist. To the degree that it exists, it achieves by itself the synthesis that the Enlightenment entrusted to critical public discourse and that early Romanticism sought in the individual's own deconstruction and re-construction of subjectivity and in an I-thou encounter made possible through the reflective medium of poetry.

Criticism loses its function where public speech and an emphatic notion of life or vitality in art are thought to oppose one another. As Achim von Arnim wrote in his essay *Von Volksliedern:* "Everyone had something to say about his life [during the period of 'universal complaint and suffering' called the Enlightenment], but no one was alive. Since no one lived according to the impulses of his nature but according to its constraints, counterfeit money and short measure were as common in thought as in the marketplace. No estate believed that its necessary origin made it as thoroughly good as the fruits of the earth, but that its worth was determined by exchange formulas having to do with the purpose of its business."[121]

"Organic individualism" was originally a concept that was opposed to the dissolving, alienating power of analytic thinking and the abstracting force of exchange. However, the notion was originally not insulated from the social process, as happened later when it was made mythical, but interpreted in such a way as to remain directly connected to reflection as a mode of cultural resistance. The metaphorical transference of the concept to the realm of art allowed for the idea of "organic" reflection, which could be cultivated in order to overcome the negative aspects of a centripetal mode of rational thinking. Transferring the concept of the organic to the notion of a people and to national history eliminated the ties that that concept had with reflection and speech or writing, making any sort of institutionalized reflective discourse impossible. And to the degree that literature's historico-philosophical dimension harks back to the static image of a regressive utopia, literary criticism's function dwindles. As a result, the late Romantics tended to dispute the value of criticism. Arnim, for example, polemicizes against the "inventors of this hellish art of reviewing and the critical babble of washerwomen."[122] In 1810 Wilhelm Grimm wrote to Brentano that he found "no immoderately severe criticism justified," because "modern art can never be absolutely perfect. . . . Only national poetry [Nationaldichtung] is perfect, because, like the laws handed down from Mount Sinai, it is written by God himself; there are no fragments as there are in human works."[123] Unfortunately, one can only wait humbly for national poetry and the conditions in which it becomes possible. Nothing is better able to illustrate criticism's loss of purpose in late Romanticism than Wilhelm Grimm's comparison of modern art with national poetry. The critique of civilization, still present in Arnim's critiques, for example, is fixed in images of a regressive utopia and thus paralyzes critical and artistic praxis: "However often these scarecrows twist about with their own un-authoritative opinions, wherever the hose of their artistic spray is directed, art seldom turns, in the face of the miseries of our times, to pure activity; art [as produced today] is almost never necessary, but for most an evil habit [compensatory institutionalization of the aesthetic realm!]. . . . The artists of the world are therefore as superfluous as they are mutually miserable."[124]

The late Romantics thus tended to discard a critical discourse that in early Romanticism was still characterized by the dialectic of negating and conserving tradition; the resultant dialectical tension between negation and conservation fostered an atmosphere of probing communication that was intended to transform society through—and in the course of—reflecting upon it. The insight that had been common since the time of Kant and Lessing, that we can "only defend and expand upon moral and political achievements" when the norms and values we use to orient ourselves "can be linked to self-evident remnants of tradition,"[125] was increasingly replaced in late Romanticism by an appropriation of the concept of tradition that excluded this dialectic.

PETER UWE HOHENDAHL

· · · · · · · ·

Literary Criticism in the Epoch of
Liberalism, 1820–70

TRADITIONAL periodizations of the history of *literature* have tended to pattern themselves on the evolution of belles lettres. They have generally traced this evolution either in terms of authorial groups—so-called "schools"—or in terms of stylistic and aesthetic characteristics common to works separated in time and space. But it is by no means certain that this mode of periodization is adequate to the historiography of literary *criticism*. Indeed, since such a historiography is almost nonexistent even today, we have only the barest conjectures as to the manner in which changes have occurred in literary criticism. The poverty of our knowledge on this point becomes particularly apparent when one does not equate literary criticism with literary theory but conceives of it as a literary institution by means of which certain practices are transformed into or subjected to the form of rules and norms. Whereas changes in literary theory can be culled from history by reading canonically central texts, changes in the much more broadly variegated object, literary criticism, are much more difficult to survey and conceptualize. One must therefore treat with some reserve the notions that historical development proceeds either continuously or discontinuously and that there exist particular historical situations in which certain tendencies have dominated while others have withdrawn into subordinate roles. Already by the early nineteenth century, the number of magazines and literary periodicals had grown to such an extent that it was no longer possible to read all published reviews, commentaries, and characterizations. The historian today is thus dependent upon the choices that were made by the readers of that time and that were thereafter adopted more or less critically by the historiographical tradition. One must keep this tradition in mind in order not to attribute its representations of evolutionary tendencies, and so on, to the historical process as such, in order to recall that these representations are merely attempts to organize and conceptualize documentary material.

It belongs to the commonplaces of today's scholarship that the literary criticism of Young Germany definitively differentiates itself from the literary criticism of Romanticism. Nearly everyone assumes the contrast to be so extreme that one can speak of a new historical phase.[1] For example, a recent study argues that the year 1830 marks an important turning point for literary criticism as well, insofar as the July revolution in Paris, together with its more distant effects, means in Germany the end of the Classical-Romantic conception of literature and thus introduces a new epoch.[2] This judgment can appeal for support to passages in Heinrich Heine, Karl Gutzkow, and Theodor Mundt, all of whom emphasize in various contexts that in Germany the age of art has come to an end. If one adds to this the polemic of Young German authors against the Romantic generation, one certainly comes up with the image of a radical turningpoint. Of course, this conception ought to be further differentiated. The literary criticism of the 1820s, determined above all by such authors as Ludwig Börne, Wolfgang Menzel, and Karl August Varnhagen von der Ense, appears as a time of preparation, in which a few advanced critics experiment with new forms and procedures. In the 1830s the Young Germans proceed to develop out of these innovations their own mode of criticism.

If one wishes to work with this hypothesis, which seems to me sensible enough, one must nonetheless not forget that it bases its understanding of change on the work of a small group of authors. It thus ignores the wide mass of critics who were regularly publishing reviews in the numerous magazines of the time. It could well be that the hypothesis thus ends by exaggerating the degree of change in the institution of criticism as a whole. Friedrich Sengle has expressed these doubts, preferring to see the time between 1815 and 1848 as a unity in which continuity outweighs discontinuity.[3] Although I am hardly inclined to agree with the particulars of his judgment on Young

Germany, I do think one should take seriously the question as to whether the history of literary criticism between the Napoleonic era and the revolution of 1848 is not to be conceived as a stable epoch with unceasing, continuous changes. In the realm of literary criticism this possibility is worthy of consideration, especially when one takes critics such as Menzel, Börne, and Heine to be forerunners of Young Germany. For it certainly would be easy to show that the critical model to which these authors appeal remains indebted to the Enlightenment conception of literature, not least in its assumption that aesthetic works have a practical effect on life. In this sense one could argue that in the early nineteenth century the Enlightenment model of literary-critical *raisonnement* by no means loses its legitimacy but maintains itself in various forms in connection with the spread of liberalism. In this context, one could well ask further whether the revolution of 1848 is in fact for literary criticism the caesura as which it has sometimes been seen in recent scholarship. Historians have rightly pointed out that the liberal intelligentsia of the period following the March Revolution contrast their work starkly with the literature of the 1830s and 1840s and develop an oppositional literary program. But even this happens in a context that modifies but by no means destroys the basic model of the Enlightenment. One can see in the literary public sphere between 1820 and 1870 a strategic reorganization of emphasis regarding certain premises and arguments within literary-critical theory and practice. But when viewed from the outside, the period retains a considerable measure of continuity. It is precisely these constants that allow the practice of literary criticism to reproduce itself. The form of representation and judgment remains in general unquestioned.

Production and Distribution

As my introductory remarks suggest, the structure and history of literary criticism can be grasped only in connection with the history of the apparatus of criticism.[4] Acts of characterization and judgment, however much they may refer explicitly or implicitly to theoretical models, are all bound to the ideological apparatus and thus to concrete organizations such as magazines, newspapers, publishing houses, government officials, and so on. What is important here is not so much the influence of individual organizations as their structure, for this structure frames and determines practice. In the early nineteenth century the literary market expands by leaps and bounds, absorbs realms that were previously untouched, and thus changes the very system of literature. This process begins, according to recent research, as early as the end of the eighteenth century and accelerates its progress with particular rapidity from the 1820s on. In economically regressive Germany, the capitalization of the publishing industry is remarkable: even before industrialization begins in the 1840s, the literary market has fully developed the structure of competitive capitalism.[5] The structural transformation palpably alters both the quantity of book production and the quality of literary interaction. The critics too are affected, even if they are only partially conscious of these alterations. By about 1800 the literary public sphere can only partially proceed in accordance with the model developed during the Enlightenment. The increasing competition between publishers has the result that what receives support and encouragement is not literature as such but the literature of the particular direction or tendency from which the publisher can promise himself the greatest gains. This manifests itself, among other ways, in the practice of literary criticism and in the new relations of competition in which critics suddenly find themselves. By means of the intimate relationship between magazines and book publishers, as Christa Bürger puts it, "competitive struggle" enters "the Republic of the Learned."[6] The practice of reviewing comes to serve less the enlightenment of the public than the production of the success of certain authors on the literary market. The founding of magazines— and that includes the most important, such as the *Horen* or *Athenäum*—is guided by strategic intentions to push particular concepts, literary tendencies, and so forth, on an already overcrowded literary market. In this situation literary criticism assumes a new function: namely, that of selecting and sorting for a reader who has become uncertain in the face of excessive supply. Contemporary critical observers of the reviewing business remark these changes and compare factual practice critically with the ideal conception developed by the Enlightenment. What will appear in later literary histories, beginning with Georg Gottfried Gervinus, under the stylized form of the Classical Age of German Literature appears to its contemporaries as the dissolution of a literary system that has attained the state of anarchy.

And what is nascently recognizable around 1800 becomes self-evident one generation later. In the face of a literary industry in which it is no longer possible to get an overview of one's situation, literary communication takes on more and more the form of a permanent struggle. In the 1820s the reviewing business has already become a secondary industry whose task is to prepare for consumption the plethora of annually appearing works. Menzel remarks in 1827: "Several hundred journals circulate daily in Germany, covering all literary subjects, being read daily by millions of readers; and the majority of German readers read more journals than independent works. . . . They cannot read all the works newly appearing on every subject, but they still want to know what's in these works, so they yearn for reviews and excerpts."[7] Precisely this situation occasions Börne's bitter remark one year earlier that "German reviews can be concisely compared to nothing so well as to the blotting-paper on which they are printed."[8] Reviewing has received such a bad name that those writers who want to make a name for themselves as critics are forced to set themselves apart from the mass of reviewers by formulating a new program (and not infrequently in a new journal).

The literary trade of the 1820s is characterized by a rapid expansion of the book market, which is in turn followed by the magazines as the necessary organs of communication. Between 1820 and 1843 the number of annually published book titles increases by 147 percent.[9] According to the calculations of Johann Goldfriedrich, in 1820 there are 4,375 new titles; in 1834 there are already more than 9,000 titles, and in 1840 there are 10,808.[10] These numbers obviously provide only a crude picture of the structural change, since they take into account neither the change in the content of the production nor the new forms of distribution. It is above all the mechanisms of distribution that change both quantitatively and qualitatively. Between 1822 and 1842, according to the calculations of Ronald A. Fullerton, the number of book-sellers rises by 183 percent. Whereas at the beginning of the 1820s there are 450 booksellers, in 1842 there are 1,247, of whom most still fulfill the functions of publishing and sales.[11] The distributional nexus solidifies within a generation in two respects. First, it expands spatially, especially by including the henceforth numerous small cities. Second, it becomes more dense, particularly in the older literary centers. Beyond the cities, bookstores are hardly to be found; the rural population remains dependent, during this period, on colporteurs.[12] And even in urban areas there are considerable differences between northern and southern Germany, the eastern provinces and Saxony. Whereas the number of bookstores rises enormously in mid-Germany, it remains decidedly lower in the North and the South.[13]

This expansion is all the more remarkable in that it is not accompanied by a corresponding expansion of the literary public. Literacy does increase but not in the same measure as the literary market. The book industry speculates on the anticipated extension of the reading public and is thus constantly exposing itself to the danger of bankruptcy. The form of competitive capitalism regularly claims sacrifices, but of course this does not prevent other entrepreneurs from establishing themselves in the market. On the whole, the consciousness of prosperity dominates the scene. In contrast to earlier decades, the book industry—especially younger firms such as Brockhaus or Meyer—is now prepared to take big risks as long as they promise sufficient profits. The nascent industrialism of publishing seeks undiscovered holes in the market that might allow for profitable mass production. Encyclopedias and the work of popular novelists like James Fenimore Cooper and Walter Scott prove to be especially profitable objects of publishers' interests.

Between 1820 and 1850 the majority of the population certainly is not buying books—for economic reasons.[14] Even the inexpensive editions of the classics and of fashionable authors remain unaffordable. The expanding book market caters to the academic or wealthy bourgeois public, which fulfills the economic and educational conditions for literary reception. The common people, too, read and even buy printed material, but their needs are covered by a separate market. Ninety percent of the population is served by publishers and booksellers with whom established firms such as Cotta or Wigand would not deign to compare themselves. This popular literature, sold by colporteurs, lies beyond the ken of the educated public as it lies beyond the ken of the reviewers. The institution of criticism comprises, in its practice, only part of the regular book market, where the capitalist mode of production applies itself—as the leading publishers repeatedly emphasize—to the task of educating and enlightening the public.

The contradictions between ideal purposes and material goals, already observable in the late eighteenth century, reveal themselves even more drastically in the 1820s and 1830s. Every attempt to formulate a new literary program, to assert a new mode of writing, or to develop a new sort of text remains dependent upon the mechanisms of the book market. The economically dependent writer has to learn to think strategically. And literary criticism assumes an important role in the writer's choice of his strategy. It takes on the task of providing orientation. The more impossible to survey the literary industry becomes, the more important become the central positions of communication: that is, the reviews in important magazines and newspapers. The meaning of a given discussion depends on the organ in which it appears; the significance of a critic depends on the instrument of publication he controls. The most obvious case in the 1820s and 1830s is that of Wolfgang Menzel's influence on literary life. This influence is rendered possible above all when the Cotta publishing firm, in 1825, grants him control over the literary supplement to the *Morgenblatt für gebildete Stände* (Morning journal for the educated professions). Menzel uses this position of power quite skillfully to push through his program of nationalist liberalism and even to attack his competing liberal critics, as when he assaults Gutzkow and Young Germany in 1835. Menzel's attack, which results in the ban of Young Germany by the Diet of the German Confederation (*Bundestag*), is the expression not only of his ideological preferences but simultaneously of his competitive relationship with his enemies. The ad hominem polemic forms part of a strategy to sweep the main competitor from the marketplace.[15] Thus, Menzel sees the younger Gutzkow—whom he has initially wooed—as a rival as soon as the latter wants to form his own critical periodical. "Science and art have ascended out of guarded chambers and entered the marketplace," writes Heinrich Laube.[16] And he means it positively, for he assumes that literature ought to democratize itself. The literary trade of the 1830s shows, of course, that this popularization is necessarily bound up with an intensification of literary competition. The cliquishness of which the Young Germans accuse the Romantics does not decline in their literary practice but in fact increases. Ideological partisanship and economic competition are becoming difficult to separate. What appears as the formation of schools is often no more than the formation of purposive contracts and arrangements of interest directed against a common enemy. "The

Young Germans produce in isolation from one another. They attempt to correct for the formation of relationships of isolated competitors in the marketplace—but manage to do this only competitively; they establish temporary arrangements of interest while maintaining, if suppressing somewhat, the competitive struggle among themselves."[17] Such behavior is in obvious contradiction to the emphatic concept—inaugurated by the Enlightenment—of the critic as judge of art speaking in the name of reason, for the task of such a judge is to discover the truth precisely beyond all special interests. The possibility of a consensus of all readers—a notion posited by the Enlightenment—is in practice unattainable in the nineteenth century, not so much for psychological reasons as for the reason that the apparatus (de)forms the behavior of the critics in a particular manner.

The Public Sphere and the Public

Jürgen Habermas has distinguished three phases in the history of journalism: the early capitalist, merely informational press of the seventeenth and eighteenth centuries; the press of rational dialogue of the late eighteenth and early nineteenth centuries; and finally the commercialized press that began to establish its hegemony after 1870 in Germany. According to Habermas, the journalism of rational dialogue is interested primarily in influencing public opinion and only secondarily in the maximization of profits. The publishers, Habermas argues, "assured the press of its commercial basis without commercializing it as such."[18] Habermas names as an example Cotta's *Allgemeine Zeitung* (Common news), which despite its great influence is not financially profitable. This characterization of the development of the press is essentially correct. For early German liberalism the emancipation of the economic system is still largely identical with the reorganization of the political system (that is, the overthrow of absolutism). Compared with the French press, in which even in the 1830s typical forms of commercialization occur, the German press remains behind the times in the years leading up to the revolution of 1848.[19] It is under pressure to conform to the political opinions of the Absolutist state, against which it must attempt to maintain its position. This struggle against the state censor does not, of course, exclude the establishment of a principle of competition between the newspapers and journals. Public opinion gets manufactured by rival journals, each of which formulates a particular standpoint and attempts to persuade others of its truth.

Since political discussion in the era of Metternich is restricted, the public sphere gets displaced into the literary sphere. As in the Enlightenment, the literary public sphere represents the forecourt of the political public sphere. Discussion about literature becomes, as Börne remarks, the means of political debate. Under these conditions the literary magazines become the carriers of specific ideological positions that struggle among themselves for hegemony. Literary journalism between 1820 and 1848 regards journals as—in Heine's phrase—the fortresses from which one can carry on the struggle against rival parties. And this continues to be true to some extent during the period immediately following the March revolution. He who has no periodical of his own is at a marked disadvantage.

The capitalization of literary journalism does not first begin when a culture-consuming public takes the place of a reasoning public. The transformation of literature into a market phenomenon takes place early in the nineteenth century through the attachment of literary discourse to an apparatus that obeys the mechanisms of competitive capitalism. Like the book market, the journal market is expansive. For the period between 1815 and 1850 there are more than 2,000 magazines.[20] The majority are short-lived, forgotten after very few years, but some, like the *Blätter für literarische Unterhaltung* (Journal for literary entertainment), the *Literaturblatt* (Literary supplement) of the *Morgenblatt für gebildete Stände,* or the *Allgemeine Zeitung* are recognized by their contemporaries as influential opinion-forming institutions. The founding of a magazine is a wager that the need for information is no longer exhausted: one either seeks a gap in the information supply or intends to displace magazines that already exist.

In 1835, introducing the journal *Literarischer Zodiacus,* Theodor Mundt formulates with striking precision the interrelatedness of ideal and economic competition: "In every general store, a moment's standstill, a moment's pause from the operation of the machines and the traffic of commerce is already considered regression and thus loss. He who *stays still* cannot survive. He who wishes to survive must keep moving [Wer *stehen bleibt,* kann nicht *bestehen.* Wer *bestehen* will, muss sich *bewegen*]."[21] The law of movement is in force, according to Mundt, not only for (the spirit of) business but for (the business of) spirit as well, and the literary periodical is the site where new trends and tendencies gain expression. It is the ideal place of turnover. Magazines represent the institutionalized opposition and are therefore for Mundt the instrument of progress. Using Menzel as an example, he explains how this works: "He possessed—and in sufficient measure—the decisive one-sidedness every man of the opposition must possess. Such a character is indispensable when in debate on vital questions conviction must be turned against conviction with the utmost intensity. . . . He stood up like a critical orator among the people, like a demagogic speaker for the people's literary cause. His critiques became masterworks of parliamentary rhetoric: they had no aesthetic-scientific basis, but historical importance and an enthusiasm of and for the people."[22] One could have said the same for Börne. The critical journalism of a Menzel or a Börne is partisan; their journals are polemical and do not obscure the differences between the various standpoints under discussion.

In the consciousness of Young German writers, the new journalism presents itself as a broadening of the literary—and in the final analysis also political—public sphere. Journals are seen as instruments of historical progress; they serve, in the industry of ideas, the same function as machines in the industry of material production. Thus, in 1834, Mundt writes in the introduction to his *Schriften in bunter Reihe* (Writings in mixed series): "What the steam-engines and railroads are for external and commercial trade, the journals have already become in the realm of thought and for spiritual turnover. Only in the 'penny-magazines' has this spiritual-industrial meaning of journalism taken on the transiently monstrous form that makes it ruin the entire state economy of literature. One must therefore see that it essentially prepares and promotes the general education of the people for the future period of cultural development."[23] The optimism of this utterance is characteristic of the early 1830s. Although Mundt is in no way blind to the potential danger of industrialized literature (he remarks upon its transience and superficiality), he nonetheless sees it as the signature of a time of transition.

The hope that through the journals literature might reach the masses turns out to be an illusion of the Young German writers. These journals never make it to the majority of the population; they remain a part of a limited bourgeois public sphere. If one looks at them more closely, it is not hard to see that they are directed at those with literary education. Their rhetoric presupposes literary experience: that is, acquaintance with the tradition, knowledge of rhetorical means, and insight into current aesthetic and literary norms. The democratization of literature they demand expresses itself finally not in an increase in the reading public but rather as a differentiation of the existing public sphere. Instead of a single center to determine norms and practices, a plurality of rival would-be centers results. Institutionalized competition comes to be understood as the motor of literary evolution, and the institution of literature appears as a theater of war in which one must assert oneself in order to fulfill one's historical mission.

The differentiation (*Ausdifferenzierung*) of the public sphere leads to an intensification of literary activity, Börne maintains—as early as 1818—in the announcement of the *Wage* (the Scale): "One takes the presence of numerous streets and canals crisscrossing a country to be the sign of a well-ordered and wealthy state, for the presence of many roads implies much movement, and through such presence great and manifold forces announce themselves. In analogous manner, it is a sign of the lively exchange of thoughts when many paths are open to their free and fast communication."[24] Börne assumes that public opinion is positively influenced by the acceleration of spiritual traffic. The journalist is charged with the task of leading scholarship out of its hothouse and into the fresh air of public competition. This polemical journalism sees itself as an ally of the public whose emancipation it strives to achieve. Its relationship to this public can be described as abstract intimacy: the public is addressed and involved in a dialogue, but it never actually enters the debate as a concrete social organization. The reader is supposed to feel himself to be represented by the critic. As various as are the images of the reader in Börne, Gutzkow, or Arnold Ruge, and as various as are the politics of information embraced by their various journals, they all adhere to a conception of the public sphere that leaves little room for the social differentiation of their readers. The public they address is simply supposed to represent the entire society. In this sense Gutzkow demands in 1831 a literary history directed not at lovers of literature or dilettantes but at the general public. Similarly, Robert Prutz says in the introduction to his

Geschichte des deutschen Journalismus (History of German journalism; 1845) that "the public [has] directed its hopes at the daily newspapers" for the reason that these papers "are supposed to provide the mouthpiece for the wishes of the nation."[25] He further argues that "of all contemporary journalism the only really lively sort, and the only sort that is really carried by the interests of its readers, is the one which, from near or far, retelling or reasoning, confuting or agreeing, deals with the political situation of the present."[26] This definition does not exclude literature. To the contrary: for Prutz, literary discussion in the 1840s is the preparation for political action.

The important literary magazines of the post-1848 period also cling to the ideal of *raisonnement*; they too see themselves as the mouthpieces of public opinion, even if they distinguish themselves more clearly from the uneducated lower classes. The first magazines to refuse this commitment are the family magazines that flourish suddenly in the 1850s and 1860s. They attempt, successfully, to address their readers quite concretely by personalizing the mode of dialogue. Significantly, they do not discuss the literary-critical tradition. The *Gartenlaube* (the Arbour) knows only biographical characterizations, which serve to inform the public. Critical reviewing is restricted to a special supplement.

The critical-polemical journalism of this period draws its life from the consciousness that it represents the public; its struggle for freedom of opinion appeals to the principle of the public sphere. And yet it cannot in practice achieve what it claims to. The critical public sphere and the reading public are no more identical than in the eighteenth century. As Prutz notes in his 1845 essay on popular literature (*Unterhaltungsliteratur*), besides the literature that criticism and literary history describe and evaluate, there exists another literature that is neither reviewed nor otherwise taken into consideration by critical journalism: "In literary history as our scholars write it, this literature has not yet played any role; they have either ignored it silently or, at best, considered it with a dismissiveness that is hardly adequate to the extraordinary scope of this literature."[27] The cleavage noted by Prutz between a canonized high literature and a barely tolerated popular literature points to a corresponding differentiation in the reading public. As a majority of belles lettres are excluded from aesthetic judgment, so a majority of readers, the users of the reading-societies and lending libraries, are not reached by critical *raisonnement*. Prutz unmasks the critical participation of the reading public as a fiction, however much he himself still may cling to the notion of a critical press. Even within the domain that we have described as the regular book market, the group that pursues critical debates in the journals is decidedly smaller than the reading public. The plethora of journals should not blind us to the fact that they were secondary channels of communication for the book market. The history of lending libraries in the nineteenth century says more about the evolution of the public than does the history of literary journalism. The order of magnitude of the critical public—that is, of the consistent readers of the journals—remains difficult to determine because empirical studies do not exist. But the scattered remarks of contemporary observers make it seem probable that not more than 10 to 15 percent of readers took an active part in the critical dialogue.[28] Even this number may be exaggeratedly high.

It seems the Young Germans had only vague notions of the composition of their public, despite their constant call for the democratization of literature. For example, Mundt remarks, "No one seems to have found out about who the public might actually be." And Laube, too, occasionally makes critical comments about the quality of the public: "The reading public and even more the buying public is hard of hearing and nearsighted."[29] In the face of this uncertainty the journals pursue an indirect strategy: they direct themselves at the smaller groups who have in fact the power to form public opinion, and hope that these then take over the task of dissemination. The other possibility consists in offering a widely differentiated program in which various segments of the public are represented and addressed.[30]

The circle of readers of the Young German journals—and one could say about the same for the periodicals of the Young Hegelians—could be described at least approximately by the use of a professional-group model. "The core of the recipients was formed by those who were professionally concerned with literature: in the realm of production and literary criticism, authors, editors, and reviewers; in the realm of distribution, booksellers and librarians."[31] Beyond this narrow circle, the readers of these journals are academics, especially professors and teachers in the academic secondary schools but also lawyers and doctors. It seems to me doubtful, in light of the small printings of these journals—apparently generally between 500 and 1,000 copies—that they reach either the teachers in nonacademic secondary schools or the lower state officials. These conditions change little in the following decades. The *Deutsches Museum* (German museum) and the *Grenzboten* (Messengers of the border)—to name just two important magazines of the period immediately following the revolution of 1848—never reach printings of more than 1,000 to 1,500. One can conclude from this that the communicative space of literary criticism does not essentially expand in these years.

The Institution of Literary Criticism

At the end of the eighteenth century in Germany, the separation of art from the other subsystems within the total social system announces a functional difference between the aesthetic realm and the sphere of social practice: literary texts are no longer to be used like pragmatic texts. The theory of aesthetic autonomy at once reflects and forces this altered situation.[32] On the one hand it gives conceptual expression to factually occurring processes and thus raises the consciousness of the general public about such processes, but on the other hand it sharpens the division it names insofar as the theory affects, by means of its normative power over the institution of literature, the production and reception of texts. The cleavage between art and social practice does indeed solve certain problems of the theory of art. For example, it disburdens the artwork from the interventions of state and church authorities. But this cleavage simultaneously obstructs the integration of art into the realm of social practice. As soon as the aesthetic sphere appears to be removed and thus no longer binding in the realms of politics and morality, it becomes impossible to assign to art any specific purpose beyond self-referentiality. Such functionlessness can of course be reconsidered as a function, but then—if one wants to continue to pursue the project of enlightenment—there arises the question as to how a relationship can be established between aesthetic freedom and political emancipation. The revolution of 1830 provided an occasion for the manifestation of this problematic, since the events in Paris awakened in Germany too the hope that political stagnation could be overcome.

Börne's and Heine's reactions serve as a precedent for the younger generation: the cleavage between art and life, literature and politics is to be overcome. Under the pressure of political events, literary discussion concentrates on articulating a refusal of the doctrine of the self-sufficiency of aesthetics, the doctrine of the autonomous artwork. Heine is by no means alone when in 1833 he advocates overcoming the difference between life and writing and demands from the writer that he be at once scholar, artist, and apostle.[33] Ludolf Wienbarg too takes this position. In his *Ästhetische Feldzüge* (Campaigns of aesthetic battle) he distinguishes between the posture of the contemporary writer—of whom Heine is exemplary—and that of the Classical and Romantic writers: "Recent writers have come down from these secure heights to constitute a part of their public; they hang out with the masses, lose their heads, rejoice, love, and rage about like anyone else."[34] The writer who is *au courant* at this time is bound to the "struggles of the times"; that is, he understands himself to be part of a politicized practical life. The young literati are conscious of standing on the threshold of an epoch in literature, of an epoch in which art will have new social meaning. Even if this evaluation proves to be only limitedly correct, because it exaggerates the significance of the change that is occurring, it still influences the self-conception of the younger generation immensely. In 1839, in the *Jahrbüch der Literatur* (Literary almanac), Gutzkow again summarizes this change: "At that time [i.e., 1830], literature took on, in nearly all its directions, the color of the spirit of the times. The harmless poetic activity that had earlier sat beneath elder branches, singing its songs only to compete with the lark, became silent or, in any case, was no longer to be heard."[35]

Scholars have rightly pointed out that the Young German writers narrow the gap between literature and criticism. It is not so much that criticism is supposed to be poeticized—this having been the case for Romantic theory—as rather that literature is to be pervaded by elements of criticism. For this reason Heine's prose becomes the model for the younger generation, for it consciously breaks through the traditionally poetic mode of representation, mixing philosophico-critical and aesthetic discourses in a provocative manner.[36] The field of criticism is thus broadened: it can no longer be satisfied with description and evaluation of artworks but must include in its considerations political and scientific literature. The cleavage between scientific and poetic text, which had surreptitiously gained plausibility in the trade of reviewing, is expressly eradicated, for it no longer corresponds to the Young German concept of literature.[37] This integration of criticism into literature gains expression in the Young German's posture of absolute distance from Romantic conceptions.

Romanticism is criticized for having remained at so great a distance from the general public. In his Heine essay of 1835, Wienbarg compares "Young" criticism with Romantic criticism: "Young criticism has new wreaths to bestow, and in this it distinguishes itself from the older criticism, whose wreaths are all bestowed and withered, pressed flat against the temples of the grandiose dead. But Young criticism celebrates no apotheoses and is considering indeed plundering the laurel trees devil-may-care and in all haste. It has an extremely simple manner of praise and blame: it calls things by their names."[38] The settling of accounts with Romantic criticism emphasizes, and not only in the case of Wienbarg, a particular moment: the alliance between the Romantics and the restoration. This alliance becomes the object of Heine's ruthless attack in the *Romantische Schule* (Romantic school). The Romantic authors have turned toward the past; they thus appear incapable of formulating a new aesthetic program. Romantic literary criticism is in Heine's judgment fruitful for the description and characterization of artworks but blind in its basic evaluations, because it lacks its own philosophical system.

Of course, this polemic does not constitute an adequate reception of the Romantic conception of literary criticism. It addresses itself only to certain aspects of the Romantic position and proceeds in general ad hominem. It is indeed quite possible to argue that the Young German literati remain much more deeply indebted to the Romantic conception of criticism than they are aware.[39] The Young Hegelians already see this quite clearly; for them Young Germany has been in many respects merely a modification of Romanticism. According to a formulation of Robert Prutz, "Young Germany was the most decided and outspoken opponent of previous Romanticisms, but in an essentially romantic form. It wanted to overcome the one-sidedness of our previous merely literary education; it wanted to close the gap between literature and life, to refresh and restore literature's exhausted body with the touch of politics, philosophy, and theology, but in order to do this it made use of exclusively literary means. It wanted, in a word, to lead literature out beyond itself, but fell prey, in the midst of this struggle, to the same clannishness in which Romanticism, too, had indulged. It wanted to be a political, social party, and only managed to become a literary coterie."[40] If the communicative structure of Romantic criticism can be described as a coterie, this is no less the case for Young Germany—or, for that matter, for the left Hegelians. The element of partisanship makes itself felt, however differently in each case, in the theory of criticism itself.

Romantic literary theory, then, not only constitutes the foil against which the Young Germans unfold their own theories; it constitutes the very material with which the Young Germans work out their conceptions. For this reason, Romantic theory is sketched here briefly.[41] I shall restrict myself to a schematic summary. Romantic theory takes as its double object both the specificity of the artwork and the manner of activity by means of which criticism acts on this artwork. It is precisely in this point that Romantic theory goes beyond Classical theory, which determined the artwork without simultaneously reflecting on the status of its own activity. The Romantic theoreticians do, however, share with the tradition of the eighteenth century the notion that it belongs to the essential tasks of criticism to make aesthetic judgments: that is, to distinguish between good and bad artworks. Criticism is for the Romantics the art of the judgment of the beautiful, and Friedrich Schlegel assumes that criticism has to do with an "absolute aesthetic evaluation."[42] We owe to Walter Benjamin the insight into the predominantly positive character of this evaluation, which is interested more in unfolding literary and aesthetic characteristics than in the discovery of mistakes and failings.[43] The critic does take his distance from bad works but only in that, ideally, he evaluates just those works that correspond to and fulfill the aesthetic demands of the critic. The silence of criticism thus contains at once the condemnation of a work. But one should not overlook the difference between the Romantic model and its Enlightenment predecessor. From the one model to the other, the function of critical judgment is displaced and the role of the critic is altered. In rationalistic criticism the judgment remains related to the public, and the critic sees himself as a judge of art who watches over literary norms and good taste. In Romantic theory—even if in practice this is not quite true—the position of the critic is otherwise invested. Neither communication with the public nor the role of judge in the public sphere is central but rather the artwork itself, the comprehension and interpretation of which become the focus of the critic's interest. This task determines at once the method and the role of the critic.

Once the poetic text has become the center of attraction—which was the case neither in the older Classicism nor in sensualist doctrines of taste—important methodological implications are introduced. The judgment of the text presupposes its characterization and this, in turn, a method of interpretation. In other words, the business of criticism is unthinkable without a hermeneutics. It is not by chance that the generalization of hermeneutics as a method of interpretation falls in this period.[44] In the Romantic period, interpretive comprehension becomes the basis of literary criticism. According to Friedrich Schlegel, one must "seize and interpret the great sense of creative works with pure, complete, and sharp determinacy, for this sense is often deeply hidden and in need of an interpreter."[45] If the value of the work in question is not already legitimated by tradition or another authority, the question presents itself as to how the act of comprehension and the act of judgment can be linked, since comprehension as such implies no critical evaluation—as Friedrich Schlegel argues in opposing Herder's historicist hermeneutics. Isn't an aesthetic theory always already presupposed, whether explicitly or not, when judgment is passed on the quality of an artwork? Such a theory was still available to Classicism. But after the historicization of both art and the standards of its judgment introduced by the "*querelle*," this path is no longer open to Romantic theory.[46] The possibility remains open, of course, that one could deduce judgments of value from historical evolution: that is, out of literary processes. Alternatively, one could ground the aesthetic norm in the work itself and in this way proceed to transhistorical judgments of value.

If for Romantic theory the artwork presents an image of the absolute, a manifestation in the most emphatic sense, it remains to be seen how the work could present itself as a structure that critical judgment could determine. Criticism must assume this structure to be present in the individual work and then proceed to demonstrate it. The structure must be found by the critic, although it is the basis that first makes the evaluation possible. In his review of *Wilhelm Meisters Lehrjahre* (Wilhelm Meister's apprenticeship) Schlegel comments upon the difference between conventional and productive criticism:

> The poet and artist, on the other hand, will want to present anew the presentation [*wird die Darstellung von neuem darstellen . . . wollen*], will want to form anew what already has form; he will supplement, rejuvenate, and newly construe the work. He will only divide the whole into limbs and masses and pieces, never dissect it into its original constituents. For the latter are dead with the relation to the work because they no longer contain unities of the same sort as the whole, even if—in relation to the cosmos—they could come alive and become limbs or masses of this cosmos.[47]

Here Schlegel is commenting on his own procedure. The characterization of the artwork which the critic assumes as his task is a productive thinking-out of the text, which always contains more than the intention of the author, more than meaning in the narrow sense. The act of criticism becomes a spiritual experiment in which the concrete work can and indeed must be destroyed in thought in order to reveal the borders of the individual and thus to effect an approximation to the thought of the absolute.

Friedrich Schlegel applies this hermeneutic procedure—differentiation between whole and part, and reconstruction of the whole out of its part and of the parts out of the whole—to the object of history as well. In his introduction to the writings of Gotthold Ephraim Lessing from the year 1803, he speaks of the "historical construction of the whole of art and poetic writing"[48] and characterizes this construction as one of the fundamental conditions of criticism: "However, this construction and knowledge of the whole has been set up by us as the single and most essential fundamental condition of a criticism that would really fulfill high destiny."[49] In this sentence, it is less remarkable that Schlegel comprehends literature historically than that he draws the relation he does between literary history and literary criticism. Romantic theory brings the two into a systematic relationship by grounding criticism in the history of literature. "Think of criticism," Schlegel writes in the introduction, "as a middle term between history and philosophy that binds both, in which both should be united into a new third term. Without philosophical spirit, it cannot flourish; everyone admits that; and just as little without historical knowledge. The philosophical purification and verification of history is incontrovertibly criticism; but such is also every historical view of philosophy."[50] As a third element hermeneutics is mentioned just a bit further on; it is considered to be the "genuine business and inner essence of criticism."[51] The site of romantic criticism is in other words the meeting point of history, hermeneutics, and philosophical aesthetics. These points of view supplement one another, but they limit one another as well: history undermines the idea of a systematic aesthetics; philosophical aesthetics, on the other hand, opposes a historical relativism; the hermeneutic method directs itself against philosophical final deductions; and historical understanding hinders the isolation of the artwork.

This constellation remains binding for the theory of criticism—and partially for its practice as well—until the middle of the century. It does not follow, however, that the solution proposed by the Romantics necessarily remains the basis for all later attempts. Rather, the Romantic model raises a series of questions and formulates a series of problems to which later theoreticians are compelled to address themselves. To these questions belong those of the relations between criticism and history (in the double meaning of literary history and general history), comprehension and judgment, and the aesthetic realm and practical life. The opposition of the younger generation against the Romantics flares up above all around the Romantic determination of practice, which the younger generation finds indeed to be less a determination than an utter absence of practice. The hermeneutic grounding of Romantic theory—that is, the conception of criticism as a dialogue between text and reader—appears to them a questionable privatization; in contrast, they are interested in regaining the public character of critical practice. As they promise themselves a greater effect of literature on the social and political realm, so they expect literary criticism to mediate between literature and life.

The Young Germans never form a single school, as has been with reason recently underlined,[52] but they are united in their common difference from common enemies. Accordingly, their literary-critical works are never fully consonant with one another; indeed, they tend rather to be mutually critical. Nonetheless, one can develop something like a model out of the corpus of discussions and statements of position. One can then compare this model on the one hand with Romantic and on the other hand with Young Hegelian criticism. In contrast to Romantic theory, the criticism of Young Germany is not work-oriented. However much authors such as Gutzkow or Mundt cling in their journalism to the current conventions of the literary trade and make single works the occasions of their reviews, they still do not as a rule place the literary text, its organization and significance, in the center of their interests. The emphasis displaces itself from interpretation to critical judgment. The work and its author get situated in a broad literary and social context out of which the judgment of value is then deduced. Problems of interpretation are placed in the background; in theoretical utterances they are seldom thematized. In this, Gutzkow is not different from Menzel, and Heine is not different from Wienbarg. Instead, the questions that become central concern the relation of art to practice: i.e., the status of art with respect to society (the question of autonomy) and the intention of the author (communication with the public). From this shifted emphasis arises the relative neglect of any formal-aesthetic standpoint, which is not to be read as a lack of sensibility but rather as evidence of a principled determination of the critic's task.

The swerve from the concept of aesthetic autonomy, the skeptical pose with respect to Classical-Romantic aesthetics, problematizes in particular the formalism of its central concepts. For these new critics, the structure of literary texts can no longer be described in traditional ways, even if new descriptive models do not immediately offer themselves. The extraordinary attention that the post-Romantic critics pay to literary criticism as a genre reveals, however, that they reflect upon the altered situation. After 1830 critics demand that the new literature become essentially a critical literature. They thus modify the Romantic notion that the development of literature could and should be furthered by criticism, that a new literature could and should be unfolded under the influences of criticism. As Heinrich Laube writes in the *Zeitung für die elegante Welt* (Newspaper for the elegant world): "We live in a critical epoch; everything is in question; the great examination of the world has finally begun."[53] With this, more is meant than that literary criticism should dominate poetry and fiction. The Saint-Simonian concept of a *critical* epoch defines itself in opposition to *organic* epochs that dispose over a closed conception of the world. Critical epochs are periods in which principles—and thus also aesthetic and poetological norms—are placed in question.

When critics between 1830 and 1835 attempt to characterize literary criticism, they begin by situating it in a broad historical context. They then attempt to demonstrate the function of a given kind of criticism in terms of the character of the epoch in which it is situated and in terms of the function of literature in general within this epoch. The problem is to define the tasks of criticism in a period of upheaval in which received categories have lost their meaning. Gutzkow circumscribes this situation concisely when he writes, "Our literature is in a period of transition."[54] He approvingly alludes to Heine's judgment that classical literature has reached its end, that already in the 1820s the glowing reputation of Weimar Classicism had been established at the cost of a lively, more recent literature, which has been incapable of unfolding its potential because of the conditions prevailing under the political restoration. Hence, it falls to criticism to introduce the new literary epoch: "It is well known that our literary revolution has been introduced by criticism. Everything that had spirit in the periods which have been carried to their graves fled into criticism."[55] The concept of criticism is thus essentially negative and polemical.

However, the evaluation of the situation both in general and for criticism has changed already by 1835. Not only Gutzkow but also Mundt announce the end of the critical epoch. Critical literature is to be replaced by a positive and productive literature. One should certainly not overestimate these short-term evaluations, but they do provide some indication of the critics' self-conceptions. Literary criticism historicizes itself to such a degree that it does not merely situate and interpret its objects historically but simultaneously relates its own function to the historical situation in which its practice is involved. "The history of German criticism," Gutzkow declares in 1831, "is nothing other than the history of the literature contemporary with it."[56] When Gutzkow revokes in 1835 his most extreme demands and relegates criticism anew to a subordinate status, he revokes a part of that program which he had formulated in 1831 together with Menzel, Börne, and Heine. In 1835 the definition reads: "Good criticism is the average opinion of the thinking people in a nation; it should not be above or below that level."[57] This sentence evokes once more the ideal of an enlightened public sphere in which the critic is neither more nor less than the mouthpiece of the public. However, Gutzkow admits that this state of affairs is attainable for German literature only under certain conditions. In Germany, as Gutzkow argues in 1835, not liberalization but the achievement of the status of science is the order of the day for criticism: "The critical school has approached to an extraordinary degree learned scholarship; it is nearly at the point of establishing an alliance with the pulpit and the universities."[58] In the face of the simultaneously developing academic literary history and Hegelian philosophico-historical (*geschichtsphilosophischen*) criticism, the prognosis is remarkably accurate.

The historicization of literary criticism which, as we have seen, gets Menzel and Georg Gottfried Gervinus involved in literary history, is not to be understood as a preference for the past but as the attempt to situate the present by setting it off against the past. The status of the present is accentuated here by reflection on its place within transformations at the levels both of literary forms and genres—which the critic has to consider in his evaluative judgments—and of literary criticism itself within the historical process. The categories of transformation, alteration, and movement serve to accentuate the dynamic character of literary experience in its historical presence. By proposing a context, the critics establish the course, goal, and relation to life of their work. Wienbarg, for example, traces the course of German literature in his *Ästhetische Feldzüge* in order to determine the contemporary situation. And Heine's struggle with the Romantic school proves by closer inspection to be a sketch of German literary history proposed as an alternative to Friedrich Schlegel's version.[59] The construction of historical spaces and sequences is indispensable to Young Germany, for only through the historical perspective can the single work and the individual author be strictly susceptible of judgment. The context, then, determines the work's status and its significance for literature as a whole. This moment of contextualization, doubtless already anticipated in Romanticism, will become ever stronger in the criticism of the 1840s under the influence of Hegel. For Arnold Ruge and Robert Prutz, literary-critical judgment is part of a historico-philosophical construction.

At this point we should distinguish more clearly between Young German and left Hegelian conceptions of criticism.[60] In spite of their temporal proximity to Hegel, it would be questionable to attribute a worked-out theory of history to the Young German writers. Heine comes closest to this goal in his *Romantische Schule* and *Über Religion und Philosophie in Deutschland* (Religion and philosophy in Germany), in which he provides a construction of the course of history. Aside from this, mostly mere slogans excite discussion in the journals and newspapers. The critics emphasize the meaning of the present and accentuate the meaning of the individual with respect to the laws of the total course of history.[61]

For Young Germany, the concept of the present is bound up with the concept of life. The emphatic evocation of life—for example, in Wienbarg's *Ästhetische Feldzüge* or in Gustav Kühne's work—provides the standpoint from which literary practice is to be judged. In other words, it is expected from literature that it open itself up to life. Of course, life is conceptualized in this period in a manner quite different from that of the late nineteenth-century philosophy of life. Life appears as the basis for a progressive process in whose course conservative political and social forces are overcome. In this process, authors and works find their places; in this context, the literary achievements of the past, on the one hand, receive their evaluation, and the tasks of the present and future, on the other hand, receive their determination.

The implication is that literary judgments are never final; they always represent an opinion that results from one angle on history. The possibility—indeed, the necessity—of revision is the result of the descriptive historicization of criticism, which, however, does not (as was the case with the Romantics) want finally to transcend history into the poetic realm but rather, conversely, wants to subordinate aesthetics to history. One could show this well by using as examples the judgments of Heine and Börne. The younger writers such as Wienbarg, Gutzkow, and Mundt are aware how much they are indebted to and stand under the influence of these authors; in their early work they emphasize the innovative character of their predecessors. After 1835 the characterization changes: Heine's and Börne's negativity, which in 1830 was highly valued as opposition to Classicism and Romanticism, appears to have been outmoded by an altered historical situation in which a positive attitude is necessary to productivity. Not much later, Heine is considered passé even by such a critic as Karl Gutzkow, who had still defended him in 1835.

In the thought of Young Germany, history and life practice are inseparable. Literary theory and literary criticism both belong in this context. It follows that one must not isolate the aesthetic theorems of Young Germany (in this respect they are hardly original) but judge them as part of a larger politico-historical theory. For the Young Germans, the field to which literature must be applied is politics in the wider sense that early liberal theory gave to this concept: namely, as the explicit formulation of ideas and programs through which the relation between state and citizen can be changed. For this reason, literary criticism is a political matter; the critic fights for progress and a new practice of life. In contrast to Romantic theory, the Young German concept of criticism is related to the addressee: that is, to the public. Public opinion itself—which one hopes to influence by means of newspapers and journals—should lead the attack on the conservative powers. Thus, Gustav Schlesier writes on the task and function of criticism: "Criticism . . . has an indescribable effect on German literature, as does literature on culture, as does culture on our history. The critic of literature is helping to get the history of his people on its feet."[62] Characteristically, Schlesier calls art and literature the only means for accelerating the emancipation of the German people.

Unmistakably, the Young German theory of criticism adopts basic notions from the eighteenth century, even if it does not formulate them as systematically as it might. The practice of criticism presents itself as a dialogue between the critic and the public, a dialogue that convenes in the reasoning of the public sphere itself. As ambivalent as the Young Germans are about the real public of their time, they nonetheless hold fast to the Classical model of the public sphere—with, of course, one significant modification: the hope for an alteration in living social relations attaches itself to faith in the poetic writer's positive influence. For example, Schlesier adopts without reservation the Romantic concept of genius and integrates it into his theory of criticism: "Why doesn't criticism purify the temple and open it for young gods, given that the old ones have outlived their time or do not want to create and that our languishing spirits are reviving? These are the gods over whom the weapons of criticism have given us power."[63] If in the eighteenth century the purpose of criticism is to promote the self-awareness and mutual understanding of its readers, Schlesier assumes that the purpose of criticism is above all to regulate literary production. This implies that the best poets have the greatest influence on the public. For this reason, Menzel is considered to have made a great contribution. He appears as a regulating force that has brought order to the diffuse literary life of the 1820s, as an author who has had the courage to distinguish between the helpful and the harmful. The authority of a critic already plays here a greater role than the reasoning of the public. The question of practice is seen from the perspective of the writer and his work: how does the work affect the public, and how can the program be translated into deeds? Wienbarg defines the work of writers as a service to the Fatherland: "The truth, reality, has imposed itself upon them with overwhelming force, and their force must wrestle with this reality—for this is the task of their destiny—until the real is no longer the mean, until the real is no longer opposed as an enemy to the ideal."[64] In the face of this emphatically stylized view of the writer, the recipients have to accept an essentially passive role: they are to be the earth in which the seed should one day ripen.

The literary criticism of the Young Germans ambivalently adopts an idealist concept of practice which ascribes to theory a power it may well not have. The question of what work is good and what work faulty depends for them on its function. In most cases, however, aesthetic and political functions are held apart. The objections to Goethe's work, as formulated by Börne, Menzel, and Wienbarg, concentrate on the conservative political effect ascribed to Goethe's *oeuvre*. Both Wienbarg and Gutzkow cut off from this the aesthetic function in Goethe's works, which they see as progressive. In contrast to Heine, who chastises Classicist aesthetics for its political indifference, Wienbarg defends Goethe's works for their literary and aesthetic innovations, which Wienbarg assumes must have a progressive moral and political effect: "Goethe carried as a youth the entire new age, the coming view of the world [*Weltanschauung*] in his breast, and what moved him in his depths, that with which he surprised the world and his contemporaries, will sooner or later move the world and recreate Germany politically and morally."[65] Gutzkow said much the same thing in 1836. He posed the rhetorical question, "Ought one to tear the poetic laurels away from Goethe and pass him off for a subordinate layman of Parnass because his patriotism lacked the excitement of a young man and because he did not approve of the haste in recent attempts?"[66]

Yet the defense of Goethe against ungenerous fanatics such as Menzel prevents neither Wienbarg nor Gutzkow from prescribing new literary tasks for their own time. Thus, in his 1837 evaluation of Theodor Mundt, Gutzkow refuses the lyric all significance and stresses instead the importance of prose: "I know that before the tribunal of aesthetics the lyric is at present the only thing in Germany that possesses a gleaming, Classical garnish; still, the lyric seems to me an interim solution, unfruitful, futureless."[67] From the present function of prose Gutzkow deduces its literary possibilities, which he sees fulfilled in Heine but not in Mundt. Gutzkow reprimands Mundt's style for being abstract and sluggish. Heinrich Laube proceeds similarly in the evaluation of Karl Immermann.[68] Laube is not interested exclusively, or even primarily, in the individual character of Immermann's single works but rather in their status within a particular historical constellation. He asks, what can the genre of drama achieve under present conditions?

Granted, categories that would be appropriate to the new aesthetic program only partially exist. Neither Wienbarg and Gutzkow nor Laube and Mundt ever propose a systematic aesthetics. They never get beyond the beginnings we can find in Heinrich Heine's work. Indeed, as a whole, the younger generation remains behind its predecessor. And even in Heine's work of the 1840s one can detect a return to central concepts of the aesthetics of autonomous art.[69] The literary criticism of the Young Germans remains for the most part dependent on Classical-Romantic aesthetics, even if they no longer share—or, rather, polemically attack—its presuppositions. This contradiction can be traced most clearly in Wienbarg's *Ästhetische Feldzüge*, in which on the one hand an antitraditional literary program is sketched out that underscores the political function of art, while on the other hand the core concepts of the "age of art" continue to be invoked. Wienbarg is capable of borrowing at once from Friedrich Schelling and from Heine.[70]

These contradictions also become apparent in the practice of the Young Germans, especially where, in order to evaluate a particular work, they retrieve criteria they have rejected programmatically in other places. The impression that the Young Germans criticize convictions more than anything else has to do with this contradiction. Wherever the functional, contextual method allows itself to get involved with a particular work, it lacks the concepts with which to grasp its changed aesthetic problems. When Theodor Mundt discusses Goethe's *Wilhelm Meisters Wanderjahre* (Wilhelm Meister's journeymanship), he points out in his introductory remarks that Goethe's writings belong to a bygone era and thus cannot necessarily satisfy the interests of a new era. But at the same time he considers the novel in terms of the concept of the organic artwork and, following Goethe, labels the *Wanderjahre* a fragment. However, since he defines the genre of the novel as an art form, he takes the *Wanderjahre* to be a failure, for it "attributed to the muse, instead of lively poetry, long treatises of the reflexive understanding."[71]

The relationship between aesthetics and literary criticism remains problematic also for the radical students of Hegel who assemble around the *Hallische Jahrbücher* (Halle almanac) and *Deutsche Jahrbücher* (German almanac). In a certain sense the contradiction indeed intensifies, for on the one hand the left Hegelians radicalize the political function of literature, and on the other hand the leading theoreticians of their group return to a Classicist position in aesthetics which refers to both Goethe and Schiller as authorities. Of course, these tensions hardly become visible to the literati involved, because the left Hegelian discussion orients itself less in terms of Hegel's aesthetics than in terms of his philosophy of history. The thesis of the end of the age of art, which was electrifying the literati around 1830, has by 1840 lost much of its initial power of persuasion. The category of the critical age has been revoked already in 1835 by the writers of Young Germany (Mundt, Gutzkow). Where the *Hallische Jahrbücher* develops a principled literary position—namely, in the essay "Der Protestantismus und die Romantik" (Protestantism and Romanticism; 1839)—they attack Romanticism exclusively, characterizing Weimar Classicism and Jean Paul as belonging to the progressive tradition of the Enlightenment.[72] By establishing a rigid opposition between Classicism and Romanticism, Ruge and Ernst Theodor Echtermeyer can attack the literary theory of Romanticism and simultaneously affirm the Classical conception of art. The criticism of Romantic ideology and its political consequences allows them to spare Classicist aesthetics, which shifts into a positive position as a result of its having been set up in opposition to Romantic aesthetics.

The criticism of Romantic subjectivity and arbitrariness can in some respects appeal to the authority of the Young Germans' polemics, but it is substantially indebted above all to Hegel. Here, however, it is a question not of indebtedness but of the systematic status of this critique. Ruge and Echtermeyer conceive the doctrine of Romanticism as the unfolding of Schelling's philosophy: "In the development of Schelling toward his unfree consequences we have seen the principle of Romanticism originate. This principle was, in a word . . . *the Schellingian arbitrary subject* and the historical course of Romanticism is the spreading of this arbitrariness over the entire world."[73] Schelling is accused, then, of straying from the path of the Enlightenment. Insofar as art is given a special place in his philosophy—namely, as the form in which the Eternal reveals itself—his philosophy takes on great importance for the Romantics. "Schelling's philosophy is nothing other than *fantasizing geniality*. This is why he places art (at least through the period of his transcendental idealism) above philosophy."[74] As Ruge argues in his sketch of the most recent German literature, the aestheticization of philosophy in Schelling leads to a reactionary notion of history in which the past determines the direction of the historical process. "History (and this is the sign of the *Romanticism* that attaches itself to this notion) becomes thus utterly a matter of Reaction."[75] Romantic aesthetics is suspected of declaring "war of the spirit of arbitrariness on the free, lawful spirit of our times."[76]

The remarkable thing about this polemic is that it barely even begins to deal with Romantic art criticism itself but concentrates on the relation of Romanticism to history. Even Friedrich Schlegel's theory of irony is here regarded above all as an ideological form of relation to the world and not as a poetological method. The manifesto of the *Hallische Jahrbücher* attempts to represent the interests of a post-Romantic situation without explicating in detail the aesthetic and literary-critical implications of this change. When Ruge and Echtermeyer borrow from the Enlightenment and Classicism, they seem to imply that it could be feasible to adopt a Classicist aesthetics and theory of literature. Schiller's aesthetic theory, especially his *Briefe über die ästhetische Erziehung des Menschen* (Letters on the aesthetic education of man), points the way because it presents an image of the fulfillment of the Enlightenment. Since Schiller's aesthetic theory is bound to a philosophicohistorical construction according to which man is on the way to his perfection as a species-being, this theory is not only imaginable but in large part to be recommended. "Thus Schiller proves to us first the realizability of the infinite within the finite and the possibility of the most sublime humanity. Whoever has followed the development of the great questions of the free, the divine, and the immortal in recent times will discover with a delighted shock in the words we have quoted from Schiller the seed of more than one epochmaking work of spirit in our times and will bring to Schiller, even in the name of the coming world, the philosophical crown."[77] Ruge advocates Classicism here while he represses both the notion that the age of art has reached its end and Hegel's critique of the claim of art to epistemological authority in the period of modernity. Like Gervinus, the authors of the manifesto propose a compound of the subjective idealism of Schiller and the more individualistic theory of self-development in Goethe. This compound does not yet have the character of a synthesis, however; the historical dialectic demands rather an intensification of the oppositions that gain expression in Jean Paul and the Romantics. The synthesis will be reached only when objective freedom has been grounded. "But this cannot manifest itself until the German state has become free and publicly accessible, until the reformative process has taken us out of the subjectivity of sensibility and the inwardness of theoretical one-sidedness, so that the spirit perceives, in the objective world, the realization of the freedom it has hitherto gained in the form of knowledge and binds itself to this objective freedom in will and deed."[78]

In his later literary history Ruge makes certain revisions in precisely this passage, emphasizing, beside the synthesis of freedom, the exemplary status of Classicism. The synthesis has indeed not yet taken place in German history, he says, but in Greek culture it has already been attained. "Beautiful humanity is Classicism. But the Classical spirit is still a private matter. If humanity becomes the universal ideal, then art becomes the people's form of religion, and poetry becomes immediately a public force and a real satisfaction in which it is impossible to stagnate in beautiful egoism or in the yearning for the freedom of the people."[79] Ruge projects the Classical humanism of Weimar into the future—there, it will attain the popularity (*Volkstümlichkeit*) that it failed to attain in the eighteenth century.

The *Hallische Jahrbücher*, as well as Ruge's later works, treats the historicity of literature not as a theoretical but as a strategic problem that can be formulated as follows: an aesthetic theory is sought which is reconcilable with the political goal of humanist emancipation. Classical aesthetics is useful in the sense that it emphasizes the formative (*bildende*) function of the artwork. In contrast, Ruge does not in these works address the systematic and historical problems of the theory of art bequeathed by Hegel. In his critical essays Ruge deals with his self-contradictory theory by suspending Classical aesthetics when discussing contemporary works. For example, in the discussion of Georg Herwegh's poems, he divides the political message from the form: "In a word, political freedom, total and without compromise, is the religion and poetry of our times."[80] While he agrees with Herwegh's political views, he criticizes Herwegh's language: "The otherwise beautiful language suffers from many faults. . . . One must warn against the stabilization of such faults as conventions in an age where it is necessary to save from barbaric reaction not only the achievements of bourgeois freedom, not only the free thoughts of our great forebears, but also their perfect forms."[81] Ruge, then, would have considered Herwegh's poems to be perfect had they clothed their progressive content in Classical forms.

When, on the other hand, critics attempt to clarify the problems of aesthetic theory in more strictly Hegelian terms, the question of the historicity of art gets suppressed by systematic problems. Exemplary is Friedrich Theodor Vischer's essay *Zur wissenschaftlichen Ästhetik* (On scientific aesthetics),[82] which provides a plan for a new organization of aesthetic theory. For Vischer, the evaluation of literature is above all an immanent problem that can be solved within the framework of a systematic organization. The application of the subject-object dialectic leads him to posit literature as telos because, being the subjective-objective form of art, it is the synthesis of the plastic arts with music. According to the same scheme, drama is granted the crowning position above both epic and lyric. The evaluation of the individual artwork is hence a question on the one hand of the deduction of aesthetic forms out of the concept of the beautiful in art, and on the other hand of the application of concepts of genres to the individual work. It is not by chance that the postrevolutionary Classicism that understood itself as realism hooked into the works of Vischer. The schematization of aesthetics corresponded to the need for rigid concepts that could be applied in literary criticism.

In his evaluation of Herwegh's work, Vischer comes to conclusions

that differ from those of Ruge on the basis of theoretical considerations. Where Ruge praises the political content of Herwegh's work
because this content harmonizes with the progressive demands of the
times, Vischer concerns himself in his 1843 discussion with the formal
possibilities of the political lyric as a genre. Since for Vischer there is a
discontinuity between politics as abstract system and poetry, he cannot simply presuppose the legitimacy of political lyric: "Politics is, in
our context, the dissatisfaction with present life in the state, the desire
for an improved future of this life, enthusiasm for great deeds to which
this dissatisfaction and desire should lead, etc. As such, politics remains a content which is . . . always . . . utterly inimical to genuinely
poetic treatment in the form of the lyric."[83] Therefore, Vischer assumes that the writer of political lyric poetry must necessarily become
a rhetorician, for rhetoric is the only means appropriate to the lyrical
expression of a not yet realized goal. Vischer's judgment of Herwegh's
poems results from the application of these general considerations:
they must necessarily remain within the prosaic realm and cannot
attain to poetic content—not merely because Herwegh lacks sufficient
talent but because the political context (the dismembered character of
modernity) does not suit itself to poetic expression.

In the Hegelian philosophy of the 1840s, two models of criticism can
be distinguished: on the one hand an intensification of historicization
which, however, can still cling to Classicist aesthetic norms; on the
other hand an attempt to deduce literary criticism from a systematic
aesthetic theory. In the latter case the social and political world becomes an externality which, in the absence of any tie to literature,
remains to be brought into relation to it. For this reason, it always
remains possible to weaken or dissolve the contact between literature
and society and thus to revoke the notion of the historicity of both
literature and criticism. The Classicism of the 1850s and 1860s adopts
this course quite consistently. It establishes the theory of art as a
systematic architecture out of which literary judgments are to be strin-
gently deduced. In the 1840s, on the other hand, there remains an
extremely strong need for historical construction, for a procedure that
allows the critic to conceptualize the accelerated alterations in the
social as in the literary sphere. Heine's *Romantische Schule* already
contains the project for a literary criticism that proceeds constructively
and not by (hermeneutic) understanding. Ruge and Echtermeyer

choose the same method for their polemic against Romanticism. At the same time, Gervinus offers fundamental methodological consider- ations about how the history of literature could be reconstructed. Of course, it would be wrong to assert simply that literary criticism and literary history approach one another. Rather, it could be argued that literary history (historiography) differentiates itself from literary crit- icism until in the 1850s it has become, even institutionally, self-suffi- cient. It is above all Robert Prutz who before 1848 reconstructs histor- ical sequences with the intent to show how the literary and political tasks of the present have developed out of these sequences.

The philosophical parallel of this project is the historicization of absolute spirit by the Hegelian left. The gradual disappearance of transcendence from Hegel's philosophy, against which the Hegelian right strives, leads to the assumption that the site on which the abso- lute appears is human consciousness. Thus, one finds in the *Deutsche Jahrbücher* of 1841: "The idea is the truth of this world, the immanent god who reveals himself as self-consciousness."[84] If art, religion, and science are grounded as forms of absolute spirit in the history of human consciousness, significant consequences result for the evalua- tion of literature. History places the destruction of theological fictions in the hands of human beings; the reconstruction of this history is part of their self-realization. If the concept of spirit is immanently inter- preted, there arises—as one can read above all in the works of Prutz— an overarching context that allows the critic to conceive of and to construct literature as an aspect of the history of spirit. The process of literary production and reception is at once the signature of reason as it comes to itself.

Robert Prutz's survey of early literary history in Germany, written in the 1850s, is simultaneously a survey of the history of literary criticism; for the Hegelian left, both undertakings are aspects of the same thing. In their thought, criticism becomes literary history and history a form of criticism. As Prutz describes the goal of this project: "It is a matter of shaking the nation out of the one-sidedly literary education and the abstract aesthetic interests in which it has moved till now, and of inducing it to enter practical, public life; it is a matter of stripping literature of the exclusive dominion it has held over us till now and of bringing theory and practice, literature and life, poetry and reality, art and the state into their proper and natural interrelation."[85] Prutz implies that this goal can be reached only if historians (and critics, too) change their attitudes toward literature. He advocates a radical historicization of criticism that must occur on two levels. On the objective level the critic must track down historical laws, even in the field of literary evolution; on the subjective level, however, one must grasp the place of the critic in the historical process in order to be able to proceed from theoretical knowledge to political practice.

The circle around the *Hallische Jahrbücher* distinguishes itself from Young Germany less in its determination of social practice than in its conception of the role and status of theory. The Young Hegelians constantly accuse Young Germany of being subjective—that is, arbitrary—and state that the correct goal is to conceive with methodical rigor the laws of history and thus of literary history. This scientific claim of literary criticism stands, of course, in the service of social practice. In this sense, Prutz notes, the goal is "to have a practical effect on our people and to prepare through literary creations the great creation of a free, truly happy age."[86] Thus, the Young Hegelian model is not less dependent on and related to its public than the Young German model, for only through recipients can thought finally become deed.

The reattainment of the public sphere was of central importance for Börne and Young Germany. The demand of the *Hallische Jahrbücher*— that criticism should be rendered scientific—carries on this tradition but alters the procedure. While Wienbarg and Gutzkow speak of the "democratization" of literature and thus also of general critical discussion, the left Hegelians emancipate their critical communication from such considerations. They turn toward the intelligentsia and presuppose for the most part that the reader is informed about current philosophical discussion. The general public is supposed to feel itself to be represented but has no right to be addressed in terms it would understand. Although Prutz bemoans the gap between canonized Classical-Romantic literature and the subliterature (*Trivialliteratur*) of his time and proposes that a popular literature (*volkstümliche Dichtung*) be produced to bridge this gap, he nonetheless fails to see that literary history (and criticism) suffer from an analogous rupture. The *Literarisches Taschenbuch* (The literary pocket-book) edited by Prutz provides indeed little evidence of any desire to keep its readers entertained. The discourse of this journal rests on theory, especially on the

philosophy of Hegel and his school. To this degree, the literary criticism of the Hegelian left separates itself from the literary public
sphere, although these critics propose the politicization of literature
and thus the passage from the literary to the political sphere with
stronger emphasis than even the radicals of the thirties.

Naturally, the reconstruction of a critical model ought not to be
confused with the empirical reality of literary criticism. The majority of
the discussions published between 1840 and 1850 certainly do not
conform to the demands of the Young Hegelians. The expansive business of reviewing, carried on by hundreds of journals, barely concerns
itself with these demands. The effectuality of the model is restricted to
a limited group of journals and literati, even if these are the ones who
assume the role of leaders within the institution of literary criticism
and determine the direction discourse takes. They lose this dominant
position after the revolution of 1848, which appears at first as the
fulfillment of their hopes and then—with the victory of the conservative forces—buries their faith in the political effectuality of literature.
The political defeat of the liberal and democratic forces places the left
Hegelian concept of theory in question. In the face of altered political
relations, the deduction of revolutionary practice from literature
seems inappropriate. Just as, during the 1850s and 1860s, political
liberalism enters the phase of its self-critique in order to come to some
sort of arrangement with the new situation, so the pre-1848 concepts
of literary criticism and literary history are submitted at this time to a
far-reaching critique. The same Prutz who in the 1840s conceived of
high literature (die schöne Literatur) as the propaedeutic to political
discussion warns in the 1850s against exaggerated hopes:

> The one-sided interest which we dedicated in the pre-1848 period
> to literary conditions and personalities was in the final analysis a
> pitiful supplement for lacking political interest. Actors and writ-
> ers shared in our culture of those days the privilege—scarcely
> enviable according to the concepts of that time—of being public
> personages and of being as such subject to public judgment,
> whether in praise or chastisement; we could not get to those to
> whom we would have preferred to dedicate the bath—the minis-
> ters and statesman—and thus we shed all our wrath and all our
> thirst for public presence on the poor actors and literati.[87]

The ironic self-criticism touches the decisive point of the left Hegelian model: the inflated significance of literary criticism arises from the necessity-turned-virtue that literature stand in for politics—in other words, that the political system be criticized and changed by means of the cultural system. The various groups after 1850 all agree that the intimate relation between literature and politics must be dissolved. The liberals want to dissolve it because the concept of practice in the pre-1848 period has not proved valid; the conservatives want to dissolve it because they hold this concept of practice to be politically dangerous and are even tempted to reintroduce the censor. The common characteristic of this criticism is the wish for a sober judgment of literature and its effects. Thus Prutz asserts in 1858 that practical interests should have precedence and that everything opposing the successful ordering of political and social conditions must be pushed aside.[88]

Recent studies of realism have repeatedly criticized the description of the year 1848 as a decisive break in the history of German literature; they argue that the literary theory of programmatic realism, however radically it may refuse Romanticism and Young Germany, still attaches itself to the aesthetic theory of the pre-1848 period—for example, to the work of Berthold Auerbach and Vischer.[89] Can one make a similar argument about literary criticism? The answer will depend on the level at which the question is posed. Any analysis of the literary programs concerned will doubtless emphasize the differences. The realists' program, formulated above all by the writers collected around the journal *Die Grenzboten*, polemically distinguishes itself from the pre-1848 period, as Friedrich Sengle has rightly underscored.[90] This new concept of literature determines also both the interpretive and the evaluative work of the *Grenzboten* critics. Their considerations of Weimar Classicism and Romanticism as well as the polemic against Heine and Börne are based on programmatically formulated principles. On this level the revolution first appears as an element of discontinuity. The realists' struggles against their predecessors leave certain realms unaltered, of course, or at least changes occur in these realms more gradually than in those explicitly thematized. In the sphere of literary theory one could show that a continuous transformation takes place. The return to Classicism—especially the search for binding aesthetic norms—can already be seen in the 1840s, not only in Vischer's work but also in that of the more radical Arnold Ruge.

But at the level of the institution, we can see no essential changes. While the rhetoric of literary criticism changes, the bases of the discourse remain the same as before 1848. The restriction of the literary public sphere—specifically, its depoliticization—does not change the fact that literary criticism is recognized as an important institution within the cultural system, whose task is to articulate public opinion. It is not by chance that one refers anew to Lessing in this period in order to explain and justify one's own practices. The beginning of a feuilleton criticism that emphasizes the subjectivity of the critic, as we see it in the work of Heine and Young Germany, does not reassert itself; in the 1840s it is already being suppressed. These tendencies do not play an important role until after the foundation of the Second Empire in connection with the transformation of the daily press. Liberal discourse, whether it leans more toward the democratic or more toward the conservative side, holds fast to the ideal of *raisonnement;* it privileges a rationally argumentative manner of dealing with literature. The appropriateness of logic with respect to literary texts remains uncontested. This is the ground shared by critics as diverse as Lessing, Börne, Ruge, and Julian Schmidt. Despite their differences, they all advocate the same model: the critic appears as a reasonable mediator between text and public, the mouthpiece of aesthetic norms and poetic rules, and the judge of their application; in each case he merely formulates what the public would have to say were it in a position to speak. Beyond this consensus there is only one position which in the final analysis does not allow of unification with the liberal discursive model: the Romantic theory of literature. The Romantic turn toward the text, which defines the literary-critical act as a process of productive understanding, explodes the liberal model. Since this foundation of criticism in hermeneutics is already condemned in the 1830s—not least by Heinrich Heine—as conservative, the possibilities of the alternative discourse are not tried out. The conservative turn in later Romanticism (religious conversion and support of the political restoration) suffices, for the liberal and democratic forces, to render the critical method of the Romantics questionable. Thus, the subversive moments of Romantic theory are blocked off until the 1860s, and then, with the salvation of Romanticism by the early Wilhelm Dilthey, the hermeneutic procedure has indeed been placed in the service of an affirmative position.[91]

In the history of aesthetic theory the decades between the revolution of 1848 and the foundation of the Second Empire would be treated only cursorily, since theoretical innovation in this period is relatively rare. The critics concentrate their energy on developing out of generally accepted aesthetic premises (on the nature of the artwork and the difference between art and reality) a new conception—that of realism. The often bitter literary feuds center on the legitimation and effectuation of this program. However various the positions of the individual critics may be, they all share the commitment to securing their judgments of works and authors by basing them on universal principles. The critical judgment should not exhaust itself in descriptive characterization but, rather, establish a relation between the text and literary norms. Whether the critic begins with the description of the work and proceeds from there to more general considerations or begins with universal aesthetic norms and relates them then to individual works, the judgment is understood to be a verdict on the quality of the text, a verdict intended to warn or encourage the public. The more strictly aesthetic norms are established (Classicism), the more strongly the critic is understood anew as a judge of art. Julian Schmidt, Rudolf Gottschall, and Robert Prutz see themselves as being in the service of the reading public, which, because it remains silent, they have to represent before the poets.

These critics speak in the name of Enlightenment in order to legitimate their work. But this recourse tends to overlook the fact that for the Enlightenment, *raisonnement* is never closed off; hence, a judgment on art can be revised whenever public opinion changes. The critical work of the realists also generally adheres to the legitimating function of the public, although there is no longer an intimate relation between critics and readers. The appeal to the public has become, in industrial society, an abstract gesture by means of which the critic enhances his authority vis-à-vis the writer. But wherever the fictions of liberal discourse are exposed, new forms of literary criticism arise that find their point of departure in the critic's subjective experience, avoid the universalities of rational discourse, and attempt to reestablish the dialogue with the reader. Before 1870 this is much more the exception than the rule. The leading critics hold to the model of argumentative critique. In the practice of the literary trade during the 1850s and 1860s, however, new tendencies do emerge: reviews that either withhold judgment (by pure description, extensive retelling of content) or seek new forms of legitimation.

Liberalism and Reaction (1815–35)

The construction of critical models is indispensable for the conceptualization of structure, but with respect to concrete historical developments such models have mainly heuristic value: they describe the dominant structures within a given epoch. In the face of the unsurveyable excess of material that renders impossible the consideration of all texts in a corpus, the establishment of a model guides us in the organization of our object. Only against the background of such constructs can one reconstruct singular deviations and changes or describe the historical individuality of particulars. So far, we have been treating the literary criticism of Young Germany as such a model, and in this interest we have stressed the configuration of elements rather than individual authors and their texts. The next step will consist in tracing in with greater distinctness—if still all too sketchily—the historical contours.

Recent scholarship has rightly warned against regarding the year 1848 as some sort of magical border in literary history. One could say about the same for the year 1830. However much the July Revolution is recognized as a significant political event that is bound to have ramifications for journalism and literature, it still does not mean an essential division between epochs in the realm of literary criticism. In this respect the July Revolution is certainly less important than the revolution of 1848. It does, of course, enhance certain already present tendencies, on both the liberal and the conservative side. The events in Paris work as a catalyst: they induce the various fronts to establish their divisions more clearly. The first great conflict comes then in 1835, when Menzel denounces Young Germany with the support of conservative forces, and David Friedrich Strauss simultaneously incites the break within the Hegelian school with the publication of his *Leben Jesu* (The life of Jesus).

The 1820s have the reputation, because they are an essentially res-
torational decade, of having contributed little to the development of
literary criticism. This lack of distinction is bemoaned repeatedly by
contemporaneous writers, especially by liberals such as Börne and
Menzel, who conclude that criticism ought to be thoroughly re-
vamped. These assessments must be understood as part of a strategy
whose undeclared goal is to transform the literary system, restricted
by Metternich, into a forum for political opposition. The strategy
proves in large part successful, despite the numerous countermea-
sures it confronts. The web of relationships between Börne and Heine,
Heine and Varnhagen, Varnhagen and the Young Germans, Menzel
and Heine, Menzel and Gutzkow, and so on, prepares the ground for
the literary journalism of the 1830s, which openly draws the appropriate political conclusions and therefore meets quite soon with the resistance of the conservative forces in state and church.

The single most important event for the situation of literary criticism
in the 1830s and 1840s is still Metternich's drastic intervention in the
institution of literature: the Karlsbad Decrees of 1819, which go into
the constitution in 1820 as part of the Final Acts of Vienna. Aside from
the ban on students' associations (*Burschenschaften*) and the strict sur-
veillance of the universities, literary communication is to be regulated
by a pre-censorship of all writings less than twenty sheets long. The
control of literature means for Metternich the guarantee that the ideological education of the public will be prevented. Indeed, merely
negative measures do not suffice. Metternich wants to carry out the
attack on liberalism and idealism by means of his own positive program. He therefore enlists in his service intellectuals of the stature of
Friedrich Gentz, Adam Müller, and for a while even Friedrich Schlegel. A method of literary-critical conservatism is thus developed. This
conservatism—a tendency apparent in Friedrich Schlegel's work as
early as 1812—wants to see literature adopt a traditional transcendent
orientation and therefore finds in the history of modern literature an
aberrant development that, misled by critical Protestantism, tends to
contradict church authority on the status and character of transcendence. The conservatives' claim that contemporary literature should
be based on Christianity is forced, in the end, to turn even against the
neohumanism of Weimar. Thus, Goethe's reputation among the conservatives is anything but assured. The precariousness of the situation

is fairly clear even before the rabid attacks of the *Evangelische Kirchenzeitung* (Protestant church newspaper) on the published correspondence between Goethe and Schiller and on the *Wahlverwandschaften* (Elective affinities) in 1830 and 1831 respectively. The conservatives revoke, explicitly or implicitly, the humanistic plea for autonomous aesthetics. The militant Protestant and Catholic restoration refuses categorically the liberal literary program and intends to replace it with a decidedly Christian one.[92]

The alliance between the political and the theological restorations solidifies itself on the basis of their common enemy—liberalism, which has been strengthening its position journalistically since the 1820s. The alliance culminates in 1835 in the campaign against Young Germany, followed shortly by the struggle between the *Evangelische Kirchenzeitung* and the *Hallische Jahrbücher* on the occasion of the religious controversies in Cologne. For the Protestant orthodoxy the evaluation of literature is never exclusively, indeed not even predominantly, an immanently literary question; both the orthodoxy's critique of liberalism and its positive program are determined by its interests in moral education. The orthodox clergy promote literary works that take an unambiguous stand in favor of belief and criticize works and authors who contradict or even merely evade (as had Goethe) the transcendent anchoring of literature.

One can gain some sense of the orthodoxy's expectations by looking at its members' polemical reviews. For example, a reviewer of the Goethe-Schiller correspondence makes these introductory remarks: "Subsequent generations prefer to truly rejoice over the greatest minds that have reigned in the realm of the high arts only when they find in the lives of these minds a harmonically developed whole wherein the ethical is bound with the beautiful in an immanent and reciprocal penetration."[93] The reviewer goes on to state explicitly that this confession of faith in the beautiful is at base a confession of faith in religion, and he proceeds to turn this doctrine against Schiller and Goethe: "The extent to which, through their adversarial relation to the Gospel and through their lack of acquaintance with its true essence, they have robbed their talent of thematic substance and their productions of inner truth—this has long been apparent to all those to whom the appearance of our savior is dear."[94] The decidedly more extreme critique of the *Wahlverwandschaften* goes so far as to deny its author the ethical stability necessary to the composition of a novel on marriage. But these orthodox opponents of Goethe, as narrow-minded as they may be in literary matters, do see the decisive point: the aesthetics of autonomy is not compatible with a didactic literary program. The same Goethe whom radical liberals such as Menzel and Börne attacked in the 1820s as the epitome of political restoration appears from the standpoint of the Protestant conservatives as a subversive element. In a letter to Prince Wittgenstein, Metternich expresses similar reservations, commenting on the *Wahlverwandschaften* in tones reminiscent of the *Evangelische Kirchenzeitung* on the occasion of Varnhagen's commemorative piece on Young Germany: "Goethe had in fact very few purely moral and religious concepts; he was a man of the senses and his 'Wahlverwandschaften' is a highly immoral book that leans toward the new religion of the flesh."[95]

It would be wrong, however, to place Metternich's literary taste on a level with the taste of Hengstenberg and the *Evangelische Kirchenzeitung*. Neither he nor his literary advisors are tempted to reduce literature to its moral-didactic content. Adam Müller speaks out early against a criticism based on rules; indeed, he speaks out against all fixed normative notions and defines the authentic task of criticism as that of mediation. He rejects among other things Friedrich and A. W. Schlegel's attempt to constitute a sphere of the absolute in the realm of criticism, a sphere from which everything would remain excluded that does not fulfill the strictest demands of authentic poetry. Against Romantic criticism, Müller objects that wherever it corresponds to its own ideal, it excludes from any serious criticism that part of literature which the broad reading public consumes. Müller argues with reference to early Romanticism: "In the absolutely scientific one-sidedness in which it has heretofore almost exclusively appeared, the critical revolution in Germany was able to have no great or immediate effect on the German nationality because it disdained, owing to a certain utterly indecorous pride, actively and insistently to enter into the essence of contemporaneous social movements both in their public and in their private relations."[96]

This wish to anchor the institution of criticism in society and open it to the needs of the public, leads not to the politicization of criticism, as one would assume, but to an organicist model that grants the state a certain influence. Adam Müller—and this distinguishes him from

Friedrich Schlegel—is interested more in the totality of literature than in the individual work. The new work is compared tellingly with the citizen who seeks acceptance in the state of literature.[97] This concern with the German nation includes Goethe, who is treated by Müller with the same attentiveness and awe as by the Schlegels'. Müller grants Goethe's works, especially *Wilhelm Meister*, a central position in German literature, but his admiration for Goethe—which concentrates exclusively on the aesthetic value of his work—does not exclude the recognition of such popular writers as August Wilhelm Iffland and August Friedrich von Kotzebue; Müller gives them, too, a modest place in the canon of German literature. His alliance with the conservative forces (he serves Austria during the wars of emancipation from French rule) is made possible by his concept of criticism, which advocates the perpetuation of the status quo by means of the hermeneutical appropriation of tradition. This alliance is bound to render suspect to liberal critics the hermeneutic procedure to which Müller is obviously indebted.

The militant restoration sees itself challenged by the various forms of liberal criticism as early as the late 1820s. In its conciliatory form, liberalism appears on the scene under the protective cloak of the extollment of Goethe in the work of Varnhagen von der Ense, the Prussian diplomat whose cautious strategy is to avoid any direct confrontation with the authorities while supporting progressive tendencies wherever possible. Varnhagen's reputation—unquestioned among his contemporaries—as one of the most important literati and critics of his time falls into obscurity during the post-1848 period.[98] Varnhagen is a master of the art of innuendo, of the hidden suggestion and the unobtrusive allusion that are bound to escape the censor. He creates a broad forum for his own effectiveness in 1827 when he founds, with Hegel and Eduard Gans, the *Jahrbücher für wissenschaftliche Kritik* (Almanac for scientific criticism). Moderate liberalism protects itself against the state here by insisting on the strict scientificity and nonpartisan attitude of its contributions: "Therefore the tone will be moderate at all costs and worthy of the dignity of science. Since the efforts of the institute are directed toward nothing but the promotion of this dignity, the negativity frequently encountered nowadays remains automatically excluded."[99] A judgment, the editors suggest, should be the result of an interpersonal and thus impersonal critical deliberation. For this reason they decide to present all reviews, before publishing them, to a circle of experts who make up an independent advisory board.

His connection to Goethe and Classicist aesthetics does not prevent Varnhagen from promoting younger authors—such as Heinrich Heine and Heinrich Laube—who pursue other directions. The younger generation is later quite conscious of this important support and points out in its own journals the importance of Varnhagen as a critic. He unmistakably belongs, with Börne and Heine, to the admired predecessors. He remains an important ally, even though he stays in the background and never breaks out of his pose of moderate liberal. A remarkable example of his advocacy is his intervention in 1835 at Metternich's court on behalf of Young Germany. As a recognized scholar of Goethe, he is in a position to use his authority to integrate the younger writers into the German tradition. For example, he writes of Heine's *Buch der Lieder* (Book of songs): "Of course there are certain [poems] among them of a more bitter taste, but the poet has organized his collection reasonably and has duly pushed aside all that is immature as well as all that is excessively bold, without however suppressing the fresh audacity and the sharp wantonness which indeed constitute an essential element of his poetry."[100] One can feel the attentiveness to the official standpoint here, and even more strongly in the following comment on the *Reisebilder:* "This book is considered irreligious and revolutionary. We admit that the words in it all too often have both of these colorations. But much would seem to be lacking which would be necessary before the *sense* would thoroughly go in this direction."[101] The circumspect diction, the distance taken from both author and public, the barely noticeable irony with respect to the state censor: these all characterize Varnhagen's liberalism, which aims at conciliation and mediation but not at compromise. In their political notions, Varnhagen on the one hand and Menzel and Börne on the other are not far apart, but Menzel's and Börne's hatred of Goethe establishes a distance in the literary sphere that prevents them from any unification with Varnhagen.

The ambivalence of early German liberalism about the authors who later enter literary history as German Classics, the wavering between admiration and indictment, has its basis in liberalism's tie to an Enlightenment literary program. This program, as it is represented by Lessing in an exemplary manner, legitimates literature as a whole—

and thus also every single work—in terms of its moral-social function. When the Classical-Romantic theory of literature cancels these notions of the goals of literature, it problematizes the legitimation of literature institutionalized by the Enlightenment. But in turn, the self-sufficiency of the aesthetic realm is exposed to the critique of trifling and frivolity, of insufficient engagement in the realm of politics. According to this logic, the decision for political-moral progress becomes at once the decision against the aesthetic programs of Weimar and Jena. In the case of the critical activities of Börne and Menzel, this logic can be shown quite clearly. Their unrelenting and also uninsightful polemic against Goethe, for which later literary history has so resented them, is based on a literary program that has no place for the concept of aesthetic autonomy, attaching itself instead to older rationalist traditions. Börne's announcement of the journal *Wage* (1818) makes this connection quite clear. The goal is not science as such but its dissemination, communication with a broader public: "One says that science in Germany has become less deep than before; this may be so, but it has become more broad."[102] The journal is supposed to provide a forum for a public discussion not limited to the circle of scholars: "In our journal, the most excellent works of our nation's science shall be judged, especially those that treat civic matters; and so that no one-sidedness of criticism should install itself, we shall seek the opinions of men of various points of view."[103] Börne insists on the exoteric side of criticism; it seeks no hidden truths but attempts to propagate open truths among the people. "Truly, the copper that by means of the daily newspapers is brought to the people is worth more than all the gold in the books."[104] He assumes, then, that critical periodicals, at least in the long term, have an enduring influence on the public and thus promote enlightenment.

He would like to overcome the sunderance of the public sphere, its fragmentation into rival factions. It is on this point that his critique of the *Jahrbücher für wissenschaftliche Kritik* concentrates.[105] The scientific reasoning of the Hegelians withdraws itself, he maintains, from the general public through its theoretical expectations. The withdrawal into the scientific or literary coterie pays, according to Börne's argument, an extremely high price: it sunders literature into one realm accessible only to an elite, and another realm abandoned to the crowd. This critique is directed quite as much against Varnhagen's Goethe cult as against the poetical criticism of the Romantics. Börne restores the rights of the *raisonneur*, whose task it is to clarify the impressions of the reader and to measure them against the purpose of literature. Since this (moral) purpose transcends the realm of the aesthetic, aesthetic judgment has in the final analysis merely strategic status. Thus, Börne's objections to Goethe and Schiller are morally-politically motivated. He views the alliance of Weimar as a literary faction that serves self-cultivation, not enlightenment. The essay "Über den Charakter des Wilhelm Tell in Schillers Drama" (On the character of Wilhelm Tell in Schiller's play) accordingly attempts to read Schiller's figure not merely as an element of the drama but against its historical background. In this context the hero proves to be an anxious German petty bourgeois who is not particularly useful for political emancipation. Börne's characterization of Tell becomes a description of German social relations; once the historical veil is torn away, Schiller's drama of freedom loses its emphatic force.

Börne divides anew what the aesthetics of genius has bound together. While the senses should deal with the beautiful, the mind (*Geist*) should take care of judgment: "The sense and the heart do not put things to the test: the senses incline toward the beautiful; the heart loves and hates. But the mind judges and distinguishes between what is worthy of love and what worthy of hate."[106] Thus, the practice of criticism does not apply itself merely to the small number of authentic works of art. Börne's *Dramaturgische Blätter* (Dramaturgical journal) treats Kotzebue and Heinrich Clauren with the same extensiveness as Franz Grillparzer and Schiller, without ignoring or forgetting the differences in stature. Börne's concept of criticism negates the authority of tradition; the literary-critical essay must, for him, characterize and evaluate its object each time anew. The historicization of criticism introduced by Romanticism is alien to him; when he makes comparisons, it is a matter of general claims to legitimacy, not of historical contexts. Börne expects from the critic that he deal with the work as if it had just appeared and needed to be explained fully to the reader. Therefore, the critical act is a dialogue with the public. Börne's style, too, is designed to accord with this goal: it is terse, sparing, but effective in the use of rhetorical figures; it avoids abstract formulations wherever an example can make a point more concretely. This style— for which even the skeptical Heine cannot refuse respect—probably affects the younger generation more than any other aspect of Börne's work. His writings are a signal: with this mode of writing, one would be able to conquer the public sphere.

The third critic who becomes exemplary for this generation is Wolfgang Menzel, who after 1825 leads the influential *Literatur-Blatt* (Literary supplement) of the *Morgenblatt für gebildete Stände* and who uses this position in order to push through his program of national liberalism. In 1831 Gutzkow expresses enthusiastically what Menzel means to the younger critics, greeting him in the *Forum der Journalliteratur* (Forum for the literature of the journals) as the critic who has controverted "the stream of public opinion."[107] Menzel, he says, "expressed freely for the first time that, in our storm-ridden times, a breath other than the artificial bellows-wind would have to stir the strings, and a fire other than the artificially fanned tinder flame [*Zunderfeuer*] flare up in us. It is of no avail now to make sacrifices to small idols in closed temples. Rather—in the great temple of the world and nature the flames must be fanned by windstorms."[108] Menzel is seen as a welcome ally. In 1831 Gutzkow attributes to him the capacity "to introduce in all respects into literature the ideal construction of the future" and concludes that with him a new period of literature begins.[109]

For Menzel, literature is the expression of life; hence, German national literature is the expression of the German malaise—not an immediate copy of political and social weaknesses but the result of a process of compensation. The extended literary production in Germany appears to him to be the signature of a national weakness. The Germans live more for their literature than it for them.

The concept of national literature is not problematic for Menzel. German literature is for him the necessary result of the German national character; the task of the critic is to inform and influence this character. As for Börne, for Menzel the concept of criticism is not limited to the evaluation of literary texts but extends to the ethical-practical evaluation of the nation. The task of criticism therefore involves quite a bit more than the announcement and characterization of books.[110] For him, criticism's purpose is to inform public opinion and to stimulate the public to take a critical stance. It is not by chance that he invokes Lessing and the tradition of the Enlightenment when he is attempting to defend the institution of criticism against commercialization and the spirit of the coterie. In retrospect, Menzel describes this task as follows: "I had to see clearly in the midst of chaos. I had to struggle against all that had caused and was daily increasing the inducement of the confusion, dullness, and desacralization of what had such majesty. I saw how a sophistry of the understanding and the heart, a spirit of the lie, an aristocratic meanness had forced its way into the highest spheres of science and art—and I could not forgive this merely on the basis that it was associated with the fame of great names."[111]

One aspect of this struggle for the purification of German literature is the unhalting polemic against Goethe that begins in 1823 and reaches its high point in 1828 in *Deutsche Literatur*. Goethe's development, which became for later literary history the center of German tradition, appears here as a pronounced aberration. Menzel labels Goethe a mere author of fashion as early as 1824, while characterizing Schiller as an author who has had to swim against the stream.[112] This opposition of Goethe and Schiller throws clarifying light on Menzel's literary program. He desires the ethical education of the nation through writing— that is, on the one hand, through the opposite of the entertainment offered by the widespread contemporary mass literature but, on the other hand, through the opposite of the poetization of practical life as the Romantics tried to imagine it. Thus, Schiller becomes the exemplary poet because he morally influences his public. The antipode would be Friedrich Schlegel, who, in Menzel's words, embraces the "most frivolous modernity" in that he believes himself "to be permitted to connect the lowest sensuous pleasure with the most sublime feelings."[113]

The liberal alliance of the 1820s is incapable of enduring because it has neither a unified ideological position nor a consistent literary program on the basis of which a common strategy could be developed. Heine is already alluding to the presence of these dangers when he writes, in his review of Menzel's literary history, that Menzel's hatred of Goethe involves an utter miscomprehension.[114] Heine knows his own literary strategy to be thoroughly distinct from Menzel's (and Börne's) conceptions. In his reconstruction of the German tradition he concerns himself more with Goethe than with Schiller, although he does not thereby include himself in the cult of Goethe worshipers. What Heine has only suggested in the review of Menzel he develops fully in the *Romantische Schule:* a historical critique that distinguishes itself on the one hand from Friedrich Schlegel's Vienna lectures and on the other hand from Menzel's *Deutsche Literatur*.

This step is extremely important for the institution of literary criticism. The reflection upon the nature of critical judgment leads here to the discovery of its necessary link to literary historiography. Characteristically, this attempt to conceptualize literature as a developmental process does not restrict itself to high literature. Under the influence of Hegel one has a tendency to comprehend and represent the evolution of literature as a part of the history of absolute spirit. Hegel himself points thus to the revolutionary content of German idealist philosophy in his lectures on the history of philosophy: "In these philosophies [of Kant, Fichte, and Schelling] revolution is laid down and spoken out as in the form of thought to which spirit in Germany has progressed in recent times."[115] As is well known, Heine adopts this conception—in this exceeding Menzel—in order to combine the history of literature with the history of philosophy in a concept of spirit destined for revolution. But the task of the formulation of this concept, as writers like Wienbarg and Gutzkow realize at about the same time, entails problems of organization that cannot be solved by traditional means. Menzel's attempt at a systematic classification is generally regarded as having failed because it organizes its material schematically and without regard for the interrelations between various works. His mixture of rigid classification and personal polemic proves inadequate to the task of leading criticism out of the ghetto of belles lettres. Heine's solution becomes as influential as it does because it promises to be able to combine "scientific" demands (in the Hegelian sense) with the demands of journalism.[116] Heine makes the esoteric language of philosophy generally comprehensible and loads his journalistic texts with philosophical content. Criticism of literature and criticism of art (which are not strictly separable) leave behind the traditional genres (reviews) and make use of both the reportage of daily events and the presentation of more distant history.

Heine's journalistic pieces for the *Allgemeine Zeitung* (from January through June 1832), later published under the title *Französische Zustände* (French situations), practice for the first time a form of critical discourse in which—mediated by the subjectivity of the reporter— social, political, and aesthetic matters are integrated. Heine's critical prose combines modes of writing that have hitherto remained sepa-

rate. The mixture of styles refuses to harmonize the dissonant, preferring instead to juxtapose heterogeneous contents and modes of writing in a kind of montage. In this manner the critical judgment on
literature is doubly broken—colliding both with social and political
themes and with the subjective reflection of the reporter, who can at
any time assert his own position. The procedure is subversive—as
indeed the state censor quite quickly understands.[117] By combining
questions of literature with questions of social practice, Heine undermines the isolation and neutralization of the aesthetic sphere instituted by the aesthetics of autonomy. What distinguishes him from
Menzel and Börne, of course, is the historical-normative insight that
criticism must not fall behind Classical-Romantic aesthetics and that
the mere reenlivening of the program of Enlightenment therefore cannot contain a progressive solution. This solution resides, for Heine, in
the consistent historicization of literary evaluation; the critic must, for
him, proceed with the understanding that the functions of art and
literature are constantly transformed by the movements of history at
large. This conception allows Heine—more decisively and clearly than
is possible for the Young Germans—to distinguish the present from
the "age of art" and its aesthetics.

Both journalistic and historiographical modes of criticism must, for
Heine, be seen together, for they deal with the same fundamental
problem: how is contemporary literature to be related to its own times,
and how can it contribute to the general emancipation? Where Heine
distances himself from the monumental literary history of Gervinus,
he makes clear what dissatisfies him: a manner of treatment devoid of
spirit and wit.[118] He does not compete with academic literary history
but transports the viewpoint of the feuilleton, its wit and subjectivity,
into historiographical representation itself. The purpose is on the one
hand to win a broader circle of readers and on the other hand—not
less importantly—to secure critical discourse against academic neutralization. While Gervinus trusts utterly in his materials and constructs the development of literature from them, Heine pairs the philosophico-historical construction that is indebted essentially to Hegel
and to Saint-Simonism with the subjectivity of the *Reisebilder* (Images
of travel). This procedure ironizes at every point the claim of facts to be
self-sufficient. The critical stand exhausts itself neither in facts nor in
philosophico-historical construction.

The Young Germans conceive of themselves as daily news reporters who intervene in the struggles of public opinion with the weapons of journalism. This image unifies their work even if they never attain a consensus on the particulars of the proper mode of combat. From the liberal criticism of the 1820s they inherit a high estimation of literature, a faith in the possibility of altering political relations by means of literary influence. The Young Germans' strategic use of literature thus enhances—at least in theory—the status of literary criticism, whose task becomes that of programmatically organizing the struggle against the forces of restoration. The younger writers adopt and further develop the journalistic means originally proposed by Menzel, Börne, and Heine. Hence, the magazine remains the most important instrument for the transportation of a literary program into the public sphere. Heinrich Laube's early attempt to establish the *Aurora* in 1829 can be seen in this context. The undertaking collapsed after a mere six months. Two other examples are Gutzkow's *Forum der Journalliteratur* of 1831 and Theodor Mundt's *Schriften in Bunter Reihe* of 1834 (which was supposed to appear as *Perspectiven für Literatur und Zeit* [Perspectives for our literature and times] but was forbidden by the censor). Examples of more successful journals are the *Phönix*, whose literary supplement is edited by Gutzkow (after 1835), and the *Telegraph*, founded in 1837 and later taken over by Gutzkow. Heinrich Laube's *Zeitung für die elegante Welt* probably reaches the greatest circulation, though critical discourse occupies only a subordinate position in its contents.

Menzel's surprising attack on Gutzkow and the authors of Young Germany, which leads at the end of 1835 to the ban on these writers, alters with one blow the entire literary and ideological constellation. The ensuing literary infighting, in which all means of polemic are employed, results in a reorganization and redefinition of the alliances and animosities involved. The liberal alliance, in which democratic, national, and Protestant-religious forces have been working together, dissolves. Menzel aligns himself explicitly with the reactionaries; Heine becomes more closely associated with the Young Germans by virtue of the fact that his name is mentioned in one breath with theirs. This infighting has exemplary significance also for reasons other than those that can be represented by a history of ideology; at the same time it pointedly reveals the possibilities and limits of literary criticism. We

have to consider two points of view in order to evaluate these occurrences. On the one hand, as competitors on the literary market the
critics attempt to suppress one another. On the other hand, it is
principled literary programs, not mere individuals, that are at stake in
this competition. Heinrich Laube openly addresses this issue of competition as early as 1833: "The writers meet on the terrain of the public
sphere not like natural allies who all steer toward the same goal of an
enhanced education of the people but like natural enemies. One main
source of this passion rests, again, on economic relations."[119] Menzel's
polemic against Gutzkow is obviously in part determined by such
motives. Simultaneously, of course, he wants to oppose his religiously
grounded nationalist liberal conception of literature to the sensualism
of Heine and his associates, such as Gutzkow.

The settling of accounts with Gutzkow, which takes as its occasion
Gutzkow's novel *Wally die Zweiflerin* (Wally the skeptic), is for Menzel
an opportunity to delimit his concepts of literature and criticism.
Patriotic liberalism cuts itself off here from radical sensualist and possibly atheistic tendencies. In order to reach his opponent, Menzel ma-
nipulates the literary program of the Enlightenment in such a way that
it is turned against Gutzkow and Young Germany. He expressly calls
on the authority of public opinion and accuses Gutzkow of abusing the
latter by introducing confusion into it: "Herr Gutzkow attempts as a
critic to thwart and confuse all opinions, to destroy every basis on
which public opinion rests, to besmirch every honorable name, to
make every noble tendency laughable, in order to swim on the surface
of his chaos and to erect in the midst of the general anarchy of minds
the throne of his godless lewdness."[120] The conservative rhetoric can
hardly be overlooked; the prosecutor warns that anarchy will ensue if
authors such as Gutzkow are not restrained. At the same time Menzel
explains the part of the Enlightenment literary program that he means
to save: the moral-didactic function of literature. When Menzel bitterly
accuses Gutzkow of irreligion and lewdness, we see the reverse side of
the same coin: the literature that does not support the positive social
task of Enlightenment should be sacrificed. Poetic writing stands for
Menzel too in the service of a politically conceived morality, but this
moral itself remains immune to critique. As soon as literary production
radicalizes itself and calls ethical conventions into question, Menzel
views it as his duty to proceed against what he sees as abuse. In his

struggle with Young Germany, he interprets the office of the "judge"—
ever since the Enlightenment, the dominant image for the function of
the literary critic—in a restrictive and repressive way. His critique of
Gutzkow's *Wally* uses as its weapon dogmatic conceptions of morals
and religion. Yet nowhere does Menzel make the attempt to show why
Gutzkow's treatment of religious and ethical questions is corruptive
and immoral. Menzel's liberalism begins to be afraid of its own consequences and would thus like to silence its younger and more radical
proponents. "His [Gutzkow's] criticism," Menzel remarks, "is as un-
ethical as his novel, but perhaps more damning. A poet may paint
filthy images, but he leaves the beautiful and holy images of the others
alone. However, when a critic undertakes to make a mockery of all that
is healthy and noble in literature with his syphilitic and blasphemous
mind, this is a much more serious offense."[121]

What Menzel objects to, in the criticism of Gutzkow and thus of
Young Germany as a whole, is the absence of principles from which an
impartial judgment may be derived. Menzel distorts the objectively
present competitive relationship between himself and Gutzkow in
such a manner as to make it seem that the suspicion of an arbitrary
marketing of personal judgments could attach itself only to Gutzkow.
Meanwhile, Menzel celebrates himself as the just and objective mouthpiece of the general public. He intends to annihilate his opponent and
to secure his own position as that of the leading critic. In order to do so,
he evokes public opinion as the legitimating final instance of criticism.
In this way, the liberal model of criticism is refunctioned so as to serve
conservative tendencies.

The opposing camp understands this strategy quite well—and it is
this understanding that renders the struggle exemplary. Heine and
Börne in particular are quite acutely aware of what is at stake, while
Gutzkow clings to the moral discourse and thus remains the prisoner
of the terms in which Menzel conducts his polemic. But we cannot
pursue the feud in its details. We shall content ourselves with emphasizing two points, for the struggle leaves its imprint on the institution
of criticism on the levels of both form and content. As concerns form,
for the first time, strategies and patterns are tried out whose politically
explosive power will become fully evident two generations later. As
concerns content, the conflict becomes so intense that neither side can
distinguish any longer between person and issue. The concept of

polemics takes on in both of these respects new meaning; in the struggle between Menzel and Young Germany it is a matter not only of books and reputations getting torn to bits but of the (even bodily) elimination of the opponent from the public sphere. Above all, Börne and Heine take on the challenge and use the form of polemics for the purposes of literary-critical execution.

The alliance between Börne and Menzel, which could have based itself on moral asceticism, breaks down as Börne comes to realize that Menzel's patriotism is taking on a chauvinistic character and playing into the hands of the conservatives. Börne's *Menzel der Franzosenfresser* (Menzel, devourer of Frenchmen) settles accounts with the liberalism of those who have remained loyal to the government. The attack is led in such a manner that Menzel is annihilated by means of wit—and this is the source of Heine's admiration. Neither Börne nor Heine, in his *Über den Denunzianten* (On the denouncer), allows Menzel's arguments to be taken seriously. Their ironic style sacrifices the opponent to his own ridiculousness. Menzel appears as the barbaric, teutono-maniacal figure who thrashes about in narrow-minded incomprehension. Heine's work treats Menzel with ceaseless irony; Börne takes a stand on the question of his patriotism. Since his concept of literature is akin to Menzel's, the need to differentiate himself is all the more pressing. "Herr Menzel says I declared German patriotism to be an idiocy while granting French patriotism its legitimacy. I am supposed to have taken to the fields of battle against the Germans in the interests of the French and to have wanted to spread French culture abroad under the mask of freedom."[122]

This accusation is quite dangerous—as its impact in later history shows—because it marginalizes Börne's critique of the German situation. Thus he chooses the strategy of making the struggle for freedom into a common German-French project: "It is the task of the French to destroy and carry off the decrepit building of bourgeois society; it is the task of the Germans to ground the new building and erect it."[123] The German and French traditions that Menzel treats as opposites belong together as a complementary pair for Börne and Heine. Translated into the terms of literature, this means that the establishment of national traditions, which would determine the horizon of criticism increasingly throughout the nineteenth century, is not merely narrow but regressive. Heine's mocking analysis of Menzel's moralism shrewdly grasps that Menzel's accusations, however much they can be derived from the Enlightenment concept of literature, would help finally not the Enlightenment but the reactionary forces. Menzel's fixation upon the French foe means the denunciation of a nation and political system that allow for more freedom than Germany. Above all, though, it is Menzel's accusation of irreligion, directed at Gutzkow and then easily extended to Young Germany as well as Heine and Börne, that proves effective, for it has the advantage of mobilizing on its behalf the powers of the church and its theologians.

Menzel's attack provides the conservative forces with the opportunity they have been seeking to reconquer lost terrain. Neither the Protestant nor the Catholic church recognizes in this period the idea of autonomous art; both evaluate the literature of their time according to whether and in what manner it promotes religion. The churches therefore support in most cases the standpoint of the state censor. The judgment of the Prussian High Censor's Collegium (*des Preussischen Ober-Censur-Collegiums*) on Theodor Mundt's novel *Madonna* makes this connection quite clear. In its conclusions one reads: "The book takes an extremely important place in a class of writings which has become prominent in recent years as in no earlier period of German literature and which threatens to have an influence that would be in high degree corruptive of morals and thus also politically dangerous."[124] In particular, Young German sensualism is singled out as a dangerous position that ought to be suppressed. The Protestant orthodoxy, grouped in Prussia around the *Evangelische Kirchenzeitung*, takes up Menzel's cause. Even before Menzel's review of *Wally*, the Berlin theologian Ernst Wilhelm Hengstenberg introduces his campaign against the "rehabilitation of the flesh" with a series of articles in that journal. He establishes without delay the connection between the incriminated sensualism and the (French) Enlightenment: "It is the last instance of Evil—that Satan, dressed as the Angel of Light, or that the materialism which, in Voltaire, raised itself in indignation against religion, begins, in Heine, to pass itself off for religion."[125] The Protestant orthodoxy forces fictional literature back into the bed of the theological discourse. Hengstenberg's polemic is unconditional; he wants nothing less than the elimination of sensualist philosophy and its proponents. Since he does not recognize the aesthetic as a special realm of its own but measures even literary writings against theological standards, there can be no compromise: "And so long as they have not given to Christian matrimony a confessional guarantee, we curse the satyrlike connotations of their doctrine of elective embrace [*der Wahlumarmung*]."[126] The standards of critical judgment are positive Christian morals. However, the orthodoxy does not content itself with condemnation. Hengstenberg expressly allies himself with Menzel's denunciations and threatens that the "powers that be" shall smash the Young Germans. This is the call for the intervention of the state: "The police will intervene and disturb these masses of the new world religion."[127] Characteristically, Hengstenberg accuses rationalist theology of excessive laxity in pursuing this struggle.

The literary feud between Menzel and Young Germany offered both factions the opportunity to undermine the opposing position. In this, of course, the chances of success were not quite evenly distributed, since the state ban on Young German writings endangered the public basis of these liberal and democratic critics. The Christian critique did not restrict itself, however, to the sphere of pamphlets, commentaries, and reviews. Popular literary history, for example, belonged equally to the forms in which the conservative message is presented and defended. The forces of restoration successfully influenced public opinion in the direction of their Christian nationalist program. Since the literary histories of Friedrich Christian Vilmar and Heinrich Gelzer did not claim scholarly status for their own discourse but rather understood themselves as popular works for educated readers, they have left no traces in the history of scholarly literary historiography.[128] A social history of criticism cannot ignore them, however, for they had considerable impact on the public sphere of their day. One can show in particular by their example that the distinction between criticism and history that is today self-evident was not yet established in the pre-1848 period.

On both the liberal and the conservative side, the genre of literary history is used in this period as an expanded form of criticism. In this respect Menzel's *Deutsche Literatur* of 1828 presumably exercises a greater influence than the later canonized literary history of Gervinus (1835–42), for which the question of historicity becomes a central problem and which is therefore and with good reason generally regarded as marking the beginning of scientific historiography. One can characterize Menzel's literary history as an extensive commentary in which critical assessment does not concern itself exclusively with a work or an author but attempts to present and classify the entire literature of a nation. In the same way, Vilmar and Gelzer concentrate on the task of critical judgment and not on the task of phenomenal description.

The distinction current today between literary criticism and literary history renders inaccessible to view both this general situation and consequently also the strength and influence of the conservative party within it. Until 1848 this party dominates the literary apparatus as a whole more strongly than do the liberal and democratic forces, which see themselves again and again threatened by exclusionary repressions. The cooperation of the conservatives with the officials of the state censor—that is, with the ideological apparatus of the state—assure them of a power that one should not underestimate in a central Europe governed by Metternich. That this influence is not adequately understood later is probably due to the fact that the Christian components of restoration conservatism are no longer utilized during the second half of the nineteenth century and so fall into historical oblivion.

Vilmar's literary history has its source in public lectures held by the author in Marburg in 1843 and 1844. The same is true of Gelzer: his literary history is based on his public lectures at the University of Basel. Gelzer's work may well be of relatively little importance for the history of historiography, but it nonetheless exemplifies the attempt of conservatism to establish a systematic position from which an assessment of the entirety of modern German literature could be formulated against neohumanism and the liberalism born of neohumanism. Gelzer speaks of a "comparative opposition of the Christian-ethical world view with the world view of modern German letters [Bildung]."[129] Thus, he concentrates his attention on those streams of literature in which Protestantism expresses itself and which he then passes off as the true goal of the German people. Gelzer's introduction underscores explicitly this religious program; poetry is once again enlisted in the service of religion. Furthermore, the national standpoint then takes sides with the religious one. Like Vilmar, Gelzer assumes that "the further development of the German spirit promises to ensure the rebirth of the political greatness of Germany."[130] Vilmar's literary history forces this national perspective and remains thus also quite popular even in the second half of the nineteenth century. The national spirit of the Germans, as he imagines it, constitutes itself both in opposition to alien—especially French—influences and in opposition to the democratic and socialist positions attributed to these alien influences. In the treatment of modern German literature Vilmar's canon does not even greatly distinguish itself from those in the work of Gervinus and other liberals. He names Friedrich Gottlieb Klopstock, Lessing, Christoph Martin Wieland, Johann Gottfried Herder, Goethe, and Schiller "the six heroes of our modern poesy,"[131] yet by his emphasis he opposes the liberal tradition. While Klopstock gains central status because of his patriotism, the enlightener Lessing is granted only a marginal position, and Wieland is finally attacked for his intimacy with French literature. The evaluation of Weimar Classicism is not unambiguous. On the one hand, Weimar is praised as the second high point of German literature; on the other, Goethe and Schiller are criticized for producing works that no longer belong within the architecture of Christianity. Romanticism is, in contrast, defended against the attacks of the radical liberals, especially where it agrees with the political and religious restoration.

The tendency of today's literary historians to view the phase prior to 1848 as the prehistory or early history of literary criticism projects the epistemological interests of a later epoch back into the early nineteenth century. For in the early 1800s, even when the procedure of historicism is applied to the history of literature, the connection with literary criticism is in general both theoretically and institutionally maintained. This nexus loosens up after 1850 and dissolves in the *Kaiserreich*, once literary scholarship has established itself in the universities.

The extent to which this connection between literary criticism and literary history seems self-evident to the contemporaries of this period can be seen in the following passage published by Robert Prutz in 1859. He is writing about the literary history of the 1820s:

> Literature and its history were the sole place of refuge open to the thought of German unity, which at that time was so heavily proscribed but which nonetheless no persecutions or bans could completely suffocate: the words themselves—"nationality" and "Germanness"—slipped by the argus-eyes of the police at that

time only when they appeared in a literary-historical work. It is highly characteristic and worthy of serious consideration in any determination of the political and ethical influence of literary history among our people that in the very time of our deepest national division and indignity—at first after the wars of liberation, when all those glorious hopes and dreams with which our fathers went into battle fluttered to bits in the pitiless air of the real—that in this very time the term "national literature" first arose and came into currency (by means of Wachler, 1818).[132]

Tellingly, there is no talk here of scientific method, only of political function. Prutz stresses the politicization of the public sphere. The same can be said of the literary criticism of the time; from it, too, the decided liberals expect a politicization of public opinion. The plan of writing the history of literature as the history of German national literature grew out of the idea of demonstrating, at least in the field of mental evolution, the progress of Germany, a progress that eventually would have to inscribe itself in the political sphere. Against this background, Heine's *Romantische Schule* appears more intimately related to Gervinus's literary history than is traditionally assumed in the historiography of literary criticism. For the former ends with remarks concerning the coming revolution in Germany, and the latter establishes a connection between the end of Germany's literary evolution and the beginning of political unification. However widely Gervinus's reflections and materials range in order to allow him to present the course of German literary history, his interest is still not directed—any more than Heine's—at a mere description of what has happened in the past. For Gervinus, the historiographer is—just like the critic—one whose task it is to reason in order to promote the self-comprehension of the public. Literary history is for Gervinus not the property of a small community of specialists but, like every scholarly activity, a concern of the general public.[133] The participation of literary history in public matters renders it partisan—and in this insight Heine and Gervinus coincide; the historian stands not outside the process he presents but takes part in its evolution and promotes it through his own activity. Accordingly, Gervinus speaks emphatically against the objectivity of the historical school.[134]

Gervinus's view of history as a unified process whose goal is human freedom already entails a determination of the position of the historian. The historian becomes a partisan of history: that is, he becomes the interested interpreter of progress and simultaneously the critic of those tendencies that resist humane progress. Hence, an ideal construction underlies Gervinus's literary history, which he himself underscores—an ideal construction that makes the development of spirit the guideline of its diachronic presentation. The individual work or author takes its place and submits to the judgment of its value on the basis of its function in the historical process. Gervinus's refusal as a historian to judge literature aesthetically does not mean that he withdraws to the more noncommittal mode of description but that he forgoes aesthetic judgment because it would introduce an absolute, transhistorical element into historiography. Since German history—at least the epoch between 1648 and the French revolution—does not allow for the constatation of a unified development, the history of literature must supplement this lack: "We have no princely dynasties that reflect for us the history of the German nation as a whole. The heroes of the intelligentsia replace them. We orient ourselves in terms of Luther, Hutten, Keppler, Herder, Schiller, Pestalozzi, Fichte, etc."[135] Here, literary history legitimates itself, much as in Heine, as the history of ideologies that accompanies material history but also drives it forward. As the history of ideologies, not as a specialist's science, literary history—which is not yet securely or exclusively anchored in the universities—attains its prominence. It owes its central position to the fact that together with literary criticism it mediates between the cultural and political systems. What is essential is not so much that it be general history as that it be critique—appropriation of the national tradition for the sake of projects to be realized in the future. In this sense, Gervinus's evaluation of Weimar Classicism as the high point of German literature on which nothing could follow but loss and deterioration functions as a polemical attack on Young Germany, the value of whose works as a substantial contribution is by implication negated. While Heine reacted to the end of the age of art by demanding that literature fulfill a new function, the responsibility for this new function shifted for Gervinus from literature to politics. In this way he was able to bind a progressive conception of history with an aesthetic that remained essentially indebted to the period of Goethe.

Criticism as Philosophy and Science (1837–48)

The tension in Gervinus's work between a progressive notion of history and a Classicist aesthetics is present in a similar form in the work of the Hegelian school, which exercises considerable influence on the literary criticism of the 1840s. This tension is present in the work of Arnold Ruge and Friedrich Theodor Vischer, for example, while Robert Prutz attempts—if in the final analysis without success—to break out of Classical aesthetics and to enhance the reputations of literary genres that have been regarded as non-art by the aesthetics of Classical and Romantic criticism. The site on which this tension gets played out is defined, on the level of theory, by the struggle over the inheritance of Hegel at German universities, which alters fundamentally the context of critical debate.

One of those involved, the young Friedrich Engels, expresses himself with extreme severity in a discussion of Alexander Jung's *Vorlesungen über die moderne Literatur* (Lectures on modern literature; 1842): "Young Germany has come and gone, the young Hegelian school has arrived, Strauss, Feuerbach, Bauer, the Almanacs have attracted the attention of the general public, the struggle of principles is in its most beautiful blossoming, it is a matter of life and death, Christianity is threatened, the political movement is pervasive, and the good Jung is still of the naive belief that the 'nation' has nothing to do but to await with bated breath a new drama by Gutzkow, a promised novel by Mundt, an expected bizarrerie by Laube."[136] Engels describes the transformation as the passage from an aesthetic-literary movement to a movement concerned with world views and politics. Under the influence of Hegelian philosophy the discourse has decidedly changed. Conceptual-systematic thought, to which the left Hegelians attribute greater clarity than to aesthetic forms, has displaced poetic literature and aphorism. Prutz expresses himself similarly when he later compares Young Germany to Romanticism.

It has become customary to read this change in literary climate as determined by the change of the throne in Prussia (1840) and the related incipient political hopes. The liberal course of the new government is supposed to have encouraged the intelligentsia. The effect, of course, was such that the government soon returned to repressive measures. Among other things, it wanted to dam up the influence of

Hegel's philosophy. The offer of positions in Berlin to Schelling and Stahl spoke quite clearly for itself. But one must not fail to recognize that the transformation of discourse described by Engels can be seen to have occurred already in the 1830s. The work that occasioned the struggles within the Hegelian school, Strauss's *Leben Jesu,* appeared in 1835; the *Hallische Jahrbücher* began publication in 1838; Feuerbach's critique of Hegel started as early as the 1830s—his essay *Zur Kritik der Hegelschen Philosophie* (Toward a critique of Hegel's philosophy) appeared in 1838 in the *Hallische Jahrbücher.* Around 1840 the new criticism was already visible. In the passage cited above, then, Engels was only formulating commonplace knowledge: the Young German writers had become silent or removed themselves from the arena of criticism. In any case, they no longer dominated as a group the literary public sphere.

Despite the fact that Gervinus cannot strictly be included within the Hegelian school, the historico-scientific structure of his project links him with this group. Both Gervinus and the Hegelians distinguish themselves from the Young Germans' style and notion of critique as individual characterization (*Charakteristik*). They give to the Young Germans' historicization of criticism a systematic and conceptually rigorous form. The literary criticism in the Hegelian circle sees itself as science and has little sympathy for the Young Germans' attempted popularizations in the feuilleton. Even the Hegelian left, which inscribes on its banners the transition from philosophical theory to political practice, moves within the frame of an academic discussion which, because of its abstract terminology, remains inaccessible to the broader public. If they believe themselves to be representing not the affairs of a coterie but the general public, this belief is based on the conviction that reason, unfolding itself in history, will attain its goal in any case.

The literary criticism of the 1840s stands unmistakably—as far as the institutionally decisive positions are concerned—under the sign of Hegel. Of course, one must not overlook that the reception and dissemination of Hegel's philosophy not only splits up into various camps (right, middle, left) but invokes certain of his writings more than others. For example, the literary theory and criticism of the Young Hegelians is much more decisively stamped by the philosophy of religion and history than by the aesthetics, which has thus less central importance for the political struggle of the 1840s. And where critics such as Ruge and Prutz refer importantly to the aesthetics, they are less centrally concerned with the systematics of the aesthetic theory (with which Karl Rosenkranz and Vischer grapple) than with Hegel's judgment of Romantic literature and especially with the question—already enunciated by Heine—of how literature can be judged beyond the end of the age of art. The conceptual frames of both these questions touch each other, of course, insofar as they both derive from Hegel's metaphysics of history, in which art, religion, and philosophy each has its place. But in the application to the contemporary situation, contradictions arise out of the fact that when the Young Hegelians infer activist political consequences from Hegel's construction of history as the unfolding of world spirit, these consequences are not easy to harmonize with the dictum on the end of art. The contradiction can be resolved only by assigning to art a new function that brings it into a more intimate relation with the process of political history. Ruge and Prutz both take this path when they declare themselves in favor of the politicization of art in their discussions of Herwegh and Ferdinand Freiligrath. This decision logically implies, however, a taking of distance both from Classical aesthetics and from the Hegelian critique of modernity. But Ruge is not ready, and Prutz is only partially ready, to take this step, while Vischer places himself squarely on the side of the aesthetics and makes clear his objections against notions of the possibility of politicization.

Hegel's philosophical interpretation of history (in contrast to both naive and critical interpretations) contains themes and motifs that can be variously interpreted. He assumes that history will prove to be reasonable as soon as it is regarded from the standpoint of reason. That is, he assumes that history can be interpreted as a total process unfolding itself according to rationally necessary principles. This assumption allows him to construe as a logical evolution the particular phases of this process, even and especially where they appear contradictory. For Hegel, world history, when it is philosophically constructed, comprehends all partial histories, hence also the history of art. Hegel provides history with a subject (world spirit) from whose standpoint historical totality can be constructed or construed, and he provides history at the same time with a goal—freedom. "World history," he writes in the introduction to the *Vorlesungen über die Philoso-*

phie der Geschichte (Lectures on the philosophy of history) "is the progress of the consciousness of freedom—a progress that we have to
(re)cognize in its necessity." The radical interpretation of the philosophy of history by the Young Hegelians concentrates above all on the
concepts of progress and freedom. The Hegelian left does not bother
itself much about the postulated reasonableness of history or the
totality of the historical process. Their objections ignite, first, around
what they feel in Hegel to be extraneous theological form and, second,
on the position of Hegel's philosophy with respect to the present and
the future. When Hegel passes the state off as "the divine Idea as it is
present on earth,"[137] he simultaneously legitimates the existing situation whose critique the Hegelian left sees as the essential task. The
dialectics of history cannot be suspended by being known philosophically; rather, philosophical theory must intervene in the historical
process. It can do this, however, with the means that Hegel has placed
at its disposal—namely, the dialectic, of which Ruge says in 1845:
"Thought is *this movement of reflection*. It is *origination* and *passing away*
in one, for each new thought is the negative survival [*die Aufhebung*] of
an old thought. The innermost core of the Hegelian system is revolutionary criticism—freedom!"[138] Thus, Ruge concludes that dialectical
thought must dissolve any system, including that of Hegel, for every
system is forced by its static character to become one-sided.

The thought of the radical students of Hegel turns, according to Karl
Löwith, around the question of how philosophy relates to the history
of the world;[139] it turns around the question of how theoretical insight
is to be united with the social practice of human beings affected by
history. Pure philosophy has, for the students of Hegel, reached its
end. In his system it has, according to its own concept, come to itself.
Reason has attained the full unfolding of itself. The only step that
remains possible is the negative survival (*Aufhebung*) of philosophy, its
passage into social and political practice. Insofar as this happens by
means of thought, a theory arises that radically forces the encounter
with social reality. When the left Hegelians give up the metaphysical-
theological foundation of Hegel's historicism, they nonetheless retain
the critical moment of historicization. Journals such as the *Hallische
Jahrbücher*, the *Deutsche Jahrbücher*, and the *Deutsch-Französische Jahrbücher* are the "fortresses" from which they launch their attacks.

By replacing Hegel's concept of reason with a concept of human self-consciousness, Hegel's radical students make man the measure of reason, and history the field in which human reason actively realizes itself. Hegel does include human activity in his philosophy of history as a decisively dynamic element: it is human passions and particular interests that the cunning of reason uses for the attainment of its own final end. But for the Hegelian left, history has become an immanent process in which human consciousness is, in the forms of religion, science, and art, the motor of a movement no longer subject to a cunning not its (nonmetaphysically) own. In order to attain the goal of freedom, human spirit must intervene; its theory must become practice. As early as 1839 this leads, in the case of the *Hallische Jahrbücher*, to a concrete struggle with the Prussian state. In their critique of Karl Streckfuss, Ruge and Echtermeyer insist that Prussian social relations by no means correspond to the Hegelian concept of the state, that the progressive Protestant tradition has been indeed broken off and suppressed. In 1840–41 the *Jahrbücher* reach the point in its criticism where the Hegelian conception of the system is rejected in favor of a negative dialectics. The consequences can be seen not merely in the realm of politics but also in the realm of art. "We can . . . recognize neither absolute religion nor absolute art, much less *absolute knowledge*, and will prove to him [Hegel] everywhere that such unfreedoms are repulsive to his own—to the eternal—principle of freedom and to the revelation of the absolute in history, i.e., to development."[140] From the historicization of absolute spirit follows the historicization and politicization of literary criticism.

For literary criticism, a double task presents itself (among others): on the one hand it must concern itself with the literary tradition; on the other hand it must—no less than philosophy—orient itself in relation to practice. The function of contemporary literature is now to be developed out of an analysis of the present. The criticism of the single work will have to invoke general historical categories in order to be able to define the work's status within the enveloping historical process.

Exemplary for this criticism of the tradition is Ruge's and Echtermeyer's treatment of recent German literature in the essay "Der Protestantismus und die Romantik" (Protestantism and Romanticism). The authors determine their task as the struggle for the "free structuring of our spiritual reality" and against "the recalcitrance of dejected spirits who are oppressed by a dark moodiness and resistant to the recently entered final phase of the Reformation."[141] When these critics, following Hegel, invoke the Protestant principle as that from which progress has emanated, they fix in advance the categories according to which they will partition the tradition and the standpoint from which they will make their judgments. Writers who can be included within the history of Protestantism are then viewed positively, for their works represent steps along the way to free maturity (*Mündigkeit*). What Ruge and Echtermeyer expect from this work is to exceed the subjective procedures of Young Germany; here, the evolution of history itself should pronounce judgment by clarifying the difference between progressive and reactionary forces. The treatment of the literature of the past should establish the foundation for the judgment of contemporary literature. The critique of political and literary Romanticism, which is what Ruge and Echtermeyer are really getting at, is thus founded in a reconstruction of German history of ideas since the Reformation, but especially since the eighteenth century.

Young Hegelian criticism attempts to address real issues rather than mere texts; the latter are merely the concrete materials of proof by means of which a thesis is proposed. For example, Romanticism is for Ruge and Echtermeyer not a literary school or movement that can be circumscribed with the help of a series of names (as it still was for Heine). It is a principle, to be sought in the concept, even before the facts of history come into view: "This entire circle of the *idée fixe*, of the Reformation principle of freedom become unfree; the circle that fixes, at its ease, the Idea in the arbitrariness of the subject, in part as mere feeling, in part as the movement of reflection, and fails to respect its objective, both historical and scientifically methodical, artistically lawful process—this entire circle we have called, not without being occasioned to this by the celebrities, Romanticism."[142] In contrast to Heine, who denounced the Romantic school as the forced return to the Middle Ages, the *Hallische Jahrbücher* insists, in Hegelian manner, on seeing modernity as the result of the subjectification of spirit that set in with the Reformation and has received its reactionary form during Romanticism. The history of German spirit determines itself in this view as the dialectical movement between irrational and rational tendencies. The high poetic literature of the age of Goethe appears then as the preliminary synthesis of this movement, while Romanticism plays anew the role of antithesis: namely, as the intuition of the absolute in the form of "fantastical and genius-addicted titillation." Hegel's philosophy then has the function of restraining Romantic subjectivity: "In this opposition of the prudent spirit to gloomy fermentation, to still-unfree self-emancipation on the ground of feeling and subjective willfulness, the developmental process of the Reformation principle lies before our eyes."[143]

Unmistakably, the logic of the development of spirit prescribes for criticism here the view it is to take of the individual text. The historical context is for Ruge and Echtermeyer less a social and political than a religious and philosophical context. The reconstruction of the history of spirit places literature and philosophy in proximity to one another as different moments of the same evolution. Critical discourse can comprehend both of them because, as a rational discourse, it carries both within itself in the form of their negative survival. In the final analysis it is the task of philosophical-critical argumentation to annihilate art as such and, by conceptualizing art in its historical development, to carry its living remains into philosophical-conceptual discourse; hence the minimal interest in hermeneutical problems, for this task is essentially a constructive one. The conceptualization of the individual text consists in demonstrating its specific logical and historical function.

For the historical criticism of the 1840s, the relationship to Weimar Classicism (Goethe and Schiller) is quite as important as it was for the Young German writers. One could demonstrate this in Ruge and Echtermeyer's manifesto against Romanticism no less than in the section of Gervinus's literary history that treats Goethe and Schiller. But the form of approach to Classicism has displaced itself. The moment of personal participation, which distinguished the assessments of Börne and Heine and also Gutzkow and Wienbarg, is lacking. Beginning with the *Hallische Jahrbücher*, the discussion centers on the status of the classics in the tradition of German literature. The problem comes to a head in the question of whether and how art could be possible after the "age of art" in Weimar. The treatment of Classicism proceeds in the context of the problematic of aesthetic theory as Hegel's lectures have defined it.

For the manifesto of the *Hallische Jahrbücher*, the treatment of Goethe and Schiller is the exemplary task of historical scholarship: "Those who have set themselves the task of knowing them aesthetically will not accomplish this task if they do not take into account the historical calling of these men and the pressure of the Protestant spirit toward this development in art."[144] Ruge and Echtermeyer already anticipate what Karl Robert Mandelkow attributes to Gervinus: namely, the establishment of a synthesis that reconciles the works of Goethe with those of Schiller instead of opposing them to each other.[145] The dualistic viewpoint is overcome. In the argumentation of the manifesto, Goethe and Schiller constitute the site on which the eighteenth century attains its closure.[146] Schiller is seen as the masculine principle, Goethe as the feminine in this internal dialectic. Goethe's subjectivity, of course, is criticized. Ruge and Echtermeyer hold against him that he merely arranges himself with the course of the world in his later period, whereas the task is to realize the "freedom of a rational totality of historical spirit."[147] Goethe's concept of renunciation (*Entsagung*) contains for the *Hallische Jahrbücher* a negative index; it becomes his confession of inadequacy for his historical task. The concept of individual self-formation (*Bildung*) appears here as an egoistical limitation, an aesthetic standpoint that fails to grasp the becoming of the absolute in time.

For Ruge and Echtermeyer, Goethe and Schiller remain at a stage that must be overcome historically. In the construction of this historical logic Jean Paul appears as the poet in whom the ideal subjectivity of Goethe and the subjective idealism of Schiller are united. Of course, this occurs not in the objectivity of a real idealism but in the extremist exacerbation of subjectivism. It is not necessary in this context to pursue the particular content of this argument, for our concern is not the history of the reception of Classicism and Romanticism but the conception of literary history as a critical procedure. The individual—either author or text— is justified as a moment in the development of reason. The objectivity of the procedure Ruge and Echtermeyer invoke consists in the mediate character of the critic's relation to the works he treats: the scaffolding of historical logic establishes the distance through which personal preferences and disinclinations are restrained. In this sense the settling of accounts with Romanticism, which remains strongly indebted to Hegel, is an attempt to demonstrate that Romantic theory and literature cannot be adequate to the goal of emancipatory history. What is said of Schelling is true of the whole movement: the principle of Romanticism is, in "a word . . . the Schellingian arbitrary subject, and the historical course of Romanticism is the extension of this arbitrariness over the entire objective world."[148]

The critical position that Ruge—whose interests lie above all in the realms of philosophy and politics—only occasionally formulates in historical essays and reviews stands at the center of Robert Prutz's literary activity. Indeed, it is he who must be seen as the authentic literary critic and historian of the Hegelian left.[149] Prutz is exemplary in several respects: first, in the uncertain status of the freelance writer who has failed to find an academic position because of the resistance of government officials; further, in the attempt to establish a connection between the academic public sphere and the broader public (in contrast to Ruge, Prutz knew how to express himself simply and clearly); and finally, in the combination of criticism with "creative" writing. Besides his historical and critical works, Prutz publishes political poems and plays that excite a certain amount of attention. Prutz considers himself a journalist, not an academic writing for colleagues and students. His conception of history and his concept of criticism is in large part indebted to Hegel. Prutz follows Hegel and Ruge in the evaluation of the Reformation as the decisive event for the development of modernity, in which "the infinite right of the individual, the autonomy, that is, the self-domination of spirit" is inaugurated as the "consciousness of the times."[150] He sees the Enlightenment in particular as the continuation of the Protestant principle that drives history onward. In the introduction to his history of the "Göttinger Hainbund" he explicitly defends the Enlightenment against its Romantic critics—without denying that the Romantics were partially justified: "Indeed, the criticism itself which turned, toward the end of the previous century, with such rigor—and certainly at the time with the fullest historical justification—against this Enlightenment, this criticism will doubtless not have fallen from the heavens like a meteorite; rather, as a historical moment in our development, as every other appearance too, the criticism of the Romantics is itself a daughter of that Enlightenment against which with a hasty hand it raised its cutting knife."[151] Prutz distinguishes himself from the editors of the *Hallische Jahrbücher* through the methodological consciousness with which from the very beginning he approaches the task of the critic and the historian, the two for him being identical. In a Hegelian manner he determines literary history as "a spiritual mirror-image, a theoretical repetition that has taken place first in the factual history of the peoples, in the practice of political being."[152] Literary history has its place in the history of spirit which, as authentic history, is played off against pragmatic history. It is worthy of note that Prutz distinguishes himself from the aesthetic viewpoint, which he accuses of an exclusive interest in the select few. When Prutz declares himself, in the introduction to his history of journalism, to be in favor of treating also minor writers, this is not so much because of piety as because of the conviction that the authentic task of the critic is to portray the course of history: that is, the process in which, indeed, also the smaller minds take part. Invoking Gervinus, Prutz asserts that the historiography of literature must portray the "continuity of spirit" as opposed to the discontinuous selection presented by aesthetic and philological approaches to the past.[153] If the latter epistemological interest is best circumscribed by the concept of commentary, Prutz postulates for scientific historiography a necessary context through which the singular is demonstrated to be a moment in the universal.

Prutz's concept of literary criticism is based on literary history; that is, his view of contemporary literature arises out of his conception of history. For him, history is not the past but the development of the past toward the present. In his words: "For this reason, the goal and focal point of contemporary literary history is not the past and its aesthetic exaltation; rather, it aims at the present, which it wishes to enlighten about itself and to stimulate to new creation, to new deeds, thereby accomplishing the highest task with which science is faced: namely this—to come alive through deeds."[154] If the purpose of criticism is the self-enlightenment of the public, the reconstruction of history is, for the left Hegelians, an essential prerequisite, because the contemporary task can be characterized only in terms of the evolution of spirit. Prutz's essay argues, of course, that this task can never be determined exclusively on the basis of the historical testimony of literature. The goal of criticism is to determine the contemporary situation, especially contemporary social practice. This historicization of criticism leads to its *politicization*, insofar as the realization of critical philosophy demands the intervention in sociopolitical relations. The critique of German conditions, especially the critique of the patriarchal state, is the prerequisite for what Prutz expects and demands from the literature of the present. When, in his essay on the opposition in Germany, Prutz defines the concept of the real state as an "organic, freely self-determinate life,"[155] he is emphatically characterizing the site of the nation's literary life. For Prutz, the concept of the people is indispensable. The real state proceeds, in contrast to the absolutist state, from the will of the people. While this critique of the political situation in Germany does not essentially exceed the demands of Ruge and Echtermeyer in the *Hallische Jahrbücher*, Prutz does infer consequences for the judgment of literature that bind him on the one hand to the strivings of Young Germany and anticipate on the other hand the efforts of the socialist movement to found an alternative culture.

According to Prutz, the legitimate opposition to the patriarchal state can express itself in Germany only in philosophical and literary terms because the political institutions are lacking that would convey this opposition more directly. But even in philosophical and literary forms, such opposition remains a matter for the educated elite, not a matter for the people. Even in literary history the German malaise mirrors itself, as Prutz emphasizes: German literature lacks a popular infrastructure. Both in the theory and practice of even its best works, as Prutz argues in his essay on popular literature (*Unterhaltungslitera- tur*),[156] it remains cut off from the needs and interests of the people. Prutz's approach can be instructive. His point of focus is not particular works and authors to whom interpretation attaches itself but general concepts applied to the historical situation—in this case, the distinction between an authentic literature and a literature of entertainment. When Prutz asserts that popular literature has not been taken seriously by historians, his critique applies also to the historians of the Hegelian school, who concentrate on authentic documents of spiritual development. Thus the vision of a history of popular literature cannot invoke idealism, for this literature represents what is precisely not essential to the development of spirit. The history of popular literature, in order to avoid becoming a mere abstract critique, must take into consideration the specific social conditions under which this literature has been produced and received. The interpretation of this literature, as Prutz shows in detail, cannot do without an investigation of its material bases.

Prutz argues for the rights of this literature by showing that the social relations of the nineteenth century, especially the intensification of the division of labor, hinders—if it does not render impossible—intercourse with authentic high literature. This legitimate argument, however, is not resolvable with Prutz's own conception of history, which ties the historian to the presentation of the essential moments of spirit. The contradiction becomes clear when one follows Prutz's argumentation further. The analysis of popular literature is the springboard from which he can introduce the concept of a people's literature (*volkstümliche Literatur*): that is, a literature that both corresponds to the needs and interests of the broad population, and can make a claim to authenticity, to philosophico-historical relevance. Prutz believes that the established division between high literature and popular literature can be overcome by the return of art, beyond the phase of its reflectedness, to a new naiveté. The concept of people's literature proposed here—and this Prutz fails to see—is not identical with the concept of popularity that he has used in the discussion of popular literature. By equating these two concepts, he apparently gains the basis for a new concept of aesthetics and criticism. In reality, however, the concept is first grounded in the left Hegelian philosophy of history and subsequently transposed as a demand into the realm of factual social relations. As the state should be grounded in the people, so literature should be grounded in the people. English and French literature provide the precedents here, just as German liberalism in general looks toward England and France to see its political demands realized. The west European literatures are, according to Prutz, in this respect superior to German literature because they are able to draw on practical life and can anticipate a public that is able to look back on its own political practice.

In Prutz's thought, political and literary innovation unite because both can be deduced from the concept of the people. But in what relation do they stand? Prutz provides contradictory answers. On the one hand he is convinced that literary opposition will remain ineffectual as long as it has no popular basis: "For our poets, however, there arises from this a special, additional disadvantage—that they never have an opportunity to get to know their people as such in great masses and to seize in a delightful image the traits of its visage. We have no public sphere, or at best a literary one."[157] On the other hand Prutz shares with the left Hegelians the hope of stimulating a political public sphere and inducing political change by means of literary-philosophical activity. The examples he uses reveal that these two strands of argument are not necessarily compatible. Where he speaks of the renewal of German letters, he points to authors like Jeremias Gotthelf and Berthold Auerbach; but where he treats the politicization of letters, he points to authors like Herwegh and Freiligrath, as well as to his own poems that deal polemically with the German situation. Prutz appears not to notice these tensions, because both political lyric and a people's literature, even if the latter should be quite conservative (as in Gotthelf), have one thing in common: they can no longer be justified in terms of Classical-Romantic aesthetics. In contradistinction to Ruge, for whom the positive evaluation of Herwegh's poems is exclusively decided by their adherence to the proper political tendency, Prutz remains aware that if measured according to the standards of Classical-Romantic theory, these poems would be denied all value.

It is appropriate to consider here Vischer's objections to the work of Herwegh. They relate to the literary form of the poems, not to the political opinions of the author. Prutz's essay on political poetry treats even the aestheticians—that is, the defenders of Classical aesthetics (the autonomy of the artwork)—as the real enemies of political lyric poetry. Since in Classical aesthetics a definite social or political purpose for the work of art is not admissible, the genre of political lyric poetry does not belong to art in the strict sense, any more than does the literature of entertainment. The politicization of art, which Prutz deduces from Hegel's philosophy of history, is not reconcilable with the Classical aesthetics that Hegel summarizes once again in his lectures. Whereas Vischer adopts at this point the standpoint of aesthetic theory and refuses for this reason the politicization of literature, Prutz is unmistakably at pains to solve the dilemma. He is searching for a new aesthetics. His critique of the traditional doctrine of art culminates in the characterization of this doctrine as the expression of political impotence. The moment a nation attains political consciousness, as Prutz's Germany has done, "this consciousness will find its poetic expression; there a political poetry will arise."[158] Of course, the decisive question is what the structure and substance of this poetic expression of the political will be. In other words, how does political consciousness translate itself into a literary text? Prutz's answer operates in terms of the all too well known: "Wherever there is really political poetry, there politics will already have become the content of the beautiful individual. The one points to the other; politics has the right to poetry, and poetry the right to politics."[159] The return to the concept of the beautiful individual leads to a familiar aesthetics, for the beautiful individual has become, through aesthetic education, the beautiful *political* individual. The gap between politics and aesthetics, which has been in the general consciousness since 1830, only gets covered up.

In his *Geschichte des deutschen Journalismus* (The history of German journalism), Prutz describes history as a series of three phases: the religious, the aesthetic, and the political. He demands that the aesthetic consciousness of the eighteenth century be replaced by a political consciousness: "Just as, previously, the abstract personality of the religious sphere had to fill itself with the content of art and thus to expand itself into the beautiful subject, so now the beautiful subject must take the content of history up into itself and extend itself thus to become the politically sanctioned, free citizen of a free state."[160] How does Prutz imagine to himself the passage from an aesthetic to a political age? The mediation lies in the notion of aesthetic education, which "makes the passage from the Idea of art to the Idea of freedom."[161] It is not by chance that Schiller's name is mentioned in this context. But as soon as it is, the aesthetic autonomy reappears to which the left Hegelian philosophy of history has denied value. Prutz is no more in a position to solve this aporia than is Ruge. Both of them fail to conceptualize with sufficient clarity the altered status of art— which is nonetheless apparent to them in a general way. As soon as they consider a literary text with a view to determining its aesthetic character, they remain the prisoners of Classical-Romantic aesthetics.

In this regard they can be seen to regress with respect to Hegel, whose lectures on aesthetics radically question the legitimacy of contemporary art. Hegel maintains that in the modern period (of Romanticism in the broad sense) there no longer exists the substantial coherence of form and content that characterized Classical art. As soon as the sphere of objects becomes infinite, as soon as any object in reality can become the object of aesthetic presentation, aesthetic interest begins to focus principally upon the (mode of) presentation (*Darstellung*) itself: "Such objects cannot satisfy a deeper sense which pursues a content truthful in itself; but if neither sensibility nor thought are satisfied, increased intimacy of (sensual) intuition reconciles one with this."[162] A "disinterested apparition" (*interesselose Scheinen*) occupies center stage—dissociated from content and from the reality that content mediates. The presentation (*Darstellung*) becomes a purpose unto itself. Through this subjectification of art the artist is granted a freedom he has never known before: he can do whatever he likes with his material.

For Hegel, however, this freedom is not a gain but merely proof that art can no longer claim the same truth-content as in antiquity and the Middle Ages. For these epochs, art could "find the appropriate artistic expression for the spirit of a people." The subjectivity of an artist merges here with the content and the consciousness of his times. In contrast, in the modern age as Hegel sees it, the mimetic content with which the artist begins is merely considered to be material in the aesthetic sense. "What we lose then is the most inner belief."[163] What is missing in modernity is the belief in the necessity of the materials as the true content of the work of art. For Hegel, it is the course of history itself that leads us into this situation—not a mere aleatory mishap that could simply be corrected. For Romantic art, which in Hegel's scheme follows upon symbolic and classical art, the external form (*Gestalt*) is arbitrary. In this epoch, the artist is "the effectively self-determinant human spirit, observing, contriving, and expressing the infinity of his feelings and situations, to whom nothing is foreign any longer which can come to life in the human breast."[164] The dissolution of this stage finally requires that, on the one hand, objectivity should be externally imitated and that, on the other hand, "in humor, the becoming-free of subjectivity" should proceed "in accordance with its inner arbitrariness." The historicization of art and aesthetics leads in Hegel to the thesis that "art is no longer the highest manner in which the truth procures itself existence."[165] This assertion, precisely understood, means not the end of art but the end of its centrality.

Left Hegelian literary criticism faces the problem of determining the contemporary significance of art in order to clarify the connection between art and politics. This problem, however, cannot be solved in terms of Hegel's aesthetic system except at the cost of important internal ruptures. The circle around the *Hallische Jahrbücher* is not in a position to offer a convincing solution to these problems. On the one hand they refuse the doctrine that art is a thing of the past in order to functionalize contemporary art politically; on the other hand they remain indebted to the Classical aesthetics of the age of Goethe. This contradiction has to do, among other things, with the fact that Ruge and Prutz adopt the Hegelian critique of Romanticism and even extend it to apply to Young Germany. The accusation of arbitrary subjectivity that they throw at all post-Classical literature invokes the objectivity of the Classical as its standard, yet they are not finally in a position to invoke this standard, because the historicization of literature has as its consequence the historicization of critical standards. The left Hegelians' partial agreement with the attempts of Young Germany does not exclude sharp criticism of these attempts. While Prutz does admit in 1847 that the young German writers have left Romantic self-sufficiency behind and want to "connect with and serve the great motive powers of life, history, politics, and the practical development of the life of peoples," he nonetheless accuses them of unclarity and immaturity.[166] Prutz sees Heine and Young Germany as the continuation of the Romantic vices of privatization and aesthetic self-sufficiency. Prutz's judgment of Heine is exemplary for the refusal of the Romantic pose: "Heine is Romanticism without romantic illusion . . . the merely genial willfulness that has nothing, wants nothing, other than itself—and even this his own self he detests, because he knows that he is worthless!"[167]

Ruge, in the *Hallische Jahrbücher*, arrives at a more positive assessment because he is more capable of appreciating the significance of wit to the prerevolutionary historical moment. But even he judges Heine by a standard in accordance with which his work must fail to suffice: "One cannot hold it against anyone that he does not want to *believe:* but it is a great failing for a poet not to see or know, in this untrue reality, the truly human world. Wherever Heine deceives himself about the true sense of reality, he falls out of poetry, and he is lucky when he falls only into prose, when he does not fall head over heels into the muck."[168] The later essay "Heinrich Heine und unsere Zeit" (Heinrich Heine and our times) intensifies this critique. Although Ruge does recognize wit as a weapon of criticism, he still accuses Heine of indifference and frivolity. Ruge underscores that the age demands satire, but he grants satire only a subordinate role. Concerning the relation between satire and the authentic literature that should master it, he writes: "For the time being the demons [of frivolity] are under our control; we have enlisted their power—that of knowledge, of persuasive form, and of a realistic beat—into the service of freedom and idealism."[169]

Between Revolution and the Second Empire (1849–70)

The revolution of 1848 was doubtless one of the decisive turningpoints in the political history of Europe. The defeat of the progressive forces assured for a while the continued domination of traditional political and social structures. In the long run it promoted in Germany a constellation in which the bourgeoisie had to renounce its radical demands in order to participate in government. But political events do not necessarily have the last word in the history of literature. What was the effect of the revolution on literature? Three aspects of the situation have to be distinguished in the attempt to answer this question: the situation of the writer, the structure of individual works and genres, and the literary system as a whole. For the radical literary intelligentsia, the political defeat meant that they lost the possibility of writing and publishing. They became silent or, like Georg Herwegh and Ferdinand Freiligrath, fled to foreign countries. Between 1850 and 1858, freedom of opinion was restricted and engaged political literature suppressed. The German governments made no bones about their intention to persecute democrats and republicans. The trial of Gervinus for high treason by the government of Baden is a case in point.[170] Still, one can observe that conservative writers like Emanuel Geibel achieved a success that had been denied them in the 1840s. The situation of the writer was, then, significantly influenced by the revolution and its aftermath. But even more important is the question of the degree to which one can draw meaningful connections between the revolution and ensuing alterations of literary norms and conventions.

Contemporary criticism is certainly convinced of the existence of such connections. In the *Grenzboten* in 1850, Julian Schmidt represents the standpoint that the revolution had been not merely a political but simultaneously a literary revolution. He distinguishes between the literature of the restoration (which he accuses of emptiness), the emphatic literature of the years of the revolution, and the postrevolutionary literature whose program he would like to propose. He says of the literature of the revolution: "But the German revolution had the strange characteristic that it was quite capable of competing with the poems of its prophets in terms of lyrical pathos, essential dreaminess, and dark and unclear longing. This is over now."[171] The connection between political and literary tendencies consists for Schmidt in this: that in political writing the division between the political and the aesthetic spheres has been removed. The consequence is dilettantism in both realms. Here, Schmidt is unmistakably attributing responsibility for the failure of the revolution to the literary intelligentsia of the pre-1848 period; its emphatic expression in literature is denounced as unrestrained and ill-behaved actionism. Eight years later Robert Prutz expresses himself in a similar vein in his literary history of the present. He too underscores that the revolution has brought a decisive literary turningpoint. The political defeat represents the end of the politicization of art and literature. For Prutz, the left Hegelian model of literature has proved to be of unsound construction, for it turns out to have overestimated the effect of literature on society.

Prutz and Schmidt draw from this insight the inference that literature will have to be placed on new foundations if it is to regain its proper significance. As Schmidt comments, "The only manner in which a rebirth of German poesy can be effected is by the removal [Aufheben] of dilettantism, not merely in art, of course, but also in life and thought."[172] This programmatic assertion entails not merely a distinction between the new program and the literature of the pre-1848 period but also the demand for a new theory of literature and a new poetics that would allow clear and distinct suggestions for future literary production.

The consciousness of an epochal turn can be seen especially in the literary criticism of this time. This consciousness expresses itself in the wish to submit literature as a whole to a new program—for which the concept of realism is introduced. Whether or not realist literary theory can make a claim to independence is doubtful, but beyond doubt is its claim to institute norms that distance themselves decidedly from the pre-1848 tradition. To these belongs among others the clear distinction between poetic writing and politics. This concerns by no means only political writing in the narrow sense; at issue rather is the hope of regenerating art by means of the regeneration of society formulated by Vischer and by the early Hermann Hettner before 1850. Hettner had expected that a healthy people's literature would arise out of the revolution. At the end of the *Romantische Schule* (1849) he had expressed these hopes quite explicitly:

> If a future blossoms for our poetry, it will be a great future. . . . Now more than ever we are on the way to this great goal. It is only a matter of turning political poetry into a historical poetry: i.e., into a poetry that is not, like the present one, composed out of the wish and the need for a beautiful reality but out of factual existence, out of the fullness and enthusiasm of this existence; we will then have attained what we want; we will have poets who move in the same element out of which Shakespeare's great poetry arose.[173]

The relation between literature and politics gets inverted here—and the later turn of liberalism already implicitly reveals itself in this. Literature is no longer the cause of political changes; rather, political revolution is the ground for a renewed writing. In the treatment of comedy, Hettner speaks of a revolutionary situation in which "unmistakably," as his quotation of a letter from Gottfried Keller puts it, "people and art wrestle together unconsciously here toward a new content and toward the emancipation of a gradually ripening ideal."[174]

The utopia of the new age of art that finds expression in Richard Wagner's essay "Das Kunstwerk der Zukunft" (The artwork of the future)—an essay that Hettner regards positively in 1850—invokes the authority of the aesthetic theory of the 1840s, especially that of Friedrich Theodor Vischer. Because contemporary society is characterized by alienation and because the reigning, prosaic social relations render a genuine literature impossible, the path to a new art must pass by way of the political alteration of social relations. Vischer refuses the literature of his time and demands instead the ethically transfigured representation of reality. According to a formulation by Willi Oelmüller: "Vischer therefore defines the beautiful as the promise of a good, perfected life. It is the 'anticipation, by means of appearance [*Schein*], of a perfect life or the highest good.' This appearance is not that of the lie, not untruth or illusion, but the project [*Entwurf*] of a successfully happy life, of a life that is reconciled with itself and the world."[175] Poetic writing anticipatorily approximates the overcoming of alienation and of contradictions. Thus authentic writing plays for Vischer the important role of preparing, by rendering reconciliation visible, an improved social situation. The demand for the idealization of reality arises for Vischer from the demand for the sensual realization of the idea. But precisely at this point the theoreticians of realism will decisively modify Vischer's construction.

The will to differentiate oneself from revolutionary radicalism can be detected both in the *Grenzboten* and in the *Deutsches Museum*. This programmatic intent does not, however, deny that the aesthetic theory—and through its mediation also the literary criticism—of the post-1848 period remains deeply indebted to the idealistic theory of the pre-1848 period. Vischer's authority—the first volume of his *Ästhetik* appears in 1846—remains uncontested even in the post-1848 period. This authority, behind which the shadow of Hegel still looms large, is owing to the fact, among other things, that in Germany a materialistically grounded theory of realism never asserts itself. For even the programmatic German realists rigidly condemn as "naturalism" the materialist realisms they observe, for example and above all, in France. On the whole it is therefore more appropriate to describe the changes in the field of literary theory as reconstruction and reinvestment of given concepts, whereas in the field of criticism the break becomes increasingly clear by means of the formation of fronts and camps. But here again we must not overlook the element of continuity. The opposition to the period of the restoration (Romanticism, Young Germany, and the pre-1848 period) attaches itself consciously to older traditions (Enlightenment and Classicism), which it then reinterprets and renders contemporary in terms of its own purposes. Even where the Young Hegelians are under attack, the historical categories that have determined the literary theory of the 1840s remain in force—though adapted, of course, for present cultural and political tasks.

The best example of this reconstruction is the critical activity after 1848 of Robert Prutz, who exercises considerable influence on the literary public sphere with the journal *Deutsches Museum*.[176] In the 1850s Prutz revokes his activist conception of literature as the vanguard of the historical process, but he nonetheless holds fast to the Hegelian model of history. Within this model, literature plays henceforth the role of a mere accompaniment, yet his criticism of the overweaning expectations of the pre-1848 period clings to the concepts of progress and humanization. The faith in historical evolution is unbroken. Indeed, it is in part even intensified by the incipient industrial revolution.

The remarkable optimism of the liberal intelligentsia, which recovers relatively speedily from its political defeat and begins already in the early 1850s to express its new demands in the cultural sphere, can be explained in part in terms of the continuity they maintain with earlier patterns of historical and literary interpretation. They do indeed modify these patterns in order to correspond to postrevolutionary relations of force, but they do not renounce the substance of liberal ideology in the cultural realm. Political liberalism does increasingly revoke its demands concerning the social totality and limit itself, criticizing its earlier expectations, to the representation of its own bourgeois class interests, but to some extent it retains and defends the legitimacy of its hopes within the realms of aesthetic theory and literary criticism. The bourgeois intelligentsia assert their leading role in the cultural sphere and attach their goal—evolution through education—to the efforts of pre-1848 liberalism (Auerbach and Vischer). The social contribution of literature lies, for the liberal theoreticians of the post-1848 period, in its educative power.

The emphatic notion of education (*Bildung*) strategically supplants in literary theory the notion of political tendency, from which the writers of this period wish to free (poetic) writing. The notion of education avoids revolutionary connotations and permits easy combination with notions of an upward technological development through which the situation of society as a whole should be improved. It has—with good reason—recently been objected to the thesis of postrevolutionary resignation that economic prosperity was in general read by liberals as a sign of social and humane progress; the political defeat of the bourgeoisie was seen as a temporary regression that could be made good again by means of economic expansion.[177] In this sense one reads in the *Grenzboten* in 1849: "It is not revolutions that build [*bilden*] the progress of humanity but what lies outside them: science, which researches the law of nature, and art in the broader sense, which reigns over nature and forces her to serve the human will. Both are as bourgeois as they could possibly be."[178] Like science, art can also serve progress. Under the sign of scientific positivism, which makes itself noticeable in literary criticism itself from the 1860s on, a positive social function can be ascribed to art—namely, as support for those tendencies from which the bourgeoisie expect progress. Art is presented with the task of confirming these forces. And realism proceeds to exclude whatever does not conform to this determination—including in particular those elements of the literary tradition in which critical reflection predominates, as in Jean Paul or in Heinrich Heine. Realism expects of the artist that he will discover in the present historical moment those tendencies that embody historical progress. The artist must have a sense for reality, not oppose the ideal to reality as the subjective idealists had done.

The realists no longer propose this task, of course, in the name of an explicit philosophy of history; rather, they see it as a moral concept centered on bourgeois virtues of honesty and the will to work. In the struggle with Georg Büchner, Julian Schmidt clarifies the appropriateness of an ethical grounding of poetic writing. If Büchner himself insists—in his review of his own drama *Dantons Tod*—that the writer not be a teacher of morality and that he not tamper with the historical figures he portrays, Schmidt rejects the notion of writing as a pure representation of reality: "The writer, who represents only a fragment of the world, cannot content himself with the empirical and imperfect. . . . Further, it is not even possible for the writer to provide a mere feeble imitation of the real; he must idealize, whether he wants to or not, and if he does not idealize in the direction of the divine, he idealizes in the direction of the infernal, as does the entirety of modern Romanticism."[179] What Schmidt misses in Büchner's work is the "healthier, more manly world view" which characterizes the realist author.[180]

The moralistic final purpose of writing leads by no means, as Schmidt's objections to Büchner indicate, to a theory of art as a mirror image of the empirically given. The realist program indeed retains from idealist aesthetics certain transcendent elements. The distinction between a true and a false realism, which assumes the abstract characteristic to be an index of truth, removes the realist program from those definitions that are motivated by sociocritique: "False realism in art lies in the incapacity to choose, even with the most glittering technical virtuosity, those moments that life brings forth: it is the same opposition as that between the artist and the virtuoso."[181] The realists demand the transfiguration of reality as the procedure through which the mimesis of reality can be synthesized with ethical engagement.

It is not our purpose here to trace in detail the theory of realism. We do have to sketch it in broad outline, for it determines in large degree the literary critical practice of the post-1848 period. The assumption of the older scholarship that there is no theory of realism in Germany, which René Wellek still repeats,[182] is due to the fact that only seldom is this theory coherently unfolded by the theorists themselves. It is most often discussed only in the context of treatments of particular works and authors. Theory and application pass incessantly into one another; the single work becomes the occasion for theoretical considerations, and questions of principle offer the opportunity for exemplary application. This interpenetration of critical theory and practice gives the post-1848 literary criticism its unitary stamp and distinguishes it from late nineteenth-century criticism, which regards programmatic theory with a more skeptical eye. Even where leading critics debate over principles and their application, they nonetheless agree that criticism is in need of theoretical foundations. Critical judgment is supposed to legitimate itself by means of the relation to *universal* aesthetic principles. Through this theoretical superstructure, realist criticism gains a prescriptive and not seldom dogmatic character: the realists approach the artwork with predetermined values and measure it, then, in terms of these values.

The realist program, represented above all by the journals *Die Grenzboten* and *Deutsches Museum,* takes a radical and polemical stance. It sees its task in the determination of a frame for the literature of the present in which this literature can fulfill its altered social function. The self-delimitation of this theory operates on the one hand against idealism, above all in its subjective variant—the tie to Hegel's aesthetics being maintained even while it is denied—and on the other hand against empiricism and its aesthetic forms, which are everywhere denounced as naturalism. The idealist tradition, of course, proves to be the stronger. The attempts to bind literature to reality and thus to gain a new point of departure for practice remain largely bound to idealist premises.[183] The moralistic foundation of art makes mimesis as the mere doubling of pregiven reality impossible from the very beginning.

Schmidt's criticism of Büchner clarifies this point. In order to reach its goal the aesthetic treatment of reality must idealize its object. The *Grenzboten* assigns to the "material imitation of nature" only a subordinate place, even where this imitation obeys the laws of poetry.[184] Nonetheless, realist theory insists that reality, not an abstract ideal, should be the object of the presentation. Julian Schmidt's formulation situates the problem quite precisely, if without providing its solution: "This extension and absorption of ethical ideals into the details of real life is the necessary, the only basis of a genuine and great poetry."[185] For how is the penetration of profane reality by ideas to be achieved without doing violence to the reality, disturbing the objectivity of the presentation? For the theoreticians of realism, the concept of objectivity contains more than the Classicist distance that had been admired in the mature Goethe. The objectivity they seek relates to a transcendently conceived, extra-aesthetic reality. Julian Schmidt says on this point: "This new principle no longer concerns inner but outer reality— not self-correspondence but correspondence with so-called reality."[186] The observation and presentation of this reality is the precondition for poetic imitation, but not more than a precondition. It is a matter not merely of the exact and objective registration of empirical materials but, beyond this, of a selection that corresponds with the ethical purpose of art. Only the essential elements of reality deserve to be taken up into the work of art: "The sharper the eye of a poet for what is essential to mind, the better he knows how to abstract from the arbitrary and inessential in his times, the more Classical he will be: i.e., the more enduringly will he remain comprehensible and valuable to humankind."[187] Certain moments of reality should be traced in such a manner as to become more than a bit of reality, in such a manner that they enclose and expose within themselves the Ideal. The Ideal should be inlaid into reality. In this way, an illusion will be created for the reader that the events have happened as they have been narrated, and that the characters have behaved as they have been described.

It is not the thought of autonomy that leads in realist theory to the demand that art not restrict itself to copying empirical reality. This theory does not satisfy itself with the formal argument of the self-legislative nature of art. For this reason, the characterization of post-revolutionary literary criticism as Classicistic is easy to misunderstand: it is Classicistic in its belief in norms and rules but not in its understanding of aesthetic production. In the background—as Otto Ludwig has most clearly expressed—looms the problem of totality. How can the totality of the real be aesthetically represented? If the totality is seen as a harmonic whole, there arises for aesthetic production the task of seizing the structure of this whole in a literary mirror image. The aesthetic world is characterized, according to Ludwig, by the fact that it is more transparent than empirical reality. It allows the order of the whole, which in empirical reality remains hidden, diaphanously to appear (*durchscheinen*): "A piece of world [is] rendered whole so that necessity and unity are not merely present but made visible. The main difference between artistic realism and artistic idealism is that the realist leaves his recreated world as much breadth and multiplicity as is compatible with the conceptual development in the work, so that the unity of the work imposes itself on the eye perhaps with greater difficulty, but only that much more majestically."[188]

Realist criticism never delivers the philosophical foundation it promises. The wish to hold solutions in abeyance is not helpful in the clarification of the problematics of foundation. A look at Rudolf Gottschall's poetics or at studies by Julian Schmidt or Robert Prutz reveals that the realists hardly even discover, never mind solve, the contradictions inherent in realist theory. The formation of opposing standpoints—for example, the frictions between Gottschall and the critics of the *Grenzboten*, or the vehement controversies between Gutzkow and Julian Schmidt—do not clarify much of anything, for they assume the concept of reality (*Wirklichkeit*) to be established from the start. For example, Gottschall criticizes Gustav Freytag and Schmidt, arguing that the presentation of labor—that is, of ordinary, everyday reality— is not appropriate to poetic writing, but in this critique Gottschall uses the very conceptuality he attacks, simply giving it a different emphasis.[189] On the level of theory, one can agree with Ulf Eisele when he argues that realism marks not so much a new beginning as a continuation of the problematic of the pre-1848 period: "One cannot speak, in the case of programmatic realism, of the sort of 'paradigm-change' that marks a genuine break in the history of theory. Rather, realism represents the last remaining resource in the struggle for the maintenance of the ruling paradigm: the traditional concept and consciousness of literature."[190] This characterization applies also to the realists' practice of literary criticism. As much as the realists attempt to distinguish themselves from the epoch of the restoration, the model with which they operate is still indebted to older traditions. Realist criticism owes its position not least to post-Hegelian idealism as represented by Heinrich Gustav Hotho, Friedrich Theodor Vischer, and Moriz Carriere.

The realist program is comprehensible only if we take into account the influence upon it of Vischer's version of idealist aesthetics. Especially the arguments for the limitation of the imitation of nature and the demand for a *transfiguration* of reality are adopted from Vischer's theory, even if they function differently there than after 1848. Vischer's distinction between the tasks of rhetorical persuasiveness and poetry, his assumption that poetry should have a special task, leads to the postulate of transfiguration: "The task of art, especially of today's art, is to stimulate to deeds by means of art, by means of the ethically transfigured mimesis of reality."[191] The ethical improvement of the world that Vischer wants to see is an immanent task; in the same manner the aesthetic critique of reality—that is, the transfiguration of the profane—is an immanent question.

Vischer's concept of reality—and this distinguishes him from the theory of the post-1848 period—remains tied to the Idea. Thus he distinguishes three stages of reality: at the highest stage, the Idea; at the lowest stage, empirical objectivity; and between these, the reality of art that rests already on a certain selection from the empirical. For Vischer, the student of Hegel, however, the reality of the Idea is the standard for all stages of reality. Therefore, art has to do not merely with the presentation of empirical reality but with the mediation between Idea and empirical reality. The presentation of reality in art may, indeed must, exclude that which is merely *aleatory*. With this, both the ugly and the ethically repulsive are clearly assigned a merely marginal position: "The ugly is allowed, if it breaks through sparingly and in the appropriate places."[192] This stance with respect to the ugly remains characteristic for German realism all the way to the late Theodor Fontane. The demand for realism must not be understood in the case of Vischer as a demand for proximity to the empirical, for in this way truth would not be gained; truth in the mode of aesthetic presentation arises rather only where this presentation goes beyond arbitrary elements and establishes an order in which the Idea becomes visible. "Like the novel, the drama must seek out the places where the prosaically understood and really prosaic order of history is broken through, discloses itself and offers an image of freer movement."[193] This sentence from the *Ästhetik* clarifies that the artist must adhere to the elements of reality that allow one to divine its inner coherence with the Idea.

Whereas the literary program of Vischer is directed essentially toward the future, the present being disqualified for him as a period of transition, this orientation disappears in postrevolutionary criticism. Anticipatory form reduces itself to the mirroring of the sensuously concrete, without of course abandoning its claim to truth. To this extent, the distinction between empirical and emphatic reality cannot be sacrificed. Both in the *Grenzboten* and in the *Deutsches Museum*, critics distinguish between phenomenal and authentic reality, the presentation of the latter becoming the task of the artwork. But even given this continued privilege of the emphatic, empirical reality has decisively greater significance for realist theory than for idealist theory. It becomes indeed the point of departure for aesthetic mimesis. Ulf Eisele has rightly pointed out that in realism the distinction in principle between literature and reality is removed: "Literature and reality [do] not coincide, but they are *partially identical.*"[194] The higher reality of art, on which realist criticism—no less than Vischer—insists, receives its foundation in empirical reality. The possible problematization of aesthetic truth, as it has been undertaken by Hegel, is not pursued further in post-1848 criticism. To the contrary, it is suppressed as an endangerment of poesy. This is the reason for the realist disinclination to reflexive and subjectivist narrative. One result of this disinclination is the dogmatic character of post-1848 criticism: it is not prepared to discuss the problematic of post-Classical art. In this way the realists attempt to forestall the threatening abstraction of the capitalist world and the loss of meaning bound up with it. The emphatic meaning that appears lost in the social world is to be saved in the work of art.

Let us illustrate this procedure with several examples. Prose and especially the novel occupy the center of critical interest in the 1850s, even if aesthetics still has not granted it equal rank with epic and drama. The critics follow with great attentiveness the production of stories about village life from which they expect the turn toward realist presentation. Auerbach and Gotthelf become witnesses of the new realist prose. Doubtless, however, the narrative of the village (*Dorf-geschichte*) cannot replace the social novel as it is represented in England by Dickens and Thackeray. In the search for models the realist critics return again and again to these English writers, even if they are not always in agreement with the realism of detail and occasionally miss the search for a higher aesthetic truth. The discussion of the novel concentrates above all on two works, Gutzkow's *Ritter vom Geiste* (The knight of the spirit; 1850–51) and Freytag's *Soll und Haben* (Debit and credit; 1855). Both become objects of heated controversies in which the critics involved attempt to determine whether or not these novels fulfill the expectations of realist theory. The situation itself is telling: the expectations exist even before the novel that should fulfill them appears. Only after the publication of *Soll und Haben* do most critics feel that they have found the paradigmatic novel capable of constituting the genre anew.

Julian Schmidt's review of Gutzkow's *Ritter vom Geiste* exemplifies the stance of the circle of critics publishing in the *Grenzboten*. The condemnation claims neither more nor less than directive control of the genre of the novel. Through his criticism, Schmidt wants to steer the form of the novel in a particular direction. He therefore accuses Gutzkow of belonging to the older tradition, especially of Jean Paul, and of attempting to present a total image of society on the basis of subjective narrative reflections and allegorical characters. Schmidt deplores the lack of plasticity in character depiction that is supposed to distinguish the realist novel: "This is a manner which has been frequently employed in recent years but which deserves the strictest censure."[195] But the accusation goes further. Gutzkow fails, as far as Schmidt is concerned, in his attempt to write a novel of the times because "he has attended throughout his entire life only to the appearances swimming on the surface, which do arise out of the general movement of spirit but do not provide an adequate expression of this movement."[196] This objection describes quite precisely the expectations of the critic: the construction of a novelistic plot in which concrete characters give the impression, through their behavior, of an order that points beyond itself to a higher truth. At no point in his extended discussion does Schmidt attempt to analyze Gutzkow's novel in terms of its own intentions or to interpret the work immanently. His condemnation invokes principles whose self-evidence he takes for granted.

Even reviewers who judge the novel more sympathetically, such as Karl Rosenkranz, prefer this stance. For Rosenkranz, the decisive question—which he asks of Gutzkow's preface—is, what should one expect of a contemporary social novel? Significantly, he grants the legitimacy of allegorical-typological presentation, to which Schmidt so strenuously objects, on condition that the author objectively present the various tendencies of his time—the political factions struggling for domination—without allowing narrative subjectivity to intrude. Rosenkranz's (Hegelian) reservation concerns instead the form of the novel, in particular the intention to create totality by operating on several levels at once—"as if," he remarks, "poetic totality lay in an encyclopedic thoroughness!" He is skeptical about the serial novel (*Feuilletonroman*), of which *Ritter vom Geiste* is in his opinion an example, because one cannot attribute to its construction any principled advantage over the individual novel (*Individualroman*). If he nonetheless praises the work it is because, despite its weaknesses, he sees realized there the higher truth toward which art should strive: the reader "can . . . everywhere sense the urge upward toward the good and beautiful."[197] Rosenkranz thus sides with Gutzkow's politics, which Schmidt refuses. In both cases one is confronted with an ideological critique; both invoke similar aesthetic principles.

The debate on *Soll und Haben* is not less ideological. For the circle around Julian Schmidt, the novel fulfills the realist program. For Theodor Fontane, too, Freytag has managed the great work that will bring international recognition to the German novel. He praises in particular the virtues of Freytag's composition: "We have spoken till now of the structure [*Bau*] of the novel and believe ourselves to have discovered the causes for the wonderful composition of the novel in the dramatic schooling and proficiency of the author. The refined precision of his motivations and a certain irresistible power of his dialogue also deserve mention at this point."[198] The closed tightness of the novel is proof for the critic that the claims of reality and art, characterization and Idea, are susceptible of unification. Fontane does not entirely fail to notice that this idealized image of the German bourgeoisie is proposed at the cost of other social and national groups; nevertheless, he does not let this substantially mitigate his positive evaluation. The critical reception of the novel substantiates the ideology of the text. As one might expect, the same is true for Julian Schmidt, who takes a stance on *Soll und Haben* in the fourth printing of his literary history in 1858. Even more clearly than Fontane, he underscores the glorification of the bourgeoisie. Further, he emphasizes the positive function of humor. Freytag, he says, "does not seek to delude as to the dangers of the conflict, but he awakens in every healthy heart the courage to struggle with the disagreeable elements of life and to emerge from them free and innocent. This healthy courage for life appears in part in the old form of humor."[199] Beyond this, Schmidt takes Freytag's novel as an occasion to establish once again the distinction between the realist novel and the false tendencies of the pre-1848 period. In lines that move toward a polemic against the 1848 revolution, he writes: "This extension and absorption of ethical Ideas into the details [of life] is the necessary, indeed the only basis for a genuine poesy."[200] Freytag's novel proves to be the fulfillment of this demand: "Freytag has exactly studied farming and business, and this is why his studies are as convincing as they are warm, and the depiction of the typical figures clear and transparent."[201]

Schmidt's judgment is utterly in accord with Freytag's political intentions. Freytag's main concern is political engagement.[202] His radiant history of a business family named Schröter underlines the claims of the bourgeoisie against the aristocracy even before the bourgeoisie have had the opportunity to formulate these claims in the political sphere. The few opponents of the novel understand this quite well. Hermann Marggraff's review in the *Blätter für literarische Unterhaltung* (Journal for literary entertainment), which repeatedly polemicizes against the *Grenzboten*, puts its finger on the novel's weakness.[203] It argues that Freytag is not the objective, realist novelist that other critics have praised but rather a prejudiced writer who presents reality in a particular way. The glorification of bourgeois labor appears to Marggraff as a philistine foreshortening insofar as this glorification concentrates on business. T. O. Schröter and Anton Wohlfahrt, the book's two positive figures, always behave honorably and capably but never disturb the established order. The critical reviewers read *Soll und Haben* as the model of a postrevolutionary existence in which the bourgeoisie have abandoned their political goals in favor of a crude materialism. As one anonymous review states, "The author has wiped away and carefully suppressed as if intentionally everything that could smell in the least spiritualistic and idealistic, and it is for this reason that his glowing book is nothing more than an apotheosis of an intrinsically crude materialism."[204] It is, of course, worthy of remark that neither the anonymous reviewer nor Marggraff takes the novel as an occasion to place the principles of the realist program in question. Even Robert Giseke, who characterizes *Soll und Haben* explicitly as a work of the restoration, uses realist theory in his critique.[205] This theory is by 1855 no longer a matter of controversy. What is debated is its application to a concrete work.

By comparison with the pre-1848 period, the literary-critical discourse in the epoch between 1850 and the foundation of the Second Empire is moderate.[206] The extreme literary feuds of the 1830s and 1840s have disappeared in connection with the transformation of the political climate. The postrevolutionary repression in general puts a damper on the tone of the literary discourse; literary criticism as a subsystem of the institution of literature has the opportunity to reconsider its role. But the sobriety of criticism is not explicable solely on the basis of the new political situation; rather, it is most intimately bound up with the function of criticism in literary life as a whole. Criticism assumes the task of regulating literature both in its production and in its reception. Thus the treatment in reviews always involves a decision as to whether an individual work should be accepted within the canon of literature or excluded from it, a decision as to what status the work has in relation to what various other works, and so on. Julian Schmidt formulates this task in the *Grenzboten* with great clarity: "What sort of aesthetic and ethical impression . . . what particular impression has the poet attempted to make on his audience? Can one grant one's approval to the intended impression or not? . . . in what relation do the work's images of the good, beautiful, and true stand to the ideals that the general consciousness already comprehends?"[207] But for Schmidt, criticism is not exhausted with the evaluation of the individual work. Criticism's essential labor consists in the mediation between the particular work and universal concerns. In this connection the theoretical system is more important than the individual text. The critic describes and evaluates the work in relation to programmatically formulated expectations and with respect to the desired reaction of the public.

Such normative discourse can become polemical if the text to be judged does not correspond to the judge's expectations. There is general agreement on the critic's right to make value judgments on failings and shortcomings; on the other hand, there is general disapproval of the subjectivity of personal feuds in which ad hominem arguments are used, because criticism is understood as an *objective* procedure where known aesthetic rules are applied to a particular thing. Under these conditions, controversies can arise when critics disagree with respect to premises or when the same text is judged in different ways. In this case, however, the personal polemic so characteristic of the pre-1848 period is inappropriate. The subjectivity of the critic—his sensibility, his preferences and disinclinations—is in this model relatively limited. It has a legitimate function in the mediation between universal and particular but is not permitted to become a purpose unto itself.

If one presupposes the theoretical program of realism as the premise of interpretation and evaluation, the business of criticism becomes a matter of logic and convention, even given the personal involvement unmistakably present in such critics as Prutz and Marggraff, Freytag and Giseke. Both the subject of judgment and the work judged are finally replaceable; the maintenance and promotion of the literary system as a whole is what matters. Although this postrevolutionary criticism still orients itself with reference to the Classical model of the literary public sphere and hence in terms of the assumption that the critic speaks for the public, professionalization is nonetheless by this point so far advanced that criticism hardly takes into account the opinions of the reading public. The regulation of the literary system is left to a small circle of writers who influence by means of their opinions both distribution and, to a certain extent, production.

The promotion of the fiction of village life is a good example of this form of literary politics. The literature of the village receives extraordinary attention from the post-1848 critics because it is thought to contain the seed of realist prose. If before 1848 the fascination of this literature for the critics resided above all in its popularity (*Volkstümlichkeit*) and in its oppositional, liberal stance, after 1848 the criteria have changed. Gotthelf's and Auerbach's prose provides the model for the new realism. In 1850 Julian Schmidt plays out—in connection still with the discussions of the 1840s—the literature of the village against the Romanticism that has allegedly proposed an idealized and false image of the people. He sees a line of development from Immermann to

Auerbach to Gotthelf, in which, finally, modern reflexivity is totally overcome. "The Swiss [Gotthelf] has no need to shake off the somnambulism of our poetry of moonlight and the gray spiderwebs of our dialectics; he is still naive with respect to overexcited sensibility and faithless sophistry."[208] This naiveté recommends the writer Gotthelf even where his critic is no longer in agreement with him. Schmidt goes so far as to accept the Christian conservatism of the Swiss because it provides literature with an ethical foundation. "But there are also healthy natures to whom heaven is only a hinge to which they attach the earth and its law. They believe in this world, in the right and good and beautiful that reveals itself within this world. And because they deduce this belief from a world beyond, it is quite natural that they attempt to give it a form as concrete, positive, determinate, and historical as possible."[209] Gotthelf's prose is exemplary for Schmidt because it knows how to depict its object, life on the farm, in a concretely intuitive manner. Still, Schmidt qualifies the exemplary character of Gotthelf's prose at the end of his discussion: although German literature can learn from Gotthelf, his work cannot become the paradigm of the new realism, for the Swiss stories are to the German reader mere idylls, not the people's literature that criticism seeks.

During the 1850s the critics adopt a new attitude toward the literature of the village. The voices denying this literature its exemplary character multiply. Whereas the reviewer of Auerbach's *Barfüssele* (Little barefoot girl) in the *Weimarer Sonntagsblatt* (Weimar Sunday Times) underscores anew the realistic character of the literature of the village,[210] other critics emphasize its idyllic character and thus negate—at least implicitly—its value as a realistic presentation of life on the farm. Such qualifications can be found in Wilhelm Hauff, but above all in Vischer, who situates the literature of the village in idyllic literature and warns against overestimating it: "Village stories definitely have their value, but one must not overestimate the entire form, and the proponents of this form must be very careful not to deceive themselves about the approval of the lorgnette-ing [*lorgnettirenden*] eye of modern society."[211] After the appearance of *Soll und Haben* (1855), the village story to a great extent loses its exemplary function for realism—evidently, not for just formal reasons: Freytag has opened up a thematic realm that stands closer to the bourgeois reading public than the world of the farm. He transfers the detailed realism of the village stories to the novel of education and society and thus constitutes the new model.

If one pursues the literary discourse of the post-1848 period in its more significant cultural journals, one can observe differences of theory and style between this discourse and the discourse of the pre-1848 period, but the basis of literary discourse remains constant. Journals such as the *Deutsche Museum*, the *Grenzboten*, the *Blätter für literarische Unterhaltung*, and the *Preussischen Jahrbücher* (Prussian Almanac), to name just the most important, are quite similar to the journals of the pre-1848 period, even though they represent different world views and literary positions. Both the realm and the structure of communication remain essentially the same. These journals address educated readers, and their printings are correspondingly small. Their editors consider themselves to be publicists who have taken up journalism in order to promote the formation of opinion, not in order to earn money. The industrial revolution that begins in the 1850s changes within a generation the structure of German society and thus the composition of the reading public, but the institution of criticism at first hardly participates in this structural change. While the literary system as a whole conforms to the new conditions, the subsystem of literary criticism maintains itself in the form that has emerged in the early liberal phase. As a rule, the critics cling to the role that fell to them in the Enlightenment. This self-confidence justifies itself in terms of the fact that the number of educated readers has markedly increased: criticism thus promises itself increasingly broad effectuality.

The development of the book market appears to confirm this impression. Between 1852 and 1871 the number of booksellers rises at a decidedly higher rate than the population. According to the calculations of Ronald A. Fullerton, the increase in booksellers between 1851 and 1861 is 14.75 percent; the increase in population 11.93 percent. The following decade sees an increase of 46.67 percent in booksellers but an increase of only 14.37 percent in population. The statistics on the geographical distribution of the German book trade are instructive. In the large cities and central Germany the book trade expands its concentration, while elsewhere, especially in the East, it is relatively inactive. The extremes lie at 1,570 inhabitants per bookseller in Frankfurt am Main and 76,500 inhabitants per bookseller in East Prussia. In

Dresden the number of booksellers increases between 1842 and 1860 by 20 businesses (about 75 percent), in Hamburg by 22 (about 90 percent), and in Munich by 15 (about 80 percent).[212] One can conclude on the basis of these figures that the number of readers expands, although the number of annually published titles in this period actually decreases. (The 1850s are a particularly crisis-ridden time for the German book trade.) One can speak with certainty of a condensation of literary distribution and hence also of literary communication, even if it is not the entire population that takes part in this process. The social borders of the literary discourse apparently change little for some time. The purchase of books, even in the post-1848 period, remains a privilege of the upper social strata, above all of the educated bourgeoisie—the group that literary criticism sees as its addressee.

Yet the general reading public does seem to change both quantitatively and qualitatively in the years after the revolution. One can see this first of all in the literacy data. The percentage of illiterates begins to drop after 1850 more quickly than before. In 1875, 2.4 percent of persons in the German Empire are illiterate; in 1880, only 1.6 percent. Naturally, one cannot conclude that the majority of the population is interested in literature. But these figures are significant, though one must compare them with the situation of the 1850s in order to estimate the tendency of the change. In 1857–58, 20 percent of the conscripts in the province of Posen are still without schooling. For the year 1851–52 the statistics on the conscripts in Prussia show that 5 percent are illiterate and 20 percent have had insufficient schooling.[213] The increase in formal literacy is the result of Prussian school politics, which, by means of compulsory schooling, wants to familiarize even the proletarian population with the basic elements of education. At the same time, the expansion of the council schools (*Stadtschulen*) and nonacademic secondary schools (*Realschulen*) is supposed to provide the petty bourgeoisie with the opportunity to gain qualifications. Students who will not later study at the university are the main target of these educational programs. The proponents of the nonacademic secondary schools argue already in the 1840s that the expansion of a nonacademic middle school is necessary in order to prevent overcrowding and excessive democratization in the academic secondary schools (*Gymnasien*).[214] The struggle beginning in the 1850s for the equal rights of the nonacademic in relation to the academic secondary schools can be interpreted as the striving of a new social group for the educational privileges of the upper bourgeoisie.

Such an interpretation gains support from a remarkable transformation of the realm of the media. While after 1848 the book market at first shrinks and does not start to expand again, slowly, until the 1860s, the newly emerging family magazine is an indication that the reading public is expanding and is in any case much larger than the circle of book buyers. The number of copies printed of the *Gartenlaube*, founded in 1853, indicates that in the late 1860s a journal can count on approximately a million readers every week.[215] One can study the interests of this mass public in the contents of the family magazines: they concern themselves, according to the empirical studies of Dieter Barth, with (1) belles lettres, (2) biography, (3) history, (4) geography and ethnology, (5) popular natural science, (6) cultural history and art, (7) trades and professions. This broad program is calculated to address a heterogeneous group of readers. Interestingly, however, there is no literary-critical discourse—or, rather, it is limited to biographical contributions to literary history. The family magazines are no longer interested in current literary discussion. Their editors define their public as a family, and the needs they assume to be proper to this institution become the standard of information. "The family-related themes were treated such that nothing exceeded the mental level of any family member and nothing came up that could disturb the order of the family."[216] The beginnings of a consumer culture, in which the needs of the public are manipulated from without, are unmistakable.

The differentiation of journalism and the simultaneously incipient commercialization of the daily press change the context of literary criticism in a manner that critics in this period do not fully comprehend. There is no lack of the traditional reservations of the literary intelligentsia concerning the superficiality of the public, but the augmentation of the reading public and the extension of secondary education make an impression of universal progress and so block off insight into the structural changes with which literary criticism is beginning to have to deal as an institution in a thoroughly capitalized industrial society. While critics like Freytag and Auerbach are still demanding that a people's literature be created, signs are accumulating on the book market that the popularization of the classics is less a question of broadened education than a question of business. The cheap editions of the classics thrown onto the market in 1867 (after the change of the copyright law) are for the most part publishers' speculations for which the enlightenment of the public is nothing but the figleaf.

The postrevolutionary model of criticism as a regulatory activity gives rise to a curious contradiction: at the moment when the potential influence of the critic rises as a result of the intensification of communication, a large part of literary production escapes his control. And this part includes not merely the popular literature, which even before 1848 has been beneath the dignity of the reviewing trade, but also such new media as the family magazines. Thus, along with the classical cultural journals it is above all the daily press that appears as the medium for literary criticism. The transregional journals increasingly assume this function, since the numerous local cultural journals of the pre-1848 period have failed to survive the capitalization of the press.[217] But here, too, the limitations of the liberal model can be seen. In the culture section of the newspapers, the feuilleton, rules are in force that diverge from those of the literary journals. The journalist who writes for a daily paper must deal with a heterogeneous public. He can presuppose in his readers neither familiarity with nor interest in aesthetic theory and poetic norms. For these readers, high literature is a mere topic of conversation. Thus the critic writing for a feuilleton sees himself either as a mediator of information or as a participant in the kind of literary chitchat that has been the rule in the French press ever since the 1830s. When the *Wiener Zeitung* (Vienna News) introduces its feuilleton in 1848, the editors remark that this section pursues other goals and must use other methods than the main part of the paper: "The feuilleton section must be absent neither from the splendorous chambers of the Duchess nor from the mansard of the grisette. In the feuilleton section the witty epicurean Jules Janin opens up his tripod and oraculates on tragedy and comedy, providing a brief but hotly desired and often expensively bought immortality. The meetings of the Academy of Science, the achievements of the annual Salons, as the Parisians name their painting exhibits, are discussed here, and the significant inventions of industry, the daguerreotype and a thousand others, announced to the public."[218] In this passage, the editors distinguish the feuilleton unambiguously from serious literary criticism: the subject of the latter is argumentative reason; the subject of the former is the associative imagination.

The structural change of the literary public sphere of which we have spoken here remains largely hidden to contemporaneous criticism. The ideal of the critic continues to be that of the free publicist who controls his own means of production. The critic steps up before his public in this role and expects from it a certain familarity with literary conventions. But this concept of the public, which critics such as Prutz and Julian Schmidt still invoke, becomes more and more abstract. The gap between the enlightened reader they postulate and the average actual literary recipient yawns ever wider. In other words, by around 1870 the liberal model of critical reasoning, of criticism as reason, has dissolved its ties with social practice. Criticism arrives at the fork in its road; it must henceforth choose one of two directions. In the realm of the press, literary criticism enters the context of the feuilleton section and receives from this context its stamp in terms of both form and content. In the realm of the university, criticism as reason(ing) attaches itself to the discourse of science. The establishment of academic departments and professional journals are indices of the insulation and isolation of academic criticism from the general public sphere; one could illustrate the consequences of this quite well by looking at the case of Wilhelm Scherer and his school. But the tendency to define the critic as an expert is not limited to positivism. It is visible also in Wilhelm Dilthey's attempts to place literary history on a firm scientific foundation by returning to the hermeneutic tradition.[219] Scherer and Dilthey are both still trying to maintain the connection with an educated public: Scherer's literary history is conceived for the educated reader, not for the professional; and in the 1860s Dilthey does not consider himself above publishing in *Westermanns Monatsheften* (Westermann's monthly—a general, not scholarly, magazine). Tendentially, however, academic criticism withdraws into its professional journals and develops a discourse that becomes increasingly incomprehensible to the general public. From the 1860s on, literary history (as an academic discipline) and literary criticism are divided.

TRANSLATED BY JEFFREY S. LIBRETT

RUSSELL A. BERMAN

. . . .

Literary Criticism from Empire to Dictatorship, 1870–1933

IN the wake of the revolution of 1848, the literary critical discourse underwent important structural changes, including economic transformations that rendered the autonomy of critical judgment increasingly questionable. The industrialization of the press commenced, leading to the consolidation of the three predominant newspaper companies of the imperial period—Scherl, Ullstein, and Mosse. Both this rapid growth of the industry and the plethora of family periodicals profoundly influenced the forms of literary life. While commercial motivation had certainly played a role in the press before 1848, it had remained subordinate to literary or political goals.[1] However, during the two decades after the revolution, commercialism effectively displaced the older political press, a process bluntly described by the sociologist Ferdinand Tönnies: "All who have written recently about newspapers agree that the newspaper—at least the large ones—is and has become a capitalist venture, whose immediate goal is therefore to make profit from the business. Consequently, writers must orient themselves in accordance with this goal and conform to it—they must assert what promotes it, keep silent about what hinders it: the understanding of the commercial interest of the paper determines the 'spirit' of its pronouncements."[2] This commercialization of the press changed the situation of the writer, including the literary critic writing for the press, who corresponded less and less to the image of the Enlightenment *raisonneur* and became increasingly a wage laborer, having no right to dispose of the means of production. The formation of the journalist-critic's judgment thus increasingly fell under the influence of external pressures. The issue is one not of individual moral corruption but of the undermining of the critic's autonomy by the capitalization of the literary public sphere. The profit-oriented press gradually commodified its own content, transforming the critic into an employee and his autonomy into an ideological illusion.

This economic process, eroding the independence of the critic reduced to wage laborer, was amplified by a second factor, an anticritical bias within the culture of realism. Both tended to restrict the free judgment of the critic and lower his social status. Indeed, the critic suffered an enormous loss of prestige during the second half of the century. His diminished power within the commercial apparatus was echoed in widespread negative designations: the realist Julian Schmidt placed the critic beneath the active politician; later, for the naturalists, he was merely the servant of the creative artist; in general, the public held him in distrust or even contempt.[3] This antagonism toward the critic was compounded by the accusation of corruption; the common belief in the critic's venality, especially characteristic of the late nineteenth century, is more significant than actual cases of demonstrated bribery.

Meanwhile, critical autonomy was under attack from still another side: after 1848 the state, particularly in Prussia, tried to control the public sphere less through censorship than through indirect influence. To be sure, state intervention in the press largely concerned political news, as the example of the so-called *Welfenfonds* makes clear. However, at least after 1866 in Prussian-occupied Hanover, the Prussian press office pursued a definite cultural policy of distributing prepared feuilleton articles to newspapers. At the same time the industrialization of the press contributed both to a centralization of journalistic production in the new news agencies and to a loss of power of the individual editor.[4] Both factors made government influence easier—influence that could scarcely have succeeded in the political press before 1848, despite all the censorship. In addition, as in the case of putative commercial corruption, the vicissitudes of criticism depended both on the actual influence exerted by the state and on its subjective correlate, the popular belief that the journalistic writer disseminated judgments only in the service of capital or the state. As the early critic of capitalist journalism Heinrich Wuttke put it:

The newspapers have been wrested from the hands of the writers. An element alien to their nature has interpolated itself and subdued them. What is meant to be literature is turned into mere business, and the individual who is supposed to be independent is nullified; he is only given the choice obediently to follow alien directives or to renounce the influence of the periodical press. . . . In this sphere too the self-reliance of the individual person retreats before the oppressive all-consuming superior power exercised by great wealth and the sovereign authority of the state.[5]

Literary Criticism around 1870

Karl Frenzel, the theater critic of the Berlin *Nationalzeitung*, also regarded the 1848 revolution as a crucial watershed. In the preface to his collection of theatrical reviews, *Berliner Dramaturgie* (1877), he interprets the failed revolution, curiously enough, not as the failure of democracy but as a turningpoint toward the political freedom that, according to him, was about to unfold in the new empire. Theater criticism before 1848 suffered, he claims, from the fact that the theater "had been the only public institution in which all could participate, against which criticism was permitted."[6] Before the revolution put an end to censorship and opened up unlimited political discussion, literary criticism provided a forum for the criticism of political matters. In the empire, however, this political discussion belonged in the Imperial Parliament, understood as heir to the earlier public sphere. This typical Wilhelmine depoliticization of literary institutions led the critic to restrict the function of contemporary theater to pure entertainment. Consequently, literary critical practice abstained from issues of contemporary relevance; it was conceived neither as engaged political agitation nor in idealistic aesthetic educational terms. Criticism could serve posterity only through a historicist recording of contemporary events: that is, descriptive accounts of theatrical performances. In the turn toward documentation the nineteenth-century predilection for concrete facts can be seen, as well as a variant of Wilhelmine discretion: the publicity-shy critic was not eager to speak his own mind but tended to prefer "only" to document.[7] This passive attitude recurred in the view of historicity typical of the time that Friedrich Nietzsche unmasked in his *Unzeitgemaesse Betrachtungen* (Untimely reflections): the linear image of time allowed the critic to subordinate himself to a longer development, to undervalue the significance of his own present, and, finally, stressing his own flaunted modesty, to claim an inactive role in the public sphere as well as in history. Love of detail, teleology, and passivity, familiar characteristics of nineteenth-century culture, indicate the institutional crisis of criticism; the erosion of critical subjectivity led to a depoliticization of criticism, which, robbed of its prerevolutionary polemical tone, tended to avoid hard confrontations.

Treating his own critical prose as documentary material toward a future theater history, Frenzel explicitly regarded the plays he discussed as historical documents. Each dramatic work is placed with scholarly precision in its historical context, while the contemporary significance of possibly topical references is not mentioned. Apart from the university philologists, almost no critic after Frenzel devoted as much attention to the historicity of the literary work. But the banishment from the critical text of all links to the present is nowhere else nearly so complete, as can be shown by the example of his discussion of a performance of *The Marriage of Figaro* in the Royal Theater on May 12, 1862. By situating Pierre Augustin de Beaumarchais's play in the French *ancien régime*, Frenzel does not intend to suggest comparisons with contemporary Prussia; on the contrary, he presents the historical distance as an unbridgeable gulf, thereby denying the drama its erstwhile political content. For Frenzel, only amusement remains: "With the Revolution Beaumarchais's comedy lost its political content, its Aristophanic aspect; it is just a comedy, no longer a tract or a political speech." Since the critic denies any historical continuity, he arrives at a completely depoliticized, purely formal judgment. This exclusion of political content is maintained despite the urgency of the conflict over the Prussian constitution, when the play's topicality must have been particularly evident: "Junkers still exist but there is no longer a Count Almaviva with medieval feudal rights. In this respect therefore *The Marriage of Figaro* now awakens only historical interest; it does not directly follow the line of Molière's comedies into the realm of charming illusion; it wears its rococo tresses, but one thing remains safe: its Figaro and its irrepressible bubbling gaiety. It overflows with the champagne foam of drollery."[8]

Instead of politics, only entertainment, not because the play was unable to arouse any topical interest—in view of the explosive domestic political crisis the opposite was more likely to have been the case—but rather because the model of literary criticism to which Frenzel was committed renounced any political claims in order to adjust to the conservative normalcy of the postrevolutionary period. Frenzel's historical discussions, characterized at times by extraordinary academic erudition, were intended above all to prevent the production of a historical continuity and to hinder any political reception. Forced into passivity, the critical subject was thereby denied the possibility of historical change, as the past degenerated into a field of completely alien controversies quite unrelated to the present.

Frenzel saw no historical continuity between drama and the present, yet there was for him another compelling ground for the discussion of literary works. The categories of Classical Weimar aesthetics, which had formed around the historical experience of the French Revolution but which in Frenzel deteriorated into epigonic conventions, gave the critic a convenient and, during the second half of the century, not infrequently used apparatus for the evaluation of new literary works. So, for example, he meets Christian Friedrich Hebbel's *Die Nibelungen* with the charge that the world of Nordic mythology, "the wild, murky, and vague," does not belong in drama: the ambivalent and secret belong to lyric poetry; heroic breadth is the concern of the epic. Mythic material is not suitable for drama, for "drama requires humans, human will, human deed and guilt; myth points beyond to the eternal and unresearchable." Evidently, Frenzel is not concerned with the success of the individual play, not to mention the quality of its performance. Instead, the critic measures each literary work by inherited categories that have collapsed into rigid formulas. He ascribes priority not to the work in question but to handed-down requirements of a normative poetics: "Tragedy requires no magic caps or mysterious potions, but only one thing: the full and complete human. And where is that in Hebbel's tragedy?"[9] Neither the impressions and feelings of the critic nor the contours of the work itself are thematized. Instead, one finds extensive commentary in the terms of the poetic code of the early part of the century—not adapted in an analytic procedure but merely applied for the dispensation of censure. Allowing himself no judgment of his own, the critic acts simply as the literary executor of a misunderstood Classicism.

The reified usage of inherited categories served, like historicism, to displace political evaluations with purely formal judgments. Frenzel rejected war dramas such as Paul Heyse's *Colberg* because, again, the breadth intrinsic to their subject matter was appropriate not to drama but to the epic. He raised a similar objection to Karl Gutzkow's *Prisoner of Metz* (which Theodor Fontane also attacked, though with a completely different critical strategy, discussed below). The play had to do with the presentation of military confrontations between Germany and France in the sixteenth century, and it opened during the Franco-Prussian War in January 1871 in an atmosphere of heightened patriotism. The public responded to the contemporaneity of the play, both intended by the author and recognized by the antagonistic critic Fontane. Frenzel, however, noticed none of it; he commented only on the action as bursting the formal bounds of the drama: "If one must duly acknowledge the felicitous idea, the inspiration of the author, to work a theme artistically that carries within itself so many and such unforced connections to the present, there does on the other hand arise as a considerable difficulty the superabundance of subject matter."[10]

The normative poetics, the view of history, and the depoliticization that characterized Frenzel's literary critical strategy resulted from an increasingly conservative culture in the decades of defeat for democracy and liberalism. The social retrenchment of the bourgeois subject determined the weakness of literary criticism that manifested itself in Frenzel as a self-inflicted attenuation of his own subjectivity and critical power. Although Frenzel long remained an important voice in the literary world, an opposing critical model soon emerged that sought to draw its critical force precisely from the reassertion of critical subjectivity.

Subjectivization of Literary Criticism: Feuilletonism

In the course of the 1860s and 1870s, a radical shift took place in the discursive structure of literary criticism. While the dominant model relied on the application of stereotyped categories in order to prevent any politicization of critical judgment, the concepts of an epigonic poetics disappeared from the new critical direction; on the contrary, an open animosity was often to be detected toward a culture felt to be old-fashioned and toward its theoretical language. Critical discussion was no longer organized around tradition and aesthetics but, instead, around a center that had been taboo for the older criticism—the subjectivity of the critic; it thus formed the journalistic correlate to Nietzsche's attack on the empty formalism of bourgeois culture. The claim to treat literary works with a fixed, systematic, and therefore purportedly objective conceptual apparatus yielded to a tendency to give precedence to the critic's own feelings and reactions, without claiming for them any universal validity. The impressions of the critic were registered, and the critic appeared accordingly as a person within the critical text. At the same time, the description of these concrete impressions required a more sensuous language, characterized by a wealth of images completely absent in the older discourse. This subjectivist literary criticism—which conservative critics pejoratively dubbed "feuilletonism"[11] in order to emphasize the distinction between mere journalism and a critical science—was thus able to thematize contents that Frenzel, for example, had sytematically excluded. Subjectivist criticism could even return, though in an indirect way, to the political themes that had disappeared since 1848. But at the same time the expanded receptivity of critical discourse involved the danger that the critic would merely dwell in passing on colorful impressions, losing any critical incisiveness. The immanent dynamic of feuilletonist literary criticism thus moved between the two poles of subjectivist politicization and uncritical chatter.

Paul Lindau, a typical representative of this direction during the first two decades of the empire, had spent the 1860s in Paris, where he began his career as a critic in the shadow of the French *prince des critiques*, Jules Janin, in whose work the typical feuilletonist features were already manifest: absence of system, thematic expansiveness, and sensual language, which evoked either admiration or (as in the case of Charles-Augustin Sainte-Beuve) the standard charge of corruption. Lindau appreciated Janin's chattiness as a capacity to incorporate broad ranges of experience that had been excluded from established criticism: "He wrote down whatever came to mind—and something always came to his mind—even if it had rather little or even nothing at all to do with the object about which one wanted to hear from him. He took his reader intimately by the arm and went for a stroll with him.

He did not stay long on the broad avenue. He soon turned down a side road, which soon led to another detour. He had to follow the detour too. And then also a narrow shady path, where one could chat nicely about all kinds of things without being disturbed. No one else knew about chatting as he did."[12] The image of the critic as flaneur, who observes and discusses the variety and randomness of the big city, indicates the potential richness of feuilletonist discourse, a discourse in starkest opposition to Frenzel's categorical criticism, at whose center was neither the work nor experience but the inherited aesthetic concepts of German idealism.

Feuilletonism's undervaluation of the theoretical moment was explicitly thematized as a hostility to theory, which fed on contemporary empiricist inclinations. For example, in March 1875, in his critique of Ludwig Anzengruber's *Hand und Herz*, Lindau stressed his own indifference to the problems of conventional poetics: "I would not think of rousing up good old Aristotle out of his retirement once again on this occasion and talking about pity and terror and the famous catharsis and testing on the touchstone of the Poetics whether Anzengruber's work is genuinely tragic or not. I rather think that when an author writes a play in which the hero or heroine meets his or her downfall, then he can in good conscience call the piece a tragedy; one should be less concerned with the question whether this designation is accurate than whether or not the play is good."[13] This was in evident opposition to established critical practice like Frenzel's. While Frenzel, who accepted as valid the classical trichotomy of genres, saw himself compelled to reject a drama whose construction was too epic, Lindau unsparingly denounced the inherited poetic requirements: only the successful work is good, not the rulebound work; consequently, the critic is not foremost a judge but a receptive connoisseur of art.

This restructuring of judgment reflected the erosion of the concepts of an old bourgeois-aristocratic culture in the context of rapid industrialization and social change following the founding of the empire, for social modernization could scarcely tolerate the hegemony of epigonic cultural forms. The feuilletonist attacked in the name of his own sensibility the cultural legacy of an ossified tradition increasingly reified as the conservative canon. Yet this program of cultural modernization was itself characterized by an implicit irrationalism: the chatting critic can distinguish between good and bad only intuitively; rules are not necessary; and the reader should ratify the judgment without being able to grasp any argument. Despite the modernizing force of feuilletonist criticism, its characteristic mode of judgment seems antithetical to the Enlightenment precept of mature self-reliance.

This paradox was repeatedly thematized in Theodor Fontane's theater criticism. The undermining of the autonomy of the writing intelligentsia can be demonstrated with virtually paradigmatic clarity in Fontane's early years as a journalist. After initial contributions to the radical *Dresdner Zeitung* in 1849 and 1850, he felt compelled to accept a secure job in the Prussian Central Office for Press Affairs, initiating a twenty-year-long association with the conservative wing of the newspaper industry. But Fontane was very well aware of the extent to which economic constraints had brought about his change of ideological camp. He wrote on November 30, 1851, to Bernhard von Lepel: "I have sold myself today to the forces of reaction for thirty pieces of silver a month and am again a paid writer (in verse and prose) in the employ of the holy 'German Reform,' the resurrected 'Adler Zeitung.' One cannot get by as a decent person. My debut is a poem in honor of [Otto von] Manteuffel. Content: the minister-president crushes the (inevitable) dragon of revolution. Very nice!"[14] Experience of the deformation of public writing by economic and state factors was still, at the beginning of his critical career, interpreted individually, as if Fontane had met a particular fate. Nonetheless, the relationship between the social status of the writer and the character of critical judgment is clearly recognized.

Forty years later, at the end of his career, Fontane could grasp this problematic in its full social scope: the impoverishment of the writer and his even more advanced loss of prestige resulted in the total dependence of the journalistic wage laborer. "The position of the writer is miserable. It is hard to determine which country takes precedence with regard to this calamity, yet it may be said that Prussian Germany has always figured in the front rank and is successfully occupied in maintaining itself on these old heights. Those who trade in literature and the politics of the day get rich, while those who produce them starve or just scrape by. From this money-misery results something worse: the ink-slave is born. Those who work for 'freedom' stand in unfreedom and are often worse off than the medieval serf."[15] The interests of journalistic capital ("those who trade in literature") and of writing labor power are irreconcilable; the capitalization of the public sphere creates, according to Fontane, the "ink-slave," fully deprived of the autonomy of critical judgment. This does not have to do with the charge of corruption against the critic, which for Wuttke still carried a strongly moralistic accent, but rather with the social-historical description of the proletarianization of the writing intelligentsia. Fontane was certainly not the only one to have this experience in the society of the late nineteenth century, for in the first decade of the twentieth century a series of trade organizations was founded to defend writers and their professional interests: the Defense League of German Writers (*Schutzverband deutscher Schriftsteller*) in 1900, the Cartel of Lyric Authors (*Kartell lyrischer Autoren*) in 1902, and the Union of Playwrights (*Verein der Buehnenautoren*) in 1908.[16]

Because the foundation of these trade-union-like structures was based on the recognition by authors of their social role, Fontane's complaints seem to have anticipated certain developments. Having referred, not without irony, to the eventual nationalization of literature as the solution to ink-slavery, he came up with a strategy in which the self-consciousness of the author was of central importance: "Approbation is the great means to help writers. If it fails we must look for something better. And that exists. It is called: greater respect for ourselves."[17] After the turn of the century, in the context of an increasingly powerful workers' movement, this "greater respect for ourselves" was able to lead to the new forms of organization. But "greater respect"—that is, a heightened awareness of social subjectivity—has a prehistory in Fontane's critical practice. There, as in the feuilletonist criticism of Lindau, the voice of the critic as subject becomes central: the subjectivization of literary criticism, breaking radically with inherited discourse, is born of a transformed self-conception of the writer, who is able to perceive both the modernity and crisis of contemporary society.

Fontane's description of English journalism, written at the end of the 1850s, shows how the experience of social modernization strongly influenced the character of his own literary criticism. Sojourn in major foreign cities was of great importance for the development of German literary criticism in the nineteenth century: Heinrich Heine and later Lindau in Paris, Fontane in London. The advanced social-historical developments and their cultural consequences made the German ob-

servers aware of social tendencies that would come to the fore somewhat later in Germany during the course of the empire. If the sojourn
abroad granted the critic a certain head start in cultural discussion,
conservatives reproached him exactly because of the foreign influence
(see below). Fontane's London experiences led to the development of
a literary critical practice much indebted to his descriptions of the
London *Times:*

> The *Times* editorial represents the complete victory of the feuille-
> ton style over the remnants of official prose and other misshapen
> sons and daughters of Latin Classicism. Long phrases are pro-
> hibited; sentences follow upon each other rapidly like revolver
> shots. The writer, if he has—as an exception—any thorough
> knowledge, is strictly obliged to bury his treasure and may at
> most intimate that he is in possession of it. Knowledge and details
> must not become tiresome. The well-written *Times* editorial is an
> arabesque that gracefully coils about a question, a bauble, an
> ingenious illustration; it is coquettish and aims to please, snare,
> subdue, but it never dreams of aiming to convince for all eternity.
> It is never an impartial judge, even if it occasionally acts like one; it
> is an advocate and fights less for truth than on behalf of its clients.
> That it adopts the pose of infallibility only goes to show how
> insecure it feels. It does not aim to be exhaustive, only to be
> stimulating; it appeals to the bribable imagination, not to the
> sober understanding.[18]

Feuilletonism is identified above all as a thoroughly modern mode of
writing; the break with "Latin classicism" corresponds to the turn
away from the inherited critical discourse of Frenzel. The new critic is
no longer a man of thorough learning but rather a savvy journalist for
whom stylistic charm is as essential as the insightful aperçu. In Fontane's description the standard charge of corruption is incorporated as
a characteristic of a critical strategy that addresses the "bribable imagination," less for the sake of truth than for that of the "clients." The
description of London prose is a song of praise for a new way of
writing that Fontane was to make his own as theater critic for the
Vossische Zeitung.

Fontane's critical strategy is marked above all by its renunciation of a
normative code that would guarantee infallibility.[19] Of course, there

are traces of contemporary aesthetic systems in his texts, but they have there precisely no systematic value. Not conceptual order but the critic's observations and feelings constitute the point of departure for the treatment of a work: "I do not go to the theater with ready-made opinions. I simply wait for the effect."[20] Thus the person of the critic as bearer of an aesthetic sensibility became the heart of the critical model that opposed itself to established criticism, that relied on an unquestioned canon and inherited poetics. The role of the observer, which Fontane claimed for himself, did imply a tendency to be hostile to theory, which still bore traces of the hostility to criticism inherent in the postrevolutionary culture of realism. Yet when in the first decades of the Empire an affirmative-representative national culture emerged, Fontane's position made possible a critical view that had to regard with skepticism the cultural-conservative rejection of noncanonical works. By placing his own feeling above systematic aesthetics, he attempted to make room for works that did not correspond to the conventions. Thus Fontane's subjectivism could both attack the conservative canon and, less progressively, contribute to the development of the culture industry. The antinomies of feuilletonism were evident in the fact that no rational grounding for the hegemony of critical subjectivity was offered: the feelings of the critic were simply asserted as valid within a discursive situation in which their validity could not be demonstrated.

As the concerns of inherited aesthetics lost their importance in the feuilletonist text, the critic gained the ability to express his opinions on nonaesthetic, even political matters. But just as the observed detail was ranked higher than aesthetic principle, so also was politics addressed only in passing—when motivated by some impression during a performance—rather than directly or systematically as an object of principles. Thus the regional accent of the actress playing Clärchen in a performance of *Egmont* occasioned the following melancholy reflection upon the cultural character of the new nation state, with its profound tensions between the Rhineland to the south and Prussia and Brandenburg to the north:

> Voice and form, that was the magic of this Clärchen. The voice. How this Rheinish-southern German wrapped itself pleasingly again around our heart! It makes us feel with a bit of pain that we

on our sandbar of the March may be Germans in a political sense but certainly not in a national one. We are something different, something peculiarly, perhaps (for those who care to hear it) something of greater intellectual potency, but we do not have the real German tone, at least not in our throats, and for the near future, Havelland and Zauche will not be the birthplaces of the Clärchens and Gretchens. The Main line still holds for them, and when they arrive here, we perceive with a sort of desire and humiliation how "she was not born in the valley." Each one of them—a maid from afar, a relative of that family, doomed to extinction, which once under the name of "Poesy" had its place in German hearts. She has now made way for the "founders." A horse, a horse! Seven Clärchens for one construction site![21]

The attention Fontane paid to questions of performance at once distinguished him from normative criticism as practiced by Frenzel, for the feuilletonist regard for the sensual detail was not exhausted in a consideration of the literary work but turned also to other things, above all to the theatrical experience. Moreover, in the foregoing passage Fontane takes up a detail that was of interest only in the political context and not because of the problematic of the work: the southern German coloration in the actress's speech brings up for him the question of national culture and Prussian hegemony in the new empire. With the help of literary allusions to Schiller and Shakespeare, he points out that the political victories of Prussia could not make up for its cultural deficiencies. For poetry—that is, for Schiller's "maid from afar"—and the actual actress playing Clärchen, home is still south of the River Main. The northern Germany of the founding years, in which industrial backwardness relative to England and France was made good with brutal rapidity, valued not beauty but only the economic development of the "construction sites." An examination of the significance of the content in this critique of prosaic Prussia would exceed the limits of this study.[22] What is important here is the typical feuilletonist strategy: the detail that catches the attention of the critic forms the center of the treatment, from which other themes are allusively touched upon without any exhaustive discussion. Such discourse either remained a chatty description of the critic's sundry impressions—one thinks of Lindau's positive account of Janin—or permitted the critic to raise the political themes that had been eliminated during the postrevolutionary repression. That this immanent potential for politicization could lead to more provocative statements than those of the Clärchen passage is evident in a revealing exchange between Gutzkow and Fontane.

As noted above, Frenzel judged Gutzkow's *Prisoner of Metz* in terms of classical poetics and came to a purely formal conclusion that because of its complexity the subject matter was not suitable for the stage. In contrast, Fontane thematized an aspect of the drama that ran counter to his own sensibility, an aspect that went beyond formal matters and raised explicitly political questions. In an autobiographical memoir he recalls his reaction to the play and the ensuing events: "Its anti-French quality was still just passable, but it happened also to be anti-Catholic, and that with a vengeance. And anti-Catholicism born of narrow-mindedness has always seemed something particularly terrible to me. And now at a time when a German army composed half of Catholics was in an enemy country, in such a time, an anti-Catholic play, or at least a main character in it who portrays Catholicism as disgusting!" The critical rejection of Gutzkow's play was evidently based not primarily on aesthetic objections but on a competing political position. As a critic, Fontane considered himself obligated to respond to the political tendency of the play. Also typical of feuilletonism was the way in which the polemic was conducted: less a principled laying-out of the underlying questions than an entertaining persiflage on the content. The background to the action is described as the "confused and intrigue-ridden feuds accompanying and following the Reformation, decades in which all kinds of things can be found but precisely not what is called, with special emphasis, 'German loyalty.'" The chauvinism of 1870–71, to which Gutzkow's play was indebted, is here unmasked in a humorous polemic, and an account of the content occasions a corresponding trivialization of the pretentious intention. In addition, Fontane explicitly thematizes the contemporary significance of the play: that is, he is ready to confront aesthetic with nonaesthetic perspectives: "The families Saldern and Ahlden-Uslar will scarcely be able to derive new aristocratic pride from the ancestors here foisted on them, and, concerning the abbot of Loccum and the prelate of Trier cathedral, we confess to having marveled at the courage of the stage to present such figures and at the forbearance of the Catholics to endure them. Even for our Protestant sensibility they were too much."[23] Aristocratic figures on the stage are thus seen in conjunction with present-day noble families; Catholic figures in the drama do not remain fictional forms but are taken to be representatives of real Catholicism. From the subjectivist point of view of feuilletonism, the distance between social reality and aesthetic appearance, between "life and art" shrinks to nil.

The radicality of Fontane's break with the earlier literary critical strategy is evident in the angry protest letter Gutzkow wrote to the editor of the *Vossische Zeitung*. Of course, the irritation of the criticized playwright may be explained in part biographically and psychologically.[24] Nonetheless, Gutzkow was able to sketch the line dividing an established literary criticism from the new feuilletonism: "Let Mr. Fontane find some small literary sensationalist rag for such a method of criticism. Objective reporting, control of his lust for personal revenge and subjective jokes are due the *Vossische Zeitung*, as is a measured and calm evaluation of what is offered on the stage in simple accordance with the laws of art."[25] Gutzkow was used to the public literary criticism exemplified by Frenzel, with his scholarly tone and dispassionate objectivity. Fontane's review startled him with a new way of writing whose central elements he was able to discern with remarkable clarity: subjectivity (that is, the starting from one's own, even eccentric, interests), a relatively informal style, and above all the contamination of literary critical discourse with extra-aesthetic questions—for the feuilletonist did not pursue an inquiry "simply according to the laws of art." Even the rather moderate politicization of criticism mediated by the subjectivity of the feuilletonist generated the vocal opposition of the representatives of the older model.

Feuilletonism and the Decline of Liberalism

Gutzkow's rejection of feuilletonist discourse was still guided by the postrevolutionary wish to restrict literary criticism to purely aesthetic questions. At the beginning of the 1880s a new element became prominent in the discussion of criticism, one that engendered a radicalization of the opposition to feuilletonism. In their journal *Kritische Waffengänge* (Critical passage of arms), the early naturalists Heinrich and

Julius Hart demanded a "Sedan of the spirit," a German victory over French culture as decisive as had been the German victory at the Battle of Sedan in September 1870. The weakness of German culture was now attributed to the literary critical practice of the feuilletonists, held to be representatives of a liberal and not adequately patriotic taste. This turn in the discussion corresponded to the first important rupture in the social history of the empire, "the big turn," as the historian Eckart Kehr puts it, that led to a deep "recasting of bourgeois society." In the wake of the introduction of the Socialist Law, which forced the Social Democratic Party (SPD) underground, the Bismarckian change of course from the liberal principles of laissez-faire to conservative protectionism, the anti-Semitism debate, and the start of the conservatively religious era of Robert von Puttkamer, a multifaceted change in the structure of culture took place. The transition from a liberal-capitalist society to one directed by an expansive state apparatus induced a crisis of legitimacy for individualism. Neoconservative ideologues, "who denied any autonomy either to economic growth or to intellectual matters and degraded them both to a function of state and military power,"[26] contested the rights of an independent intelligentsia. In imperialist society, the subjectivity of the feuilletonist seemed to constitute an enclave of potential opposition, which the antagonists of liberalism sought to eliminate.

The early naturalist polemic against feuilletonism manifested many features of the neoconservatism of the 1880s. For example, the absence of a normative poetics in Lindau was treated as an expression of a dangerously liberal culture, embodying "that indifference that embraces the principle of *laisser aller* in literature as well without realizing that the critic's right to exist is thereby denied." This conservative attack on subjectivist irrationalism did not denounce the feuilletonist for failing to engage in a rational debate that could establish legitimate norms; the point was rather that the feuilletonist refused to assert arbitrary norms at all. Thus the shortcoming of the feuilletonists lay less in the insistence on personal taste than in the refusal to make objectivist claims, in the rejection of the position of "truth" and "infallibility" that Fontane missed in the London *Times* editorials. The brothers Hart thought much of such eternal laws of art, which had allegedly been disregarded by liberal criticism: "Of course aesthetic ideas are formed, modified, and changed from one epoch to the next just like everything else, but there are nonetheless principles that no one dares to contradict openly, but which critics have been regularly ignoring."[27] This dogged clinging to the idea of incontrovertible laws conformed to the central tendency of postliberal culture: the elimination of autonomous criticism. The image of laws of art to be applied logically—though arbitrarily set up and not to be questioned—corresponded to the basic form of Wilhelmine legality: rational regulation without a reasonable foundation.[28]

According to the Hart brothers, the absence of authoritarian laws in liberal feuilletonism ran the risk of inducing a cultural catastrophe. As soon as subjectivity becomes paramount, all tastes come to have equal rights—a horrifying image for the early naturalists searching for a collective culture for the nation: "Once subjective feeling is considered the only norm, then there is no basis to condemn a work that lacks all poetic quality; there are people who even value Japanese idols and motley Chinese art. And it is to these consequences that Lindau's view of the subjectivity of criticism leads, to consequences that must make criticism seem an intellectual game; art, a mere plaything; and the public, a mindless herd."[29] The displacement of the image of the enemy from the European opponent in the Fontane-Gutzkow confrontation of 1871 to the Far East nations, on which in 1882 imperialism was already setting its sights, is noteworthy. The social shifts corresponding to such turns of foreign policy made a disciplined organization necessary, which, at least in the view of the brothers Hart, could not be supported by the laxity of liberal feuilletonism. Only a criticism that was stronger and stricter than the chattiness of a Lindau would be commensurate with the task of a national rebirth, a genuine "Sedan of the spirit."

The feuilletonist, ignorant of all laws of art and unashamedly fixated on his own subjectivity, was said to fail in his actual role of critic in another way, too: instead of insisting narcissistically on his private opinion, Lindau ought to have exercised an educational function. The early naturalists looked to the critic as expert, as higher authority. They reproached the feuilletonists for lack of interest in the fate of the nation: the feuilletonist is corrupt, materialist, and egoistic; the authentic critic must be pure, idealistic, and ready to make sacrifices. So for the early naturalists the feuilletonist constituted a countermodel against whom they could elaborate their own conception of criticism:

"It is time that the better among us rouse ourselves against the men who write only in order to write, who cavil only in order to make money, for whom the development of our nation's literature is not a holy matter, in the name of which one sacrifices favor and pleasure, in the name of which one trustingly endures the most petty attacks and all the rage of the clique. But for these there is nothing higher than their pitiable self, even if its pedestal is a dust heap."[30] The vocabulary of sacrifice and attack, of holiness and nation, again makes clear the imperialist character of the neoconservative turning-away from feuilletonism. Independence of judgment was defamed as self-obsession, and tolerance of a diversity of opinions as chaos; openness to feelings and even to entertainment were characterized as weak hedonism. In their place the early naturalists demanded a pedagogical literary criticism that would aggressively pursue the creation of a national culture for the whole people. Authoritarian antiliberalism evidently coexisted with a democratic ethos—not, of course, in the sense of self-determination based on open discussion but rather as the vision of a culture in which critics and artists would participate in a collective consciousness corresponding to the imputed character of the nation.

Naturalist Literary Criticism

The proponents of early naturalism developed their model of literary criticism, with respect both to the polemic against the subjectivity of feuilletonism and to an assumed addressee: the folk, which, though neglected and deceived, needed only a reliable aesthetic leadership in order to achieve a new cultural flowering. The first issue of the literary periodical of the brothers Hart, *Kritische Waffengänge*, put it like this: "Two words will do to characterize the tasks of the farmer and of the critic: to plow and to cultivate [*Pfluegen und Pflegen*]. To furrow the ground, to free it from rocks, and to pull out the weeds, that is the one duty; to tend and protect the sprouting plants is the other."[31] It is to be noted at once that here the critic is in no way meant to function as representative of the public. The critic neither engages in a public reasoning nor pedagogically introduces the work to the readership. While the Harts treat the folk as the addressee of criticism, in the last instance it figures only as a passive spectator, for the critic must dedicate himself in the first place to the bringing forth of new works: to plowing and cultivating.

Alongside this displacement of the balance between author, critic, and reader to the disadvantage of the reader, a certain privileging of the critic is evident in the metaphor. The process of creation, which is pushed out of the realm of society into a sphere governed by an unquestionable natural law, has its inexplicable origin outside critical discussion but thereafter remains fully dependent on the preparatory plowing and protective cultivation. The valuable works of art will not come to be by themselves; according to the views of the Harts, the intervention of the critic remains a necessary component. Against the background of the early naturalist attack on the liberalism of feuilletonism and its laissez-faire perspectivism, this characterization of the critic evidently mirrors the emergence of monopoly capitalist forms of social organization. Natural occurrences—whether in the market economy, industry, or the arts—seem to have lost their credibility, and the interventionist critic is called upon to stimulate literary production from without. This model explains the passive role assigned by the Harts to the public, which is no longer an active participant in cultural production but rather an object of pedagogic governance by a literary leadership.

The correspondence pointed out here between the early naturalist critical project and monopoly capitalist transformation of society is confirmed in an exemplary way by a cultural political suggestion of the Harts. In an "Open Letter to Prince Bismarck" in 1882 they propose the foundation of a special "Imperial Office of Literature, Theater, Science, and Art." Unlike Fontane, who called upon the state, albeit ironically, to alleviate the poverty of writers, the Harts ignore economic matters, appealing to the state instead for ideological reasons: a decidedly national literature is indispensable for the new nation. Since the shallow taste of self-obsessed critics and the superficial kind of entertainment afforded by the popular French writers are still dominant in the German literary scene, intervention by the state is apparently needed in order to elicit adequate works. Only through such an intervention can the disproportionately strong influence of particularist forces be broken; only the state can guarantee an authentically national literature: "The history of recent years should have made one thing clear, that it is time to see in the state something higher than a coercive institution that seeks to suppress all individuality; at any rate, even assuming the worst, a state literature offers the possibility of a further, freer development than a court literature that lives by the grace of the Medicis, Estes, etc."[32] The historical experience to which reference is made is the defeat of liberalism in the late 1870s and the increased importance of the state—no longer the strictly limited political institution of laissez-faire but an interventionist power, actively shaping society. The family names from the Italian Renaissance are meant to indicate that without a strong state only the private interests of ruling families, whether aristocratic or bourgeois-capitalist, will determine the character of culture. Only if the state replaces the "court" as bearer of culture can a national literature be brought forth that will do justice to the fundamental national identity.

While the naturalists repeatedly invoked the folk as the genuine form of the public, that invocation functioned only as a structuring moment within the polemic. References to the folk served to underscore the alien character of established literature, the necessity of a new literature, and the function of the critic as educator. Thus the concept "folk" legitimated the critic as a separate power, and the absence of any genuinely democratic characterization confirms that the early naturalist understanding of the people corresponded to the transition to a monopoly-capitalist public sphere. The folk was not a sovereign nation but the bearer of an essence that only the writer (and not the folk itself) could express: the "spirit of the nation hidden beneath the surface, deep and still, subject to no change, always at one with itself." The fixing of the folk as an unchangeable quantity corresponded to its ascribed passivity: the folk cannot act, for it does not change: hence the insistence on an immutable identity as the basis for the nationalism that often characterized naturalist literary criticism. "The nation will brace itself, and what is called 'national spirit' will no longer be an empty word! We all feel ourselves to be Germans, representatives of Germanness in opposition to the haughtiness of Rome and the expansive Slavs. The blood in our veins flows with more energy, and after the languid after-dinner hours of the past decade, after the mere ecstacy of enjoyment that one sought in art, as in all aspects of life, we again feel the need for great ideals, which can ennoble us and raise us above trivial tasks."[33] In its early phase, naturalist literary criticism saw itself as part of a national rebirth and consequently adopted this xenophobic tone. This nationalism had important ramifications for the literary critical model: the critic, who claimed to speak as educator of the nation and guardian of poetry, could regain the objectivity that the subjectivist feuilletonists had surrendered.

Yet the literary critical program of naturalism did not only correspond to the collapse of laissez-faire liberalism; it also bore witness to an avant-gardist claim and to the close link between naturalism and twentieth-century modernism. Like the later modernists, the Hart brothers were gripped by a vision of a social crisis to which they responded with a program of aesthetic renewal: they experienced a growing gap not between the mass of the folk and the literary world (hardly a new problem) but rather between the carriers of innovative literature and the literary public. The midcentury realist writers were on a relatively peaceable footing with the hegemonic bourgeois readership, but with naturalism the bitter tension between avant-garde and public, typical of modernism, emerged. However much the Harts strove to talk in the name of the folk, they were basically struggling for the position of the modernist critic, oblivious to social pressures but anxious to maintain his own privilege.[34] This hidden modernity explains the emphatic voluntarism with which the Harts joined in the literary debates. Although eager to provide an objective grounding for their judgments in the concept of the folk, they remained—like their enemies the feuilletonists—subjectivist critics. Their subjectivity took another form, however, than that of personal-privatist feuilletonism and was directed toward another goal: instead of the expression of individual experience, the construction of a future literature whose emergence would also signify the resolution of the social crisis. The belligerent tone of their polemics indicates that the early naturalist literary critics never pretended to be judges "simply in accordance with the laws of art" but acted instead as engaged agitators for a modernization of literary life.

As the naturalist movement gradually consolidated during the 1880s—for example, around the journal *Die Gesellschaft* (Society; 1885–1902), the organ of the Munich wing—the focus of literary critical discussion shifted. The nationalist coloration remained, but the purportedly pedagogic role of the critic became less prominent. Nevertheless, the polemic previously conducted against Lindau intensified and was redirected against the entire institution of literary criticism. The characteristic move of the naturalist literary criticism of the Munich school involved a constant attack on hostile critics, which displaced any substantial evaluation of contemporary writers. This curious lack of interest in making judgments about artworks can be explained in part by basic elements of naturalist ideology: the creative process was still stylized as a phenomenon of nature and thereby placed beyond the purview of rational analysis; the established critical discourse, in contrast, was fair game. This polemic drew on two familiar components: hostility to criticism, now in the form of a hostility to critics, and avant-gardist antipathy toward dominant taste.

As an example of naturalist literary criticism, Hermann Conradi's essay "Das sexuelle Moment in der Literatur" (1885) exemplifies the dialectic of modernism and the anticritical stance. In response to critical annoyance at allegedly graphic novellas printed in *Die Gesellschaft*, he defends artistic freedom against the "delicate little souls, naturally stuffed to the gills with the purest idealism, these champions of 'good taste' and similar beautiful things." For Conradi, the artist as genius stands beyond the range of rational scrutiny. Consequently, the critic may at most judge whether an artist has successfully fulfilled a project, but he may never question the legitimacy of the project itself. Conradi proceeds to assert that the critics of his day had transgressed this narrow limit: "Just as there are particularly finely strung and delicately built spirits that feel well only with the elegy and the idyll, with the soft, reserved, 'atmospheric' sounding of a tone, there are in truth also strong, pithy, manly souls with a sizable portion of healthy sensuality that has not been neutered, who deeply hate anything smelling of crippled middle-of-the-road feelings, who have strongly expressed sympathies and antipathies—and should such a full nature, rich in blood and muscle, bend to the pipings of hysterical half-men? should he swear allegiance to a code nicely and cleanly concocted by a bunch of dwarfs in a broken-down age bent on making everything the same?"[35] The priority of the artist thus leads to the opposition of the healthy artist, distinguished by sensual masculinity, and the critic, presented as a "half-man" whose delicacy and refinement are signs of effeminacy, whose judgments are hysterical, and who is denounced as the bearer of an antiquated taste (elegy, idyll). Critical speech is discarded as irrelevant, and the critic sorely defamed: the defense of aesthetic innovation turns into a radical denunciation of critics. Conradi adds, "My speech is not exactly very parliamentary"—clearly an ironic comment on his own style but actually revealing the social-historical content of naturalist literary criticism.

The devaluation of criticism in the literary realm corresponded to the undermining of parliamentarism, as several articles in *Die Gesellschaft* praising Bismarck indicate. A system of historical signs was superimposed on the opposition of critic versus artist, belying the immanent political message: "It is enraging to watch how the most decrepit and pedantic mediaevalisms rise up against and hinder our literature, just as it is about to sprout a new, vital, succulent branch, just as it is attempting to become an authentic national power by casting off its lacquered decorative costume."[36] The critic is now identified with a past characterized as elitist and unfree, which is about to give way to a national literature disguised as an irresistible organic force. The equation of the critic with prenational "medievalisms" has the same value as the Harts' talk about the "Medicis, Estes, etc": the nation needs a national literature, and the same critics, who merely talk and who once tried to obstruct the blood and iron of Bismarck's national unification, are also the opponents of a strong national literature. Hence the imperative of eliminating critical judgment, and replacing it with a polemic against representatives of anachronistic cultural tendencies and internationalist sympathies.

This polemic against obsolete taste was able to formulate certain cross-connections between literature and society and thus to extend the scope of literary criticism. If Conradi focused on established critics, the reviews of Conrad Alberti considered a literary work in its social-historical context: writer and text were set on a common plane with the public, against which the full force of a brute naturalist tirade (it found its peak of intensity in Alberti) was mercilessly directed. The activity of the literary critic shaded into social criticism, whose tendentious assertions exhibited all the features of naturalist ideology. Thus, for example, Alberti's discussion of a successful author of the time was occasion for wide-ranging cultural criticism: "Paul Heyse is not a single individual—he is a symbol, the plastic embodiment of the entire moral degeneracy of the German bourgeoisie, for which vulgarity, prurience, cheekiness, and shamelessness constitute the ideal of beauty."[37] While Conradi combined a hostility to critics with an aesthetic avant-gardism, Alberti linked a similar avant-gardism with cultural conservatism. His polemic against the bourgeoisie mixed a radical critique of the capitalization of literary life with a commitment to backward-looking ideals of bourgeois propriety. This double character of naturalist literary criticism is a consequence of the contradictions in the social historical setting. On the one hand the eruption of an early phase of modernism required a more polemical tone than the chattiness of feuilletonism could support; on the other hand a sharp rejection of the forms of bourgeois culture followed; hence the denunciation of liberal criticism as much as of bourgeois morality. But even where the folk was invoked with an apparently democratic insistence, the antibourgeois position could still be understood as the correlate of social transformation. The literary critic no longer conceived of himself as a participant in a public exchange of opinions among equals. He knew best and was obliged to proclaim this unquestionable knowledge in aesthetic as well as in moral matters: administration could consequently replace the mediations provided by a public discourse.

Berlin Naturalism

Corresponding to the specific character of modernism in Berlin, naturalist literary criticism developed differently in the imperial capital than it did in Munich. While a thorough discussion would exceed the scope of this chapter, the most important aspect was certainly the fact that Berlin quickly developed into the center of political activity, while Munich tended rather to attract the antibourgeois bohemians of the Wilhelmine counterculture.[38] In addition, Berlin naturalism started relatively late, around 1890, when the new literary movement had already won a certain legitimacy. In the context of the initial populism of Wilhelm II, the removal of Bismarck, and the repeal of the Socialist Law, the Berlin avant-garde could envisage a different, more integrated social role than did the authors writing for *Die Gesellschaft*.

The alternative concept of criticism in Berlin modernism can be traced in the program of the *Litterarische Volkshefte*, the organ of a group of literati founded in 1886, the "Verein Durch" (Breakthrough club): "The *Litterarische Volkshefte* wishes to awaken and nurture with regard to topical literary questions the sense for true criticism and the understanding for true poetry in the widest circles. The *Litterarische Volkshefte* fights accordingly no less against dilettantism and refinement than against epigonic classicism; for modern content and modern form in literature. The *Litterarische Volkshefte* is meant for the entire public, to the extent that it reads books and goes to the theater. The *Litterarische Volkshefte* will accordingly, while maintaining a pronouncedly polite attitude, be written in a lively way and so as to be understood by all."[39]

Unlike the Munich naturalists, this program ascribes to criticism a mediating role: a literary public is perceived, to which the periodical should make new works accessible. But criticism is not the midwife of the heroized artist: nothing remains of the "plowing and cultivating" of the *Kritische Waffengänge*. The folk, previously conjured from mystic depths, now appears in the form of the readership, and the nationalist substratum is absent. In the *Litterarische Volkshefte* the focus is not on a forced folkishness but rather on an emphatically historical consciousness: "topical questions" should be discussed because an explicitly modern literature—that is, one that does justice to contemporary circumstances—should be encouraged. At issue is neither the subjectivity of the critic nor the salvation of the folk from an alien canon but rather the culture of the historical moment—what was characterized soon after the founding of the Verein Durch as "modern life."

Through his essays and reviews of the 1880s and 1890s, Otto Brahm became the most important representative of the literary criticism of Berlin modernism. For Brahm, as for other critics whose careers begin around 1890 (Paul Schlenther, Alfred Kerr), the influence of positivism on the universities is an additional important factor. Although epigonic idealist aesthetics were not dispelled, they were nevertheless jeopardized by the new conception of literature modeled on the natural sciences, which was then gradually gaining ground. The shift of interest at German universities toward the natural sciences, which accompanied the rapid industrialization after the founding of the empire, generated this positivist literary scholarship. The academic-aesthetic foundation of normative poetics underlying the literary criticism of Frenzel and Julian Schmidt was thus systematically destroyed: aesthetic principles ceased to be of paramount importance and were replaced by an objective observation of the work. The leitmotif of academic positivism, in conjunction with elements of Berlin modernism, were embodied in the literary critical model of Brahm.

Brahm's criticism and reviews, which appeared in the *Vossische Zeitung*, the *Nation*, and later in the *Freie Buehne fuer modernes Leben* (Free stage for modern life)—founded in 1890; after 1904 published as *Die neue Rundschau* (New review)—offered neither a description of personal experience nor a tendentious polemic in the manner of Alberti. Instead, works were treated with an objectivity that betrayed its positivist lineage: not the objectivity of generally binding norms but a descriptive objectivity that discussed aspects of a work and pointed out causal connections. Brahm did of course consider the form of a work, but he also regularly mentioned a series of other themes (which, though connected to the work, would scarcely have been touched upon by a representative of the old guard like Frenzel): dramaturgical adaptations, reaction of the public, reception history. Brahm called for an integration of works of drama into modern life; instead of presenting historical distance as unbridgeable, his remarks on the genesis of a work served to demonstrate the legitimacy of a modern appropriation. His positivist literary criticism thus contained, alongside a purely descriptive element, an engagement on behalf of a modernization of literary life, and his success as a critic depended on this often labile balance between descriptivism and aesthetic renewal.

Brahm's attempt to encourage literary modernization did not only anticipate his later activity as the most important theater director of naturalism; his interest in works that could be relevant to the contemporary public pointed as well to his understanding of the critic as mediator between work and public. In the debates about Henrik Ibsen and Gerhart Hauptmann, during which Brahm proved himself champion of modernism, he confronted conservative critics who still worked normatively with unquestioned aesthetic ideals: "One believes that a critic is someone who ascertains that this is praiseworthy and that is objectionable . . . but that the critic is also the one who seeks to reveal to the audience the intentions of uncomprehended art like an honest broker—the gentlemen have never heard of this."[40] Thanks to the sharpness of the confrontations, he felt forced again and again in the essays on Ibsen and Hauptmann to respond to the critics of the conservative camp. Such discussion of a contemporary controversy—in the Verein Durch it was referred to as "topical literary questions"—belonged to the mediating role, of course, but this was no innocent mediation by an objective third party. Brahm was naturally a supporter of the naturalist literature that he discussed as a critic. His public judgment was also part of his campaign of promoting the avant-garde; as a critic he tried simultaneously to be a positivist observer and an engaged modernist.

The paradox that Brahm, the critical spokesman of the naturalist avant-garde, did not acknowledge as valid any aesthetic principles could be resolved only by means of historicizing his literary critical strategy. Modern life—that is, contemporary society—became the central concept of his account. Even naturalism itself was accorded only a temporary validity, as Brahm put it in a programmatic essay in the *Freie Buehne:* "We swear by no formula and do not want to dare to bind in the rigid chains of rules that which is in eternal motion, life and art. . . . As a friend of naturalism we want to accompany it a good stretch of the way, only it should not surprise us if, in the course of the walk, at a point that we cannot today yet see, the road suddenly bends and surprising new views of art and life open. For the infinite development of human culture is bound by no formula, not even by the most modern."[41] Brahm's critical activity owed its strength to a brief historical moment in which his principle-free positivism converged with principled modernism. As long as an explosive avant-garde was in conflict with established culture, the positivist critic, who did not express his own opinions and relied upon a descriptivist prose, could play an active role in critical controversy. But as soon as naturalism had carried the day, this descriptive strategy could no longer be supported by public tension, and a passivity inherent in the literary critical model emerged. Brahm's descriptivism, which fostered a polemical but not a judgmental criticism, ultimately remained linked to the early naturalist hostility to criticism, for it continued to discriminate against independent judgment. Thus the limitations of Brahm's literary criticism come into view: it was effective only as long as it was carried on the literary wave that it itself applauded. The positivist poverty of theory and the objectivist skepticism about autonomous judgment reflected yet again the institutional crisis of criticism: both bourgeois tradition and the modernist program required a critical agency, while the transformation of the public sphere in postliberal culture greatly restricted its effectiveness.

Aestheticization of Literary Criticism: Alfred Kerr

Around the turn of the century the intelligentsia began increasingly to function as vanguard of an advanced aesthetic movement. The avant-garde version of criticism was already evident in naturalism, but because of the peculiarities of naturalist ideology it played a subordinate role there. Vanguard criticism implied either a commitment of the critic to a specific program or the ascription to criticism itself of the character of art. Such an aestheticization of literary criticism reflected the instability of the institution of criticism, since the critic was able to legitimate himself in the eyes of the public not as a rational judge but only as a modernist artist. The plausibility that criticism, defined as a work of art, could claim corresponded to a quietist though social-critical opposition of art and society: the gray, everyday life of high capitalism was confronted with an emphatic concept of art as the site of beauty and sensuality. While cultural conservatives opposed democracy with an ossified notion of culture (that is, the aestheticization of politics that was realized in proto-Fascist literary criticism), avant-garde bohemianism carried art on its banner against an establishment it decried as philistine. This aesthetic engagement changed gradually into an explicitly political engagement on the part of the literary intelligentsia, especially after the revolution of 1918–19 seemed to raise the prestige of public discussion. The space in which the poet was permitted to intervene in politics, as a slogan of the day put it, was extended in the Weimar Republic, which led to the articulation of a further revaluation of the intellectual: the literary critic as political critic.[42] Of course, the call for the man of letters to confront the concerns of society completely contradicted the idea of the poet held by the educated middle class, but in social-historical terms it signified an attempt by the stratum of bourgeois intellectuals to guarantee themselves a legitimate role in the postliberal social order.

That Alfred Kerr, whose theater critiques appeared in *Der Tag* and later in the *Berliner Tageblatt*, well appreciated the difficulties that weighed upon any attempt at critical discourse in the first decades of the century is demonstrated by his reflections upon the grounding of his own work. For him, criticism should neither mediate between aesthetic work and the literary public nor serve to encourage the aesthetic production of others, as the Harts had intended with their horticultural metaphor. Criticism was rather an art form equal in status to the classical triad: "Henceforth one must say that poetry is divided into epic, lyric, drama, and criticism." This aestheticization of criticism functioned as a guarantee of its priority: "In this world it is the highest, if it is also art." The privileging of criticism as art was based on a conception of the artwork peculiar to the *boheme* of the turn of the century, including the privileging of the artist, whose typical features, productive heroism and creative irrationality, could now be taken up by Kerr for himself. The artist whom the critic had to match was neither classicist nor realist but a force endowed with features of the Nietzschean superman, one who could qualitatively bring forth new creations through the strength of his own character. In this way the critic was able to overcome the broad disparagement of an autonomous intelligentsia, prevalent since 1848. Kerr's hypertrophic self-conception was far removed from Gutzkow's cozy domesticity of the 1850s and the modesty of Fontane's judgments, which claimed merely to be private: "But I myself say what I as an honest man must in truth say: that I have brought sounds into the world which did not exist before; that I made possible a more unbounded humanity; that I built upon a certain wood, which no one before me had; that I, bud of the future, have drawn essence from waters, meadowland from seaweed and salt, and blossoms of the sea with my arms."[43] Here, the critic as artist himself claimed to be the redeeming hero for whom the naturalists were waiting, whom they posited as counterimage to the despised representatives of established literature.

But in his attempt to lend legitimacy to critical discourse through a strategy of aestheticization, Kerr did not fully succeed in overcoming the thematized antinomy of criticism and art. In terms of literary history, it was rooted in the rival models of feuilletonism and naturalist polemic; in terms of social history, in the isolation of the critic from a reasoning public. A critic could either entertain or publicize the avant-garde in the public sphere of cultural consumption, but a discursive reciprocity with the readership could not be attained, and criticism kept falling back into the immanent dichotomy: "It is the singing of a harp that is a slingshot; the noise of a slingshot that becomes a harp."[44] That Kerr identifies himself in this well-known passage with the biblical King David—who vanquished the giant of the Philistines with his sling and who recited the lyric psalms with his harp—points again to his exalted self-esteem. It also indicates the hybrid character of the conception of criticism which sought to unify art as subjective lyric with militant polemic but which in fact merely held the two near each other. The basic plan of an oscillation between art and life, between sense and sensuality, corresponds to a critical model according to which the artist-critic stands over against social life in order repeatedly to intervene effectively but, as bearer of a superior intelligence, actually belongs to a higher sphere. In Kerr's early work during the last decades of the empire, this strategy continued to be colored by bohemian aestheticism; after the revolution of 1918–19, in the politicized public sphere of the Weimar Republic, this *fin-de-siècle* metaphysics was refashioned into a particular program for the left-liberal intelligentsia.

But the consequences of the unresolved antithesis in Kerr's understanding of criticism point to the enduring instability of the institution of literary criticism, despite the support provided by the strategy of aestheticization. Kerr continues the sentence cited above about the harp and slingshot as follows: "And everything lies in what I hear: the indifference to objections; the insignificance of art; and the joy, the joy, the joy of being." Despite the attempt at a synthetic resolution, slingshot and harp, life and art, consistently fall apart in Kerr, and so in the final instance the critic stands there facing his object quite helplessly. To be sure, the formulation bears witness to an aestheticist optimism, but beautiful appearance is not able to hide the irreconcilability of the imperial "indifference to objections." Criticism as an institution is still illegitimate, but this critic, who aggrandizes his own subjectivity to mythic dimensions and thus becomes the paragon of what came to be known as a "great critic," possesses a privileged position from which he can look down upon the "insignificance of art." Kerr's literary critical strategy thus serves to displace aesthetic objects and to produce the critic himself as central, as the star: "My work does not offer 'The History of Drama in the Period from —— to ——,' but rather critiques in the period from the beginning of the author's career until his acme."[45] Criticism, disqualified in social-historical terms, now survives as a public production of the critical personality; the bourgeois institution of literary criticism saves itself by fleeing into a system of famous personalities.

The potential politicization of the aestheticized critic became noticeable in Kerr even during the empire. As editor of the literary periodical *Pan* (1910–15), he attacked Traugott von Jagow—president of the Berlin police and infamous in liberal and left circles—when Kerr heard of his attempt to use his office as theater censor to help him initiate a relationship with the actress Tilla Durieux. With articles in *Pan*, Kerr set off a scandal that ended with Jagow's transfer to Leipzig. Through this politicization of the literary public sphere, Kerr won not only praise but also the reproach of sensationalism; especially the Viennese language critic Karl Kraus found in Kerr the appropriate target for a bitter polemic against what he saw as a corrupt press. The conflict between Kerr and Kraus, nourished by the Jagow affair and, after 1914, by Kerr's nationalist war poems, continued into the last years of the 1920s and constitutes a very revealing sideshow of the literary public sphere of the Weimar Republic.[46]

The actual politicization of Kerr occurred during the republic, for the tensions of the years of revolution and the increased importance of public discussion in a parliamentary state caused a broad turning to topical themes among literary figures. Kerr himself was at least temporarily interested in being considered a leftist. For example, in the *Rote Fahne* he characterized the Communist politician Karl Liebknecht (who was murdered in 1919) as "a man of infinitely high spiritual stature" and claimed "never to have forgotten the wonderful purity of this high spirit." The added note that he wanted "to play absolutely 'no role' in politics" certainly expressed an antipathy to partisan affiliations (the *Rote Fahne* was the official organ of the Communist Party) but not to the participation of literati in political controversies. A short article with the remarkably clear title "For the Soviet Union" in *Das neue Russland* (New Russia) similarly exemplified an attempt of the literary critic to express himself directly about a political matter. Written during the violent political debates of 1932, the explicit defense of the Soviet Union constituted a reply to the anti-Communism of the Nazis. Kerr had for years been one of the best-known public opponents of Hitler; his statement on the U.S.S.R. should make clear with what decisiveness Kerr, who has often been misrepresented as merely an impressionist aesthete, concerned himself with a central political issue in contemporary debates. So he declared, "The fact 'Soviet Republic' is to my mind one of the greatest and most joyous facts. Because here for the first time in two thousand years the honest attempt is being energetically made to bring justice into the world. Were I to die tomorrow, the thought of this single phenomenon within a timorous and backward world would be the last, the only solid consolation."[47]

The literary critical counterpart to this political stand is the essay "Lunacharsky in Berlin" that Kerr wrote on the occasion of the production at the Volksbuehne of the Soviet dramatist's *Don Quixote Unbound*. Characteristic of Kerr's wide-ranging critical strategy is the diversity of objects he mentions: Anatoly Lunacharsky himself, the content and form of the work, its Russian context, the political implications of its message. Kerr in no way restricts himself to formal-aesthetic perspectives; on the contrary, he goes to lengths to highlight topical aspects so as to express in the end his own political opinions. He is not even afraid to take up truly peripheral aspects for the purpose of formulating a political statement; for example, although Lunacharsky used the Cervantes material only as a vehicle for his thoughts about revolutionary politics, Kerr allows himself the following critical comment on the contemporary situation in Spain: "This play is set in a Spanish world. Not in the Spain of Primo de Rivera. For two reasons. First: the play is older than the dictatorship of the general—and will, one hopes, stay on the scene longer. Second: the eponymous hero, Don Quixote, should be notably skinny—while General Primo de Rivera, as a heavenly Madrilenian assured me, is less loved by the women because he has a paunch. (All this in confidence.)" This passage recalls Fontane's critique of *Egmont*, though the connection between Lunacharsky's drama and Spanish politics is actually even more arbitrary than the link Fontane makes to the southern German accent of the actress playing Clärchen. But in both cases an incidental moment of the dramatic performance is taken up in order to contaminate the literary critical text with political—that is, extra-aesthetic—material. The entertaining tone of the excerpt soon gives way to a more serious interpretation of the play, which sees Don Quixote as the paradigm of the person who must suffer political defeats because of his ethical conduct.

Kerr summarizes: "The quintessence of this drama is: a man of action cannot always act justly. A politician cannot necessarily be a moralist. And it is precisely in this open non-ethics that the ethical quality of the play lies. . . . The knight of La Mancha always acts in

Lunacharsky's drama as a pure idealist—and thereby brings about misery, sorrow, misfortune, political retreat." It is hardly surprising that the critic distills the thematized message of the work under consideration, but what is noteworthy is the fact that these themes now become the center of the critical text. Kerr therefore engages less with the play than with the question of revolutionary ethics. This occurs of course via literary material. *Don Quixote Unbound* is compared to Ernst Toller's *Masse Mensch*, but the comparison concerns the political positions of the two works, which Kerr sees as opposed, not their character as art: "These two dramas, the drama of the Russian Lunacharsky and of the German Toller, are the two poles of political ethics"[48] but not, we may add, of political dramaturgy, with which Kerr is not concerned— which means that criticism is undergoing a transformation from an aesthetic to an explicitly political discourse.

As has been shown, the politicization of the content of literary criticism can also be found in rudimentary form in Fontane and follows from feuilletonist subjectivization. In Kerr, however, the political object is not merely mentioned in passing but made the main concern of the essay. Instead of objectively explicating the polarity Lunacharsky-Toller, Kerr himself takes a stand and opts for the ethical message of Lunacharsky's drama, which he recognized earlier in the essay as a justification of Bolshevik politics. Consequently, literary critical discourse serves to announce the political opinions of the critic. The paradoxical consequence of the aestheticization of the critic becomes strikingly clear here: the revaluation of the critic as artist did not by necessity lead to an aestheticist foreclosure of social controversies; it functioned rather as a claim to priority in the public sphere. The critic, who claimed to be an artist and demanded artistic freedom, tried thereby to escape any limitations on the scope of his pronouncements.

Despite the apparent radicalization (compared with his earlier phase) evident in the Lunacharsky essay, Kerr remained bound to his vitalist heritage throughout the Weimar Republic. The aestheticization of criticism was able to effect a politicization of the critical discourse, but it did not mean a politicization of aesthetics. Art and life were not dissolved into one another; they remained ultimately in opposition. The artist might certainly intervene in life—that is, in politics; Kerr's readiness to engage in politics explains the admiration that the young generation of expressionists felt for him during the years just before the First World War[49]—but these interventions were not motivated by any systematic program. For Kerr, literature, like literary criticism, was only on occasion political; its true character remained primarily aesthetic. This explains why he did not understand the dramaturgy of Bertolt Brecht, whose very project was the politicization of aesthetic form; his inability to grasp the real meaning of the Brechtian renewal directly indicates the limits of his literary critical model. Just as the theater could address political questions while seeming to retain an apolitical character as art, so could the critic certainly intervene in social life without radically calling into question the form of literary criticism as art. As bearer of a superior intelligence, the aestheticized critic occupied a privileged position from which he could descend into the realm of politics (to do him justice, one must stress that on occasion Kerr virtually demanded such engagement), but the priority of the critic, grounded in the claim to be an artist, was always to be maintained. For only through this superiority was the critic in a position to intervene on behalf of enlightenment in the chaos of "life" conceived in vitalist terms: only the critical intelligentsia could give the world meaningful form.

Kerr therefore underscored Gotthold Lessing's critical capacity "to erect signposts in the confusion of human brains; to lay out guidelines; to achieve order, order, order. That is to do exactly that which distances us from the unconscious, from only-chaotic drives, from the intelligent animal—even from the poet. And further: to do that which directs man to the goal bearing the Kantian prescription: *aude sapere*— have courage to make use of your understanding."[50] The definition of the critic that Kerr develops in his work on Lessing was based on a new version of his turn-of-the-century metaphysics. The intellectual as bearer of enlightenment and understanding still stands over against an irrational life, which is, however, no longer transfigured into the "ecstacy of being." In the context of the social tensions of the Weimar period, "life" appears rather as a threatening chaos, in absolute need of leadership by a bearer of higher knowledge in order to be saved from catastrophe. Kerr does not demand aesthetic laws from the critic—in this he remains loyal to his own avant-garde origins—but guidelines for the life of society, which he sees as incapable of authentic self-determination and doomed to continue to err unguided unless endowed with a consciousness brought to it from without.

Kerr's transformation of the early art-life antithesis into a program of social engagement for the critical intelligentsia was expressed most clearly at the end of the Weimar Republic in an important radio talk on the occasion of the visit to Berlin of the editor of *Nouvelles litteraires*. Here the subjectivity of the critic is still made the object of the literary critical text: Kerr stresses that there can be found in "certain theater reviews of Martin du Gard all kinds of things out of his own life." The vitalist Kerr still presents the realm of actual aesthetic production, once dismissed as "insignificant," as less worthy of admiration than a natural life: Du Gard "considers peasants to be in general more reasonable than writers." Nonetheless, an enlightening function is ascribed to the writing intelligentsia because of its greater knowledge. According to Kerr, the critic may proclaim a knowledge that the addressee, left to himself, cannot attain. His definition of the critic thus depends on the claim to a privileged position, emphasized again and again despite the modesty indicated in the following image: "Yes, we intellectuals are at best the electricians on the gallery of a dark hall in which a terrible confusion reigns, a black thronging, a jumble of pressing, groping, and squeaking people, in which the one steps on the feet of the next and they aimlessly squash and trample each other instead of systematically looking for a door—we intellectuals could at least light the place where the carpenter has left a hole."[51] The imputed ignorance of the recipients is the correlate of the priority of the critic; a clearly political knowledge is to be conveyed to a public which, however, is itself not considered able to participate as an autonomous partner in dialogue in a public discussion. Thus the critic functions as an authoritarian educator, not as reasoning representative of the public, though he is still meant to be the bearer of reason, a reason that it is the task of the intelligentsia to proclaim as revelation.

Kerr's critical discourse may therefore be accused not of turning away from politics but instead of a heteronomous dichotomization, absolutely dividing the critical specialist and the passive recipient. Kerr's message may well have possessed democratic content, but its mediation by the mass media and the state radio monopoly was based on a strict division between the independent speaker and the structurally dependent addressee. Although the ideological trimming of this critical program, derived from vitalist philosophy, could tolerate political speech, it could not tolerate equal rights for the audience.

Genuine public discussion was displaced by the public self-presentation of the critic.

Literary Criticism and the Labor Movement

The process of industrialization that commenced during the 1850s reached a high point in the Empire, transforming Germany into the leading economic power in Europe by 1900. In the increasingly urbanized population the number of industrial workers doubled between 1887 and 1914. At the same time social legislation, advanced for the epoch, was gradually extended. Nevertheless, the conditions of life and habitation of the proletariat were anything but satisfactory: "An industrial worker family in 1914 was generally not able to eat enough, to live healthily, and to have sufficient clothing at the same time."[52] During the 1890s, in the context of the emergence of the proletarian masses in the industrial centers, their economic misery, and the absence of subjective hopes for upward social mobility, a labor movement developed in which a Marxist anticapitalism spread, displacing the heirs of Ferdinand Lassalle and Mikhail Bakunin. Marxism, which articulated a radical critique of the bourgeois mode of production, addressed the psychological needs produced by the class divisions of the empire: the social *déclassement* of the worker was now disguised by an emphatic class consciousness. The proletariat could consider itself the bearer of a future society in which it would inherit the bourgeois culture that the ruling class, in its decadence, was only able to fritter away. Radical social criticism coexisted with a longing for integration and social reform. This contradiction was evident in the Social Democratic Party (SPD) debates as the polarity between Karl Kautsky's ideology of revolution and Eduard Bernstein's evolutionary socialism.

The behavior of the labor movement with respect to the nation-state was equally contradictory. Though in 1848 the Communist Manifesto had proclaimed the homelessness of the proletariat and the international nature of its struggle, a unified Germany remained an unquestioned desideratum for the early labor movement, as it had been for the liberals and democrats of the midcentury. Only a democratic Germany promised to break the power of the aristocratic dynasties; particularism could be overcome only through a pan-German parliament. Thus, democratic revolution and national unification were indivisibly united. In fact, the foundation of the empire in 1871 brought unity only under the dominion of Prussia, the bulwark against democratizing tendencies. In addition, the new empire sought to secure its inner cohesion through the ideological exclusion of putative "enemies of the empire." Although the labor movement had supported national unification, its members were discriminated against as "unpatriotic ruffians." The introduction of the Socialist Law in 1878 led to massive persecutions: many were condemned to prison; others were expelled or forced to emigrate.[53] This political bias against the workers left deep scars, and the antagonism toward "Prussia-Germany" constituted a second motif of proletarian culture along with the actual critique of capitalism.

Both elements—Marxist social criticism and hostility toward Prussia—were crucial to the literary criticism of Franz Mehring, which exemplifies the proletarian public sphere between the repeal of the Socialist Law and the outbreak of the First World War and at the same time constitutes a pinnacle of critical writing at the turn of the century. Mehring's journalistic activity began at the time of the founding of the empire in the camp of the bourgeois left. Around 1890 his experience in the increasingly capitalist press of the Bismarck period and the retreat of liberalism from its earlier ideals led him to the Social Democratic Party, in whose left wing he played an important role up to his death in 1919. The immediate occasion of his turn to socialism was the so-called Lindau affair: an actress was allegedly boycotted in all the Berlin theaters on the instructions of Paul Lindau, her former lover. As editor of the left-wing *Volkszeitung*, Mehring took on her case, publishing Lindau's letters to her and implicating other theater critics, (including Otto Brahm) as possible participants in the boycott. In what followed, Mehring presented an image of theater life corrupted by capitalism, which he lashed with his sharp polemic in the brochure *Der Fall Lindau*. The interests of money had banished authentic culture; current theater criticism was little more than advertising whereby the real character of art was being undermined: "I believe that the director, the dramaturge, the critic, the press, and the theater can and should pursue more general and higher goals than 'business.' If I'm wrong, all the worse—not for me but rather for present-day art, for the present-day press, for present-day society, and not least also for the present-day state."[54]

After the Lindau affair, Mehring quit the established press, whose capitalization he thought hindered true criticism, and took up his work in the periodicals of the socialist movement. Aspects of his literary critical articles are characteristic both of the worker movement of the period and of his experience with mainstream literary criticism. This is especially clear in his unyielding opposition to the expansion of a Prussian-colored chauvinist ideology. The glorification of the Hohenzollerns was based not only on the dominance of Prussia within the empire but rather more generally on the aristocratic, antidemocratic orientation of society. The literary consequences included the dramatic work of Ernst von Wildenbruch, whose epigonic dramas depicted a glorious Hohenzollern past; when he died, the conservative press attempted to protect him from the reproach that he had been an opportunistic "court poet" by pointing to his own Hohenzollern ancestry.

At this point Mehring joined in with a humorous article published in the Neue Zeit, the theoretical journal of the SPD: " It was only so-so with this ancestry. Wildenbruch was certainly a grandchild of Prince Louis Ferdinand, but it was all the more doubtful whether Louis Ferdinand was a Hohenzollern. The mother of this prince had not sworn by Zelinde's motto: I only want a little child the legitimate way. Most dear to her heart was Count Schmettau, whom his comrades in the Guards used to call 'Minna von Barnhelm or Soldiers' Fortune.' " Mehring's objection strikes not so much at Wildenbruch himself as at his public, distinguished by a servile loyalty to the Kaiser. The critic does not directly denounce Wildenbruch's dramas but dismisses his work as a whole as an expression of the culture of the authoritarian state: "He was honestly infatuated with Prussianized Germany, and this object of his love is reflected all too faithfully in his works: in their sober ecstacy, in their blooming senility, in the rustling train of their form, which always swept up the common dust of the street, in the fuss of words without a trace of thought, in the conceit without creative power." The disappointed radical Mehring, who had experienced the political misery in the empire of the 1870s and 1880s, was now writing for a socialist public that could remember the persecutions of the Socialist Law; all the failings of the state were consequently rediscovered in the official literary life. The "Sedan of the spirit" once demanded by the Harts was for Mehring all too clear in the work of Wildenbruch: "If after a hundred years free and happy people cannot imagine how things were in Prussianized Germany, then they need only to open Wildenbruch's works to encounter, with a yawn, the entire spiritual barrenness of the new German imperial splendor."[55]

But Mehring's most important attack on the Hohenzollern ideology of the empire occurred right at the beginning of his socialist period. In June 1891 he began to collaborate regularly on the *Neue Zeit* (New times) and in 1892 launched a series of twenty-one articles on the treatment of Lessing in official literary historiography. Later published as *Die Lessing-Legende: Eine Rettung* (The Lessing legend: A rescue), the study embodies various moments of Mehring's literary critical project: the demolition of the idealized image of Prussia, the emphasis on democratic elements in earlier German literature, the attack on established literary criticism and on the German philology of the Wilhelmine university system. Like Otto Brahm, Mehring integrated reception history into the literary critical discourse: the critic does not judge merely a work but also its influence. Yet while for Brahm this extension of the discussion remained within the aesthetic sphere, despite his frequent invocations of "modern life," the Marxist Mehring attempted to integrate economic and political material.

Ostensibly a response to Erich Schmidt's biography of Lessing, *Die Lessing-Legende* formulates the socialist critique of positivist literary scholarship fostered by the influential critic Wilhelm Scherer. In the preface to the second printing (1906) Mehring notes: "Great diligence and other achievements must be granted the Scherer school. It has achieved a good deal in the field of aesthetic-philological footwork and is fine at the critical analysis of poetic texts, as long as it adopts aesthetic-philosophical points of view. . . . But its understanding vanishes, as if cut off with a knife, where the literary comes in contact with the economic and political, with general historical development: If it tries to write literary history, its presentations lack the historical perspective and its figures lack historical depth. It collapses into empty phrases that are nothing less than prettified by an embarrassing touch of loyalty and subservience." The value of the positivist research of literary history in the narrowest sense is acknowledged, but the inability to present literary development in a social-historical context makes the results pale, their only color coming through the imposition of Prussian ideology. So in Scherer and Schmidt, "Alexandrian learning" and "Byzantine attitude" determine each other reciprocally.[56] The restriction of the critical regard to literary facts excludes political history and replaces it with Wilhelmine "phrases," whose antidemocratic ideology necessitates the exclusion of progressive elements in the German past.

Thus the Scherer school became for Mehring the index of the capitulation of progressive bourgeois culture to the imperial power establishment. His main objection to the positivists had to do with the transfiguration of the role of the Prussian court in the development of German literature in the eighteenth century. For the socialist critic, that poetic flowering counted as an expression of an earlier bourgeois striving for emancipation, while Scherer and Schmidt saw in it the fruits of royal favor. Though they generally ignored the political and especially the economic background, "as soon as the Brandenburg-Prussian state comes into view—heaven help us! a phrase must be called into service, like a little piece of soap with which the Byzantine foam can be beaten." Mehring shows how Scherer tried to reclaim other figures besides Lessing, like Friedrich Klopstock and Johann Winckelmann, for the glory of Prussia. He then immediately tests such distortions and confronts them with contrary statements by those same writers, such as Winckelmann's "better a circumcized Turk than a Prussian."[57]

In the development of bourgeois literary historiography Mehring recognized the gradual demise of liberal principles and the establishment of the ideological hegemony of the Wilhelmine class-state. Yet the ideals given up by the bourgeoisie could be effectively preserved in the socialist public sphere. Mehring's critique of university literary scholarship was therefore not fundamentally different from his diagnosis of bourgeois literary criticism with respect to the Lindau affair. Though the commercial element predominated in the Lindau affair and the ideological element in the critique of Schmidt, both asserted a falling-away from authentic judgment. Critical autonomy had been bought off in the bourgeois public sphere either by capitalism or by the state. According to Mehring, only outside the commercial press, in an international socialist movement immune to chauvinism, could a true criticism find its place.

Indeed, a specific strategy can be found in Mehring's critical practice, in which the thematization of reception history did not foster a new literary movement, as with Brahm, but actualized the contents of literary critical argument and thematized politically the main points of dispute. In this strategy, literary history and literary criticism are not pursued solely from a naive interest in inherited cultural material; instead, they sharpen the confrontations of the day via the images of the past. Walter Benjamin describes the actualization of the past in the literary critical project of historical materialism—"To put the historical experience that is at the origin of each present into the work—that is the task of historical materialism. It turns to a consciousness of the present that breaks the continuum of history"[58]—in the context of evaluating Mehring's Lessing book. The polarity Benjamin describes between a merely passive historical contemplation and the active-critical task of historical materialism corresponds to the distinction between the positivist cult of the classic and Mehring's historiography of reception.

In addition to criticizing Hohenzollern ideology, Mehring addresses the commercialization of contemporary literary life, drawing on both his own experiences of corruption in the press and the implications of Marxist social criticism. The former is evident in the discussions of contemporary drama as complaints against the "organized clique" and the "humbug of business advertising," terms he uses to characterize bourgeois theater criticism. Mehring explicitly attacks this commercial criticism, since "unmasking the deceptions of advertising belongs among the first tasks of criticism."[59] Thus he repeats the claim raised frequently after the 1860s regarding the prevalence of corruption in the institution of literary criticism.

Mehring also used Marxist social theory to explain that the historical changes in the theater after 1890 were a consequence of the contradictory class interests of the bourgeois public. He provided particular insights into the fate of naturalism, as in his diagnosis in 1901 that the naturalists were forced to find dramatic solutions to problems that could have been genuinely solved within the existing social order. He also described there the two alternatives open to the naturalists: first, that of Hauptmann, who "soon enough went in for little compromises" such as joining the neo-Romantic movement, which avoided the socialist problematic; and second, that of Max Halbe, whose attempts "to drive naturalism beyond itself" not only put too great a demand on his artistic talents but also met with the rejection of a public that would not put up with a writer who dared "to press home the conflicts of capitalist society."[60]

Although both political tendencies—the attack on Prussian ideology and the Marxist critique of capitalism—dominated Mehring's literary critical discussion, he also staked out an aesthetic dimension beyond political or social tensions. This realm of beauty, in which every successful work of art participated, never represented a concrete alternative to social reality, however; Mehring was not propounding an escapist aestheticism, but he was prepared to discriminate between the social-political elements of any work and its actual character as art. Georg Lukács attributed this feature of Mehring's literary criticism to his closeness to a putative line of influence from Kant to Lassalle, one that diverged sharply from the Hegel-Marx tradition.[61] Lukács's historico-philosophical gloss pointed up certain features of Mehring's aesthetics, but it was also closely bound up with Lukács's own ideological needs in 1933. In social-historical terms, Mehring's discrimination of a purely aesthetic dimension can be understood as a correlate of the heterogeneous character of contemporary social democracy with its mix of revolutionary rhetoric and integrationist reformist practice. Mehring never eschewed radical political analysis of a work, yet even when he rejected that work's political implications, he would be ready to grant it a formal-aesthetic greatness, as if real aesthetic questions lay beyond the social realm. Thus the foundation was laid for a depoliticized reception of bourgeois art by a proletariat eager for integration, especially during the Weimar Republic.

The contradiction between politics and aesthetics in Mehring's work is clearly embodied in an essay of 1895 about Franz Grillparzer's *Traum ein Leben*. Here the fact that Grillparzer "remained more or less distant from great strata of the German nation, namely, the working classes" is attributed to the reactionary character of the Metternich period. Life and work bore witness to a spirit that must seem completely alien to the modern, class-conscious proletariat: "He was the son of his time, a miserable, useless, decrepit time, from which he could not completely free himself. Revolutionary titans could not flourish in Metternich's Austria." This would constitute the first step of the treatment of a work on the basis of the base-superstructure schema. But for Mehring,

Grillparzer's significance is not exhausted in the quietist features whose social-historical genesis he is able to explain. Alongside the restorationist tendency, which he ascribes to a failure of political history, he emphasizes a definite aesthetic success that he finds lacking in, for example, the north German contemporary Ernst Raupach, who had been working in an equally conservative context: "One may compare the melodic and gentle flow of Grillparzer's dramas with the dreadful logroads along which Raupach drives the Prussian court tragedy." Grillparzer's advantage over Raupach is for Mehring a purely artistic one: political judgment is distinguished from aesthetics, and a contradictory image of Grillparzer emerges, acknowledging both his regressive message and his work's irreproachable quality as art. Consequently, Mehring can cite approvingly the comments of bourgeois critics like Heinrich Laube and even Karl Frenzel on the beauty of Grillparzer's drama, though the message of the content of the play—a "return from the raging world to the peace of home" (Frenzel)—calls forth Mehring's displeasure: "It is scarcely necessary here to stress that this bourgeois philistine conception is completely at odds with the proletarian ethic."[62] Political rejection and aesthetic enjoyment—this duality reflected the social composition of the worker movement of the prewar period with its critique of bourgeois society and its simultaneous yearning for integration into bourgeois culture. The activist acuity of Mehring's literary criticism could still mediate between the two contradictory elements. But in the course of the 1920s, after the split in the labor movement, this balance broke down: the literary criticism of the proletarian public sphere divided into a depoliticized-aesthetic discourse and a scientific Marxism-Leninism.

Following the collapse of the Empire, the social democratic labor movement during the Weimar Republic continued to suffer from a relative underdevelopment of its literary and cultural theory. This subordination of aesthetic questions to economic problems was a consequence of the productivist reduction of Marxism, which limited the critique of capitalism to laws of economic development. Furthermore, after 1919 the SPD became the most important supporter of the state and consequently tended to foreground more practical considerations. Since the party saw its main goal in the extension of social legislation, it did not emphasize the development of a decidedly socialist culture. In this, the prewar skepticism about demands for an independent proletarian culture, which had also colored Mehring's program, certainly continued to play a role. The fact that such demands could not find much resonance among either party theoreticians or workers corresponded to the widely held wish for social advancement and integration into the petty bourgeoisie in order to escape the misery of the conditions of proletarian life. After the revolution, which brought the establishment of a democratic republic but was not able to break the power of conservative forces in the army and heavy industry, a mood of resignation set in. The alliance between the SPD and the Wilhelmine general staff at the foundation of the Republic further impaired the already labile self-understanding of the class and thus called into question the desirability of a proletarian literary public sphere.[63] The possibility of linking antipathy to the state with social-revolutionary content consequently disappeared. The SPD renounced plans for an explicitly proletarian culture, and bourgeois aesthetic ideals came to dominate the socialist literary discussion.

Basic to the critical discussion in the SPD organ *Vorwärts* during the 1920s was the supposition that culture offers a class-neutral dimension outside the sphere of production. In art and literature, questions of class are not relevant; through aesthetic experience the worker can therefore transcend his proletarian existence in order to attain an authentic humanity. In 1929, for example, the writer Gerrit Engelke was praised for having shed his proletarian background, for no longer being a "workers' poet, but instead a poet *tout court* and an artist." The opposition of a specific social affiliation to a general human character to be attained only through art signifies the adoption of an element central to bourgeois aesthetics in Germany since Weimar Classicism: depoliticized poetry was ranked above any tendentious literature, and political writing was discredited in the eyes of a working class that had in any case been disappointed with politics.[64]

The bourgeois transformation of the critical discussion in the SPD press was carried out in the shadow of competition with the commercialized mass media. The beginnings of that press, whose influence on the status of the journalist has already been mentioned, lay in the founding years of the empire and were based on three innovations: a technological one, the introduction of the rotary press, first used at the London *Times*; an economic one, the increase in advertising revenue as a source of finance and the consequent loss of importance of subscription revenues; and a legal one, the first permit to sell newspapers on the street (Leopold Ullstein's *BZ am Mittag*), starting on November 22, 1904. Despite the liberal commitment of Ullstein and Rudolph Mosse, among the most powerful press magnates of the empire, a depoliticized mass press thoroughly loyal to the government was built up by August Scherl; in 1883 he founded the *Berliner Lokal-Anzeiger*, which simultaneously propagated conservative respect for authority and manipulated mass taste.[65] This loyalist mass press presented the liberal firms with strong competition and was gradually built up into a newspaper empire that Scherl sold in 1913 to a group "friendly to the government"; it became the foundation of the operations of the radical rightist media magnate Alfred Hugenberg.

The Hugenberg press contributed greatly to the weakening of the Weimar Republic. It exercised an inestimable attraction on the mass public, which put great pressure on an SPD press that had hoped to be equally effective among the masses, though with the opposite political position. Demands were therefore raised to depoliticize the SPD press somewhat in order to make it more entertaining and thus keep the mass readership from the influence of the commercial press. Such considerations led the *Vorwärts* to introduce theme-based supplements—the "Book World Review," "Film World," "Home World," and the like—which, though they certainly did not completely renounce political perspectives, were separated from the central social political themes, as if the cultural realm lay beyond urgent questions of class struggle. This segregation of the aesthetic dimension corresponded to a change within the socialist feuilletons, which traded in their political edge for the kind of entertainment found in the mass press. "In the realm of cultural politics the trend away from articles about basic principles prevailed just as did the increasing abandonment of polemical agitation. In their place . . . came announcements and reviews of performances, glosses, stories, poems, theater and book reviews, reports and commentaries on current events, a 'Puzzle Corner,' caricatures, and so forth."[66] The trend toward depoliticization of cultural discussion in the SPD press thus converged with the dreams of upward mobility in the proletarian readership; both factors led to a divorce of culture from social confrontation—whether "culture" implied mere entertainment or the ethereal dimension of authentic humanity.

In stark contrast to the bourgeois orientation of social democratic

literary criticism, the discussion in the press of the Communist Party
(KPD) and the syndicalist Communist Workers Party (KAPD) was
strongly antibourgeois. Naturally, a different estimation of the Weimar
Republic found expression there: while the SPD considered the democratic state the suitable context for promoting social progress, the
Communists saw it merely as a capitalist state to be overthrown by
proletarian revolution. The KPD first called for a general boycott of all
cultural activity. This demand corresponded to the program of the
party to pursue its battle in parliament and through the trade unions,
where participation in literary life represented a distraction from social-political confrontations. In relation to the same historical situations, the left Communist KAPD came to a completely different cultural
political position. It stressed the absence of subjective readiness for
revolutionary action in the proletariat despite the presence of objectively revolutionary conditions. "The problem of the development of
the self-consciousness of the German proletariat" thus gained central
significance, whence followed an emphasis on cultural questions. The
correlative openness of the KAPD to bourgeois writers, who, radicalized by the war, formulated an expressionism with revolutionary
trimmings, soon led on the one hand to tensions between the divergent goals of the leftist workers and the aesthetic avant-garde; on the
other hand, left-wing Communism's identification with modernist
experimentation had an indirect influence on Communist criticism
because the KPD was eager to distinguish itself from the KAPD in order
to make way for the union with the more moderate Independent
Social Democratic Party (USPD), which occurred in December 1920.
This political constellation within the left explains the fact that up until
1924 Gertrud Alexander, the anti-avant-garde student of Mehring,
played a determinant role in the feuilletons of the *Rote Fahne:* not
because of an explicit discussion in the party about literary politics but
because the direction of her criticism converged with other party
goals.[67]

Alexander's programmatic article of 1921 on the criticism of bourgeois art shows to what extent her literary critical practice shaped the
identity of the KPD by demarcating it from other proletarian tendencies. She polemicized against the leftist "cultural anarchism" of the
"representatives of the cult of the proletarian," which meant primarily
Erwin Piscator's Proletarian Theater, while her demand for a clear

position on class conflict clarified the divergence from the SPD. The pressure to imitate the commercial mass press (discussed above with respect to *Vorwärts*) she decisively rejected: "Certainly those must be granted their rights who demand entertainment. But it must also be said here that today it is more important to fight than to 'enjoy art,' even in the feuilleton." Although serialized novels did take up a lot of space in the cultural pages of the *Rote Fahne,* in fact it always incorporated a political dimension. Literary questions remained closely tied to topical social political controversies; they did not disappear in a separate aesthetic sphere. Thus Alexander inherited Mehring's engaged legacy: "It is absolutely necessary to take a critical position with regard to bourgeois art, theater, etc. It is the indispensable appendix to our political development. It is necessary at every step to show—and to explain—the decay and uselessness of most bourgeois art events and offerings. It is necessary to destroy that illusion of a 'revolutionary' bourgeois art, which expressionism and dadaism and everything 'modern' pretend to be. It is necessary that the proletariat take a public stand on all these things, in contrast to the bourgeois and social democratic press."[68]

The situating of Communist literary criticism as "appendix" to the actual political activity of the party makes clear the continuity with Mehring's linkage of political tendency and aesthetics. The unmistakable disappointment with the state of bourgeois literature also recalls Mehring's analyses, in which the decay of the stage is derived from its capitalist character. Thus in the background an aesthetic ideal is postulated which the bourgeois literature industry, not to mention the avant-garde, is no longer in a position to realize. To expose this crisis of bourgeois cultural production, the critic was called upon to function as an agent of enlightenment, who, with his aesthetic and theoretical training, could educate the proletarian readership.

In this sense, the *Rote Fahne* undertook to present a variety of literary objects. The public homages on the occasion of Ibsen's one hundredth birthday in 1928, for example, occasioned Paul Braun's portrait of the dramatist, which explored the social background and political content of his work while avoiding formal aesthetic issues. A similar example of the mediation of literary works by investigation of their political implications is Karl August Wittfogel's essay on novels about the "Imperialist War," which dealt with "class conflict in war literature from 1914 to 1930." There, a multiplicity of works—from Walter Flex and Ernst Jünger to Erich Maria Remarque and Johannes Becher—is virtually catalogued, chronologically ordered, and classified in terms of the Communist understanding of the imperialist character of the war.[69] Other issues include the many articles on Piscator's drama-turgy, which after Alexander's replacement in 1924 took on a positive tone, and also the commentaries on the contemporary German debate about radio and literary developments in the Soviet Union.

The defeat of the left-wing governments in Thuringia and Saxony in 1923 led to a general revision of Communist strategy, and the preced-ing phase of politics was rejected as rightist and opportunist. This change of course had major consequences for literary politics and literary criticism, which had either been based on an inconsistent program or, as in the case of Alexander, had expressed an antipathy toward an independent proletarian culture. "One began to grasp artis-tic activity as a part of the overall propaganda work of the party that was still to be integrated. The guideline was no longer an abstract concept of art but rather the question of functionality with respect to the strategy and tactics of the party. The basis of cultural work should be the cultural activities of the workers themselves." Particularly after 1927 it became possible to speak "of a planned development of cultural politics in the various sectors" without any homogeneous, centrally planned organization.[70] For example, the novels of the League of Proletarian-Revolutionary Writers (BPRS) could be reviewed in dif-ferent ways in the various KPD periodicals. The principled promotion of a proletarian culture led to two separate tasks for literary criticism. First, the traditional deficit in theory had to be overcome through the development of a Marxist aesthetic. In this, references to literary de-velopments in the Soviet Union played an increasingly important role, which reflected the growing dependency of the KPD on the Commu-nist Party of the Soviet Union and on the Comintern. Second, grass-roots literary activity in the party was fostered through the worker-correspondent movement; the literary critical corollary imitated forms of bourgeois journalism (as evidenced by the founding of a "Pro-letarian Feuilleton Correspondence" after the party conference in Es-sen in 1927), while also developing a qualitatively new discourse, "mass criticism." When at the end of the 1920s there were signs of a new change of course in Communist politics, eventually leading to the replacement of the proletarian direction of the mid-1920s by an anti-Fascist popular front, these two literary critical types came into conflict.[71] The transition can be traced in a controversy in 1931–32 in the *Linkskurve* (Left curve; 1929–32), which permits a reconstruction of the literary and social character of mass criticism in the proletarian public sphere.

In this context, the aesthetic content of the conflict over the proletarian-revolutionary novel cannot be examined here; it has been treated often in the scholarly literature. For our purposes it is more important to delineate clearly the two literary critical models associated with Lukács's critical rejection of the novels of Willi Bredel, who had emerged out of the worker-correspondent movement. Lukács's initial essay appeared in 1931 in the November issue of *Die Linkskurve*; Bredel's response in the January 1932 issue conceded much to his critic, arguing from a developed Marxist-Leninist theory. The discursive structure remained similar to that of the bourgeois public sphere: the critic as privileged bearer of a poetological foreknowledge censured the artwork available to a public with literary interests.[72]

Only in the April issue did a rival critical mode emerge, in Otto Gotsche's comments on "the question of the qualification of our literature." Gotsche concedes at once that Bredel's novels lack "the application of dialectical analysis, the application of the science of Marxism-Leninism in the definition of the persons and the coexistence of the most various social levels." These are some of the criticisms that Lukács himself had made, but although Gotsche seems to agree with Lukács, the question remains how this deficit in the "application of dialectical analysis" and so on can be made good. In addition, despite the apparent concessions, Gotsche emphasizes the success of Bredel's novels: they "do not seem artificial, they are life." Gotsche thus comes to the defense of proletarian-revolutionary literature, despite its evident flaws, and he accuses Lukács of an erroneous criticism that fails to support this nascent literary culture: "Lukács correctly points out the positive sides of Bredel, but has applied a destructive method of criticism to the weaknesses in Bredel's books. It is not and cannot be the case that proletarian literature will develop without stumbling and bungling. The breakthrough of our literature has occurred; its perfection will come about only in the continuous up and down of the total process of development."[73] Gotsche asserts that the mistakes as well as the achievements of Bredel's work result from the objective "process of development" of proletarian-revolutionary literature. The effect of Lukácsian criticism is dubbed destructive, an apparent allusion to the critic's demand to adopt the artistic forms of traditional bourgeois literature as normative models.

If the critical objection of the literary expert is thereby disqualified, the question still remains how the flaws in the proletarian-revolutionary work are to be addressed. Gotsche answers with a strategy of "mass criticism." He reports that he discussed the essay of the critic "with a group of comrades" who were "worker readers, from the very milieu that Bredel had represented"; they all disputed the validity of Lukács's complaints and expressed their satisfaction or even enthusiasm for the novels. This, for example, was the response to Gotsche's question whether the characters seemed "artificial," as Lukács had claimed: "In *Rosenhofstrasse* everything is written as it really is. People really are so erratic and unpredictable in their actions." Just as the closeness of the novel to reality was valued, so also was its significance for practical political work: "What is important for us is not 'artistic' form but the value of the book in class struggle: and in that, *Rosenhofstrasse* has a hundred times better effect than do ten leaflets."[74] Literary theoretical suppositions are, to be sure, implied by these two statements—a certain conception of realism and the demand for an operative literature—but the issue here is not to prove their incompatibility with Lukács's aesthetic. The point is rather that Gotsche's reference to the reactions of a proletarian readership serves to exemplify and document a collective literary critical strategy. Through the direct interrogation of recipients, substantive moments of the proletarian experience of life—sensual concreteness and collective solidarity—are meant to be integrated into literary critical discussions.[75]

If the aestheticization of literary criticism in the bourgeois public sphere signified a mixing of poetic elements into the image of the critic, mass criticism aimed at transforming the reader into a critic. A new reception attitude was to be produced, one that would replace a passive enjoyment of art with active participation—a clear parallel to Piscator's and Brecht's reform of the theater. In addition, the relationship between literary progress and critical judgment was revised. For Gotsche, the weaknesses of proletarian-revolutionary literature are to be corrected not by the intervention of a theoretically privileged individual critic but through public proletarian debate in Communist Party cells, at the workplace or in the local community. His attack on the priority of the critic obviously had nothing to do with bourgeois hostility to the critic as manifested in naturalism or in Kerr's "indifference to objections." For Gotsche, the author certainly requires critical responses; the bearer of such criticism, however, is not a distinct stratum of the intelligentsia but the mass of proletarian readers: "We have learned endlessly from Bredel—not from Lukács—and tomorrow Bredel will learn from us. Our literature must become mass literature, our criticism, mass criticism."[76] So it is precisely the desired reciprocal relationship between the critical mass-reader and the proletarian-revolutionary writer that determines the attack on the priority of the critical agency. This characterizes the grassroots democratic character of Gotsche's mass criticism, which refused to privilege any theoretical leadership and spoke out on behalf of the development of a genuine proletarian culture without guardians or tutors.

In his response, arguing against "theories of spontaneity in literature," Lukács insists on the legitimacy of the critical specialist, who alone has command of the theoretical and literary historical knowledge necessary to promote the development of a revolutionary literature. Not the layman but only the critic can, "if need be, independently recognize the necessary developmental tendencies of the epoch," which a mere reportage of empirical facts would tend to overlook. "Independently" refers especially to cases where the eventual addressee of criticism does not attain any corresponding insight, implying that proletarian authors left to themselves cannot advance beyond an underdeveloped understanding of literature and society. Only through the knowledge imported from without by the critic can the leap be made to the valid consciousness necessary for the revolutionary labor movement. The critic gains legitimacy because he knows how to "fight, if necessary, against the given practice of the writers."[77] Lukács thereby explains precisely why his position on Bredel did not have the "destructive" effect Gotsche had imputed to it but, on the contrary, had contributed to the progress of proletarian literary production.

Lukács's insistence on the necessity of a knowledge brought to bear from without betrays the Leninist component in his model: just as the labor movement cannot do without the leadership of a revolutionary party, so does the success of its class-combative literature remain dependent on a superior critical agency. But it is noteworthy that despite its partisanship, Lukács's criticism is surprisingly similar to Kerr's contemporary critical model. Of course, the differences in style and political tendency are great, but Lukács as much as Kerr conceived the critic as bearer of an enlightening knowledge and as one who was to intervene from above in social reality—for Kerr, it was "life"; for Lukács, "the labor movement"—because social reality was not able to reform itself without the leadership of the intelligentsia. This shared concept of criticism also throws light on their common rejection of the forms of political-literary modernism, which, as in Brecht's case, questioned the priority of a univocal artistic message addressed to a passive recipient.

Political Criticism and the Weimar Left

The emphatic insistence on the privileged position of the critic, evident in the models of both Kerr and Lukács, is symptomatic of a structural legitimacy crisis of the institution of literary criticism. There no longer existed any apparently natural or unquestioned role for the critic to play, and every critical practice consequently required an additional legitimation, which in turn overdetermined the treatment of literary texts: Kerr's bohemian pathos or Lukács's claim to a Marxist science. The two figures also shared a political coloration of discourse, indicative of a significant change in the self-conception of the German intelligentsia, above all in leftist circles. The growing dissatisfaction after 1916 with the political and military leadership, the demands of the revolutionary period, and the transition to a republic led to a politicization of the intellectuals, who now saw themselves in a position to participate actively in public life. For the bourgeois writer this change signified a rejection of aestheticist escapism and a recognition of the intermeshing of literature and social processes. Thus, for example, Thomas Mann emphasized in his speech on the founding of the section for poetry of the Prussian Academy of Arts (1926) that the writer, now discovering his "sociality," had discovered "that he was an expression, a mouthpiece; that he spoke for many when he believed he was talking for himself, only about himself." He had discovered "that works of art and spirit are not only enjoyed socially, but are also already initiated and conceived socially."[78] The traditional bourgeois conception of culture, based on the postulate of an aesthetic dimension divorced from social reality, was apparently no longer credible even in influential bourgeois circles in the Weimar Republic. A politicization of literary criticism ensued, which derived, however, from a deep loss of certainty about the social status of the writer. The representational claim that the author "spoke for many when he believed he was talking for himself, only about himself" masked a real sociohistorically determined isolation; the new specification of the intellectual amounted to a compensatory appropriation of an apparently more plausible identity.

This newly assumed political identity permitted intellectuals to attack cultural phenomena that did not correspond to their avant-garde political and aesthetic expectations. For example, shortly after the end of the war, Kurt Hiller attacked the perpetuation of a liberal bourgeois hegemony, which in his opinion had long been discredited: "In the feuilleton of the 'large-scale' press, in the pay of advertising capital, the feuilletonist rabble continues to ravage the spirit with all its mendacious chicanery; Herr Georg Bernhard, renegade, publisher, director, political dilettant, and mass murderer, still considers himself—with success—to be someone who has the right to exist; the Sudermanns and cohorts still dare to open their mouths. And this is supposed to be a revolution?" Hiller's criticism is based on the assertion that bourgeois culture has failed to achieve a spiritual ideal either in literature or in politics. Only the intellectual is in a position to do so; hence Hiller's attribution of the great political event, the collapse of the empire in the revolution, to the prowess of the intellectual leadership. The participation of broad strata of the population seems to have been of secondary importance for him: "The will to shake off the oppressors had grown slowly, systematically nourished by those whose task was the revolutionizing of minds; explosive energies had accumulated. The long-nurtured thought of the leaders suddenly became the deed of the masses. The proletariat proved itself to be the great executor." Hiller is here remarkably close to Lukács on the privileging of the intelligentsia, which allegedly directed a proletariat unable to make spontaneous revolution. Hiller developed this intellectual priority into his program of "logocracy"; that is, rule by the intellectuals, corresponding to the basic activist position, intervention in the political sphere out of the security of a superior class-neutral standpoint. The heroization of the writer as critic was coupled to a political naiveté, a combination characteristic of leftist criticism in general. The invocation of the republican context allowed for a politicization of the discourse, but the understanding of politics remained very limited and was never systematically thought through; rather, it was merely invoked repeatedly whenever the opportunity arose.[79]

The problematic character of this politicization is particularly clear in the literary critical work of Kurt Tucholsky, published in *Die Weltbühne* (1905–33). Marked by an idiosyncratic mixture of romantic pessimism and an antimilitary radicalism, Tucholsky never drew up any consistent program for politicizing literature but took each discussion to be the occasion for criticizing authoritarian or reactionary features of society. Thus he in fact returned to the central tactic of feuilletonism, for it was the subjective impressions of the critic, not any aesthetic or social-political theory, that made possible the integration of extra-aesthetic elements into critical discourse. The political coloration of a review depended mainly on references to elements of content of the work in question. For example, in an essay about Heinrich Mann's *Der Untertan* the attention of the reader is directed toward the obvious social-critical relevance but not to its character as a novel. As a critic, Tucholsky made no pretense of promoting avant-garde innovations, nor did he thematize the mechanisms of the social effect of literature; he mentioned the reception of a recent publication either not at all or only in passing in order to make a political point, as his discussion of James Joyce's *Ulysses* reported its censorship in Britain and the United States. Tucholsky foregrounded whatever aspect of a book best permitted a political account. Ernst Ottwalt's *Denn sie wissen, was sie tun* was certified to be "a good help in the battle against the legal system," but Tucholsky drew no further consequences from his aesthetic objections; in contrast, Lukács's account of the same novel turned into a major theoretical pronouncement. This difference is all the more telling because Tucholsky and Lukács displayed similar responses, both comparing Ottwalt's text to the normative model of the nineteenth-century novel.[80] While Lukács referred to Leo Tolstoy's *Resurrection*, Tucholsky invoked Stendhal, but the contrast, which for Lukács embodied an important moment in the development of socialist-realist aesthetics, functioned for Tucholsky as merely a question of taste, whose significance could never overshadow the consideration of political implications.

Tucholsky's version of a politicized literary criticism never went beyond an ultimately personal comment, a strategy strongly reminiscent of Fontane. It is therefore not surprising to find Tucholsky commending an anthology of Fontane's criticism. But while Fontane's feuilletonism exploded an epigonic critical discourse with new contents, the subjectivism of the leftist critic in the Weimar Republic functioned as a compensation for the lack of social significance. The political gesturing could not undo the profound transformation of the public sphere. For this reason, after Tucholsky's suicide in 1935, Hiller was able to comment: "It is very possible that Tucholsky suffered deeply in his last years from his, let us say, impressionism or feuilletonism, and that a more grounded, systematic, and methodical way of writing hovered as an ideal before his eyes, but he no longer trusted in his power to realize it."[81]

The leftist intellectuals, who as "free-floating intelligentsia" claimed to stand above the actual party struggle, chose a political path that led at best to a politicization—itself restricted—of the content of criticism. The social historical situation of the intelligentsia itself was not thematized, either in the form of a self-critical analysis of the claim to leadership in politics or as a concrete linkage to the actual political powers in the republic. Basically, this politicization mediated the constitution of an identity, perhaps also the construction of a public image, but not the development of a decidedly political praxis, which would have had to consist of more than a melancholic bemoaning of social grievances. At its best, this politicized literary criticism amounted to tendentious reviewing, casting barbs against a political opponent but achieving no lasting influence. Walter Benjamin wrote of the "proletarian mimicry by the dilapidated bourgeoisie" that the politicization of the intelligentsia was based above all on an imitation of the radical proletariat, not on any genuine motivation of the intellectuals themselves to engage in politics. Since the critical intelligentsia could no longer play an active social role, it adopted a political disguise, as much an alibi as was the strategy of aestheticization pursued by Kerr. At the same time, the content of this "left-wing melancholy" guaranteed that such politicization would never result in authentic politics.[82]

Benjamin's complaint that leftist journalism ends up as entertainment and amusement recalls similar attacks on the feuilletonism of the empire. Indeed the causeries of the 1870s and the satires of the Weimar Republic were not unrelated. But the feuilletonists had taken a stand, in their historical context, against a conservative and depoliticized criticism, while the left bourgeois intelligentsia, despite or precisely because of the nature of their political claim, transformed politics into mere feuilletonism. In this way criticism certainly secured a social prominence and public notoriety, but it remained politically irrelevant. The ostentatious political identity was meant precisely to veil this political inconsequentiality: that is, to maintain the priority of the critic despite the crisis of the literary public sphere. Meanwhile, several other models of criticism took shape toward the end of the Weimar period, some of which, though with widely disparate intentions, recognized the crisis of the institution of criticism and therefore tried to reshape the social relationship between critic and public.

Criticism and Its Addressee

In the middle of the nineteenth century, literary criticism was still able to address the social stratum of the educated bourgeoisie and civil servants, which conceived itself simply to be "good society" and for which discussion of literary objects provided a desirable form of sociability. Continuing the traditions of the reading societies of the eighteenth century and the salons of the early nineteenth, the participants in literary life commanded a homogeneous canonical education, while literary conversation excluded matters of practical interest and therefore seemed to embody a general human significance. Furthermore, the gradually emerging professional critic, who merely published what could be discussed in the public realm of sociability, functioned as an equal representative of the public.

Yet in the course of the second half of the century this bourgeois ideal was undermined by various social-historical developments: the capitalization of literary life and the commercialization of literary criticism put in question the credibility of the critic; the emergence of an artistic *boheme* and the avant-gardist claims of the critic led to a rift with the broad public; and the political developments after the founding of the empire induced a discrediting of bourgeois ideals and social forms. In addition, the burgeoning labor movement, especially following its turn to Marxism after 1890, appeared to refute the universalist self-understanding of the bourgeois public sphere. The bourgeois literary discussion, which still provided Frenzel with a sounding board of interested recipients, forfeited its credibility. Moreover, the dissemination of an ideal of natural science, which accompanied industrialization, displaced art from the center of bourgeois attention. Consequently, the precondition of a homogeneous education, which had characterized earlier bourgeois discourse, was no longer guaranteed.[83] The audience that once reasoned in public about cultural objects disappeared, and the consumers of a commercialized culture took their place. Lacking a public sphere with a critical capacity, they remained dependent on the statements of professional critics. The reflection of this development in, for example, Kerr's critical model was the construction of a chaotic "life" in which the critic alone was capable of intervention. To the extent that the critic lacked reasoning recipients, he became a "great critic," free of the constraints of logical argumentation and relying increasingly on the impressionist reproduction of his own arbitrary reactions.

The greatest opponent of this aestheticized journalism and in particular of Kerr was Karl Kraus, in whose periodical *Die Fackel* (The torch; 1899–1936) a polemic battle against feuilletonism and its representatives was conducted over several decades. Almost all articles were by Kraus himself; only in the period before 1911 did some few articles appear by other writers, such as Carl Bleibtreu and Peter Altenberg. According to Kraus, the project was, on the one hand, to unmask the corruption that arose out of the collusion of the commercial press and special-interest politics, and, on the other, to combat this press and its language as a factor in the destruction of culture:

> So why have I chosen to attack the *Neue Presse* as my main target? because I consider it to be more than a newspaper that serves its buyers with news and advertisements. Because the faith in revealed truth with which our citizenry greets each of its assertions seems to me to be an evil that paralyzes any development here in our country. The press in Germany, France, and England is also corrupt, as it is in all other countries that, proud of their culture,

stand on the auspicious threshold of a century of the three-column nonpareil line. But what a difference! The public lady who, abroad, serves public needs without resistance but without great feeling either, here at home clothes herself in the garb of the priestess who gives indulgence with dicta of virtue and wisdom to those who have paid in cash. If our press presented itself as what it really is, as an element of the capitalist world order, how much better for us![84]

It was precisely the pretentious cultural claims of the Austrian press that stirred Kraus to his feud, for the confusion of reporting with literary goals evidently ruined both journalism and literature. In an open letter to Maximilian Harden, therefore, Kraus contrasted the aestheticization of the Viennese press with the merely political papers of Berlin: "Free writing has delivered up its best juices to the feuilleton section, on occasion even to the editorial pages. Our newspapers, to whose wanton glitter I still prefer the barrenness of reportage in the Berlin papers, are gracious enough to give the theater its dramatists every year, after they have subdued the novelists."[85]

Kraus traced this feuilletonist "amalgamation of the intellectual and the informational" back to Heine's reports from Paris.[86] In a 1911 essay on "Heine and the consequences" he combined two basic strands of thought: as expression of the commercial press, feuilletonism serves corruption, and, just for that reason, it takes on an opaque literary appearance in order to obscure the actual state of affairs. The criticism of corruption thus blended into the rejection of a merely ornamental literature, which was no longer conscious of its own task of enlightenment. The proximity to the critique of ornamentation by the radical modern Viennese architect Adolf Loos was highlighted by Kraus himself; nevertheless, his stand against Heine lost him many left and liberal supporters in Berlin, who were shocked by his proximity to the right-wing attacks on Heine. Kraus, however, was less concerned with the overall literary phenomenon of Heine than with the development of a culture industry that blocked the growth of an authentic literature. His recurrent critique in *Die Fackel* of journalistic language—often only in the form of reprinted excerpts from articles published elsewhere, with his own mordant comments—constituted a fundamental settlement of accounts with feuilletonism and the press: literary criticism as critique of the journalistic literature business.

In contrast to the combative and satirical *Fackel*, which Kraus used as a polemical organ, *Die literarische Welt* (The literary world; 1925–33) was founded in order to provide a nonpartisan overview of events in the world of letters. Initiated by the publisher Ernst Rowohlt and modeled on the Parisian *Nouvelles littéraires*, it was edited by the former film critic Willy Haas. Haas was not eager to promote any particular literary or political program, as he later emphasized in his memoirs: "I just put in whatever seemed good or important or even just funny and witty or irritating." This pluralism corresponded to the emphasis on innovation in literary life: not only new publications but also current literary affairs were discussed; Haas polled well-known writers of all persuasions, from the Communist Johannes Becher to the Fascist Ernst Jünger, for their uncensored views on topical themes. His only programmatic commitment was to report on new developments: "The *Literarische Welt*," he recalled, "was a newspaper, not a periodical. . . . The greater part of each number was simply filled with the latest news, literary news, news of theater life and art life, and not just in Germany but throughout the world." Consequently, the *Literarische Welt* was able, for example, to play an important role in advancing the German reception of Marcel Proust. While it always brushed topical political themes, it did so only to the extent that politics had itself taken on a literary coloration. Thus, in the spirit of the Locarno Treaty, the first number ran an article by Thomas Mann on the idea of cosmopolitanism, and short statements by foreign writers, including Henri Barbusse, Paul Claudel, Jean Cocteau, and Ilya Ehrenburg on their connection to German culture. The second number of the *Literarische Welt* examined Italian Fascism but, typically, only with respect to a conflict between Benedetto Croce and Benito Mussolini in which the dictator was accused of literary plagiarism. In this way the periodical remained true to its title: world events were treated only as literary events. Similarly, after a long interview with Paul von Hindenburg had been published in Paris, the journal published a translation only of the excerpts relating to the president's literary preferences.[87] This narrowness of perspective points up the real character of the organ. Despite its claim to pluralism, the *Literarische Welt* expressed the very particular experience of a distinct literature industry: here writers spoke about the writing trade. This literary-aesthetic orientation diverged from the project of the publications of the genuine avant-garde in that no program was advocated except the establishment of literature as a distinct realm of interest.

The contemporary multiplicity of literary periodicals corresponded to the juxtaposition of competing critical models and the loss of security about the inherited relationships between author, critic, and public. The heterogeneity of literary life characteristic of the first third of the twentieth century explains the coexistence—albeit rarely peaceable—of different types of criticism: subjectivist feuilletonism next to avant-garde polemic, the impressionism of the "great critics" beside objective literary analyses. No single type of periodical could have encompassed all these tendencies; hence the dispersion of literary criticism among different kinds of publications: the large daily press; general panoramic reviews such as the *Deutsche Rundschau* (German review; 1874–1964) and the *Süddeutsche Monatshefte* (South German monthly; 1904–36); the programmatic journals of political, ideological, or aesthetic interest groups. Criticism ran the risk of losing any institutional cohesion and becoming a mere function of the site of its publication or the particular addressee.

Literary Criticism and Fascism

In the context of this crisis of the bourgeois public sphere, a Fascist populist or *völkisch* literary criticism emerged, which played a central role in the radical right-wing movements that led to National Socialism. While traditional criticism insisted on a strict division between literature and politics, and various versions of leftist criticism treated literature as a possible field of political practice, *völkisch* critics brought culture into the very center of political interest. This aestheticization of politics fueled a polemic against modernism, decried as an expression of liberalism and a threat to a purportedly authentic culture. Such dire predictions struck a responsive chord in the educated middle class, summoned to the defense of culture against the "civilizational" power of democracy. The social function of culture was transformed from an object of public discussion into a sign of membership in a certain social group. This shift paralleled the adoption of bourgeois ideals of art in the proletariat: for both classes the emptied objects of culture provided a semiotic display of the signs of a desired social standing.

The program for the defense of an idealized culture can be traced back to Richard Wagner's essays of the 1850s and their conservative critique of capitalism. Wagner envisioned a distant past in which the nation was united around the authentic work of art; he contrasted this utopia with the atomization of modern society. The reconstitution of the original community was declared the goal; liberalism, capitalism, and Judaism were the enemies. Despite rejection by large parts of the bourgeois public, including Nietzsche, who clearly recognized the regressive moments in Wagner's work, this critique of culture was systematically developed and disseminated through the *Bayreuther Blätter,* after Wagner's death in 1883, by the members of the Bayreuth circle, such as Hans von Wolzogen and Houston Stewart Chamberlain. But long before Chamberlain's public backing of Hitler in 1923 boosted the prestige of National Socialism in the eyes of the educated middle class, the ideological struggle of the Wagnerians for a cultural "regeneration" came together with other cultural reform movements of the turn of the century. In particular, a widespread resentment of industrial modernization and the spread of the natural sciences— despised as "civilization"—was linked to the *völkisch* program of a nationalist definition of culture.[88]

The first literary consequence of the *völkisch* program was an irrationalist attack on positivist literary historiography, which was criticized for ignoring the genuine creativity of culture. The separation of specialized academic scholarship from a bourgeoisie eager to maintain its identity as the bearer of culture generated a bitter resentment and an anti-intellectualism, as for example at the beginning of Julius Langbehn's best seller *Rembrandt als Erzieher:* "Moreover, education in the present is entirely historical, alexandrian, retrospective: it aims much less at the creation of new values than at the registration of old values. And this altogether demonstrates the flawed nature of modernity; it is scientific and wants to be scientific; but the more scientific it becomes, the more uncreative it becomes."[89] This polarity between a scientific and a creative view of education corresponded to a distinction between the restricted specialist and the creative personality, the agent of the *völkisch* renaissance. The critique of positivist scholarship implied the renunciation of an allegedly shallow "culture of understanding" in favor of an irrationalism tied closely to the erosion of liberal ideals in the empire. Thus the *völkisch* literary historian Adolf Bartels, whose activities stretched from the 1890s into the Third Reich, attacked the positivism of the Scherer school: "Its 'spirit' [is] nothing more than the mediocre old Enlightenment . . . baptized as humanism." Bartels attacked philology at the universities with decidedly anti-Semitic arguments, despite the restrictions on Jewish scholars in the empire; for him, Jewish literary historians and critics brought to bear "on our literature the fatal influence of Judaism, which begins in Rahel Varnhagen's salon and has grown progressively." Consequently, he not only conducted a journalistic campaign against the erection of a monument to Heine but also demanded "legal measures" to rescind the civil equality of Jews and exclude them from the literary public sphere.[90] These anti-emancipatory proposals had first been made during the anti-Semitism debate of 1880 and were eventually put into effect in 1935 with the exclusion of Jews from the Nazi Chamber of Writing.

In addition to his attacks on positivist scholarship, Bartels turned to feuilletonism, which he treated as part of the "literature of corruption" of the early 1870s and as a consequence of Jewish participation in literary life; the Jews represented "a powerful clique that could not be resisted." Bartels also stressed Wagner's argument that only Jews were prepared to gain commercial benefit from cultural goods. That they did not belong to the German nation explained their responsibility for the "French enslavement" of the German stage; their lack of respect for authentic culture furthered shallow journalistic criticism. In this way *völkisch* literary criticism defined itself against two competing models: positivist literary science, which was not willing to function "creatively," and feuilletonism, which was too creative to treat culture seriously. The unity of the nation as one race was postulated and the influence of other races characterized as negative. Superiority was ascribed to the German nation as part of an "Aryan" race, and Bartels complained that literary criticism had failed to carry out a cultural regeneration of the nation.[91] The proximity to the naturalist "Sedan of the spirit" is obvious.

The rival schemes for a *völkisch* aesthetic cannot be discussed in detail here, but attention must be drawn to three elements that decisively influenced the development of the literary critical discourse.

First, the claim of the superiority of German literature (the concept "Germanic" could be stretched to include figures like Shakespeare) led to a sharp rejection of foreign cultures and to the demand for a national rather than universal "literary science." Second, despite this nationalism, the biologistic doctrine of race at the root of *völkisch* thinking implied an emphasis on subnational—that is, regional—aspects. To Bartels, for example, Wolfram von Eschenbach was a representative of a Bavarian tribe, Lessing was an Upper Saxon, and Schiller a Swabian "with, perhaps, a drop of Celtic blood." Third, the view of literature of the *völkisch* literary critics had a strongly antibourgeois character, despite its proximity to the educated middle class. Once the concept of culture was lodged in a biologistic racialism, the traditional notion of autonomy gave way to pragmatic considerations and the identification of literature with radical right-wing agitation: a politicization of culture in the name of the defense of culture. For example, Bartels could set himself apart from the established Germanist Richard M. Meyer by judging the latter's posthumously published *Die deutsche Literatur bis zum Beginn des neunzehnten Jahrhunderts* (German literature through the beginning of the nineteenth century) as merely idealistic and lacking any concept of race. Against Meyer's sketch of a "history of literary ideas" Bartels claimed that "all literature, at least all poetry, comes out of life, that it is born by personalities, that behind every development stands the folk."[92]

The bourgeois conception of the autonomy of art was thus replaced by a cult of the creative personality, seen as an expression of the folk. Out of this grew claims directed against both literature and literary historiography: namely, that "every art and every science that does not immediately serve present needs is superfluous." Hans Grimm's 1932 demand for a literature that would fulfill a function in the current political struggle parodies the operative literature of the left. Grimm also raised the demand in an important literary critical interpolation in his novel *Volk ohne Raum* (Folk without space), where he rejects Thomas Mann's *Buddenbrooks* not primarily for aesthetic or ideological reasons but because the bourgeois novel cannot be of immediate use in the practice of life. The same postulate of the primacy of a literature that was practical in terms of the *völkisch* movement underlay Paul Fechter's review of Grimm's book: it is "not just a novel" and "more than merely a piece of art." Far from bourgeois-idealist disinterestedness, the *völkisch* ideal of literature was meant to function as a primer in the disputes of the day: "Hans Grimm's book is above all a leader and beacon of clarity for future generations about our urgent needs."[93]

This short outline of central elements of *völkisch* aesthetics explains certain features of literary critical practice. The nationalist component restricted attention to native authors, although great Englishmen or Scandinavians could be appropriated as "Aryans"; Bartels even claimed that "the great works of world literature are in fact all essentially Aryan."[94] Since the concept of nation was abridged in *völkisch* biological terms, authors of Jewish ancestry were rejected. The regionalism of the *völkisch* literary ideal directed the attention of critics mainly to local figures, which dovetailed with the National Socialist hostility to the urban centers.

But it was the third component of the *völkisch* ideal of literature that significantly determined the structure of literary critical discourse. Literary criticism, like literature, was to be mobilized with the Fascist movement. While leftist intellectuals considered intervening in the struggles of the day from an extrapolitical position, in the *völkisch* view the dimension of culture was collapsed thoroughly into Fascist politics. The literary critic did not just participate in current controversies on occasion but drew his entire identity from his engagement; a non-political realm of cultural autonomy ceased to exist. In Langbehn this displacement was still draped in his characteristic mystical aesthetic vocabulary: "The new-forming spirit can . . . only be the one that lives in German artists, this word being understood in the widest and best sense; they are the German prophets; they are the representatives of a culture of the heart, while scholars pay exclusive homage to a culture of reason. Professors look into the past; prophets look into the future; average German education, to the extent that it is alive, will have to turn away from the former and toward the latter."[95] The significance of the passage does not lie simply in Langbehn's repeated invocation of an anti-academic irrationalism. The image of the prophet anticipates the *völkisch* concept of the critic; the primacy it claims with respect to the recipient is not, as for Kerr, that of the *boheme*, defending the subjectivity of the critic, but rather that of a religious calling. The *völkisch* critic does not propagate his own private taste; instead, he comes forth as the charismatic champion of a cultural renewal, a return to the imputed essence of the folk. By placing himself in the service of regeneration, he acquires an apparently objective legit- imacy, derived from the tenets of *völkisch* ideology.

In contrast to Communist literary criticism, which repeatedly at- tempted to elaborate a Marxist aesthetics, the *völkisch* critics made no corresponding theoretical efforts. The reader was not called upon to follow substantial controversies about questions of principle; *völkisch* literary criticism lacked both consistently articulated principles and authentic debate, for real differences in direction were hardly ever publicly formulated. The single goal of literary critical practice re- mained the inculcation of the recipient with *völkisch* literature, and the reader was transformed into an object of administration. So in 1931, for example, Otto Forst de Battaglia enjoined the right-wing press to treat the review consistently as advertising for a book the message of which it considered worth supporting. The ensuing strategy of dis- cussing a work, leading to a "domination of the customers," would "combine a little animal training, a little political leadership, a lot of the secret of the father confessor, and above all pedagogy."[96] The reader of *völkisch* literary criticism is hardly envisioned as a subject capable of aesthetic or even political judgment, not even as a recipient of enlight- ening reportage, but merely as the object of a political marketing strategy. Reading behavior should be directed in the interest of the *völkisch* camp with the goal that Forst de Battaglia openly describes as the "spread of the good book, and thereby the economic strengthen- ing of the author and publishers."

Such a sales-oriented book-reviewing strategy is also evident in Paul Fechter's essay on Grimm's *Volk ohne Raum*. Fechter manifests his view of the anti-autonomous ideal of literature in his attestation that this novel is not merely literature; it possesses the ability "to collaborate in the creation of this folk, which is the task still facing us." But in the foreground of the essay (which appeared in 1931 as the most promi- nent article in the October issue of Will Vesper's periodical *Die neue Literatur*) is a simple exhortation to buy the new popular edition pub- lished by Albert Langen: "Everyone who was unable to own or per- haps even to read this book because of its price now has the oppor- tunity to buy it. One should do so, despite the bad times; for this book really belongs—the phrase for once applies literally—in every house whose inhabitants want to take part in the destiny of the nation in its most difficult time."[97] The marketing character of the *völkisch* literary criticism proposed by Forst de Battaglia is here clearly evident. The movement that set out to combat the commercialization of culture ended by addressing the reader simply as a customer. The crisis of the literary public sphere, manifested in the growing rift between public and critic, was superficially solved in the critics' conscious and manipulative turn against the readers—a social relationship continued later after 1933 in the various mechanisms of the state or party management of literary life.

It would be a mistake, however, to reduce *völkisch* literary criticism to this one commercial tendency. What was decisive was rather the goal of an organized management of the antimodernist readership, a goal that since the 1870s had led to the founding of a series of public organizations: the Wagner Societies of the Bayreuth establishment, the Dürer Association of Ferdinand Avenarius, and Alfred Rosenberg's Militant League for German Culture. Certainly, the nature of each cultural conservative group was different, but the constant common feature was the organization of the public under a regenerative or *völkisch* vanguard. In the name of antiliberalism, early naturalism had reproached the feuilletonists for failing to proclaim clearly delineated and unquestionable principles instead of merely reproducing impressionistically their personal opinions. In the *völkisch* literary criticism of Bartels any trace of private subjectivity disappears; the critic becomes an administrator, the "manager of the spiritual fortune of the nation, above all the manager of living values." A certain relationship to the public follows from this often-stressed administrative function: the public is invited not to participate in discussion or consensual deliberation but only to receive clear and definite instructions about national literature: "Literary science has the task of clarifying for contemplation and thought the driving forces of literature and, further, of the creative organism of one's own nation, and thereby to determine more and more exactly the essence of one's own nationhood and the course of its development. Therefore, it is national, like all human sciences. It must at all times aid the folk to gain a clear self-consciousness and thereby influence healthy development." The claims to clarity and precision characterize the critic as the agent of a univocal message, transmitted as effectively as possible. The relationship to the reader remains authoritarian and pedagogical: he or she is to assimilate simple statements without questioning them. The crisis of the literary public sphere is suppressed, insofar as readers are "instructed" and "inspired" to conceive of themselves as members of the folk but not as autonomous participants in a literary discourse.[98]

The Public as Critic: Bertolt Brecht

In Bertolt Brecht's reflections on the structure of literary life, it was precisely this enforced passivity of the public, the very goal of Fascist literary criticism, that constituted the starting point of his project of a revolutionary transformation of the public sphere. Contemporary literary life seemed to lead to a loss of the autonomy and maturity of the recipient: "We have . . . simply not noticed in one single case that the public that fills the theater today wants anything."[99] Brecht argued that the inability of the public to speak for itself was a consequence of the institution of criticism, which had contributed considerably to the stabilization of establishment theater. An alternative program for critical discourse, pointing to a fundamental transformation of reception patterns, developed through the critiques of the two opposing theater critics of the Weimar Republic: Alfred Kerr—from the start, hostile to Brecht—and Herbert Ihering, who endeavored to explain and propagate epic theater as an innovation of the stage.

Brecht treated Kerr's subjectivism as irresponsible: the feuilletonist critic was never concerned with the dramatic performance but merely with his own self-presentation by means of an ostentatious stylization of language. The asserted lack of interest in the aesthetic object and the privatist coloration of the critical text were for Brecht symptomatic of contemporary bourgeois literary criticism. Kerr was the paradigm of the so-called "culinary critic" who, concerned only with his own taste, could not defend his judgments with satisfactory arguments and therefore remained content simply to publicize his own reactions. Such descriptivism might have been compatible with naturalist theater but became helpless in the face of the modern stage after 1918. Since Brecht recognized the anachronism of Kerr's literary critical strategy, he was also able to perceive the actual function of aestheticization as an attempt at legitimation: Kerr, he said, was selling "his own criticism as poetry" because he had "apparently admitted to himself that it is the only way it will find any recognition."[100]

According to Brecht, culinary criticism corresponded to a two-track strategy to secure the capitalist character of the theater. First, Kerr's criticism provided aid and comfort to the bourgeois public: "I am convinced that Mr. Kerr's effectiveness consists in the fact that he has the taste of his public and that this public, by means of the ability to buy tickets and to prevent everyone else from buying tickets, keeps the theaters occupied. It is a society that demands as much of the theater as the cashier gets out of it and understands of it." The naturalists had already denounced Lindau and Heyse, for example, by identifying them with a bourgeois commercial stratum of recipients. Brecht's account of bourgeois criticism resulted in an equally pejorative equation: criticism confirms established taste because the critic simply acts as "taster," but thanks to the trust the bourgeois public places in Kerr's taste, the critic can fulfill his second and more important task—to guarantee the theatrical enterprise an unbroken flow of paying customers. Behind the poetical claims on which the culinary critic always insists, Brecht perceived a concrete socioeconomic function in the financing of the commercial culture industry: the critic was able "to pump the public into the entertainment and cultural apparatus of the theater." Established theater criticism was merely advertising, its social role that of "the entertainment advertiser. The theaters sell evening entertainment, and criticism sends the public to it."[101] Brecht's distrust of criticism grew stronger as he became more familiar with Marxism, a corollary of Mehring's confrontation with journalistic corruption and his move toward the socialist movement: Mehring's Lindau anticipates Brecht's Kerr. But while Mehring tried to find a completely valid standpoint for the specialized critic outside the culture industry, Brecht envisioned a profound transformation of the critical function as a differentiated moment of the literary public sphere.

In reviews in the *Berliner Börsen-Courier* from the early 1920s on, Herbert Ihering regularly championed Brecht's dramatic work. His critical ethos, somewhat reminiscent of Otto Brahm's, was based on the importance of a serious investigation of the performance and the aesthetic form. Theater criticism could provide analytic reflections crucial to the progress of dramatic developments. On no account should criticism make do with privatist impressions; it was not an "end in itself for feuilletonist tricks." Ihering thus decisively set himself apart from the subjectivism of Kerr: "Criticism is not there for its own sake, but for the sake of its object." Nevertheless, Brecht repeatedly expressed discontent with Ihering's critical project of trying to win epic theater for the bourgeois theater, for as Brecht complained, the goal of epic theater was the destruction of that very bourgeois stage. Ihering continued to make aesthetic judgments, while Brecht was waiting for decidedly political reactions. As he wrote to Ihering, "In bad times, to improve a bad thing means to save it. Your struggle for the theater is conducted on bourgeois aesthetic terrain: you distinguish between 'good' and 'bad.' Why do you not distinguish between 'right' and 'wrong?' "[102]

While Kerr's strategy of aestheticization transformed the critical text into literature, Ihering offered theoretical reflections that discerned progressive trends in order to nurture them. Critical discourse nevertheless remained an aesthetic discourse in that it was limited to aesthetic issues. Brecht demanded a social-political judgment: "Criticism should adopt the sociological, scientific point of view instead of the aesthetic culinary one. It must simply investigate entire complexes of artistic representations from the perspective: who benefits?" Such an unambiguously social perspective was foreign to Ihering. Like Brecht, he wanted to break with traditional theater life; like Brecht, he aimed at a turn toward the proletarian public and a dismantling of the bourgeois institution of art.[103] But such a transition would have signified for Ihering an aesthetic renewal; his quest sought a modern art, which would in part have needed stimulus from the working class. In contrast, Brecht advocated social change and for that reason demanded a criticism that would not primarily investigate the artistic quality of a modern work but could first and foremost thematize the social function of any work—*cui bono.*

Through the polemic against Kerr, Brecht made clear the dependency of subjectivist criticism on the commercial theater industry. Through the confrontation with Ihering, he made apparent the limits of an objective and theoretical but ultimately aesthetic discourse. For the Marxist Brecht of the later Weimar Republic, any work and any critical practice played a role in the social struggles of the time. Therefore, he demanded of a new criticism not some class-neutral position beyond the corruption of the culture industry but rather a programmatic acknowledgment of the political function of literature. The leading propositions of Marxism should be applied, but not in order to create a Marxist aesthetics. Instead, criticism should reveal the "complex of artistic representations" inherent in any work of art and test it for ideological content in order to ascertain its social standpoint. The only aesthetic problem would be the determination of the social genesis of various artistic forms.[104]

Though Brecht did not absolutely exclude the possibility of a discrete institution of criticism able to articulate political positions, he introduced a new bearer of critical discourse: the public. While the intended activation of the recipients constituted the heart of the program of epic theater, it also led to important consequences for the reconstruction of criticism. Once the public was no longer supposed to be forced into an empathetic emotional identification with dramatic materials, it could begin to articulate an independent critical stance. The culinary posture of the solitary critic would be replaced by the collective practice of the vocalized audience: "We are not concerned with the stand the professional taster takes when we talk of criticism. We are talking about the stand of the audience; our interest is in its emancipation, in particular its emancipation from the 'total' art experience." This collective criticism would still concern itself with the success of a performance but would foreground its political problematic. The public as critic in Brecht's model would consider the work only as the occasion for a public consideration of extra-aesthetic themes, for it is "not the artistic presentation of the world, but the world itself that should be grasped with criticism, contradiction, and detachment."[105] Brecht's politicization of literary criticism is therefore substantially different from alternative versions: Mehring's dualism of aesthetics and politics, or the occasional politicizing of the left-wing intellectuals. For Brecht it was the public as collective that had been politicized and could be directed toward particular political discussions.

Brecht's plan for a new literary criticism reflected various social-historical developments—especially the change in the bourgeois public sphere, which ascribed to the public an increasingly consumerist posture, and the growing interest of the more radical parts of the labor movement in participation in cultural life, embodied in the phenomenon of "mass criticism." Völkisch literary criticism attempted to stabilize the cultural hegemony of the educated middle class through its emphasis on an inviolable canon and the consolidation of the recipients' passivity in relation to the dictates of critical authority. Brecht's model of the critical agency of the public took the opposite route. The point was not, as with Bartels, to inoculate the audience with a definite line but to stimulate it to an active and ultimately autonomous participation. In addition, Brecht expected that this involvement in theater criticism would expand into a social criticism and, more important, into a transformed practice: "This criticism of the world is an active, acting, positive criticism. To criticize the course of a river means to improve it, to correct it. Criticism of society is revolution."[106] Only if criticism ceased to be the distinct privilege of a professional specialist could it become the project of the social collective and the concretization of an enlightenment autonomy. Late bourgeois criticism, whether in its fascist (Bartels), aesthetic (Ihering), or aestheticized (Kerr) version, claimed a privileged standpoint for the individual speaker and thereby disenfranchised the public. Brecht called for the abolition of the individual critic, not in order to do away with criticism (as Goebbels attempted to do in 1935) but in order to democratize it.

Literary Criticism as Literary Self-Criticism: Walter Benjamin

As much as Brecht's plan for public criticism differed from Walter Benjamin's reviews of the 1920s, they nonetheless shared a fundamental rejection of established criticism and its discursive structure; both challenged especially the privilege of the individual speaker. While Brecht envisioned the negation of departmentalized criticism through a collective practice, Benjamin was not at all concerned with the sort of popular accessibility that had characterized the entertaining feuilletonism of Kerr and the informal impressionism of Tucholsky. Instead, he turned—with an elevated writing style and a plethora of cultural allusions—to the stratum of the literary intelligentsia. He treated it, however, not as the carrier of a universal culture but as a particular social group whose behavior and potential in contemporary social conflicts he tried to describe and influence. Through a new understanding of its target group, literary criticism also gained a new function: it no longer served to make aesthetic judgments about important new publications or to further avant-garde aesthetic trends or to educate the nation. It served instead to clarify the sociopolitical role of writers in the widest sense: it was literary criticism as the self-criticism of literature.

Two aspects of Benjamin's early work decisively shaped his critical practice after the failure of his university career and after his turn to a wider public in 1924 in the *Frankfurter Zeitung*. Influenced by the neo-Romanticism of the youth movement and religious metaphysics—in particular, Jewish mysticism—he directed his early literary critical writings toward the small group of intellectuals who had command of similarly esoteric philosophical material. Since he never envisioned a broad public, his early writings—such as the important essay on Goethe's *Elective Affinities* of 1921–22—are characterized by an extremely hermetic style; Benjamin's plans for his own periodical recall Stefan George's *Blätter für die Kunst*, the prototype of the literary organ aimed at a small circle of cognoscenti. After economic necessity and a concomitant politicization induced him to break out of this isolation and to work as the reviewer for a newspaper, he reached wider circles but still only among the intelligentsia. Thus his literary critical strategy represents the opposite pole to that which Bartels, eager for a wide effectiveness, praised as "easy readability."[107] The public sphere to which he appealed was that of the literati, a group understood not as the vessel of a privileged culture but as a historical potential within the political tensions of contemporary society.

His early concepts of literature and criticism strongly colored his later work, after 1924. Like Kerr, the young Benjamin addressed aesthetic questions of German Romanticism in his dissertation. While both consequently treated the critical text as a literary art form, the similarity ends there; in his study of Clemens Brentano, Kerr developed a model of a subjectivist writing easily reconcilable with the feuilletonist tendencies of the turn of the century, while Benjamin concentrated on the philosophical principles of Friedrich Schlegel's theory of art. Benjamin adopted the Romantic concept of art especially in one point: that is, the claim that the work is a vessel of a truth which develops progressively but which the work can never complete. Rather, "the task of criticism is the completion of the work." Criticism functions as a continuation of the work: hence its own artistic character. Criticism therefore has nothing to do with the informative descriptiveness of positivism, nor does it serve to communicate knowledge to the reading public. The critic is neither a pedagogue nor a champion of better works (and it is in this last point that the real difference from Ihering's conception of criticism as agent of aesthetic renewal lies); instead, he carries out "an experiment" conducted on the work of art, which "his reflection unfolds," in order to attain "the completion of the good and thereby the annihilation of the worthless."[108]

Benjamin adopted the truth claim from the Romantic theory of art, but while Romantic criticism was concerned with the completion of an ultimately only aesthetic truth, his conception of criticism enlarged during the early 1920s: the truth immanent to the work is not aesthetic but eschatological; its reference to a messianic redemption is opposed to the realm of appearance and the fallenness of nature. Such a truth-content exists in the work alongside its manifest content: the latter constitutes the object of commentary; the former is investigated by criticism; the two diverge in the course of history. This account clearly anticipates Benjamin's thematization of reception history, which forms a central motif in his later reviews: "The history of the works prepares their criticism, and therefore historical distance increases its force." To indicate the truth that each work carries in itself and that constitutes its affinity to philosophy is the fundamental determination of criticism, which thus turns against the merely aesthetic character of the closed work. This criticism does not complete the work as does Romantic criticism, but rather reaches into it in order to emancipate the truth: "Criticism is the mortification of the works." Through the confrontation with the symbolic work in Goethe and his own occupation with the fragmentary constructions of Baroque allegorical drama, Benjamin developed a literary ideal which, by combining a didactic motive with an open form, led to a rejection of verisimilitude and facilitated a link to the avant-garde.[109] In his later reviews and essays about surrealism, Dada, or epic writing, which were considered antithetical to the bourgeois tradition of aesthetic autonomy, there still remained his early metaphysical orientation toward a truth that promises redemption as the heart of an authentic work of art.

To the extent that Benjamin's literary critical praxis derives from his early concept of the work, the continuity in his writings is as important as the break of the mid-1920s. It was precisely the anti-aesthetic bias of his early metaphysics that converged with the anti-aesthetic construction of criticism in Brecht. Thus Benjamin the reviewer challenged the critic not to succumb contemplatively to the aesthetic pleasure of interest-free satisfaction but to seize the work under discussion in the light of the truth, which is always a historical one: "Enthusiasm for art is alien to the critic. The artwork is in his hand the shining weapon in the battle of the spirits." Critical discourse is not made up of aesthetic judgments; it is the field of historico-philosophical battle. The failure of criticism is therefore a matter not of bad taste but—here Brecht would concur—bad action: "Criticism is a moral affair. If Goethe misjudged Hölderlin and Kleist, Beethoven and Jean Paul, that does not have to do with his understanding of art but with his morality."[110]

The critic to whom enthusiasm for art was alien therefore did not concern himself exclusively with literary artworks in the narrow sense. Certainly one finds among Benjamin's reviews essays on contemporary novels—especially Russian and French works, although Edgar Allan Poe and Goethe, Hugo von Hofmannsthal and Brecht were also treated. But Benjamin regularly discussed books that did not at all correspond to the established concept of art: travel books and descriptions of cities, Lenin's letters to Maxim Gorky, new scholarly publications, as well as books about the history of toys and children's books, and even a treatise on graphology. The breadth of the selection is a consequence of his shift away from aesthetic issues; he was concerned to investigate the function of the literati's nonaesthetic kinds of writing, where each object of investigation occasioned intervention "in the battle of the spirits."

For example, in a 1926 review of Fritz von Unruh's *Flügel der Nike* (Wings of Nike) containing certain aesthetic complaints about style and narrative structure, the focus is above all on the nature of Unruh's ostentatious pacifism. For Benjamin, Unruh is paradigmatic of the German writer who, after a warmongering chauvinism before 1918, now demonstrates a superficial desire for peace during a trip to Paris and thus hinders a real reconciliation between French and German intellectuals. Benjamin charges Unruh with opportunism when "in 1922 as an urban traveler, he pumps the Pariser Platz for the sake of eternal peace," in order to be sent as cultural emissary into the former enemy land. All his activity is pointless, and he contributes nothing substantive to peace: "On the contrary, the grand dinners are the only international facts of which his new pacifism takes account. His International is hatched in the peace of shared digestion, and the gala menu is the Magna Carta of future peace among the nations." To question the authenticity of such pacifism, Benjamin reviews Unruh's political past, confronting the reader with his agitatorial "Knight's Song" of 1914. Kraus similarly lambasted Kerr for contributing in his trivial verse to an exaggerated patriotism at the beginning of the war, only to resurface during the 1920s as a prominent bearer of the conciliatory Spirit of Locarno. But Benjamin was concerned not only to unmask this sort of mendacity but to attack the quality of the peace that had broken out, a peace emphasized in order to mask the lack of social peace: "The much invoked peace that is already with us turns out, in the light, to be the one—and only 'eternal' peace we know so well— enjoyed by the erstwhile warmongers who now want to set the tone at the peace celebration. So this is what Mister von Unruh has also become. 'Woe,' declares his Cassandran jargon, to all those who did not realize at the right time—approximately between the fish and the frying—that an 'inner conversion' is the only passable revolt and that the 'revolution of bread' . . . and the machinations of the Communists must give way to a community of 'communionists' that is rising up, purified, from a light supper, whose guild escutcheon—no doubt about it—will bear the champagne glass."[111] Benjamin, who was slowly drawing close to Marxism, polemicized in this way, on the occasion of reviewing Unruh's travel book, against a conservative conception of peace that precluded a solution to the social question. His account corresponded to the view, widely held in leftist circles of the Weimar Republic, of the Versailles Treaty as an alliance of Western powers directed against the Soviet Union. Literary criticism now meant an appropriation of literary phenomena for the purpose of articulating political material with particular reference to the role of the literati.

The emphasis on an explicitly political issue, like the peace question in the Unruh review, was less characteristic of Benjamin's literary critical strategy than was the investigation of the social function of the institution "Literature." His reviews could expand into social-historical reflections, as, for example, in the discussion of Karl Hobrecker's *Alte vergessene Kinderbücher* (Old forgotten children's books) of 1924; going beyond Hobrecker's bibliophilism, Benjamin sketched out a history of the children's book, especially the consequence of the industrialization of production in the late nineteenth century. Similarly, in

1931, he directed his attention to a book that could scarcely have awakened the culinary interest of establishment criticism but had been a great success among peasant readers in Switzerland, *Chrut und Unchrut* (Herbs and weeds), an herb book by Pastor Johann Künzle. For Benjamin the critic it was a social phenomenon of extraordinary importance, allowing him to develop an image of peasant ideology and the function of the writer—here in the guise of the "herbman" as "natural philosopher." When, at the end of the review, he stressed the "applicability that one can grasp with one's hands in this lowbrow domestic treasure," he was alluding to his own critique of the bourgeois concept of art.[112] Instead of a poetry of aesthetic autonomy alien to society, he demanded an operative literature that would stand closer to practical truth than to beautiful illusion. Books like *Chrut und Unchrut* "can show the critic whose teeth are getting loose on all the novelistic porridge what really belongs between them." Thus, Benjamin's reflections on the social function of literature, here in a case of massive reception, led to a polemical intervention in contemporary debates about the concept of literature and the role of criticism.

Indeed, Benjamin prefaces the actual discussion of the herb book with a sharp attack on establishment criticism, in which the contours of his strategy are articulated with admirable clarity. Ordinary book criticism is "stuck to new publications"; it instructs the public about them and expresses the impressions of the critic. Against such literary evaluation Benjamin demands a cognitive "utilization," in which the enduring influence of the polarity of aesthetics and philosophy of the early 1920s is still evident. The critic should neither mediate information nor express personal preferences; instead, Benjamin insists on a sociological analysis of the effects of a literary phenomenon, including the role of criticism itself. Of course, there had been an earlier turn toward reception history within literary critical discourse, as with Otto Brahm, but it had mainly to do with the rejection of new kinds of artworks on the part of conservative critics; Brahm thematized such opposition in order to give support to naturalist dramaturgy. For Benjamin, the aesthetic orientation disappears, and reception is treated as a social phenomenon, not just as a fissure in the aesthetic battles of the day. He demands a literary criticism that can emancipate itself from the traditional understanding of literature as autonomous art. It should not concentrate on the work in order to experience its beauty feuilletonistically, to describe it positivistically, or to analyze it in avant-garde terms in the interest of aesthetic progress. It should rather overcome the bourgeois concept of the work of art by dissolving the unified work into a multifaceted network of social force fields—between producer and reader, critic and industry, convention and tradition—and, as a politicization of the Romantic point of departure, finally "annihilate" it.

Parallel to this program for literary criticism, Benjamin developed a critique of literary scholarship in the universities. As discussed above, the middle of the nineteenth century witnessed a split in public literary discussion that led to a sharp division between the journalistic critic and the academic scholar. Many critics, to be sure, prepared for their eventual career with university training, and some scholars tried occasionally to address a wider public. Nevertheless, a fundamental division of labor between criticism and scholarship was established. Consequently, scholarship tended to surrender its critical potential while devoting itself to the establishment of a conservative canon, and criticism as feuilletonism renounced theoretical reflection and scientific validity. Just as Benjamin was concerned to win back for criticism a certain seriousness by replacing personal judgment with social analysis, he also demanded that scholarship direct its attention toward social history. He accused idealist scholarship in the mid-1920s of blocking its own way to the object of study, whether through a hypertrophic grid of concepts or through subjectivist "empathy"; it is "always more important for itself than is any one of its objects." Established scholarship turns out to be incapable of a "pertinent investigation" of literature: "Such criticism will always give itself away through the 'grandeur' of its objects or its 'synthetic' demeanor. The lustful urge for the 'great totality' is its misfortune." Instead of the academic tendency to occlude the work by imposing irrelevant questions, he advocated a "creative point of indifference," from which one could identify "the radical singularity of the artwork" in order to call forth the truth hidden in it, rather than project truth into it.[113]

Benjamin's alternative program points toward social history and the contemporary character of the institution of literature, which embraced more than did the traditional concept of art. Through an investigation of the social dimension of literary life—for example, the public, bookselling, and writers' organizations—literature could be made the "organon of history," though not through the usual constructs of a sequence of great literary figures. However, Benjamin also critiqued positivist accounts that were not burdened with the ballast of *geistes-geschichtliche* metaphysics but that merely collected facts and recited chronicles, "a comfortable presentation of the lives and works." In his review of such a treatment of the Silesian Baroque, he formulated a program for a sociological literary science that was to present literary institutions in the framework of sociohistorical relationships. Its center of interest would be such questions as "the genesis of the baroque Trauerspiel in close connection to the emergence of bureaucracy, the unity of time and action in close connection with the dark offices of absolutist administration, lascivious love poetry with the inquisitions about pregnancy of the emerging police state, the final apotheosis in dramatic opera with the jurisprudential structure of sovereignty."[114] Once the social origin of aesthetic forms was presented, aesthetics would cease to constitute an autonomous dimension untouched by practical life interests. Literary scholarship might be saved only if the bourgeois concept of art were relinquished. A literary science for which literature was not an aesthetic fact but primarily a social one would have lost its muselike character and thus have achieved a function which, no longer limited by the compensatory needs of the educated middle class, could lead to genuine scholarship and serious research.

Benjamin applied his proposal for scholarship—the social genesis of aesthetic form—in his own reviews of contemporary literature. For example, in discussing the narrative prose of such German authors as Marieluise Fleisser, Alfred Döblin, and Oskar Maria Graf, he foregrounded not political tendency (as Mehring might have done) but rather the form of "epic" narration as expression of a new, socially motivated concept of literature that broke through the limits of bourgeois aesthetics. Instead of contenting himself with the contents of the fabula, the critic directed his attention to the social constitution of the language in which a historical truth was found, which—so he claimed—opened the way to a collective practice. Thus he stressed Fleisser's presentation of "populist speech" not as a naturalist reproduction of Bavarian dialect but "as social magic, linguistic fetishism, determined by a series of invocatory formulas that make the walls give way that stand between the classes." In intercourse with language the literary critic encountered sociopolitical reality; conversely, language now seemed not to be a transparent medium but a literary institution in which two competing modes of narration could be discerned, the epic and the novelistic. The polarity traversed the reviews of Graf and Döblin. For Benjamin, both authors represented the epic, in whose language a collectivity objectively comes to speech, whereas the novel, as the voice of the isolated individual, is characterized by being "turned in upon itself": "The birth chamber of the novel is, considered historically, the loneliness of the individual who can no longer speak out in an exemplary fashion about his most important concerns. He lacks good counsel and can give no advice. The capacity to reproduce what one has heard and to awaken in one's experience the spirit of history, that which can be told, this simple gift of being at once objective and interesting, is linked to the pure openness of the inner person." These remarks are, of course, the rudiments of an aesthetic theory of narrative prose but one that is based on a foundation of social-theoretical premises and ultimately constitutes a critique of the privatist forms of bourgeois literature: "Any self-consciousness robs the storyteller of some piece of his fluency, and not merely, as one might like to believe, of some theme. It is also a condition of existence of the epic in the new sense to liquidate this privacy that nourishes the novel." The distinction between novel and epic is in fact political before it is aesthetic. Benjamin is concerned not with promoting an epic literature against a novelistic one but with strengthening a collective practice against individualism. The social implications of bourgeois literature remain for Benjamin just as immoral as they were for him in his early phase; the moralizing critic pronounces: "Nothing contributes so to the dangerous silencing of the inner person, nothing kills off the spirit of storytelling so thoroughly, as the shameless expansion that novel-reading is undergoing in all our lives."[115]

Benjamin's demand that literary criticism address social themes culminated in a thematization of the social function of the intellectual. Rather than writing from a privileged standpoint for a lay public (as had Kerr and, with some modification, Lukács), he addressed the proletarianized intelligentsia in order to stimulate it to self-reflection. This presupposed a theory of the intellectual, which Benjamin integrated as a central issue in his reviews. In 1929 he took the narrative work of Pierre Mac Orlan as occasion to treat the history and social situation of the bourgeois intelligentsia. An interest in the "world of the lumpen proletariat" and in "the rarest, most difficult class mixings," not uncommon in the 1920s, pointed in his opinion to a "decay of the 'free' intelligentsia," for "the bourgeoisie is no longer strong enough to support the luxury of a 'classless' intelligentsia." On the one hand, the dynamic of class conflict required a partisan intelligentsia, whether for or against the bourgeoisie. There is no class-neutral position, as Benjamin put it in his critiques of Hiller and Tucholsky. On the other hand, writers were being increasingly proletarianized, both in the dependency on the capitalist means of production and in the pauperization of the economic crisis. Nevertheless, they were not prepared to acknowledge their actual class character; at most they imitatively adopted a proletarian mien in order to distance themselves from the bourgeoisie, but without entering into conscious solidarity with the working class. Benjamin situated the malaise of the intelligentsia in this unwillingness to recognize the actual tension that divides society in two: "For no existence is more chimerical than existence between the class fronts in the moment at which they are preparing to crash into each other."[116]

In his reviews Benjamin constantly returned to the social role of the intelligentsia. The real purpose of his literary critical discourse was worked out in the face of the indecisiveness of the Weimar literati: namely, "the politicization of one's own class," which Benjamin characterized in 1930 in his review of Siegfried Kracauer's *Die Angestellten* (White collar) as the only effect "that a writing revolutionary from the bourgeois class can today intend."[117] The critic could be politically effective, but not in calling on the heterogeneous public sphere of the mass press; the point was rather for the writer to address the literati in order to influence the position of other intellectuals. Thus, priority was no longer ascribed to the writer, a priority with which the bourgeois literary public sphere had always privileged the poet. Instead, the writer was conceived as a producer; literary criticism, which was directed at the critic's own class, functioned as a force in the formation of a political class-consciousness.

Benjamin's literary criticism was therefore designed for a political impact among the writers by itself thematizing the politics of literary production. So, in the year following the National Socialist seizure of power, in a speech made in Parisian exile, Benjamin summarized: "An author who teaches the writers nothing teaches no one. What is decisive, therefore, is the model character of production which, first, can initiate other producers into production, and, second, make available to them an improved apparatus."[118] Literary criticism became the conversation of literary producers among themselves, once they grasped their social position; it represented an inversion of Brecht's critical public. In both cases there was an essential revision of the bourgeois discursive structure of a privileged expert.

But this dissolution of a privileged criticism was not a sudden turningpoint at the end of the Weimar Republic, for the crisis of the bourgeois institution of literary criticism had been evident for at least half a century. Feuilletonist discourse had implicitly already renounced a public in that it was organized around personal impressions. Naturalist literary criticism manifested a fundamental hostility to critics, which led to the need for legitimation hidden in Kerr's aestheticization of criticism. Certainly, the institution of literature kept producing professional critics who played an indispensable role in the functioning of the culture industry, but the lability of the institution could be readily perceived in their strained attempts to justify critical activity. A literary public that could appreciate criticism in a rational manner, not merely from the standpoint of consumerism, was lacking. Because criticism was no longer able to contribute to the judgments of a general public, Benjamin addressed the critics themselves as a public. In the context of this radical transformation of the public sphere, actual criticism developed in various directions: into the unabashed manipulation of advertising, the isolation of private impressions, tendentious engagement, and the search for other discursive forms with new speakers and new addressees.

TRANSLATED BY SIMON SREBRNY

BERNHARD ZIMMERMANN

. . . .

Literary Criticism from 1933
to the Present

THE number of swastikas scrawled with chalk in my entrance hall increased from then on, and a few times I found a gallows sketched on the floor in front of my studio door, accompanied by the words *Drawn especially for you.*"[1] This is how Oskar Maria Graf in retrospect describes the response to his autobiographical novel *Wir sind Gefangene (We are prisoners)*, to which the *Völkische Beobachter* reacted with a public murder threat. Such reactions to literature in 1927 make it plain that it was not only after Hitler's assumption of power that the much-vaunted artistic freedom was exposed to threats of various kinds and not infrequently suspended: this is proved as much by the ban on performances of such plays as *Die Mutter* (by Bertold Brecht) and *Cyankali* (by Friedrich Wolf) and such films as *Im Westen Nichts Neues (All Quiet on the Western Front*, based on Erich Maria Remarque's novel) and *Kuhle Wampe* (by Brecht and Slatan Dudow) as by the occasional arrest of writers like Johannes R. Becher, Willi Bredel, and Carl von Ossietzky. Besides literary criticism that dealt with literature argumentatively or polemically, there already existed in the crisis-torn Weimar Republic that "criticism" which is carried out not with the pen but with the nightstick and the office of the public prosecutor.

But in spite of these symptomatic threats to literary freedom, the artistic forms of expression were considered free in principle under the conditions of the Weimar Republic and its constitution. Their relative autonomy made them appear as acceptable areas of contradiction wherein the existing social order could be criticized without exposing art as such to the totalitarian grip of the state. The civil public sphere—and within it the subsystems of the literary public—served until 1933 as the basis for a lively coexistence and confrontation of literary currents and literary critical positions. That a broad stream of anti-democratic and chauvinistic literature was able to gain acceptance with the middle-class mass reading public not only illustrates the impotence of the literary press but also highlights the inner contradictions of this highly selective literary public and the already advanced parceling-out of the available areas of literary communication. The esotericism of the avant-garde movements of the early twentieth century (not always brought about by their own fault), the limited habits of artistic perception of the mass public, and the elitist self-perception of the institutionalized critics involuntarily favored the cultural-political campaigns of the German-national and pre-Fascist right-wingers, who were able to rely on widespread resentments in their fight against modernism and intellectualism. The fundamental revision of cultural politics after 1933; the devaluation of literary modernism as "degenerate," "decadent," and "un-German"; and the simultaneous revaluation of German-national and Fascist culture to represent presumably "genuine," "substantial," and "characteristic" German art could also make use of the deep-seated identity crisis within journalistic and academic literary criticism.

The relative loss of the functional role of middle-class literature and the vacuous officiousness of a criticism whose phrases and judgments were often interchangeable signaled an advanced crisis in literary life, which did not remain hidden to sensitive observers of the literary situation before 1933: "There were few things more rotten than art criticism in the last segment of the bourgeois era, few so eager to please, so irresponsible, so influential and irreversible at the same time."[2] This verdict from 1927 was articulated not by Hanns Johst but by Ernst Bloch, who did not succumb to the obvious temptation of a nostalgic transfiguration of bourgeois cultural life in his analysis of the National Socialist "interdiction of art criticism" of November 26, 1936, but mercilessly diagnosed the symptoms of an art and literary criticism absolved of responsibility, as well as the splendid misery of the unrestrained opinion peddlers. The young Georg Lukács had described in his early work *Geschichte und Klassenbewusstsein* (History and class consciousness; 1923) the "prostitution" of artistic experiences and convictions as "the culmination of capitalist reification *[Verdinglichung]*" and thus had left the level of a moralizing and personalizing discussion of the phenomena of bourgeois literary criticism. Like him, Bloch also saw the condition of bourgeois criticism as the mirror image of a declining capitalist society: the perception of culture as a commodity was not only conveyed in the literary works themselves but was also characteristic of the critical works. Its availability for sale—in the double meaning of the term—guaranteed its freedom. Free circulation of literary goods, the competition of currents, opinions, and judgments, and the predominance of the exchange value over the intrinsic value of cultural products appeared as expressions of the assimilation of the cultural sector to the socioeconomic basis of capitalist society. If it is indeed the task of a social history of literary criticism to demonstrate how criticism as an institution (as a subsystem of art as an institution) "changes not only in its outward manifestations (attitudes, judgments) but also in its basic structure (organization, social institutions, character of the public)—and moreover in conjunction with the changing conditions of production"[4]—then German social and literary history with its historical caesurae in 1933 and 1945 offers especially abundant supporting material. At both of these turningpoints in German social history the reorganization of intellectual and literary life was determined by historical and intrasocial power configurations. Hitler's assumption of power, the military defeat of German Fascism, the partitioning of Germany, and the creation of two German states with contrasting social systems are at the same time dividing lines between periods in literary history.

Literary Life and Literary Criticism in the Third Reich

To the cultural-political harbingers of the Fascist revolution—for instance, to the "Task Force for German Culture"—the intellectual life of the Weimar Republic appeared to be the mirror image of the Jewish-Bolshevik conspiracy that was branded by Hitler's followers as the presumptive root of all evil. The concept of literature of those pre-Fascist right-wingers was characterized by a resentful anti-intellectualism that considered the artistic developments of the late nineteenth and early twentieth centuries as expressions of biological decline and intellectual decadence—in short, as "degenerate" art. Of all the traditional formal expressions of modernism that had developed in the German-speaking countries since the turn of the century, only the elitist antimodernism of Stefan George, whose heroic cult of the artist showed similarities to the restorative features of the German-nationalist literature movement, was spared the label "decadent" by the pro-Fascist right.

The intellectual battle lines of the times were reflected not only in the literary criticism of the late 1920s but also in such cultural institutions as the Department for Poetry within the Prussian Academy of the Arts. On the literary scene before 1933, the proponents of the nationalist–National Socialist ideology also had to deal with the relatively strong resistance of their opponents and of a public that had not yet been brought completely into the official line. The voices that made themselves heard in the journalistic organs of their literary policies (for instance, in the *Deutsches Volkstum,* edited by Wilhelm Stapel; in Willi Vesper's *Die neue Literatur;* or in the *Nationalsozialistische Monatshefte*) could make a valid claim—based on their use of rhetoric, which modeled itself after the demagogy of Joseph Goebbels—not to be criticism in the traditional sense, particularly since a rationally based critical judgment could not be generated on the pages of such militantly biased journals. Only the fact that before 1933 the literary ideologues of National Socialism still had to prevail by linguistic means against their opponents makes it appear legitimate to circumscribe with the term "criticism" the function of publications integrated into the party apparatus of the National Socialist German Workers Party (NSDAP); the aim of this criticism was not—as the following example shows—a discursive argument with the opinions of the adversary but rather his destruction: "We are at war, engaged in the grim defense of our holiest treasures, of the substance and the way of life of our nation. We are confronted . . . by an impertinent, shameless, murderous fellowship of rootless literati and Asians who poison and corrupt everything. And so we have no choice but to fight to the destruction of their spirit or ours, their way of life or ours here in Germany."[5]

This exemplary quotation from the journal *Die neue Literatur* presages in 1932 the indeed novel self-concept of Fascist literary criticism, which is the prelude to its unavoidable self-termination under the Fascist regime. It is no longer satisfied with unsettling the intellectual positions of its opponents but demands the actual liquidation of all literature not commensurable with its own stated goals. These demands were fulfilled, and not only by cultural-political measures *after* 1933. How much of a public menace the utterances of the National Socialist critics really were becomes clear not only in their resorting to sewer language, in the rhetorical transformation of their opponents into criminals, and in the branding of any opposition as "subhuman" and "scum" to be eliminated, but also in their self-interpretation. National Socialist criticism sees itself as the place for the articulation of a Germanic national soul to whom "criticism" is ultimately alien because it is said to be of Jewish origin. National Socialist critics attack these signs of "Jewish subversion" in a jargon that has the characteristics of a call to duty and considers itself a propaganda weapon. The functional framework of National Socialist literary criticism changes in step with the three phases that Rolf Geissler distinguishes in the development of increasing National Socialist regimentation of literature: "(1) the militant period, during which German-nationalist writers and journalists before 1933 combat democratic literature with anti-Semitic and chauvinistic phrases; (2) the period of purging and supervision from 1933 to 1936; (3) the period of one-sided appreciation, praise, and regulation of subject matter after 1936."[6] In the context of our presentation the most interesting developmental steps after 1933 are those that contribute to the dissolution of the framework of literary criticism and lead to its total conversion into a part of the totalitarian propaganda apparatus.

In spite of their Fascist sense of mission, the defamatory critics and the militantly polemical press of the radical right before 1933 were confronted with the necessity of facing the critical judgment of readers and the public at large. While they could fight for the adoption of their views with all means at their disposal, they could not yet give their opinions the force of an official decree. Thus National Socialist criticism—even where it had linguistically and ideologically long been outside the scope of criticism—remained, through its alliance with art, an institution, part of a debate conducted according to the laws and customs of public life. It conducted its appraisals and pronounced its verdicts publicly, understood its activities as part of a comprehensive cultural-political battle, but could still be controlled and combatted under these conditions.

The operating conditions of pre-Fascist literary criticism were suspended not by the official ban on literary criticism but already in the period from 1933 to 1936, when criticism was de facto deprived of its function to pass aesthetic judgment and its role as a filter—its selective and evaluative function—was no longer conducted in public but *in camera*. The official tools for the regulation and supervision of intellectual life took over the screening and selecting of literary products; the state-controlled critic ultimately was left with only the task of post-rationalizing and spreading the officially decreed value judgments in the appropriate publications.

Numerous examples attest to the fact that this new distribution of responsibilities could not be put into operation without contradiction. When Alfred Karrasch's novel *Parteigenosse Schmiedecke* was reviewed negatively in the *Deutsche Allgemeine Zeitung* of August 29, 1934, one of the leading literary officials of the National-Socialist regime, Hellmuth Langenbucher, objected indignantly to the "defamation of a National Socialist working-class novel" and uttered these threats against the reviewer (who signed himself "Kn"): "We will know how to deal with Kn's continuing to do violence, under the disguise of critical judgment, to books that have great merit. In addition, the novel carries the seal of approval of the PPK [the party's board of examiners] . . . and thus any attack on the book must be considered at the same time an attack on an official department of the National Directorate of the party."[7] It is not the threat as a form of criticism, which we already know from the pre-Fascist press, but the undisguised appeal to the critical primacy of the pre-censorship of the National Socialist Party that is striking in this context, since it brings into the open the long-completed debilitation of literary criticism by which even Langenbucher's statement is affected. The authority of the critical judgment is vindicated only by its appeal to the "higher party authorities." It is not without a certain irony that Langenbucher himself, as occasional chief reader in the State Department for the Promotion of German Literature, represents those "higher state authorities" to which he appeals in his argumentation as a critic. And even the threat as a form of criticism reached a new level of meaning in the changed conditions of literary life after 1933, because the National Cultural Chamber Law of September 22, 1933, obliged all creators of art to serve the state in the framework of their cultural activities. Those who did not want to accept this obligation or could not prove an Aryan background usually had no prospect of being admitted to the chamber with jurisdiction over their profession.

One look at the powers of the National Literature Chamber, the central institution within the organizational framework of Fascist literary life, makes it plain that even as early as the period of "purging and supervision" between 1933 and 1936, literary criticism was of marginal importance in view of the increasingly effective administrative regimentation of literary life.

Under the supervision of Goebbels's "National Ministry for Popular Enlightenment and Propaganda," hundreds of reviewers, serving on numerous committees after 1933, established "blacklists" that covered all fields of knowledge and served as the basis for subsequent bans and confiscations. A "regulation governing damaging and undesirable publications" of April 25, 1935, gave two of those blacklists the power of law and made the distribution of books and pamphlets that did not conform to "National Socialist cultural intentions" a criminal offense. From then on, publishing houses were obliged to register their new publications with the "counseling office" of the National Literature Chamber. The GESTAPO (*Geheime Staatspolizei*, or secret police) monitored the observance of these regulations. Violations could lead to drastic sanctions—from a warning to "removal from the list of members of the profession" (equivalent to being prohibited from working as a writer and thus deprived of one's livelihood) to being sent to a concentration camp.[8]

When Hanns Johst became the president of the National Literature Chamber on October 3, 1935, the process of bringing the literary branch into the party line and of filling all the crucial positions in the cultural area with loyal followers of the NSDAP had been essentially completed. Only those works that made it past this preventive censorship of the party and the state were available for evaluation in published criticism—but were largely immune to criticism by virtue of the official stamp of approval they already bore. After the discrediting and liquidation of their political enemies within the country and after the exodus of its cultural opponents into exile, the suspicion of the Fascist cultural politicians focused primarily on the remaining elements of bourgeois life and worked industriously for their elimination. Included among these elements were the cultural press and its traditional special status, whose content and editorial independence from the other parts of the newspaper had no justification whatsoever in the totalitarian concept of the role of journalism. The often maligned "cultural discussion section" of the middle-class press, which had preserved elements of the classical model of public life, was considered an expression of Jewish lack of character and of officious cliquishness that had no place for strong intellectual positions.[9] The open competition of opinions and not least of all the analytical procedures of criticism were incommensurable with the main cultural-political theories of the National Socialist system; this is why the elimination of the cultural press of the old school had already been largely carried out, not only in the party press but also in the rest of the papers, before the official ban on art criticism. The cultural press was to be subservient to the same goals that governed the formation and direction of political opinions. This was designed to lead to the conformity of cultural journalism and make it useful for ideological mobilization in the spirit of Fascism; at the same time it accomplished a revaluation of the cultural segment of the newspapers that led, among other things, to the demand to move book reviews to the front page and to lay them out as lead articles. The figleaf function of the liberal cultural section in conservative newspapers, the lack of commitment of the radical cultural criticism in the vicinity of stock market reports and advertisements—in short, the illusion propagated by the bourgeois cultural press that the ruling thoughts were not necessarily those of the rulers—lost its foundation in the wake of the conformity and increasing involvement in politics of the cultural press.

Just as officially supported art was supposed to aid the development of a Fascist public consciousness and to legitimize the national and international policies of the National Socialist regime, the cultural press was expected to assimilate its form and content to the daily political demands and also, in this sense, to assume strategic and tactical assignments within the total scope of party propaganda. At the same time, the cultural-political planners of the state hoped, with the help of the cultural press, to win over those apolitical circles within the traditional bourgeoisie who faced the new state without resistance but with partial reservations or with an inner distance: "There are many readers who are particularly receptive to cultural matter by virtue of their profession or their inclination. . . . in the planning of the cultural section of the papers it is important to remember that this section is the gateway to an understanding of events and developments in politics for many readers."[10]

That this cultural-political offensive met with many obstacles is underlined by the complaints of many National Socialist journals which discovered that the literature they promoted was being received with little enthusiasm by the reading public.[11] While it was possible to ban the total literary production of exiled authors from the active consciousness of the public by prohibiting the publication as well as all reviews of their works, it was not possible in the short run to fill the remaining vacuum with a propaganda campaign for a National Socialist literature only partially commensurable with the apolitical concept of literature traditionally held by the educated bourgeoisie. These difficulties, as well as the fact that in the cultural pages of the remaining "independent" publications the books of the officially "undesirable" but still tolerated "inner emigrants" were reviewed sympathetically, may explain why—in the period from 1933 until the official banning of criticism in 1936—the notion could gain acceptance among the leading echelons of the propaganda apparatus that ultimately it was only the clever obstructionism of the cultural press that prevented the public from responding more favorably to National Socialist literature: "One of the bastions where the intellectual enemies of the new Germany have sought shelter is literary criticism . . . the godforsaken, instinctless hoards of nonbelievers should not bother us, so it should be our duty not to rest until literary criticism also is cleansed of everything and everybody who is not in tune with our National Socialist ideals."[12]

These massive polemical attacks against the intellectual pockets of resistance in the cultural columns of the "independent press" cannot gloss over the fact that despite the common cultural-political goals to which the party spokesmen appealed, grave discrepancies in literary judgment appeared at times, even in the pages of official publications. This should hardly be surprising in view of the nebulous definitions by which the leading cultural authorities attempted to circumscribe the "nature" of the new National Socialist literary criticism. It was supposed to "grow from instinct," to be "the voice of racial destiny," and to need no "rational rules or laws"; it would be "National Socialist as a matter of course, since it is subject to the law of all profound relationships that characterize and form the new life style created and demanded by National Socialism."[14] Such empty macro-ideological clichés obviously could not provide valid guidelines for practical literary criticism. Thus the literary journals of the official party press often arrived at completely contrary evaluations, especially of fellow travelers and officially "undesirable" authors such as Ernst Wiechert or Hans Fallada; sometimes even contributors to the very same magazine disagreed completely. Willi Vesper, one of the most prominent party poets, found it necessary to defend emphatically Fallada's novel *Kleiner Mann, was nun?* (Little man, what now?)—in the April 1933 edition of his journal *Die neue Literatur*—against an abusive review penned by one of his own staff members the previous November 1932, in spite of the fact that the novel did not at all correspond to the artistic concepts of the National Socialist regime: "Fallada's political stance is not our own—still, this novel about a small tormented and harassed employed and later unemployed worker of our time is, beyond all temporal and political intentions of the author, an honest piece of writing. . . . The hand of the poet has made a hymn to love and steadfastness out of a musty story."[15] Yet in the same journal Vesper harshly rejected Fallada's novel *Wer einmal aus dem Blechtopf frisst* (Who has eaten from the tin cup once), published in 1933, even though the author paid homage to the new regime in his preface. Vesper sharply rejected opportunistic accommodation and political lip service by fair-weather National Socialists like Hanns Heinz Ewers—as evidenced by his devastating review of Ewers's novel *Horst Wessel: Ein deutsches Schicksal* (*Horst Wessel: A German Destiny*). The Ewers case, however, as well as the example of best-selling author Fallada, is testimony to the basic ineffectiveness of literary criticism as a means for influencing the actual reading preferences of the public at large. Ewers's novel sold 130,000 copies; Fallada's books remained best sellers even during the Third Reich and became popular abroad as well—in stark contrast to the officially promoted works.

The official critical publications noticed the actual lack of success of their efforts with considerable unease. Since they could not question the basic cultural-political concepts, they interpreted this failure as a failure of criticism and its methods. The allegedly growing number of complaints about art criticism, which came from the ranks of National Socialist hack writers as well as from all other segments of the population, in addition to the claim that the unsatisfactory condition of art criticism had not improved after four years, was reason enough for Propaganda Minister Goebbels to decree the prohibition of art criticism on November 26, 1936. In its place there was to be from then on "the National Socialist contemplation of art," which only especially authorized persons were allowed to engage in, as was announced in the *Börsenblatt des deutschen Buchhandels* of August 19, 1937: "The president of the National Press Chamber once more points out that on June 30, 1937, the provisions governing the ban of art criticism of November 26, 1936, have been put into force. Therefore, only those discussions of art may appear in the German press whose authors have received permission to contribute occasionally their evaluations of art as temporary members of the German press."[16] Whoever wanted to publish art criticism in the press had to be listed in the "Professional Register of the German Press." Apart from political criteria, this listing was conditional on the writer's having reached thirty years of age—an additional requirement designed to guarantee that only "mature" persons would voice their opinions on cultural topics. These executive orders governing art reviews, announced in December 1936, were intended to make sure that any discussion of art would from then on be totally devoted to the appreciation and presentation of the contents of the work. Since the right to criticism was granted only to the official supervisory organs of the state, the function of the art reporter was circumscribed by the euphemistic term "art servant." Besides the technical regulations, which governed the mailing of review copies and the deadlines by which a book review had to appear in the various media, there were also very explicit guidelines for its internal structure. The review should have a plot summary and should give an appreciation of the political merits of the book. In the case of mediocre books and works that might give rise to objections on political grounds, the approval of the Propaganda Ministry was suggested before publication of the review. According to this model, the new form of the appreciative book review could be subdivided into the following categories, as illustrated by the examples in Dietrich Strothmann's study: "(1) Analysis of the contents of the book in the form of a detailed plot summary, supplemented by direct quotations from the text; (2) examination of the ideological conformity of the work with the prevailing world view; (3) comments on style and form; (4) formulaic statement of recommendation or rejection; (5) indication of the potential use for the book."[17]

The prohibition of criticism and the strict regulation of the art review process had created an instrument with which the state propaganda authorities were able to control effectively the spreading of cultural opinions, particularly since the authorities had the final word on the publication of controversial reviews. This assured that inner ideological controversies and competing trends within cultural politics did not reach the public—as they had between 1933 and 1936—and therefore a picture of cultural unity could be presented to the world. Numerous examples of literary criticism can be cited for the period between 1933 and 1936—for instance, Alfred Rosenberg's journal *Die Bücherkunde* of 1934—that expose the poor literary standard of literature beholden to the regime in style and content. One of the regular critics of that journal even reached the following conclusion in 1934: "In the past [i.e., in the literary life of the Weimar Republic], many a writer failed not because he was a German-nationalist, but because he was incompetent." In a commentary on *Einer baut den Dom*, a volume of poetry by Carl Maria Holzapfel, the reviewer warned in 1934 that if things went on in this manner for long, the fledgling National Socialist poetry might end in a few years with a huge hangover or become downright ridiculous.[18]

On the one hand the National Socialist concept of literature emphasized the predominance of subject matter; it understood literature as an expression of an "ethnic" racial identity and presupposed its direct and immediate connection with practical life. The literature of the militant period, which is dominant between 1933 and 1936, corresponds to this concept. It perpetuates the myth of the Führer and the ideology of an ethnic community from the perspective of those who had "experienced" the heroic fight of Hitler and his early followers and had even to some degree participated in it. On the other hand, the cultural-political ideologues of the state, who considered themselves called upon to build a new millennial culture, could not overlook the amateurish nature of this poetry of Fascist experience, and they objected—like Hellmuth Langenbucher—to books that combined the predominance of plot with artistic incompetence: "A book that contains no mention of the SA [storm troops] of the Third Reich, or of National Socialism can still be more National Socialist than a novel that teems with 'brown' experiences."[19] Although prominent role models and cultural officials could and did here and there make critical comments about the standard of extant National Socialist literature even after the banning of criticism in 1936, the wider public was barred from such discussions by the strict regulation of the review process. At the same time, the ban on criticism soon had consequences that surely could not have been in the objective interest of its originators, since the methods of the state propaganda machine were not entirely useful for the journalistic-psychological campaign against its own public. Just as censorship can function effectively only when kept from the scrutiny of the public, the regimentation of literary reviews can work only when it is hidden from the public and the censored material appears in the guise of products of free speech. But the exaggerated conformity under the heading of "art contemplation" after the ban of criticism, the pedantic observance of guidelines for an appreciative literary review, and the extreme fear of critical appraisal led to an ossification of the press, whose sycophantic praise missed the mark and proved to be an inadequate tool for mobilizing the public. In an account to the Ministry of Propaganda, these inopportune effects of the suppression of criticism are listed with great insight: "(1) The judgment of the public becomes insecure. (2) The difference in quality between artistic efforts is no longer sufficiently apparent. . . . The most capable artists in particular are dissatisfied with this undiscriminating treatment. . . . (3) There is the danger that the contemplation of art will be looked upon as an advertising tool by the producers of art. It is therefore not appropriate to force upon the art observer the function of an advertising executive, with an allusion to the fact that criticism is prohibited."[20]

Even such artistic or linguistic-structural criteria carried little weight in the reviewing system of the National Socialist press of the following years. In the course of war preparations, and increasingly after the outbreak of World War II, the cultural press absorbed the phrases of daily political events; only following the military defeat of Hitler's legions at Stalingrad did the importance of the cultural press grow again, in conjunction with the rise of that Nazi literature of end-of-an-era introspection, designed to take the reader's mind off the impending military catastrophe and to give sustenance to the guilt-ridden. Another indication of the immediate adjustment to the psychological demands of the worsening war situation was the amazing increase in the production of popular entertainment literature after 1942, which Goebbels defended against the champions of a "pure" literature. "Adventure and eroticism," instead was the slogan that Goebbels in 1943 considered vital for coping with the psychological situation at the front. It was an obvious attack against Alfred Rosenberg and the literary policies he represented when Goebbels remarked: "There are still ideologues among us who believe that the member of a submarine crew prefers to reach for "The Myth of the 20th Century" when he comes out of the engine room, covered with dirt and oil. That is utter nonsense."[21] The pragmatic concept of literature that predominated in literary politics formed the basis for changes of this kind in the course of literary policy: those books that had been branded "trash" before were now considered an appropriate means of psychological relief for the troops; the presumably apolitical now carried out the duties of everyday politics and could thus be exempted from ideological judgment. (That this mobilization of the apolitical in the service of genocide is no monopoly of the National Socialist regime was illustrated only a few decades later by the "operational use" of entertainers in Vietnam.)

Anti-Fascist Literary Criticism in Exile

Like most liberal writers and intellectuals, prominent literary critics of the bourgeois-republican camp and of the Marxist-oriented left made their way into exile after 1933; Kurt Tucholsky, Georg Lukács, Walter Benjamin, Kurt Kersten, and Kurt Hiller may here suffice as examples. The anti-Fascist literary critics who remained in Hitler's Germany were subjected to harsh persecution—as the biographies of Werner Krauss, Victor Klemperer, Wilhelm Girnus, and Carl von Ossietzky clearly show—and confronted with the reality of Fascist "cultural politics" in concentration camps and jails. While the basis for a workable literary criticism was thus removed inside Germany in the course of the intellectual and literary leveling-out, the exiled literary intellectuals also faced the problem of having been, for the most part, deprived of the support of a German-speaking reading public. The geographical diaspora of the exiled critics to highly dissimilar countries and linguistic areas—not least the daily fight for survival to which many of them were exposed and which drove such important figures as Kurt Tucholsky and Walter Benjamin to suicide—posed tremendous challenges to the exiled writers and critics and their efforts to build an anti-Fascist reading public outside Hitler's Germany. It was difficult enough for most writers who had been deprived of their German-speaking audience to make a living from the revenues of their literary work, but it was even more difficult for the literary critics. The most important outlets for anti-Fascists, the exile journals, were not often able to remunerate their contributors adequately, which led, for example, to the situation that such high-powered documents of exile criticism as Walter Benjamin's review of Brecht's *Dreigroschenroman (Three-penny novel)* remained unpublished or appeared only after the death of the critic: Benjamin had not released his completed review for publication in Klaus Mann's *Die Sammlung* because of the minimal honorarium the journal offered him. Aside from novelists of the Weimar Republic who were well known abroad, only those Marxist writers and critics who had chosen exile in the Soviet Union were spared this struggle for existence. They found at first better conditions for contributing to the creation of an anti-Fascist readership, but by the end of the 1930s quite a few were facing survival problems of a different kind in the era of the Stalinist terror. The fate of Communist writers and critics like Ernst Ottwalt, Hans Günther, and Karl Schmückle may here represent the victims of that excessively autonomous political power, which discredited the goals of the October Revolution in the name of socialism and which has done the gravest damage to the reputation of socialism right up to the present.

The increasing acrimony of the class struggles had already accelerated the polarization of literary intellectuals even in the years of the Weimar Republic and had confronted writers and critics with the necessity of making political decisions that had grave consequences for their intellectual lives. The process of attempting to arrive at personal ideological positions, which was already of vital concern before 1933 and which included the debate about the function of literature and art, was continued in exile with somewhat changed historical premises. While in Germany the role of the writer in the intellectual life of the National Socialist state was mainly determined by Fascist cultural policies, and writers opposed to this situation could only retreat into silence or various forms of "inner emigration," the creation of an anti-Fascist literary criticism in exile was closely connected with the task of clarifying the role of literary production and the work of the critic in exile. Literary criticism in the exile journals is thus characterized by a synthesis of critical analysis and creative anticipation: a critical ideological (including formal) analysis of National Socialist literature was a permanent conceptual part of the exile journals; the critical analysis of literature created in exile and the literary-critical discussion of an aesthetic theory appropriate for the battle against Fascism was probably the most important component of their content.

In the Marxist-oriented exile journals—such as *Internationale Literatur* and *Das Wort*, edited by Lion Feuchtwanger, Willi Bredel, and Bertolt Brecht—the question of the adoption of the cultural heritage became important after 1936. This newly fanned debate about the bourgeois cultural heritage focused on the "popular front" program of the Marxist left as well as on the attempts at usurpation of the National Socialist literary politicians who tried to represent themselves as executors of Faust's testament. Not only the discussion about cultural inheritance but ultimately all literary debates in exile were characterized by the fact that the *literary* problems discussed included *ideological* questions: questions of style and literary form were treated from the standpoint of their usefulness for the creation of an anti-Fascist consciousness; at the same time, political content and tendencies were no longer debated separately from aesthetic criteria. This was equally true for the examination of the literary potential of the historical novel in exile and for the debate about expressionism in 1937–38, as well as for the discussion of Marxist realism that developed after the First Union Congress of Soviet Writers in 1934.[22]

The history of the generally short-lived exile journals points out clearly that the most perceptive positions in the literary-critical debate did not prevail automatically and that prominence as a critic was conditional on various external factors. Nothing demonstrates this fact more convincingly than the influence and hegemony of Georg Lukács's critical opinions on the one hand, and the ineffectiveness of the views of Walter Benjamin in the critical circles of the exile on the other. Even more than under the conditions of bourgeois literary life, connections to a journal and possibly adherence to a critical concept were preconditions for an effective literary criticism in exile. Whereas Georg Lukács had an excellent outlet for the development and dissemination of his theoretical and critical concepts in the Moscow journal *Internationale Literatur*—published from 1931 on and appearing in Russian, German, English, and French—one of the reasons Benjamin remained an outsider was that he could not form a lasting alliance with an exile journal. Although Benjamin's theoretical stance is diametrically opposed to that of Lukács, he can be ranked, like Lukács, with those exile critics who based their positions and judgments on a coherent theoretical concept that emphasized a strong synthesis of social and aesthetic theory. In this sense, too, Benjamin belongs to a minority group because most literary critical essays published in exile journals were furnished by exiled writers who entered into a critical debate with each other: Lion Feuchtwanger reviews Ernst Toller's *Jugend in Deutschland* (Youth in Germany); Arnold Zweig reviews Heinrich Mann's *Jugend des Henry IV* (The youth of Henry IV); Heinrich Mann writes about the poetry of Max Hermann Neisse; Hugo Huppert discusses Brecht's *Dreigroschenroman;* F. C. Weiskopf reviews Willi Bredel's *Die Prüfung* (The Test); Willi Bredel reviews Friedrich Wolf's play *Beaumarchais;* Anna Seghers discusses Bodo Uhse's *Leutnant Bertram.* The critical essays became a means for clarification of the author's own positions; there they could reflect on the fundamental intentions of their own works with a view to the historical situation and the objectives of literary activity.

The growing divergence of creative and critical activity and the specialization of the role of the writer and the critic, which Lukács had interpreted as a product of capitalist division of labor, appear to have been suspended temporarily in the exile journals. When authors make critical statements, they not only do so in the form of an exchange of roles that enables them to answer literary questions from the perspective of the readers but develop independent demands for a criticism that might be useful for literary practitioners:

Criticism stops with admirable courage where the poem proper begins. Poetry remains substantially untouched by it. The scheme of such a criticism can be described as follows: (1) long announcement of the publication of a new book, mention of earlier works, biography; (2) listing of titles; (3) general plot summary; (4) detailed plot summary with a descriptive commentary on a number of selected poems; (5) 'particularly successful is . . .' or 'Less successful appears . . .'; (6) general ideological praise or reproof; (7) patting on the back, 'looking forward to future efforts.' Such praise is of course interesting to the ('highly talented' or rather 'highly poetic') author only as an extension of his cumberbund. Criticism provides advertising. But the author who wants to make progress . . . dreams of a critic who speaks to him as a human being, who is an expert, who loves poems and even shares his home with them outside of his work as a critic. . . . This kind of criticism would inform about metrics, symbolism, metaphors, about the relationship between theme and rhyme . . . anybody would love to learn from such a critic.[23]

Isolated from its historical context, this could be misunderstood as the echo of a traditional poetic nostalgia for the congenial criticism that sees itself as the servant of poetic production and can to some degree take the lead in the development of literature. However, in addition to their general validity, the significance of these demands lies in the fact that they were delivered by Johannes R. Becher as part of a speech to the plenary session of Soviet writers in Minsk in February 1936, and that they are part of a cultural-political discussion that touches on the fundamentals of anti-Fascist literary criticism in exile. The rejection of an arbitrary external inspection and the verdict against review practices that are predominantly content-oriented and give top priority to ideological criteria gain status particularly because they do not advocate an empty formalism and because they defend the intrinsic value of aesthetic categories in the name of a partisan political concept of literature: "Where is the place of the poet? Where he stands as a *poet:* amid the best he has created and not where he puts his signature and where he confesses his political convictions," Becher argues in the same speech and thereby certainly approaches the critical position of Georg Lukács. And Brecht's reflections on a "realistic criticism" accentuate—as shown by his own critical method in the analysis of Fritz Brügel's poem "Flüsterlied" (Whisper song; *Das Wort*, no. 1, 1936)— the significance of the poetic process for a form appropriate to the demands of a political battle. At the same time, however, Brecht turns against the formalist use of formal criteria in Marxist criticism, particularly against those of Lukács: "The description of a world in a state of constant change demands constantly new means of depiction. These new means of depiction must be judged according to their success with the respective object, not as such, detached from their object, by comparison with former methods. Literature must be judged not from the perspective of literature but from the standpoint of the world—for instance, from the standpoint of that part of the world with which it deals. What sense will all this talk of realism make when nothing real appears in it any longer?"[24]

Brecht's critical works written in exile strikingly illustrate his preconceived notions of literary criticism, which are completely contrary to the rules of the bourgeois popular press. Not only his published but, even more, his unpublished contributions to the realism debate make it clear that Brecht always checked his own critical statements for their pragmatic worth in the battle against Fascism. Although his unpublished writings voice a theoretical stance with regard to realism that can bear comparison with Lukács's critical essays in intellectual rigor and precision of expression, Brecht did not think it made sense to push the public debate about realism too hard, particularly because he was afraid to damage existing alliances; from the standpoint of the creative artist he recognized the danger that would threaten the realism discussion should it turn into a purely theoretical debate. His unique pragmatic conception of literature and criticism is made plain in more than this restraint. Even in exile, Brecht polemically and mercilessly attacks the symptoms of a helpless anti-Fascism that demonizes the reality of the Third Reich rather than penetrating to its foundations:

> The truth must be spoken because of the actions that result from it. . . . How can somebody now speak the truth about the Fascism he opposes when he won't say anything about the capitalism that causes it? How can such a person's truth lead to practical action? Those who are against Fascism without being opposed to capitalism are like those people who want to eat their share of the calf but object to the calf's being slaughtered. They want to eat the calf but do not want to see blood spilled. . . . They are not opposed to the social conditions that result in barbarism, only to barbarism itself.

> They raise their voices against barbarism, and they do it in
> countries where the same social conditions still exist but where
> the butchers still wash their hands before they serve the meat.[25]

The inner contradictions of a militant middle-class humanism here are
criticized polemically without regard to any alliances; the aim of the
polemic is to arrive at an analysis of Fascism that is appropriate to
historical reality and will have practical consequences. The critical
controversy about Ernst Bloch's work *Erbschaft dieser Zeit* (published in
1935 in Zurich), which was carried on in 1936 in the journal *Internationale Literatur*, must be seen against this background. It is true that
these are more or less inner-Marxist ideological battles, not free of
dogmatic tendencies in spite of the significance of their subject matter.
In the discussions about the role of the petty bourgeoisie in Hitler's
Fascist regime, about the asynchronism of its thinking, and about the
fitness to inherit of a petty-bourgeois anticapitalism, we are reminded
of the unconquered problems of the pre-1933 theory of Fascism, which
knew how to localize the economic foundations of Fascist supremacy
but was not able to provide an adequate explanation for the mass
support of the Fascist movement.

The critical self-concept of the exile authors, the discursive clarification of their theoretical positions, and the debates about the formal
expression of anti-Fascist exile literature tend to be the main ingre-
dients of criticism in exile. The various forms of criticism can also be
put into the following framework: there is the theoretical essay; the
review and discussion of literature created in exile; and the "portrait of
the author." Usually, the portrait of the author has the formal features
of an extensive panegyric but does not in principle exclude critical
traits. The aggressive, polemical tone typical of the theoretical debates
in exile is almost totally absent from the reviews of exile literature, but
here also the exception proves the rule. Balder Olden's review of
Melodien—Alfred Kerr's collection of poetry, published in Paris in 1938
in the journal *Die neue Weltbühne* (vol. 1, 1939)—is one of these exceptions; the reviewer's personal aversions against the conceits and the
lyrical transgressions of the author are vented without restraint and
prevent historical-critical access to the text itself. As a scathing polemical attack, Olden's review is directed less against the text than against
the author, whose integrity is put in doubt: "Kerr at least did not look

out for the rest of the world, but only for himself. The screams of abused creatures, of Ossietzkys tortured to death, of all the hardships of all the hundreds of thousands . . . [these do] not reach the ears of the hero of a gallant episode."[26]

Olden's review sparked off an agitated debate in subsequent issues of *Die neue Weltbühne*, in which not only Alfred Kerr himself but also Egon Erwin Kisch participated in order to protect the author against Olden's rude critical manner. F. C. Weiskopf's review of Joseph Roth's novel *Tabaras*, published in the Prague exile journal *Neue Deutsche Blätter* (vol. 10, 1934), is also burdened with this method of ad hominem critical attack, which does not concentrate on discovering the shortcomings of the literary method but establishes close relationships between the biography of the author and his work: the critic wants to expose the weaknesses of the character of the author through the shortcomings of the works. In contrast to Becher, who in 1939 recognized the importance of Roth's work with great sensitivity for the tragic circumstances of the author's life, Weiskopf was not satisfied merely to point out the novel's lack of political perspective but in his concluding sentences depicts Roth as a more or less second-class emigrant: "He did not leave Germany in order to fight. He emigrated. A traveler who goes round in circles. On an escape without end." The reviewer does emphasize the artfully simple, noble, beautiful language of the narrator and recognizes the integrity of Roth's character and his honest opposition to National Socialism, but he discredits these positive features largely because they are based on a misguided conservatism and on the posture of an Austrian monarchist. The critical review by Viktor Röbig (that is, Alfred Kurella) of Emil Ludwig's biography of Cleopatra, published in 1937 in Amsterdam, also belongs to these exceptions that prove the rule, even though this perspicacious review attacks not the author but the literary methodology of a psychological biography.

The fundamental problems of a literary anti-Fascism in exile[27] surely constitute the most important focus of literary criticism in exile, but the argument with the cultural policies of the National Socialist state and with the formal expressions of Fascist culture and literature also continued. The earliest documents of this concern with the cultural reality of the Third Reich often take on the nature of a personal disagreement with a fellow writer who, like Gottfried Benn, blindly toadied up or subjected himself to the new regime; or who, like Hanns Johst, rose to the top of the ranks of its cultural officials. Klaus Mann's article "Gott-fried Benn; oder, Die Entwürdigung des Geistes" (Gottfried Benn; or, the debasement of the mind), which appeared in 1933 in the Amster-dam journal *Die Sammlung*, is one example. The problem of personal integrity and professional artistic ethics necessarily becomes the focus of such critical position-fixing. But as the expressionism debate of 1937, which was also prompted by the "Benn case," demonstrates, such discussions could broaden into an axiomatic debate in which the person under attack becomes identical with the aesthetic problems of the work and is then only a code for transcendent societal aesthetic questions that largely evade personal analysis.

In spite of all the personal dismay expressed in Klaus Mann's article about his former poetic idol, his critique of Benn aims beyond the framework of a personal definition to illustrate—in the analysis of Benn's essay "Der neue Staat und die Intellektuellen" (The new state and the intellectuals; 1933)—the tragic situation of the artist who ruins himself artistically by prostituting himself. Klaus Mann considered Benn's affirmation of the Fascist state "intellectual treason," but his interpretation still belongs conceptually to a way of thinking to which Benn himself had adhered until 1933. Mann's critical style presup-poses an intimate acquaintance with Benn's intellectual state of mind. In contrast to the work of Marxist contributors to the expressionism debate, who considered Benn's intellectual development from expres-sionist to apologist of the Fascist mind not an aberration but a logical radicalizing of the latent Fascistoid potential of his aesthetic beliefs, Mann's critique is characterized by its high level of sympathetic under-standing. It is not only the indignation of the disappointed admirer but also a sympathetic view of Benn's artistic stance before 1933; it puts Benn the literary critic before the man who is now classified as a "traitor." Not only the highly emotional tone of the review—which describes Benn's relation to the Fascist state as "monstrous," "crimi-nal," "base," and "hysterical"—but precisely the fact that the reviewer resorts to the use of pathological terminology to illustrate the phenom-enon under attack is a certain sign of the deficiencies of an analysis that cannot only be attributed to dismay and indignation but corresponds to the "logocracy" advocated by Klaus Mann and other bourgeois authors. Walter Benjamin exposed this dilemma with unrelenting incisiveness: "The spirit that voices support of Fascism *must* disappear. The spirit that opposes it, trusting in its own magical powers, *will* disappear."

The critical style of which Klaus Mann's Benn review is an example is, however, hardly representative of exile criticism in general merely because of the immediacy of its situation. It shares the bondage of exile criticism but also its consistency in separating itself from all those intellectuals who had remained in Germany and had submitted to the demands of Fascism. Just as no sympathetic dialogue is possible between victim and executioner, no critical intercourse in cultural journals could exist between the lackeys and journalistic stooges of the Third Reich and those who had escaped its murdering grasp by fleeing into exile. This was true not only for the critical discussion of authors who had, like Benn, openly declared themselves apologists of Fascism but also for dealing with such authors as Rudolf Borchardt, who had ideologically been unjustly exiled so to speak: he had to leave Germany because of his race (thus outwardly sharing the fate of the exiled authors) but remained associated with the stench of Fascist ideology in spite of his expulsion. Borchardt's novel *Vereinigung durch den Feind hindurch* (Unification all the way through the enemy), published by Bermann-Fischer in Vienna (1937), was used by Fritz Brügel as a paradigm for an "aristocratic Fascism" that could not be put into practice in Hitler's Germany but whose opposition to the real thing is based not on an anti-Fascist ethos but on a competing Fascism that could not be put into practice in practical politics. With the help of many quotations from the text, Brügel illustrates his critical verdict, not only relying on the biography and literary past of the author but using the text to make visible the crystallization of a Fascistoid mode of thinking that had been banned from its intellectual motherland only by accident. The paradoxical conditions of Fascist everyday life, which in 1933 caused Oskar Maria Graf to ask for the burning of all his works because as an opponent of Fascism he did not want to be disgraced by being an author tolerated in the Third Reich, created a complex complementary phenomenon in the case of Rudolf Borchardt, which Brügel sums up in one sentence: "The first writer who has recommended the burning of books cannot be published in Germany!"[29] But Brügel's review of Borchardt's novel does not intend to illustrate the paradoxical conditions of Fascist everyday life to the readers in exile.

Rather, it wants to make a contribution to Borchardt's repatriation to that homeland where he and his writings really belong, and it objects to a paradox of a totally different sort: that is, to the fact that Borchardt's Fascism, masquerading as aristocracy, can be articulated in an exile publishing house, in the catchment area of exile literary life, so to speak: "Rudolf Borchardt to this day still has a sort of congregation, even outside Germany; he is, for instance, one of the leading contributors to the elegant Swiss journal *Corona,* and he is considered an important author by those people who collect but do not read luxury editions. Therefore, it is necessary to mention Borchardt's silly new book, which is a renewed affirmation of German Fascism and Fascism in general. . . . the strange fact that a publisher who was forced to leave Germany by the bookburners now presents to the world a man who has called for the burning of books and for the torturing of human beings and, to make matters worse, did so even before the Fascist writers had such criminal ideas . . . we cannot pass over such a strange fact in silence."[30] This example of Brügel's critical method belongs to the category of "demarcation criticism": the critic presupposes insurmountable and irreconcilable differences between Borchardt's literary and ideological positions and the basic concepts of anti-Fascist literature as represented by the critic himself. The expressions of the Fascistoid consciousness that Brügel documents in Borchardt's writing are not commensurable with this value system. Since the exile publisher Bermann-Fischer is classified as a part of this non-Fascist literary public, Brügel takes the side, somewhat in absentia, of the anti-Fascist intellectuals who had been expelled "for good reasons" and against an editorial policy that opens its pages to Fascism and thus undermines its own foundations.

The critical struggle of the exile critics with literature published in Hitler's Germany is carried out predominantly but not exclusively within the framework of this "demarcation criticism." That it is not limited to this model is demonstrated by the critical work of Kurt Kersten: for instance, by his review of Hans Fallada's novel *Wolf unter Wölfen* (Wolf among wolves), published in the journal *Das Wort* (no. 2, 1938). Kersten points out the obvious shortcomings of Fallada's surface realism, his selective and falsifying presentation of social reality, his opportunistic maneuvering in the adaptation of his material, and the constant willingness of the author to please the ruling authorities of the day. Kersten's critique reveals how ideological opportunism and lack of creative self-confidence affect the literary form; how Fallada, by trying to accommodate himself politically, ruins himself as an author; how the beginnings of a realistic writing style dissolve in the wake of preventive self-censorship to which the author submits in order to become a successful writer. Kersten argues that Fallada should not be measured by the standards of anti-Fascist literature:

> It is not possible to predict how low Fallada will sink. Since he lacks interaction with the readers and with criticism, since he does not exercise self-criticism but suppresses it because of the lack of freedom in his country, Fallada's development seems to continue on its downward path. He attempts to evade a direct confrontation with topical themes and phenomena by escape into the past but at the same time falsifies that past. A few items in the book betray that Fallada even now still struggles against National Socialism within himself; others are proof of his capabilities, of his outstanding power of observation and his intuitive sense of reality. But Fallada is incapable of developing any further; totally unknown and a mystery to him is the skill to speak the truth even under the condition in which he prefers to live.[31]

Despite the firmness of the verdict, Kersten's critical method is characterized by its variety of shades, its multiplicity of perspectives, and its vigilant interest in the forms of literary life in Hitler's Germany. His critical essays in *Das Wort* are not limited to verdicts based on ideology; on the contrary, they grope with great intellectual effort, supported by relevant material, for the truth and try to provide authentic standards for an informed judgment to the readers in exile. His observations in "Leser und Kritiker im Dritten Reich" (Readers and critics in the Third Reich) in *Das Wort* (no. 5, 1938) are examples of his critical method.

The comprehensive "demarcation criticism," whose moral-ideological legitimacy is beyond doubt, had primarily an affective and group-dynamic function with regard to the self-definition and stabilizing of the exile reading public. Its cognitive value emerged predominantly within this functional framework. More important for the creation of a collective consciousness in that exile reading public, however, were those forms of literary criticism—such as Brecht's conceptual sketches of an anti-Fascist populism or his discourse on the "difficulties in writing the truth" under the conditions of Hitlerian Fascism—that responded concretely to the challenges of the historical situation and developed the aesthetics for the immediate future from the battle conditions of the present. Other examples are Paul Kersten's detailed analyses and many micro-analyses of Fascist cultural politics that appeared in *Das Wort* in the column "An den Rand geschrieben" (Written in the margins). They composed a mosaic of Fascist everyday life and partially counteracted a dangerously oversimplified view of Hitler's Germany that no longer registered its internal contradictions and passed off the Fascist regime as the collective effort of the "German people." This view of Hitler's Germany was quite influential within the anti-Fascist exile population, as is documented by Thomas Mann's public statements and his activities in his American exile. The political upshot of this view was the "collective guilt" theory, which suited the ideological interests of the western Allies, inasmuch as it helped to veil the capitalist class foundation of Fascist rule and exonerated the economic and political leadership of the system at the expense of its henchmen and collaborators.

Paul Kersten's "Leser und Kritiker im Dritten Reich," which pays attention to the phenomenon of the essential failure of the literary policies of the National Socialist regime, also objects to the demonizing of Fascist everyday life: "We can and regrettably must notice that a certain 'know-it-all attitude' appears also outside the Third Reich; these 'know-it-alls' totally ignore the opposition inside the country . . . which does not always appear in the form of traditional resistance."[32] Kersten draws his supporting material from the National Socialist press: from the diagnoses and the research of the journal *Die Bücherkunde*, which in 1937 helplessly confronted the phenomenon that all strategies so far developed for making National Socialist literature more popular among factory workers had been almost totally unsuccessful—a finding that, like the rejection of "Blubo" literature (*Blut und Boden* = blood and soil) in the rural population, caused widespread discussions about the suitability of the hitherto subsidized publications. Kersten's critical attention particularly focuses on all forms of passive resistance accessible only to those readers and critics with a comprehensive grasp of the conditions of literary production in the regimented literary life of the Third Reich. He does not consider the reading of the literature produced within the Third Reich superfluous, but he demands of the exiles a highly sophisticated form of reading, capable of deciphering even the forms of meaningful silence and the codes of intended forms of expression in certain works: "Jokes and satirical asides will not be enough. . . . Beyond the 'oddities,' beyond the agents, the bullies, the block wardens, the sergeants . . . the spies and the informers, there live millions of people with sorrows and cares, who have to work 80 hours and more each week, there live disappointed, betrayed former supporters. . . . All these events must sublimate themselves in literature and indeed are reflected there."[33]

To be able to detect these reflections requires a way of reading that is able to fathom the secondary levels of meaning of literary forms and that reads between the lines and makes the necessary interpolations. Kersten uses as an example the novel of a younger author who describes the life of a young married couple in the time of crisis: "They are totally left to their own resources but defend themselves as individuals against hunger, need, landlord, bailiff . . . but the narrative takes place in the period long after 1933, and there is still the same state of exigency. . . . This man and this woman whose marriage is described in the book do not expect anything from others but rely only on themselves. In the 'Third Reich' such a description will be understood, while it is not only incomprehensible in other circumstances and under different social conditions but even looks reactionary and counterrevolutionary. If one does not start with the conditions under which an author works, it will be impossible to understand the meaning and the nature of his work."[34] This claim set a standard for the literary critics in exile to which they could frequently not measure up in practice, particularly since the everyday life of the National Socialist regime became more and more closed to the view of the exiled writers and critics the longer the exile lasted. In addition, the phenomenon of the "language of slavery" became a difficult problem for the critics and led to many misinterpretations both inside and outside the Third Reich. One example among many is Werner Bergengruen's novel *Der Grosstyrann und das Gericht* (The great tyrant and the court), which was praised as a "Führer-novel of the Renaissance" in the *Völkische Beobachter*; among many exile readers, however, it was considered proof of a successful camouflage that really expressed intellectual opposition to the Fascist dictatorship.

Because the anti-Fascist critics were shut off from an essential ingredient of literary criticism—that is, an immediate experience of the intellectual life to which it responds—the dissemination and analysis of information about cultural life in the Third Reich became especially important. Karl Obermann's inventory of four years of National-Socialist literature, published in *Das Wort* (nos. 4–5, 1937), can be viewed as a prototype of this form of literary criticism. The author evaluates a survey of Berlin book dealers, conducted by the *Deutsche Allgemeine Zeitung* in the period before Christmas of 1936, which provides information about the actual preferences of the reading public and documents the failure of the National Socialist book promotion campaign. The findings produced by critical essays in the exile journals, with the help of such structural analyses, are confirmed by Obermann's data on the state of the paper industry and the printing business, and their socioeconomic basis as well is made plain: the index of book production, which declines synchronously with the acceleration of the arms production, poignantly characterizes the priorities of a political system that needed bombs more than books for the retention of its capitalist social conditions.

Besides the discussion about the present reality of the Third Reich, the quest for preconditions and possibilities of a cultural reconstruction following the military defeat of Hitler's Fascism moved into the center of the critical debates after 1937—particularly in the publications of the Marxist left, the journals *Das Wort* and *Internationale Literatur*. The contributions to the debate about the literary heritage must be viewed from the same perspective. They were directed equally at the present and at the future: they looked to the present insofar as they intended to highlight the manipulation and desecration of the cultural heritage by the cultural policies and the literary scholarship of the National Socialist state; they were directed at the future insofar as they tried to uncover the cultural traditions that would underlie a future literature and culture unburdened by the legacy of Fascism. The glance into the future, the theoretical anticipation of the cultural-political problems of a new beginning, made visible the intellectual contradictions and political conflicts within the exile reading public. F. C. Weiskopf considered especially problematical the "Germanophobia" of those exiled writers "who did not cross the borders to fight but did so in order to emigrate."[36] His individualistic psychological approach hits on only one aspect of a much more complex state of affairs and simplifies the problem in the sense that he represents the difficulty of national identification in the exile as applicable only to the cosmopolitan segment of the exile intelligentsia.

In a review of Johannes R. Becher's collection of poetry, *Der Glück-sucher und die sieben Lasten* (The fortune seeker and the seven burdens), Alexander Abusch approaches the problem of a destroyed national identity among the exiles more self-critically and with greater consideration of the historical conditions of the socialization of the literary intellect: "Had we not abandoned our native country and our fatherland too lightheartedly? Yes, we correctly agreed with working-class Germany that proletarians do not have a fatherland. They do not have one as long as private property prevails. But does that mean that they do not even wish to have a fatherland? . . . We remained at the surface or chased phenomena and thus became prisoners of the bourgeois ideology that stopped to be interested in its own country with the beginning of imperialism. We drifted in the stream of a wretched cosmopolitanism that is characteristic of the whole literature of the imperialist era."[37] The look forward to the difficulties of a future cultural reconstruction directed the attention of the literary intelligentsia to the damage done, even to some of its adversaries, by the society that had given birth to Fascism; and it confronted the exile intellectuals with the question whether and how far the existing language, whose concepts had been distorted beyond recognition by Fascism, was still operational for the battle against Fascism. The dispute about cosmopolitanism, anti-Fascist patriotism, humanism, and the central ideological concepts of the cultural heritage thus had to be in a sense a dispute about language, which centered on the question whether the anti-Fascist intellectuals could help the despoiled, eroded language regain its historical birthright and liberate it from these distortions, or whether the traditional notions and ways of thinking bore the permanent defects of the ideology that culminated in Fascism.

The continuity of the process of literary elucidation in exile was not assured, primarily because of the geographical fragmentation of the exile public and the ephemeral nature of most journals. Nothing can make the overwhelming force of existential threats and their consequences for the basic conditions of exile criticism more obvious than the fate of Walter Benjamin, one of the most discerning literary critics and theoreticians of the first half of the century, who in 1940 took his own life at the Spanish border while trying to escape from the Gestapo. The still unexhausted potential of his critical work had only marginal influence on the reading public of the exile and became the focus of increasing critical attention only at the end of the 1960s. Although his works written after 1933 were hardly noticed by the exile reading public and were without impact on the most important critical debates between 1933 and 1939, they probably provide us with the most perspicacious critical interpretation of "epic theater" in the manner of Brecht. His most important critical essays of that era—an address delivered in Paris, "Der Autor als Produzent" (The author as producer); and the article "Das Kunstwerk im Zeitalter seiner technischen Reproduzierbarkeit" (The work of art in the age of technical reproduction)—are distinguished by a concept of art that abandons the adherence to the traditional notion of the work of art, opens the way for a functional analysis of art, and accentuates a systems approach to the understanding of artistic perception. Propped up by the theoretical foundation of a historical-materialist interpretation of history and in determined opposition to the aesthetic and critical positions of Georg Lukács, Benjamin's theoretical ideas work toward an "operational aesthetics" that questions the basic tenets of the traditional art concept based on contemplation and confronts the historically exhausted traditional art concept with the notion of an operational art that not only reflects the contemporary class struggles but actively takes part in them. It is therefore no accident that his most radical publication, "Der Autor als Produzent," contains a fundamental critique of the artistic currents defined as the "New Realism" and of the sort of intellectual who made the class struggle the object of consumption and accelerated the transformation of the political battle from a decisionmaking force into an object of contemplative contentment. Starting from Brecht's concept of the "restructuring" of existing forms and means of production, Benjamin sets up the New Realism as an example of the decisive difference between the mere supplying of a system of production and the actual changing of that system: "We are indeed confronted with the fact . . . that the bourgeois machinery of production and publication can assimilate astonishing numbers of revolutionary themes and even propagate them, without seriously putting in question its own existence and the existence of the class that owns this machinery. . . . And I maintain further that a substantial segment of the so-called left-wing literature had no other social function but to continue producing new effects for the entertainment of the public out of the political situation."[38] The fundamentally different emphasis of Benjamin's ideas does not, however, consist in the demand for a tendentious or partisan literature in the service of the proletariat, because the merely ideological solidarity with the proletarian class struggle does not, according to Benjamin's analysis, at all guarantee the emergence of a literary production appropriate for the demands of the class struggle. On the contrary, the organizing role Benjamin demands from art is closely tied to literary *technique*. He sees in the type of the "operational writer," as personified by Sergei Tretyakov, the best example of the "functional interdependence between the right political tendency and the progressive literary technique." The kind of literary activity Benjamin demands

> will never be only an occupation with the products but will always include involvement in the means of production. In other words . . . products must have an organizing function besides and before their role as literary works. And in no way must the organizational usefulness be limited to a propaganda function. The best political tendency is wrong if it does not show the posture that is necessary for following it. And the writer can demonstrate this posture only in his only field of activity: as an author. . . . *An author who teaches nothing to other writers does not teach anything to anybody.* Therefore the role model character of literary production is important first of all because it will give guidelines for production to other producers, and second because it can make improved means of production available to them. The quality of this system is determined by the number of consumers it supplies for the producers: in short, by how many readers and spectators it can turn into active participants.[39]

In Benjamin's opinion, the prototype for such a production system is the epic theater developed by Brecht, and the majority of his critical writings after 1933 deal with this topic. The nucleus of the concept of art he advocates is the organizing role of art that revokes the role of the recipient and transforms him into a co-producer of the discovery of truth and the cognitive process that social necessities demand. But the discovery of truth that is the aim of the activity of the "operational writer" has as *its* aim not truths without consequences but truths that have practical consequences, that make action for change unavoidable. This aspect of his later critical writings in the long run differentiates his critical method from that of the Frankfurt School, which had a decisive hand in his rediscovery in the 1960s. Benjamin's controversial "Kunstwerk" essay, which tries to explain the systematic change in artistic perception as a result of the fundamental changes in the social forces of artistic production and the new media it produced, is distinguished—in spite of all the speculation it contains—by a bold synthesis of philosophical and social-historical concepts, which is fundamental to Benjamin's whole critical work and gives him a special place among the literary critics of the exile. His writings are examples of a kind of art and literary criticism that reflect the historical circumstances of their own practices, make the medial constraints on artistic perception and their social and class-specific dependency the center of the critical discussion, and thus anticipate developments that the broad literary public did not recognize until decades later.

Developments after 1945

The military defeat of Hitler's Germany and the collapse of Fascism demolished the intellectual and ideological foundations that had for twelve years defined literary life on German soil. The intellectuals who had paved the way for Hitler—the conceptual ideologues of Fascism at the universities and the journalist henchmen in the editorial offices— at first seemed totally discredited by the roles they had played in the regime and thus unfit to serve as the intellectual support structure of a post-Fascist social order. The National Socialist state had left behind a wretched intellectual legacy: the anti-Fascist intelligentsia within Germany had, with few exceptions, been driven out or fallen prey to the terror of the system. Non-Fascist intellectuals still existed in the context of the "inner migration"; their apolitical shadow existence at the far end of Fascist cultural politics was not only due to political conditions but was also reflected in the nature of their art, a nonpractical end-of-an-era introspectiveness that offered a rather meager beginning for an anti-Fascist cultural reorientation. At first, however, most problems connected with the ailing cultural life had to take a back seat to general survival problems. Books and culture remained luxury items, and the literary public regimented by the National Socialist state was not immediately replaced by an unconstrained anti-Fascist literary market but by a public regimented by the victorious occupation powers. This system was governed by the idea of "reeducation"; it was designed to guarantee that adequate information about the crimes of Hitlerian Fascism, long concealed by propaganda, would be provided to the population, and that not only the intellectual henchmen of Fascism but suspected fellow travelers who tried to present themselves as secret dissidents would at first have no influence whatsoever on the formation of public opinion. Besides those published by the Allies themselves, the only periodicals subsequently allowed to appear were those licensed by the Allied occupation authorities and edited only by persons who had not been actively involved in the criminal activities of the National Socialist regime. In the dire economic straits of the postwar period, publications were controlled by paper allotment: "Everything then had to be licensed: the German press and the publishing business; foreign printed material; theater and film performances, even the actors themselves. By controlling the allotment of paper, the Americans controlled (until the currency reform) the editorial policy of all German printed matter. Paper was available only to those who published material conducive to 're-education.' "[40]

In neither the first cultural journals to appear in the Allied occupation zones nor in the general press of this period between the end of World War II and the creation of two separate German states did literary criticism reach an important position.[41] This was caused not only by the fact that very few (and hardly any new) books appeared in German but more by the fact that the national future of Germany had not yet been decided; it had still not been determined in what social framework cultural life was to have its new beginning. The provisional decisions about Germany's political future turned out to be significant for the creation of the model of public life within which literary communciation was to take place. The reconstruction of a capitalist social and economic order in the Federal Republic of Germany and the political framework of a bourgeois democracy became the basis for a form of public life in which artistic and literary statements could from then on be articulated. The construction of a "socialist democratic republic" in the Soviet style determined the functional framework of literary communication and the status of literary criticism in the eastern part of Germany. Although the historic encumbrances of the past were a cultural-political challenge for both remaining parts of the former Third Reich, the cultural and literary assimilation of this past was achieved in markedly different fashions in the two German states. The majority of the exiled anti-Fascist intellectuals and writers settled down east of the Elbe River after their return. But this was not the only reason the intellectual life in the Adenauer Germany of the 1950s was not given its peculiar character by intellectuals who came from the ranks of the active anti-Fascist opposition.

The most influential literary critic in the press of the Adenauer era was Friedrich Sieburg, an emigrant who had fraternized with Nazi collaborators during the occupation of France by Hitler's troops.[42] What held true for the law and for economics was reflected in cultural life as well: in the wake of militant anti-Communism and of rearmament, not only those persons who had financed Hitler's plans and had given legal formulation to his racial laws but also those misguided spirits in the realm of literature who had erred to the bitter end became socially acceptable again. Gottfried Benn was belatedly accorded the praise for his poetry that he had refused to accept all his life. This tardy renown cannot be separated from his role as literary rebuttal witness in Konrad Adenauer's state. The partitioning of Germany and the establishment of two contrasting social systems on German soil undoubtedly hindered the emergence of a journalistic literary criticism that was up to its genuine task. The separation of Germany led, within the German Federal Republic, to the predominance of a critical self-image that considered itself apolitical but still paid lavish tribute to the climate of the Cold War. In view of the compromised position of a politically controlled literary scholarship and criticism in the Third Reich, the pronounced political indifference of West German literary criticism of the 1950s and the predominance of the ahistorical concept of literature typical of its methodology can be interpreted as logical reactions to an unconquered past. But this explanation would take into account only one single—although admittedly very important—aspect of the phenomenon, because the critical paradigm for the developments in West Germany in the 1950s was not at all limited to West Germany but corresponded to developments in the French and

Anglo-American linguistic areas, in spite of differing intracultural conditions.

The antagonism between academic and journalistic criticism, which has had a long tradition in Germany, proved damaging to both institutions even during the first half of the century: the elimination of the critical component in literary scholarship turned out to be an opportune precondition for the political commissioning of the tenured literary scholars in the service of Fascism. But the unscholarly subjectivity of the journalist critics and their arrogant aesthetic verdicts were a welcome pretext for the National Socialist regime to eliminate the critical activity of the press. Between 1933 and 1945 the qualitative, if not the institutional, differences between academic and journalistic *contemplation* of literature were suspended: "Whereas the *scholar* in his role as National Socialist civil servant measures the literature of the past by the standards of the official policies of the state, the tenured *contemplator* of art does the same for the literature of the present."[44] The triumph of the New Criticism in the 1950s contributed to the consolidation of this anachronism. The New Critics' claim of abstinence from critical judgment turned out, on close inspection, to be mere lip service, because they did not reveal the criteria for the selection of their subjects.

Both Walter Muschg's *Tragische Literaturgeschichte* and Ernst Robert Curtius's *Europäische Literatur und lateinisches Mittelalter* are witnesses to a trend toward conciliation between scholarship and criticism in the 1950s. Curtius explains his intentions in the preface to the second edition of his highly erudite work: "I have written this book not only from purely scholarly motives but because I fear for the preservation of Western culture."[45] Curtius was not to remain the only scholar to consider his work a form of cultural and historical criticism and to want to contribute to the preservation of the occidental cultural traditions against the corruption of the times. The elitist concept of culture and literature represented by Curtius catered to the lack of orientation of the postwar period and largely determined the self-concept of both academic and journalistic critics. The renunciation of a systematic investigation of the problem of literary valuation on the part of the scholars and the guidelines of a new body of works of literary modernism whose basic tenets were still not accounted for in the 1950s resulted in the same "subservient" critical approach to literature in the cultural press that Goebbels had demagogically turned against so-called "destructive" literary criticism. The erudite, often perspicacious reviews of Egon Holthusen reveal even rhetorically a strong affinity for criticism that attempts to follow the postulate of the teacher, Curtius, who defines criticism as "that form of literature whose subject is literature."[46]

Holthusen's ambitious use of language indicates his claim to an aesthetic-critical position normally not open to the communicative and journalistic function of criticism. The conservative critical ethos of his reviews combines with a critical method that does not see the contemporary literary output in the light of its historical background but measures it by the standards of the presumably time-proven classics and finds it sadly lacking. That Holthusen's critical work remained generally without consequences and that West German literature did not produce any new poets of the stature of T. S. Eliot or Rudolf Alexander Schröder may serve as evidence that Holthusen's hope, expressed in 1951, for a possible revival of the glorious past had little chance for success: "The time appears to be ripe to think our disjointed world back into order and to withdraw from circulation those parodies of the traditional truth and the perversions of revealed and traditional wisdom."[47] The discrepancy between the stated intellectual claim and the profane reality of the publishing conditions of cultural journalism certainly cannot be blamed on the critics; however, it becomes by necessity grotesque when criticism no longer has any concept of its position in society or loses sight of its intellectual foundations because of excessive self-examination.

The dominant concern with the "classics of modern literature" in Holthusen's critical essays reflects the ubiquitous search of the 1950s for literary models and standards for contemporary literature and ultimately also for literary criticism. The ahistorical establishment of a canon with the label "classics of modern literature" is contestable because it largely ignores the tradition of realist literature in the twentieth century. It is also questionable as a critical method because it ultimately serves Holthusen as an excuse to avoid a discussion of contemporary West German literature in its historical context. The aesthetic inferiority of contemporary German literature is indisputable for Holthusen because it cannot measure up to the literary master-pieces of James Joyce, Marcel Proust, T. S. Eliot, and Paul Valéry. The internal logic of this "rapidly spreading bad habit of proving one's literary cosmopolitanism by accusing German postwar literature of provincialism in comparing it to the untested canon of 'classics of modern literature'"[48] is described very accurately by Franz Schonauer's retrospective comments:

> That was more noncommittal than to investigate the origins of such 'provincialism,' since that would have necessarily raised extraliterary, e.g., political and social, questions. In other words, a specter of unquestioned literary stature—a stature either derived from the Western tradition or explained by [Arnold] Toynbee's cultural morphology—was to be the measure of everything that looked like innovation. . . . But at the same time this specter was used as an ideological pretext by the neoconservative critics, because they insisted that their standards had been derived exclusively from masterpieces, although in view of the conditions in Germany during the first decade after the war, the construction of a flawless aesthetic system was certainly not the most important for the critics, except that it might have been vital to consider political and social aspects within the framework of literary criticism.[49]

This lack of any reflection of political and social aspects in literary criticism can be interpreted as a reaction to the elimination of the institutional autonomy of the National Socialist regime. But the strict rejection of extraliterary factors, though designed to prove the institutional autonomy of literary criticism, only contributed to the generation of a new myth of officially protected introspectiveness and intensified the identity crisis of criticism—as demonstrated by the Benn boom and the uncritical admiration of poets like Eliot and Ezra Pound, who had shown sympathies for Fascism. By seeing itself as a form of literature, literary criticism divested itself of its public mission. Although it was published in newspapers and journals and although it was written for readers who participated in the public literary scene, criticism did not define itself by its public mission but derived its task from literature itself.

This self-image of criticism appears paradigmatically in the person of Günter Blöcker, who was, next to Sieburg, the most prominent literary critic of the *Frankfurter Allgemeine Zeitung* in the 1950s and

1960s. In contrast to his famous colleagues, Blöcker touches on the pragmatic and economic side of criticism in his remarks on the role of the critic: one would search the writings of Sieburg, Max Rychner, or Holthusen in vain for the revealing comment that the book critic is the "victim of a seasonal rush business" (spring and fall) and thus more an appendage to the book industry than its conductor. But this insight into the economic base of the book industry never decisively influences Blöcker's understanding of the role of the critic. He resolutely defends an ideal concept of criticism that defines the work of the critic as the expression of noninterchangeable individualities: "We have critics, but we have no criticism . . . we have critics, but they remain individuals each of whom has to bear the risk of his critical existence by himself."[50] This strict individualistic view of the institutional role of criticism has methodological consequences at all levels. The fragmentation of criticism corresponds to the atomizing of literature: "More than ever before, contemporary literary criticism has to deal with the individual literary work."[51] But when literary criticism in practice concentrates on the encounter of two unexchangeable individualities, there arises the hermeneutical problem of interpretation as well as the problem of critical and interpretive competency. The competence of the critic, according to Blöcker, is based "on his talent, his specific aptitude, on his affinity to literature."[51] Thus, competence cannot be taught, particularly since it has to be demonstrated by dealing with a subject that is equally unteachable: "Poetry cannot be explained, it can only be grasped."[52] This concept of literature, which is based on the theoretical position of Emil Staiger, and the intense mystification of critical competence lead to Blöcker's definition of the role of literary criticism: its relation to its subject matter manifests itself in a congenial interpretation; its relationship with the readers consists in the "communication of the reading experience."[54]

Blöcker pays attention neither to the conceptual framework of mediation by the publishing mechanism nor to the problem of reader-oriented presentation. He does concede that the "communication of the reading experience of the critic" might make it easier for the reader (of the critical analysis) to gain access to the interpreted work; but since for the reader, too, literature is an immediate experience, the critic can only present his own experiences with the same subject, in relation to which the reader can then compare, or even broaden, his own experience. The main difference between the artistic experiences of the public and the critic is limited to the critic's greater competency of critical judgment (which, however, cannot be explained) and to the public's articulation of the critical verdict: "It is the ultimate goal of criticism to recognize the poetic work, to comprehend it as adequately as possible, and to assess its nature and its form publicly. Everything else is of secondary importance."[55] The standards for this evaluation, which are not supposed to be discussed, turn out to be the fundamental problem for turning these critical theories into practice. The standards are not—as Blöcker supposes—excluded from the cognitive act but indeed guide and direct its formal expressions. His critical premise that criticism performs interpretive rather than judgmental tasks hides the fact that interpretation has always been preceded by a valuative decision, which manifests itself as an act of selection with regard to the established literary tradition and the literary output of the present. This filtering function of criticism becomes the center of attention only when one accentuates the reader orientation of critical activity, something Blöcker does not do. His understanding of the role of the critic is caught in the same contradiction as that of his neoconservative colleagues: criticism wants to create responses in the public without in practice adjusting itself to the task of establishing a critical reading public: "Criticism strove for public recognition but, at the same time, increased the distance between itself and the public. It cited the public nature of critical reasoning and removed the criteria for its judgments from public discussion."[56]

When critics base their expertise on a not further defined "talent," when they lay claim to a public office on one side but on the other side consider their judgments legitimate because they are supported by a proven refinement of taste, the suspicion arises that the actual social importance of criticism is minimal. Thus Friedrich Sieburg's critical writing in the daily press combines a high measure of literary erudition and aesthetic sensitivity with an arbitrariness of the critical judgment and a shocking absence of theoretic knowledge; these enable him to think of himself as the navel of the literary world and to make his own doubtlessly refined taste the guiding principle for contemporary literary life. His blanket condemnation of the West German literature of the 1950s and the early 1960s—in spite of his sound sense of its shortcomings—is a sign not so much of the superiority of his critical position as of a concept of literature that derived from the past, glorified the past, and was no longer appropriate. Although Sieburg defines his own critical work as a service to a literary culture that aids in humanizing the social sphere, his notions of "humanizing" are located in that realm of "twilight introspection" which creates a kingdom of Truth, Virtue, and Beauty far away from the reality of practical social existence.

Sieburg's opposition to the kind of literature connected with the *Gruppe 47* (the best-known group of young West German writers after World War II) and its largely abstract-humanistic social criticism is thus not really a contradiction but rather a logical consequence. His objections to the social-critical literature of the Adenauer era, which rely on aesthetic arguments—that is, on objections having to do with "good taste"—confirm the resentment of an educated reading public that wanted to be spared a confrontation with "politics" in dealing with literature or, as followers of Gottfried Benn, expected from literature the evocation of a fictional "counterworld" against the corrupting world of political concepts. In this sense Sieburg, with his own critical idiosyncrasies, participated in the spirit of social restoration and of the Cold War; the fact that he had few influential opponents among the critics of the 1950s is an interesting ideological piece of evidence for the state of public opinion during the Cold War.

"Every society has the critics it deserves."[57] This dictum, directed by Franz Schonauer at Friedrich Sieburg and the society of the Adenauer era, is valid mainly in the sense that Sieburg's practical critical work generally corresponded to the intellectual predisposition of that part of the public which was served by the journalists of the *Frankfurter Allgemeine Zeitung*. As a newspaper critic, Sieburg was prevented from taking the drastic steps taken by Emil Staiger (a professor of German at the University of Zurich) because of his aversion to the pen-pushing age in which he was forced to live: in his acceptance speech upon being awarded the Zurich Literature Prize—which started the so-called Zurich Literature Feud—Staiger publicly explained the reasons that militated, in his opinion, against a critical occupation with contemporary literature, which no longer conformed to the classical ideals of Beauty, Truth, and Virtue. Sieburg did, in fact, acknowledge the most significant new publications of his time—for instance, the novels of Heinrich Böll and Martin Walser and the poetry of Hans Magnus

Enzensberger—but did not consider them worthy objects of serious critical debate; he used them more as a means for discharging his duty as a chronicler of literature from an ironically detached position. No other critic of that era is Sieburg's equal in wit and stylistic brilliance: his critical writing is a treasurehouse for the educated German who feels only scorn for literary life and for literature that deals with contemporary problems. But the literary objects of such impressionistic criticism serve only as a pretext for a witty self-portrayal—which is not without entertainment value for the "in-group" readers who can conserve and enjoy their own prejudices in identifying with his ironic style. The following may serve as an example:

> When the book was put into my arms like a newborn babe, very gently and with an almost religious, whispered comment that asked me for reverence, the sycamore still carried its leaves. . . . Today, when I finished the book, the trees stand bare and dead leaves pile up between the shrubbery. Almost 900 pages had to be conquered; over and over again I lost the thread when I allowed myself to get carried away by the dismal verbal wit of the author, who did not seem to have fun at all with this whole story. . . . God knows that I was diligent. . . . If my notes don't deceive me— right now I am checking those of October 17—it is one Anselm Kristlein who tells the confusing and not-at-all entertaining story of his life. . . . The landscape is barren; almost 900 pages have been honestly finished. It was butchery, not a battle. I was never able to identify this Josef Heinrich clearly: is the narrator in the textile business or does he deal in oil heating systems; yes, I know it is not really important but then the novel talks about it constantly.[58]

This is Sieburg's review of Walser's novel *Halbzeit* (Halftime; *Frankfurter Allgemeine Zeitung*, December 3, 1960). The novel's problems of epic integration, its tremendous wealth of characters, the wide-branching episodes, and the breadth of variation of Walser's language are wittily insinuated; the reader is confronted with reading impressions that could also indicate problems of the literary object. But this method totally lacks any of the analytical dimension—in either the sense of giving a close interpretation of the text or the sense of a discussion guided by literary theory—that could have put the novel into the context of the contemporary literary scene or even brought in extraliterary topics.

In stark contrast to Sieburg and the educated detractors of the postwar literature that was influenced by the *Gruppe 47*, the critics close to the *Gruppe 47*—for instance, Walter Jens, Joachim Kaiser, Hans Mayer, and Marcel Reich-Ranicki—concentrated their critical attention on newly published works and in a sense participated in their creation. Although their critical verdicts and standards were radically different from those of their opponents—indeed, often diametrically opposed—their critical method was not nearly so different from that of their adversaries as one might be led to believe. They, too, insisted on the right to bring their personal convictions to bear, but they saw themselves as journalists and stressed the reader orientation of literary criticism—at least in the definition of their own roles—although that is seen as only one of many points of reference. The catchy phrase "Better Books for Better Readers" with which Reich-Ranicki characterized his intentions shows that his self-image and his claims were the legacy of the European Enlightenment but suggests at the same time that the critical model of the Enlightenment could be transferred without break into contemporary literary life. In contrast to his historical models, whose educational optimism was supported by the ethos of the bourgeoisie about to emancipate itself, Reich-Ranicki and his colleagues in the bourgeois press jungle no longer had much justification for such an optimistic attitude. In exceptional cases their actions produced a rustling in the leaves of the press, but usually they did not even achieve that. If one adjusts the historical proportions and takes into consideration the fact that the socially dominant literature was disseminated for the happy few, untouched by literary criticism and away from the belletristic boutiques, and that the potential consumers of the utterances of Reich-Ranicki and his colleagues constituted hardly more than 4 percent of the population, one must surely concede that the critics associated with the *Gruppe 47* contributed more than their opponents to the stimulation of public interest in the problems of contemporary literature.

Reich-Ranicki's published criticism is not at all limited to the production of aesthetic judgments about newly published works but reflects to some degree the social and political framework of these works. It vaguely allocates them a sociocultural rank in the intellectual debates of the day as Reich-Ranicki surveys the literary landscape from his own combative personal perspective. At a safe distance from the real social controversies and, unlike the political and economic journalists, freed from the obligation to represent the existing social order as the best one possible under the given circumstances, the critic of the cultural press could not expose himself to the suspicion of political partisanship, but he could take up courageous positions in the cultural battle of opinions. It is in this sense that Reich-Ranicki takes sides. He is against the troubled relationship between leading Christian Democratic (CDU) politicians and contemporary literature (key word: *Pinscher*, vocabulary); against the usurpation of literary discussion by political terms and criteria (the campaign against Brecht under the banner of the Cold War); against playing down the impact of National Socialist literature; against the critical campaigns of Rudolf Krämer-Badoni, who exhorted the West German authors of the day to participate in the propaganda crusade against East Germany led by the Axel Springer Press; against the literary policies in East Germany. But he is *for* certain trends for which he wanted to prepare the way with his critical activity: the intellectual confrontation with the literature of the other German state (strictly avoided by the phraseologists of "reunification"); for the rehabilitation of the realistic style of narration at a time when the death of traditional narrative technique was eagerly predicted in Brecht's fictional "Tui republics" and when the depictability of reality was denied under the influence of Absurdism. Reich-Ranicki had faith in the power of criticism and considered it an effective weapon in the battle of public opinion whose functional competence he took for granted. He hoped that criticism would encourage certain kinds of literature and prevent others from coming into existence. Thus he created a fictional literary republic whose citizens—the reading public—seek access to literature under the guidance of critical opinion leaders and more or less dictate their aesthetic desires to the producers.

The overestimation of the importance of their role, which manifests itself in many literary critics of the older generation, is probably less an attribute of vanity than the immediate expression of their idealistic concept of a literary life where the operating conditions of criticism are not at all taken into account. It is significant that the institutional base of criticism was still passed over in silence at the beginning of the

1960s, when the literary public began to become more conscious of the problems of contemporary criticism. The critical colloquium organized by the West Berlin Academy of Arts in 1963 focused mainly on the examination of critical standards whose adequacy for the evaluation of contemporary literature was to be the subject of debate. The problematic premises of the leading critics—for instance, the exclusive concentration on "highbrow" literature and the esoteric rhetoric of criticism—did not become the center of the discussion, nor did the entire complex of problems surrounding the actual critical publishing conditions within the media. The cultural status quo, the cultural dichotomy of "highbrow" and mass literature, was accepted without question by the participants in the colloquium. Their discussions mainly revolved around the objective adequacy of criticism. More than fifty participants supplied evidence, of sorts, for Blöcker's thesis that there is no criticism, only individual critics. The pluralism of critical positions and the heterogeneous nature of the standards were not disguised but neither were they ever addressed as serious problems; rather, they were taken as the expression of a lively diversity of opinion appropriate to the heteronomy of literary creations.[59]

It was only in the second half of the 1960s that the discussion of practical literary criticism reached a new level and that the social foundations of literary criticism as an institution became central to the critical debate, not only within the radical cultural criticism of the New Left but also among those critical minds who strove for a reform of the institution. Thus, for example, Peter Glotz's critical analysis *Buchkritik in deutschen Zeitungen* (Literary criticism in the German press; 1968) disassociated itself categorically from the cultural critics of the Frankfurt School and from the conclusion that Jürgen Habermas had reached in his pioneering study *Strukturwandel der Öffentichkeit* (Structural changes in the reading public). Glotz refutes Habermas's central thesis that the development of bourgeois society in the nineteenth and twentieth centuries coincides with the progressive disintegration of the literary public and that the latter has been replaced by the "pseudo-public and pseudo-private sphere of cultural consumption."[60] Glotz juxtaposes this finding with his own thesis that the literary audience has not disintegrated at all but merely changed its social composition and that the position of the literary elite has changed as well. Glotz conducts his altercation with Habermas and the cultural critics of the Frankfurt School with the aim not of justifying the existing status of literary criticism but rather of calling it into question. His inquiry into the state of literary criticism in the German newspapers culminates in the diagnosis that the functional literary elite hardly accomplishes its journalistic mission. He accuses it of cementing the cultural status quo by its self-definition and its critical practices and of inadequately utilizing its power for the bridging of cultural chasms. Glotz regards the split between elitist and popular culture and the extreme fragmentation of the spheres of literary communication—which partially overlap in the existing "cultural landscape"—as historical fact but considers the condition changeable even within the existing social structural framework. In a certain way he thus shares Reich-Ranicki's critical self-image, which concedes substantial influence to literary criticism. He shares this image particularly in the sense that he has high hopes for lasting positive consequences for the receptive behavior of the reading public from a "change in attitude" by the critics. His critique is predominantly directed against the esoteric habits of communication of elitist criticism, but it also turns against a narrow concept of literature that leaves popular literature out of the realm of criticism and thus completely removes it from critical control. Glotz's expectations for literary criticism are best summed up as the popularization of "representative culture" by reader-oriented critical guidance and critical inspection of popular culture without resorting to methods inadequate for this task.

When Glotz pleaded for a democratization of culture that becomes reality in the duty "to make the representative cultural goods generally accessible,"[61] his approach still ultimately neutralized the social and historical substance of culture and became subject to a charge of confusing a merely quantitative broadening of the object area of journalistic literary criticism and a modification of its mode of communication with real democratization. The merit of Glotz's study lies in its impact as a critical corrective to the manipulation theory that was beginning to gain ground among the New Left, a theory that ultimately promoted the idolatry of the culture industry and proved to be theoretically vulnerable. In fact, however, Glotz evaded the question of the function of the culture industry in the context of contemporary conditions of communication and the exercise of power. His demands were quite sensible, but the expectations he based on them were unreasonable.

From the perspective of the 1980s we can see that his demands had some impact: mainly, that the newly created cultural and literary sections of the audiovisual media, but also the cultural section in many newspapers, extended their critical efforts to popular literature in the course of the 1970s and developed more public-oriented modes of mediation in the presentation of "representative culture"—but without an accompanying change in the basic structure of literary communication.

In contrast to Glotz's reform attempts, the critics of the New Left did not strive for a reform of existing practices but questioned the legitimacy of the institution of criticism as such. On the one hand, their radical doubts about the possibility of finding a viable alternative to the compromised bourgeois literary review procedures were based on their view of the culture industry, whose power the critics could no longer neglect. On the other hand, they were based on the New Left's social theory—strongly indebted to Herbert Marcuse—which no longer permitted a look at the subject of social change and abetted an illusory self-enthronement of the critical mind to become the revolutionary subject of the present. The thesis of the death of criticism, proclaimed in 1968 in *Kursbuch 15* by Walter Böhlich, Karl Markus Michel, Yaak Karsunke, and Hans Magnus Enzensberger, signaled the New Left's renunciation of the theory of art it had championed as the most progressive form of contemporary cultural criticism during the first part of the 1960s: the aesthetic theories of Theodor W. Adorno, which had been developed to counter the "operative" concepts of literature of the Marxist left in the 1920s and 1930s. Adorno firmly stood by the autonomy of the aesthetic experience and defended an emphatic concept of art—modeled after the ideas of postsymbolist modernism—which was interpreted as a negation of the advanced social alienation in the period of "waning capitalism." To insist on the autonomy of the work of art means to decline to serve the existing evil: the opposition to reality of works of art grew from their autonomous condition, from their dissociation from social practice. It was this detachment of the arts from practical life, their abstract negation of reality, that by the end of the 1960s was interpreted as the key element of Adorno's theory of art, the element that connected his theories to the bourgeois art ideologies of the past and put them into a historical context that made them look outdated. In a time of growing political engagement of the literary mind, of spreading extraparliamentary protest movements against the Emergency Powers Acts and the genocidal U.S. military campaigns in southeast Asia, the theoretical positions of the "Critical Theory" and Adorno's theoretical ideas lost more and more influence to the competing materialistic notions in art and social criticism.

The New Left combined a partial renunciation of Adorno with an exaggerated activism that generally questioned the social function of literature: "An essential social function for literary works of art in our present situation can no longer be maintained," Enzensberger felt justified to proclaim in 1968.[62] The congruence of formal innovation and social progressiveness, of artistic autonomy and emancipatory potential, was denounced as illusory; the suspicion of ideological bias, from which art had been exempted by Adorno's aesthetic theory, now fell on art as well, since it had no demonstrable practical consequences and, indeed, could be said to function as immunized contradiction, as a liberal alibi for the existing social order. The overtaxing of literature, the disappointment with the impossibility of cracking social practices by genuinely literary means, turned into that undialectical thesis of the death of literature that necessarily included the demise of criticism:

> Criticism is dead. What criticism? The bourgeois criticism, the ruling criticism. . . . Bourgeois criticism is no longer effective beyond the first day. It causes its own oblivion. . . . It still believes that the mind is the highest authority . . . that intellect is power; it has gratefully accepted its own debilitation. It has allowed itself to be banned to the last pages of the weeklies, of the journals. It accepts that the politics made on the front pages even in its own view contradicts the critics of the last pages. Critics, however, still believe that they can exert influence. Criticism has resigned itself to being the liberal tinsel of an authority that has long ceased to be liberal. It submits to daily humiliation because it is permitted to express its opinions daily. Its bourgeois opinion. Would it be allowed to express its civil opinion? Are we not allowed to have a form of criticism that will throw the threadbare notion of the work of art overboard and will finally accept that the social function of literature is paramount and will therefore recognize the function of art as incidental?[63]

Böhlich's *Autodafé* addresses several issues on which the radical questioning of literary criticism is concentrated: the concept of the work of art as a museum piece, to which many academic and journalistic critics still adhere and which obscures the social function of literature and its socially pragmatic uses in the context in which it appears; the ideology of a classless, nonutilitarian art that denies its roots in the bourgeois class ideology; and, not least, the liberal fairytales that bourgeois criticism spreads about itself, the ambivalence of that freedom which was relegated to the playground of the cultural pages and could serve as the fig leaf for illiberal critical practices. The attack of the New Left is directed less at the thematic than at the institutional side of literary criticism. Its ideological critique is designed to unveil the protective function of the "acceptable spheres of contradiction," where critical thinking could have the illusion of freedom as long as it did not ask for any practical consequences. But where it begins to become pragmatic, the same thinking that had been rewarded with literary prizes inside these "spheres of toleration" is soon punished by prohibitions and bans, and the liberal facade turns out to be a part of that ideology used by the social system to disguise its real character.

The New Left's critique of the institution of literary criticism is indeed highly contradictory, particularly where it takes concrete form. This is made apparent in its ambivalent appraisal of the role and function of the literary critic: on the one hand he is described as an appendage of the system, a meagerly remunerated "stimulator of sales"; on the other hand he is presented—in the persona of the much-maligned "megacritic"—as a "manipulator" of public opinion, since he has access to the opinion-forming media. The ambivalence of this image is related to the inner contradictions of the New Left's critique of ideology (influenced by Herbert Marcuse), which abruptly juxtaposes materialist and left-Hegelian theoretic elements. The materialist analyses cannot overlook the economic aspect of the activity of the literary critic: "Since critics need their salaries to make a decent living, they are forced to become quill drivers—superficial reading is followed by superficial criticism. The system keeps its employees from producing more thorough analyses to which, ultimately, it might be subjected itself."[64] Karsunke's approach directs attention to the working conditions of criticism in the press and does not overlook the condition of the end product: that is, the literary review. The reference to the economic base of criticism, which describes the average critic as a journalist wage-earner, undercuts the illusory self-image that critics have presented to the public and makes the status of criticism in the literary marketplace a relative one: its institutional working conditions but also its close ties to the seasonal rush periods of the book business identify it as an "appendix of the book market."[65]

Had they followed this materialist analytical approach to its logical conclusion, Karsunke and the New Left would hardly have sought refuge in the thesis of the death of criticism but might have come to the recognition that a fundamental change of the working conditions of literary criticism is an unalterable precondition for a criticism that can effect social change, as postulated by the New Left. The conclusions that Brecht in his radio theory and Benjamin in his later works summed up in the concept of "re-direction" were still far from the New Left's thoughts in the late 1960s; like Karsunke, it considered the culture industry a tool for the ideological securing of bourgeois class rule, as well as for a highly developed organizational structure of late-capitalist manipulation of the public mind—an appraisal that logically attributed the position of greater importance to the manipulators. This is the reason the New Left's strict rejection of the agents of literary criticism—discredited as they were by their collusion with the machine of the culture industry—could be combined with an involuntary overestimation of their real social power. Although the New Left saw through the illusory self-image of liberal criticism and recognized the critic's relative loss of social status due to his growing economic dependence on the new organizational structures of the culture industry, the most prominent critics were included in the "establishment," that illustrious group which harbored all system-supporting forces—from Rockefeller to firefighters. This revaluation of the opposition in the hostile area of the critical "establishment" is to a certain degree logical, since it turned out to be a useful tool for an indirect revaluation of the New Left's own position and could be used to justify a leadership role in the political controversies of the day, a role that the literary intellectuals claimed for themselves. At the same time, this monolithic image of the enemy absolved the New Left from going to the trouble of dealing seriously with the contradictory reality of contemporary literary criticism, which was not at all as unanimous as Böhlich implies in subscribing to a concept of art that had turned its back on politics and society.

The anticriticism of the New Left continued to concentrate on the object of criticism but showed a lack of interest in a more thorough analysis of the conditions of media communication and in a strategy for changing them. The gravest deficiency of its fundamental critique, however, was the fact that it conducted its discussions about criticism in the late 1960s as if behind closed doors and thus undermined its own claims. Research into the nature and composition of the reading public was left to the disparaged culture industry, which considered reading—as shown in a study commissioned by the Bertelsmann publishing house—a form of leisure activity and was interested less in the manipulation of public consciousness than in the lucrative profit from the limited cultural maturity of the broad reading public. The rhetoric of anticriticism alone—indebted to that of the Frankfurt School—guaranteed that this critique of criticism found its way into the cultural press, since it competed with its opposition for essentially the same reading public. That the New Left's anticriticism—as well as criticism like that of Peter Glotz, which was informed by a "democratization of culture"—had some impact on future critics can be documented by the theoretical debates and partially by the practical work of the critics of the 1970s. The theoretical discussion of the function and conditions of critical communication in the media focused attention—thus following Glotz—on the reader-orientation of criticism and designed models for dealing effectively with the opportunities for communication in today's mass media.[66]

Criticism in the press and in the universities in the 1970s is characterized by the overcoming of the concept of art as a museum piece, which the anticriticism of the New Left had polemically attacked. However, this revision of the traditional concept of literature is not only rejected by the conservative guardians of Virtue, Truth, and Beauty but also by the Marxist critics. Although the New Left's predictions of the demise of the "megacritic" and the bankruptcy of criticism have proved premature and partially untenable; although the traditional animosity between academic and journalistic criticism undoubtedly diminished in the 1970s and has given way to various attempts at a productive dialogue, the problems of criticism as an institution, accumulated over the years, cannot yet be considered solved. The disintegration of the reading public and the subdivision of the literary sphere of communication have grown worse in the 1980s. The cultural and political secession movements that came into prominence in the 1970s in the wake of the depoliticization of the intelligentsia then developed their separate reading publics and, combined with these, separate forms of criticism that predominantly employ "in-group" rhetoric and thus intensify the lack of communication between the various groups. But even criticism that has access to the media and reaches a broader, more varied reading public remains subject to the laws of the "insider discussion" because of the need of the media critic to establish a distinct individual profile: "In the literary papers and journals the exclusion of the public is publicly demonstrated: the small circle of connoisseurs is all by itself. Here we can see the repressive spectator status of competent criticism; there we witness the literary public that had once been declared to be of age reduced to a mass of slavish consumers of culture."[67]

It is true that the concept of culture has been updated and modernized, as even a cursory look into the cultural pages of *Die Zeit*, the *Frankfurter Allegemeine Zeitung (FAZ)*, or the *Frankfurter Rundschau* reveals: not only Thomas Bernhard and Peter Handke but also Heinz G. Konsalik, Johannes Mario Simmel, and the Anglo-American best sellers are now exposed to the probing of the critics. More exacting films (mainly from the studios of the domestic *auteur* filmmakers and from abroad) and television productions for more demanding viewers can be certain of being reviewed on the cultural pages. There is also no shortage of clever background studies into developments in media politics, and there are many attempts to show individual phenomena in their larger sociocultural context. The death of Keith Moon, the drummer of the legendary British rock group "The Who," leaves traces even in the cultural section of the *FAZ* in the form of a well-informed eulogy that makes insightful comments about the musical impact of the group. More examples could easily be cited, but here they are of interest only as an indication of the changing concept of culture and literature that became obvious in the 1970s and appears in the cultural pages of the newspapers. These changes might be summed up in the thesis that an elite few are today better informed about literature and the culture of the masses, both quantitatively and qualitatively; "bet-

ter" also in the sense that criticism is no longer limited to the confirmation of ingrained prejudices about a supposedly preestablished cultural value system.

When Reich-Ranicki, seemingly renouncing the traditional self-concept of the committed literary critics, pleaded in 1962 for a good (that
is, witty, entertaining, critical) German popular prose[68] and also wrote
critical reviews of contemporary popular novels such as those of Hans
Habe, he did so in the certain knowledge that there were objectively
established literary strata, extending from "popular trash" to "high
art." The middle stratum of this system should, according to his concept, be filled with "high-level popular literature." However, his call
for such literature (for instance, in the tradition of Bernhard Keller-
mann), as well as his critical practices in dealing with it, really only
confirmed the established value scheme, which was considered practicable. This is why Reich-Ranicki, in reviewing what he considers
popular literature, suspends the critical standard he considers fundamental in appraising Gunther Grass, Martin Walser, and others—a
procedure that makes its judgments by classification without even
stopping to demonstrate why Habe, Simmel, and Willi Heinrich belong in the category of popular literature while Grass and Walser
should be ranked with the "great artists"; a procedure that is satisfied
to modify its critical tools according to the different strata of the literary
system. It is not by virtue of his critical value judgments that Reich-
Ranicki differs from those of his colleagues whose elitist sense of
mission excludes any dealings with popular literature. He shares their
prejudices but not their conclusions; he justifies the existence of different kinds of literature by pointing out their differing functions. Far
be it from him to agree to the thesis that the two poles of the literary
system are mutually contingent, that the various kinds of literature
have a common socioeconomic base veiled by the dichotomous value
systems. Still, a "great literature" without a "substructure" appears
problematical to him: "Nothing is more dangerous than a no-man's-
land between trash and great art. And just that phenomenon is noticeable in frightening measure in German literature. From time imme-
morial the German author has been inclined either to strive for an
earthshaking philosophy or to locate his book a priori on a level that is
really outside literature."[69] But where might that "outside" be if not

outside a preestablished notion of literature to which the critic sub-scribes?

Reich-Ranicki's plea for "high-quality popular literature" ultimately confirms the traditional definition of literature. This makes his critical work different from other tendencies that also appeared on the cultural pages in the 1970s and began to compete with the traditional self-concept of the newspaper critics. For example, when Peter W. Jansen presents the musical film *The Kids, They Are All Right* in the cultural program of the ZDF (the Second Channel of German television), when he praises the unspent energy of the rock group "The Who" and emphasizes its inherent utopia of rebellion against petrified social conditions, his positive evaluation of the film may be disputed: one could point out to him its aesthetic conventionality, the problem of filmed music, and much more. It is decisive, however, that Jansen, against the undisguised skepticism of the moderator of the program, presents a music film outside the operatic genre as a document of contemporary popular culture and does not try to defend it against the predictable objections of cinema scholars and the members of the aesthetic "in-clique." He considers the film the product of a contemporary commercial culture industry and an object of entertainment; as such, he takes it just as seriously as the *aspekte* editorial office takes its young prizewinners, whose literary products hardly have a more authentic claim to recognition than the symbolic rebellion that Jansen finds in the music of the film. Like his fellow cultural critics in the *Frankfurter Rundschau* (Henryk M. Broder, Michael Rieth, Wolfram Schütte), Jansen does not suspend his critical standards when dealing with popular culture in his film reviews for the *aspekte* culture program on television, but neither does he lapse into a denunciation of popular culture.

But even a criticism that has as its goal the education of critical consumers of culture is not suitable, in the form of individual contributions, to question substantially the traditional concept of culture; this is demonstrated by the structure of the cultural programs on television.[70] "Viewer-oriented" criticism—Jansen's film reviews, but also notices of exhibits and tour announcements, which are usually supplemented by an appetizer in the form of film clips or a personal appearance by the artist—takes place in the information segment of the program, whose basic function demands a consumer-oriented communication technique. In contrast, the rest of the cultural program sections (the worst are without question the "Imperial court reports" from numerous domestic and international festivals, but also the worship of individuals: the cult around star conductor Herbert von Karajan and the like) retain a largely uncritical way of dealing with representative culture. It critically illuminates details but really suggests to the public that the Suhrkamp publishing house is synonymous with progressive contemporary literature (even if it is by novelist Karin Struck), that Salzburg is synonymous with musical events of the century, and that the public which has access to these events is indeed the cultural elite of the present time. This intimidation by "classicism" is often accompanied by an intimidation by "progressivity," which applauds with equal euphoria, as a sensational step in the direction of "culture for everybody," such alternative cultural spectacles as the "World Theater" in Cologne. The critical claim of this cultural journalism obsessed with making headlines is brought into disrepute by its imitation of the star cult of the tabloids on the level of elitist culture; it does not dare to make any social demands on literature and presents the crisis of the culture under review as a harmless, authentic reflection of a world in crisis.

There can be no doubt that the ideological critique of popular culture, advocated by the Frankfurt School, is no less important today than before. But since it is carried out on the cultural pages of the newspapers, surrounded by critical reviews that do not investigate elitist culture with the same ideological perspicacity, it often turns into its opposite and degenerates into a tool of affirmation. In relation to the contemporary theater this means that the plays of Botho Strauss and Thomas Bernhard deserve the same critical inspection with regard to the function they assume as the productions of the Ohnsorg Theater in Hamburg (which produces folk plays), although they have been tailored for a different audience. The standards for dealing with the "folk theater" tradition of Ohnsorg and the actor Millowitsch's company in Cologne have been established by Melchior Schedler in his television feature "Are the Folk Really That Folksy?" The study investigates the stereotypes and the impact of the "Theater of Stultification" from the perspective of the audience it addresses and militates against the reactionary "folksy by decree from above" by letting members of the audience speak up and giving them the opportunity of seeing the logic that informs all this rumpus, appearances to the contrary. It makes use of the potentialities of the medium to make self-confident recipients out of victims of cultural incapacitation, who will recognize the reactionary fluff that is produced for them as the expression of the daily disregard and degradation to which they are subjected.[71] The established critics of the newspapers and the media rarely set such standards for dealing equally critically with the culture of the "happy few"—positive exceptions are the reviews of Wolfram Schütte and Wilfried F. Schöller.

The situation of literary criticism in the Federal Republic of Germany in the 1980s is certainly more controversial than at the end of the 1960s, when the New Left questioned its legitimacy. The "megacritic" that the New Left attacked has not disappeared from German cultural life, however, but has become more influential in a highly limited literary public—because of the expansion of the media and the subsequent increase in status of individual critics. Although the institutional independence of critical judgment is still by and large guaranteed, clever analysts can discover the following phenomenon in the cultural pages of an "opinion-forming supraregional" daily newspaper: in Munich the cultural editor of newspaper Z moderates a panel discussion on problems of contemporary literature, about which journalist B subsequently writes a report in newspaper Z. The chief of the literature section of Z publishes a book about theme N, some chapters of which are previewed in Z. Z-employee C reviews the book and has particular praise for the contribution of the chief of literature of Z. On the Third Channel, Z-employee F is on a discussion panel. Z-editor K writes about it in Z. In cultural journal Q the chief of literature of Z reviews the latest book of author M, which has just been chosen book-of-the-month by a panel of critics of radio station S; the chief of literature of Z was a member of that panel. This example is not designed to suggest that all cultural reporting in the papers is manipulated, but it serves to illustrate the ways in which, on the most elementary level, media presence can be manufactured and critical opinions can be multiplied. Still, it would be an inadmissible simplification to start from the assumption that the selection and appraisal of books by the critics also decides the fate of the literature under review on the literary market. Klaus Ramm has used the books of Herbert Achterbusch to refute this assumption with persuasive data.[72]

According to Monika Dimpfl, the actual function of published literary criticism can be summed up in the following statements:

1. "Since the volume of the current book market hardly permits comprehensive announcement and simultaneous critical appraisal of all new publications, the selection of the review material becomes the primary function of literary criticism."[73] The content of criticism is secondary to its selective function. We must see the phenomenon of the "sales stimulation through negative criticism" in this context. At the same time, this does not imply that the primary function of criticism has immediate effect on the market—the material under critical review, positive or negative, does not gain acceptance with the public simply because it has been reviewed—but it does allow the function of criticism to take effect only in collaboration with other conditions of literary reception.

2. "Readers of critical reviews belong on one side to a socially limited and relatively small group of recipients who are interested in literary life; on the other side they come from that circle of experts who have mainly a commercial interest in the literature 'business' (authors, book dealers, librarians, editors, and other critics) and for whom literary criticism is a means of 'in-house' business communication."[74] On this functional level of literary criticism can be located part of that institutional power which is attributed to critics with reference to their gaining reader and publisher acceptance for new authors and literary trends. Here we have to differentiate as well: even the most defamatory review by the renowned critic X has only very limited influence on the sales of a book whose author has already gained a following among the readers; sophisticated expert readers can form their own judgment without previous direction by the critics. For the elite reading public, book reviews are more subject matter for conversation and discussion than they are "direction" in the narrow sense. The relationship of this elite group to literary criticism does not suffer the lack of direction that would make it receptive to a rhetoric of intimidation. As a rule, such readers have their own standards for dealing with literature, although these standards are open to correction from the judgment of literary critics. This elite also includes those literary intellec-

tuals who help form the trends of contemporary culture in their positions as media professionals or who have selective functions in editorial offices and publishing houses. For professional reasons, they cannot afford to ignore the verdicts of literary criticism, even when they consider them without basis; they must include those verdicts in their calculations as one directional element in a whole bundle of factors that permit them to make inferences about the cultural force field. However, the audience with literary interest which seeks direction from newspaper and journal critics is not identical with this functional elite but, as an educated minority, far exceeds it. The critics of the press are valuable in gaining acceptance for new literary trends or even in presenting the traditional in the guise of innovation, even when they cannot achieve this acceptance all by themselves and remain dependent on extraliterary factors of cultural life in their role as "trend setters."

3. "Literary criticism that does *not* see itself as a broadly effective instrument of popularization, and that absorbs and articulates the thematic trends and tendencies of literary production, becomes—where there is no longer (or not yet) a 'literary public' in the traditional sense—a part of the 'internal' communication between the agencies of production and distribution."[75] It is difficult for criticism to see itself as a "broadly effective instrument of popularization," given the condition of the field of literary communication and the antagonism stemming from the social structure. Where it is "broadly effective"—as in the announcements of the book club magazines—it immediately turns into advertising and rejects its critical stature. The broad effectiveness that criticism can claim depends less on its self-definition or—as Glotz argues—on its rhetoric than on the priorities of the society in which it is articulated. Where the slogan "Bombs instead of Education" determines daily social life, a literary criticism that wants to be broadly effective without doing away with that which blocks its mass effectiveness is fighting a lost cause. The intentional renunciation of mass effectiveness by the cultural section of the *FAZ* is therefore logical and in affinity with the role of the newspaper.

4. "We have to investigate the influence and the effects of literary criticism from the perspective of 'meta-communciation': during the discussion of literature, short-term literary norms and judgments are formed that can give direction to the participants in the process of

literary communication."[76] These norms and judgments of short-term validity produced by criticism must, however, be seen less as a symptom of its failure than as an assimilation of its functions to those laws guaranteeing the ability of the literary production apparatus to function and assuring that the culture industry can work at full capacity.

5. "Generally, we will have to start from the assumption that the influence of metacommunicative functions in the area of distribution and production increases where the recipients have less immediate access to literary production and literary works and, conversely, the authors to their readers; it is in proportion, therefore, to the incisiveness of certain barriers to communication within the literary field of communication. Mass communication as institutionalized in literary criticism becomes the reference point of literary communication when clear-cut and lasting social conditions and relations begin to dissolve in the matrices of primary communication. The relationship between real literary communication and the derivative metacommunicative functions of the area of the sphere of communication will be reversed: the establishment of the process of literary communication between author, text, and reader becomes dependent on metacommunicative processes of mediation, which thus become preconditions of literary mass communication."[77] The growing dependence of literary communication on metacommunicative processes makes a revitalization of literary life appear unlikely; instead, we can expect a further decline in the collective social estimation of that kind of literature which depends on critical intervention.

Literary Criticism in the German Democratic Republic

"Re-education," even though under different premises, was also the order of the day in the eastern part of Germany—that is, the Russian occupation zone—after the collapse of the Hitler regime. Even in the territory of the German Democratic Republic (D.D.R.), just emerging from the Soviet occupation zone, large segments of the middle class and of all social strata had been compromised by their active or passive involvement with Fascism. The anti-Fascists returning from exile or from the concentration camps were a small minority of the total population. The presence of Soviet occupation troops had decided the power struggle in favor of a social order that did away with private control over the means of production. The fact that Fascism and capitalism had not been removed from the inside—that is, by the people themselves—but had been terminated as a consequence of the postwar global power constellation turned out to be a heavy burden on a new political and cultural beginning under the banner of socialism. This study is particularly interested in the effects of such a situation on the cultural-political reconstruction as far as they were significant to the critical debate.

It was an omen of the way the cultural reconstruction would be conducted in the Soviet occupation zone (S.B.Z.) and later in the D.D.R. that in the period immediately after the war not only were the exiled anti-Fascists received with open arms and the prominent representatives of bourgeois humanism wooed intensely, but even authors like the venerable Gerhart Hauptmann (who had been able to hibernate literarily in Hitler's Germany and had not exposed himself as an anti-Fascist) were now emphatically persuaded to move to the S.B.Z. As early as the summer of 1945 the "Cultural League for a Democratic Renewal in Germany" was formed and elected Johannes R. Becher, later to become Minister of Cultural Affairs of the D.D.R., as its first president. It was the aim of this league to establish a broad cultural popular front which—in the vein of the popular-front strategy of the Brussels conference of the German Communist Party (KPD)—was to unite all anti-Fascist intellectuals and prepare them for their contributions to the construction of a "socialist democratic republic." The popular-front concept of the 1930s, which the KPD used to revise its previously held thesis of "social Fascism," had been devised in a time of expanding Fascism and was meant to help extend the base of the anti-Fascist struggle all the way into the bourgeois camp. In cultural politics the concept corresponded to a notion of humanism that combined the revolutionary traditions of both the middle class and the working class and that leveled out the differences between bourgeois and proletarian humanism. By resorting to this concept, "anti-Fascist humanism" was to become the basis for the cultural reconstruction within the S.B.Z./ D.D.R., with the following goals: "Elimination of the National Socialist ideology and modification of those social conditions that might lead to a reemergence of Fascism. In the attempt to establish a democratic republic in the eastern part of Germany, the bourgeois humanism of the eighteenth century regained an important role: the works of the classics provided models with whose aid post-Fascist Germany could cleanse herself. This model of humanist renewal was not so much directed at a revolutionary Marxist party any longer . . . as at a defeated nation whose social classes had been compromised in various ways."[78]

The appeal to the bourgeois cultural heritage did not merely serve tactical purposes—as the Marxist discussion of this heritage had already proved in exile—but was able to base itself on a genuinely Marxist theory of history that describes the decline of bourgeois culture in the Age of Imperialism as the reflection of a class that had betrayed its revolutionary tradition and abandoned its emancipatory ethos. On the basis of this interpretation of history, the revolutionary working class could claim to be the heir of these revolutionary traditions and of the historical force that translates the basic tenets of a degenerated bourgeois revolution into reality and thus deprives it of its bourgeois features. This "executor thesis" was supported by the tradition of the early social-democratic labor movement as well as by Lenin's "heritage theory," which, however, emphasized the selection of the bourgeois cultural heritage by the party. Lenin had developed this theory—which accentuated the irrefutability of the proletarian class perspective in the inheritance process—in polemical debate with left-radical movements that denied the vital role of "knowledge" and "education" and advocated the sequestration of proletarian literature into a "literature for workers"; he had also developed it in rejection of social-democratic views that had reduced the cultural emancipation of the proletariat to a taking-over of cultural products whose social class content was no longer relevant. In these debates about the cultural heritage, which were of crucial importance for the cultural life in the D.D.R. during the 1950s and 1960s, the aspects emphasized by Lenin were pushed into the background. This may have been related, particularly during the 1950s, with the fact that the literary intellectuals who were the carriers of the academic and critical debates of the period did not generally have the necessary Marxist tools for an analysis of literature but often adhered to approaches that could not meet the demands of a materialist analysis of cultural phenomena; they compensated for these shortcomings by methodically unsupported quotations from the Marxist classics.

In addition, Lenin had arrived at his heritage theory in historical circumstances quite different from the social conditions that were to lead to a cultural reconstruction in the S.B.Z./D.D.R. In this period of radical change the concept of cultural heritage that first became dominant selected its heritage of the past not from the standpoint of proletarian class logic in a capitalist social system but from the standpoint of a class-transcending alliance that had to prove itself in the social framework of a noncapitalist society. The cultural identity of the developing postcapitalist society was to be nurtured by all progressive traditions of the cultural past. This conception remembered at most subliminally that even in the "heroic phase" of the bourgeoisie the class interest of the middle class had not coincided with the emancipatory claims of the Fourth Estate. The harsh attacks on Hanns Eisler's *Faustus* libretto (culminating in the accusation that the work propagated an "antinational" and "unpatriotic" view of history) and the harsh rejection of Brecht's 1953 *Urfaust* production (which stressed the contradictory nature of Faustus—he is at once hero and black-magician/charlatan—and made it difficult to view him from the traditional perspective of bourgeois interpretive history) make it plain that the concept of literary and cultural heritage had extraliterary and, in the widest sense, political significance. To illustrate the connections between a central character of the cultural heritage and the present German miseries was, in view of the tense internal and international political situation, a cultural-political provocation that had to be answered sharply. At a historic moment, when the integration of the intelligentsia that was needed for the construction of the new state was the focus of the cultural-political efforts of the East German Socialist Party (SED); at a moment when the members of the scientific-technological and cultural elite were encouraged even with material privileges to participate in the social reorganization,[79] an approach to the classical heritage that exposed it to the "plebeian eye" had to appear "sectarian." Speaking to representatives of the intellectual elite in May of 1953, chief-of-state Walter Ulbricht sharply denounced such tendencies: "In my view the position of the intellectuals to great questions of our nation is quite clear. We do not only struggle for the development of science, of technology, etc., but lately also for a whole series of cultural decisions by not allowing one of the most important works of our great German poet Goethe to be formalistically deformed and the great ideas in Goethe's *Faust* turned into a caricature, as has happened in a few instances, even in the D.D.R., for instance in Eisler's so-called Faust and in the production of the *Urfaust*."[80]

Both Brecht—criticized implicitly by the reference to the *Urfaust* production of the Berlin Ensemble—and Eisler categorically rejected the accusation that the intention of their productions was to reject the cultural heritage. Brecht's remarks about the problems of heritage stressed the necessity of investigating the process of cultural inheritance and deriving the conditions for a productive adoption of the cultural heritage for the present from the reality of the social life in which the inheritance process takes place. Therefore, he did not simply postulate that the aesthetic habits and cultural demands of the inheritors could be free from all those elements of bourgeois ideology that blocked the development of the new system, particularly such a short time after the deposing of the old order: "It is a great misfortune in our history that we have to build the new without having achieved the destruction of the old. The Soviet Russians have done the latter for us by defeating Fascism. This is probably why we look at the reconstruction so undialectically. And doing so has in turn the disadvantage that we do not give sufficient expression to the daily battle against the old order. We constantly try to shape the 'harmonious' and 'beauty per se' instead of the struggle for harmony and beauty."[81]

Beyond the respective arguments and themes, the debate about the cultural heritage reflects the forms of communication and the discursive models peculiar to literary criticism in the D.D.R. Institutionalized literary criticism there has a social status different from that in the German Federal Republic. Whereas the institutional operational framework of literature and criticism within bourgeois-capitalist society forms a more or less accepted sphere of contradiction—as long as the processes taking place within that sphere do not have practical consequences and do not suspend the condition of art—art and literature are socially "productive forces" in the view of the socialist system, and artistic and literary creativity is seen as an activity that can and should radiate opinion- and personality-forming effects and impulses for the development of society. The fact that the social mission of literature and art is indisputable has grave consequences for the social role and status of the creator of cultural products. Since no "free" literary market (in the Western sense) exists, one guided by a constant fluctuation in the supply of goods and by the maximization of profits, the function of the creator has different features from those in evidence in a capitalist book market. Whereas the "free author" in the Western mold produces for a theoretically unlimited demand and whereas the fate of his books is decided in a marketplace that not only satisfies demands but constantly creates and produces new ones, art production in the centrally planned socialist economic system not only is "work for hire" in the sense of the role of the artist as described above but, from an economic standpoint, has the characteristics of limited production that often lags behind the articulated demand of the reading public—even though first editions of fictional material are, as a rule, published in substantially larger editions than in the German Federal Republic.[82] "Limited production" is an economic reflection of the conditions of production of a planned economy where contact between literature and readers is made less by way of secondary stimuli (advertising, marketing, and the like) than by reliance on a relatively close relationship between author and reading public. Since all printed material in the D.D.R. is subject to printing permits by the state, and since the system of planned paper allocation requires, in addition, the establishment of priorities and forces pre-selection, literature submits not only to the control of readers and critics but also to that of the state authorities, whose right to censorship can keep the public away from books classified as questionable, reactionary, or antisocialist. It is common knowledge that these labels are often used to discriminate even against books and authors whose critique of the contradictory claims of socialist everyday life and of the discrepancy between socialist claims and social reality is not at all prompted by anti-Communist motives. The expatriation of Wolf Biermann is an example of the incompetent and doctrinaire treatment of authors and intellectuals who refuse to give in to the pressures of the official literary policies.

Since the state has a de facto monopoly in the area of information and formation of opinion, the debate about public problems, where they are not completely withdrawn from public discussion, is also conducted differently from that held in a capitalist society where diverging class and group interests can be articulated more clearly (even though the discretionary power of the private sector generally guarantees a hegemony of opinion multiplication that benefits the ruling class). The regimentation of the political public in the D.D.R. is mirrored in the language of journalistic forms of presentation where the official semantic regulation is quite important. The political world view creates—as is demonstrated by the editorial and linguistic layout of *Neues Deutschland*—its own nomenclature and thus insulates itself to a certain degree against outsiders. Whoever participates in the public debate has to identify himself by proving his mastery of this nomenclature and is thus recognized as a loyal participant. The literary public is not entirely exempt from the idiosyncrasies of this regimented public mode of reasoning. The discussions about the cultural heritage, about contemporary socialist realism, about a socialist view of man or the fully developed socialist personality and its reflection in literature all revolve around norms and formulas of cultural politics whose content can be modified by history, since they have not been established ahistorically and can be completed in differing ways in the course of history. It may suffice here to point to the changing appraisal of Romanticism in the first half of the 1970s to illustrate changes in the evaluation of the cultural heritage. The changing attitude toward the historical avant-garde movements of the first half of the century, beginning during the late 1970s, is an indication of the possibility of significant shifts in literary evaluation, even in a rigid theoretical framework, without the abandonment of substantial aesthetic norms. To the cultural critics in the D.D.R., the 1950s rock-and-roll music, for instance, was simply an expression of cultural barbarism that appeared to fit neatly into the stultifying cultural tendencies of U.S. mass culture. Two decades later, D.D.R. criticism—without surrendering its socialist partisanship—arrived at a vastly differing estimation of rock music: it was now, not in toto but in many of its forms, positively contrasted with other phenomena of Western mass culture that were seen as intensifying and commercially exploiting the stupidity of the public. The geographical position of the D.D.R., the possibility of importing Western mass culture and ideology through radio and television, made the analysis of such culture a necessity. This analysis often remained caught up in a mechanistic theory of manipulation that failed to give an adequate explanation of the unquestionable mass impact of certain forms of imperialist mass culture.

The first and foremost goal of literary criticism in the D.D.R., however, is not the discussion of cultural and literary trends in the German

Federal Republic—though these have always been followed with great interest—but the discharging of the duties it has to perform within East German society. Criticism is defined as "one of the essential driving forces of total social development."[83] According to the *Philosophisches Wörterbuch* (Philosophical dictionary) of the D.D.R.: "The nature of criticism and self-criticism as a method for changing existing conditions in the interest of total social progress cannot be reduced to the changing of the views of individuals or whole collectives but includes the changing of practical forms of behavior and of historically outmoded conditions. . . . In this sense criticism is the creative, positive participation in the shaping of socialism which seeks and promotes innovation. A creative, critical approach to the problems related to the shaping of socialism is incompatible with the stance of a detached or skeptical observer."[84] This general definition of criticism in a socialist society requires a commitment to the goals set by that society. Only the acceptance of these goals creates the conditional possibility of criticism, which is always understood as criticism in support of the continued development of the existing order. That reality does not always correspond to this definition, that not all "creative, positive participation in the shaping of socialism which seeks and promotes innovation" has been seen and praised in this sense as a positive driving force of total social progress, is proved by the already mentioned attacks on Brecht and Eisler, whose creative activity did complete justice to the definition quoted above. The operational definition of criticism as a constructive attitude that excludes skeptical detachment from and rejection of the existing social order is based on the premise that in actuality, not only has socialism conquered all antagonistic contradictions typical of capitalist societies, but all conceivable and existing contradictions are no longer antagonistic and can be solved in the context of the existing social order. Consequently, criticism has duties that differ from those in social systems characterized by a fundamental antagonism between capital and labor.

This definition and demarcation of criticism—which is problematic (not only from a Western perspective) and whose right to exist in a society convinced of the practicability of its tasks still has to be determined—is constitutive for the form and the functional framework of the literary and political public in the D.D.R. The *Kleine Politische*

Wörterbuch (Short political dictionary) describes the role of literature in East Germany as follows: "Literature published in the D.D.R. is humanist. It serves the ideas of peace and friendship among all people. Books help the workers achieve a high level of education; they impart moral and ethical values for character development. They are used for the dissemination of the progressive knowledge of mankind and to penetrate the emotional and intellectual world of our time and of the past. They are mediators of education, knowledge, and patriotic consciousness, of aesthetic adventures, entertainment, and relaxation. Socialist society thus encourages creative public debates about literature and generates the enjoyment of reading and good books."[85] Since, according to the self-concept of socialist society, literature is no longer the privilege of the educated elite but has become the concern of society as a whole, literary criticism in its role as mediator has to assume important functions within "literary society": it should contribute to the solution of literary problems in the shaping of the present—that is, it should not only describe and appraise literature and give it a secure position in the public consciousness but also exert a positive influence on the development of literature. Its public mission also includes the encouragement of broad public participation in literary life, the improvement of the receptive capabilities of the public for an intensive exchange of ideas between production and reception, and the elimination of the cultural barriers typical of capitalist society. Like the literary creators, the literary critics should also feel bound by the principle of socialist partisanship and become educators in the service of this principle. It is true that the resolution of the politbureau of the Central Committee (ZK) of the SED "concerning the improvement of literary criticism, bibliography, and the advancement of progressive books" (1953) demanded that "reader reactions to individual books" should be published in greater numbers. But on the basis of socialist society organized according to the principle of a division of labor, literary criticism too was classified as an activity for specialists which had a lasting foundation in society. That a truly mass-effective criticism—one that educates its public to become mature and critical experts, and helps to establish literature as an organic ingredient of social everyday life—might eventually render itself superfluous was not envisioned, in view of the manifold cultural-political "troubles with leveling," as the objective of cultural development; such an outcome would probably appear as a spontaneous aberration from the perspective of the cultural-political rulers and leaders.

The ZK resolution of 1953 must rather be seen as a reaction to a cultural-political situation in a period when the new critical directions were only beginning to take form and when a broad-based criticism interested in socialist social reform did not yet exist. This is one reason the resolution mentions the obvious abstinence of academic criticism with regard to contemporary literature. The high priority that the SED gave to the cultivation of the cultural heritage should not obscure the fact that the emerging literature of socialist reconstruction took its bearings no longer from the aesthetic models of Weimar Classicism but from the traditions of socialist realism, and that the Marxist appropriation of the cultural heritage could not replace or make redundant the formation of new, independent literary traditions. The alliance policies of the SED and its attempts to win over wide sections of the intelligentsia for socialist social improvement had to counteract the possibility that the scientific-technological and literary intellectuals might totally isolate themselves from the developing socialist system in highly specialized functional spheres. Thus, the resolution particularly stresses the immediately relevant and necessary requirements in the area of literary criticism: "The Secretary of State for Higher Education is ordered to take the appropriate measures for the education of literary critics in the universities. The trend to shy away from dealing with contemporary literature, which can be observed in many scholars of German literature, must be combatted energetically. We must take care that literary doctoral theses do not deal with irrelevant topics but contribute to the solution of topical, burning problems of our literature."[86] Next to organizational measures designed to create qualified critics and to give criticism broader social effectiveness, the resolution focuses on the topical function of critical activity: "We have to direct our special attention to the task of raising the ideological and literary level of these reviews, to support all progressive elements of literature, and to combat mercilessly the enemy ideology in whatever disguises it may appear."[87] The reference to the effectiveness of the ideology of the enemy must ultimately be seen against the background of national borders that were still open and that exacerbated the confrontation of the two contrasting social systems on German soil while impeding the economic development of the D.D.R.

East German criticism in the 1950s was characterized by the search for standards appropriate for the newly emerging literature. To this end the authors returning from exile—as evidenced by Brecht's *Katzgraben-Notate* or the critical work of Johannes R. Becher, Anna Seghers, and F. C. Weiskopf—again became the leaders in the development of sound critical standards for academic criticism, which only in the 1960s established the basic tenets of a contemporary socialist culture. If one disregards outstanding critics like Paul Rilla and the influential—but unproductive for a detailed poetics—critical essays of Alfred Kurella and Alexander Abusch, it can be shown that the fundamental critical impulses for the literary debate of the 1950s were predominantly introduced by the authors themselves. This held true for the discussion about a dramatic theory appropriate to a socialist society, which juxtaposed Brecht's model of the epic theater and Friedrich Wolf's theory of empathy. This debate about "formal problems of the theater caused by new themes" also became an explosive cultural-political question because it implicitly called into question the fitness of certain traditional aesthetic conventions of socialist realism: for example, the positive hero as a medium for the creation of a socialist consciousness. Both models had the same goal: to make the audience socially active in the advancement of socialist society. The pragmatic nature of the debate ensured that it was free from that unproductive dogmatism which characterized the discussion about the cultural heritage. F. C. Weiskopf's description of the condition of D.D.R. criticism in 1953 documents the fact that the authors themselves introduced literary-aesthetic standards into the critical debate: "Examine the book reviews published last year in our important journals and calculate the percentage of those reviews that deal, even superficially, with the language of the work; I could not find more than one in twelve. And is it not revealing that the editors of *Neue Deutsche Literatur,* in their otherwise laudable attempt 'to help' a 'young, still inexperienced writer' with his partially completed manuscript by a broad critical response from the readers, list a number of possible themes for discussion but forget to ask one question: 'What about the language of the manuscript; how has the author mastered this element which is of paramount importance for his work and all literary works in general?' "[88] Weiskopf's critical approach introduces a focal dimension of the "heritage theme" which had been accentuated in Lenin's heritage theory but had remained peripheral to the cultural-political debates in the D.D.R.: the recognition that cultural progress has to manifest itself also in the literary material and that socialist literature could be a substantial building block in the construction of a socialist society only to the degree in which it realized its creative potential *qua literature.* Dispensing with all cultural-political slogans and clichés, Weiskopf's criticism is still cultural-political in the wider sense of the term, because it sees the literary shortcomings in socialist society as political shortcomings as well: what could be denounced as dilettantism in a capitalist literary market turns into a social failure according to the self-definition of a socialist literary public. Weiskopf's approach emphasizes the social responsibility of writers and artists by concentrating on genuinely literary standards and by asserting the importance of formal artistic criteria in relation to the thematic content.

Wherever the critical debate of the 1950s becomes specific and not limited to the development of aesthetic postulates and programs, it best fulfills the role it was asked to assume with respect to the advancement of contemporary literature. Even before the workers had been exhorted to objectify their experiences as producers of the material fundamentals of socialist society—in connection with the Bitterfeld Conference of April 24, 1954, and in the context of a broad cultural-political initiative—workers and industrial activists had already articulated their demands on contemporary literature in the so-called *Nachterstedter Brief* (Nachterstedt letter) to the Union of German Writers of the D.D.R.; they complained that there were "too few books by far in which our writers describe the reconstruction in the factories and life in the D.D.R."[89] In a letter published in the trade union paper *Tribüne,* they demanded an authentic presentation of everyday life in the developing socialist society: "Write more novels and reports about this theme; come to our publicly owned factories—there you will find ample inspiration and material for creative work. . . . Write more works about our new people . . . about the innovators in economic production, who deliberately work and fight for the laborers, for the people, for the state of workers and farmers."[90] The central postulates of socialist aesthetics—for instance, the principle of solidarity with the people—first had to prove their pragmatic worth in practical critical and literary life if they did not want to give up their Marxist claim to be the self-dissolution of theory into practice. And literature incapable of giving form to the everyday life of the people and the sphere of material production under the influence of the imposed division of physical and intellectual labor could hardly claim to show "solidarity with the people." The demand for a depiction of a socialist society under construction turned out to be an inescapable challenge for contemporary literature and was very difficult to answer, since it presupposed the overcoming of separate experiential areas, not only on the theoretic level but also on the level of artistic subjectivity.

Hans Marchwitza, an author with a working-class background, in a response to the Nachterstedt letter poignantly described the formal problems many writers faced in coping with this task, problems that could not be solved simply by familiarizing writers with the conditions of the workplace *in loco*. The task of creating authentic portraits of social innovation confronted creative intellectuals with a learning process that reversed the point of departure of the heritage problems. It could not be limited to the task of "guiding" the workers closer to literature; first, they themselves had to be guided closer to their new duties:

> It is commonly thought that workers are so busy with their daily work, with deliberations of production and competition, with their rolling-mills . . .that they cannot be bothered with such difficult problems as literature. They would have to be gently 'led' closer to these strange matters. It seems to me, however, that our writers are no less in need of guidance with their own problems and thus with their real work. . . . This disdain is made obvious by the fact that many writers pretended to be able to write a novel about our new society, after only a cursory and superficial look at a factory. . . . They had observed work at the lathe and in the rolling-mill, but their working-class characters still turned out weak, boring, wooden—sometimes even caricatures. The conflicts were ill conceived or nonexistent; love, the conversation of two lovers, resembled the talks at a production meeting. Sometimes the proletarian heroes were even allowed to dance and to be happy. All of this remained without flesh and blood. . . . The world of work and the world of the mind of the worker is in most cases limited to too small a functional sphere. In reality the world of work is powerful and its sphere unlimited . . . it is so vast and

rich in ideas, adventures, and incidents that all senses must be strained to grasp and comprehend its true greatness.[91]

Marchwitza's observations, like Brecht's critical works, are distinguished by genuine interest in the depiction of a new reality, one that could no longer be grasped adequately with traditional methods.

Even with this recognition the academic critics of the 1950s already lagged behind the critics of the press, mainly because academic criticism was largely dominated by the aesthetic theories of Georg Lukács. That the cultural and literary problems debated by the critics also became a focal point of public political discussion is documented in the proceedings of the Fifth Party Congress of the SED in July 1958, where the demand "to overcome the separation of art and life, and of the artist and the people" was established as an immediate cultural objective and led to the cultural-political initiatives of the "Bitterfeld Way."[92] These initiatives were even more ambitious than Marchwitza's intentions; they were not satisfied to demand of professional art products a greater solidarity with the people but also demanded, as a complement to the works of professional writers, the development of a proletarian lay art that was expected to provide valuable impulses for the full blossoming of contemporary socialist literature. The literary activities associated with the "Bitterfeld Way," which became stagnant after 1963, had only limited impact on the development of literary criticism in the 1960s, especially because the exploration of the traditions of socialist literature stressed by the scholars and the theoretical clarification of the term "socialist realism" provided more differentiated norms for the future and counteracted the narrow concentration on workplace literature and proletarian lay art.

During the Sixth Party Congress of the SED in 1963, and the Second Bitterfeld Conference in 1964, a different emphasis was given to the current problems of cultural development: the emphasis was no longer on proletarian cultural work but on the development of a qualitatively improved entertainment literature, particularly since the cultural demands of the broad reading public were not substantially different from those that determined the cultural consumption of the "best seller country" across the border. The scholar-critics, however, began to investigate the phenomena of popular literature only toward the end of the 1960s. It was only through the study of aesthetic-cultural needs, conducted with growing intensity after 1968, and through the analytical studies of literary reception of the 1970s that popular literature received increasing attention; these studies also corrected misleading fantasies stimulated by the thesis that the receptive standards at all social levels had already been largely equalized under the conditions of socialism.

Literary criticism in the 1970s was generally distinguished not only by a more differentiated approach to contemporary literature and a sounder theoretical approach to the tradition of socialist realism but also—in comparison with the 1950s—by an astonishing heterogeneity of critical positions that leave their mark in the appraisal of the emerging contemporary literature. The construction of the Berlin Wall, the visible demarcation line in the West, stimulated new discussions within the D.D.R.—particularly in the sphere of literature and culture; the mood of the discussion was more relaxed and allowed for a greater visibility of differing positions than the tense atmosphere of the 1950s had permitted. This is shown by the lively critical debate centering on Christa Wolf's novel *Der geteilte Himmel* (Heaven divided). In the course of this debate, critical stances of the 1950s (partially derived from an unrefined definition of socialist realism) appeared outmoded in the critical altercation with a differentiated formal-aesthetic approach to the novel (as represented, for instance, by Dieter Schlenstedt),[94] because they contributed nothing new to the adequate reception of the novel and to a present-oriented understanding of literature. The literature of socialist reconstruction had not at all suppressed the many contradictions of socialist everyday life but had interpreted them as retarding elements of social growth that would nevertheless be unable to stop the triumph of the new, that could at most delay the positive solution of the conflicts. Christa Wolf's novel helped to gain acceptance for a kind of realistic literature that seeks out the contradictions of social development at the subjective experiential level of the individual and describes the suffering caused by the discrepancy between social ideal and reality; it also showed the hero/heroine as destroyed by these contradictions and refused in principle to accept a mere superficial reconciliation of ideal and reality. Those critics who approached the novel with the theoretical attitude of the 1950s felt offended mainly by the individualizing tendencies in the world view of the novel; they missed the optimism based on the experience of changing social conditions and on the certainty that the future belongs not only to socialism but also to the people who translate it into reality. Their critical method, however, remained caught up in a formalism that judged the text by predetermined norms of form and content and no longer saw those prescriptive norms in their historical context; thus it overlooked the practical function of literature in the process of history.

The repudiation of positions that had little value for the development of literary life in the 1960s did not proceed without objections; rather, it was accompanied by cultural-political doubts and by the fear that the ideology of imperialism might spread in the guise of literature not yet concentrated on the unsolved problems of socialist everyday life. This is documented by Alfred Kurella's critical reaction to the revaluation of Franz Kafka by Western marxists that was articulated during the 1963 Kafka Conference in Prague. Kurella's reaction was provoked mainly by the fact that such ideological diversity was allowed to grow within a friendly party, the French Communist Party, thus apparently signaling the rehabilitation of "decadence" with Marxist features; Kurella made this process into an ideological test of loyalty of the highest importance. Without any doubt the argumentation of the French Marxist Roger Garaudy had gone beyond a threshold of tolerance and had questioned the basic ideological assumptions of D.D.R. criticism, because Garaudy had included Kafka in the acceptable cultural heritage on the basis of precisely the same elements in his work that discredited the author in the eyes of the D.D.R. critics: "To claim that he is of current interest and to maintain that he has valuable ideas to communicate to us means to become aware of the fact that the battle against alienation does not end with the assumption of power but takes on a new shape and real significance from that point on. This awareness revives, within the revolutionary movement, Kafka's concept of the negative as well as the wish to grant a place to subjectivity and not to deprive man of any of his dimensions."[95] Kurella's sharp critique was not provoked only by the thesis that capitalist alienation is not eliminated by the socialist conditions of production but is continued at a higher level of quality, and by the certainly questionable hope that the revolutionary movements of the present need Kafka's world view to recognize their own nature; it relied also on the historical experience that the global hegemony of the social order whose forms Kafka describes in his literary works were destroyed by a force of logic different from the one Kafka could appeal to. Kurella's tirade aimed beyond Garaudy's argumentation to its functional role, or maybe to the role Kurella imputed to these arguments: that is, the undermining and depletion of the Marxist concept of realism and the ideological convergence of two contrasting social systems. "The main issue in this debate about Kafka is the question whether or not the peaceful coexistence of states with diverging social regimes should be 'supplemented' by various playforms of ideological coexistence, in this case by the coexistence of Marxism and existentialism . . . or even more precisely: an 'extension' or 'redefinition' of Marxism by a variation of existentialism."[96]

Kurella's cultural-political demarcations illustrate that the internal changes in critical positions did not weaken the delineation from the outside but rather contributed to their intensification, particularly where the ideological altercation did not center on openly antisocialist positions but—as in the case of the Frankfurt School—focused on critical positions that saw themselves as neo-Marxist and were given this epithet by their conservative opponents with the intent to disparage them; these neo-Marxist theorists could justly claim to have contributed to the undermining of the official anti-Communism in the Federal Republic of Germany more than any of the competing philosophical-intellectual movements and to have had significant impact on the political consciousness of the public.

One sign of the intensification of the ideological demarcation against the West was the growing attention D.D.R. critics paid to West German critical trends that registered the proliferating examples of social criticism in East German literature of the 1960s and precipitously painted a picture based on the juxtaposition of "critical" D.D.R. literature and conformist propaganda literature. Hermann Kähler polemically attacked this trend in his otherwise highly debatable review of Hermann Kant's novel *Die Aula:* "Literary critics, even those for whom there is not, nor ever can be, a good work of socialist realism, have reacted to this phenomenon for a long time. There grew the thesis of the integration of our literature into the true, the one homogeneous, nonconformist contemporary literature. This thesis offers two highly practicable elements: it defuses West German nonconformism by changing a concrete critique of a concrete society into a general literary position; it defuses socialist literature by trying to create a contradiction between that literature and the true socialism in the D.D.R."[97] Apart from the validity of this appraisal, Kähler's review of Kant's novel is a good illustration of the cramped style of East German criticism, which is reinforced by the outside pressure from West German criticism. His interpretation of *Die Aula*, labeling the novel as simply a hymn of praise to the D.D.R., closes its eyes to the artistic possibilities that this novel opens up for socialist realism in the 1960s; it contributes to an a posteriori hardening of the front lines that had been established from across the borders by classifying Annemarie Auer's interpretation (which emphasized the book's innovative formal-aesthetic techniques) and Silvia and Dieter Schlenstedt's review as critical approaches that missed the main point of the book—that is, its "socialist partisanship, its socialist pathos," its "partisanship not only in the sense of taking the ideological side of socialism but in Lenin's sense of being in direct solidarity with and consciously subordinated to the revolutionary ideals of the party of the working class. This novel is the aesthetic expression of the self-confident youth, raised and brought up by the party, who join productively in the construction of the republic."[98] Kähler's critical approach is symptomatic of the rigidity of D.D.R. criticism in the 1960s, which obstructs fruitful approaches to emerging D.D.R. literature because its frame of reference pays too little heed to the determination of literary production by inner laws.

The intended function of literary criticism, to foment literary life and stimulate literary growth, remained largely unfulfilled in the 1970s despite its qualitative improvement. It mainly *reacted* to literary trends. Thus it is hardly surprising that in 1973 the shortcomings of literary criticism became the focal point of a theoretical debate during the Seventh Writers Congress. During the Eighth Party Congress of the SED, in 1971, Kurt Hager had already anticipated some of the key terms that dominated the critical debate of the following years. His cultural-political demands stressed the individuality of creative activity and the irreplaceability of artistic effects on the development of socialist life. Literary activity had to unfold, in full utilization of its artistic potential, on the "inalienable basis of socialist-realist art—firm socialist perspective, partiality, and solidarity with the people." D.D.R. society values "art in its total aesthetic nature and in its specific personality-forming mode of action."[99]

These cultural-political demands had an effect on the internal literary production of the 1970s and found expression in a greater variety of artistic positions. The emphasis of the individuality of artistic creation worked counter not only to the literary but also to the critical formalism that had been made the center of attention by Franz Fühmann during the Seventh Writers Congress in 1973. Fühmann's remarks about the relationship between literature and criticism culminated in the accusation that existing critics largely misunderstand the "nature of the literature" they are supposed to judge. They see themselves as contributors to a form of criticism that does justice to its socialist mission, and they sum up the shortcomings of the prevailing critical method in a critical list of negatives but emphatically stand up for the necessity of criticism as an institution: "Criticism *should be* a public force and only thus, as a social authority, can it ban administrative provisions from literary life and I am in favor of that. . . . In any case, it should achieve one goal: i.e., to make society conscious of *literature*. If criticism loses its grip on one of those key elements, society *or* literature, then it will lose its way in sterile extremes: in arbitrary aesthetic judgments on one hand, on the other hand in a regimentation that the author considers foreign to his nature."[100] Above all, Fühmann misses a feeling for the specific nature of literary cognition in the total critical system and laments the cleft between aesthetic and ideological criteria in applied criticism. From the perspective of the producer of literature, he exposes and resists the false expectations critics have of contemporary literature, "as if the hardships and burdens . . . the tragic features of our present life could be removed by not being mentioned or spirited away by literature."[101] His remarks gain substantial cultural-political significance not only by his insistence that "critical standards for the appraisal of literature . . . can only be derived from literature itself—existing as well as emerging,"[102] but also by his insistence on conducting criticism in public and on clearly separating criticism and administration: "Appeals to extraliterary authorities should cease."[103] Thus Fühmann not only addresses immanent functional deficits of criticism but also focuses on the external problems of not having an institutional separation of the politics of culture and literary criticism. Moreover, his demand that "literature, society, and even the critics should learn to be able to stand criticism—at first maybe as an evil, then as a necessary evil, and later, perchance, not even as an evil at all"[104] reminded the public that—contrary to official announcements—the public application of reasonable criticism and a productive relationship with it were not among the practiced virtues of socialist life. He focused attention on an important social learning process that might be practiced in the field of literary communication.

Even more than in the 1960s, the leveling trends of criticism appeared dangerous from the perspective of the 1970s because they created an illusory unity of contradictions while suspending all contradictions and thus were no longer able to cope with contemporary cultural-political controversies. Therefore, Kurt Blatt remarked with some justification during the Writers Congress of 1973, "such a method is sensible only in the constitutive period of socialism; it soon loses its justification and even becomes fraught with danger as soon as socialist literature is recognized worldwide (even when it is not loved). For in that fashion we limit ourselves to declaring the unity of unity, and we leave it to our opponents to exaggerate the contradictions."[105] The intensive pursuit of socialist literature by the academic critics and a critical approach that gives greater attention to the individual author illustrate the fact that the D.D.R. critics of the 1970s self-critically put the attacks on their own shortcomings to good use. In this sense, criticism ultimately followed in the footsteps of literary production without detriment to its own development. That D.D.R. criticism is not subject to the tyranny of the capitalist book market and that it does not have to praise every old-fashioned "innovation" as a breakthrough to new territories does not keep it from committing follies but does protect it from the dilemma of literary review procedures that specialize in the production of ephemeral key terms and verdicts and cannot have any hope for long-term impact.

The debate about Ulrich Plenzdorf's play *Die neuen Leiden des jungen W.* (The new sufferings of young W.), which reverberated all the way into the trade union papers, highlights the contrasting conditions of literary communication in the two cultural systems. Freed from its historical context and transported to the contemporary sphere of West German communication, the attraction of the play is limited mostly to the highly amusing parody of Goethe's *Werther*, modestly provocative for the expert; to its short-term topicality for an audience suffering from chronic amnesia; and to its exotic appeal for the rest of the population. One may justifiably doubt that the highly unusual reaction of the D.D.R. press to the play was appropriate to the literary quality of the piece, but one should not doubt that the play expresses an experience of socialist everyday life that was realistic and could be sure of a response—positive as well as negative. The debate equally testifies to a change in the literary atmosphere (the play could not have succeeded without such a change), as well as to the continuing traditional expectations of socialist contemporary literature, particularly where it deals with the literary heritage without respect.

Sometimes, however, the total incommensurability of the contrasting social systems produces comparable failures—against the will of the planners and rulers. This is indicated by the judgment of a certain Ludwig Rücker in the December 1982 edition of the D.D.R. journal *Theater in der Zeit*. Rücker states, as a representative of the organization of theatergoers and supported by the utilitarian point of view of the audience: "When performances are poorly attended it is predominantly a symptom of the theater's inability to respond to the audience's needs. It does not help to appeal to so-called 'cultural-political necessities.' What sort of cultural policies are those that year after year led to a decrease in theater attendance? . . . I maintain that a substantial reason for the alienation between theater and audience is the high educational level of the theater people. I know that this sounds paradoxical; therefore, I have to explain. This high level the theater people have reached through their studies after years, often decades, of work in their profession, through talent and hard work, all of this should really serve to make it as easy as possible for the audience to understand what goes on. Instead, one often has the impression that everything becomes more and more impenetrable. This is because they all want to show off their qualifications. And so they pile all their wisdom and ability on top of each other: the author, the director, the producer, the conductor, the designer, the actors, and finally even the critic. The poor spectator in the audience who does not have a clue does not understand a thing, does not see the forest for the trees. I am sure that such a state of affairs is quite attractive for the expert when he later sits in the orchestra and witnesses such a performance, and it surely is very flattering when another highly qualified expert critic praises him in public, and without any doubt it is beneficial for the qualitative development of art when it is produced and reviewed entirely from such expert perspectives. Only: one can no longer call this a popular theater when it no longer appeals to the masses and when this art does not at the same time convince the nonexpert and cannot be grasped by him."[106]

That such views can find a forum in the 1980s in the most reputable theater journal in the D.D.R. is evidence of the fact that this cultural-political tragedy may well be an optimistic tragedy whose heroes do not necessarily stumble toward a catastrophe.

TRANSLATED BY FRANZ BLAHA

Notes

· · · · · · · ·

Introduction

1 Cf. Peter Uwe Hohendahl, "Vorüberlegungen zu einer Geschichte der Literaturkritik," in *Literaturkritik—Medienkritik,* ed. Jörg Drews (Heidelberg: Quelle und Meyer, 1977), 68–83.

2 See also Hartmut Steinecke, *Literaturkritik des Jungen Deutschland* (Berlin: E. Schmidt, 1982), esp. 9–13.

3 The English term "literary criticism" covers two domains that are held terminologically apart in the German literary institution. In German, the term *Literaturkritik* refers to the reviewing of contemporary literature and the mode of cultural reportage encountered in popular magazines and newspapers, whereas *Literaturwissenschaft* refers to the scholarly, philologically, and methodologically weighted considerations of literature (of the past) published in academic journals and books and pursued within the university.—TRANS.

4 Cf. Gerhard Sauder, "Fachgeschichte und Standortbestimmung," *Erkenntnis der Literatur,* ed. Dietrich Harth and Peter Gebhardt (Stuttgart: J. B. Metzler, 1982), 321–43.

5 Cf. Walter Hinderer, "Zur Situation der westdeutschen Literaturkritik," in *Elemente der Literaturkritik* (Kronberg: Scriptor Verlag, 1976), 191–218; Peter Uwe Hohendahl, "Das Ende einer Institution? Der Streit über die Funktion der Literaturkritik," in *Literaturkritik und Öffentlichkeit* (Munich: Piper, 1974), 151–86.

6 Cf. *Kritik/von wem/für wen/wie. Eine Selbstdarstellung der Kritik,* ed. Peter Hamm (Munich: C. Hanser, 1968); and *Ansichten einer künftigen Germanistik,* ed. Jürgen Kolbe (Munich: C. Hanser, 1969). See also Bernhard Zimmermann in this volume.

7 Cf. Norbert Mecklenburg, "Wertung und Kritik als praktische Aufgaben der Literaturwissenschaft," in *Literaturkritik und literarische Wertung,* ed. Peter Gebhardt (Darmstadt: Wissenschaftliche Buchgesellschaft, 1980), 388–411.

8 Cf. Niklas Luhmann, *Zweckbegriff und Systemrationalität* (Tübingen: Mohr, 1968);

Louis Althusser, *Ideologie und ideologische Staatsapparate* (Hamburg: Verlag für das Studium der Arbeiterbewegung, 1977).

9 Cf. Peter Uwe Hohendahl, "Literaturkritik und Öffentlichkeit (1971)," in *Literaturkritik,* 7–49; Peter Gebhardt, "Friedrich Schlegel und Ansätze: Aspekte zur Literaturkritik und literarischen Wertung," in Gebhardt, *Literaturkritik und literarische Wertung,* 412–69, esp. 452; Reinhart Koselleck, *Kritik und Krise: Eine Studie zur Pathogenese der bürgerlichen Welt* (Freiburg: K. Alber, 1959). For a critique on Habermas, see Hohendahl, "Kritische Theorie, Öffentlichkeit und Kultur," *Basis* 8 (1978): 60–91.

10 Esp. Wolfgang Jäger, *Öffentlichkeit und Parlamentarismus: Eine Kritik an Jürgen Habermas* (Stuttgart: W. Kohlhammer, 1973).

11 Jochen Schulte-Sasse, "Kritisch-rationale und literarische Öffentlichkeit," in *Aufklärung und literarische Öffentlichkeit,* ed. Christa Bürger, P. Bürger, and Jochen Schulte-Sasse (Frankfurt am Main: Suhrkamp, 1980), 18.

12 Annette Leppert-Fögen, *Die deklassierte Klasse: Studien zur Geschichte und Ideologie des Kleinbürgertums* (Frankfurt: Fischer-Taschenbuch-Verlag, 1974).

13 Norbert Mecklenburg, "Die Rhetorik der Literaturkritik," in Drews, *Literaturkritik— Medienkritik,* 36.

14 Heinrich Vormweg, "Der Verlust der Theorie: Zur Situation der Literaturkritik," in Drews, *Literaturkritik—Medienkritik,* 28–33; Peter Glotz, *Buchkritik in deutschen Zeitungen* (Hamburg: Verlag für Buchmarktforschung, 1968).

15 Cf. Matei Calinescu, *Faces of Modernity: Avant-Garde, Decadence, Kitsch* (Bloomington: Indiana University Press, 1977).

16 Karl Heinz Bohrer, "Die drei Kulturen," in *Stichworte zur "Geistigen Situation der Zeit,"* ed. Jürgen Habermas, 2 vols. (Frankfurt am Main: Suhrkamp, 1979), 2:636–69.

17 Cf. Monika Dimpfl, *Literarische Kommunikation und Gebrauchswert* (Bonn: Bouvier, 1981).

18 As to the task of literary criticism, see also Peter Gebhardt, "Literarische Kritik," in Harth and Gebhardt, *Erkenntnis der Literatur,* 79–109, esp. 104ff.

From Classicist to Classical Literary Criticism, 1730–1806

1 Albert Dresdner, *Die Entstehung der Kunstkritik im Zusammenhang des europäischen Kunstlebens* (Munich: Heimeran, 1915), 17.

2 René Wellek, *A History of Modern Criticism* (New Haven, Conn.: Yale University Press, 1955), 1:v.

3 Hans Mayer, ed., *Deutsche Literaturkritik,* 4 vols. (Frankfurt: Fischer, 1978); Peter Uwe Hohendahl, *Literarturkritik und Öffentlichkeit* (Munich: Piper, 1974), 131.

4 *Reallexikon der deutschen Literaturgeschichte,* ed. W. Kohlschmidt and W. Mohr, 2d ed. (Berlin: De Gruyter, 1958), 2:63.

5 Wellek, *Modern Criticism,* 1:v.

6 The following widely used textbooks on literary criticism agree with this concept:

A. H. Gilbert, *Plato to Dryden* (Detroit, Mich.: Wayne State University Press, 1940); and G. W. Allen and H. H. Clark, *Pope to Croce* (Detroit, Mich.: Wayne State University Press, 1941).

7 John Dryden, foreword to "State of Innocence" (1677).

8 René Wellek, "The Term and Concept of Literary Criticism," in *Concepts of Criticism* (New Haven, Conn.: Yale University Press, 1963), 21, 25, 26, 28.

9 Ibid., 30.

10 Wellek, *Modern Criticism*, 1:8, 9. He adds: "Yet it seems harder to associate particular doctrines with particular social and historical changes."

11 Immanuel Kant, *Kritik der reinen Vernunft* (Hamburg: Meiners, 1956), 7.

12 *Was ist Aufklärung? Beiträge aus der "Berlinischen Monatsschrift,"* ed. N. Hinske (Darmstadt: Wissenschaftliche Buchgesellschaft, 1977), 455.

13 Reinhart Koselleck, *Kritik und Krise* (Frankfurt am Main: Suhrkamp, 1976), 81, 89, 93, 94, 100.

14 Friedrich Schiller, "Was kann eine gute stehende Schaubühne eigentlich wirken?" in *Sämtliche Werke*, ed. F. Fricke and G. Göpfert (Munich: Hanser, 1960), 5:823.

15 Koselleck, *Kritik und Krise*, 83.

16 Jürgen Habermas, *Strukturwandel der Öffentlichkeit* (Wiesbaden: Luchterhand, 1971). While it is true that Koselleck's work is not cited and there are only two references to it, the notes contain an acknowledgment: "To R. Koselleck's excellent study I owe many suggestions" (p. 319 n. 2). And so he does.

17 Cf. Koselleck's polemics against criticism, emancipation, and utopia, which accompany his presentation as a leitmotif. It is after all a "study of the pathogenesis of the bourgeois world."

18 *G. E. Lessings sämtliche Schriften*, ed. K. Lachmann, cont. F. Muncker (Leipzig: Göschen, 1886–1924), 9:239.

19 Habermas, *Strukturwandel*, 42, 40, 58, 44, 58.

20 Ibid., 58.

21 Wellek may have neglected this viewpoint because from his understanding of "literary criticism" he takes more interest in the theory of literature, but perhaps also because the history of journals and of book criticism had not then been sufficiently investigated and even today remains in its infancy.

22 Cf. H. Kiesel and P. Münch, *Gesellschaft und Literatur im 18. Jahrhundert* (Munich: Beck, 1977); W. von Ungern-Sternberg, "Schriftsteller und literarischer Markt," in *Sozialgeschichte der deutschen Literatur*, ed. R. Grimminger (Munich: Hanser, 1980), 133–85.

23 Quoted in Habermas, *Strukturwandel*, 36.

24 Kiesel and Münch, *Gesellschaft und Literatur*, 159.

25 In Prussia in 1717.

26 Rudolf Schenda, *Volk ohne Buch* (Munich: Beck, 1977), 444.

27 Kiesel and Münch, *Gesellschaft und Literatur*, 161.

28 Friedrich Nicolai, *Das Leben und die Meinungen des Herrn Magister Sebaldus Nothanker*, ed. F. Brüggemann (Leipzig: Göschen, 1936), 72.

29 Habermas, *Strukturwandel*, 52.

30 Likewise, Gottsched's literary journal *Beyträge zur kritischen Historie der deutschen*

Sprache emerged from the "Deutsche Gesellschaft" in Leipzig; and the "Berlin Wednesday Society" made the *Berlinische Monatsschrift* into its organ.

31 Cf. Kiesel and Münch, *Gesellschaft und Literatur*, 124ff.

32 Immanuel Kant, "Über die Buchmacherei," in *Sämtliche Werke*, ed. K. Vorländer (Leipzig: Göschen, 1913), 6:213.

33 Johann Goldfriedrich, *Geschichte des deutschen Buchhandels, 1740–1804* (Leipzig: Teubner, 1909), 248.

34 Kiesel and Münch, *Gesellschaft und Literatur*, 196.

35 Cf. M. Beaujean, *Der Trivialroman in der zweiten Hälfte des 18. Jahrhunderts* (Bonn: Bouvier, 1964).

36 Jochen, Schulte-Sasse, "Das Konzept der bürgerlich-literarischen Öffentlichkeit und die historischen Gründe seines Zerfalls," in *Aufklärung und literarische Öffentlichkeit*, ed. Christa Bürger, P. Bürger, and Jochen Schulte-Sasse (Frankfurt am Main: Suhrkamp, 1980), 100.

37 Cf. Jochen Schulte-Sasse, *Die Kritik an der Trivialliteratur seit der Aufklärung* (Munich: Fink, 1971).

38 P. Raabe, "Die Zeitschrift als Medium der Aufklärung," *Wolfenbütteler Studien zur Aufklärung* 1:99ff.

39 Robert E. Prutz, *Geschichte des deutschen Journalismus* (Hanover, 1845), 7.

40 Jürgen Wilke, *Die literarischen Zeitschriften des 18. Jahrhundert* (Stuttgart: Metzler, 1978).

41 Kiesel and Münch, *Gesellschaft und Literatur*, 165.

42 Georg Forster, "Über die öffentliche Meinung," in *Werke*, ed. S. Scheibe (Berlin: De Gruyter, 1974), 8:364.

43 Wilke, *Literarischen Zeitschriften*, 1:8, 16, 54–63.

44 In England, moral weeklies like the *Spectator* (1711–12, 1714) and the *Guardian* (1713) are prototypes.

45 Habermas, *Strukturwandel*, 60. He uses the English paradigm.

46 Wolfgang Martens, *Die Botschaft der Tugend: Die Aufklärung im Spiegel der deutschen moralischen Wochenschriften* (Stuttgart: Metzler, 1968).

47 Wolfgang Martens, "Bürgerlichkeit in der frühen Aufklärung," in *Aufklärung, Absolutismus und Bürgertum in Deutschland*, ed. F. Kopitzsch (Munich: Nymphenburg, 1976), 357.

48 E.g., *Briefe die neueste Literatur betreffend* (1759–65) and *Allgemeine Deutsche Bibliothek* (1765–1805).

49 Habermas, *Strukturwandel*, 58.

50 Cf. Walter Jens, "Rhetorik," in Kohlschmidt and Mohr, *Reallexikon*, 2:432ff.

51 G. Ueding, *Einführung in die Rhetorik* (Stuttgart: Metzler, 1976), 226.

52 *Anleitung zur Poesie* (Breslau, 1725).

53 J. W. von Goethe, *Gedenkausgabe*, ed. E. Beutler (Zurich: Artemis, 1948–60), 15:1035.

54 W. Rieck, *Johann Christian Gottsched: Eine kritische Würdigung seines Werkes* (Berlin: Aufbau, 1972).

55 H. P. Hermann, *Naturnachahmung und Einbildungskraft: Zur Entwicklung der deutschen Poetik, 1670–1740* (Bad Homburg: Athenäum, 1970).

56 H. Freier, *Kritische Poetik: Legitimation und Kritik der Poesie in Gottscheds Dichtkunst* (Stuttgart: Metzler, 1973). This study interprets Gottsched's poetics "between Classicistic and systematic aesthetics" (p. 2). Freier relies on Habermas's model of the bourgeois public sphere (pp. 96ff.), but he knows full well how problematical it is to speak of a literary public sphere as early as during the Gottsched phase (p. 122).

57 Wellek comments on Gottsched merely that his *Critische Dichtkunst* "established a ponderous and pedantic local version of French neoclassicism" *(Modern Criticism,* 1:144).

58 On this, see the index of his sources in the preface of the first edition of Johann Christoph Gottsched, *Critische Dichtkunst* (Leipzig, 1730), xxvii.

59 One can identify shifts in his theory of style also: he assigns the high style to poetry but takes special interest in the middle "witty" style. See P. Böckmann, *Formgeschichte der deutschen Dichtung* (Hamburg: Hoffmann/Campe, 1965), 512ff.

60 Gottsched, *Critische Dichtkunst,* 2d ed. (Leipzig, 1737), xxx.

61 *Critische Dichtkunst* (1st ed.) preface (not paginated).

62 Hohendahl, *Literaturkritik,* 12.

63 Gottsched, *Critische Dichtkunst,* pp. 202, 204, 123, 132.

64 Ibid., 123, 132.

65 *"Beyträge zur kritischen Historie der deutschen Sprache, Poesie und Beredsamkeit"* 8:155.

66 Mayer, *Deutsche Literaturkritik,* 25, 26f. Mayer asserts that this "judicial literary criticism" is in force for the entire Enlightenment. While he concedes that this does not hold for the criticism of the "Storm and Stress" period without reservation, he overlooks the consequences of the taste debate that led to a separation of the rules of poetics from the aesthetics of effect.

67 See the article "Geneigter Leser," *Beyträge* 1 (1732).

68 Gottsched, *Critische Dichtkunst,* 118, 135. Here, "the taste of the world" still stands for a public that was not yet available to Gottsched as a concept.

69 J. B. Dubos, *Réflexions critiques sur la poésie et sur la peinture* (1719), 2:301.

70 Gottsched, *Critische Dichtkunst,* 125. Gottsched knew of the debate between Dubos and Rollin, and he rejected Dubos's famous "sixth sense" (p. 123).

71 *Spectator,* no. 592 (Sept. 10, 1714).

72 *Beyträge* (1742): 146.

73 Gottsched, *Critische Dichtkunst,* 123.

74 *Sammlung critischer, poetischer und anderer geistvoller Schriften, zur Verbesserung des Urtheils und des Witzes in den Werken der Wohlredenheit und Poesie* (1741–44), preface.

75 *Briefwechsel von der Natur des poetischen Geschmacks* (1726; published 1736), 12f., 44, 45f.

76 Quoted in A. Baeumler, *Das Irrationalismusproblem in der Ästhetik und Logik des 18. Jahrhundert* (Halle: Niemeyer, 1923), 98.

77 Hohendahl, *Literaturkritik,* 13.

78 Quoted in Baeumler, *Irrationalismusproblem,* 265.

79 H. G. Gadamer, *Wahrheit und Methode,* 3d ed. (Tübingen: Mohr, 1972), 33.

80 See Ueding, *Rhetorik,* 58f.

81 Cicero, *De Oratore* 21.71; Ueding, *Rhetorik,* 39.

82 A. von Bormann, ed., *Vom Laienurteil zum Kunstgefühl: Texte zur deutschen Geschmacksdebatte im 18. Jahrhundert* (Tübingen: Niemeyer, 1974), 2.

83 Gadamer, *Wahrheit und Methode*, 32f.

84 In France *gusto* was transformed into a social-aesthetic *bon goût* that allowed the *honnêt homme* to move with delicacy and ease in courtly society; thus taste is integrated into the courtly culture.

85 Here I follow Freier's considerations, *Kritische Poetik*, 114 n.56.

86 The aristocratic taste ideal was still very strong in the eighteenth century and even influenced bourgeois aesthetics.

87 *Spectator*, no. 409 (June 19, 1712), and no. 411 (June 21, 1712).

88 Dubos, *Réflexions*, 2:301, 303, 336, 312.

89 Hohendahl, *Literaturkritik*, 15.

90 Baeumler, *Irrationalismusproblem*, 50.

91 Dubos, *Réflexions*, 2:339, 310: "Without knowing the rules, the *parterre* judges a theatrical production just as well as a judge of art."

92 Johann Ulrich König, *Untersuchung vom guten Geschmack* (1727), quoted from Canitz, *Gedichte* (Berlin: Nicolai 1765), 321.

93 It is not necessary to deal with König's treatise in more detail, because Gottsched took up his ideas and expanded on them.

94 Quoted in Baeumler, *Irrationalismusproblem*, 94.

95 Ibid., 231.

96 Ibid., 265.

97 Immanuel Kant, *Kritik der Urteilskraft*, ed. K. Vorländer (Hamburg: Meiners, 1961), 148.

98 Ibid., vii, 127.

99 Ibid., 39, 48.

100 Ibid., 49, 48f.

101 Ibid., 78, 146.

102 Ibid., 145, 146.

103 Hohendahl, *Literaturkritik*, 15.

104 Quoted in R. Daunicht, *Lessing im Gespräch* (Munich: Heimeran, 1971), 42.

105 *Herders sämtliche Werke*, ed. B. Suphan (Berlin: Nicolai, 1877ff.), 15:486.

106 Friedrich Schlegel, *Kritische Schriften*, ed. W. Rasch (Munich: Hanser, 1964), 390.

107 This caesura is also emphasized by Wellek (*Modern Criticism*, 1:151–75), but his presentation of Lessing's achievements is in part captious (esp. pp. 151–58) and in part self-contradictory. On the one hand he complains that Lessing discusses individual problems in too much detail instead of engaging in "practical criticism" (p. 152); on the other hand he praises Lessing for being "far more than just a practical critic" (p. 158). Further surprise is offered by the judgment that in Lessing's work one finds "little literary criticism in the strictest sense" (p. 159). Such a comment can be explained only if one assumes, along with Wellek, that "practical criticism" is the interpretation of a single work, whereas "true criticism" is literary theory. Correspondingly, Wellek is again in his element when he explains Lessing's theory. Those who want to learn about the "professional critic" (p. 158), however, which Lessing after all was for more than two decades as a

freelance writer, or about the public function of Lessing's criticism, will inevitably be disappointed.

108 *Lessings sämtliche Schriften*, 9:3.

109 Ibid.

110 Ibid., 10:187, 188.

111 Ibid., 8:237.

112 Cf. I. Strohschneider-Kohrs, *Vom Prinzip des Masses in Lessings Kritik* (Stuttgart: Metzler, 1969). Taking a different view is A. Nivelle in his article "Lessing im Kontext der europäischen Literaturkritik," in *Lessing in heutiger Sicht*, ed. E. P. Harris et al. (Bremen: Jacobi, 1977), who calls the distinction between inductive and deductive method "a rather primitive opposition" (p. 102). H. Steinmetz, "Der Kritiker Lessing," *Neophilologus* 52 (1968), stresses not only the importance of Lessing's inductive method but also the difference between literary theory and review (as practical literary criticism).

113 G. E. Lessing, *Gesammelte Werke*, ed. K. Rilla (Berlin: Aufbau, 1968), 3:158.

114 E. Keller, *Kritische Intelligenz: Lessing, Friedrich Schlegel, Börne* (Bern: Francke, 1976), 78.

115 *Lessings sämtliche Schriften*, 9:335–99.

116 Ibid., 9:390, 10:190, 97.

117 Cf. K. Bohnen, *Geist und Buchstabe: Zum Prinzip des kritischen Verfahrens in Lessings literarästhetischen und theologischen Schriften* (Cologne: Böhlau, 1974). "The method of criticism is to think within the ambivalence of spirit and letter" (p. 7).

118 *Lessings sämtliche Schriften*, 9:239, 10:32, 123.

119 Schlegel, *Kritische Schriften*, 390; W. Jens, "Feldzüge eines Redners," in *Von deutscher Rede* (Munich: Piper, 1969), 52.

120 Cf. W. Barner, "Lessing und sein Publikum in den frühen Schriften," in Harris et al., *Lessing in heutiger Sicht*, 323ff.

121 See also W. Bender's selection of Lessing's contributions to the *Literaturbriefe* (Stuttgart: Reclam, 1972).

122 *Lessings sämtliche Schriften*, 9:182, 10:213.

123 Schlegel, *Kritische Schriften*, 430.

124 *Lessings sämtliche Schriften*, 9:105.

125 In *Lessing—Ein unpoetischer Dichter*, ed. H. Steinmetz (Frankfurt: Athenäum, 1969), 74.

126 *Lessings sämtliche Schriften*, 10:105, 437, 84; 7:431.

127 Ibid., 10:213.

128 See documentation in Bender, (n. 121 above), 344.

129 *Literaturbriefe*, nos. 48–51, 98, 99.

130 Cf. M. Torbruegge, "On Lessing, Mendelssohn, and the Ruling Powers," in *Humanität und Dialog: Lessing und Mendelssohn in neuer Sicht*, ed. E. Bahr et al. (Detroit: Wayne State University Press, 1982), 305–18.

131 M. Fuhrmann, *Einführung in die antiken Dichtungstheorien* (Darmstadt: Wissenschaftliche Buchgesellschaft, 1973), 272.

132 *Lessings sämtliche Schriften*, 9:318, 10:127.

133 Whether even earlier reviews of Gottsched's works, which appeared between 1748

and 1750 in the *Berliner Privilegierte Zeitung*, can be attributed to Lessing has been debated many times, most recently by K. S. Guthke, "Der junge Lessing als Kritiker Gottscheds und Bodmers," in *Literarisches Leben im 18. Jahrhundert in Deutschland und der Schweiz* (Bern: Francke, 1975), 48ff.

134 *Lessings sämtliche Schriften*, 4:301f, and 1:248f.

135 A detailed interpretation of this forgotten poem can be found in Guthke, "Der junge Lessing," 39.

136 Letter to Gottsched, July 9, 1754 (see ibid., 28).

137 *Bibliothek der schönen Wissenschaften und freyen Künste* (1757ff.) and *Briefe die neueste Literatur betreffend* (1759ff.).

138 Just Riedel, *Briefe über das Publikum* (1768), 168f.

139 *Lessings sämtliche Schriften*, 10:190; 9:210; 10:190, 215.

140 On the journals named here and their editors, see Wilke, *Literarischen Zeitschriften*.

141 Thus, it is stated in the "Vorläufige Nachricht" of *Bibliothek der schönen Wissenschaften und freyen Künste* 1 (1757): 3, that "the judgment of our taste must at all times be confirmed by the reason of criticism."

142 Friedrich Nicolai, *Briefe über den itzigen Zustand der schönen Wissenschaften in Deutschland*, ed. G. Ellinger (Berlin, 1884), 41, 116, 141.

143 Lessing's letter to Eschenburg, Oct. 26, 1774.

144 Cf. K. Scherpe, *Werther und Wertherwirkung* (Bad Homburg: Athenäum, 1969).

145 Friedrich Nicolai, *Beschreibung einer Reise durch Deutschland und die Schweiz* (Berlin: Nicolai, 1783–96), 11:200ff; Friedrich Nicolai, *Anhang zu Schillers Musen-Almanach für das Jahr 1797* (Berlin: Nicolai, 1797), 11f.

146 Schiller, *Sämtliche Werke*, 5:868.

147 Schiller's letter to Cotta, March 3, 1795.

148 Ibid.

149 Nicolai, *Sebaldus Nothanker*, 72.

150 Nicolai's preface to vol. 1 of the *ADB*, p. 1. For the history of the *ADB*, see Günther Ost, *Nicolais Allgemeine Deutsche Bibliothek* (Berlin: Nicolai, 1928).

151 In this connection, the changes within the most important areas of knowledge between 1750 and 1800, as reflected in the *ADB*, are interesting:

	Theology	Philosophy	Belles lettres
1750	28.9%	26.7%	8.7%
1775	19.9%	34.1%	14.3%
1800	6.0%	39.6%	27.3%

152 Thus Johannes Biester, co-editor of the *Berlinische Monatsschrift*, in an evaluation of the *ADB*.

153 He was thus reproached by both Goethe and Schiller (*Xenien*, 1797), as well as by Kant ("Über die Buchmacherei," 1799), all of whom mistook his merits. See K. L. Berghahn, "Masslose Kritik: Friedrich Nicolai als Kritiker und Opfer der Weimarer

Klassiker," in *Kontroversen, alte und neue*, Akten des VII, Internationalen Germanisten-Kongresses Göttingen, 1985 (Tübingen: Niemeyer, 1986), 2:189ff.

154 Nicolai to Herder, Dec. 24, 1768.

155 Hohendahl, *Literaturkritik*, 17.

156 Quoted from *Gelesen und geliebt: Aus erfolgreichen Büchern 1750–1850*, ed. H. Kunze (Berlin: Aufbau, 1959), 27.

157 Schulte-Sasse, "Das Konzept der bürgerlich-literarischen Öffentlichkeit," 99.

158 Schenda, *Volk ohne Buch*, 57ff.

159 *Lessings sämtliche Schriften*, 10:190.

160 *Herders sämtliche Werke*, 1:245.

161 Ibid. The triple relation to art—namely, as a "man of feeling" (connoisseur), philosopher, and critic—is strongly reminiscent of the beginning of Lessing's *Laokoon*, which had just appeared.

162 Ibid., 246.

163 *Herders sämtliche Werke*, 1:242, 247, 250, 255.

164 Ibid., 5:219.

165 Ibid., 210, 645, 646.

166 Besides the editors J. H. Merck and J. G. Schlosser, Goethe and Herder were also on the editorial board. Although the attribution of anonymous reviews is very difficult, these writers must have contributed the greatest share. See H. Brüning-Octavio, *Herausgeber und Mitarbeiter der Frankfurter Gelehrten Anzeigen 1772* (Tübingen: Niemeyer, 1966).

167 *Goethes Werke*, ed. E. Trunz (Hamburg: Wegner, 1949ff.), 10:430.

168 *Frankfurter Gelehrte Anzeigen vom Jahre 1772*, ed. W. Scherer (Heilbronn, 1883), 664, 665, 666, 446, 670.

169 Ibid., 379f.

170 Goethe to Kestner, Oct. 2, 1772.

171 Scherer, *FGA*, 596.

172 · Mayer, *Deutsche Literaturkritik*, 1:28.

173 *Grimms Deutsches Wörterbuch*, 12:499.

174 *Goethes Werke*, 9:408f.

175 *Bürgers Werke*, ed. L. Kaim and S. Streller (Weimar: Aufbau, 1956), 328, 341, 338, 321.

176 The first edition had already appeared in 1778, the second came out in 1789, and Schiller published his review on Jan. 15 and 17, 1791, in the *Allgemeine Literatur-Zeitung*.

177 Thus the commentary of the Hanser edition (Schiller, *Sämtliche Werke*, 5:1223), which can represent many similar simplifying interpretations.

178 Ibid., 980, lines 29f.

179 Mayer, *Deutsche Literaturkritik*, 1:32.

180 For interpretations of Schiller's Bürger review, see W. Müller-Seidel, "Schillers Kontroverse mit Bürger und ihr geschichtlicher Sinn," in *Formenwandel: Festschrift für Paul Böckmann* (Hamburg: Hoffmann und Campe, 1964), 294ff; K. L. Berghahn, "Volkstümlichkeit ohne Volk?" in *Popularität und Trivialität*, ed. R. Grimm and J. Hermand (Frankfurt: Athenäum, 1974), 51ff.

181 Schiller, *Sämtliche Werke*, 5:970, 973.

182 Cf. K. L. Berghahn, "Ästhetische Reflexion als Utopie des Ästhetischen," in *Utopie-Forschung*, ed. W. Vosskamp (Stuttgart: Metzler, 1983), 3:148ff.

183 Schiller, *Sämtliche Werke*, 5:971, 973, 974, 975.

184 Ibid., 972. Cf. G. Ueding, *Schillers Rhetorik* (Tübingen: Niemeyer, 1971), 16ff.

185 Schiller, *Sämtliche Werke*, 5:979.

186 E. Wilkinson, "Über den Begriff der künstlerischen Distanz," in *Deutsche Beiträge zur geistigen Überlieferung* 3 (1957): 69ff.

187 Schiller, *Sämtliche Werke*, 5:282. Oscar Wilde's observation that "all bad poetry springs from genuine feeling" (quoted in Wilkinson; see n. 186) captures this point exactly.

188 Schiller to Christian G. Körner, March 3, 1791.

189 *Goethes Werke*, 12:30.

190 Schiller to Körner, Feb. 28, 1793.

191 "Über die Gegenstände bildender Kunst," *Weimarer Ausgabe* 45:94.

192 *Goethes Werke*, 12:471. For Goethe's concept of symbol, see W. Emrich, "Das Problem der Symbolinterpretation im Hinblick auf Goethes 'Wanderjahre,'" *DVjS* 26 (1952): 331ff.

193 Thus Schiller's formulation of the problem in his review of Friedrich von Matthisson's poetry. For Schiller's use of symbolic language, see K. L. Berghahn, "Schillers mythologische Symbolik: Erläutert am Beispiel der 'Götter Griechenlands,'" *Weimarer Beiträge* 31 (1985): 1803ff.

194 *Goethes Werke*, 12:471.

195 Cf. Christa Bürger, *Der Ursprung der bürgerlichen Institution Kunst: Literatursoziologische Untersuchung zum klassischen Goethe* (Frankfurt am Main: Suhrkamp, 1977).

196 Mayer, *Deutsche Literaturkritik*, 1:32.

197 An interesting recovery of this author, who otherwise is mentioned only in a footnote to Goethe's essay, is undertaken by Christa Bürger, "Literarischer Markt und Öffentlichkeit am Ausgang des 18. Jahrhundert," in Bürger, Bürger, and Schulte-Sasse, *Aufklärung und literarische Öffentlichkeit*, 179–82.

198 *Goethes Werke*, 12:240.

199 Cf. D. Borchmeyer, *Höfische Gesellschaft und französische Revolution bei Goethe* (Kronsberg: Athenäum, 1977).

200 Ironically, the honorary citizenship document reached Schiller only after he had already fundamentally changed his attitude toward the Revolution.

201 Schiller to Körner, Dec. 21, 1792, and Feb. 8, 1793.

202 Schiller to F. C. von Augustenburg, July 13, 1793.

203 Schiller to Herder, Nov. 4, 1795.

204 Schiller, *Sämtliche Werke*, 5:593, 535.

205 K. Vorländer, "Über Goethes Exemplar der 'Kritik der Urteilskraft,'" in Kant, *Kritik der Urteilskraft*, xxvff.

206 Goethe to K. F. Zelter, Jan. 29, 1830.

207 Cf. H. Marcuse, "Über den affirmativen Charakter der Kultur," in *Kultur und Gesellschaft* (Frankfurt am Main: Suhrkamp, 1965).

208 Draft of a letter to J. G. Fichte, Aug. 3, 1795.

209 Schiller, *Sämtliche Werke*, 5:764–68.

210 E.g., Körner's detailed critique in a letter to Schiller (Nov. 5, 1796), which Schiller published subsequently in the *Horen*.

211 Goethe, Wilhelm von Humboldt, K. L. Woltmann, and (until his withdrawal) Fichte belonged to the inner circle of co-editors.

212 Schiller, *Sämtliche Werke*, 5:868.

213 *Horen*, ed. P. Raabe (rpt.; Darmstadt: Wissenschaftliche Buchgesellschaft, 1959), postscript, p. 9.

214 Schiller to C. G. Schütz, Sept. 30, 1794.

215 Schiller to J. F. Cotta, Oct. 2, 1794. Cotta was even willing to pay 100 thaler to the *ALZ* for paper and printing costs.

216 Schiller, *Sämtliche Werke*, 5:870. Along the same line, Goethe states in his *"Unterhaltungen deutscher Ausgewanderten,"* first published in the *Horen*: "Let us agree to ban all conversation regarding the interest of the day."

217 Quoted from O. Fambach, ed., *Schiller und sein Kreis in der Kritik der Zeit* (Berlin: Aufbau, 1957), 152.

218 Advertisement of the *Propyläen*, in *Goethes Werke*, 12:581.

219 Goethe to H. Meyer, May 20, 1796.

220 Goethe, Weimar, ed., 48:23, 45:250.

221 Schiller to Goethe, June 25, 1799.

222 C. Bürger, "Literarischer Markt," 167 n.35.

223 Goethe to Schiller, Nov. 15, 1796.

224 D. Borchmeyer, *Tragödie und Öffentlichkeit: Schillers Dramaturgie* (Munich: Fink, 1973), 115.

225 Hohendahl, *Literaturkritik*, 19.

226 Schiller, *Sämtliche Werke*, 2:819, 817, 818.

227 Ibid., 816, 819, 820.

228 Borchmeyer, *Tragödie und Öffentlichkeit*, 19.

229 Georg Lukács, "Schillers Theorie der modernen Literatur," in *Goethe und seine Zeit* (Berlin: Aufbau, 1955), 88.

230 To the suppressed (and repressed) past of German literary criticism belongs the republican and Jacobin journalism that decisively pushed for a political public sphere and a public opinion. As political journalism, it would be the counterpart to the apolitical and aestheticized literary public sphere of Weimar Classicism. That it could not prevail vis-à-vis the Classic-Romantic criticism has less to do with its intrinsic quality than with the fact that the political conditions, the censorship, and the dominant aesthetics delayed its reception. Cf. I. Stephan, *Literarischer Jacobinismus in Deutschland, 1789–1806* (Stuttgart: Metzler, 1976).

The Concept of Literary Criticism in German Romanticism, 1795–1810

1 This chapter is a free adaptation rather than a translation of my German original, expanding the essay more often than abridging it. I am very grateful to my

research assistant, Brent Peterson, who provided me with a first-draft translation and who made many helpful suggestions to improve the final version stylistically.

2 Ludwig Tieck, *Werke in vier Bänden*, ed. M. Thalmann (Darmstadt: Wissenschaftliche Buchgesellschaft, 1963–66), 1:718–19. Unless otherwise indicated, all translations are original.

3 Ibid., 746.

4 Ibid., 807–8.

5 Friedrich Schlegel, *Friedrich Schlegel's Lucinde and the Fragments*, trans. Peter Firchow (Minneapolis: University of Minnesota Press, 1971), 229. Further translations from this source are cited in the text as FS, plus the page number.

6 Wilhelm Heinrich Wackenroder, *Werke und Briefe* (Heidelberg: Lambert Schneider, 1967), 80, 112, 114.

7 In the last three decades of the eighteenth century, the German book market had exploded into a mass market for fiction. The publication of new plays, the traditional narrative genre, increased tenfold in the second half of the century (from 125 to 1,029 newly published plays per decade). Once the novel was accepted as an equally valuable genre aesthetically, the number of newly published novels increased even more dramatically. Between 1751 and 1760, 73 new novels were published in Germany. In the last decade of the century that figure increased more than twentyfold, to 1,623. Simultaneously, the share of fiction among all books published rose from 5.8 percent in 1740 to 21.5 percent in 1800. Writers of so-called high literature reacted to this development with horror; they introduced dichotomous categories to comprehend and criticize the development of a mass market, the accompanying bifurcation of the reading public, and the increasing economic pressure they felt, and they rearranged their aesthetic theories accordingly (the dichotomy of *Kitsch* and *Kunst*, pulp and art, has its roots here). Cf. Jochen Schulte-Sasse, *Die Kritik an der Trivialliteratur seit der Aufklärung: Studien zur Geschichte des modernen Kitschbegriffs* (Munich: Fink, 1971).

8 Kurt Röttgers, *Kritik und Praxis: Zur Geschichte des Kritikbegriffs von Kant bis Marx* (Berlin: De Gruyter, 1975), 21.

9 Friedrich Schlegel, *Kritische Friedrich-Schlegel-Ausgabe*, ed. Ernst Behler et al. (Munich: Ferdinand Schöningh, 1958ff.), 3:83. Quotations translated from this German edition are cited in the text as KA, with volume and page numbers.

10 See Oscar Fambach, ed., *Ein Jahrhundert deutscher Literaturkritik, 1750–1850* (Berlin: Aufbau, 1963), 5:603.

11 Clemens Brentano, *Werke*, ed. F. Kemp (Munich: Hanser, 1963), 2:1135f.

12 Walter Benjamin, *Gesammelte Schriften*, ed. Rolf Tiedemann and Hermann Schweppenhäuser (Frankfurt am Main: Suhrkamp, 1974), vol. 1, pt. 1, p. 109.

13 See in this connection Schulte-Sasse, *Kritik an der Trivialliteratur*, 113–26.

14 Friedrich Schlegel, *Friedrich Schlegel, 1794–1802: Seine prosaischen Jugendschriften*, ed. J. Minor (Vienna, 1882), 1:95.

15 Jürgen Habermas, "Der Eintritt in die Postmoderne," *Merkur* 37 (1983): 751.

16 Jürgen Habermas, *Legitimation Crisis*, trans. Thomas McCarthy (Boston: Beacon Press, 1975), 78.

17 Habermas, "Postmoderne," 759–60.

18 See, e.g., Gisela Dischner, *Bettina von Arnim: Eine weibliche Sozialbiographie aus dem 19. Jahrhundert* (Berlin: Wagenbach, 1977), 64, 41.

19 Henri Brunschwig, *Enlightenment and Romanticism in Eighteenth Century Prussia*, trans. Frank Jellinek (Chicago: University of Chicago Press, 1974), 183.

20 Quoted in Hans Mayer, ed., *Meisterwerke deutscher Literaturkritik: Aufklärung, Klassik, Romantik* (Berlin: Rütten und Loening, 1956), 1:759.

21 Quoted in Mayer, *Meisterwerke*, 1:659.

22 Joseph Freiherr von Eichendorff, *Werke und Schriften*, ed. G. Baumann with S. Grosse (Stuttgart: Cotta, n.d.), 2:1072.

23 Fambach, *Jahrhundert*, 206.

24 Novalis, *Schriften*, ed. P. Kluckhohn and R. Samuel (Stuttgart: Kohlhammer, 1960–75), 4:333. Hereafter cited in the text as N.

25 August Wilhelm Schlegel, *Vorlesungen über schöne Literatur und Kunst* in *Deutsche Literaturdenkmale des 18. und 19. Jahrhunderts*, ed. J. Minor (Stuttgart: Heinemann, 1884), 17:8.

26 Cf., e.g., Jochen Hörisch, "Herrscherwort, Geld und geltende Sätze: Adornos Aktualisierung der Frühromantik und ihre Affinität zur poststrukturalistischen Kritik des Subjekts," in *Materialien zur ästhetischen Theorie: Th. W. Adornos Konstruktion der Moderne*, ed. B. Lindner and W. M. Lüdke (Frankfurt am Main: Suhrkamp, 1980), 397–414.

27 See Panajotis Kondylis, *Die Aufklärung im Rahmen des neuzeitlichen Rationalismus* (Stuttgart: Klett-Cotta, 1981), 58.

28 Cf. Klaus Michael Wetzel, *Autonomie und Authentizität: Untersuchungen zur Konstitution und Konfiguration von Subjektivität* (Frankfurt am Main: Peter Lang, 1985).

29 In Mayer, *Meisterwerke*, 1:761.

30 Johann Gottlieb Fichte, *Sämmtliche Werke*, ed. J. H. Fichte (Berlin: Veit, 1846), 7:66, 26, 29–30.

31 In Mayer, *Meisterwerke*, 1:559.

32 See Jochen Schulte-Sasse, "Das Konzept der bürgerlich-literarischen Öffentlichkeit und die historischen Gründe seines Zerfalls," in *Aufklärung und literarische Öffentlichkeit*, ed. Christa Bürger, P. Bürger, and Jochen Schulte-Sasse (Frankfurt am Main: Suhrkamp, 1980), 83–115; and Schulte-Sasse, *Kritik an der Trivialliteratur*.

33 The quotations in the remainder of this paragraph are from Fichte, *Sämmtliche Werke*, 7:87–89.

34 Gerda Heinrich, *Geschichtsphilosophische Positionen der deutschen Frühromantik (Friedrich Schlegel und Novalis)* (Berlin: Akademie, 1976), 74.

35 Karl Marx and Friedrich Engels, *Collected Works* (New York: International Publishers, 1976), 6:50; 5:195. Quoted in Heinrich, *Geschichtsphilosophische Positionen*, 74.

36 Heinrich, *Geschichtsphilosophische Positionen*, 13.

37 Brunschwig, *Enlightenment and Romanticism*, 105.

38 Geraint Parry, "Enlightened Government and Its Critics in Eighteenth Century Germany," *Historical Journal* 4, no. 2 (1963): 182.

39 In Mayer, *Meisterwerke*, 1:552.

40 Johann Heinrich Gottlob von Justi, *Gesammelte Politische und Finanzschriften*, 3:86–87. See Parry, "Enlightened Government," 182.

41 See in this connection my drama chapter in Rolf Grimminger, ed., *Sozialgeschichte der deutschen Literatur* (Munich: Hanser, 1980), 3:423–99.

42 Christoph Jamme and Helmut Schneider, eds., *Mythologie der Vernunft. Hegels "ältestes Systemprogramm" des deutschen Idealismus* (Frankfurt am Main: Suhrkamp, 1984), 11–12.

43 Brentano, *Werke*, 2:999.

44 Reinhart Koselleck, *Preussen zwischen Reform und Revolution: Allgemeines Landrecht, Verwaltung und soziale Bewegung von 1791 bis 1848* (Stuttgart: Klett, 1967), pp. 24–25, 118, 60.

45 Quoted in ibid., 49.

46 Fichte, *Sämmtliche Werke*, 7:30.

47 Eichendorff, *Werke und Schriften*, 2:1040, 1043.

48 Immanuel Kant, *Critique of Judgment*, trans. J. H. Bernard (New York: Harner Press, 1951), 165 (B206, A204).

49 See Albert O. Hirschman, *The Passions and the Interests: Political Arguments for Capitalism before Its Triumph* (Princeton, N.J.: Princeton University Press, 1977), and the excellent study by Hans-Jürgen Fuchs, *Entfremdung und Narzissmus: Semantische Untersuchung zur Geschichte der "Selbstbezogenheit" als Vorgeschichte von französisch "amour-propre"* (Stuttgart: Metzler, 1977).

50 Niklas Luhmann is an important German sociologist whose major works have only recently begun appearing in English. In this context his *Love as Passion: The Codification of Intimacy* (Cambridge, Mass.: Harvard University Press, 1986) is the most pertinent one.

51 Mayer, *Meisterwerke*, 1:xviii.

52 Friedrich Schlegel, *Literarische Notizen 1797–1801/Literary Notebooks*, ed. Hans Eichner (Berlin: Ullstein, 1980), LN 286f.

53 The scurrilous pun *zur Notdurft* is very characteristic for the Romantics' notion of the function art serves in modernity; the phrase designates a bodily necessity, such as having to go to the bathroom.

54 Brentano, *Werke*, 2:992.

55 F. Schlegel, *Literarische Notizen*, LN 714.

56 Dieter Arendt, *Der poetische Nihilismus in der Romantik. Studien zum Verhältnis von Dichtung und Wirklichkeit* (Tübingen: Niemeyer, 1972), 1:12.

57 In Fambach, *Jahrhundert*, 193.

58 Dischner, *Bettina von Arnim*, 133.

59 In Mayer, *Meisterwerke*, 1:612f.

60 Mayer, *Meisterwerke*, 1:615–16, 624, 621, 612.

61 Ibid., 547.

62 Ibid., 619.

63 Hans-Joachim Mähl, *Die Idee des goldenen Zeitalters im Werk des Novalis: Studien zur Wesensbestimmung der frühromantischen Utopie und zu ihren ideengeschichtlichen Voraussetzungen* (Heidelberg: Winter, 1965), 357.

64 See the interpretation of the historical avant-garde in Peter Bürger, *The Theory of the Avant-Garde*, trans. Michael Shaw (Minneapolis: University of Minnesota Press, 1984).

65 Dischner, *Bettina von Arnim*, 133.

66 Eichendorff, *Werke und Schriften*, 2:506.

67 Johann Gottlieb Fichte, *Grundlage der gesamten Wissenschaftslehre, 1794* (Hamburg: Meiner, 1979).

68 Immanuel Kant, *Critique of Pure Reason*, trans. Norman Kemp Smith (New York: St. Martin's Press, 1965), 601–2 (A751–52, B779–80). I have changed the translation slightly: to translate *eines gesetzlichen Zustandes* as "of a legal order" narrows the meaning of *gesetzlich* considerably.

69 See in this connection Jochen Hörisch, *Die fröhliche Wissenschaft der Poesie. Der Universalitätsanspruch von Dichtung in der frühromantischen Poetologie* (Frankfurt am Main: Suhrkamp, 1976), 80.

70 Ludwig Tieck, "Briefe über W. Shakespeare," *Poetisches Journal* 1 (1800): 24–25.

71 Kant, *Critique of Judgment*, 157 (A190, B193).

72 Cf. my essay "Imagination and Modernity; or, The Taming of the Human Mind," *Cultural Critique*, no. 5 (Winter 1987): 23–48.

73 Kant, *Critique of Judgment*, 157–58.

74 Mayer, *Meisterwerke*, 1:627.

75 Ibid., 607.

76 Heinz-Dieter Weber, *Über eine Theorie der Literaturkritik: Die falsche und die berechtigte Aktualität der Frühromantik* (Munich: Fink, 1971), 55.

77 Friedrich Wilhelm Joseph Schelling, *Philosophie der Kunst* (Darmstadt: Wissenschaftliche Buchgesellschaft, 1976), 3.

78 See my *Kritik an der Trivialliteratur*, 33–34.

79 In this connection, see Jochen Schulte-Sasse, "Literarischer Markt und ästhetische Denkform: Analysen und Thesen zur Geschichte ihres Zusammenhangs," *Zeitschrift für Literaturwissenschaft und Linguistik* 2 (1972): 11–33.

80 Schelling, *Philosophie der Kunst*, 5.

81 Ibid., 3.

82 Mayer, *Meisterwerke*, 1:581.

83 Benjamin, *Gesammelte Schriften*, vol. 1, pt. 1, 67.

84 Ibid., 26, 29.

85 Mayer, *Meisterwerke*, 1:555, 561.

86 Ingrid Strohschneider-Kohrs, *Die romantische Ironie in Theorie und Gestaltung* (Tübingen: Niemeyer, 1960), 233–34.

87 Quoted in Benjamin, *Gesammelte Schriften*, vol. 1, pt. 1, 93.

88 Ibid., 51.

89 Carl Schmitt, *Politische Romantik* (Berlin, 1919), 104.

90 Ibid., 226.

91 Lothar Pikulik, *Romantik als Ungenügen an der Normalität: Am Beispiel Tiecks, Hoffmanns, Eichendorffs* (Frankfurt am Main: Suhrkamp, 1979), 88.

92 A. W. Schlegel, *Literatur und Kunst*, 17:93.

93 Schelling, *Philosophie der Kunst*, 273.

94   Fambach, *Jahrhundert*, 197–98.
95   In this connection, see also Weber, *Theorie der Literaturkritik*, 44–45.
96   See Hörisch, *Fröhliche Wissenschaft*, 135.
97   In Mayer, *Meisterwerke*, 1:630.
98   *Leibniz: Selections*, ed. Philip P. Weiner (New York: Scribner, 1951), 544.
99   In Mayer, *Meisterwerke*, 1:760.
100 Schlegel, *Jugendschriften*, 95.
101 In Mayer, *Meisterwerke*, 1:566, 576.
102 Ibid., 629, 569.
103 Ibid., 592–93.
104 A. W. Schlegel, *Literatur und Kunst*, 19:9.
105 In Mayer, *Meisterwerke*, 1:550.
106 Ibid., 557.
107 Ibid., 550.
108 Fichte, *Sämmtliche Werke*, 7:77.
109 See the research carried out by José Antonio Maravall, esp. *La Cultura del Barroco* (Barcelona: Ariel, 1975), trans. Terry Cochran as *Culture of the Baroque: Analysis of a Historical Structure* (Minneapolis: University of Minnesota Press, 1986).
110 In Mayer, *Meisterwerke*, 1:697–98.
111 Ibid., 709.
112 See Manfred Frank's outstanding book *Der kommende Gott: Vorlesungen über die neue Mythologie* (Frankfurt am Main: Suhrkamp, 1982).
113 Ibid., 234.
114 In Fambach, *Jahrhundert*, 587.
115 Josepf Freiherr von Eichendorff, *Werke* (Munich: Winkler, 1976), 3:153.
116 Achim von Arnim, in Mayer, *Meisterwerke*, 1:717.
117 Ibid., 691.
118 Fambach, *Jahrhundert*, 13, 33, 42.
119 Achim von Arnim, in Mayer, *Meisterwerke*, 1:717.
120 Joseph Görres, review of *Des Knaben Wunderhorn*, 1809–10, in Fambach, *Jahrhundert*, 454f.
121 Mayer, *Meisterwerke*, 1:704.
122 Ibid., 723n.
123 In Fambach, *Jahrhundert*, 604.
124 Achim von Arnim, in Mayer, *Meisterwerke*, 1:701f.
125 Willi Oelmüller, *Die unbefriedigte Aufklärung: Beiträge zu einer Theorie der Moderne von Lessing, Kant und Hegel, mit einer neuen Einleitung* (Frankfurt am Main: Suhrkamp, 1979), xxxi.

Literary Criticism in the Epoch of Liberalism, 1820–70

1   René Wellek, *A History of Modern Criticism: 1750–1950*, 4 vols. (New Haven, Conn.: Yale University Press, 1965), 3:201–4; Peter Uwe Hohendahl, "Literarische und politische Öffentlichkeit: Die neue Kritik des Jungen Deutschland," in *Literaturkritik und Öffentlichkeit* (Munich: Piper, 1974), 128–50.

2 Hartmut Steinecke, *Literaturkritik des Jungen Deutschland* (Berlin: E. Schmidt, 1982), 15–57. Also see Bernd Witte, "Literaturtheorie, Literaturkritik und Literatur-geschichte," in *Deutsche Literatur: Eine Sozialgeschichte*, ed. Bernd Witte, 10 vols. (Reinbek: Rowohlt, 1980), 6:63–82; Hohendahl, "Literaturkritik und Literatur-geschichte," in *Deutsche Literatur*, ed. Horst Albert Glazer (Reinbek: Rowohlt, 1982), 7:47–58.

3 Freidrich Sengle, *Biedermeierzeit*, 3 vols. (Stuttgart: J. B. Metzler, 1977), vol. 1; esp. for Young Germany, see Petra-Sybille Hauke, *Literaturkritik in den Blättern für literarische Unterhaltung 1818–35*, 3 vols. (Stuttgart: J. B. Metzler, 1972); Sabine Peek, "Cottas Morgenblatt für gebildete Stände (1827–65)," *Archiv für Geschichte des Buchwesens* 6 (1966): cols. 1427–1659.

4 Peter Uwe Hohendahl, *The Institution of Literary Criticism* (Ithaca, N.Y.: Cornell University Press, 1982), 11–43; also Hohendahl, "Beyond Reception Aesthetics: The Institution of Literature," *New German Critique* 23 (Winter 1983): 108–146.

5 Christa Bürger, Peter Bürger, and Jochen Schulte-Sasse, eds., *Aufklärung und liter-arische Öffentlichkeit* (Frankfurt am Main: Suhrkamp, 1980), esp. articles by Schulte-Sasse, Christa Bürger, and Onno Frels; Ronald A. Fullerton, "The Development of the German Book Markets, 1815–1888" (Ph.D. diss., University of Wisconsin, 1975), 86–114.

6 Christa Bürger, "Literarischer Markt und Öffentlichkeit am Ausgang des 18. Jahr-hundert in Deutschland" in Bürger, Bürger, and Schulte-Sasse, *Aufklärung und literarische Öffentlichkeit*, 170.

7 Wolfgang Menzel, *Die deutsche Literatur*, 2 vols. in one (Stuttgart: Gebrüder Frankh, 1828), 1:73.

8 Ludwig Börne, "Einige Worte über die angekündigten Jahrbücher der wissen-schaftlichen Kritik," in *Kritische Schriften*, ed. E. Schumacher (Zurich: Artemis, 1964), 53.

9 Fullerton, "Development," 86.

10 Johann Goldfriedrich, *Geschichte des deutschen Buchhandels*, 4 vols. (Leipzig: Börsen-verein der deutschen Buchhändler, 1913), 4:199.

11 Fullerton, "Development," 86. The available statistics make it clear: that the num-ber of traders rises steadily in old literary centers such as Berlin and Leipzig (Berlin: 51 in the year 1822, 81 in 1832, 106 in 1842), and that stores are being opened in small cities that previously had few or none: e.g., Stettin had no bookstore in 1822, three in 1832, no less than eight in 1842—or, at this point, a bookstore for every 3,750 inhabitants. This ratio is worse than that of Stuttgart (1,083) but better than that of Hamburg (5,000) and Bremen (10,000). Cf. Fullerton, "Development," 87.

12 See Fullerton, "Development," 174–222; and Rudolf Schenda, *Volk ohne Buch*, paperback ed. (Munich: Deutscher Taschenbuch, 1977), 228–70.

13 Fullerton, "Development," 92.

14 Schenda, *Volk ohne Buch*, 441–66. W. Fischer, J. Krengel, J. Wietog, eds., *Sozial-geschichtliches Arbeitsbuch I* (Munich: Beck, 1982), 147–72, has material concerning wages and incomes.

15 Ingrid Oesterle and Günter Oesterle, "Der literarische Bürgerkrieg. Gutzkow, Heine, Börne wider Menzel," in *Demokratisch-revolutionäre Literatur in Deutschland:*

Vormärz, ed. Gert Mattenklott and Klaus R. Scherpe (Kronberg: Scriptor-Verlag, 1973), 151–85.

16 Quoted in *Das Junge Deutschland*, ed. Jost Hermand, (Stuttgart: Reclam, 1966), 104.

17 Oesterle and Oesterle, "Der literarische Bürgerkrieg," 158.

18 Cf. Jürgen Habermas, *Strukturwandel der Öffentlichkeit*, 2d ed. (Neuwied: Luchterhand, 1965), 201.

19 Cf. Hohendahl, "Kunsturteil und Tagesbericht: Zur ästhetischen Theorie des späten Heine," in *Heinrich Heine: Artistik und Engagement*, ed. Wolfgang Kuttenkeuler (Stuttgart: J. B. Metzler, 1977), 207–41.

20 Franz Schneider, *Pressefreiheit und politische Öffentlichkeit* (Neuwied: Luchterhand, 1966); Kurt Koszyk, *Deutsche Presse im 19. Jahrhundert*, Geschichte der deutschen Presse II (Berlin: Colloquium Verlag, 1966). See the bibliography of Alfred Estermann in *Die deutschen Literaturzeitschriften 1815–1850*, 10 vols. (Nendeln: KTO Press, 1978–80).

21 *Literarischer Zodiakus* 1 (1835): 1.

22 Ibid., 9.

23 *Schriften in bunter Reihe* 1 (1834): 5.

24 Börne, *Kritische Schriften*, 306.

25 Robert Prutz, *Geschichte des deutschen Journalismus*, (Hanover: C. F. Kius, 1845), 16.

26 Ibid., 15.

27 Robert Prutz, "Über die Unterhaltungsliteratur, insbesondere der Deutschen," in *Schriften zur Literatur und Politik*, ed. Bernd Hüppauf, (Tübingen: Niemeyer, 1973), 10.

28 Steinecke, *Literaturkritik des Jungen Deutschland*, 32; Walter Hömberg, *Zeitgeist und Ideenschmuggel: Die Kommunikationsstrategie des Jungen Deutschland*, (Stuttgart: J. B. Metzler, 1975), 122–46.

29 *Schriften in bunter Reihe* 1 (1834): 7; Heinrich Laube, *Ausgewählte Werke*, ed. Heinrich Hubert Houben, 10 vols. (Leipzig: Max Hesse, 1906), 8:321.

30 This is the way in which, e.g., the *Phoenix* is edited, which from 1835 competes with magazines such as the *Morgenblatt* or the *Zeitung für die elegante Welt* on the market. While Eduard Duller, the editor of the journal, follows a moderate course, encouraging both liberals and conservatives, Gutzkow, the editor of the supplement, which is concerned with literary criticism, takes a more radical stance. This supplement addresses a smaller and more select audience (see Hömberg, *Zeitgeist und Ideenschmuggel*, 123–29). Wienbarg does the same thing a few years later with the *Deutsches Literaturblatt*, which appears as supplement to the *Kritische Blätter der Börsenhalle* (1840–42).

31 Hömberg, *Zeitgeist und Ideenschmuggel*, 94.

32 *Autonomie der Kunst: Zur Genese einer bürgerlichen Kategorie* (Frankfurt am Main: Suhrkamp, 1972), esp. the contribution by Berthold Hinz; Peter Szondi, *Poetik und Geschichtsphilosophie*, 2 vols. (Frankfurt am Main: Suhrkamp, 1974), vol. 1.

33 Heinrich Heine, *Sämtliche Schriften*, ed. Klaus Briegleb, 6 vols. (Munich: Hanser, 1971), 3:468.

34 Ludolf Christian Wienbarg, *Ästhetische Feldzüge*, ed. Walter Dietze (Berlin: Aufbau Verlag, 1964), 188.

35 *Jahrbuch der Literatur* 1 (1839): 12.

36 Cf. Wolfgang Preisendanz, "Der Funktionsübergang von Dichtung und Pub-lizistik," in *Heinrich Heine* (Munich: Fink, 1973), 21–68.

37 Steinecke, *Literaturkritik des Jungen Deutschland*, 26–33; Hohendahl, "Kunsturteil und Tagesbericht."

38 Wienbarg, "Heinrich Heine. Salon. Zweiter Teil," in *Ästhetische Feldzüge*, 267.

39 Hohendahl, "Geschichte und Modernität: Heines Kritik an der Romantik," in *Literaturkritik und Öffentlichkeit*, 50–101.

40 Robert Prutz, *Die deutsche Literatur der Gegenwart*, 2 vols. in one (Leipzig: Voigt und Günther, 1859), 2:6.

41 See Walter Benjamin, *Der Begriff der Kunstkritik in der deutschen Romantik* (1920; rpt., Frankfurt am Main: Suhrkamp, 1973); Armand Nivelle, *Frühromantische Dichtungstheorie* (Berlin: De Gruyter, 1970); Peter Szondi, "Friedrich Schlegels Theorie der Dichtarten," in *Schriften II* (Frankfurt am Main: Suhrkamp, 1978), 32–58.

42 Hans Dierkes, *Literaturgeschichte als Kritik: Untersuchungen zu Theorie und Praxis von Friedrich Schlegels frühromantischer Literaturgeschichtsschreibung* (Tübingen: Niemeyer, 1980), 89.

43 Benjamin, *Der Begriff der Kunstkritik*, 24, 72, and 103.

44 See Hans-Georg Gadamer, *Wahrheit und Methode*. 2d ed. (Tübingen: Mohr, 1965), 162–83; trans. and ed. Garrett Banden and John Cunning as *Truth and Method* (New York: Seabury Press, 1975), 153–72.

45 Friedrich Schlegel, *Kritische Ausgabe*, ed. Ernst Behler, 24 vols. (Paderborn: F. Schöningh, 1967), 2:14.

46 Hans Robert Jauss, "Schlegels und Schillers Replik auf die 'Querelle des Anciens et des Modernes,'" in *Literaturgeschichte als Provokation* (Frankfurt am Main: Suhrkamp, 1970), 67–106; Hohendahl, *Literaturkritik und Öffentlichkeit*, 81–101.

47 "Über Goethes Meister (1798)," *Schriften und Fragmente*, ed. Ernst Behler (Stuttgart: Kroener Verlag, 1956), 37.

48 Ibid., 51.

49 Ibid.

50 Ibid., 54.

51 Ibid.

52 Steinecke, *Literaturkritik des Jungen Deutschland*, 39–42; Oesterle and Oesterle, "Der literarische Bürgerkrieg."

53 Quoted in Steinecke, *Literaturkritik des Jungen Deutschland*, 182.

54 Ibid., 77.

55 Ibid., 79.

56 Ibid., 76.

57 Ibid., 80.

58 Ibid., 81.

59 Hohendahl, *Literaturkritik und Öffentlichkeit*, 69–82.

60 Cf. Jost Hermand, "Der deutsche Vormärz," in *Von Mainz nach Weimar* (Stuttgart: J. B. Metzler, 1969), 174–210.

61 Wulf Wülfing, *Schlagworte des Jungen Deutschland* (Berlin: E. Schmidt, 1982). Terms such as "Herkommen" and "Tradition" have therefore, as Wülfing has shown, a

negative connotation. Gutzkow talks about a despotism of tradition and argues, against Görres, that one has to live against history instead of "inside" history. Gutzkow insists on self-determination and is against tradition (Wülfing, *Schlagworte*, 99f.). The past gains a positive meaning only in connection with the present and the future. Hence, Laube noted: "The ultimate goal of knowledge is the *present* and the *future*—the past is no more than a *means*. By inverting this relationship one has created a dismal and dead kind of erudition" (*Zeitung für die elegante Welt*, May 14, 1833, p. 375).

62 *Zeitung für die elegante Welt*, Jan. 2, 1834, p. 1.

63 Ibid., 2.

64 Wienbarg, *Ästhetische Feldzüge*, 188.

65 Ibid., 173.

66 Gutzkow, "Über Goethe im Wendepunkt zweier Jahrhunderte," quoted in *Goethe im Urteil seiner Kritiker*, ed. Karl Robert Mandelkow (Munich: Beck, 1977), pt. 2, p. 126. As to Gutzkow, see Peter Demetz, "Der Literaturkritiker Karl Gutzkow," in *Karl Gutzkow, Liberale Energie: Eine Sammlung seiner kritischen Schriften*, ed. Peter Demetz (Frankfurt: Ullstein, 1974), 10–33.

67 Theodor Mundt, *Die Kunst der deutschen Prosa*, quoted in Steinecke, *Literaturkritik des Jungen Deutschland*, 117.

68 Ibid., 185–86.

69 Cf. Hohendahl, "Kunsturteil und Tagesbericht."

70 Rainer Rosenberg, *Literaturverhältnisse im deutschen Vormärz* (Munich: Damnitz Verlag, 1975), 123.

71 Hartmut Steinecke, *Romantheorie und Romankritik in Deutschland*, 2 vols. (Stuttgart: J. B. Metzler, 1976), 2:85.

72 Later, Ruge notes: "I refer to our romantics as those writers who, using our present erudition, oppose the period of Enlightenment and Revolution and attack in the spheres of science, art, and ethics the principle of a self-determined humanity." See Arnold Ruge, *Sämtliche Werke*, 2d ed., 10 vols. (Mannheim, 1847), 1:11.

73 *Hallische Jahrbücher* (1839): col. 2400.

74 Ruge, *Sämtliche Werke*, 1:285.

75 Ibid., 287.

76 Ibid., 301.

77 Ibid., 182.

78 *Hallische Jahrbücher* (1839): col. 2120.

79 Ruge, *Sämtliche Werke*, 1:212.

80 Ibid., 2:271.

81 Ibid., 273.

82 Theodor Vischer, *Kritische Gänge*, 6 vols. in three (Tübingen: J. G. Cotta, 1844), 2:343–96.

83 Vischer, "Gedichte eines Lebendigen," in *Kritische Gänge*, 2:286.

84 *Deutsche Jahrbücher* (1841): col. 609.

85 Robert Prutz, *Die deutsche Literatur der Gegenwart*, 2 vols. in one (Leipzig: Voigt und Günther, 1859), 1:4.

86 Robert Prutz, *Kleine Schriften. Zur Politik und Literatur*, 2 vols. (Merseburg: L. Garcke, 1847), 1:66.

87   Prutz, *Die deutsche Literatur der Gegenwart*, 1:63.
88   Ibid., 19.
89   Hermann Kinder, *Poesie als Synthese* (Frankfurt: Athenäum, 1973); Ulf Eisele, *Realismus und Ideologie* (Stuttgart: Metzler, 1976).
90   Sengle, *Biedermeierzeit*, 1:257–84.
91   Cf. Hohendahl. "Von der politischen Kritik zur Legitimationswissenschaft: Zum institutionellen Status der Literaturgeschichte," in *Zum Funktionswandel der Literatur*, ed. Peter Bürger (Frankfurt am Main: Suhrkamp, 1983), 194–217.
92   Cf. Sengle, *Biedermeierzeit*, 1:144–54.
93   *Schiller—Zeitgenosse aller Epochen: Dokumente zur Wirkungsgeschichte Schillers in Deutschland*, pt. 1, ed. Norbert Oellers (Frankfurt: Athenäum, 1970), 246.
94   Ibid., 260.
95   Quoted in *Goethe im Urteil seiner Kritiker*, pt. 2, ed. Karl Robert Mandelkow (Munich: Beck, 1977), 76.
96   Adam Heinrich Müller, *Vermittelnde Kritik*, ed. Anton Krättli (Zurich: Artemis, 1968), 54f.
97   Ibid., 61.
98   See Klaus F. Gille in his introduction to Karl August Varnhagen von Ense, *Literaturkritiken* (Tübingen: Niemeyer, 1977), viiif.
99   Notice in *Morgenblatt für die gebildeten Stände*, quoted in Estermann, *Die deutschen Literaturzeitschriften*, 4:251.
100 Varnhagen von Ense, *Literaturkritiken*, 50.
101 Ibid., 44.
102 Börne, *Kritische Schriften*, 311.
103 Ibid., 312.
104 Ibid., 307.
105 Börne, "Einige Worte über die angekündigten Jahrbücher der wissenschaftlichen Kritik," in ibid., 52–62.
106 Ibid., 121.
107 *Forum der Nationalliteratur* 1 (1831): 56.
108 Ibid., 57.
109 Ibid., 59.
110 Where Menzel is concerned with contemporary reviewing, he complains about the consequences of a commercialized literary system: "Most journals [with the exception of those edited by universities] are primarily founded by publishers who are interested in the profits. Hence, the reviewers are treated like factory workers who have to do their job." See Menzel, *Die deutsche Literatur*, 4 vols., 2d ed. (Stuttgart: Gebrüder Frankh, 1836), 4:349f.
111 Menzel, *Die deutsche Literatur*, 4:358.
112 *Goethe im Urteil seiner Kritiker*, pt. 1, 367.
113 Menzel, *Die deutsche Literatur*, 4:162.
114 Heine, *Sämtliche Schriften*, 1:454f.
115 G. W. H. Hegel, *Werke* (Theorie-Werkausgabe), 20 vols. (Frankfurt am Main: Suhrkamp, 1970), 20:314; trans. E. S. Haldane and F. H. Simson as *Lectures on the History of Philosophy*, 3 vols. (London: Kegan Paul, 1892; rpt. 1974), 3:409.
116 Wolfgang Kuttenkeuler, *Heinrich Heine: Theorie und Kritik der Literatur* (Stuttgart: W.

Kohlhammer, 1972); Günther Oesterle, *Integration und Konflikt* (Stuttgart: J. B. Metzler, 1972).

117 Judgment of the Prussian *"Oberzensurkollegium"* concerning Heine's "Salon," in Hermand, *Das Junge Deutschland*, 323f.

118 Jürgen Brummack, ed., *Heinrich Heine: Epoche—Werk—Wirkung* (Stuttgart: J. B. Metzler, 1980), 180.

119 Quoted in Steinecke, *Literaturkritik des Jungen Deutschland*, 202.

120 Alfred Estermann, ed., *Politische Avantgarde, 1830–1840*, 2 vols. (Frankfurt: Athenäum, 1972), 1:48.

121 Ibid., 47.

122 Börne, *Menzel, der Franzosenfresser und andere Schriften*, ed. Walter Hinderer (Frankfurt: Insel Verlag, 1969), 126.

123 Ibid., 127.

124 Estermann, *Politische Avantgarde*, 1:193.

125 Ibid., 195.

126 Ibid., 212.

127 Ibid., 224.

128 Cf. Reinhard Behn, "Aspekte reaktionärer Literaturgeschichtsschreibung des Vormärz: Dargestellt am Beispiel Vilmars und Gelzers," in *Germanistik und deutsche Nation 1806–1848*, ed. Jörg Jochen Müller (Stuttgart: J. B. Metzler, 1974), 227–71.

129 Heinrich Gelzer, *Die neuere Deutsche Nationalliteratur nach ihren ethischen und religiösen Gesichtspunkten*, 2 vols. in one (Leipzig: Weidmann, 1847), 1:ix.

130 Behn, "Aspekte reaktionärer Literaturgeschichtsschreibung," 328f.

131 Friedrich Christian Vilmar, *Geschichte der Deutschen Nationalliteratur* (Marburg, 1845), quoted from 11th ed. (Marburg: Elwert, 1866), 404.

132 Prutz, *Die deutsche Literatur der Gegenwart*, 1:3.

133 Georg Gottfried Gervinus, *Kleine historische Schriften* (Karlsruhe: F. W. Hasper, 1838), 315f.

134 Ibid., 320.

135 Quoted from Karl-Heinz Götze, "Die Entstehung der deutschen Literaturwissenschaft als Literaturgeschichte," in Müller, *Germanisitik und deutsche Nation 1806–1848*, 179.

136 Friedrich Engels. "Alexander Jung und das junge Deutschland," in Hermand, *Das Junge Deutschland*, 358. See also Else von Eck, "Die Literaturkritik in den Hallischen und Deutschen Jahrbüchern (1838–1842)," *Germanische Studien* 42 (1926).

137 Hegel, *Werke*, 12:32, 57; *Lectures on the Philosophy of World History*, trans. H. B. Nisbet (Cambridge: Cambridge University Press, 1975).

138 Ruge, "Unsere letzten zehn Jahre (1845)," in *Die Hegelsche Linke*, ed. Karl Löwith (Stuttgart: F. Frommann, 1962), 42.

139 Löwith, *Die Hegelsche Linke*, 7.

140 *Hallische Jahrbücher* (1840): col. 1211.

141 Ibid. (1839): col. 1953.

142 Ibid., cols. 1962f.

143 Ibid., cols. 1965f.

144 Ibid., col. 2113.

145 Karl Robert Mandelkow, *Goethe in Deutschland* (Munich: Beck, 1980), 1:120–25.

146 "Schiller and Goethe mark a closure in the cultural formation of the last century. As we indicated in our first essay, they achieve a moment of reconciliation in the dualism and the process of fermentation—Schiller by rendering the moral principle, which Kant had defined as an abstract norm in his categorical imperative, through a rich world of images and metaphors, through a world of plots and characters, and by visualizing this in a way that affects the soul; Goethe, on the other hand, by subjugating the false pathos of the subjectivity and self-referentiality of Jacobi and his circle, a pathos and subjectivity that are empty yet claim to be absolute and thus try to impose themselves on reality—through the energy of his talents and by purifying and aesthetically transfiguring the objective laws of art": *Hallische Jahrbücher* (1839): cols. 2113f.

147 Ibid., col. 2115.

148 Ibid., col. 2401.

149 Ingrid Pepperle, *Junghegelianische Geschichtsphilosophie und Kunsttheorie* (Berlin: Akademie-Verlag, 1978), 109–32; Reinhard Lahme, *Zur literarischen Praxis bürgerlicher Emanzipationsbestrebungen: Robert Prutz* (Erlangen: Palm und Enke, 1977).

150 Robert Prutz, *Vorlesungen über die Geschichte des deutschen Theaters* (Berlin: Duncker und Humblot, 1847), 45.

151 Prutz, "Der Göttinger Dichterbund," quoted in Huppauf, *Schriften zur Literatur und Politik,* 2.

152 Robert Prutz, *Geschichte des deutschen Journalismus* (Hanover: C. F. Kius, 1845), 2.

153 Ibid., 5.

154 Ibid.

155 Prutz, "Über die gegenwärtige Stellung der Opposition in Deutschland," in *Kleine Schriften,* 1:59.

156 Prutz, "Über die Unterhaltungsliteratur, insbesondere der Deutschen," 10–33.

157 Ibid., 23.

158 Prutz, "Die politische Poesie, ihre Berechtigung und Zukunft," in *Kleine Schriften,* 1:129.

159 Ibid.

160 Prutz, *Geschichte des deutschen Journalismus,* 69.

161 Ibid., 71.

162 Hegel, *Werke,* 14:226; trans. T. M. Knox as *Hegel's Aesthetics,* 2 vols. (Oxford: Clarendon Press, 1975).

163 Ibid., 14:232, 233.

164 Ibid., 238

165 Ibid., 239; 13:141.

166 Robert Prutz, "Vorlesungen über die deutsche Literatur der Gegenwart," in *Zu Theorie und Geschichte der Literatur,* ed. Ingrid Pepperle (Berlin: Akademie-Verlag, 1981), 338.

167 Ibid., 323.

168 Ruge, *Werke,* 2:38.

169 Ibid., 60.

170 Walter Boehlich, ed., *Der Hochverratsprozess gegen Gervinus* (Frankfurt: Insel, 1967).

171 Julian Schmidt, "Die Märzpoeten," in *Realismus und Gründerzeit: Manifeste und Dokumente zur deutschen Literatur 1848–1880*, ed. Max Bucher et al., 2 vols. (Stuttgart: J. B. Metzler, 1975), 2:78.

172 Ibid., 80.

173 Hermann Hettner, *Schriften zur Literatur*, ed. Jürgen Jahn (Berlin: Aufbau-Verlag, 1959) 164.

174 Quoted in Hettner, "Das moderne Drama," in *Schriften zur Literatur*, 258.

175 Hettner, "Die romantische Schule," in *Schriften zur Literatur*, 160f.

176 Cf. Eisele, *Realismus und Ideologie*, 1976; also Hans-Joachim Kreutzer's instructive afterword to a facsimile edition of Prutz's *Geschichte des deutschen Journalismus* (Göttingen: Vandenhoek und Ruprecht, 1971), 423–56.

177 Helmuth Widhammer, *Die Literaturtheorie des deutschen Realismus, 1848–1860* (Stuttgart: J. B. Metzler, 1977), 1–6.

178 *Grenzboten* 4 (1849): 288.

179 Julian Schmidt, "Nachgelassene Schriften von G. Büchner (1851)," in *Roman und Romantheorie des deutschen Realismus: Darstellung und Dokumente*, ed. Hans-Joachim Ruckhäberle and Helmuth Widhammer (Kronberg: Athenäum, 1977), 83.

180 Ibid., 88.

181 Schmidt, "Schiller und der Idealismus (1858)," in Ruckhäberle and Widhammer, *Roman und Romantheorie*, 92.

182 As to the state of research, cf. Widhammer, *Die Literaturtheorie des deutschen Realismus*, 23–41; Wellek, "The Concept of Realism in Literary Scholarship," in *Concepts of Criticism* (New Haven, Conn.: Yale University Press, 1963), 222–55.

183 Cf. Kinder, *Poesie als Synthese*; Eisele, *Realismus und Ideologie*; Widhammer, *Die Literaturtheorie des deutschen Realismus*.

184 *Grenzboten* 4 (1854): 45f.

185 Schmidt, "Die Märzpoeten," in Bucher et al., *Realismus und Gründerzeit*, 2:82.

186 Schmidt, "Die neuesten englischen Romane und das Princip des Realismus (1886)," in ibid., 2:90.

187 Schmidt, "Neue Romane (1860)," in ibid., 2:96.

188 Otto Ludwig, "Shakespeare-Studien," in ibid., 2:102.

189 Rudolph Gottschall, *Poetik: Die Dichtkunst und ihre Technik*, 2 vols. (Breslau: E. Trewendt, 1858), 1:98–100.

190 Eisele, *Realismus und Ideologie*, 46.

191 Kinder, *Poesie als Synthese*, 83.

192 Quoted in Kinder, *Poesie als Synthese*, 95.

193 Friedrich Theodor Vischer, *Ästhetik*, 3 vols. in five (Stuttgart: C. Mäcken, 1857), 3:1414.

194 Eisele, *Realismus und Ideologie*, 56.

195 Schmidt, "Karl Gutzkow: Der Ritter vom Geist," *Grenzboten* 1, no. 2 (1852): 44.

196 Ibid., 62.

197 Rosenkranz, "Gutzkow's Ritter vom Geist (1852)," in Steinecke, *Romantheorie und Romankritik*, 2:235, 236.

198 Theodor Fontane, "Rezension zu Gustav Freytags Soll und Haben," in ibid., 2:252.

199 Schmidt, "Geschichte der deutschen Literatur seit Lessing's Tod. 4th ed. vol. 3, 1858," in ibid., 2:344.

200 Ibid., 345.

201 Ibid.

202 Cf. Franz Röhse, *Konflikt und Versöhnung: Untersuchungen zur Theorie des Romans von Hegel bis zum Naturalismus* (Stuttgart: J. B. Metzler, 1978), 127.

203 Hermann Marggraff, "Ein Roman, 'der das deutsche Volk bei seiner Arbeit sucht,'" *Blätter für literarische Unterhaltung* 25 (1855): 445–52.

204 Quoted in Röhse, *Konflikt und Versöhnung*, 133.

205 Gieseke's review appeared in the *Novellen-Zeitung* 3, no. 1 (1855): 311–18.

206 See Peter Uwe Hohendahl, *Literaturkritik: Eine Textdokumentation zur Geschichte einer literarischen Gattung*, ed. Alfred Estermann, 4 vols. (Vaduz, Liechtenstein: Topos Verlag, 1984), 4 (1848–70): 1–78.

207 *Grenzboten* 2 (1850): 431.

208 Schmidt, "Jeremias Gotthelf (1850)," in Ruckhäberle and Widhammer, *Roman und Romantheorie*, 118.

209 Ibid., 119.

210 *Weimarer Sonntagsblatt* (1857): 161–66, partially reprinted in Bucher et al., *Realismus und Gründerzeit*, 2:182–85.

211 Hauff, "Über Dorfgeschichten (1859)," in Bucher et al., *Realismus und Gründerzeit*, 2:190.

212 Fullerton, *Development*, 230.

213 Rolf Engelsing, *Analphabetentum und Lektüre* (Stuttgart: J. B. Metzler, 1973), 97.

214 Detlev K. Müller, *Sozialstruktur und Schulsystem: Aspekte zum Strukturwandel des Schulwesens im 19. Jahrhundert* (Göttingen: Vandenhoeck und Ruprecht, 1977), 200ff., esp. 202.

215 Dieter Barth, *Zeitschrift für alle: Das Familienblatt im 19. Jahrhundert* (Münster: Institut für Publizistik der Universität Münster, 1974), 437: 1861, 105,000; 1865, 150,000; 1866, 230,000; 1871, 310,000. *Über Land und Meer* and *Illustrirte Welt* have equally large editions.

216 Barth, *Zeitschrift für alle*, 182f., 207.

217 Rolf Engelsing, *Massenpublikum und Journalistentum im 19. Jahrhundert in Nordwestdeutschland* (Berlin: Duncker und Humblot, 1966).

218 Quoted in Wilmont Haacke, *Feuilletonkunde* (Leipzig: Hiersemann, 1943), 120.

219 Cf. Bernd Peschken, *Versuch einer germanistischen Ideologiekritik* (Stuttgart: J. B. Metzler, 1972); also Hohendahl, "Von der politischen Kritik zur Legimationswissenschaft."

Literary Criticism from Empire to Dictatorship, 1870–1933

1 Cf. Hans Erman, *August Scherl: Dämonie und Erfolg in wilhelminischer Zeit* (Berlin: Universitas, 1954); Isolde Rieger, *Die wilhelminische Presse im Überblick: 1888–1918* (Munich: Pohl, 1957); Hermann Ullstein, *The Rise and Fall of the House of Ullstein*

(New York: Simon & Schuster, 1943); Wilhelm Bauer, *Die öffentliche Meinung und ihre geschichtlichen Grundlagen: Ein Versuch* (Tübingen: Mohr, 1914), 293.

2   Ferdinand Tönnies, *Kritik der öffentlichen Meinung* (Berlin: Springer, 1922), 179–80.

3   Cf. Peter Uwe Hohendahl, "Prologomena to a History of Literary Criticism," *New German Critique*, no. 11 (Spring 1977): 163.

4   Cf. Wolf-Arno Kropat, "Obrigkeitsstaat und Pressefreiheit: Methoden staatlicher Propaganda und Pressegesetzgebung im 19. Jahrhundert am Beispiel der preussischen Pressepolitik in Hessen-Nassau (1866–1870)," *Nassauische Annalen* 77 (1966): 233–88; Eberhard Naujocks, "Bismarck und die Organisation der Regierungspresse," *Historische Zeitschrift* 205 (1967): 46–80; Dieter Brosius, "Welfenfonds und Presse im Dienste der preussischen Politik in Hannover nach 1866," *Niedersächsisches Jahrbuch für Landesgeschichte* 36 (1974): 192; Heinrich Wuttke, *Die deutschen Zeitschriften und die Entstehung der öffentlichen Meinung: Ein Beitrag zur Geschichte des Zeitungswesens* (Leipzig: Krüger, 1875), 126–27.

5   Wuttke, *Die deutschen Zeitschriften*, 186.

6   Karl Frenzel, *Berliner Dramaturgie* (Erfurt: Bartholomäus, 1877), 1:1.

7   Cf. Bernd Peschken, *Versuch einer germanistischen Ideologiekritik* (Stuttgart: Metzler, 1972), 88–104.

8   Frenzel, *Berliner Dramaturgie*, 1:26.

9   Ibid., 31, 33.

10   Ibid., 87–88, 230.

11   Adolf Bartels, *Die deutsche Dichtung der Gegenwart: Die Alten und die Jungen* (Leipzig: Avenarius, 1901), 172–73.

12   Pierre-Georges Castex, et al., *Jules Janin et son temps: Un moment du romantisme* (Paris: Presses Universitaires de France, 1974), 8; Paul Lindau, *Nur Erinnerungen* (Stuttgart: Cotta, 1919), 1:101.

13   Paul Lindau, *Dramaturgische Blätter: Neue Folge 1875–1878* (Breslau: Schottlaender, 1879), 1:1–2.

14   Cited in Hans-Heinrich Reuter, *Fontane* (Munich: Nymphenburg, 1968), 260.

15   Theodor Fontane, *Literarische Essays und Studien*, ed. Kurt Schreinert, vol. 22 of *Sämtliche Werke* (Munich: Nymphenburg, 1963), 491.

16   Cf. Wolfgang Martens, *Lyrik Kommerziell: Das Kartell lyrischer Autoren 1902–1933* (Munich: Fink, 1975); Susanne Jährig-Ostertag, "Zur Geschichte der Theaterverlage in Deutschland bis zum Ende des Dritten Reiches," *Archiv für Geschichte des Buchwesens* 16 (1976): 143–290.

17   Fontane, *Literarische Essays und Studien*, 494.

18   Theodor Fontane, *Politik und Gesellschaft*, ed. Charlotte Jolles, vol. 19 of *Sämtliche Werke* (Munich: Nymphenburg, 1969), 242–43.

19   Cf. Levin Ludwig Schücking, *Die Soziologie der literarischen Geschmacksbildung* (Munich: Rösl, 1923), 125.

20   Theodor Fontane, *Theaterkritiken*, ed. Siegmar Gerndt, vol. 3 of *Sämtliche Werke* (Munich: Hanser, 1969), 642.

21   Ibid., 68–69.

22   Cf. Kenneth Attwood, *Fontane und das Preussentum* (Berlin: Haude und Spener, 1970).

23 Theodor Fontane, *Von Zwanzig bis Dreissig: Autobiographisches nebst anderen selbstbio-graphischen Zeugnissen*, ed. Kurt Schreinert and Jutta Neuendorff-Fürstenau, vol. 15 of *Sämtliche Werke*, (Munich: Nymphenburg, 1967), 392; Fontane, *Theaterkritiken*, 19, 21–22.

24 Cf. Heinrich Hubert Houben, *Karl Gutzkows Leben und Schaffen* (Leipzig: Hesse, 1908), 197.

25 Quoted in Fontane, *Von Zwanzig bis Dreissig*, 649.

26 "Das deutsche Theater," *Kritische Waffengänge*, no. 4 (1882): 3; Eckart Kehr, *Der Primat der Innenpolitik: Gesammelte Aufsätze zur preussisch-deutschen Sozialgeschichte im 19. und 20. Jahrhunderts*, ed. Hans-Ulrich Wehler (Berlin: De Gruyter, 1966), 65–66, 72.

27 "Paul Lindau als Kritiker," *Kritische Waffengänge*, no. 2 (1882): 15–16, 17.

28 Kehr, *Der Primat der Innenpolitik*, 68–71.

29 "Paul Lindau," 17.

30 Ibid., 43.

31 "Wozu, Wogegen, Wofür," *Kritische Waffengänge* 1:7.

32 "Offener Brief an der Fürsten Bismarck," ibid., 2:7.

33 "Wozu, Wogegen, Wofür," 8.

34 Cf. Schücking, *Soziologie*, 99–100.

35 *Die Gesellschaft* 1 (1885): 751–52.

36 Ibid., 752.

37 Ibid., 976.

38 Cf. Helmut Kreuzer, *Die Boheme: Beiträge zu ihrer Beschreibung* (Stuttgart: Metzler, 1968).

39 Quoted in Katharina Günther, *Literarische Gruppenbildung im Berliner Naturalismus* (Bonn: Bouvier, 1972), 51.

40 Otto Brahm, *Kritiken und Essays*, ed. Fritz Martini (Zurich: Artemis, 1964), 439–40.

41 Ibid., 318–20.

42 Cf. Ludwig Rubiner, "Der Dichter greift in die Politik," *Die Aktion* 2 (1912): 642–52, 709–15.

43 Alfred Kerr, *Die Welt im Drama* (Berlin: S. Fischer, 1917), 1:vi, xix.

44 Ibid., 15.

45 Ibid., 15, 7.

46 Cf. Tilla Durieux, *Meine ersten neunzig Jahre* (Munich: Herbig, 1976), 107–13; cf. Karl Kraus, "Der grösste Schuft im ganzen Land . . . (Die Akten zum Fall Kerr)," *Die Fackel* 30 (Sept. 1928), 1–208.

47 Alfred Kerr, "Eine Erklärung," *Die Rote Fahne*, Aug. 8, 1925; "Für die Sowjetrepublik," *Das neue Russland*, November 1932, p. 12. On the origin of the *Rote Fahne*, see Manfred Brauneck, *Die Rote Fahne: Kritik, Theorie, Feuilleton 1918–1933* (Munich: Fink, 1973), 9–19 (hereafter cited as Brauneck).

48 "Lunacharsky in Berlin" (typed manuscript in the Alfred Kerr Archive of the Akademie der Künste, West Berlin), 1, 3, 5.

49 Cf. Kurt Hiller, "Ein besserer Mitteleuropäer," *Die Aktion* 1 (1911): 172–75.

50 "Lessing Heute," 2d version (typed manuscript in Kerr Archive), 2.

51 ["Maurice Martin du Gard"] (typed manuscript in Kerr Archive), 1, 6.

52 Helga Grebing, *Geschichte der deutschen Arbeiterbewegung* (Munich: Nymphenburg, 1980), 95.

53 Alex Hall, "The Kaiser, the Wilhelmine State and Lèse-Majesté," *German Life and Letters* 27 (1973–74): 102; Grebing, *Arbeiterbewegung*, 87–93.

54 Franz Mehring, *Der Fall Lindau* (Berlin: Brachvogel, 1890), 56.

55 Franz Mehring, "Der Klassiker des verpreussten Deutschlands," in *Aufsätze zur deutschen Literatur von Hebbel bis Schweichel*, ed. Hans Koch, vol. 11 of *Gesammelte Schriften* (Berlin: Dietz, 1961), 109.

56 Franz Mehring, *Die Lessing-Legende*, ed. Hans Koch, vol. 9 of *Gesammelte Schriften* (Berlin: Dietz, 1963), 9, 8, 185.

57 Ibid., 186, 189.

58 Walter Benjamin, "Eduard Fuchs, der Sammler und der Historiker," in *Gesammelte Schriften*, ed. Rolf Tiedemann and Hermann Schweppenhäuser (Frankfurt am Main: Suhrkamp, 1977), vol. 2, pt. 2, p. 468.

59 Mehring, "Ein Märchendrama," in Koch, *Aufsätze*, 313; Mehring, ["Fuhrmann Henschel"], in Koch, *Aufsätze*, 319, 318.

60 Mehring, ["Max Halbes, 'Haus Rosenhagen'"], in Koch, *Aufsätze*, 376.

61 Georg Lukács, "Franz Mehring (1846–1919)," in *Probleme der Ästhetik*, vol. 10 of *Werke*, (Neuwied: Luchterhand, 1969), 368–78.

62 Mehring, "Grillparzers 'Traum ein Leben,'" in Koch, *Aufsätze*, 503, 504, 505, 508.

63 Cf. Grebing, *Arbeiterbewegung*, 162, 168.

64 *Vorwärts*, March 7, 1921, cited in Christoph Rülcker, "Arbeiterkultur und Kulturpolitik im Blickwinkel des 'Vorwärts' 1918–1928," *Archiv für Sozialgeschichte* 14 (1974): 139; see also p. 143.

65 Hans Dieter Müller, *Der Springer-Konzern: Eine kritische Studie* (Munich: Piper, 1968), 18, 23–24.

66 Rülcker, "Arbeiterkultur und Kulturpolitik," 125.

67 Herbert Scherer, "Die Volksbühnenbewegung und ihre interne Opposition in der Weimarer Republik," *Archiv für Sozialgeschichte* 14 (1974): 222; cf. Hanno Möbius, review of Manfred Brauneck, *Die Rote Fahne*, in *Archiv für Sozialgeschichte* 14 (1974): 692; Scherer, "Volksbühnenbewegung," 223, 224, 230 (program of KAPD cited p. 223).

68 Gertrud Alexander, "Zur Frage der Kritik bürgerlicher Kunst," *Die Rote Fahne*, Jan. 4, 1921 (cited in Brauneck, 89); Brauneck, 88.

69 Paul Braun, "Henrik Ibsens hundertster Geburtstag. 20 März 1828–1928," *Die Rote Fahne*, March 20, 1928 (cited in Brauneck, 338–47); Karl August Wittfogel in *Die Rote Fahne*, July 26, 1930 (cited in Brauneck, 397–404).

70 Scherer, "Volksbühnenbewegung," 237, 238; Möbius, review of Brauneck, 692.

71 Cf. Hanno Möbius, "Der Rote Eine-Mark Roman," *Archiv für Sozialgeschichte* 14 (1974): 176, 167, 199.

72 Cf. Helga Gallas, *Marxistische Literaturtheorie* (Neuwied: Luchterhand, 1974); Georg Lukács, "Willi Bredels Romane," *Die Linkskurve* (reprint 1970) 3, no. 11 (1931): 23–27; Willi Bredel, "Einen Schritt Weiter," *Die Linkskurve* 4, no. 1 (1932): 20–22.

73 Otto Gotsche, "Kritik der Anderen—Einige Bemerkungen zur Frage der Qualifikation unserer Literatur," *Die Linkskurve* 4, no. 4 (1932): 8.

74 Ibid., 29.

75 Cf. Oskar Negt and Alexander Kluge, *Öffentlichkeit und Erfahrung: Zur Organisationsanalyse von bürgerlicher und proletarischer Öffentlichkeit* (Frankfurt am Main: Suhrkamp, 1972).

76 Gotsche, "Kritik der Anderen," 30.

77 George Lukács, "Gegen die Spontaneitätstheorie in der Literatur," *Die Linkskurve* 4, no. 4 (1932): 31.

78 Thomas Mann, "Rede zur Gründung der Sektion für Dichtkunst der Preussischen Akademie der Künste," in *Reden und Aufsätze* 2, vol. 10 of *Gesammelte Werke* (Frankfurt: S. Fischer, 1960, 1974), 213.

79 Kurt Hiller, "Wer sind wir?" in *Geist werde Herr: Kundgebungen eines Aktivisten vor, in und nach dem Kriege* (Berlin: E. Reiss, 1920), 77, 73–74; Walter Benjamin, "Der Irrtum des Aktivismus: Zu Kurt Hillers Essaybuch 'Der Sprung ins Helle,'" in *Gesammelte Schriften*, ed. Hella Tiedemann-Bartels (Frankfurt am Main: Suhrkamp, 1972), 3:351; cf. Heinrich Mann, *Ein Zeitalter wird besichtigt* (Stockholm: Neuer Verlag, n.d.), 339.

80 Kurt Tucholsky, "Der Untertan," in *Gesammelte Werke*, ed. Mary Gerold-Tucholsky and Fritz Raddatz (Reinbek: Rowohlt, 1975), 2:63–67; "Ulysses," in *Gesammelte Werke*, 5:379; "Auf dem Nachttisch," in *Gesammelte Werke*, 10:26–27. Cf. Georg Lukács, "Reportage oder Gestaltung? Kritische Bemerkungen anlässlich des Romans von Ottwalt," *Die Linkskurve* 4, no. 7 (1932): 23–30; no. 8: 26–31.

81 Kurt Tucholsky, "Der alte Fontane: zum hundertsten Geburtstage," in *Gesammelte Werke*, 2:235–39; Kurt Hiller, *Köpfe und Tröpfe: Profile aus eine Vierteljahrhundert* (Hamburg: Rowohlt, 1950), 292–93.

82 See Walter Benjamin, "Linke Melancholie: Zu Erich Kästners neuem Gedichtbuch," in *Gesammelte Schriften*, 3:281.

83 Schücking, *Soziologie*, 59–60, 64–65.

84 *Die Fackel*, no. 28 (Jan. 1900): 6.

85 Ibid., no. 2 (April 1899): 6.

86 Ibid., nos. 329–30 (Aug. 31, 1911): 13.

87 Willy Haas, *Die literarische Welt* (Munich: List, 1957), 158, 153; *Die literarische Welt* 1, no. 3 (Oct. 23, 1925): 4.

88 Winfried Schüler, *Der Bayreuther Kreis von seiner Entstehung bis zum Ausgang der wilhelminischen Ära: Wagnerkult und Kulturreform im Geiste völkischer Weltanschauung* (Munich: Aschendorff, 1971), 126–27; cf. Adolf Bartels, *Heine-Genossen: Zur Charakteristik der deutschen Presse und der deutschen Parteien* (Dresden: Koch, 1907), 126.

89 Julius Langbehn, *Rembrandt als Erzieher* (Leipzig: Hirschfeld, 1891), 1.

90 Adolf Bartels, *Geschichte der deutschen Literatur* (Leipzig: Avenarius, 1905), 2:418; Bartels, *Heine-Genossen*, 124.

91 Bartels, *Geschichte der deutschen Literatur* (1905), 2:457, 458.

92 Adolf Bartels, *Nationale oder universale Literaturwissenschaft? Eine Kampfschrift gegen Hanns Martin Elster und Richard M. Meyer* (Munich: Callwey, 1915); Bartels, *Ge-*

schichte der deutschen Literatur (1905), 1:6–7; Bartels, "Vorwort von 1919," in Geschichte der deutschen Literatur (Braunschweig: Westermann, 1943), v.

93 Hans Grimm, "Von dem 'politischen' Amte der Dichtung: Brief an einen Liter-
arhistoriker," in Forderungen an die Literatur: Aufsätze zur Verantwortung des Dichters
und Schriftstellers in unserer Zeit (Lippoldsberg: Klosterhaus, 1977), 45–46; Hans
Grimm, Volk ohne Raum (Munich: A. Langen, 1926), 2: 254–55, 278–79; Paul Fechter, "Ein deutsches Volksbuch," in Die neue Literatur 32 (1931): 466.

94 Bartels, Nationale oder universaler Literaturwissenschaft? 138.

95 Langbehn, Rembrandt, 175–76.

96 Otto Forst de Battaglia, "Unkundige Trojaner: Eine Kritik der Buchkritik," Die neue
Literatur 32 (1931): 527.

97 Fechter, "Ein deutsches Volksbuch," 467, 466.

98 Bartels, Nationale oder universale Literaturwissenschaft? 134, 135; Bartels, Geschichte
der deutschen Literatur (1905), ix.

99 Bertolt Brecht, Schriften I: Zum Theater, ed. Werner Hecht, vol. 7 of Gesammelte
Werke in acht Bänden (Frankfurt am Main: Suhrkamp, 1967), 82.

100 Bertolt Brecht, Schriften II: Zur Literatur und Kunst; Zur Politik und Gesellschaft, ed.
Werner Hecht, vol. 8 of Gesammelte Werke in acht Bänden (Frankfurt am Main:
Suhrkamp, 1967), 96, 97; cf. Berthold Viertel, Schriften zum Theater, ed. Gert
Heidenreich (Munich: Kösel, 1970), 474–75; Brecht, Schriften II, 100.

101 Brecht, Schriften II, 99; Schriften I, 377; Schriften II, 98, 109.

102 Herbert Ihering, Der Kampf ums Theater und andere Streitschriften 1918 bis 1933
(Berlin: Henschel, 1974), 15; Brecht, Schriften II, 103.

103 Brecht, Schriften II, 106; Ihering, Der Kampf uns Theater, 32.

104 Brecht, Schriften II, 114.

105 Brecht, Schriften I, 377, 378.

106 Ibid., 378.

107 Bernd Witte, Walter Benjamin: Der Intellektuelle als Kritiker. Untersuchungen zu seinem
Frühwerk (Stuttgart: Metzler, 1976), 32; Bartels, Geschichte der deutschen Literatur
(1905), vi.

108 Benjamin, Gesammelte Schriften, vol. 1, pt. 1, p. 108.

109 Ibid., 125–26, 172–73; cf. Norbert W. Bolz, "Walter Benjamin," in Klassiker der
Literaturtheorie: Von Boileau bis Barthes, ed. Horst Turk (Munich: Beck, 1979), 263–
64; Walter Benjamin, Briefe, ed. Gershom Scholem and Theodor W. Adorno
(Frankfurt am Main: Suhrkamp, 1964), 323; cf. Peter Bürger, Theorie der Avantgarde
(Frankfurt am Main: Suhrkamp, 1981), 92–98.

110 Walter Benjamin, Einbahnstrasse (Frankfurt am Main: Suhrkamp, 1962), 52, 51.

111 Benjamin, Gesammelte Schriften, 3:610, 23, 22, 25.

112 Ibid. 13, 297, 300.

113 Cf. Norbert Mecklenburg, Kritisches Interpretieren: Untersuchungen zur Theorie der
Literaturkritik (Munich: Nymphenburg, 1972), 16; Benjamin, Gesammelte Schriften,
3:50, 51.

114 Benjamin, Gesammelte Schriften, 3:290, 193.

115 Ibid., 190–91, 309, 309–10, 231.

116 Ibid., 174–75, 176.

117   Ibid., 225.

118   Ibid., 2:696.

Literary Criticism from 1933 to the Present

1   Oskar Maria Graf, *Gelächter von aussen: Aus meinem Leben, 1918–1933* (Munich: Desch, 1966), 413.

2   Ernst Bloch, "Deutschfrommes Verbot der Kunstkritik," *Literaturkritik und literarische Wertung*, ed. Peter Gebhardt (1937; Darmstadt: Wissenschaftliche Buchgesellschaft, 1980), 120.

3   Georg Lukács, *Geschichte und Klassenbewusstsein* (1923; Neuwied: Luchterhand, 1968), 111; trans. Rodney Livingstone as *History and Class Consciousness* (Cambridge, Mass.: MIT Press, 1971).

4   Peter Uwe Hohendahl, "Vorüberlegungen zu einer Geschichte der Literaturkritik," in *Literaturkritik—Medienkritik*, ed. Jörg Drews (Heidelberg: Quelle und Meyer, 1977), 75.

5   *Die neue Literatur* (1932).

6   Rolf Geissler, "Form und Methoden der nationalsozialistischen Literaturkritik," *Neophilologus* 51 (1967): 264f.

7   See Dietrich Strothmann, *Nationalsozialistische Literaturpolitik: Ein Beitrag zur Publizistik im Dritten Reich* (Bonn: H. Bouvier, 1960), 270.

8   Cf. Hildegard Brenner, *Die Kunstpolitik des Nationalsozialismus* (Reinbeck bei Hamburg: Rowohlt, 1963), 192ff.

9   Cf. Strothman, *Literaturpolitik*, 259.

10   Ibid., 261.

11   Cf. Gisela Berglund, *Der Kampf um den Leser im Dritten Reich* (Worms: Heintz, 1980), 2.

12   *Die Bücherkunde*, 4th ser., 1(1934): 10.

13   Cf. Strothmann, *Literaturpolitik*, 263.

14   Ibid., 266.

15   *Die neue Literatur* (1933): 209f.

16   Josef Wulf, *Literatur und Dichtung im Dritten Reich* (Gütersloh: S. Mohn, 1963), 270.

17   Strothmann, *Literaturpolitik*, 328.

18   Cf. ibid., 394.

19   Cf. ibid., 393.

20   Cf. ibid., 292f.

21   Cf. ibid., 188.

22   Cf. the documentary work of Hans-Jürgen Schmitt, ed., *Die Expressionismusdebatte: Materialien zu einer Marxistischen Realismuskonzeption* (Frankfurt am Main: Suhrkamp, 1973); and Hans-Jürgen Schmitt and Godehard Schramm, eds., *Sozialistische Realismuskonzeptionen: Dokumente zum 1. Allunionskongress der Sowjetschriftsteller* (Frankfurt am Main: Suhrkamp, 1974).

23   Johannes R. Becher, "Aus der Welt des Gedichts," in *Kritik in der Zeit: Anti-*

faschistische deutsche Literaturkritik 1933–1945, ed. Klaus Jarmatz and Simone Barck (Halle: Mitteldeutscher Verlag, 1981), 51f.

24　Bertold Brecht, "Realistische Kritik," in ibid., 519.

25　Bertold Brecht, *Gesammelte Werke* (Frankfurt am Main: Suhrkamp, 1967), 18:226f.

26　Balder Olden, "Gedichte von Alfred Kerr," in Jarmatz and Barck, *Antifaschistische deutsche Literaturkritik*, 519.

27　Cf. the instructive study by Gunther Heeg, *Die Wendung zur Geschichte: Konstitutionsprobleme antifaschistischer Literatur im Exil* (Stuttgart: Metzler, 1977).

28　Walter Benjamin, "Der Autor als Produzent," in *Versuche über Brecht* (Frankfurt am Main: Suhrkamp, 1966), 116.

29　Fritz Brügel, "Aristokratischer Faschismus," *Das Wort* 12 (1937): 98f.

30　Ibid., 101.

31　*Das Wort* 2 (1938): 138.

32　Paul Kersten, "Leser und Kritiker im Dritten Reich," *Das Wort* 5 (1938): 143.

33　Paul Kersten, "Von den Methoden der Schriftsteller im Lande," in Jarmatz and Barck, *Antifaschistische deutsche Literaturkritik*, 327.

34　Ibid., 326.

35　Cf. Alexander Abusch's programmatic essay "Die Verteidigung der deutschen Kultur und die Volksfront," *Die Internationale* (1937).

36　F. C. Weiskopf, "Zwei Soldaten," *Die neue Weltbühne*, May 9, 1935, p. 363.

37　*Internationale Literatur* 9 (1938), quoted in Jarmatz and Barck, *Antifaschistische deutsche Literaturkritik*, 512.

38　Benjamin, *Versuche über Brecht*, 105.

39　Ibid., 110.

40　V. Wehdeking, "Eine deutsche 'lost generation'? Die 47er zwischen Kriegsende und Währungsreform," *Literaturmagazin* 7 (1977): 147.

41　Cf. Franz Schonauer, "Literaturkritik in der Bundesrepublik Deutschland," in *Deutsche Gegenwartsliteratur*, ed. Manfred Durzak (Stuttgart: Reclam, 1981), 406f.

42　Cf. Wulf, *Literatur und Dichtung*, 289f.

43　For the reception of Benn after 1945, cf. the documentary by Peter Uwe Hohendahl, *Benn—Wirkung wider Willen* (Frankfurt am Main: Athenäum Verlag, 1971).

44　F. Nemec, "Tendenzen der Literaturkritik seit 1945," in *Kindlers Literaturgeschichte der Gegenwart* (Munich: Kindler Verlag, 1976), 5:433.

45　Ernst Robert Curtius, *Europäische Literatur und lateinisches Mittelalter*, 2d ed. (Bern: Francke Verlag, 1953), 9; trans. Willard R. Trask as *European Literature and the Latin Middle Ages* (New York: Pantheon Books, 1953).

46　Ernst Robert Curtius, *Kritische Essays zur europäischen Literatur*, 2d ed. (Bern: Francke Verlag, 1954), 33; trans. Michael Kowal as *Essays on European Literature* (Princeton, N.J.: Princeton University Press, 1973).

47　Hans Egon Holthusen, *Der unbehauste Mensch: Motive und Probleme der modernen Literatur* (Munich: Piper, 1951), 33.

48　Schonauer, "Literaturkritik," 417.

49　Ibid.

50　Günter Blöcker, "Literaturkritik," in *Kritik in unserer Zeit*, ·2d ed., ed. Günter Blöcker et al., foreword by Karl Otto (Göttingen: Vandenhoeck und Ruprecht, 1962), 13.

51 Ibid., 17.

52 Ibid., 18.

53 Ibid., 15.

54 Ibid., 16.

55 Ibid., 15.

56 Peter Uwe Hohendahl, "Das Ende einer Institution," in *Literaturkritik und Öffentlichkeit* (Munich: Piper, 1974), 164f.

57 Schonauer, "Literaturkritik," 415.

58 Friedrich Sieburg, *Zur Literatur* (Stuttgart: Deutsche Verlagsanstalt, 1981), 2:196f.

59 For the documentation of the Berliner Kritiker-Colloquium, cf. *Sprache im technischen Zeitalter* 10/11 (1964).

60 Jürgen Habermas, *Strukturwandel der Öffentlichkeit*, 5th ed. (1962; Neuwied: Luchterhand, 1971).

61 Peter Glotz, *Buchkritik in deutschen Zeitungen* (Hamburg: Verlag für Buchmarktforschung, 1968), 7f.

62 Hans Magnus Enzensberger, "Gemeinplätze, die neueste Literatur betreffend," *Kursbuch* 15 (1968): 187ff.

63 Walter Böhlich, "Autodafé," *Kursbuch* 15 (1968).

64 Yaak Karsunke, "Uralte Binsenweisheiten," *Kritik/von wem/für wen/wie: Eine Selbstdarstellung deutscher Kritiker*, ed. Peter Hamm (Munich: C. Hanser, 1968), 46.

65 Hohendahl, *Literaturkritik und Öffentlichkeit*, 183.

66 Cf. Olaf Schwencke, ed., *Kritik der Literaturkritik* (Stuttgart: Kohlhammer, 1973); and Drews, *Literaturkritik—Medienkritik*.

67 Norbert Mecklenburg, "Die Rhetorik der Literaturkritik," in Drews, *Literaturkritik—Medienkritik*, 42.

68 Marcel Reich-Ranicki, "Deutsche Unterhaltungsliteratur," in *Literarisches Leben in Deutschland* (Munich: Piper, 1965), 78–82.

69 Ibid., 80.

70 Cf. also Peter Seibert, "Die Musen, das Medium und die Massen," in *Fernsehsendungen und ihre Formen*, ed. Helmut Kreuzer and Karl Prümm (Stuttgart: Reclam, 1979), 377–90.

71 Cf. also Bernhard Zimmermann, "Das 'Hofbräuhaus' der Unterhaltung: Volkstheater im Fernsehen—Typen, Strukturen und Tendenzen," in Kreuzer and Prümm, *Fernsehsendungen und ihre Formen*, 126–39.

72 Klaus Ramm, "Unverbundene Materialien zur Diskussion über den Zusammenhang von Literaturkritik und literarischem Markt am Beispiel von Herbert Achternbusch," in Drews, *Literaturkritik—Medienkritik*, 1–11.

73 Monika Dimpfl, *Literarische Kommunikation und Gebrauchswert* (Bonn: Bouvier, 1981), 106.

74 Ibid.

75 Ibid.

76 Ibid.

77 Ibid., 107.

78 Peter Uwe Hohendahl, "Theorie und Praxis des Erbens: Untersuchungen zum Problem der literarischen Tradition in der DDR", in Peter Uwe Hohendahl and

Patricia Herminghouse, eds., *Literatur der DDR in den Siebziger Jahren* (Frankfurt am Main: Suhrkamp, 1983), 17.

79 Cf. Wolfram Schlenker, *Das 'kulturelle Erbe' in der DDR: Gesellschaftliche Entwicklung und Kulturpolitik 1945–1965* (Stuttgart: Metzler, 1977), 49ff.

80 Cf. W. Zobl, "Die Auseinandersetzung um Eislers revolutionäre Umfunktionierung des Dr. Faustus," *Das Argument*, spec. vol. 5 (1975): 251.

81 Brecht, *Gesammelte Werke*, 17:1154.

82 Cf. also Hans Jürgen Schmitt, "Die literarischen Produktionsverhältnisse in Becher's 'Literaturgesellschaft'" in *Einführung in Theorie, Geschichte und Funktion der DDR-Literatur*, ed. Hans Jürgen Schmitt (Stuttgart: Metzler, 1975), 165.

83 Georg Klaus and Manfred Buhr, eds., *Philosophisches Wörterbuch* (Leipzig: Verlag Enzyklopädie, 1972), 2:628.

84 Ibid.

85 Waltraud Böhme et al., eds., *Kleines Politisches Wörterbuch* (Berlin: Dietz Verlag, 1973), 125.

86 Cf. Klaus Jarmatz, ed., *Kritik in der Zeit-Literaturkritik der DDR 1945–1975*, 2d ed. (Halle: Mitteldeutscher Verlag, 1978), 1:185.

87 Ibid., 184.

88 F. C. Weiskopf, "Bermerkungen über die Verrottung von Sprache und Stil," in Jarmatz, *Kritik*, 1:194.

89 Cf. Jarmatz, *Kritik*, 1:215f.

90 Ibid.

91 Hans Marchwitza, "Die Literatur und ihr natürlicher Boden," in Jarmatz, *Kritik*, 1:218.

92 Walter Ulbricht, from the *Protokoll des V. Parteitags der SED* (1959): 1401.

93 Cf. the documentation by Martin Reso, ed., *'Der geteilte Himmel' und seine Kritiker* (Halle: Mitteldeutscher Verlag, 1965).

94 Dieter Schlenstedt, "Motive und Symbole in Christa Wolfs Erzählung 'Der geteilte Himmel,'" *Weimarer Beiträge* 1 (1964): 77–104.

95 Alfred Kurella, "Der Frühling, die Schwalben und Franz Kafka" in Jarmatz, *Kritik*, 1:383.

96 Ibid., 389.

97 Hermann Kähler, "'Die Aula,'—eine Laudatio auf die DDR," in Jarmatz, *Kritik*, 2:27.

98 Ibid.

99 Kurt Hager, "Literatur und Kunst bereichern das Leben," in Jarmatz, *Kritik*, 2:174.

100 Franz Fühmann, "Literatur und Kritik," in Jarmatz, *Kritik*, 2:240.

101 Ibid., 243.

102 Ibid., 245.

103 Ibid., 246.

104 Ibid.

105 Kurt Batt, Voraussetzungen der Kritik," in Jarmatz, *Kritik*, 2:258.

106 *Theater in der Zeit*, Dec. 1982.

Index